Also by Jane Bryant Quinn

Everyone's Money Book

MAKING THE
MOST
OF YOUR
MONEY

*Smart Ways to Create Wealth
and Plan Your Finances in the '90s*

—

JANE BRYANT QUINN

SIMON & SCHUSTER
New York · London · Toronto · Sydney · Tokyo · Singapore

Simon & Schuster
Simon & Schuster Building
Rockefeller Center
1230 Avenue of the Americas
New York, New York 10020

DESIGNED BY BARBARA MARKS
Manufactured in the United States of America

11

Library of Congress Cataloging in Publication Data
Quinn, Jane Bryant.
Making the most of your money: Smart ways to create wealth and plan your finances in
the '90s/Jane Bryant Quinn.
p.   cm.
Includes index.
1. Finance, Personal.   2. Investments.   I. Title.
HG179.Q57   1991

332.024'01—dc20   90-25050

CIP
ISBN 0-671-65952-9

FOR DAVID

and all the joys that money can't buy

CONTENTS

FOREWORD

Any era can be described as "uncertain," but this one more than most. Housing values aren't as solid as we thought. Jobs vanish even from profitable companies. College tuitions rise faster than a parent can save. An offer of early retirement may carry the subliminal message, "take it or else." We dare not count on being safe.

Yet neither can we put our lives on hold. Our days progress toward personal goals that are deeply held and widely shared: to enjoy our homes, raise and educate our children, and provide for our futures. We hope to improve our standard of living and secure our older age. We have choices to make about when to borrow, what to save, and where to invest. A shiver of doubt may urge more caution than we felt ten years ago. But life is long, and assumptions change. In good years, we should build safety nets, in case our prospects take a turn. In bad years, we should be laying plans for the better times that lie ahead.

This book was designed to help find a balance point between safety and enterprise, to address our fears without putting limits on our hopes. It's an eight-step system for being your own financial planner. By working with these chapters, one by one, you will master the fundamentals of money, build a base to keep you and your family safe, then begin to buy the kinds of investments that best suit your age, goals, and circumstances. Don't hesitate to make these decisions by yourself. The chief difference between you and a professional planner is information. This book, I hope, will close that gap. Some of the details will change, over the years that you use these facts. But the broad principles of personal finance will stay the same: save money, borrow intelligently, invest for growth.

Even in a chancy economy, I urge you not to hunker down and play it absolutely safe. Making a judicious stretch is the classic path to high reward. The error of the 1980s was to jump without a parachute. The wisdom of the 1990s is always to know where the ripcord is. That's one of this book's major themes: how to reach for growth while still protecting what you have.

Holding on to a ripcord—a fallback position—carries a price. You'll be spending less in order to save a little more. But postponing consumption isn't so bad. There's more to life than credit cards can ever buy.

At a dinner party I went to last year, the hostess gave the guests little wind-up toys, one at each plate. We had just begun a somber conversation about the postponements that the risky 1990s might bring when suddenly a cheery blue drum sashayed across our table, bouncing a cymbal and waving tiny yellow hands. The message on the drum restored us: "Don't postpone joy."

JANE BRYANT QUINN
North Salem, N.Y.
May 1991

1 BUILDING YOUR BASE

If I could have lunch with anyone, whom would I choose? Shakespeare, for sure. Cleopatra—to see how compelling she really was. Virginia Woolf. Bill Cosby. (Bill, call me at 212-350-4000). Archimedes.

Okay, Archimedes isn't someone you would think of, right off the bat. But I have a special feeling for the Greek mathematician. Aside from his theoretical work, he constructed ingenious mechanical devices. He showed that great weights could be moved with small effort, provided that the lever was long enough. "Give me a place to stand," he said, "and I will move the world."

Our world could stand a little shove—especially the world of money. Each new generation staggers forward under the weight of old ideas. We "know" too much that isn't true, or isn't true for the 1990s. This is a lean and wary time (I would explain to Archimedes, over sandwiches). The extravagant eighties are history. We're looking at security now, a return to first principles of family economics and finance. Our minds need moving, as well as our money.

That's a job for a lever. This book was written to help you find a place to stand.

1

WHAT ARCHIMEDES
WOULD HAVE DONE:

Where You Stand on the Money Cycle

—

The finest of all human achievements—and the
most difficult—is merely being reasonable.

All of our deepest beliefs about
money are formed in the years when we grow up. We learn the great
lessons of our era and set out to put them all to work.

But time is a trickster. Just when you think that you've learned all
the rules, some hidden umpire changes the game.

Think about the Depression Kids. Those woeful years left a legacy of
fear. Forever after, the generations marked by the thirties and early
forties saved compulsively. A loan made them feel sick to their stom-
achs. They took no risks. When the Great Prosperity swelled around
them, they mistrusted it. They knew in their hearts it wouldn't last.

Now think about the Inflation Kids, raised in the 1960s and 1970s.
They saw in a flash that a dollar saved was a dollar wasted because
inflation ate it up. A dollar *borrowed* was a dollar saved. You could use it
to buy a car or a stereo before the price increased.

The Inflation Kids felt sorry for the codgers who saved so fruitlessly and lost so much. In the 1970s, the value of fixed savings, pensions, and insurance policies fell apart.

But what does that younger generation know about money, in its heart? As adults, they all "know" that real estate will always go up. They "know" that it's smart to borrow because loans will be repaid in cheaper dollars. They are wrong—but to act on any other belief goes against their grain. They haven't yet caught on to the new facts of the 1990s.

The next turn of the wheel is bringing us the Compression Kids. They're seeing a very different world. Living standards, flat. Real estate, undependable. Wages, not rising fast enough to cover the compounding interest on loans. Money in the bank, looking good again. This generation will watch its elders struggling to carry debts and be appalled.

Can the Inflation Generation change *its* approach to money any better than the Depression Generation could? Can you find a better place to stand? On the answer to those questions, everything depends.

A CYCLE OF SPENDING AND SAVING

Money comes and goes in your life at different times. Mostly goes, when you're young. Those are the spent years. Maybe the *mis*spent years. But never mind. As you grow older, the urge to save creeps up on you. Here's the typical cycle of wealth:

AGES 20 TO 30. You establish credit, buy your first furniture and appliances, take your first auto loan, learn about insurance and taxes. Maybe (here I'm dreaming) you save a little money—in payroll savings or an Individual Retirement Account. IRAs are money machines for young people, because you have so many years to let them grow untaxed. By the end of the decade, you might get married, have a baby, buy a house. (Yes, I know. You'll borrow the down payment from your parents.)

AGES 31 TO 45. You don't know where your money goes. Bills, bills, bills. College is a freight train headed your way. You start a tuition savings account and pray that your house will be good for a second mortgage. Maybe (here I'm dreaming again) money still dribbles into retirement savings. This is a good time to start a business. Invest in yourself and hope for a payoff.

AGES 46 TO 55. You *do* know where your money goes: to good old State U. At the same time, you get the creepy feeling that maybe you won't live forever. You thrash around. You buy books about financial planning. You have an affair. When all else fails, you start to save.

AGES 56 TO 65. These are the fat years. You're at the top of your earning power, the kids are gone, the dogs are dead. Twenty percent of your salary can be socked away.

AGES 66 TO 75. How golden are these years? As rich as your pension, Social Security, and the income from the money you saved. Start out by living on the first two. Let the income from savings compound for a while, to build a fund for later life.

AGES 76 AND UP. Quit saving. Spend, spend, spend! Forget leaving money to your kids—they should have put away more for themselves. Dip into principal to live as comfortably as you deserve. This is what all those years of saving were *for*.

WHEN YOU FALL OFF THE CYCLE

You say you can't find your place on the cycle? That's no surprise. Almost no one lives exactly to order anymore. Still, we all come to the same place in the end. If you fall behind during any decade, you'll need a plan for catching up.

YOU HAVE YOUR CHILDREN IN YOUR THIRTIES. It seemed like a smart idea at the time—diapers tomorrow but never today. No one told you that, in your fifties, you'd be paying for college just when you were trying to save for your own retirement. (And even if they told you, you'd never have believed you would ever be that old.) You might have to choose between sending your children to a low-cost college or shortchanging your own future. The moral, for those who can think ahead: Save more in your twenties, using the discipline of tax-deferred plans, like IRAs and company 401(k) plans, that penalize you for drawing the money out.

YOU GET DIVORCED AND START OVER. Divorce costs you assets and income, with the greater loss usually falling on the woman. She rarely can earn as much money as her ex-husband takes away. For the man, a new wife and new babies might mean that college-tuition bills will arrive in the same mail as the Social Security checks. Unless you're rich or remarry rich, divorce may be a decision to cut your standard of living, sometimes permanently.

YOU DON'T MARRY. You lack the safety net that a second paycheck provides. On the other hand, there's usually no other mouth to feed. You can start saving and investing earlier than most.

YOU'RE MARRIED, WITH NO CHILDREN. You've got nothing but money and plenty of it. You are one of the few who *really* can retire early, not just dream about it.

YOU'RE GIVEN THE GOLDEN BOOT. A forced retirement. Sometimes you see it coming, sometimes it catches you blindside. You get a consolation prize, in extra pension or cash. But you lose 5 to 10 years of earnings and savings. This risk is the single strongest argument for starting a retirement-savings program young.

LIFE DEALS YOU AN ACCIDENT. A crippling illness. Early widowhood. A child with anguishing medical problems. An economic depression in your industry that costs you much of what you worked for. A family that has always saved can make it through these tragedies. A family in debt to the hilt cannot.

WHO NEEDS WHAT WHEN

The number of financial products on the market today—bank accounts, insurance policies, investment funds—I estimate, conservatively, at two zillion point three (2.3Z). Most of them, nobody needs. You *do* need a few simple things, matched to your age, your bank balance, and your responsibilities. The rest of this book tells you how to choose them. Here, I offer a general framework for your thinking.

YOUNG AND SINGLE. Admit it—you are living your life on "hold." Cinderella, waiting for Prince Charming. Peter Pan, not wanting to grow up. You are serious only about your work. Everything else is temporary. There is nothing in your refrigerator and nothing in your bank account. "Wait until I'm married," you say. But what if you don't marry? Or marry late? Looking back, you'll see that you lost ten good years. *Your* future starts now. As a young person you should:

• Establish credit, with a low-cost bank card. Practice on one card before getting two. Debt tends to rise to the highest allowable limit.

• Get disability insurance coverage. It pays you an income if you're sick or injured and can't work.

• Get health insurance if you don't have a company plan. No one wants a charity patient. If you can't afford a policy, maybe your parents will buy it for you. They would probably pay for an operation if you needed one, so buying your health insurance is really a way of protecting themselves.

• Invest in your own education and training. Your earning power is your single greatest asset.

• Start saving money. Put away 10 percent of your earnings. I hear you saying, "I can't do it"—so sneak up on it. Start with 5 percent. I guarantee that you'll be up to 10 percent within the year. Where should the money go? For starters, part to a bank and part to a retirement plan.

• Start a tax-deferred retirement plan: an Individual Retirement Account or a savings plan through your company. Put the money into stock-owning mutual funds and leave it there.

• Rent, don't buy an apartment. Condominiums and cooperative apartments may not hold their value. The money you'd spend on a down payment is better invested somewhere else. Buy only when you've definitely put down roots.

• Buy property insurance to cover your possessions and to cover your liability if anyone is hurt on your premises.

• Make a will, unless it's okay for your parents to inherit everything. If you die will-less, that's where your property will probably go.

• Do a power of attorney and a living will. That's basic protection in case you meet with a horrible accident that leaves you alive but not alert.

OLDER SINGLES. You might be your own sole support for life. But don't let that scare you into playing your hand too conservatively. Stocks do better than bank accounts, over long periods of time. You need, for financial self-defense:

• A good credit record—good enough for a mortgage or a business loan.

• Enough education and job training to keep your income moving up.

• Good health and disability insurance. The older you get the greater your risk of illness or injury. When you pass 60, consider nursing-home insurance. *You don't need any life insurance, unless someone depends on your income for support.*

• A home of your own. Living will be cheaper and expenses more predictable if you own a house or apartment free and clear when you retire.

• A habit of saving. Try for 15 to 20 percent of your income. No, that's not too much.

• More than one retirement plan: a pension, a company savings plan, an Individual Retirement Account, a Keogh plan for the self-employed, a tax-deferred annuity.

• A mix of investments in your retirement plans: some U.S. and foreign stocks or stock-owning mutual funds; some Treasuries or other bonds.

• An interest beyond your regular job—a pastime or charity. It may open the door to a second career.

• A will, a living will, and a durable power of attorney.

• A good attorney or other surrogate, who will manage your money if you can't do it yourself.

MARRIED COUPLES. You have a lot of responsibilities. Your mate needs security if you die. Children have to be set up, too. After that, the big question is how to handle the family money. You need:

• A cost-sharing system. If you are a two-paycheck couple, will you split the bills or pool your money in one account? If you are a one-paycheck couple, will you start a savings account for the nonearning spouse? Financially speaking, there is no best way, only *your* way.

• Credit cards in the names of both spouses. You both should be legally liable for the debt. A wife without joint responsibility could have her cards yanked if her husband dies or leaves.

• Disability insurance. Each income-earning spouse needs it, to cover the lost paycheck if he or she becomes too sick to work.

• Health insurance. Don't be without it, especially between jobs. When you're out of work, you're under a lot of stress—which can lead to accidents and poor health. Working couples should try not to duplicate benefits in their company health plans.

• Life insurance. If your family depends on your income for support, you need life insurance. If your family can get along without your income, you don't. Working couples alone may do just fine with whatever group-term insurance they get from their companies. But you'll need much more coverage if children arrive. Buying insurance on a nonearning spouse is a luxury purchase. Buying it on a child is a waste.

• A will, so that beneficiaries will inherit exactly as much as you intend.

• A power of attorney, so someone can manage your finances if you can't.

• A living will, if you don't ever want to spend your life in a coma, hooked up to life supports.

• A premarital agreement, if you don't want your spouse to inherit (see page 121). Premarital agreements generally limit what each spouse can get from the other, at the time of death or divorce. They are mostly used by people of vastly unequal wealth; the previously divorced who swear that they won't be "burned again"; and older people, with children from previous marriages to protect. There are postmarital agreements, too, for arrangements you wish you had made earlier.

• Your own home. It should still be a good investment, if you own it long enough. It's also a form of forced saving and nice to have free and clear, when you retire.

• Regular savings. Sprinkle 10 percent of every check among ready savings, his-and-hers tax-deferred retirement plans, and college savings. Come to think of it, sprinkle more. You'll never catch up with college costs on a mere 10 percent.

• Job skills. A wife without them is asking for trouble. Life is not fair. Death or disability occurs. Breadwinners lose their jobs. Not all spouses love each other until the end of time. As the poet said, "Provide, provide."

• Nursing-home insurance, once you pass 60.

BLENDED FAMILIES. Life gets expensive when both bride and groom come with children attached. You need everything that any other married couple does, plus extra protection for stepchildren. Check:

• Whether all the kids are covered by health insurance.

• Whether your will needs changing, to include the stepchildren.

• Whether you need trusts, to insure that the children of the former marriages inherit the property that they're due.

• Whether all the kids will have enough money for college.

YOUNGER WIDOWS, WIDOWERS, AND THE DIVORCED. Maybe you're just plain single again. More likely, there are children to support. It's harder alone. You'll need a substantial safety net:

• Buy as much disability insurance as you can get. If you can't work and can't support your children, the family might break up.

• Don't be without a family health policy for a moment.

• Buy a lot of life insurance, if your children's future depends on you. Stick with low-cost term insurance and cancel it when the kids grow up.

• Write a will—especially to name a guardian for your children. Add a living will and a power of attorney.

· Call Social Security. Unmarried children under 18 or 19, or children disabled before age 22, whose mother or father is dead, can get a monthly Social Security payment on that parent's account. So can widowed people (including divorced spouses whose ex-spouse dies), if their child is disabled or under 16.

· If you're divorced, report your new status to everyone who gave you credit. You don't want your ex-spouse's new charges to show up on your personal credit history. If the credit card was granted on the basis of both your incomes, you may have to prove that you're still creditworthy. But that usually doesn't happen unless you run into trouble paying your bills.

· If you're widowed, maybe you want to report your new status to credit granters. Then again, maybe you don't. If the card was based on two incomes, or on the income of the spouse who died, you may not be able to keep the card unless you can prove that you're creditworthy. If the family credit history is good and you have an income, the card will doubtless be reissued. But if you have only a small income, it might not be. In that case, nothing in federal law stops you from keeping your old card and keeping mum.

· Find work. Or find better work. Train for a higher-paying job. You can't afford to coast.

· If you collect child support, take out a term insurance policy on your ex-spouse (this should be part of your divorce agreement). The insurance proceeds will make up for your lost child support, if he dies.

· Save money, even at the cost of your standard of living. Maybe you will remarry, but you can't count on it.

· Consider trading down to a smaller house.

· Keep your home if you're rooted in place or have children. Otherwise, hang loose and rent, on a short-term lease. Your next life may lie somewhere else.

· Take no quick advice about money. Not from your brother. Not from your friends. Above all, not from anyone selling financial products. Salespeople love widows, for their ready cash and their presumed dependence on a sympathetic man. Keep your money in the bank until you've learned something about managing it and know exactly what you want to do.

· Don't automatically turn your life-insurance proceeds into an annuity. Inflation will gradually wipe out the value of a fixed monthly income. You might want to take a lump sum instead, and invest it conservatively.

OLDER WIDOWS, WIDOWERS, AND THE DIVORCED. You have great freedom, if your children are grown. Your life can be reconstructed from the ground up. Your check list includes "cancels" as well as "buys":

• Cancel your life insurance. Use the money to add to your savings and investments.

• Cancel your disability insurance, if you have retired and no longer get a paycheck. The insurance company won't pay when you have no earnings to replace. So you're wasting the money you spend on premiums.

• Keep your health insurance. At age 65, get a Medigap policy, to cover what Medicare doesn't.

• Call Social Security. The widowed who reach age 60 (50 if disabled) may be entitled to payments. If you were married for at least 10 years and are now divorced, you're probably eligible for benefits from your ex-spouse's account if (1) you've reached 62, (2) you are not now remarried, and (3) your ex-spouse has also reached age 62 or is receiving Social Security disability payments. Even if you have remarried, you may get benefits from your ex-spouse's account if (1) your new spouse is receiving Social Security payments and (2) your benefits on your new spouse's account would be less than you're getting from your former spouse's account. If your ex-spouse dies, your benefits can start when you reach age 60 (50 if you're disabled). Incidentally, a new wife often worries that Social Security payments to an ex-wife will reduce her own benefits. They won't. Each gets a full payment, as if she were the only wife around.

• Study up on money management. If you've never handled investments before, this is the moment that nature has chosen for you to learn. In the meantime, keep your money in the bank. *Don't give it to anyone else to manage for you until you know a lot about money yourself.* Otherwise, your "expert" might manage it right into his or her own pocket.

• Write a will or change your old one. A living will and a power of attorney grow even more urgent as you age. You need someone to speak for you, if you become incapable.

• Call your late spouse's (or ex-spouse's) company. You may be due some employee benefits, including up to three years of health insurance at group rates. The employer is supposed to notify you about the group health policy. To get it, you have to apply very soon after the death or divorce.

· Find work, if you need it, perhaps through a temporary help agency.

SORT-OF-MARRIED. More than single but less than married, you have only to change the locks to "divorce." You need:

· Separate bank accounts. Contribute to common bills in proportion to earnings. If one of you earns only 30 percent of the total, that person should pay only 30 percent of the expenses. It's not fair to hit him or her for 50 percent.

· Separate property. One buys the lamps, one buys the couch, so that ownership is clear.

· Written agreements for property bought together. What happens to it if you split up? If one of you dies?

· A will, to be sure that the other gets—or doesn't get—what you intend. With no will, everything goes to your family, not to your partner.

· The same health, disability, and living-will protection that you'd give yourself as a single person. If you both work, you need no life insurance, unless there are children. If you decide that one of you won't work, protect that person with an insurance policy. In a few jurisdictions, a "domestic partner" might be covered by the other's employee-benefits plan.

These lists tell you generally what you need. The rest of this book tells you how to get it. As you read, you can construct your own financial plan, chapter by chapter—adding, subtracting, revising, updating—one step at a time.

2
THE ULTIMATE WISH LIST:

What You've Got and Where You're Going

———

Need rises with income. What was out of the
question when you made $25,000 becomes
urgent at $40,000 and indispensable at
$70,000.

Your own financial plan starts with a wish list. Write it all down, every single thing. A speedboat. A week in Barbados. State U for two children. Enough money to retire early. Forget that you can't afford it. More likely, you only *think* you can't. The whole reason to have a financial plan is to focus yourself on what matters most and work out a strategy for getting it.

So get out a yellow pad and a pencil and start dreaming. On the left side of the pad, write "What I want." On the right, side write "When I want it"—next summer? 1994? 2001? In the middle, write "How I get there from here." That middle column is the *terra incognita* that this book will fill in. You are going to develop some real numbers and a real timetable, so you won't still be dreaming five years from now.

Once you've listed all your material wants, stare off into space and think. You can have it all, but the cost of getting it might be an extra job, working nights and weekends, working to a later age than you'd intended, or hanging on to a job you hate. Is it worth it? Or would you rather take that speedboat off your wish list?

When reflecting on this question, take another piece of paper and write down your personal goals. Don't kid yourself. If money and status are important, say so. Do you want to write a book by the time you're 30? Start a business? Spend more time with the kids? Move to the country? Become a top officer of your corporation? Give more time to charity? All the things you most care about are likely to affect how much money you'll have, which in turn will shape your financial plan. The planning process asks you to set priorities and make trade-offs.

The plan you finally develop may not work—at least, not exactly. Some things may go better than expected, others may go worse. You may fall behind schedule. You may filch money for a new car that should have gone into the education fund.

But the point is, *you'll know it.* You'll see the hole in your kids' tuition account and you'll figure out how to make it up. The reason financial plans succeed is almost stupidly simple. It's their specificity. Instead of vague hopes, you have hard targets—something concrete that you're working toward every year. Once you *see* it, you can get it.

YOUR BASIC SECURITY PACKAGE

Back to your yellow pad. I know you've remembered to list "Barbados vacation." But one or two other things might have slipped your mind, without which your prettier plans might be undone. Here is your basic security package:

1. *Life insurance.* Do you have enough? If you die, your spouse needs enough to support himself or herself. Your children need support and education. Part of that money will probably come from the surviving spouse's earnings. You need just enough insurance to cover the rest. For how much life insurance to buy, see Chapter 12.

2. *Disability insurance.* Most people are covered if they die. But what if you fall off a ladder, break your back, and live? That's the risk nobody thinks about (or wants to). You need two levels of disability coverage: (1) for a short illness of 6 to 12 months, during which you'd try to keep your way of life intact, and (2) for a permanent disability, usually requiring a drop in your standard of living. For how large a policy you need, see Chapter 14.

3. *Health insurance.* You probably get it from the company you work for. If not, call Blue Cross or a health maintenance organization—and don't leave home without it. Nursing-home policies are improving rapidly, but they're not yet for younger people. Shop for this coverage when you pass 60. See Chapter 13.

4. *Repaying debt.* It's pointless to save money at 7 percent interest while you're still supporting a Visa Card habit at 18 percent. Pay off the Visa first. Often, the best use of savings is to pay off the debts that are costing you more than the savings earn. For ways of saving more money, see Chapter 9.

5. *Owning a home.* How much do you need for a down payment and how will you raise it? The lucky ducks go to the Daddy Bank. Failing that, you will have to throw every resource you have at the problem. For ways of finding the money for a home of your own, see Chapter 17.

6. *College.* How much will college cost when your children reach 18, and how long do you have to accumulate the money? Four years at the average public college cost around $33,000 this year. For the average private college, it's around $63,000. The most selective and expensive schools are nearing $100,000. You'll find a list of college saving and investing plans in Chapter 20.

7. *Fun and games.* Put some luxuries on your list. A new kitchen. An RV. Skiing in Aspen. August at the race track. Estimate what they will cost (except for the race track, where you'll *make* money, right?), and when you will want them. Chapter 8 tells you how to fit them into your plan.

8. *Retirement income.* How much will you need to retire on? A younger person hasn't a clue. Too many incalculables exist, in the economy and your personal life. Still, you ought to make a start. By your late forties, the picture should be coming clear. For the book on retirement planning, see Chapter 29.

For your pains, you now have a daunting list of expenses:

1. The price of more life insurance.

2. The price of a disability policy.

3. The price of health insurance, if you don't have a company plan.

4. The extra monthly payments needed to reduce your consumer debts.

5. How much you'll have to save each month for a down payment on a home.

6. The cost of your children's college and the length of time you have to raise the money.

7. The price of anything special you want for yourself, and how long you have to save for it.

8. The amount of money you'll need for a decent retirement.

Some of you are starting out at the top of this list; others are already partway down. In either case, the total may look unattainable. But I promise it's not. It's like running a marathon: You do one mile at a time until you finish.

FINDING THE MONEY

Winning a lottery would be nice. Maybe you could marry a rich Texan (there *are* some left). An inheritance is dandy, the drawback being how you get it.

Windfalls aside, there are only three ways of getting the money you need to underwrite a financial plan: culling current income, taking loans, and using the gains from your savings and investments. But everything ultimately springs from income, which sets up your savings and pays off your debts.

No plan will succeed if you live to the brink of your income and beyond. You *must* hold back something for savings and investments. "No way," you say? "It takes $50,000 just to pay the grocer?" Sure, but only if you build your life that way. Every single one of us can look down the street and see someone living well on $5,000 less a year than we make. That's $5,000 we could be saving every year and still hold up our heads in the neighborhood. Only by living on less than you make will you ever be able to live on more than you make.

KEEPING SCORE

Start our your plan by figuring your present net worth. Recalculate it once a year. These figures, and the changes in them, will show you a lot of interesting things:

· Whether your debts are under control. Is your indebtedness growing faster than the money you're saving?

· How well you're investing the money you save. Does your investment account generally rise in value? Or are you losing money faster than you're putting it away?

· How much money you could lay your hands on in an emergency. Do you have a enough readily salable assets to help you through a bad patch, or are too many of your assets tied up?

· Whether you need more life and disability insurance. What income could you get from your assets compared with how much you need to live on?

To find your net worth, add up the value of everything you own (your *assets*), figured at what you could reasonably sell each item for. Then subtract everything you owe (your *liabilities*). The remainder is your net worth. It's the money you'd have if you converted all of your property into cash and paid off your debts. If you owe more than you own, you have a "negative net worth," and maybe an ulcer. ("I'm going to be a millionaire," a friend of mine who was a gambler used to say. "I'll die owing a million dollars." He came close.)

Your aim is to raise your net worth every year, through a combination of new savings and sound investments.

Just as important, you need a good balance between assets that are tied up, like your house, and assets that can quickly be turned into cash.

Those parts of your net worth that are always on tap are your *quick assets*, like cash, mutual funds, stocks, bonds, and life insurance cash values. You fall back on your quick assets in an emergency

Those parts that might take a long time to sell are the *slow assets*, like most real estate. Don't load up on slow assets until you have plenty of quick assets on tap.

Some of your net worth is effectively frozen. I'd include here that portion of your home equity against which the bank won't make a loan; an interest in a limited partnership that can't be sold easily; money owed to you at some point in the future; a lump sum due from your pension plan. Mentally, you might also add a pending inheritance, although it doesn't belong on your personal balance sheet until it's actually yours.

Yet another part of your net worth is *restricted*, in that it can be reached only by paying a penalty. This includes most unmatured certificates of deposit; a tax-deferred company 401(k) plan; certain retirement-savings annuities used by employees of public schools and some nonprofit organizations; various other forms of pension savings—like Individual Retirement Accounts, Keogh plans, and tax-deferred annuities—if you're younger than age 59½.

When figuring your net worth: (1) You don't have to know the exact value of everything. A ballpark estimate will do. (2) To find out what your bonds and unit trusts are currently worth, ask your stockbroker to price them for you. They will bring more or less than face value, depending on market conditions today. (3) Sherlock Holmes couldn't ferret out the value of limited-partnership shares, unless they're traded publicly. Ask your stockbroker whether he can sell them and for how much. If no one is biting, list the shares at zero. When the partnership dissolves, thank the gods for every dollar you get back. (4) In a pinch, you could sell your cars and jewelry. But you won't, so they're not truly part of your usable net worth. You need to know their current value only to keep them well insured.

YOUR NET WORTH
Date _____

WHAT YOU OWN (Assets)

	Amount
Quick Assets	
Cash in checking, ready savings, and money market mutual funds	$____
Other mutual funds	____
Stocks, bonds, government securities, unit trusts	____
Publicly traded partnerships	____
Other easily salable investments	____
Money due you for work you've done	____
Life insurance cash values	____
Precious metals	____
Easily salable personal property: jewelry, silver, cars	____
Restricted Assets	
Certificates of deposit, if they have early withdrawal penalties	____
Retirement accounts: IRAs, Keoghs, tax-deferred annuities, company thrift accounts, deferred salary	____
Current worth of your vested pension, if payable in a lump sum	____
Executive stock options	____
Slow Assets	
Your home	____

Other real estate   ____
Art and antiques   ____
Other valuable personal property: furs, boats, tools, stamps,
   coins   ____
Restricted stock, not readily salable   ____
Limited partnerships, not readily salable   ____
Money owed you in the future   ____
Equity value of a business   ____
TOTAL ASSETS   ____

WHAT YOU OWE (Liabilities)

	Amount	Interest Rate
Current bills outstanding: this month's rent, utilities, medical bills, insurance premiums, etc.	$____	
Credit card debt	____	____
Installment and auto loans	____	____
Life-insurance loans (if you're paying them off currently)	____	____
Home mortgage	____	____
Home equity loan	____	____
Other mortgages	____	____
Student loans	____	____
Loans against investments, including your margin loans	____	____
Other loans	____	____
Income and real-estate taxes due	____	____
Taxes due on your investments if you cash them in	____	
Taxes and penalties due on your retirement accounts, if you cash them in	____	
TOTAL LIABILITIES	____	
NET WORTH (Assets minus liabilities)	____	

PATCHING YOUR SAFETY NET

Optimist: "This is the best of all possible worlds."
Pessimist: "That's right."
So far, you've been thinking like an optimist. You're worth more

than you thought! Your pencil is flying! Your stock options will pay off your loans and then you'll be on easy street! All it will take is a few more years.

But what if you don't have a few more years?

Here's where the average plan comes a cropper. How would your family manage if you died? How would you live if you had an accident and couldn't work anymore? There would be some income, from disability insurance, Social Security, spouse's earnings, and so on, but not enough. You'd also have to live on your savings.

To measure the real strength of your position, you have to look at your net worth in another way. How much cash would be available to you or your family, if you had to marshall all of your assets to live on?

Start with the figures you reached above, and assume three things: (1) You (or your survivor) would not sell your house, one car, and personal property; (2) all other slow assets would be converted to cash; (3) your restricted assets would be freed up for use.

YOUR SURVIVOR'S USABLE CASH
Date _____

ASSETS
Quick Assets (not counting life-insurance cash values, one car,
   and other personal property) $____
Restricted Assets   ____
Slow Assets (not counting your house and personal property
   that your spouse would want to keep)   ____
Proceeds from Life Insurance   ____
TOTAL USABLE ASSETS FOR SURVIVOR   ____

LIABILITIES
Loans Against Insurance Policies $____
Death Costs, including funeral and estate administration, up to
   5 percent of assets   ____
Taxes, including final income tax return and estate taxes, if
   you're wealthy enough to owe them   ____
TOTAL   ____

MONEY LEFT FOR SURVIVOR (Usable assets minus
   liabilities) $____

You need a large enough nest egg so that—when it is combined with other sources of income—your dependents will have enough to meet their expenses. If your savings fall short, fill the gap with more life insurance. If your household depends on two paychecks, make these calculations twice—first assuming that the husband dies, then assuming the death of the wife.

If you think that your family would move to a smaller house at your death, they would net some money from the sale of the house you own now. Add those funds to their assets.

DISABILITY IS ANOTHER STORY. There's no life-insurance payoff, so your usable assets are much smaller. I've shown few liabilities here, because you can't predict your lump-sum expenses. Even the size of your uninsured medical bills is a question. You have three ways to prepare for a disability: Get a better disability insurance policy, save more, or invest better.

Use this same calculation for early retirement.

YOUR USABLE CASH, IF YOU'RE DISABLED
Date _____

ASSETS
Quick Assets (except for one car and personal property) $____
Restricted Assets   ____
Slow Assets (not counting your house and any personal
   property you want to keep)   ____
TOTAL USABLE ASSETS   ____

LIABILITIES
Taxes on funds you withdraw from retirement accounts $____
Uninsured Medical Bills (make a guess)   ____
TOTAL   ____

MONEY ON TAP (Usable assets minus liabilities)   ____

There is one more way of measuring your personal security. Do you have enough quick assets to cover all the bills coming due this year? That would give you a 12-month breathing space, if you lost your job. Figure it this way:

1. How much has to be paid on your debts over the next 12 months? Call this your Current Debt. $____

2. How large are your quick assets, not counting personal property and life-insurance cash values? Call this your Ready Money. $____

3. Your Ready Money should be greater than your Current Debt. If not, you are living with a lot of risk. As time passes, your Ready Money should grow larger and larger than your Current Debt.

ROUNDUP DAY

Once a year, sit down with your spouse (if you're single, sit down with yourself) and see where you stand. Go over everything. Are you spending too much? Did you save enough money? Should you change your investments? Did your net worth improve? Do you need more insurance? What financial goal will you shoot for in the next 12 months? What personal purchases would you like to make?

I call this annual accounting *Roundup Day.* A good time for it is the week between Christmas and New Year's, when things are slow. Another good time is the week you do your income taxes, when every money nerve is tingling. Working couples need this day, to tally their separate investments. Spouses who don't handle the family money need this day, to keep in touch. *Everyone* needs this day, to gloat over triumphs, fix mistakes, remember what you're doing, and freshen your resolve.

HOW MUCH IS ENOUGH?

You don't have to get richer every year. At some level of personal security, all you need is enough growth to keep your assets even with inflation. Knowing when to quit and go fishing is just as important as knowing when to keep your shoulder to the wheel.

My job is to help you grow wealthier and more secure. But not everyone is so lucky. Accidents happen. Investments fail. Companies fold. So here's a heretical thought: If your income drops, is that so bad? Is it so terrible to live in a cheaper place with fewer clothes and luxuries? People live happy lives who earn $5,000 less than you, and so do people who earn $5,000 less than they.

I wish you every increase. But if the gods frown, there are worse things in life than stepping down.

3

I HAVE IT RIGHT
HERE SOMEWHERE:

The Right Way to Keep Records

———

(Don't go away. I'm still looking.)

Okay, I confess.

Sitting here, right now, I can't remember the name of my life insurance company. My husband has both keys to the safe deposit box in his office but I'm not sure where. In the pile of papers on the floor to the left (I think) there's the booklet explaining the changes in my group health insurance. In short, I am often a slob about my own financial records.

But I am reforming. Writing this chapter has embarrassed me into reorganizing the Quinn family's scattered financial files. And take my word for it: When you finish this kind of job you feel clean—as if you had shined all your shoes and cleaned up the cellar.

With good records:

YOU CAN FIND THINGS. I estimate 84 hours saved per year, right there.

YOU CAN REMEMBER WHAT YOU HAVE. Did you sign that power of attorney? Did you fill in the form that lets you take money out of your mutual fund by phone? Now you'll know.

YOU CAN REMEMBER WHAT YOU DON'T HAVE. No, you didn't sign that power of attorney, because you kept misplacing it. Now that you're putting your records together, you'll get it done.

YOU CAN SAVE MONEY FOR YOUR HEIRS. They will be able to find things, too, without paying a lawyer to do detective work for them. They won't shake their heads and mutter, "What a mess."

YOU CAN FEEL TERRIFICALLY SMART AND WELL-ORGANIZED.

YOU WILL KNOW THAT, IF A CEILING FELL ON YOUR HEAD THIS VERY MOMENT, YOUR HEIRS WOULD GET EVERY DIME THAT WAS COMING TO THEM. Sometimes, a deed, a contract, or a bankbook is hidden away and never found. Lawyers tell story after story about stumbling across a stray piece of paper that entitled a widow to money that she didn't know anything about. Think of the numbers of widows who throw those pieces of paper away.

WHERE TO KEEP RECORDS

Invest in a file cabinet. It doesn't have to be steel; cardboard works fine. You can tuck a two-drawer cabinet under a table. Or use it as a table. Don't put it in the attic or behind the tennis rackets under the stairs! Unless your cabinet is so handy that you practically trip over it, you'll put off filing your records, which means that your system will fall apart.

Eventually, back tax returns and old bank records will overflow your file drawers. Don't compulsively save everything with your name and a dollar sign on it. Some records can be thrown away (see "What to Keep, What to Toss," below). Put beloved old statements that you can't part with into labeled boxes on closet shelves.

What? You had a fire? I forgot to tell you . . . invest in a fireproof home safe or locked file, or a bank safe deposit box, for records that are a pain in the neck to replace. Throw in pictures of all your clothes and furniture. After a fire, you'll have to prove to a fish-eyed insurance investigator that although you lived modestly your possessions were worth a fortune.

A home safe should be rated for fire resistance by the Underwriters Laboratory. You need a class 350 safe, which protects paper documents against high heat for at least half an hour and perhaps up to four. If you keep computer records on floppy discs, you'll need a class 125 safe. An unrated metal box won't do anything except keep incurious children out; in a fire, the heat would scorch to ashes any documents inside.

These safes, incidentally, won't stop a burglar for a moment—they're only for papers. You might as well write the combination on the top, to save a thief the trouble of whacking off the lock. To protect valuables at home, you need a much more expensive vault. When you go on vacation, put good jewelry and silver into a safe deposit box.

Safe deposit boxes are normally rented from a bank, although they are increasingly being offered by S&L's and even a few credit unions. Small boxes, for holding papers and a little jewelry, cost around $10 to $50 a year. For a lot of valuables, or your irreplaceable hubcap collection, the bank has larger boxes at a higher price.

Sometimes there's a waiting list, especially for the bigger boxes. As an alternative, you might look at a private vault company. It charges more than banks but is supposed to follow bank security procedures and may even offer 24-hour access—handy for dropping off your diamonds after the ball. If you have something to hide, it will interest you to know that most private vaults let you open an account under a false name (banks require identification). On the downside, private vaults may not provide all the security that customers were promised. Many have gone bankrupt. Personally, I wouldn't go near one.

When you rent a safe deposit box, you sign a card. The bank or vault will also need the signatures of anyone with access to the box—your spouse, your secretary, a friend. Every time you visit your diamonds or hubcaps you sign again, so that your signature can be checked. It takes two keys to open the box, yours and the bank's. You get two copies of your own key. If you lose one, no problem; it costs maybe $5 to $10 to replace. But it might cost $75 to $100 if you lose both. The bank doesn't keep a copy of your key, so it has to drill into your box and start you out with a brand new lock.

What to keep in your safe deposit box depends on how easy it is to enter the box right after you die. About half the states allow your executor free access to the box. Even more states let your spouse in, if the two of you owned the box jointly (although other joint owners may be kept out). The rest of the states seal the box until the contents can be inventoried—just in case you were hiding millions in cash. The bank may be allowed to search a sealed safe deposit box for a will, military discharge papers, or a cemetery deed. In a few states, only the will can be removed immediately.

If all you keep in your safe deposit box is some jewelry, your marriage license, and old Topps baseball cards, state laws are no problem. Nor are they a problem in the states that don't seal boxes at death. But where boxes are sealed, don't use them for papers that your survivors will need right away. Ask the bank or private vault company what the rules are.

If you and your spouse keep separate boxes, give each other access, just in case something happens. Consider putting a friend's name on the signature card, too, so someone else can enter in an emergency. You don't have to give your friend (known as your "deputy") a key, but tell him or her where you keep it.

Don't count on your deputy to clean out the box before the taxman cometh. A deputy's access ends when you die, whether the state seals the box or not. It also ends if you become mentally incapable. With a jointly owned box, access terminates if both joint owners die. So your deputy doesn't have much wiggle room. He or she can get into the box only if you keep all your marbles, if one joint owner stays alive, and if the box remains unsealed.

If you own a business, get a company safe deposit box. These boxes are never sealed at death, so you and your spouse can keep your wills and insurance policies there.

Unfortunately, nothing in this world is 100 percent secure, not even safe deposit boxes. If a thief breaks in, the bank or vault company is not responsible for your losses, unless you can prove negligence. Federal deposit insurance isn't responsible, either. It covers only your deposit accounts. But your homeowners or tenants insurance should pay, up to the limits of your policy (see page 363). After a theft, you do have to prove what you kept in the box, which is not always an easy job. Keep receipts, appraisals, and photos, including a photo of your box with the valuables in it.

Tell your heirs where the box is and where you keep the keys. If you keep a home safe, note the combination to the lock in your personal-money file.

WHAT TO KEEP, WHAT TO TOSS

Clarity, clarity. A filing system should be so logical that anyone who opens the drawers can find exactly what he or she wants. Label every folder, choosing titles that are sensible, not cute. If a financial document doesn't fit exactly into one of the categories you have already, start a new file for it. Keep weeding out documents that don't apply any longer. No sense sending your heirs on wild goose chases.

The Will

You have one, of course. A good-looking, clever, glowing social success like you wouldn't be so dumb as to go without. The only reason I even put Chapter 6 in this book (it's about writing wills) is that that was the only way to get from Chapter 5 to Chapter 7. Chapter 6. It's on page 96. Just in case.

It is simple and safe to leave the will with your lawyer, keeping a copy for yourself. On your copy, put the lawyer's name, address, and phone number. The drawback—if you see it that way—is that your family might feel forced to use that particular lawyer to handle your estate. They don't have to. They can retrieve the will and pick a different lawyer. If you think that would embarrass them, keep the will yourself.

Keep it somewhere safe and accessible. Maybe a fireproof home safe. Maybe a safe deposit box. Before putting the will into your safe deposit box, find out from the bank what happens to the box when you die. Is it sealed? Can it be opened only in the presence of a tax agent? Can it be opened instantly, to retrieve the will? If there might be some delay, don't put it in your box—or in your spouse's box, either. The two of you might die together. Put it in someone else's box—your executor's, a family member's, your company box if you own your own business. If none of these solutions make sense, keep it with your lawyer. Whenever you make a new will, destroy the old one along with all copies.

The Power of Attorney

Put it in a fireproof home safe (as long as the person you named knows the combination). Or give it to that person for safekeeping in his or her safe deposit box (I assume that you trust her; otherwise, you wouldn't have given her the power). Don't put this important document into your own safe deposit box. Your friend can't get into it if you become mentally incapable—which is just when the power of attorney may have to be used. If you own your own business, you could keep the document in the business's box and give your friend access. Keep your copy in your file at home.

The Living Will

This is the piece of paper that says, "If I'm in a permanent coma, pull the plug." Keep it in your fireproof home safe where people can find it. Give executed copies to the people who will make those ultimate choices in accordance with your wishes: your spouse, a friend, your doctor (see page 118).

Life Insurance Policies

Keep them in your safe deposit box only if the bank assures you that, under state law, your beneficiary can get them immediately. Include all correspondence affecting the policy, such as change-of-beneficiary notices or proof that ownership of the policy has been transferred to someone else. Add the name, address, and phone number of your insurance agent.

If your box will be sealed at your death, keep the policies and supporting material in your file cabinet or fireproof home safe. As backup, put the name and address of your insurance company and insurance agent, and your policy number, on the Master List (page 49) that's kept in your safe deposit box.

In the same file, include a note about any insurance you have through your employer and how to claim it. File your receipts for mortgage-life and credit-life insurance, if you've bought any. These policies pay off your loans if you die. If your executor doesn't know about them, money will be wasted paying off those loans out of your estate.

You probably have some other forms of coverage that your executor should know about. For example, if you charge a travel ticket to a credit card, it may generate $100,000 or more of life insurance. You might be covered for accidental death and dismemberment, whether you travel by plane, train, bus, or ship. Ditto if your accident occurs in an airline terminal or while traveling on public transportation to or from the terminal.

The government will cancel your guaranteed student loan, your PLUS loan, or your Supplemental Loan to Students if you die or become permanently disabled.

Credit union members sometimes have small life-insurance policies linked to their savings accounts.

If you belong to the American Automobile Association, you may be covered if you die in an auto accident.

Other clubs and organizations sometimes offer small policies as part of your membership package.

Clues to any payments of this sort should be kept in your life-insurance file.

Health and Disability Insurance Policies

You say you have a pain in your side? Your doctor wants your gall bladder out? If you don't get a second opinion and an okay from your insurance company, your health insurance might not pay. Keep the insurance policy, or the booklet explaining it, in your file cabinet. Ditto your disability-income policy. As backup, keep the names of your health-insurance companies, the policy numbers, the phone number of your company's employee-benefits office, or the name of your insurance agent in your home safe or safe deposit box, as well as on your Master List (page 49).

Homeowners, Tenants, and Auto Insurance

You usually get a new policy every 6 or 12 months, but don't throw the old ones out. If someone was injured on your property 18 months ago and develops back pains from a previously undiscovered crack in a spinal disc, you'll want to be able to prove that you were insured at the time. Your insurance company should have all the records. But you need backup, just in case the computers have lost track. Furthermore, the language of insurance policies changes over the years. It could be important to know exactly what you were covered for when an injury occurred.

Keep recent policies in your safe deposit box. Your insurer can re-place them if they're burned, but it might take a week or a month. Also you can't rely on the company's computer to pick up all of the special riders you carry.

Keep old policies in a dead file (attic; closet shelf; junk room). State statutes of limitations normally run for two or three years from the time the medical problem is discovered. So you could be sued for an injury years after it happened.

As usual, put the names of these insurance companies, the policy numbers, and the name of your insurance agent in your home safe or safe deposit box. If you bought special riders for things like furs, art, jewelry, and silver, include appraisals of their current value or sales slips showing what you paid for them.

Household Inventory

I'm not your mother, I don't care that your room is messy and that you don't write. But you still haven't done your household inventory, and how many times do I have to tell you? I know it's boring. I know that you started out in the living room, put your pencil down while you made some coffee, and never got any further. That's because you were using a pencil. The simple way is to use a camera. Take pictures of every room, every open closet, every open drawer. Keep sales slips for anything that's unusually expensive. Otherwise, you'll have to compile an inventory of all your possessions from memory if your house burns down.

Put your pictures and records in your safe deposit box. If you use a home safe instead, stash copies at a friend's house, in case your safe isn't quite as fireproof as promised.

Personal Papers

Anything you need to prove who you are, how long you've been around, and what you've been up to belongs in a fireproof home safe or safe deposit box. This includes birth certificate, marriage certificate, all documents relating to separation and divorce, military-service records, citizenship or adoption papers, diplomas, licenses, passports, permits, union cards, Social Security cards, and family health records such as vaccinations and dates of operations. Keep a passport that has expired. It makes it easier to get a new one. Don't stash your military records before checking with the service to be sure that its dates agree with yours. If the service has them wrong and your survivors don't realize it, they might not get all the benefits they're due.

Tax Records

Yes, I know. You accidentally added the veterinarian's bill to your deductible medical expenses. How long does the IRS have to catch you and fine you? Three years—during which time you'd better keep not only your tax return but all supporting data. After that, you're in the clear and can toss the return—unless the vet is the least of it. The government has six years to audit you if you underreported your income by more than 25 percent. If it pursues you for fraud, or if you filed no tax returns at all, there is no statute of limitations; you can be hit for back taxes anytime. If you lose any federal tax return for the past six years, the IRS charges only $4.25 to replace it (although it can't replace your supporting data).

Keep the tax return that shows the capital gain you're carrying forward on your house. You'll need that information when you sell.

And keep the returns that show any contributions you made to an

Individual Retirement Account that were not tax deductible. You'll need these records to establish your tax when you finally take the money out.

History buffs keep tax returns for many years, because of the personal information in them—like who you worked for and what you earned—and as proof that you filed, should the IRS ask.

Bank Records

Some people keep all their canceled checks: Some weed them out, keeping only those they might need for tax or insurance purposes. I favor weeding your older checks (starting three years back), to keep the paper storage down. But I keep the newer ones. You never know when they'll come in handy. Here are eight good reasons to keep canceled checks:

1. If you want to make a budget, old checks are a roadmap to what you've been spending.

2. The IRS might disagree with your version of life and ask for proof. Canceled checks can sometimes stand in for receipts, in substantiating tax deductions (although usually the IRS wants receipts).

3. Old checks show the names of the people you've done business with and might want to find again.

4. It's easier to collect in full on a property-insurance claim if you can show the company what you paid for your rugs, furniture, and other damaged items.

5. When you sell your house at a profit, every nickel you spent improving the property cuts the size of your taxable gain. Canceled checks remind you of what everything cost. What's a tax-saving improvement? Anything that raises the value or lengthens the life of your house—adding a room, putting on a new roof, remodeling the kitchen, landscaping. You can even count repairs and maintenance, like patching the roof and painting, as long as it's done to fix up a house in the 90 days before it's sold.

6. Your ex-spouse might claim that you missed some child-support payments. If you didn't, your canceled checks will prove it.

7. You might have to prove to one of your creditors that a bill was paid. For this purpose, keeping checks for six months should be enough.

8. If you're one-half of an unmarried couple, and own property jointly, the checks prove what you paid for, which could be important if you split or your mate dies.

Some banks don't return canceled checks anymore. They just send you a statement showing which checks were cashed, which is easier to file.

If you also have loans or certificates of deposit, keep the most recent statements showing their status (old ones can be tossed.) When you make new deposits, keep the receipts until the monthly statement comes in, so you can check that they were entered correctly. Keep loan agreements and any passbooks for open savings accounts. Keep copies of letters that confirm the instructions you gave about your accounts or CDs. Throw these records out when the loan or account is closed. Keep all disclosures you get from the bank about its fees and interest rates, so that you can check any changes you question.

Be especially meticulous about record keeping if you have any money in a bank or S&L that's known to be troubled. If it fails, your federally insured deposits are always safe, but the institution's records might be a mess. You may have to prove how much money you deposited, when, and at what interest rate.

Paycheck Stubs

If you trust your employer to add up your earnings correctly (as I do), you can throw them away.

Receipts for Paid Bills

In your file cabinet: Keep receipts for every expense that is tax deductible—ideally, clipped to the check you paid it with. The IRS prefers both, if you're ever audited. (Some expenses that aren't deductible on your federal return might still be on your state return.)

In your fireproof safe or safe deposit box: Keep receipts for high-cost purchases like furs and antiques. They'll prove your claim, if you have to dicker with the insurance company after a fire or theft. Also keep receipts and canceled checks for home-improvement expenses (see "Bank Records," page 43).

In a box on your bureau or desk: Keep receipts for gifts until you know that you won't have to take them back. If you pay in cash, keep the receipt long enough to be sure that the item is in good working order. Throw other receipts out. Your canceled check is normally proof enough of payment.

Medical and Drug Bills

Keep them for a year. Any uninsured bills exceeding 7.5 percent of your adjusted gross income are deductible on your tax return. But you have to be pretty sick, and pretty poorly insured, to qualify for this writeoff. If you get no tax deduction, throw the bills away. (The super-cautious keep medical bills for three years. If something should change on their tax return that lowers their income—don't ask me what—a borderline miss could turn into a deduction.)

Monthly Credit Card Statements

Check every one, as soon as it comes, to be sure that every bill is actually yours. A thief needs only your credit card number and a telephone in order to buy goods and charge them to your account.

Keeping these statements is optional. Personally, I hang on to them for two or three years. Who knows when an item charged and paid for will erroneously pop up on my bill again? Who knows what will break and need returning—and how else will I remember the name of the store? Who knows when I'll want to look up the name of that great Cajun restaurant in Biloxi? Back bills also help you track your spending and draw a budget. But if you never use these records, toss them. As of 1991, you don't even need them for income-tax reasons because the personal deduction for credit card interest has expired. You now need to keep records only of the interest you paid on business purchases.

When you take something back to a store, you'll get a return receipt. Keep it right where you open your mail, to remind you to check that the money was actually credited to your account. Then throw the receipt away.

Deeds, Titles, Title Insurance, Surveys

Records of purchase, property descriptions, and proofs of ownership —including the title to your car—belong in your fireproof home safe or safe deposit box. Copies are available, if you lose the originals. But it's simpler to protect the records you have.

Debts

In the file cabinet: Your mortgage, bank-loan records, contracts for installment purchases. No problem, if a fire burns them up. Your creditors will remember. They'll even have copies.

But paid-off debts are another story. Get a receipt for the canceled note and keep it in your safe deposit box. Proof of payment is especially important when you borrow money from an individual. She may note the debt in her records and forget to erase it. When she dies, her heirs might ask you (or your survivors) for payment. The receipt shows that you're clean.

Money Owed to You

Keep the note in your home safe or safe deposit box. Keep the repayment records in your file cabinet. When you get all your money back, cancel the note.

Employee Benefits

They've gotten so complicated that companies often publish them in loose-leaf notebooks. File everything. Keep the annual statements on the status of your pension, profit-sharing, salary-deferral, or employee thrift plans, so you can follow their progress. Keep employment contracts in your home file, safe deposit box, or the office of the lawyer who negotiated them.

Retirement Plans

Write down the numbers and locations of all your retirement accounts—Keogh plans, Individual Retirement Accounts, tax-deferred annuities—and put them in the safe deposit box. Keep the plan documents in your file cabinet along with the annual reports showing how your investments are doing.

Investments

Your safe deposit box is the right place for the following items.

Stocks and other securities. Keep a list of their names, denominations, certificate numbers, and CUSIP numbers (for Committee on Uniform Securities Identification Procedures). If you lose a security, those numbers get you a duplicate. (The transfer agent who sent you the security should also have a record of its numbers.) Take great care with your securities. It's costly and time consuming to replace them (page 559).

Bonds and Treasury securities. All new U.S. Treasury securities exist only as blips in the mind of a government computer, so you have no actual certificates to store. Most corporate bonds and some municipals are also issued this way. But keep all your purchase records. You may need them to prove your ownership if an interest or principal payment goes astray.

A list of your U.S. Savings Bonds, showing their denominations, serial numbers, and issue dates.

Gold, silver, or platinum bars or coins that you want to hold personally.

The original prospectus and sales material for any limited partnerships you own. They may contain misrepresentations. If a deal goes bad, your prospectus could help establish grounds for a lawsuit. Also keep the quarterly and annual reports that chart the partnership's progress. They might be needed for a lawsuit, too.

The names and account numbers of your mutual funds and unit trusts.

What about all the informational material you get from your mutual fund or unit trust? In your file cabinet, keep the original prospectus and sales literature. They tell you what you bought, how to redeem shares, and the services offered to investors. Keep any letters that say the fund has changed its rules. Whether to keep the quarterly and annual reports depends on how closely you follow your investments. If you only check prices, throw out the reports. But a continuing series of letters from management is valuable to investors who compare promise with performance. When you finally sell out, dump all but the buy-and-sell records, which you'll need for income-tax purposes.

If you trade through a stockbroker, you have three choices: Keep the securities in a fireproof safe at home, in a safe deposit box, or at the brokerage house. For investors who buy and sell a lot, the broker is probably the best choice. It saves mailing securities back and forth. Brokerage firms insure accounts for at least $500,000 and sometimes much more. But if you trade only occasionally, you might prefer having the securities under your control. For more on this issue, see page 558.

File your brokerage house agreement, annual statements, and dividend reinvestment statements. Keep all confirmations of trades. You have to know exactly when each security was bought and sold, the price, and the commission you paid, in order to figure out your income tax. When you get your annual statement of account, which summarizes all transactions, keep it and throw the monthly statements out.

Take notes of all conversations you have with your broker. Put all your instructions in writing, including follow-up letters after a phone conversation. Keep copies. If you get into an argument about how the broker handled your account these records can support your case.

If you're a casual investor, betting your money on someone else's say-so, there's no point cluttering your file drawers with the quarterly and annual reports sent by companies whose stocks you own. But at least read them before tossing them out. Maybe you'll learn something. If you're really following the company, you'll keep these reports in your files until you sell.

Rental Properties

For reference, keep a couple of years' worth of income and expense records in your current files. Older receipts belong on the shelf with your back tax records.

Business at Home

There you are, in the spare-bedroom-turned-office, trading currency futures for all the parents at your day care center. You know you can write off your telephone expenses (a separate phone line is best) against the potloads of profits you're making. But what else? For a home-based business, take a lesson from an accountant on how to keep track of income and expenses and what your tax deductions are. For example, you may be able to depreciate that part of the house that serves as your office. You might also write off a pro rata portion of your mortgage interest and real estate taxes, and even part of what you pay to heat, light, clean and insure your house. So you'll need to keep all those bills and canceled checks. Keep current bills in the filing cabinet and old bills with the tax records. Carry a business diary, to record tax deductible expenses for travel, entertainment, supplies, and so on. The IRS gets dark under the eyes when your diary reads as if you composed it just in time to make the audit.

Trust Documents

Keep the originals with your lawyer or in a safe deposit box. Put copies in your files.

Gifts

Keep receipts for tax-deductible charitable gifts with your tax records. Keep records of important gifts to friends and family members in your safe deposit box, if the gifts will affect the size of your estate tax or to keep the peace in a squabbling family.

In Case of Death

Keep a "last wishes" file. Include the cemetery deed, if you have one; material for your obituary (relatives often get things wrong); a list

of final instructions about your funeral, if it matters to yo.
of your living will, if you don't want to be kept alive by "ex
means. Don't bother including an Organ Donor card; by tl
found it will be too late. Keep the card in your wallet and   your
doctors and relatives that you want your organs to be used. Also tell your
relatives and executor about your living will and last-wishes file, and
where to find them. President Franklin D. Roosevelt made detailed notes
about how his funeral was to be conducted and put them in the White
House safe. They weren't found until after he was buried.

Safe Deposit Box Key

Drop it into a tool box. Keep it with the handkerchiefs. For obscurity
—the usual fate of a key to a safe-deposit box—those places are as good
as any. In my dreams, however, I see the key resting in your top desk or
bureau drawer, labeled, with the bank's name attached (what's the good
of a key if your survivors don't know which bank to take it to?). I see a
note on your Master List, telling everybody where it is. Ditto for the
combination to the lock on your home safe.

The Master List of Where Everything Is

Record the results of your masterful filing system on a couple of
sheets of paper and leave this Master List in your file for your executor
and heirs. If you have a home computer (that someone besides you
knows how to operate), keep it there, too. Tell your family where to find
it, so they won't tear the house apart looking for your records. List:

   · Your insurance policies and insurance agents.
   · Employee benefits and the phone number of the office that handles
them.
   · Bank accounts and any particular banker you deal with.
   · Where to find your safe deposit box and keys.
   · Where you keep your will, and the lawyer who drew it up.
   · Your executor.
   · Where trust documents are.
   · Where all your personal papers are.
   · Your brokers or investment advisors—names, addresses, and
phone numbers.
   · Your accountant.
   · Where to find your securities and retirement accounts.
   · Where your tax records are.

- What properties you own and where the deeds are.
- Your debts and any money owed you.
- Your Social Security number, and that of every family member.

Tell someone where you hide your home safe and give that person the combination to the lock.

Make a list of all your credit cards—account numbers, addresses, telephone numbers—in case your wallet is stolen and you have to cancel them.

Personal Spending Plans and Net Worth Records

You say you don't have any? Ah, but you will. Read on.

4
YOUR BASIC BANKING:

Finding a Bank That Even Your Mother
Would Love

———

Everyone needs a small-town banker. Especially
in a big town.

When you look for a bank, pick a
small institution. Or a small branch of a large institution. You get a lot
of personal help in a place where you're known, and the smaller the
place the sooner you're known. Small, independent banks and S&L's
may also charge lower fees than large ones. My small branch:

· Pushes the buttons for me when I mess up the automated teller
machine.

· Doesn't care whether I use the automated teller or not.

· Pays my young son's checks when they're written against funds
that haven't cleared yet, and waives the fees.

· Answers questions in a flash. If I ask the wrong person, the right
person answers from the next desk. Or hollers out the answer from the
vault room. Everyone always pays attention.

· Answers questions by telephone.

· Returns my calls.

· Fixes what's wrong.

· Calls to ask questions, if something happens in the account that they don't understand.

· Negotiates interest rates on mortgages and personal loans.

· Looks for ways to say yes.

· Goes to bat for me, against the parent company's bureaucracy.

"Aha," you say, "that's only because you write about this stuff." It's not. Only a handful of people operate my branch, and they know their customers—every one of them. The character of the manager is important. The manager sets the tone of any office, and mine goes out of the way to please. Not that big banks, or big branches, can't do a good job. Some have created a private-banking division for their big-bucks customers, which amounts to a small bank-within-the-bank. But in general, big banks try harder for corporate customers than for just plain folks. Individuals can't make the personal contacts that grease the wheels when you need a favor done.

Savings and loan associations work the same way: Smaller is usually better. S&L's may charge lower fees and pay higher interest rates than banks.

On the niceness scale, credit unions are often at the top. Enough of them offer better interest rates and lower banking fees to make it worth your while to take a look. Write to the Credit Union National Association (P.O. Box 431, Madison, WI, 53701) for the address of your state association. That association, in turn, will give you the names of credit unions that you might be able to join.

Some credit unions offer a limited fare: only checking accounts (known as share-draft accounts), savings deposits, and consumer lending. But others also offer mortgages, credit cards, and stockbrokerage at a discount. At the end of each year, a well-run credit union often has a surplus to distribute to members, either as a rebate of loan interest or as an extra dividend on savings.

But follow the rules below on judging interest rates and fees; the rates that some credit unions advertise aren't as generous as they sound. *And avoid any credit union that doesn't carry federal deposit insurance.* Around 10 percent of them still carry private coverage, which, as previous banking debacles show, can buckle under pressure.

Banklike services can also be had at large brokerage firms, through their asset-management accounts (page 548). But those are best used as convenience accounts for heavy investors. For everyday transactions, you still need a bank.

OPENING AN ACCOUNT

Don't just stop by a bank and wait to see someone who's free. Make an appointment with the person in charge of opening new accounts. That starts you out as a client, not just a customer.

Before going to the meeting, pick up the brochures that the bank stocks by the front door, describing its many services. Read them to see what you might want; write your questions in the margins.

At your meeting, get all your questions answered. And go further than that. Explain to the banker the kind of customer you expect to be. How much money will be flowing through your checking account. How much saving you expect to do. What services you will need. Find out who to call if you have a question or need some help. Above all, talk about the loans you might want. A home mortgage? Money for investments or for starting a business? What does the bank offer? What does it take to get a lower interest rate? Bankers love to make loans; that's how they make their money. They're especially attentive to potential borrowers, who can help them meet their loan budgets for the year.

Take the measure of the person you're meeting with. Is he or she helpful? Knowledgeable about the bank's products and services? Willing to answer your questions in detail? Ready with good ideas? Interested in getting your business? A banker who starts out gruff, impatient, vague, supercilious, or ill-informed will not improve with time—and what is tolerated in one bank officer will be tolerated in others. If you have a choice, go to a place that makes a better first impression.

Compare the fees and interest rates offered by two or three institutions. They're a statement of business philosophy. High-fee banks are likely to charge even more in the future; low-fee banks are dedicated to holding down overt costs. High savings-interest banks are telling you that they'll always be competitive; low-interest banks aren't. Those are messages to pay attention to.

DON'T SETTLE ON JUST ONE BANK. TAKE TWO. Different banks have different virtues. Each institution will want to get some of your business from the other, giving you a chance to negotiate lower fees and lower interest rates on loans.

WHICH CHECKING ACCOUNT?

No need to wander through the wilderness, wondering which of half-a-dozen checking accounts is best. Your choice is simple, because it hangs on a single test: What is the lowest average balance you will leave on deposit every month? If it's small, you'll probably get a checking account that pays no interest. To earn interest, you have to maintain an average of $1,000 or $2,500 on deposit, depending on the bank. The higher your minimum balance, the higher the interest rate you'll get.

There are two ways of figuring your minimum balance—one favorable to you, and one not.

You want a bank that uses the *average-daily-balance* method. This takes the amount you have in your account each day and averages it across the entire month. If you keep $5,000 there for 29 days, and on the thirtieth day write a $5,000 check, that month's average balance would be $4,833.

This is the truest way of figuring the value of your account to the bank and gives you the best chance of earning interest on your deposits. In arriving at your average daily balance, some banks will count both your checking and your savings deposits.

With the *low-balance* method, by contrast, the bank looks only at the lowest point in your account that month. If you held on to $5,000 for 29 days and then emptied your account, the bank would call your balance "zero." You would earn no interest. Worse, you would pay a fee for falling below the minimum balance.

When choosing among banking institutions, ask which of these two calculations is being used. If the banker doesn't know, he or she should make a phone call to find out. Reject the low-balance method. Smile at the banker, put down the brochures, and leave. Low-balance accounts don't pay you fairly. They may even force you to accept a checking account that pays no interest at all.

Besides interest rates and minimum deposits, look at the schedule of fees: monthly fees, per-check fees, ATM fees, and others. Don't let your banker's hand be quicker than your eye. A checking account might deliberately carry a low monthly fee, in order to make it look cheap to price-shoppers. But the bank might recoup by charging you extra for processing checks or using the ATM machines. This is especially true of banks that tout gimmicks, like extending the manufacturer's warranty for any product that you buy by check.

You want an account that pays the highest interest rate possible, on the balances you can afford to keep, while not breaking your back with extra fees. So look around. At GoodGuy S&L, your checking deposits might earn $75 a year. At BadGuy, exactly the same account might *cost* $150. Here is a general idea of what's around.

IF YOU KEEP A SMALL BALANCE AND WRITE IT DOWN ALMOST TO ZERO EVERY MONTH, LOOK AT:

NO-INTEREST CHECKING. These accounts carry one of two fee schedules: (1) a monthly maintenance charge and a charge per check, but no minimum balance, or (2) no maintenance charge and no charge per check, but a minimum balance of $300 to $500 and a fee for falling below the minimum. In either case, no interest is paid on your idle balances.

IF YOU CAN MAINTAIN A DECENT MINIMUM BALANCE AT ALL TIMES, LOOK AT:

NOW ACCOUNTS. You generally earn 5 to 5.5 percent interest on your idle balances and pay no check-processing charges or monthly fees. Average minimum balances run in the area of $500 to $1,000. But if you fall below the minimum or, in some cases, write more than a specified number of checks, fees start to mount.

SUPER-NOW ACCOUNTS. You earn a variable rate of interest, which is set by the bank. It's a little higher than the interest rate on the NOW account, and could be quite a bit higher in inflationary times. But you'll also face higher penalties for falling below the average minimum balance, which runs around $1,000 to $5,000.

TIERED ACCOUNTS. Many banks have dropped the distinction between NOW and Super-NOW accounts in favor of a single interest-paying checking account. The interest you earn, and the fees you pay, depend on how much money you keep there, and may vary from month to month.

BUNDLED ACCOUNTS. Your checking account may be "bundled" with other banking services, like free travelers checks, a line of credit at no annual fee, a credit card with a one-year waiver on the fee, discounts on loans, and a quarter-point interest bonus on various savings deposits. You get the whole package for a single low fee or no fee at all.

ASSET-MANAGEMENT ACCOUNTS. These are for active investors who want an easy way to keep track of their cash. They generally combine an interest-paying checking account with a brokerage account and a credit card. With asset-management accounts:

• Your cash earns money market interest rates.

• You can draw on your money with a special checkbook or a debit card.

• You may get a credit card, which can trigger a loan against any stocks you own.

• A single monthly statement shows all your investment and banking transactions.

• All dividends and interest are automatically reinvested at money market rates.

The minimum deposit (including the value of your stocks and bonds): $1,000 to as much as $25,000. Annual fees run from zero to $125. Asset-management accounts are offered by a few big banks, brokerage houses, some mutual funds, and a few insurance companies.

IF YOU HAVE A LOW INCOME AND WRITE ONLY A FEW CHECKS EVERY MONTH, LOOK FOR:

BASIC OR NO-FRILLS CHECKING. These accounts are for people who keep low average balances and write just a few checks a month. There's usually a small monthly fee and, often, access to your account by way of an automated teller machine. The first 10 or 15 checks (or more) may be free. This simplified service is offered by about half the banks—although it may be restricted to students or the elderly.

IF YOU SOMETIMES BOUNCE CHECKS, OR WANT TO HAVE INSTANT CREDIT ON TAP, GO FOR:

OVERDRAFT CHECKING. This is a line of instant credit. It lets you write checks for more money than you have in your bank account. The excess is a loan, on which you're charged a high rate of interest. Monthly repayments are often deducted from your account automatically. The right to use overdraft checking may cost you $10 or so a year.

TEST YOUR BANKER'S IQ

A good banker can answer all seven of the following questions. If you get a blank look—or a gentle drift of oral fog—ask again. You're entitled to a clear and simple statement that makes sense. If you don't understand what the banker is saying, don't blame yourself. Blame the banker, who probably doesn't have all the facts (and is covering up). If I had $10 for every "expert" who wasn't, I'd be rich.

1. *Ask:* With interest-paying checking, what does the bank pay interest *on?* Some pay on all the money that's in the account at the end

of each day, which is the fairest way. Some pay on the average daily balance for the month. Some pay on the average "collected" balance, which means that interest payments don't start until the checks that you deposit clear.

Some pay only on the lowest balance, which is a gyp. Here's why: If you had $3,000 in the account all month and wrote a $2,500 check at the very end, you'd receive monthly interest only on the $500 that remained. A number of credit unions that advertise high interest rates pay only on the lowest balance, so they are not as good a deal as they sound.

Some banks advertise more than one rate, depending on the size of your deposit. They might pay 5.5 percent on checking or savings deposits up to $1,000 and 7 percent on larger amounts. But what exactly does that mean? There's a good way and a bad way to figure it.

Say, for example, that you deposit $2,500. You might get 7 percent on the whole amount, usually called a *tiered* rate. That's good. Or you might get 5.5 percent on the first $1,000 and 7 percent only on the remaining $1,500, usually called a *blended* rate. That's bad. In fact, it's a clip job. Avoid blended rates.

2. *Ask:* What is the penalty for falling below the average minimum balance? Is it large enough to eat up the interest that your account is likely to earn? A 5.25 percent checking account might earn zero if you drop below the minimum. It might even wind up costing you money. If you can't be sure of maintaining the minimum deposit, go with a no-interest-paying account.

3. *Ask:* Can the bank *truncate* your checking account? With truncation, you get a monthly list of the checks you wrote but not the canceled checks themselves. If you need a copy of a check to prove that you made a particular payment, the bank might send it to you free —or it might charge one to five dollars. Most customers like to get canceled checks, but you rarely need them. Truncated accounts are often cheaper, because the bank may waive the monthly fee and minimum balance.

4. *Ask:* What fees might you have to pay with this account? You should get a list, including charges for maintaining the account, processing checks, bouncing checks, using an automated teller machine, using a human teller, buying checks printed with your name and address, confirming your current bank balance, buying certified checks, stopping payment on a check, and transferring funds by telephone.

5. *Ask:* Will the bank reduce the interest rate on your loans if you keep a checking account there and allow the loan payments to be deducted automatically?

6. *Ask:* If you buy a certificate of deposit or take out a loan, will the bank eliminate the fees it charges for your checking account? Most institutions give their better customers special breaks. Some tie-in deals, however, are not worth having. You might save yourself a quarter point on an auto loan by taking out a certificate of deposit. But that's no bargain, if cheaper auto loans are available somewhere else.

7. *Ask:* When you deposit a check, how long do you have to wait before being able to draw against the funds? By law, your bank has to tell you exactly what the rules are.

HOW FAST WILL YOUR CHECKS CLEAR?

There you stand, like a kid with his nose pressed against a pet-store window. Your money is romping behind the glass and you can't get at it. Any checks you deposit may be held by your bank until they clear.

If you write a check against deposited funds too soon, it will probably bounce. You'll pay $3 to $30 for the error. To bounce-proof your checks, sign up for overdraft checking (page 56). Alternatively, move your account to a small, friendly bank that will honor checks written against uncollected funds—although you'll probably be charged for the service. A *really* friendly bank will waive the fee.

Under federal law, banking institutions *must* give you access to at least $100 of your deposit on the next business day, and generally *must* clear the rest of your deposit on the following schedule:

1. One business day for federal, state, and local government checks, electronic payments (like direct deposit of a paycheck or Social Security check), postal money orders, cash, personal checks drawn on the same bank, cashier's checks, and certified checks.

2. Two business days for local checks.

3. Five business days for out-of-town checks.

4. On deposits fed into a bank's own ATM machines before noon —two business days, for cash, cashier's checks, and state and local government checks; one day for federal government checks; three days for local checks, and seven days for out-of-town checks. Add one day for deposits made after noon.

5. Seven business days, for all deposits made before noon in ATMs not owned by your bank; eight days for deposits after noon.

6. On deposits made by mail or in the bank's night depository—two days after receipt by the bank for cashier's checks and state and local government checks; three days for local checks, seven days for out-of-town checks.

These rules exist solely to whip reluctant banks into line. Many institutions cheerfully offer one-day clearance for almost all checks. And even the banks that hold your checks for two to eight days might credit interest to your account from the day of deposit.

Is a bank ever allowed to hold checks longer than usual? Absolutely. It needs at least some weapons against the risk of dishonesty and fraud. Expect a delay in drawing against deposited checks if:

1. You're a brand new customer. The bank gets 30 days to take your measure, during which time you might have to wait longer than usual for checks to clear. But even new customers can draw, the next business day, on the first $5,000 of funds from a government, cashier's, or travelers check, or from deposits made electronically. So if you move, transfer your bank account by wire.

2. You repeatedly overdraw your checking account, or are redepositing a check that bounced. In this case, a local check can be held for 7 days and an out-of-town check for 11 days.

3. You deposit more than $5,000 in checks in a single day. Part of your money will be released on the normal schedule; part can be held up to four days longer.

These rules all apply to withdrawals by check or to cash withdrawals through a human teller. Limits are allowed on cash withdrawals through an ATM.

MORE CHECK FACTS

To cash checks at a branch other than your own, get a signature card.

When you endorse a check (that is, sign your name on the back) it becomes as good as money and can be cashed by anyone who finds it. To prevent that, endorse it with instructions: "Pay to the order of Tiny Tim" or "For deposit only." When accepting an endorsed check from someone else, ask him to write "pay to the order of (you)," so that if you lose it neither of you will be out the money.

Endorse checks on the back, at the left-hand end (when viewed from the front), in the first inch and a half of space. If your signature is anywhere else, the bank may ask you to sign again. Most checks now carry a line to show where your signature goes.

Technically, a check may be good for years. But in practice, the bank might refuse any check that is more than one year old. That is, if the bank notices.

If you write a check and wish you hadn't, call your bank and ask that payment be stopped. Your account should be flagged right away, but you have to follow up with written authorization—usually by filing a stop-check form. The cost: $3 to $20. A stop-payment lasts for a limited period of time but can be renewed. If the check slips through, the bank takes responsibility for it. The stop-check form should spell out the rules.

You can arrange for regular, automatic transfers from your checking to your savings account. Interest on your certificates of deposit can be deposited into either account.

If someone forges your signature on a check and the bank cashes it, you are entitled to 100 percent reimbursement. It doesn't matter that you failed to report that your checkbook was stolen (although you should have). It doesn't matter that you kept your checks with your credit cards, which carry your signature. In most cases, it is the bank's absolute responsibility to guard against forgery. But you have a responsibility, too. If you don't report a forgery within 14 days after the bank mailed your statement, and fraudulent checks continue to be cashed by the same person, the later losses are all yours.

Use a *certified check* when the person you're paying wants a guarantee that the check will be good. The bank certifies that the check will be paid, by withdrawing the money from your account when the check is issued. A *cashier's check* can be used by people with no checking account. You give the money to the bank and it issues a check on its own account. Banks, S&Ls, money-order companies, and the Post Office also issue money orders, payable to specific people. Keep all receipts. They're your only proof of payment. File them as if they were canceled checks.

If you have a checking or savings account that you haven't touched for a while, check into its status. Some banks stop paying interest on quiescent accounts. Some even start charging fees. You can usually return to claim an old account, but you won't receive any interest for the years it lay dormant or get back any of the fees you were charged.

If your bank accounts lie untouched for three to seven years (and sometimes longer, depending on your state), the money will be turned over to the state treasury. Ditto for property in safe deposit boxes, certificates of deposit, even property held by the bank in trust. The bank, S&L, or credit union first has to try to reach you by writing to your last known address and by putting a notice in the newspaper. The state may have to advertise, too. If you don't show up, the money goes. You (or your heirs) can usually get it back by going to the bank with proof of ownership. But you won't be paid the interest you lost.

If you owe the bank money and haven't paid, it can generally dip into your other accounts—savings, checking, sometimes even a trust account, depending on the trust document—to satisfy the debt. Some states put modest limits on which accounts can be seized for what. Federal law prevents banks from taking money to satisfy a disputed credit card bill. But otherwise you are at risk, for your own unpaid debts and any loans you cosigned. If you lose your job and foresee a problem paying your mortgage, prudence dictates moving your savings to another bank.

BALANCING YOUR CHECKBOOK

Good news: *You don't have to.* The Rockies won't crumble, Gibraltar won't tumble, if you take the bank's word that your balance is right. Personally, I'm not happy unless my checkbook adds up—but that's easy for me to say; I let my husband do it. If you are allergic to arithmetic, here's the minimum you can get away with:

• Enter every deposit and withdrawal on your check register as you go along—not forgetting your dealings with ATMs or money withdrawn when you paid for something with a debit card. You need a running total so you won't overdraw. Also, you don't want to fall below the minimum balance your account requires.

• When the statement comes in, check every deposit and withdrawal against your check register, to be sure that the bank got everything right. If you wait a year or more to report a mistake, the bank might not make good. This system also catches alterations that a dishonest clerk might have made to your check.

• Put a check on each check that was cashed.

· If you have an interest-paying checking account, add the interest the bank paid that month to your checkbook balance. Then subtract all the fees. (These items show on your monthly statement.)

Assuming that nothing feels wildly out of line, it's okay to leave it at that. I don't trust a bank to enter checks correctly but I do trust its addition. (My own addition isn't so hot.)

Every six months or so, purge your math errors. Take the current balance, as reported by your bank; add all new deposits; subtract all uncashed checks; enter the result as the new balance in your checkbook, and start over.

Mind you, I don't recommend that you leave your checkbook a mess. But getting it in balance isn't the end-all of good financial planning.

AUTOMATED TELLER MACHINES

The ATM machine is McBanking at its easiest. You insert a card and punch a few buttons. Instantly, you're in touch with your bank account—to confirm your checking-account balance, withdraw or deposit funds, or at some machines, switch money from one account to another. Thanks to these fast-cash machines, you can get money whenever you want: on your way to work, in the middle of a holiday weekend; late on Sunday night. Banks hook up their ATMs to national networks, so funds are even available if you run short while you're out of town.

But ATMs are sometimes a nuisance—for example, when they make mistakes. When you ask for $100, only $70 might show up in the drawer. For information on correcting these errors, see page 74.

Around half of the banks now charge you for using their own ATMs —usually around 25 cents to $1 per transaction. It's sometimes more expensive than visiting the human teller. More than two-thirds of the banks charge if you reach your account through an ATM owned by another institution—maybe 75 cents to $2. The fee is usually for withdrawals. Deposits and balance inquiries may be free.

Most ATMs also accept credit cards. You use them to take out a loan against a line of credit. Debit cards, by contrast, withdraw money directly from your account (page 193).

IF THE BIG ATTRACTION OF ATMs IS CONVENIENCE, THE BIG RISK IS CRIME.
When you slip your card into an outdoor ATM, you're a sitting duck for a cruising crook. He knows that you've just picked up some cash. If

he has the time, he might force you at knifepoint to tap your account for even more. Then he might steal your car and drive away.

ATM crime is growing, although no one knows by exactly how much. Banks don't like to report it, for fear of scaring you away. Also, full disclosure of the risks of using ATMs might give victimized customers stronger grounds for suing the banks to recover their losses. So the bankers keep mum.

Under the Electronic Fund Transfers Act, your bank has to reimburse you for all but $50 of an unauthorized withdrawal, provided that you report the loss immediately. So you're covered if a thief swipes your card and drains your account. You are also covered if you're persuaded by a gun in your back to empty out your account. Some institutions have tried to avoid paying customers in this situation, but the law says you're owed.

It is not at all clear, however, that the bank has any liability for your losses if you're knocked on the head as you're leaving the machine. Customers have sued their banks, but most of the cases are settled out of court. In at least one case, a bank argued successfully that the customer was himself negligent for using a poorly lighted ATM at night. Here's how to play it safe with an ATM:

• Don't use ATMs at night, even if they are located on bank property. A survey by the Bank Administration Institute discovered that most ATM crimes take place between 7:00 P.M. and midnight, on bank premises.

• Don't use ATMs in isolated areas at any time.

• Don't use ATMs that are badly lit or readily accessible to a quick-hit thief in an automobile.

• Don't be the only person at an ATM.

• Don't use ATMs that are hidden by shrubbery.

• Don't use a drive-up ATM without first locking the car doors.

• Don't use ATMs that lack a permanent surveillance camera that could identify an assailant. (During a Florida lawsuit, it was discovered that, although a sign at an ATM said the machine was under surveillance, no camera existed.)

• Don't write your personal identification number (PIN) on your ATM card. The PIN tells the bank machine that you're really you. If your card is lost, that number is an open door into your account.

• Don't give your PIN to a stranger. If the stranger claims to be a cop or a banker, he's lying. No one but a crook would ask.

FOR FAST, FAST, FAST RELIEF

When you have to get money to someone in a hurry, a check might serve if it's delivered fast. But there are even better ways. The quick-delivery systems include:

1. Use the Post Office's Express Mail service. Your check can be delivered overnight to all major cities and many smaller ones in the United States.

2. Use postal money orders sent by Express Mail, if the recipient has nowhere to cash one of your checks. But you can count on rapid delivery only within the United States. International money orders are governed by country-to-country agreements, and may take four to six weeks to arrive.

3. Use Western Union. Call toll-free 800-325-6000 and charge up to $2,000 on your Visa or MasterCard. Or take cash (sometimes a cashier's check is okay) to a local Western Union agent. Some agents, and the 800 service, are available 24 hours a day, seven days a week. Cash can be transferred within the United States, Canada, Puerto Rico, and a limited number of foreign countries in as little as 15 minutes. Funds wired elsewhere usually take at least two business days, because delivery goes through local banks. The local agent or the 800 operator will tell you where the recipient can claim the money.

4. Use American Express MoneyGrams. You can wire money to and from any Amex office or agent in the United States, as well as agents in around 42 foreign countries. At this writing, Amex accepts only cash and the following credit cards: Optima, Discover, Visa, and MasterCard. Transfers may take less than 10 minutes, even to locations abroad. To locate a MoneyGram agent, call 800-926-9400.

5. Use the State Department. It's the agency of choice if your son has to get his motorcycle repaired in Bangladesh. In an emergency it will send cash within 24 hours to any American embassy or consulate, for a fee of $15. All you have to do is get the money to the State Department —using Western Union, bank wire, overnight mail, or regular mail. For details, write to the Overseas Citizens Services, Consular Affairs, Room 4800, Department of State, Washington, DC 20520, or call the Citizens Emergency Center, 202-647-5225.

6. Use your bank for big-money transfers within the United States. It can wire money to another bank for pickup the same day or one day

later. But mistrust banks for international transfers. Unless the foreign bank pays a lot of attention, a transfer that ought to take a day can take a month.

Ask what identification the recipient will need in order to pick up the money. Usually two proofs are needed, like a passport or driver's license, with picture attached. Sometimes he or she will also need a code word or authorization number that you furnish.

TO GET EXTRA MONEY WHEN YOU'RE OUT OF TOWN: If you run short of cash or travelers checks, or your wallet is stolen, there are several ways to rescue yourself.

1. Get someone at home to send you money, using one of the techniques above.

2. If you know your Visa or MasterCard number, you can call Western Union at 800-325-6000, charge your card for up to $2,000, and send the money to yourself.

3. If at least one of your cards wasn't stolen (just in case, travelers with two cards should keep them in two different places), you have some choices.

Your ATM card will probably plug into one of the national ATM networks. You can generally withdraw $200 to $600 a day from your account at home. You might also be able to get a cash advance against your overdraft checking. Transaction fee: usually 75 cents to $2. Many ATM webs have toll-free numbers that you can call to find cash machines wherever you go.

The leading credit cards are also widely accepted by ATM networks: Visa, MasterCard, and the travel-and-entertainment card, American Express. If you sign up for American Express's Express Cash service, and have a green card, you can use an ATM to tap your checking account for up to $500 a week in cash and $500 in American Express travelers checks. With a Gold Card you can get $500 in cash and $2,000 in travelers checks from your card's line of credit. MasterCard and Visa holders can get loans against their lines of credit, through ATMs or banks—domestic and foreign—affiliated with the card's sponsor.

4. Take your checkbook when you travel. Many stores, hotels, and restaurants accept personal checks from tourists. American Express holders can cash personal checks (up to certain limits) at any Amex office, as well as at some hotels and airlines.

WHICH SAVINGS ACCOUNT?

Where you put savings depends on how much you have and what you plan to do with it.

For Only a Small Amount of Money

With less than $200 to $500 or so, you've got problems. Hardly anyone wants your money. Banks might let kids have a small, free savings account. But as an adult, you will probably pay service charges, and they might exceed the interest you earn. Some banks won't pay any interest at all. So instead of growing, your savings account would gradually shrink. One solution: Add that money to your checking account *and don't spend it.* The extra $500 might give you enough to qualify for interest-paying checking. Another solution: Try a credit union, which is more likely to accept small savings accounts without charge.

A *statement savings account* might pay interest on small deposits (over $200 to $500) and still charge no fees. You don't get a passbook. Instead, you get a statement every month. I like the convenience of statement savings. You don't have to remember where you put the passbook and can usually handle the account through an ATM. You'll earn around 5 percent interest and can withdraw your money at any time.

A *passbook account* might require a higher minimum balance. Then again, it might not. Everything depends on the bank. Deposits and withdrawals are recorded in the passbook; interest rates run in the area of 5 percent.

For larger amounts of money

A *money market deposit account* pays a variable rate of interest—and I do mean variable. The bank has the right to change it at will. In high-rate periods, this account should pay much more than passbook savings; in low-rate periods, it pays about the same. You get unlimited deposits and withdrawals, although there may be a rule on how much you have to withdraw at once. Usually, only three withdrawals per month can be made by check. You'll be charged monthly fees if your deposit falls too low.

Money market accounts are a good place for money you're likely to need pretty soon, like rainy-day money, money waiting to be invested somewhere else, money you'll need to live on for the next six months, earmarked money, like a tuition payment due in a few weeks. It is *not* a good place for longer-term savings. Even if interest rates are high today, they'll be low tomorrow.

Savers tend to use money market deposit accounts because they're there. But a smarter buy is often a money market mutual fund (page 164). The mutual funds have been paying 1 to 1.5 percentage points more than the bank accounts.

Certificates of deposit commit your money for anywhere from six months to 10 years. Some institutions set fixed terms, like one year or two years; others let you pick the exact number of days, weeks, or months you want. Normally, the longer the term, the higher the interest rate.

CDs are for money that must be kept safe, like your daughter's tuition for next year, funds that you'll need next year to pay your bills, money you're saving for a new house, some of your retirement money, or all of your savings, until you learn how to invest.

You normally pay a penalty (of one to six months' interest, and sometimes more) for withdrawing funds before the term is up. But don't let that scare you. If you're forced to break your CD before maturity and pay the penalty, so be it. That won't be the first bit of money you've frittered away. The chances are, however, that you'll keep your CD for the full term and earn more interest than you'd have gotten from short-term savings.

CDs FOR SOPHISTICATES

You can earn the highest possible interest on CDs, without surrendering easy access to your money, by using a simple strategy called *laddering*. Here's how it works, assuming an initial pot of savings of $6,000.

You start out by splitting that money among bank deposits of varying maturities: $1,000 into a money market account, for cash on hand; then $1,000 each into a one-year, a two-year, a three-year, a four-year, and a five-year CD (or different maturities, depending on what you find). Normally, the longer the maturity, the higher the interest rate.

One year later, your first CD will mature, paying $1,000 plus interest. If you don't need the cash, reinvest it in a new *five-year* CD, which pays a higher interest rate. You can risk putting money away that long because, in another year, your next CD will mature—once again, giving you cash on hand. If you still don't need the money, it, too, goes into a five-year CD.

If you do this each time a CD matures, all your money will soon be earning five-year interest rates. Yet a $1,000 certificate will come due every 12 months, providing ready cash if you need it. Result: You will earn much more on your money without having to tie it all up for five years at a throw.

HIGH-YIELD CERTIFICATES OF DEPOSIT

High-yield CDs pay about one percentage point more than the national average. Whether to buy one depends on why the institution is being so nice to you.

Some high-raters are strong institutions. Typically, their local economies have been booming. Quite likely, too much money has been lent and the banks have had to raise interest rates in order to keep on attracting deposits. These economies and institutions may weaken, but that's not your problem as long as your deposits are federally insured. The CDs are good buys.

Other high-raters are insolvent but haven't yet been taken over by the government. As long as they're operating on their own, your high interest rate is safe. But as soon as they pass into federal hands, their attractive CDs may not last very long. If a new investor buys the institution from the government, your rate will probably be reduced. For a free list of the S&Ls and savings banks already under government supervision, write for the Conservatorship List, Resolution Trust Corp., 801 17th St. N.W., Washington, DC, 20429. There's no point in buying a one-year certificate of deposit from an institution that's not likely to last that long.

To locate solvent, top-yielding, federally insured CDs, subscribe to the publication *100 Highest Yields* (at this writing, it costs $34 for an eight-week trial subscription, from Box 088888, North Palm Beach, FL, 33408) or to *Rate Watch* ($39 for a three-month trial subscription, from P.O. Drawer 145510, Coral Gables, FL, 33114). They both tell you the names, addresses, and latest interest rates of the best-paying institutions in the country. *Rate Watch* surveys only those institutions that meet its credit standards. *100 Highest Yields* marks the very soundest banks and

S&Ls on its list with three stars. (Both also list the highest-paying money-market deposit accounts—page 164.)

To make a long-distance deposit in a high-rate bank or S&L, call the institution that interests you and ask for the person in charge of new accounts. Get the deposit forms and a conditional account number. Fill in the forms and, using the conditional account number, mail the bank a check. You can transfer large amounts of money by wire, directly from your present bank.

Alternatively, you can buy insured CDs through one of the major stockbrokerage houses. The minimum investment is generally $1,000. Stock brokers may not offer the very top-yielding CDs in the country, but they deal with institutions that pay above average.

Yield-shoppers beware: One CD's yield can be made to sound a few tenths of a point higher than a competitor's when it's actually not. That's because there are different ways of calculating a rate of return and each of them gives a different answer. A given payment sounds the highest when it's quoted on a "CD basis," the next highest when it's quoted on a "bond-equivalent basis," and the lowest when it's quoted as "simple interest."

For the most honest comparison, forget the stated yield. Ask each broker how much you will earn, in dollars and cents, on $1,000 invested. The CD that pays you the most has the highest true yield.

DESIGNER CDs

Hungry bankers respond to every fresh scent on the wind. Show them a new market, a new worry, a change in the economic outlook, and they will design a certificate of deposit to match. Not all banks and S&Ls offer exotic CDs; those that do may call them by different names than I have used. But if these ideas interest you, watch for them in the newspaper ads. The better the deal, the larger the minimum deposit the institution will want. Always compare the annual percentage yield with that being offered by standard CDs of the same term. Sometimes the designer CDs pay less.

FREE-RIDE CD. If you think you might need some of the money before maturity. You're charged no penalty for early withdrawal of up to half your funds. Or you can withdraw all your money without penalty midway through the term.

BUMP-UP CD. If you expect higher inflation. If interest rates rise, the bank will—at your direction—raise the rate you are earning on your CD once or twice during its term. There is usually a cap on how high the rate can go.

ANYTIME CD. If you want your money back on a specific date. The bank will construct a CD that exactly matches the maturity you want.

VARIABLE-RATE CD. If you expect inflation. Your interest rate rises and falls with the general level of rates. Buy only if the CD guarantees a floor below which the interest rate cannot fall.

RELATIONSHIP CD. If you are trying to lower your banking costs. Opening a CD may entitle you to a lower loan interest rate at the same institution, or fewer fees on your checking account.

TIERED CD. If you have substantial savings. The larger your deposit, the higher your interest rate.

BITTER-END CD. If you know you can last for the full term. You get a bonus for keeping your money in the CD for a full five years.

ZERO-COUPON CD. If you want to make a gift of money look extra good. You put down a small sum now, at a guaranteed interest rate. It will grow to equal the CD's face value in a given number of years. (Each year's increase in value is taxable, so zeros are best given to a child or kept in a tax-deferred retirement account.) Always ask for the annual percentage yield and compare it with regular CDs of the same maturity. Some institutions clip you a little on their zeros.

JUMBO CD. If you (or a group of investors) have more than $100,000. Banks pay higher interest rates on large amounts of money. But choose a safe institution. If your bank fails, and the government can't find a buyer for it, your deposits over $100,000 may not be fully reimbursed.

ASSET-LINKED CD. If you want to speculate a little. CDs have been linked to the stock market, gold, and real estate. Part of your yield is guaranteed; part is hostage to fortune. Normally, federal deposit insurance covers only your principal and the guaranteed portion of your return, up to $100,000.

TAX-DEFERRAL CD. To bring down your tax bill. This 12-month CD is bought at a discount in the current calendar year, to mature next year. No interest is paid until the CD matures, which puts all of your income into the next tax year.

ABSOLUTELY FAKE CDs

Are you looking for higher interest rates than CDs will pay? Some banks and S&Ls sell an instrument called a "subordinated debt note" or "lobby note." It has also gone by other names, like "retail debenture." When you buy it, you are lending money to the institution, unsecured. Lobby notes don't carry federal deposit insurance. If the institution goes broke, your investment will probably be worthless.

Many of the banks and S&Ls that sell these notes are not in the greatest financial shape. To raise money, they shamelessly peddle "junk notes" to savers who can't evaluate the risk. Not only are you shafted if the institution fails, you are also shafted if it succeeds. The fine print of a lobby note usually allows the bank to redeem it before the full term is up. So you might lose the high interest income you expected to have.

I say, don't buy. If you're still tempted by these 5- to 20-year wonders, call Veribanc for a financial-soundness rating on your institution (page 78). If it's anything less than three-star (for "tops"), steer clear. You can get the ratings for the current quarter and for previous ones. If any one of them falls below three-star, don't buy. In 1989, investors lost $250 million in the lobby notes of the holding company for Lincoln S&L in Irvine, CA, whose reports had been wavering back and forth between "high" and "medium." Later, it turned out that behind its occasional "high" rating lay some doubtful accounting methods.

WHEN YOUR CD MATURES

When you open a CD, ask the bank what happens when the certificate matures. What instructions do they need from you, and how soon do they need them? Can you give instuctions now? All this information will be in your CD contract, but it's important that you understand it exactly.

Each institution handles things a little differently. Normally, there is a short grace period after maturity—maybe 7 to 10 days, but sometimes as little as one day—during which the bank waits to hear from you. Do you want the money moved to another account? Another bank? Invested in another CD? Interest may or may not be paid during this period. If the grace period expires, and you haven't told the bank what to do, your money will probably be reinvested in another CD of the same term. If you then decide that you want the cash, you might be able to break the CD without penalty. Then again, you might not.

Banking institutions generally write to you shortly before your CD matures. But keep track of the payment date yourself, in case the letter gets lost in the mail. Don't leave your decision to the last minute. The bank might want written instructions, and you'll have to allow enough time for them to arrive.

TEST YOUR BANKER'S IQ

Interest-rate maven Richard Morse, professor emeritus at Kansas State University, finds 7.8 *million* different combinations of factors used to calculate the dollar amount of interest paid. The language of savings rates itself demands an Einstein. For example, banks might advertise "Current Rate," "Annual Rate," "Interest Rate per Annum," "Simple Interest," "Average Daily Rate," and a dozen others. What do they mean? How do they differ? Who knows? I have learned the hard way that the highest advertised interest rate doesn't always yield the highest return in dollars and cents—because so much depends on how that interest rate is massaged. So:

1. *Ask:* What does the bank pay interest *on?* The answer should be the balance accumulated in your savings account every day, normally known as *day of deposit to day of withdrawal.* Some institutions pay on your *average deposit* over the month, which generally yields less. Be wary of an institution that pays only on the *lowest balance* each month—an arrangement most often seen in credit unions. If you had $5,000 in the account almost all month, then drew out $4,500 on the last day, you'd earn interest only on the remaining $500. Also, beware the bank that pays interest only on your *investable balance,* which might be only 88 percent of your deposit. That lowers your yield.

2. *Ask:* How often does interest compound? "Compounding" means that the bank adds the interest you earn to your account, and then pays interest on the combined interest and principal. The more often your interest is compounded, the more money you make. Daily or continuous compounding (they're just about the same) yield the most, followed by quarterly, then semiannual, then annual compounding. With "simple" interest there is no compounding at all. What difference does it make? Plenty. At 8 percent interest, compounded daily, your savings are worth 9 percent more after six years than if you had earned only simple interest.

COMPOUND INTEREST: THE MAGIC MONEY MACHINE

Compounding Method	A $10,000 Deposit, at 8 Percent After:		
	One year	Three years	Six years
Daily	$10,833	$12,712	$16,160
Monthly	10,830	12,702	16,135
Quarterly	10,824	12,682	16,084
Semiannually	10,816	12,653	16,010
Annually	10,800	12,597	15,869
Simple interest	10,800	12,400	14,800

Source: Richard L. D. Morse.

3. *Ask:* How often is interest credited to your account? Most banks that compound interest daily do not actually give you the money until the end of the month or the end of the quarter. So then ask: What happens to that last bit of interest if you close your account before the end of the period? Normally, you will lose it, even though the bank claims that it's paying you right to the day of withdrawal.

4. *Ask:* What is the *annual percentage yield* on your savings? This yield takes all kinds of mathematical quirks into consideration—not only interest rate and frequency of compounding, but also such technical details as how many days the bank counts as a year. (Some banks use 366 days, some use 365, some use 360. For reasons only Computerman would believe, 360 yields more interest.) In general, the higher the annual percentage yield, the better the deal. Still, two institutions can offer the same annual percentage yield yet pay different amounts in dollars and cents.

5. *Ask:* If you put $1,000 into this account today, how much money —in dollars and cents—will it earn in one year? *This is the only true way of comparing one savings account with another.* Some bankers don't like to answer the question, because it takes a little time. Some don't even understand what you're asking. But their attitude tells you how cheerfully a bank will accommodate you, which ultimately matters more than a minor difference in interest rates.

6. *Ask:* What is the *periodic payment rate?* That's the rate the bank applies when figuring how much interest you have earned. Knowing it, you can check the bank's calculations to see if it paid you properly. Mistakes are not uncommon. A good bank will give you its periodic payment rate and show you how to use it.

FIXING BANK MISTAKES

CASH. How many times have you cashed a check in a hurry, then walked away without counting the money? Maybe you think the teller is always right. Maybe you are intimidated by a line of grumpy people behind you. But if you count the money at the bank door and find that you're $20 short, you might be stuck. Tellers aren't allowed to hand over extra money on a customer's say-so. (After all, you could have slipped the missing $20 into your pocket before you went back to the teller's window.)

RULE 1. Always count your money before leaving the window. If you discover an error later, give your name, address, and account number to the manager. If the teller winds up the day with the right amount of extra cash, you'll be reimbursed.

DEPOSITS. Tellers sometimes err when crediting deposits; for example, entering $100 when you actually put in $1,000.

RULE 2. Double-check every transaction for accuracy before leaving the window. What if the teller credits $1,000 to your account when you gave her only $100? Don't spend the money. The mistake will be found, and in banking, there's no finders keepers.

AUTOMATED TELLER MACHINES. ATMs goof, just as people do. They short-change the occasional customer, giving you $70 when you asked for $100. Sometimes they accept cash and checks without crediting them to your account.

RULE 3. Never deposit cash in an ATM. It's impossible to prove how much you put into the envelope, so losses are sometimes hard to recover. Checks are easier to find or replace.

RULE 4. Report mistakes right away. Some banks install telephones next to their ATMs for that purpose, although they may be answered by bank personnel only during banking hours. When you call, leave your name, address, account number, the amount of the loss, and the location of the ATM; then put the same information into a letter. You will have to wait until the accounts are balanced, but if the machine is over by the sum you reported, you will get your money. At the bank's own ATM machine, the error might be fixed at the end of the day. But it will take an extra day or two (and sometimes weeks) if you used an ATM at another bank.

DEPOSIT SLIPS. It always astonishes me to see the trash baskets near

ATMs overflowing with deposit slips. If the deposit is entered wrong, would those customers know it? (I don't remember the exact amounts of all the checks I get.) Withdrawal slips are also dumped—by people who aren't balancing their checkbooks, I guess.

RULE 5. Keep all deposit and withdrawal slips until your bank statement comes in, to be sure the transactions were entered right.

CERTIFICATES OF DEPOSIT. Your bank might automatically renew your CD when it expires, even though you told it not to.

RULE 6. Keep a copy of the instructions you gave when you opened the CD, and mark the due date on your calendar. If an error is made, hustle to correct it. Too long a wait may cost you your chance to get your money out.

FEDERAL DEPOSIT INSURANCE

It will pay.

Don't waste your time searching through subclauses, thinking to find a loophole in the coverage. The government will meet every obligation of the deposit insurance funds, period. The S&L bailout is proof of that.

Federally insured money is entirely safe up to $100,000—and more, depending on how the accounts are held. Safe, in a lousy S&L. Safe, in a bank paying cockeyed interest rates. Safe, even with a crook or incompetent at the helm. So don't worry, be happy, and collect the highest interest rates that you can find.

Congress is considering cutting down on the number of insured accounts you can have. But at this writing, you get $100,000 worth of deposit insurance for *each* of the following, held in a single institution:

1. All the accounts in your own name, added together.
2. All your company pension accounts, added together.
3. A Keogh plan and an IRA, each with separate coverage.
4. Each account held in trust for a member of your immediate family —child, spouse, grandparent. (There must be a trust document filed with the bank. *Revocable* trusts usually are *not* insured separately.)
5. Your incorporated business or partnership account.
6. Each account you hold jointly with different people.

Joint money is split evenly among the account holders, provided they have signature cards on file. For example, say you have three joint accounts—one with your spouse and one with each of your two children.

Each account contains $100,000. Your spouse and two children are fully insured for their $50,000 share. But your share totals $150,000 (half of each account). Only $100,000 of that is insured.

What if you have two joint accounts with your spouse, one listed Husband/Wife (with the husband's Social Security number), one listed Wife/Husband (with the wife's Social Security number)? You don't have double coverage. Where the names on various accounts are the same, they are all lumped together and treated as one.

What happens to your money if your institution fails depends on which of four ways the collapse is handled.

THE FIRST WAY. The dead institution is sold to, or merged with, another one. Both insured and uninsured deposits are transferred intact. High-rate CDs are usually knocked down to a lower interest rate, on 14 to 30 days' notice (although some institutions let you keep that high rate until your certificate matures). If you don't like the new bank, you can close the CD without penalty. If the bank gets no instructions from you at all, it may roll your CD money into a 5 percent passbook account.

THE SECOND WAY. No one wants to buy the dead institution, but another bank or S&L takes the insured deposits. All accounts of $100,000 or less are transferred immediately. So are the insured portions of multiple accounts, like pension accounts, held in the same name. High-rate CDs are usually cut back, as outlined above. Dissenters can move their CDs to another institution, without penalty. If your S&L fails on a Friday (the usual situation), your insured deposits should be available the following Monday, with no break in your interest payments.

Sometimes, however, there are delays. If the institution's records are bad, you may have to prove what your account was worth. Multiple accounts may need sorting out. If you bought your CD through a stockbroker (page 69), the broker may have to show that the money was placed on your behalf.

Any uninsured money stops earning interest and becomes a claim against the assets of the failed bank or S&L. As the assets are sold, the proceeds are distributed among all the creditors, on a pro rata basis. Whatever you ultimately recover will be mostly paid in the first year, although additional payments may dribble in over the next several years.

THE THIRD WAY. No one wants any part of the dead bank or S&L. The institution fails and stops paying interest. Typically, it closes on a Friday and opens on Monday to pay off the insured depositors. If you go in person, you can collect your money right away. Or you'll get a claim form in the mail that has to be signed, notarized, and returned. Your check will be mailed a day or two later. The majority of accounts clear in the first week, and almost all of them within four weeks.

As for uninsured deposits, there's no telling how much you'll recover. The failing bank's assets first have to be sold. The proceeds will then be parceled out, pro rata, among all the creditors.

THE FOURTH WAY. An insolvent S&L is taken over by the federal government's Resolution Trust Corporation. High-rate CDs usually won't be tampered with, but you'll be offered a lower rate at maturity. The interest rate on money market deposit accounts may also go down. The S&L will stay open for business until the RTC disposes of it, using one of the three methods outlined above.

Customers of tipsy institutions should take three precautions: (1) Check each statement, to be sure that the bank or S&L has entered all your deposits correctly. (2) Keep copies of all your correspondence with the institution and your most recent statements. If the institution's records are in a mess, you may have to prove the size of your deposit. (3) Deposit less than $100,000 so that, even with the interest received, you will never exceed the insured ceiling. Insured depositors always get all of their money back, right away.

NEVER RELY ON STATE OR PRIVATE DEPOSIT INSURANCE. This includes the private insurance carried by many credit unions. If just one institution collapses, the fund may be unable to pay. When that happens, customers often make a run on other institutions insured by the fund, even the sound ones. That may force them to close, too. The only safe bet is Uncle Sam.

WHAT HAPPENS TO YOUR LOANS WHEN YOUR BANK OR S&L GOES BUST? You keep making the payments, to whoever takes over the loan portfolio. In almost all cases, no one can force you to refinance on different terms, as long as your payments are up to date.

What happens to an unused credit line? It may be sold to a new institution as is. If no institution buys the credit line, however, it will be terminated.

There's one important exception to the rule that loans in good standing are left alone. If you opened a home-equity line of credit prior to November 7, 1989, it will probably contain a "call" clause, allowing the lender to cancel your loan for any reason. In 1990, the failed Savers Savings Association of Little Rock, AK, called in about 135 home-equity loans, forcing the borrowers to refinance at other institutions.

For anyone behind on a loan, the jig is up. Bad loans often go to the federal deposit insurance fund, which will want a settlement or else.

FINDING A SOUND BANK

Don't rely on financial statements from your own institution. They're always self-serving and may be deceptive. Instead, call the rating service Veribanc in Woburn, MA (800-442-2657). For $10, it will tell you whether the bank or S&L ranks three-star (for "tops"), two-star, one-star or no-star for financial soundness. Ratings for additional institutions cost $3 each, as long as you ask for them during the same phone call. The fee is charged to your Visa or MasterCard. Veribanc also rates institutions as "green" for good, "yellow" for doubtful, and "red" for lousy. You want a three-star green.

Two problems with Veribanc: (1) Its reports cover only the most recent quarter for which it has data. The situation might have deteriorated since. (2) Crooked institutions dress up their financial statements so that they'll look better than they really are.

Still, you can't hide all traces of a skunk in a rose garden. The telephone operators can give you the previous quarter's rating at no extra charge. Ratings for earlier quarters are also available. If they're not all three-star, something may be amiss.

WHAT'S THE SMARTEST WAY OF SETTING UP
BANK ACCOUNTS?

Use a convenient bank for your checking account, with acceptable interest rates and well-located ATMs. Keep enough savings there to lower the service fees you're charged. But for substantial savings deposits, mail your checks to one of the nation's sound, high-rate institutions. The extra percentage point you earn is worth the stamp.

5

POOLERS, SPLITTERS, AND KEEPERS:

Who Should Own the Property—Me? You? Us? Them?

———

To the question of who should own the
property in your household, no answer is right.
But then again, no answer is wrong. Who ever
said this was going to be easy?

Get out your yellow pad again, and
buy some more pencils. Write down all the serious property you have:
house, bank accounts, cars, mutual funds, beach house, oil wells, insurance policies, stocks, gold coins. Who owns each piece? Whose name is
on the deed, title, or purchase order? Whose money bought it? Is it yours
alone, or is it jointly held? Is that okay, or should it be owned in some
other way? You can keep the property or share it. You can give it away.
With a trust, you can give it away and still keep it. (Like the economics
of the oldest profession in the world: "You get it; you sell it; you still got
it.")

Federal taxes used to have a bearing on who owned what, but now
they matter only if you're worth more than $600,000, or if your estate
plus the taxable gifts you make during your lifetime will exceed

$600,000. For everyone else, ownership depends on personality and circumstance. Almost every choice has its points.

ONE FOR THE MONEY

Whether never married or formerly married, your singleness defines the rules. You are a *keeper,* because you can own everything yourself, no fuss, no muss. All you need is a reliable friend to hold your durable (or springing) power of attorney (page 117). That person could write checks on your bank account or manage your investments if you're incapable (say, in a coma after the auto accident, God forbid).

That's when you're young. When you age, you may not be quite so independent and sometimes ownership enters in. For example: You might give half of your house to your son and his family, if they will live there with you. Or you might put your niece's name on your bank account, if she helps you do your taxes and pay your bills. If your son is a good egg and your niece is a doll, joint ownership can work.

But what if your son gets a new job and moves? The house might have to be sold to give him the money to buy a new one. What if he gets divorced? His half of *your* house might have to be divided with *his* ex-wife. What if your nice niece falls for a freeloader, who persuades her to nip a bit of your money? A joint owner of a bank account can take every penny unless you specifically require both signatures for withdrawal, which, for daily bills, gets tiresome. You can sue a joint owner for withdrawing more than he or she deposited—but the last thing you want, late in life, is to get tangled up in lawsuits with your relatives.

You can escape from a joint bank account that you've come to regret just by taking your money out. But it's a lot harder to get back your house, once you've given half of it away.

Then there's the fairness issue. A joint owner gets the property, regardless of what it says in your will. Say, for example, that your will leaves everything equally to your children, Tammis and Christopher. Then you add son Christopher to your bank account. He gets every penny of it when you die. You have cut Tammis out. By naming a joint owner with the right of survivorship, you took your bank account out of your will and Tammis won't be able to touch it. The same is true for anything else you put in joint names with a right of survivorship. The other owner walks away with the prize.

There *can* be a way around this problem: Both of you sign a notarized agreement that joint ownership is for convenience only, not for inheritance. But this might not work—because the bank might pay over to the other owner anyway, or Christopher's creditors might try to move in on the money. Why run the risk of having to start a lawsuit? Give Christopher a power of attorney to manage your affairs and hang on to the ownership yourself.

TWO FOR THE DOUGH

A married couple is a pushmi-pullyu, a two-headed animal with two minds of its own. You have to figure out how to pull together.

WHEN YOU BOTH HAVE PAYCHECKS: *Poolers* put all the money into a common pot. *Splitters* keep their own separate accounts. Which you choose is a matter of soul, not of finance. Poolers think that sharing is what a marriage is all about. Splitters hold to their own independence within the marriage. The previously married often split but sometimes pool. The first-time married often pool but sometimes split. It's so unpredictable that even your best friend might surprise you. Over time, and if the marriage goes well, splitters usually turn into *spoolers,* splitting some, pooling some, and growing less antsy about who pays for what.

The challenge for poolers is the checkbook and the bank ATM cards. How do you know what's in the bank when both of you draw from the same account? You can:

· Write no checks away from the checkbook. Use credit cards instead.

· Use only ATM cards for getting cash. Return the receipts to the central checkbook and enter your withdrawal.

· Take two or three checks to walk around with. When you use one, enter it into the check register. A big balance in the checking account prevents overdrafts.

· Use checks backed by carbons. Return all copies to the central checkbook.

· Let just one of you handle the bills. The other hangs on to two or three checks and reports whenever one is used. As in *She:* "Honey, I need more checks." *He:* "How's that? You still have two." *She:* "No, I'm out." *He:* "What did you write the last two for?" *She:* "Didn't I tell you?" *He:* "No." *She:* "Oh." It's the only truly romantic system. Once a month, you kiss and make up.

Poolers usually have *some* separate money, probably in pension accounts. There is also something about an inheritance that often resists the impulse to share. But the house, the savings, and the investments are kept routinely in joint names, even if just one of you makes all the investment decisions.

The challenge for splitters lies in keeping track of who pays for what. As in *She:* "I bought the groceries for two weeks running." *He:* "But I got your laundry and paid the sitter." *She:* "But you already owed me two sitters from last month." *He:* "Those sits were short so they just count for one." You never finally kiss and make up because you never figure it out.

For clarity, you can:

• Split everything right down the middle, even putting down two credit cards when you eat out. (No kidding. I know a couple that does this.)

• Where earnings are unequal, split accordingly—say, 60 percent him, 40 percent her.

• Make a list of "his" and "her" household expenses and take turns treating each other to dinners out.

• Toss receipts for cash payments into a box and settle up when the box overflows.

• Use the same box for "loans" you make to each other.

• Write memos about property bought together, spelling out who owns what percent.

• Keep three checking accounts—his, hers, and ours. Each pays into the "ours" account for common household bills or for the children. (Don't miss the fiendish cleverness of this arrangement. You get the mysteries of separate accounts *plus* the headaches of a joint one.)

Splitting teaches each person how to handle money and take responsibility for decisions. It also serves couples with different investment styles—say, one a speculator and one a hoarder. Nevertheless, when it comes to major financial decisions, splitters usually make them together. You are still a single financial unit, regardless of how you handle the money.

And then there's the Old Dispensation: The wife's paycheck is "hers" while the husband's is "ours." I hold with this arrangement only if the husband is well paid and the wife is truly earning peanuts. Otherwise, they're in it together and both should pay.

IF ONLY ONE OF YOU HAS A PAYCHECK. Splitting is Out. Pooling is In. Your basic contract is money-for-services, and everything tends to be jointly owned. If it's all in one name and you divorce, the courts are supposed to treat it as mutual, marital money, although sometimes the homebody gets short shrift. If the husband keeps bank and investment accounts in his own name, the wife should similarly possess her own funds. (It reminds me of what my grandmother used to call "garter money": "Pin two dollars to your garter, dear, and if he reaches for it, take a taxi home.") One fair way for couples to manage: Each year's savings, after the bills are paid, are divided 50-50 between husband and wife.

IF OLDER PEOPLE REMARRY. Your friends will be enchanted. But don't be surprised if your children aren't. It's usually not the "pater" they worry about, but the patrimony. If your new spouse gets your property after your death, he or she is free to cut your children out. Even if you own assets separately, state inheritance laws usually require that the spouse get one-third to one-half.

To prevent this, you need a premarital agreement (page 121)—truly important in senior marriages. You agree in advance not to inherit each other's property but to leave most or all of it to your respective children, instead. To provide for each other, you might take out life insurance policies, or make each other the beneficiaries of policies you own already. Or you might agree that you each get the income from the other's property for life, with the children getting the principal only after the death of the surviving spouse. A premarital agreement also settles your rights in case of divorce.

IF YOUR NET WORTH EXCEEDS $600,000. You have a high-class problem. Your estate may owe federal estate taxes, after you both die. You can reduce these taxes with bypass trusts (page 115). To make the trusts work, however, husband and wife have to own property separately, as community property, or as tenants in common without right of survivorship. Bypass trusts can't be funded with property that is jointly owned.

LOVERS AND OTHER ROOMMATES

You are splitters. Each handles personal expenses and you work out a system for paying joint bills. A 50-50 split is fair only if your incomes are roughly equal. If one of you earns two-thirds of your combined income, that person should assume two-thirds of the rent and two-thirds of the grocery bills. Otherwise, the one with the smaller paycheck is subsidizing the other. If there's going to be any subsidy at all, it should be from the richer to the poorer, not the other way around.

Long-time lovers drift toward pooling some of their money. Still, you often live on the tips of your toes, almost ready to run. So for property that is hard to unwind, separate ownership is best.

If you buy a piece of real estate together, do it as tenants in common (page 85) and write an agreement for getting your money out if the relationship fails. Will you put the house on the market and divide the proceeds according to the original contribution? Will one person buy the other out and if so, which? How will you determine the price? How will you divide the taxes, insurance, and mortgage payments? What happens if one person quits paying his or her share?

Ever since the famous Marvin case, which raised the possibility of suing for "palimony," that issue has hung over live-in relationships. If, say, the man works and the woman gives up her job to follow him, does she have a right to support if they fall out? Should one partner get some of the money that the other accumulated during their relationship? Denver lawyer Bill Cantwell has been thinking about this problem for a while and offers you his "Wallet Card Non-Marvinizing Agreement," to be signed by both parties to the relationship. It reads like this:

"We have decided to live together beginning on _____. We do not intend that any common law marriage should arise from this. We have not made any promises to each other about economic matters. We do not intend any economic rights to arise from our relationship. If in the future we decide that any promises of an economic nature should exist between us, we will put them in writing, and only such written promises made by us in a written memorandum signed by us in the future shall have any force between us. Signed at _____ on _____."

FOUR WAYS TO OWN PROPERTY TOGETHER

JOINT OWNERSHIP WITH RIGHT OF SURVIVORSHIP. The owners (there can be more than two) hold the property together. If one dies, his or her share passes automatically to the other owners in equal parts. This form of ownership is for married couples, for any two people who live together and need a convenient household account, and for truly committed unmarried couples. It protects gay couples whose relatives might attack a will.

To put something in joint ownership, you register it as such on the deed, title, or other ownership document, specifying "with right of survivorship." That's important. Otherwise, it might be argued that you held the property only as tenants in common (below).

Joint ownership isn't an inescapable trap. You can generally get out of it—although not always easily—even if the other owner objects. The ways of doing this vary, depending on your state's laws. When a jointly owned property is sold, the proceeds are normally divided equally. If you all agree, however, you can make an uneven division (in which case, if you're rich enough, gift taxes might be due).

TENANCY IN COMMON. This is a good way to own a beach house or a snow blower with a friend. Married couples use this method when they want to leave their share of a jointly owned property in trust. So do unmarried couples who can imagine an end to their relationship.

Each tenant in common has a share in the property, although not necessarily an equal share. You can sell or give away your share at any time. In the case of a house owned in common, for example, your partner could sell his piece to his brother and suddenly you would have a new roommate. If the owners fall out, one might buy the other's share. Or one could file a partition lawsuit, that might force the property to be sold.

You can pass your share to anyone at death; it doesn't automatically go to the other owners. If you die without a will, your share of the property will be distributed to your relatives, according to state law.

TENANCY BY THE ENTIRETY. This arrangement, for married couples only, must be established in writing and is recognized by 24 states. It's similar to property owned jointly with the right of survivorship but gives each of the owners more protection. Neither of you can break it up without the other's consent. In many cases, the property is protected against one spouse's creditors (assuming that only one spouse signed the debt).

COMMUNITY PROPERTY. Nine states (Arizona, California, Idaho, Louisiana, Nevada, New Mexico, Texas, Washington, and Wisconsin) declare that most property acquired by either spouse during the marriage is owned by both, regardless of whose name is on it. This rule affects anyone who ever lived in a community property state. Even if you move away, your community property keeps its character. It is always 50 percent owned by each spouse (although, as a practical matter, these ownership rights can be lost if you don't document them when you move to a non–community property state). The portion of a private pension earned during a marriage is usually community property, but Social Security isn't.

During life, it is hard to dispose of your half of the community property without the other's consent. At death, however, you can generally leave it to whomever you want; it doesn't have to go to your spouse. Unlike jointly owned property, community property goes through probate, although some states create ways for you to avoid it.

All the states have slightly different rules about what is *not* community property. They generally exempt inheritances, gifts, and property acquired before marriage. Most (but not all) states exempt property acquired before moving to the state. However, to stay solely yours, separate property has to be kept apart from the property you own together. If you inherit money and want to maintain sole ownership, put it into a bank account in your own name. If you put it into a joint account, you might turn it into community property, like it or not.

You can get out of community property, if you'd rather hold your assets in some other way. Each state runs its own escape routes. For example, you might make a gift of your community-property interest to your spouse. You might sign an agreement, specifying what is community property and what isn't. In most of the states (but not all), you can annul the community property rule with a premarital or postmarital agreement. Noncommunity property can be owned separately or jointly, as you prefer.

WHY MOST MARRIEDS LOVE JOINT OWNERSHIP

1. It makes marriage a partnership, share and share alike.

2. When one of you dies, the other automatically gets the goods. No doubts, no tears, no probate.

3. The other owner can't wheel and deal the money away. As a practical matter, most joint property cannot be sold or borrowed against unless both of you sign. This applies especially to real estate and securities registered in your personal names.

Securities held in the name of a brokerage house are another story. It normally takes only one of you to buy and sell, even if they're jointly owned. Similarly, mutual funds usually allow either of you to make telephone switches. But be it a mutual fund or a brokerage account, neither of you should be able to take the money and run. A check for the proceeds of any sale will be issued in joint names. (This doesn't prevent some spouses from forging the other's signature!)

Your most vulnerable property is a jointly owned bank account, which your spouse can easily clean out.

4. In divorce, you are a more formidable force. Under state laws,

the marital assets are supposed to be divided fairly, without regard to who holds title. But possession might still be seven-tenths of the law. If you hold the property, or at least have your name on it, your bargaining position is stronger than if you don't.

5. Out-of-state property passes to the other owner, without probate in that state. This saves your survivor some time and some money.

6. Say there's a debt that you're not responsible for—like a judgment levied against your spouse. If he or she dies, those creditors usually can't collect a dime from joint property. During your spouse's lifetime, however, joint property is vulnerable—to what extent depends on the laws of your state. You get the most protection in a tenancy by the entirety (page 85).

WHY SOME MARRIEDS HATE JOINT OWNERSHIP

1. If one of you splits, he or she can clean out the bank accounts and safe deposit box. You can file a lawsuit to get your money back, but the effort might cost more than it's worth.

2. Some investments can't be sold if one of you is too sick or senile to sign the papers, or too sore to cooperate. A durable power of attorney solves the first two problems. The third is all yours.

3. You can't set up a bypass trust with jointly owned property that provides for a right of survivorship. So if you're worth more than $600,000, this form of ownership lays higher taxes on your estate.

4. Your kids might lose money if you marry more than once. Say you put all your property in joint names with a new spouse, and die. That spouse gets everything, and can cut out the children of your previous marriage. Not that such an awful thing will actually happen, but it could.

5. Joint property can be tied up for a long time in divorce, because it often can't be sold until both spouses agree to sign. Separate property can be sold anytime you want.

JOINT PROPERTY FOR UNMARRIEDS?

The Weak Case in Favor

1. It passes automatically to the other without a will and without probate. This helps gay couples whose families might attack a will (although a good will can't be broken).

2. It's a sign of good faith.

3. It's convenient. A mother and daughter living together may want a joint account for household bills.

The Strong Case Against

1. If you want to take your property out of joint names and the other person refuses, you may have the devil's own time getting it back. Only bank accounts are simple to reclaim. You just take the money out (unless . . .

2. . . . the other person got there first). Either owner can empty a joint bank account. You'd have to sue to get your money back.

3. You might need both signatures to sell an investment, or to cash a check for the proceeds of a sale. What if your ex-mate gets sore or leaves town?

4. Say you put your investments in joint name with your son, who manages them for you. His business goes broke. His half of your property could be attached to pay his debts. (He can manage your money just as well with a power of attorney or through a trust.)

5. Assume the same story as in item 4, only your son gets divorced. Part of your property might go to his ex-wife.

6. Same story, only you have two sons. When you die, Son One inherits your investments and Son Two gets nothing. Joint property usually goes to the surviving joint owner, cutting other beneficiaries out. (A few states, however, might allow you to designate that your joint account goes half to Son One and half to all your other beneficiaries).

7. If you're rich enough to owe federal gift and estate taxes (net worth over $600,000), you can trigger a tax liability when: (1) Stocks or real estate go into joint names and the owner doesn't pay for his or her half share. (2) The noncontributing owner takes money out of a joint bank account or U.S. Savings Bond. (3) One of you dies. All joint property is taxed in the estate of the first owner to die, except for anything that the survivor can prove he or she paid for. (These rules, incidentally, apply only to joint owners who aren't married. Married couples can give, or leave, each other property without tax.)

In Either Case . . .

OWN YOUR CARS SEPARATELY. If you cause an accident and are hit with a judgment that exceeds your insurance, your other property can be attached—and so can the property of the car's joint owners. If you own the car alone, no one else will be affected.

SHOULD YOUR KID OWN IT?

Sure. A kid is still a walking tax shelter, assuming that his or her bracket is lower than yours. Money put into a child's name will be worth more, after tax, than if you keep it in yours.

How much income can be tax sheltered? That depends on when you read this. The amounts are indexed to inflation, so they'll probably rise each year. Here's the general concept, using income limits for 1991.

For a child under 14: (1) Up to $550 of the child's unearned income (from sources like interest and dividends) passes tax free. (2) The next $550 in unearned income is taxed in the child's own bracket—probably only 15 percent. So the family gets a tax break on up to $1,100 a year. That's the return on $13,700 invested in an 8 percent certificate of deposit, or $27,000 invested in stocks that pay 4 percent dividends. (3) Any unearned income over $1,100 is taxed in the parents' highest bracket. (You can hold down taxes on a child's unearned income up to $5,000 by creating a "minor's trust," but the savings may not be worth the expense of setting it up.)

These income levels rise for 1992 and will rise again in later years. Check a recent tax guide for the latest dope.

Once the child passes 14, all the unearned income is taxed in his or her bracket. So at that point, you might shift even more of your savings into the child's name.

But any gift has to pass through these four wickets:

1. You won't need the property back. This isn't Ping Pong. Whatever you give your child is his or hers to keep.

2. You have the sort of kid who won't take the money and blow it. At age 18 or 21, depending on state law, the property belongs to the child, unless it's protected by a trust.

3. The tax savings are worth the loss of flexibility. In 1991 the most a straight gift could save you, with a child under 14, was $259 a year if you were in the 31 percent tax bracket, and $226 a year if you were in the 28 percent bracket.

4. You know that your child won't be eligible for college aid. If you

are, you'll get larger grants or loans if the savings are in your name rather than in the child's (see page 435).

There are better and worse ways of giving money and property to a child under 18. Here are your choices.

1. *Outright ownership.* You hand the money to the child, with a ribbon around it. That's okay for a $100 birthday present or a $50 Savings Bond at a Bar Mitzvah. But not for larger sums. Sometimes access is too easy: The child can pillage bank accounts or Savings Bonds whenever he or she wants. With stocks and real estate, on the other hand, access is too strict: It's tough, sometimes impossible, for your son or daughter to sell the property while underage. If the stock market crashes, you can only sit there and weep.

Some people think they have given money to a child by opening a bank account in trust for him or her. Not so. You still own the money and pay taxes on the interest. It doesn't pass to the child until you die.

2. *Joint property.* Forget it. Putting property in joint names with a child is even worse than giving it outright. You can't sell the whole property without the child's consent. If the child is underage, he or she usually can't give consent without a court order. You still owe taxes on at least part of the income. If you die rich enough to owe estate taxes, the entire property will be taxed to your estate (because you paid for it). The only joint property that you can liquidate easily is a joint bank account. But that doesn't even count as a gift, or save you taxes, unless the child withdraws the money.

3. *Uniform Gifts to Minors Act.* For most people, UGMA is the ticket. Use it for anything more than a few Savings Bonds. Cash, stocks, mutual funds, bonds, and in some states, insurance policies can be given to an adult acting as custodian for the child.

The custodian—who can be you or your spouse—manages the money and can spend it on things like college tuition. When the child reaches 18 or 21, depending on state law, he or she gets the remaining money free and clear.

You generally can't give real estate and other complicated kinds of property under UGMA. For this, you need the newer—and better— Uniform Transfer to Minors Act, now in effect in around 30 states. Under UTMA, the assets don't necessarily have to be distributed by age 18 or 21, although at this writing only California has extended the age (to 25).

UGMA and UTMA gifts can be made with no muss and no fuss. Your bank, stockbroker, or insurance agent can give you the papers and tell you where to sign. In fact, it's almost too easy. Without legal advice, you might make a gift that you'll regret. Don't name yourself custodian, if your net worth exceeds $600,000. If you do, and die before the child becomes a legal adult, the money will be taxed in your estate just as if you hadn't given it away.

4. *Trusts.* To give a child a large sum of money, see a lawyer experienced in trusts. A trust can do almost anything you want it to: accumulate the income or pay it out; pay out income but not principal; hand over the money at whatever age you think your child will be grown up (no, don't wait until 50; if the child doesn't grow up earlier, he or she never will).

Don't use trust income for the child's support. Support is your legal obligation. If the trust picks up your obligation—by paying for your child's food and clothing—that income can be taxed back to you. So here's the big question, for well-to-do parents: Can trust income be used to pay for college? In divorce courts, college is increasingly considered a legal obligation for parents with money. But so far, there has been no tax attack on the many trusts that pay college bills.

SHOULD A TRUST OWN IT?

Maybe. A lot of people set up living trusts, principally to avoid probate. But probate isn't always the black hole it used to be (page 94). Take a look at the uses of a trust, and ask yourself which of them really matter. You might prefer a durable power of attorney.

A *revocable living trust* is not unlike a mirror maze in a funhouse, where you see yourself in every glass. When you set up the trust, you give some or all of your property to yourself as trustee. *You* no longer own it; your trustee, who happens to be you, does. (I told you this was done with mirrors.) You and your spouse can be co-trustees.

As trustee, you run the money just as if you still owned it in the old-fashioned way. You can move assets in and out of the trust, as you please; invest them as you like; use income and principal; juggle the terms of the trust and the beneficiaries; even revoke the trust altogether. You need a successor trustee, however, to manage the money if you become incapable and to distribute the assets when you die.

If you name someone else as your trustee and he or she won't follow orders, you can fire that person and install someone else. In other words, you're completely in charge.

Why you might want a living trust:

1. *To avoid probate.* Property in trust goes directly to the beneficiaries when you die, without pausing in the probate court. It is often a fast and cheap way of distributing an inheritance (although distribution can be held up for reasons other than probate). The value of the property can be divided in any way you like. Say, "one-third to each of my three children" or "80 percent to my husband and 10 percent to each of my children." You aren't required to leave specific properties to specific people (although you can, if you like).

2. *To have someone on tap to handle your money if you're incapacitated.* You might be ill. You might have grown permanently vague. If you made no provision for managing your money, your family will ask a court to name a guardian. But it's better to choose someone yourself. You can handle this with a durable power of attorney, which names an agent to act for you. Alternatively, if you set up a trust, you pick someone to succeed you as trustee (page 93).

The trust should specify when your trustee can move to take over your affairs. Give yourself a lot of latitude, to throw money at a gigolo or hunt for gold in Alaska. The law lets you waste your assets however you like, as long as you know that you may be doing something dumb. It's only when your capacity goes that your trustee is empowered to act.

3. *To test the ability of a professional money manager.* If you don't feel good about running money yourself, or don't have the time for it, an investment-management firm or bank trust department will handle it for you. The bank can act simply as a money manager while you remain trustee—usually, the best arrangement. Or you can name the bank trustee.

Banks take almost any sum of money. Amounts exceeding $150,000 to $300,000 can be managed individually, if that's what you want. Smaller amounts (and larger ones, too) can go into pooled accounts that work like mutual funds. Make sure that your arrangement allows you to switch to a different trustee if you don't like the personal treatment you get, or the investment results.

4. *To thumb your nose at disinherited relatives.* It is harder to upset a trust than a will.

5. *To keep matters private.* Wills are public documents, and so are court hearings to establish mental incompetence. Trusts aren't.

6. *To try to avoid creditors.* In some states, funds in a living trust that haven't been pledged to secure a debt might not be available to pay your creditors after your death. But this common-law protection is crumbling. For the best protection against creditors after death, use joint property.

One thing a trust won't do . . .

A living, revocable trust won't save income or estate taxes. As long as you control the property, the income will be taxed to you. To avoid the tax, you'd have to give away the property, permanently. That's an error for anyone but the very rich.

CHOOSING A TRUSTEE

If you go for a trust, your toughest decision will be choosing an outside trustee. Someone has to be ready to step in, if you or your spouse can no longer serve.

A dependable grown child will see to your welfare, but might have bad financial judgment.

A business associate might be good at managing your money, but help himself to it.

A bank has investment experience, won't skip out or steal, and will handle the paperwork. But it's not cheap. And it may not knock itself out to keep you happy.

Co-trustees often work well—a family member and a bank or investment advisor.

In the end, you can only go for integrity and keep your fingers crossed. And, of course, provide a method for kicking out a trustee whom the family doesn't like.

DON'T TRY TO SAVE MONEY BY SETTING UP A TRUST WITHOUT A LAWYER. Books with tear-out forms for doing trusts are not your friend. You might misunderstand the instructions, which are complicated. You might fill in ambiguous forms ambiguously. You might think you've put property into trust when you haven't, because you didn't transfer the title to yourself *as trustee.* Do yourself a favor and see a lawyer. If it's worth avoiding probate, it's worth doing the job right.

THE POOR MAN'S LIVING TRUST

This is the *durable power of attorney* (page 117). You name someone to manage your affairs if you become incapable, without bothering to set up a trust.

Another approach to the incapacity problem is to set up a "standby" living trust without putting any money in it. This saves you the occasional paperwork problem of selling assets held in trust. If you ever become mentally incompetent, the person holding your durable power of attorney could activate the trust, put your property into it, and arrange for it to be properly managed.

SAVINGS ACCOUNTS "IN TRUST FOR"

These are the simplest living trusts. You register the savings account in trust for one or more beneficiaries. Control stays with you—to buy certificates of deposit, switch to a money market account, change the beneficiary, even cancel the trust by taking every penny out. You haven't made a gift. The beneficiary can't touch the money until you die.

The same result can be achieved through a POD—Payable on Death —account. Which arrangement you use will depend on your state. One possible drawback: When you do die, the beneficiary gets the money immediately, ready or not. So don't put a big bank account in trust for a minor child.

THE LEGAL COMMUNITY IS WORKING ON A TRANSFER-ON-DEATH FORM FOR SECURITIES. If accepted by your state legislature, it would let you pass stocks, bonds, and other securities to a beneficiary, without going through probate and without the need for a trust or joint ownership. It's a great idea. Write to your state representative and say that you want it.

DOES PROBATE REALLY MATTER?

Hardly anyone is noticing. But for the average person, passing property to new owners at death is not always the struggle it used to be. So avoiding probate doesn't matter so much.

Probate means "prove." It's the system that assures that your will is valid and that your property passes to the person who is supposed to get it. Scandals have swirled around the process. Survivors have sometimes waited years for their money while judges dithered and greedy lawyers bled the estate.

In recent years, however, many states have passed probate-simplification laws, especially for small estates or estates in which everything passes to the spouse. There may also be speedy procedures for estates that aren't contested. Odds and ends of personal property, including a car, rarely have to go through probate. They're divided as your will directs, or by private agreement among your heirs. Families can handle the paperwork themselves; they just go to the probate court and let the clerk tell them what to do. Or a lawyer can handle it for you. With simplified procedures, he or she shouldn't charge too much (show the lawyer this sentence!).

THERE ARE THREE MAIN WAYS OF AVOIDING PROBATE: (1) putting property into joint names; (2) naming a beneficiary for a particular piece of property, like a life-insurance policy, bank account, or Individual Retirement Account; (3) putting property in trust. Each method runs a risk. The joint owner might take your money and run. Naming individual beneficiaries for each of your properties might accidentally bequeath one of your children less money than another. Do-it-yourself trusts might not work out. Lawyer-drawn trusts need, well, a lawyer. When there's a trustee involved, it can be a bit more complicated to sell stocks or real estate than when there isn't.

Ask a lawyer whether your state allows simplified probate and whether your courts are efficient. If so, it may not be worth setting up a trust just to avoid them. The rule is: Handle the property in the best way for you and your family. If it happens to avoid probate, fine; if not, don't worry about it.

6
WILLING MAKES IT SO:

Wills and Trusts—For Everything You Can't Take with You

The three immutable facts: You own stuff. You will die. Someone will get that stuff.

Everyone has a will. If you don't write your own, you get the universal will that your state wrote for you. The state means well but it's not too clever, brooks no appeal, and makes no exceptions to its rules. All your nearest relatives get a piece of your property, but no one else does—and no one gets more than the state-allotted share, even if it's unfair. Spouses usually suffer the most.

The tangled tales from probate court would tantalize the brothers Grimm. Yet many people who know better still don't write wills, and are not moved by the mess they're likely to leave behind. Maybe they don't intend to die. Neither do I, but I have a will anyway, just in case.

While I'm here on my soapbox, let me also nag at those of you whose wills are out of date. Old wills, written before your income went up or before family members married, divorced, or died, can wreak just as much havoc as no will at all.

Making a will is so engrossing that it beats me why anyone has to be dragged to it. You imagine their gratitude, as you assign your jewelry to Sylvia and your antique clock to Sam. You feel like God; you arrange everything.

I've heard plenty of excuses for not writing a will. To answer some of them: You can write a will even though your financial affairs are a mess. You don't have to have your property appraised. No one has to know what you own (although you'll get a smarter will if you list your major holdings for your lawyer). The witnesses to the will never know what is in it. Your property isn't locked up in any way. You can change things as often as you want.

WITHOUT A WILL...

• Depending on state law, not all of the property may go to your spouse.

• Your grown children may get some of the money that was meant for your spouse, leaving your spouse with too little to live on.

• A court will choose your children's guardian.

• Stepchildren usually get nothing.

• Neither do your friends or your roommate.

• Your family might battle with the courts.

• A fight might break out among your relatives over who gets the children and who runs their inheritance.

• There probably won't be a trust to take care of your young children's money.

• Part of the money that you meant for your spouse may go to your young kids. Your spouse, as guardian, can use it only for their support. The court will have to approve certain expenditures, and will require an annual accounting.

• Part of the family might be cut off from the family business.

• You can't leave your favorite things to your favorite people.

• The state bends over backward to keep money safe for young children—then hands it all over to them when they reach majority, usually age 18. If they're not ready for the responsibility, too bad.

• You can't leave a contribution to a church or charity.

• A closely held business will have to be sold fast, because the estate might not be permitted to run it.

• Your retarded or handicapped child may inherit money, disqualifying him or her from government aid.

• Everyone will be sore at you.

If you're married, wills sometimes seem to be beside the point. You simply put all the property into joint names so that your spouse will inherit. But what if you die together in an accident? Who gets the property then, and how are your children taken care of? You wouldn't go out at night and leave your youngsters without a babysitter. Why would you go out forever and leave them without a guardian? If you have no children and the wife dies five days before the husband (or fewer, depending on the state), everything passes to his relatives, leaving hers out. And vice versa.

Single people may not care that everything goes to their parents. But it takes a will to include a friend, a roommate, a charity, or in some states, a brother. A will is especially important for live-in couples, straight or gay. If your parents hate your way of life, they may vent their anger on the survivor, seizing property he or she ought to have.

Innocents think that, even without a will, property passes to the person who most ought to own it. How mistaken they are. What's "right" under state law may be all wrong for your family and friends. Laws vary, but the following table gives you a general idea of what could happen if you die *intestate* (will-less).

If you're	*And die without a will, your property will go*
Unmarried, no children, parents living	To your parents. In some states, they split it with your brothers and sisters.
Unmarried, no children, parents dead	To your brothers and sisters; if you were an only child, to other next-of-kin.
Unmarried, with children	To your children, but probably not to step-children. The court appoints a guardian for your minor children and their funds.
Unmarried, no relatives	To the state.
Married, with children	Depending on the state and the size of the estate, all to the surviving spouse, or part to the spouse, part to the children. The spouse may get one-third to one-half of your separately owned property, part or all of the community property, and all of the joint property you held together.

Married, without children	Depending on the state and the size of the estate, all to the surviving spouse, or part to the spouse, part to your parents, and perhaps even part to your siblings. The spouse may get one-half of your separately owned property, part or all of the community property, and all of the joint property. Some states give everything to your spouse; others divide it among spouse, parents, and siblings.

WHAT PASSES BY WILL?

One bright spot, for the families of will truants, is that so little nowadays may be covered by a will. A will dictates only what happens to property that you own individually (including your half of community property and property held as tenants in common) *and* that does not have a named beneficiary.

A lot of your property may get to its rightful owner without the intercession of your will. For example:

· All joint property automatically goes to the other owner.

· Property disposed of by contract, like a partnership with buy-sell provisions, goes to the person named.

· So does property with a named beneficiary, like life insurance, Keogh plans, Individual Retirement Accounts, employee pension and profit-sharing plans. U.S. Savings Bonds, tax-deferred annuities, and bank accounts in trust for others.

· Property put into a revocable living trust goes to the beneficiaries of the trust.

· The usual sort of personal property that we all own—the clock, the sugar bowl, the TV set—is often divided by private agreement, without a will, assuming that no one in the family lodges a formal protest. Many states even let you transfer title to an automobile without cranking up the probate machine.

To a surprising degree, we are seeing the rise of what University of Chicago Law School professor John Langbein calls "the nonprobate estate" ("probate" meaning anything covered by your will). By accident or on purpose, people are leaving their probate estates almost dry. If most of your financial assets pass outside your will, your state might not require probate for the little personal property that remains.

• • •

Some people go out of their way to avoid probate (for the pros and cons, see page 94). Others find it easier and simpler to handle everything by will. Even so, *the way you hold property may accidentally frustrate the intent of your will.*

For example, you might say in your will, "Divide my estate equally between my beloved children, John and Jane." Later, you put John's name on your bank account so that he can help you pay your bills. When you die, the account will probably go to John. Too bad for Jane. (Instead of using joint ownership, give John your power of attorney. That frees him to write checks for you. On your death the remaining money will still be split between John and Jane.)

Or your will might order that your Individual Retirement Account be paid to your sister. But what if, when you started the IRA, you named your brother as beneficiary? He'll get the money. Your sister is cut out. (You should have changed the name of the beneficiary on the IRA account itself.)

Or your will might set up a tax-saving trust to hold $600,000 of your assets. But your major asset is your mansion, which you keep in joint names with your spouse. You also have a life-insurance policy, naming your spouse as beneficiary. When you die, your spouse gets the home and the life insurance. There may not be enough in your probate estate to fund the trust. Several thousand dollars worth of estate planning will have gone down the drain. (You should have kept at least $600,000 in your separate name, or named your estate the beneficiary of your life insurance.)

Nothing can be passed by your will unless (1) it is held solely in your own name, is your half of community property, or is your half of property shared as tenants in common, and (2) it does not carry someone else's name as beneficiary.

IF VIRTUALLY ALL OF YOUR PROPERTY IS DISPOSED OF IN OTHER WAYS, WHY BOTHER WITH A WILL? Several reasons:

• To name a guardian for your children and your children's inheritance.

• To dispose of property you didn't expect to own. *This especially affects married couples.* Say that a husband with no will inherits from his wife. If he himself dies soon thereafter (perhaps because they were both in the same auto accident), the property and the children are left in the arms of the state.

• To dispose of any property you get after your death. You actually can get rich posthumously. For example, if you die in an accident, a court might bring in a big judgment payable to your estate.

• To avoid fierce family arguments over who gets the painting of Uncle Harry.

• To avoid all the problems of joint ownership and named beneficiaries (page 100). Single people, in particular, are better off with wills.

• To dispose of your half of jointly owned property, if both you and the other owner die in the same accident.

• To make sure that your probate-avoiding tactics work. If you set up a living trust, you need a so-called "pour-over will." It guarantees that any property you forgot, or that comes to you after your death, will be added to your trust.

DO YOU NEED A LAWYER?

Strictly speaking, no. You can draw your own will. But a lawyer who represents himself is said to have a fool for a client. I think the same about people who handwrite their wills and stick them in desk drawers.

Years of tradition and legal precedent stand behind the formalities of wills. The words are precise, to avoid ambiguity. The procedures are as orderly as a ballet, to make it irrefutably plain that these indeed are your intentions. Homemade documents—clear to you—may be so vague to others that your heirs have to get a reading in court. The will may even be thrown out and your property distributed according to state law. Books do exist that guide you through writing a valid will, but they take a lot of time and study. A lawyer shouldn't charge more than $300 or so for a very simple will (although you can pay in the thousands for a document that is long and complex).

Here's why you need an attorney.

TO SAY EXACTLY WHAT YOU MEAN. If you leave money to "Barbara and her children," do you mean "Barbara, if living, and if not, to her children"? Or do you mean, "divided in equal parts among Barbara and her children"? Or "one-half to Barbara and one-half to her children"? Who knows? Depending on the state, Barbara and her children may become joint owners; or Barbara may get the income from the property for life, or Barbara may be able to occupy the land for life, with the children inheriting it after her death.

TO CLUE YOU IN TO YOUR STATE'S WEIRD INHERITANCE LAWS. For example, if you leave someone a house with a mortgage on it, your estate might have to pay off the loan unless you specifically indicate it shouldn't.

TO ADVISE YOU ON HOW TO HOLD YOUR PROPERTY—jointly? individually? in trust?

TO REDUCE FEDERAL DEATH TAXES, if your estate is larger than $600,000. Even smaller estates may be subject to death taxes at the state level.

TO SEE THAT YOUR HEIRS ARE NOT ROBBED OF THEIR SHARE OF YOUR CLOSELY HELD BUSINESS. Unless someone agrees, in writing, to buy out your interest, it may be worthless to the family you leave behind.

TO ASK QUESTIONS THAT MIGHT NOT OCCUR TO YOU. For example, what if one of your children should die before you? Would you want a share of your property to go to that child's spouse? Or not? If no alternative beneficiary is named, the share may go to your child's children.

TO MAKE YOUR WILL CHALLENGE-PROOF. All the formalities have to be followed. You need the right number of witnesses, all of whom can testify that you knew you were signing your will, that you were competent to do so, and that the signatire on the will is yours.

HOMEMADE WILLS

You don't believe me. You think you're smarter than a lawyer, and don't see why you should pay him or her to complicate your life. So . . .

YOU HANDWRITE A WILL, SIGN IT, DATE IT, LEAVE IT UNWITNESSED, AND PUT IT IN YOUR DESK DRAWER. Is it valid? Yes, in some states; no, in others. The bad news is that you have to ask a lawyer what your state allows. Even if the will is good, its terms may be fuzzy. That doesn't matter as long as your heirs agree on where the money should go. But if they disagree, your "will" could set off a terrible fight. People who boast that they've done their own wills wouldn't be so smug if they saw what often happened to them later.

YOU TYPE A WILL, SIGN IT, DATE IT, AND PUT IT IN YOUR DESK DRAWER. It's invalid. It is not considered a handwritten will. To validate it, you need the signatures of the right number of witnesses. And you have to follow your state's procedures for having the will signed and witnessed.

YOU GET WITNESSES. The will might still be thrown out of court, unless you follow the specific procedures that your state requires. The witnesses may have to see you sign, or hear you acknowledge your signature to them. Or you may have to see the witnesses sign. Or they may have to sign in the presence of one another. Whatever the rules, states generally agree that a minor technical failure invalidates the will. Who witnesses the will may also be critical. Many states put limits on what a witness can inherit. A few states don't let a witness inherit anything.

YOU FILL IN THE STANDARD DO-IT-YOURSELF WILL FORM THAT A FEW STATES PROVIDE. These forms are fine, in theory, for simple wills ("everything to my spouse" or "everything to my child"). But they don't allow for many choices. Like a typed will, they need witnesses. If you misinterpret the instructions and make just one mistake in getting the will signed and witnessed, it probably won't be valid.

YOU TELL PEOPLE, ORALLY, WHAT YOU WANT. Sometimes that's a valid will—but only if you're in imminent danger of death, not much property is involved, and several witnesses hear you. Some states allow oral wills only to servicemen in combat. If you survive longer than a certain period of time, your oral will evaporates.

YOU VIDEOTAPE YOURSELF RECITING YOUR BEQUESTS. You do *not* have a will. The tape has no formal standing in law. A videotape of you signing the will, however, can prevent unhappy relatives from charging that you were too woolly to make decisions.

YOU GET A BOOK ON HOW TO WRITE YOUR OWN WILL AND FOLLOW DIRECTIONS. CAREFULLY. If you're patient, and there aren't too many mistakes in the book, maybe it will work out. One guide to try: *Nolo's Simple Will Book* by Denis Clifford, at this writing, $17.95. It's available in many bookstores or directly from Nolo Press, 950 Parker St., Berkeley, CA, 94710.

JOINT WILLS

This is a single will for two people, usually a husband and wife. They might each leave all the property to the other, and to the children equally when the second spouse dies.

I believe in sharing secrets, sharing beds, and sharing property—but not in sharing wills. Don't do it. A joint will can be hard to change without the consent of your spouse. After your death, a court might decide that it's a contract, not a will. In that case, the property left to your spouse might not qualify for the marital deduction.

What's more, your spouse may not be able to change the terms. Say, for example, that your joint will leaves money to the children equally after you both die. But after your death, one child goes blind and your spouse wants to leave that child something extra. If your joint will were read as a contract, that couldn't be done. It would be impossible to alter the terms.

NAMING AN EXECUTOR

The executor sees that your will is carried out. It's a tiresome, detailed, time-consuming, thankless job. You're doing no favors for the person you name. All the property has to be tracked down and assembled. Creditors notified. Heirs dealt with tactfully. Arguments settled. Lawyers pushed. Bills and taxes paid. Property appraised and sold. Life insurance claimed. Investments managed until they can be distributed to their new owners.

The executor usually works with a lawyer, so you don't need an expert in estate law or high finance. You need virtues that are much harder to find. An executor has to be willing, reliable, well-organized, honest, responsible about money, fair-minded, and sensitive to the worries of the heirs. The usual practice is to ask an able heir (or friend) to do the job. If you name a professional executor—a bank or a lawyer—include a family member as co-executor, just to keep things moving along. Get permission before putting down someone's name. If money is misspent or errors made, the executor can be held personally responsible.

A friend or family member usually doesn't ask for compensation. A bank or attorney, on the other hand, will charge, and charge, and charge—sometimes by the hour, sometimes a fixed fee, sometimes a percentage of the assets, not counting life insurance. In a state with simplified probate laws, your family may not need an attorney at all. The job may be easy enough to do themselves. They should go to the courthouse and ask the clerk of the probate court what's involved.

WHO GETS THE ANDIRONS?

"How nice. Mommy Dearest left me a nice, round $1 million . . . but what did you say? Jimmy took the andirons? They were supposed to be mine! I'll sue!"

And so it goes. Personal property is generally lumped together and left to your main beneficiary, who divides it among all the family members. Or it's divided equally among your children, leaving it up to them to decide. If your heirs fall out, money may not be the issue. They're more likely to fight about all the things that can't be split—the grand-father's clock, the opal earrings, the china, the antique pool table.

The easiest way to make special bequests is by letter attached to your will—the andirons to Jimmy, the feather boa to Liz. You can then change your mind about the andirons without having to reexecute your will. In some states this letter has the force of law, *if* your will states that you'll leave a letter and *if* the letter is properly written (for example, it should say specifically that these are the people who should get your personal property when you die). In other states, you're simply depend-ing on your family and executor to cooperate.

The letter might also tell your heirs which items are of special value. If you collect Batman comics or Japanese netsuke, leave the name of a dealer who might buy them back. Guns should be left to a person who can possess them lawfully.

Pets—or "heirdales," as rich dogs are called by Lawrence Waggoner of the University of Michigan Law School—are not allowed to inherit. You can leave a trust for their upkeep, as long as the trustee is willing to carry out its terms. But the trust isn't enforceable, if the trustee you name doesn't want to bother. So settle with your Good Samaritan in advance.

SETTLING SHARES

Unequal shares, to people who feel that they ought to be equals, become an eternal thorn in the side. Aunt Dora's last revenge on an irritating nephew is to leave him only $1,000 while his brother gets $2,000.

For the sake of family relations, equal shares are politic—with a few exceptions. If you've already put two kids through college and have one to go, that child deserves something extra for his education. He shouldn't have to spend his inheritance on a college degree that, for everyone else, was financed out of family funds. If one daughter married in state, the other should be able to afford the same. If one adult child is rich and the other poor, you might all agree to help the one who really needs it.

Don't keep your kids in the dark about the will. Explain the provi-sions, by letter or in a tape—especially if you've left them unequal shares. You want them to understand your reasoning, to avoid bitterness and deflect a challenge to the will.

PICKING A GUARDIAN

If you die, who better than Grandma to look after the children? The answer to that question is: practically anyone you can think of. Grandma paid her dues. She shouldn't have to gear up for child rearing all over again. Furthermore, if your parents are named guardians, you are setting up your children to lose a mom and dad all over again.

A brother or sister is a better choice. So is an older, married child, or a close friend who shares your values and way of life. The guardian should, of course, be willing to undertake the job. If you name a friend instead of a family member, spell out your reasons in your will. The family might challenge your choice and you want the court to understand your thinking.

If your children are old enough to understand the question, ask them where they'd like to live if anything happened to you—and let them in on what you decide. Don't be afraid to raise the issue. Children are often better able to cope with thoughts of dying than adults—maybe because to them death seems so remote. The older the child, the more important that he or she be part of the decision.

Besides a guardian for your children you need a guardian for their inheritance. Usually, the same person does both. But if your loving brother is an airhead about money, pick someone else to look after the child's property. You don't need a financial genius, just a conscientious person with common sense. Leave enough money—if not in property then in life insurance—so that your child can be properly raised and educated. You don't want him or her to be a burden on the guardian.

If you're divorced, the guardianship normally goes to your ex-spouse, as long as he or she wants it. A court will step in only if the parent is clearly unfit (say, a drug addict) or has legally abandoned the child. If you don't think your ex-spouse is interested, name someone else and explain in your will why you made that choice. Your ex-spouse still gets first crack. But your candidate should come in ahead of all other contenders.

WAYS TO LEAVE MONEY TO YOUNG CHILDREN

1. *Name a legal guardian for the children's funds.* State law determines what can be spent on the children and what investments can be made.

The guardian makes an annual accounting to the court. When the child comes of age—at 18 or 21, depending on your state—he or she gets the money.

2. *Use the Uniform Gifts to Minors Act (UGMA).* In many states, you have to make the gift during your lifetime, rather than by will. The funds are left to an adult who acts as custodian for the child. The law determines how the money can be spent and invested. A custodian may have more flexibility in handling money than a guardian does. The funds go to the child when he or she comes of age, usually at 18.

3. *Use the Uniform Transfers to Minors Act (UTMA),* if your state has adopted it. UTMA allows transfers by will, as well as gifts during your lifetime. The custodian can hold the assets until the child is 18 or 21 (25, in California).

4. *Leave the money in trust.* This is the best solution for sums over $20,000 or so. Your trustee—a relative, friend, attorney, or bank—manages the inheritance and pays it to the child according to your instructions. He or she can dole out income and principal as needed for the child's education and living expenses. The remainder is turned over to the child at the age you set—maybe 25 or 30. You can provide that the child gets the money all at once or in installments—say, at ages 25, 30, and 35. The trustee can be told to withhold payments, if it seems to be in the child's best interest. (Do you want the child to inherit if he or she has just joined a religious cult and will give it every penny?) You might make the child co-trustee at, say, age 23. That allows him or her to share in investment decisions without yet having to handle the money alone.

Set up a single trust for all the children. If one child has big medical bills, they can be paid out of common funds without pillaging that child's basic inheritance. Typically, all the money stays in trust until the youngest child reaches, say, 25 (although, at your death, a nominal payment might be made to the older children). Then the trust dissolves and everyone gets his or her appointed share.

LEAVING PROPERTY TO A LOVER

Since families often hate these relationships—especially gay ones—the loving couple can't be too careful. After the death of one, the parents might make a strong effort to carry everything away. If you want your mate to get your money, you need a will. And spell out, specifically, why you chose your lover to inherit rather than your family. "Mickey, who has lived with me faithfully for seven years . . ."

HOW TO RUIN A RELATIONSHIP

Your nieces, Mary and Martha, love your antique grandfather's clock so you leave it to both of them. Your 1957 black Thunderbird with tailfins goes to your two grandsons. Three of your children inherit the beach house.

Is this generosity? Will it bring the new owners together in an orgy of sharing? Not likely. You have created a monster that will eat your family up. Your nieces, once in perfect sympathy, will fall out over whose time it is.

Few people can reach perfect accord over what to do with mutually owned property. Their personal and financial situations are different. So are their attitudes. What if Martha moves to a distant state and takes the clock with her—how does Mary get her share back? What if your older grandson is a demon driver and racks up the car—can the younger one force him to put it back into prime condition? What if the beach house needs a new roof but one of the owners can't afford to pay? What if one owner wants to sell?

Anything that can't be divided should either be left to one person or sold and the proceeds split.

MORE WILL FACTS

Execute only one copy of your will. If you sign more, the court will hold up probate until they're all found. For extras, make photocopies.

Have your will checked when you move to a new state. A properly signed and witnessed will is usually valid everywhere. But ownership rights differ from state to state, which might make a difference in how your property is held.

Two ways to cancel a will: (1) The only sure way is to make a new one, specifically revoking all wills and codicils that have come before. (2) You can tear up your old will. But you had better do so in the presence of several witnesses, and say specifically that this will is no longer valid. Otherwise, an heir might argue successfully that your will is merely missing. A photocopy in the lawyer's keeping might then be accepted as a valid will.

The *only* way to make a small change in a will is to execute a formal *codicil,* amending it. Don't ink out an old provision or insert a new one. In some states and with some provisions, that works; in others it doesn't. Any change should be signed, dated, and witnessed according to your state's procedures. Otherwise, the court will ignore the change or revoke the entire provision. Extensive changes might invalidate the entire will.

Say you leave your spouse money, get divorced, and die before you change your will. Does the ex-spouse collect? Generally, no. The rest of the will is usually valid, but your ex-spouse will be cut out. However, exceptions exist—so change your will as soon as the divorce negotiations get underway. If you haven't changed your will, and die when you're legally separated but not divorced, your spouse *will* collect.

If you're getting divorced, *immediately* drop your spouse as beneficiary on your life-insurance policy, employee-benefit plans, and revocable trusts. If you don't, and die, most states allow your ex-spouse to collect, even if you have married again.

Say you leave half of your property to "my dear children Justin and Matthew." Then Sally is born, but you die before specifically including her in your will. Is she disinherited? No. But how much she gets will depend on your state. She might get exactly what the other children do. Or she might be given what she'd have received if you had died without a will—which could be more, or less, than the other children inherit. The same is true for an adopted child, but not a stepchild. Unless specifically mentioned, a stepchild is out.

Say you get married but your will still leaves everything to your pals. Is your spouse disinherited? No. The inheritance depends on state law and the size of the estate. It might be one-third or one-half. Some states give the spouse everything, if the estate is not large. Moral: Execute a new will on the way out of church.

Say you get married and regret it. Your will leaves nothing to your spouse. Tough luck—the spouse still collects something (unless you are legally separated).

A spouse won't inherit, however, if you both signed a valid premarital contract to that effect, exerting no unfair pressure to sign, and disclosing all assets. You can write a postmarital contract, too (page 122).

When leaving money to charity, check that you have the legal name and address. Many charities have similar names and might mount a fight over the bequest. Name an alternative charity, in case the first one is out of business.

If you own homes in more than one state, establish one of them as your legal residence (by voting there, paying taxes there, listing that address on your credit cards, getting a driver's license in that state, and so on). Otherwise, both states might try to tax your estate.

You can disinherit a child in every state except Louisiana. Your will should state specifically that you are leaving that child no money, or leaving a nominal sum like one dollar. If the child isn't mentioned, and was born after the will was executed, the court will treat it as an oversight and restore his or her inheritance.

Small bequests are usually stated in dollar amounts—like, "$1,000 for my friend, Lynn ————." But it's generally better to state other major bequests in percentage terms rather than in dollar amounts. Consider what might happen if you leave $30,000 to each of three nieces and the remainder to charity—expecting the charity to get a large share. If the stock market crashes and your estate winds up with only $90,000, your nieces will get theirs and the charity will get nothing. So instead, say "40 percent for the charity and 20 percent for each of my nieces."

Your will can forgive debts. In a community property state, however, you may be able to forgive only half of the debt. Your spouse would have to forgive the other half.

Some reasons to change your will: (1) a big rise or fall in your net worth; (2) a new child, by birth, adoption, or marriage; (3) marriage, separation, or divorce; (4) a child's marriage, separation, or divorce; (5) a child's college graduation; (6) the death of an heir; (7) an illness in the family that may go on for life; (8) a change in the property or inheritance laws.

Are you holding investment real estate? If your heirs aren't capable of managing real estate, leave a letter for the executor giving all the details about the investment, what it should be worth, and who is most qualified to sell it.

If estate taxes will be due, and your estate is made up mostly of illiquid real estate, leave enough life insurance to cover the bill. When considering how large a policy to buy, remember that the policy itself may increase the value of the estate.

Are you holding old tax shelters, such as partnerships to invest in real estate or oil drilling? Large payments may be due for several years into the future—payments that your spouse could not meet. The units may be taxable but not salable. If you manage to sell, the accumulated tax liability may be greater than the shelter's current value. Examine your exposure, and leave extra life insurance if necessary.

Does your net worth depend on a closely held business? Get buyout agreements with your partners, enough life insurance to cover estate taxes, and agreements to protect your family's interests. Otherwise, the business might prosper while your heirs get nary a penny.

If you're married and made your will before September 13, 1981, revise it. Under current law, no gift or estate taxes are due on property left to a spouse. But wills drawn before that 1981 date may be subject to an older law, which could leave some of the money open to tax.

Five grounds for challenging a will: (1) a procedural flaw, like an unwitnessed change in the text; (2) too young (the will was made when the person was still a minor); (3) undue influence or duress (the will was signed under pressure); (4) fraud (the person thought he or she was signing a contract rather than a will); (5) mental incapacity (the person was too senile to change his or her will). But you have to raise your objection quickly. If you miss the deadline set by your state, you won't be allowed to make your case.

SEXISM AND WILLS

It lingers on. Fathers may leave less to their daughters than to their sons. Daughters may be shut out of the family business. Wives may not be consulted on the will. Money for a wife may be left in trust, forcing her to live on a banker's dole for the rest of her life. The wife might even have agreed to the trust, because she took no interest in money management when her husband was alive. But when a wife becomes a widow, things change. She often discovers the lovely little secret that conservative investing isn't hard. She may come to resent her dependency on a bank trust department.

In the case of a long-time marriage, especially a first marriage, all questions about what happens to the money when the husband dies should be resolved on the side of the widow's freedom to act. If she eventually decides that she doesn't like handling money, she can give

it to a bank trust department herself. But the issues may be different
with second marriages, especially second marriages later in life. Each
spouse may want to leave money in trust for the children of a former
marriage.

LEAVING MONEY IN TRUST

A *testamentary trust* is set up by your will. Instead of leaving money
directly to the beneficiary, you leave it in trust, to be managed by a
trustee. Funds can be paid out for various purposes. At some point, the
trust dissolves and the money is distributed.

A TRUST CAN HOLD MONEY UNTIL A CHILD GROWS UP (page 107). But don't be a
dead hand from the grave, holding on to the child's inheritance for years.
By the time he or she is 30, the child should be able to get the money
and take his or her chances.

A TRUST CAN SAVE ESTATE TAXES. If your net worth is over $600,000, talk to
a lawyer about how to cut federal taxes. Often, you can do it without
using a trust (page 114). Your state may levy taxes on amounts smaller
than $600,000.

A TRUST CAN MANAGE MONEY LEFT TO A SPOUSE. A trustee runs the money. The
spouse receives the income and, if needed, payments out of principal.
When the spouse dies, the remaining money goes to whoever is named.
A family member, bank, or investment advisor is generally the trustee.
The spouse should be able to change trustees if the relationship isn't
working. But don't lock up *all* of a widow's money in trust. Maybe she
didn't take much interest in it while her husband was alive, but in
widowhood she might turn into a demon money manager. I've seen it
happen. Leave her free to run at least part of her funds as she pleases.

A TRUST CAN PROVIDE FOR RETARDED OR HANDICAPPED CHILDREN. State and federal
programs cover basic medical and residential care, but only if the child
has almost no money. This presents parents with a dilemma: Money left
to the handicapped child will be consumed by the institution. But without that money, the child will get only bare-bones support.

Middle-income parents may feel that they have little choice. They
leave their modest assets to their healthy children and let the handicapped one get government aid. In this case, you should specifically
disinherit the handicapped child (and tell your relatives to do likewise).
You hope that your healthy children will provide any extra comforts that
their institutionalized sibling needs.

Higher-income parents, however, might set up a trust. The handicapped child (possessing little or no money) can often qualify for government aid, while the trust supplies extra maintenance and support. For advice on how to do this, call your state or local Association for Retarded Citizens. Ask for the names of lawyers experienced in your state's public-assistance laws. For the booklet *How to Provide for Their Future*, send $8 to the Association for Retarded Citizens, P.O. Box 1047, Arlington, TX, 76004.

A TRUST CAN ASSURE THAT THE CHILDREN OF A PRIOR MARRIAGE WILL INHERIT. If you leave all your money to a second spouse, he or she can do absolutely anything with it. For example, it can all be left to charity, cutting all your children out. A trust prevents this. You can give your second spouse an income for life while guaranteeing that your children will ultimately inherit.

But whatever you do, don't lock your heirs into a planner's prison. It's not worth saving the taxes, if your trust will completely inhibit your family's freedom to act.

CHOOSING A TRUSTEE

The average trust does just fine with an individual trustee—a family member, friend, lawyer, or business associate. His or her powers are outlined in your will or in the trust document. Fundamentally, you want the trustee to do what you would have done, had you been alive.

Give your trustee wide latitude. You don't know what's going to happen 10 or 20 years hence and shouldn't try to guess. Write a letter to all the trustees (including successor trustees), with copies to all beneficiaries, explaining what you want the trust to accomplish and what the money can be distributed for. That way, everyone understands exactly what you have in mind.

Your risk is that the trustee will slip. His judgment may go. He may steal. He may disapprove of one of your children and deny that child funds. He may grow senile. Your will or trust document should provide for a substitute if the family demands it.

The alternative to a friend or relative is a bank or trust company. It's a professional money manager and experienced estate administrator, which won't move away and won't steal. If your family hates its trust officer, it can ask the bank for another one. But this choice has some drawbacks, too. The bank charges money. It takes only larger trusts (generally, $150,000 and up). It is often too busy to take a personal interest in the family (although this can be solved by naming your spouse or another relative co-trustee). Include an escape clause in the document, so your family has the option of moving the trust to another bank.

AVOIDING TAXES

At this writing, federal gift and estate taxes apply only to estates larger than $600,000 that are not being left to a spouse. On a $610,000 estate, you pay 37 percent on the $10,000 over the exempt amount. Top rate: 55 percent on taxable transfers over $3 million (with an effective rate of 60 percent on transfers between $10 and $21.04 million).

Some states also levy taxes, often on amounts smaller than $600,000 —so you may not be out of the woods just because your estate won't owe the federal tax.

It takes a lawyer to cut your tax bill without mishap. Among his or her bag of tricks:

1. *Make gifts while you're alive.* Up to $10,000 a year can go to each of as many people as you like, tax free. (That sum includes small gifts like $50 at Christmas). If your spouse joins in the gift, you can give up to $20,000. Larger gifts may trigger taxes, but probably not until you die. The rule is: A gift is taxable only if its value, when added to the value of your estate, turns out to exceed $600,000. Even if the gift will lead to taxes, the price may be worth it. If you give, say, $30,000 worth of stock, the dividends and capital gains will accumulate in your child's name instead of in yours, saving you taxes in the end.

2. *Give away your life insurance policy*—to your spouse, your child, or an irrevocable trust. That takes the proceeds out of your estate (unless you die within three years of making the gift; then the proceeds, and taxes, come back). To keep the policy out of your estate, you can't continue to pay the premiums. Instead, the new owner has to pay.

The new owner can change the beneficiary, and has the right to withdraw the cash value or even cancel the policy. If you give the policy to your spouse and then divorce, tough luck.

If your spouse owns the policy, his or her will should leave the policy to the children or another beneficiary. Otherwise, if your spouse dies, the policy might come right back to your estate. If your spouse leaves the policy to your children in trust and you're the trustee, it could also be taxed in your estate. (You see why I told you to see a lawyer.)

If your spouse owns the policy, he or she should be named beneficiary. If the children are the beneficiaries, and you die, the IRS may say that your spouse made the children a taxable gift of the insurance proceeds.

To give away your policy, ask the insurance company for an *assignment form*. You can also give away a group policy that you hold through your employer.

3. *Marry.* No estate tax is levied on property given or bequeathed to a spouse. However, whatever is left (over $600,000) can be taxed in the spouse's estate when he or she dies. Unless, of course, the spouse remarries and passes the tax deferral on.

To avoid a tax when the surviving spouse dies, the wills of married couples should create *bypass Trusts*. Each trust can hold up to $600,000 in assets. That money is left to the children, although the spouse has the use of it for life. Here's how this strategy plays out if the husband dies first (reverse it, if the wife dies first):

a. The husband dies.

b. Up to $600,000 of his assets go into a trust for the children. This money passes estate-tax free, because it's protected by the husband's estate-tax credit.

c. The wife gets the income from the children's trust for life, *plus the right to receive funds directly from the principal if needed.* That's a key point. She always has access to all of the money. It's never "locked away" from her. The trustee has to agree, when she draws on the principal. But that shouldn't be a problem, as long as the husband names a sympathetic trustee and makes it clear that the spouse should be given whatever she wants. The trust document should broadly provide that the money be used for her happiness and general welfare.

d. After benefitting from the trust for many years, the wife dies. All the remaining money is distributed to the children, tax free.

e. The wife leaves the children another $600,000, sheltered by her own estate-tax credit.

f. A total of $1.2 million has been left to the kids tax free. That's twice the amount that the kids could otherwise get untaxed.

For this to work, each spouse has to have enough assets in his or her separate name (or in community property, or tenancy in common without rights of survivorship) to fund a trust. If you own everything jointly, your tax-saving trust will fail. If your house is a substantial part of your net worth, consider owning it as tenants in common (page 85). Your half of the house can then become part of the trust.

4. *Give money to charity.* Money given—or left—to charity reduces your estate, hence your estate tax.

5. *Disclaim.* Let's say that your uncle David died and left you some money. But you're well off, and your son in college is next in line to inherit. You can say no to the bequest, letting it go directly to your son. That saves your estate from paying taxes on that money when you die.

A last word: It isn't graven in stone that you have to avoid estate taxes for the sake of your heirs. You come first. Don't give away so much property, or put so much in trust, that you become dependent on others, even if they're your own children. And *don't undertake your own tax planning.* To explain all these concepts, I have made a meadow out of what is actually a briar patch. Only an experienced estate-planning attorney can walk you through unscratched.

WHEN ARE INHERITANCES PAID?

Probate can go quickly, if your lawyer hustles, the courts are efficient, there aren't a lot of distant heirs to notify, and no one challenges the will. A will might be admitted to probate in anything from a couple of days to a couple of weeks and declared valid almost immediately. A surviving spouse can generally start taking modest sums from the estate right away, in order to meet living expenses. Life insurance is paid out pronto. In most cases, so is jointly owned property. If you wait for months, it means either that your lawyer isn't paying much attention or that you had the bad luck to land in a lousy court (New York City's comes immediately to mind).

Some executors start distributing the property without delay. Others prefer to wait for four to seven months, which is the time generally allowed for creditors to file claims against the estate. Stocks, cars, and bank accounts can be distributed as quickly as title can be passed. Other property—real estate, for example—takes longer to transfer because of the paperwork or the need to sell at a reasonable price. Valuable personal property can't be divided until it's appraised.

Executors usually hold back a little money until the final tax return is accepted (if there's a deficiency the executor is personally responsible). The average estate might be fully distributed in six months to a year. Large estates can take several years.

GRANTING THE POWER

Everyone needs a backup—a person to act for you if you're away, if you're sick, if you get hit by a car and can't function for a while, or if you grow senile. That means giving someone—a spouse, a parent, an adult child, a trusted friend—your power of attorney. A lawyer can get this document together in a jiffy. It's doubtless in his word processor and just needs printing out. Young people need a power of attorney as well as the old.

Limited powers of attorney grant narrow rights, like: "Martha can write checks on my bank account, to pay my bills while I'm out of the country for six months." *Ordinary* powers of attorney give broader powers over your finances. But both limited and ordinary powers expire if you become mentally disabled—which is exactly when you need the help the most.

So protect yourself against doomsday by asking a lawyer to draw up a *durable* power of attorney, recognized in most states. It lets someone act for you even if you're judged senile or mentally disabled; if you fall into a coma, or if illness or accident damages your brain. A durable power lasts, while other powers don't. As long as you are mentally capable, you can revoke a durable power whenever you like.

The person who holds your power of attorney could, theoretically, exercise it at any time, even if you're healthy. He or she could sell your investments and clean out your bank account. But it's not as easy as it sounds. Banks and brokers normally check on what has happened to you, before accepting a power of attorney. Besides, you wouldn't give the power to someone you didn't trust.

You have to execute a new durable power every four or five years, to show that your intention holds. Insurance companies and financial institutions probably won't honor an old power. A few won't honor any durable power of attorney at all. *Always* ask your bank, broker, or insurance company what its policy is, so you'll know for sure that the power you've signed is going to work. If your bank or broker won't accept the power you show them with the provisions you want, move your money somewhere else.

If you'd rather not trust anyone until you absolutely have to, write a *springing* power of attorney. It doesn't take effect unless you become mentally incapacitated, and the document defines exactly what that means. For example: "I shall be deemed to be disabled when two physicians licensed to practice medicine in my state sign a paper stating that I am disabled and unable to handle my financial affairs." The same language can be used to determine when your disability has passed.

How do you cancel a durable power of attorney? Tell the person holding it that he or she is out; get the copy of the power back; just in case there are duplicate copies, write to the institutions holding your money telling them not to accept that person as your agent.

A LIVING WILL AND HEALTH-CARE POWER OF ATTORNEY

Anyone who has seen a dying or comatose parent or spouse hooked up fruitlessly—sometimes painfully—to life-support machines understands the issue of the right to die. Many of those ending their lives on a tube have been forced to it by state law or custom, or because they have no one to issue the humane order to pull the plug. Maintaining a comatose person can also strip the family finances bare.

Your best hope of avoiding this fate yourself is to write a *living will*, exercising your right to refuse treatment that artificially prolongs your dying. Such wills have been ratified by law in 40 states and the District of Columbia. Several of the remaining states have legal precedents— some stronger than others—recognizing similar rights.

But even with a living will, your wishes might not be carried out. A son might say, "I don't care what my father thought he wanted, go ahead and treat him," and the doctor probably would. States also differ about whether someone in a permanent coma can be removed from life-support systems, and whether removing a feeding tube is legally and ethically any different from removing a respirator.

The surest way of having your own wishes carried out is to appoint someone to speak for you. You can name a surrogate or proxy in your living will. But for stronger protection, where state law allows, execute a health-care durable power of attorney. Many states specifically authorize a surrogate to issue the order ending life-support treatment. In the other states, a health-care power of attorney can't hurt and might help.

What happens if you fall into a permanent coma or terminal illness without having written a living will? In many states, courts have ruled that family members or a legal guardian can "stand in the patient's shoes," to make the life-or-death decision that the patient would probably make, were he or she awake to do so. The same thing happens on an informal basis in most of the other states, unless the doctor or hospital forces the issue into court. Two exceptions are New York and Missouri, where no surrogate decisions can be accepted unless there's clear evidence that the patient—while still functioning—expressed a wish not to be artificially kept alive.

A living will is the clearest expression of your intent. You can get the appropriate documents free, by sending a self-addressed, stamped envelope to the Society for the Right to Die, 250 West 57th St., New York, NY, 10107. A donation is suggested but not required.

A health care power of attorney is best drawn up by a lawyer, to conform to your state's laws and court precedents. Lawyers advise that you name two stand-ins to act for you, in case one isn't around when critical decisions have to be made. Your spouse and your doctor are two good choices. To avoid inaction or delay, either one should be able to act alone.

Let everyone know about your decision—children, spouse, doctor, friends. It isn't enough to sign a living will. You have to go out of your way to be sure it's honored.

THE WRITER'S MALPRACTICE AVOIDANCE PARAGRAPH

Writers are licensed only by the First Amendment. We can be as pigheaded and opinionated as the vocabulary allows, but we don't practice law. This chapter should give you a general understanding of wills and estate planning. But in actual practice, the field is pocked with traps that you've never heard of and wouldn't believe if you did. So when I write "see a lawyer" I really mean *see a lawyer*. That's the only way to do this right.

7

ALL IN
THE FAMILY:

Seven Checklists for Life's Milestones

———

Learn from the mistakes of others. You won't
live long enough to make them all yourself.

A PREMARITAL CHECKLIST

1. *Talk money.* It's the last taboo. Get a loaf of bread, a jug of wine, and your net worth statement, and make an afternoon of it. What does each of you earn? What do you own? What do you owe? Are there any other sources of income, like a trust? After the marriage, will one spouse quit work? How about after a baby is born? In a two-paycheck marriage, who pays for what (see page 81)? Will you invest separately or together? One bank account or two? Has either of you ever gone bankrupt? Full disclosure is in order. You might bring a copy of your credit history and maybe a second jug of wine.

2. *Talk life insurance.* Who needs it and how much (page 245)? You may have some automatic coverage from your company. If you die, is that enough to support your spouse? If not, buy more coverage right after the wedding. Two-paycheck professional couples may not need extra life insurance until they buy a house or have a baby.

3. *Talk health insurance.* Will you keep separate policies or can you consolidate? Compare costs and benefits, to see what's best. One of you needs family coverage, in case of pregnancy. At some companies, one spouse can drop health insurance entirely and choose another benefit instead. Or one spouse might go for the employer's health-maintenance organization (HMO), while the other takes a traditional fee-for-service plan (see page 297).

4. *Talk savings.* Be idealistic; assume that you'll have some. How much can you put away each year and how will you do it? Go for automatic payroll deduction, if your company provides it. Fund to the full any plan where the company matches the contributions you make.

5. *Talk commitments.* Does one of you have an aging parent to care for? Is one of you paying alimony and child support? Does one of you want to go back to school? These will all become joint responsibilities, so walk in with your eyes open. An older man marrying a younger woman will probably have to postpone his retirement. That younger woman can expect to nurse him through his last illness and spend many years a widow.

6. *Talk houses.* If you each own a house, ask an accountant how to handle the sale of one or both of them. Taxes will vary, depending on which house you sell when.

7. *Talk prenuptial agreement.* On the other hand, don't. Lawyers adore these contracts because they simplify divorce, but they're often the enemy of love.

The purpose of most prenups is pretty obvious: One spouse (usually, but not always, the man) wants to guarantee that in case of death or divorce the other spouse doesn't get his money. In bad prenups, he plays the bully, she plays the martyr, and they wonder why their honeymoon isn't a joy. A few agreements are signed on the eve of the wedding, under the threat that the bridegroom won't show. Brides should always call the bluff. Better to learn the bad news now than to start a marriage with a mortal wound. A nice way of putting it is, "I'm sorry, but I couldn't sign an agreement that's unfair to me and to your future children." And who knows? Maybe the groom will come around.

Prenups are dandy arrangements only when:

· Both parties want them, because both have good incomes and property to protect.

· Both parties want to preserve their own wealth for the children of their previous marriages.

• The agreement specifies property to be shared as well as property to be kept by one spouse or the other.

• The spouse in the weaker position is guaranteed a decent settlement.

• Neither spouse is left high and dry, without an income.

• If it's a one-sided deal, it will self destruct within a limited period of time, like a year.

• The agreement covers only money, not where to live or who washes the dishes.

• You have a closely held business and don't want to lose part of it in divorce.

You each need a lawyer to protect your interests; one lawyer can't ethically represent you both. You have to disclose all your assets, understand all the consequences, and sign the prenup freely, without being forced. Once you put your name on the agreement, it's tough to break.

A POSTMARITAL CHECKLIST

1. *Change the beneficiary on existing contracts.* Do this for life insurance, pension plans, annuities, living trusts, and Individual Retirement Accounts. You don't have to leave all this money to your spouse, but most people do.

2. *Redo your will.* Or make one.

3. *Settle on your name.* Women can keep their last name or change it. If you make a change, tell Social Security, all your creditors, and anyone else you do business with. If you don't, just leave things as they are. No law requires a Mr. and Mrs. to have the same name.

4. *Set up a joint financial file* (see Chapter 3). You each should know where the other's personal records are.

5. *Open a joint bank account.* It's useful for household expenses, even if you keep separate his-and-hers accounts for personal spending (page 51).

6. *Give each other a durable power of attorney.* That lets each of you act for the other, in an emergency (page 117).

7. *At some point in the future, you might want a postmarital agreement.* It suits a few circumstances, like the couple with children from earlier marriages, who couldn't afford to leave them separate property when the new marriage started. Or the person who starts a successful business and

wants to be sure of retaining all the stock, even if the marriage blows up.

A NEW-BABY CHECKLIST

Before Your Pregnancy

1. *Check your medical insurance.* Insurers generally require that you buy the policy three months or more before the start of your pregnancy. Otherwise, you won't be covered. How much of the cost will you have to pay? With some group plans, no more than $500 or so—but that's the ideal. More likely, your policy will pay, say, $1,000 toward the pregnancy, leaving the rest of the bills to you.

2. *Check your other employee benefits.* You may find some gems. For example, if your company employs 15 or more people and covers its workers with disability insurance, you're entitled to payments while you're on maternity leave. Those payments, combined with vacation pay, might give you an income for many weeks. Another example: Some companies give fathers an unpaid parenting leave.

3. *Save money.* In most cases, you'll have to pay part of the medical bill. Even if you don't, most insurance policies don't pay a dime until after the baby is born. Your doctor, by contrast, might require you to pay as you grow. Some insurers offer interim payments to consumers in these situations.

During Your Pregnancy

1. *Buy more life insurance.* That's not just a baby you're getting, it's bicycles, braces, and a college tuition bill.

2. *Call the hospitals in the area and make an appointment to see the birthing facilities.* There's a lot of competition for maternity business. Some hospitals offer package plans: bedroomlike birthing rooms, pre-natal exercise classes, and a candlelit meal with your spouse. To save money, ask about short-stay programs. They send you and the baby home in a day, with a follow-up visit from a nurse.

3. *Think carefully before choosing a separate birthing center instead of a hospital's birthing rooms.* Centers may charge half the price, and are great for women with normal deliveries. But they have no high-tech operating rooms or intensive-care facilities. If something suddenly goes wrong, you're zipped to a hospital—but how long is the ride? Ten minutes? Fifteen? That's not good enough.

Take my friend Judy, whose second baby got into trouble at the very last minute. Her doctor slammed her wheeled bed into the operating room and did a Caesarian in two minutes flat. Being in a hospital saved her baby's life. Or take my friend Angela. Right after the normal delivery of her third baby she started to hemmorhage. She might not be alive today if, five minutes later, she hadn't been in the operating room, stanched and sewn up. Some birthing centers are built right into hospitals, which is another matter. But if you're a few minutes away and something goes wrong, the lives of mother and baby are on the line. I wouldn't take the chance.

4. *If you have a job, be frank with your boss about what happens next.* Some women come right back to work within a few weeks. Some want part-time jobs while their children are small. Some aren't yet sure what they want. No law guarantees you reemployment after a maternity leave —although the company usually holds your job if your leave is short. It's not fair to your boss to delay a decision or to keep mum about what your plans really are. If you'll want a part-time schedule for two or three years, be up front about it. A growing number of companies make part-time deals with valuable employees.

5. *Write a will or update the will you have.* You'll need a guardian, both for the child and for the child's inheritance. Otherwise, the court might put a stranger in charge of the money—and who knows how honest that stranger will be?

After the Birth

1. *Notify your health plan of the new arrival within 30 days.* Otherwise, the baby might not be covered. Employer-paid plans usually cover new babies automatically, but the baby needs to be registered if you pay part or all of the premium yourself.

2. *Don't lose sight of your own employee benefits.* If the mother quits work, and the family was covered by her company group-health insurance, she can probably keep it for a while. As long as her company has at least 20 employees, it has to include her in the group-health plan, at the family's expense, for up to 18 months. But you get this cheap group insurance only if you ask for it within 60 days of leaving your job. So don't miss the deadline.

3. *Start saving for college.* It's not a moment too soon.

A DAY-CARE CHECKLIST

1. *Don't kid yourself about the cost.* Children aren't cheap, at any age. Working parents might pay 10 to 20 percent of their income for day care, with infant care the most expensive and hardest to come by.

2. *See what your company has to offer.* Some companies run an information service about the day-care centers in town. Some subsidize places for employees' children. Some provide flexible employee benefits, with day care as an option. Some help with emergency care when your regular sitter calls in sick. A few even run a center of their own. If your company has its head in the sand about child care, form a committee, find out what forward-looking companies are doing (your public library can help), and make a proposal to management.

3. *If your company's flexible-benefits plan includes day care, take it.* You're one of the lucky ones. Part of your pretax salary (up to $5,000) goes into a special day-care account. The company often contributes, too. That account is then used to pay the babysitter's bills. This is the cheapest way of paying for day care, because you are using pretax dollars.

4. *If both parents work, and you have no flexible-benefits plan, use the child-care credit on your income-tax return.* You can subtract from your income taxes a portion of your child-care expenses: day care, babysitters, day camp, even the price of room and board at boarding school. Tax credits are normally available for the care of children under 13. But there's an exception. If you have a company flexible-benefits plan (above), you have to choose between it and the income-tax credit. You can't use both. For most people, the flexible-benefits plan is better.

5. *Here are your day-care choices, ranked by cost.*

• Your own full-time housekeeper or nanny. Sleep-in help costs about the same as someone who works from 9 to 5. Besides salary, plan on paying for health insurance, half of the Social Security tax, unemployment taxes, worker's compensation in some states, and a paid vacation.

• Day-care centers. They cater principally to toddlers and up.

• Family day care. This describes the neighborhood mother who takes care of several children in her own home. Infants are more likely to be accepted here.

• After-school care for older children. You might find it at day-care centers or in the neighborhood. Expect to pay no more than half the cost of full-time care.

• Grandma. But give her a break, if you can. She has already raised one set of children. Why should she be saddled with another?

6. *Some things to look for in a day-care center or a family day-care home*: a state license, if one is required; a stable workforce; clean, happy children; plenty of clean, appropriate toys; a safe place to play, indoors and out; an organized daily child-care plan; friendly people; at least one adult for every four infants and one adult for every six toddlers; references, so you can ask other parents how they like the center; organized games, rather than care-by-TV; after-hours care, if necessary; a connection with a doctor or nurse, for medical emergencies; your own child's attitude— does he or she seem to be having fun?

A "MOMMY TRACK" CHECKLIST

Corporate women who leave the full-time workforce while their children are small are said to be on the "mommy track." They're willing to settle for part-time or lower-rung jobs, in order to spend more time with their kids. But with a little planning, the mommy track can lead back to the "fast-track" when your children are older.

1. *Be honest with your boss about your choices.* It's not fair to dither. Corporations need to know whether or not to hold your job. Tell your boss that you plan to stay home with your baby but want to negotiate some form of part-time work.

2. *Develop a part-time work plan.* Show your boss what kinds of jobs you can handle from home or by going to the office just three days a week. If you're a valuable employee, something will be worked out.

3. *Plump for job sharing.* At a few companies, two mommy-track employees are allowed to share a single job. Teaching is easily divided in half. So are jobs involving client services. It's the job-sharers' responsibility to keep each other up to speed. Sometimes you get reduced employee benefits; often you get nothing. At present, that's one of the prices of the mommy track.

4. *Develop a home-based business.* But don't expect to work with your children playing silently at your knee. Take my word for it: Children don't play silently. While you're on the phone, at the drafting table, or at the word processor, you'll need a babysitter to keep the kids out of your hair.

AN ELDER-CARE CHECKLIST

1. *Don't swoop down on a capable parent.* Most older people are perfectly able to manage themselves. In fact, their finances may be in better shape than yours. When help is truly needed, don't go overboard. It might be enough to find a good home health service or make a suggestion about certificates of deposit. If your parent loses track of the bills or won't see a doctor, however, don't hesitate to take more responsibility.

2. *Don't miss any of the tax writeoffs.* If you support (or help support) a parent, you may be entitled to a dependency exemption. If you have to hire help to take care of your parent so that you can go to work, you get the tax credit for dependent care (which is the same as the child-care credit).

3. *Check your employee benefits.* Some companies allow personal days off for attending to an elderly parent. If there's a flexible-benefits plan, you can generally arrange to pay for elder care with pretax dollars (it works like child care; see page 125).

4. *Call your city's social-service office or office for the elderly.* (Look for them in the Yellow Pages, under "Elderly" or under the city-government listings.) You'll usually find many useful services that you didn't know about: cooked meals brought to the home; income-tax help; legal aid; home health care; adult day-care centers, and many others.

5. *Square away the finances.* If you're going to handle your parent's money, you'll need a durable power of attorney (page 117) and the right to write checks on his or her account. Arrange for the bills to be sent to your address (the bank might pay regular bills automatically). Income—like pension and Social Security—could be paid directly into your parent's bank account. Reorganize the investments, to produce maximum income with minimum risk. Find all the financial documents, like stocks, deeds, and life insurance policies. See to the income taxes and get your parent an up-to-date will. These matters are best settled while your parent is sound of mind. If confusion ever descends, so may suspicion about money and an instinct to shut you out.

6. *See to your parent's health.* Make sure that he or she eats. Help arrange regular medical checkups. If you can, see that doctor's orders for taking pills and other medications are carried out. If your parent moves slowly, suffers pain or forgets things, don't write it off as "old age." Many such physical problems can be corrected.

7. *Deal with Medicare.* This is a kindness that will qualify you for

sainthood. Doctors and other providers of medical services submit your parent's Medicare claims. But if a check will go to your parent rather than to the doctor, it's important to see that the claim was paid properly. You always have the right of appeal, when Medicare rejects a bill that it shouldn't. But the process is aggravating and time consuming. Sometimes the doctor or hospital makes an error when a bill is submitted, but when you call the hospital, someone in the billing office may blandly deny it. I've known of cases when it took a call to a congressman's office before Medicare would pay attention.

To back up Medicare coverage, be sure that your parent has a single, comprehensive Medigap policy if needed (page 324). Cancel any duplicate policies.

8. *Shoot down the scams.* The elderly are to crooks as red meat is to a shark. Some older people will send money to every "charity" that asks, buy a dozen worthless health insurance policies, and fall for any quick-buck or free-gift scheme that comes along. Work with your parent to solve the problem. Maybe you or a neighbor can help your parent go over the mail. Maybe your parent will agree not to make a donation without telling you. Maybe you should handle the checking account.

9. *Get help from the neighbors.* Line up a teenager to mow the lawn, weed the garden, and shovel snow. Line up a neighbor to check on your parent if he or she doesn't answer the phone when you call. Line up someone to run the little errands that you can't, if you live far away. Offer to pay a caregiver who will drop in, shop, do a wash, and fix a meal.

10. *Don't shrink from the nursing-home decision.* This may be your best option if your parent can't manage alone, can't afford a companion, and —for any number of reasons—can't move in with a family member. Make the same decision for a parent who already lives with you, if his or her physical or mental problems exceed your ability to cope. Nursing homes are not snake pits. Although some are indeed mediocre, you'll also find some marvelous places, where the patients are clean, cheerful, mentally and physically active, and watched over by caring staffs. Ask a doctor, a nurse, or the social-service worker at a hospital for a recommendation. Don't feel guilty about it! Many parents who fight the idea find a nursing home congenial once they've settled in and made some friends.

11. *Bring up the question of a living will (page 118).* What is your parent's opinion about artificial life supports if he or she is terminally ill?

12. *Collect information for the obituary.* Many families put out wrong information, because they're hazy on the details of their parents' lives.

A DIVORCE CHECKLIST

1. *Follow the money.* Modern divorce is not about who's the meanest or who slept where. It's mainly about money—how to split up the property and what to allocate for alimony and child support. The division won't be fair unless all the income and property is on the table.

If you don't know much about your spouse's finances, and fear that he or she won't say, go ahead and snoop. Any financial document can be a clue to income, assets, and debts. Look for:

• Your spouse's payroll stubs. They show whether money is being deducted for savings and retirement accounts.

• Five years' worth of state and federal income-tax returns. If you can't find your copies, get them from the IRS or the state tax office.

• A copy of the financial statement that was filed with the bank for a recent mortgage or a business loan. You can tell the bank that you're updating your personal financial statement and have lost the original.

• Copies of appraisals done for insurance purposes.

• Deeds, bank statements, check registers, loan documents, credit-card statements, mutual fund reports, statements from stockbrokers, statements of employee benefits, insurance policies.

• A copy of your credit report, which will show transactions on jointly held accounts. Some credit bureaus will also send your spouse's report, so you can look for separate accounts. But don't ask to have your spouse's report sent to a different address; the credit bureau won't do it.

Each spouse should have a copy of these records. Neither one of you should spirit them away. If one of you plays nasty so will the other, and you'll wind up testing the limits of your mutual capacity to hurt.

2. *Don't borrow against your house, if your marriage isn't going well.* Your house is often your major asset. What happens if a wife (for example) agrees to sign for a home-equity line of credit, and her husband (for example) takes the money and spends it? Her share of the home equity has been eaten up, and she might not be able to get it back. In a case like this, the judge should order the husband to repay, but you can't assume that's going to happen. Take big loans only if you're sure that

you'll both be there to pay them off. If the marriage looks shaky, you'd be smart to freeze or cancel the credit line. Either one of you can usually do so unilaterally.

3. *Don't forget the pension.* In many marriages, the only assets are the house and the pension plan. You're generally entitled to a share of each, although not necessarily an equal share. Get copies of the statements for Individual Retirement Accounts, Keogh plans, and company pension and profit-sharing plans. In most cases, you won't get a piece of the pension itself. Instead, you're given property of equivalent value. If each of you has a pension, you may agree to call it a wash.

4. *Don't forget the professional degree.* Remember the Ph.T. (Putting Hubby Through)? If the wife worked in order to get her spouse through medical or law school, she may, in some states, be entitled to share in the income likely to be produced by that degree.

5. *Protect your flanks.* You'll need personal money to tide yourself over the months it takes to reach a settlement. So start putting some paychecks into a separate account. Move half of the money from joint accounts into your separate name (don't grab it all; civility will pay in the end). Tell your stockbroker and mutual funds, in writing, not to sell jointly owned investments unless your signature is on the order. Tear up the power of attorney that gives your spouse power over your assets, and tell your banks and brokers, in writing, not to accept any copies. Don't co-sign any new loans with your spouse. Open your own safe deposit box and keep your valuables there.

If you have no income of your own you're at a disadvantage. Every nonworking spouse needs personal savings for just such emergencies as this. You might be able to stake yourself by pulling cash from a credit card or home-equity line of credit. But don't be surprised if your spouse refuses to make monthly payments on those loans.

6. *Don't hit below the belt.* Only the lawyers have something to gain from a nasty divorce. Don't cancel all the joint credit cards, unless your spouse has a card of his or her own. Assure your spouse that, during the divorce negotiation, you'll continue to cover the household bills that you've always paid. Don't hide or destroy financial records. Don't hijack valuables out of the house and claim they've been lost. Don't steal money. Good manners not only facilitate the divorce, they also help the children recover. Remember that divorce, unlike marriage, lasts until death you do part.

7. *Wives without paychecks shouldn't expect permanent alimony.* At

best, most ex-wives get a few years of temporary support while they go back to school or learn a job skill. This is tragically unfair to middle-aged homemakers, who cannot hope to support themselves at anything close to their former standard of living. In several states, older women who appeal temporary alimony awards to a higher court are winning the right to permanent support. Even so, the wife's standard of living usually falls after a divorce while the husband's improves. (Occasionally, a dependent husband gets temporary alimony from a wealthy wife.)

8. *Count on a reasonable share of the property.* Everything acquired during the marriage is supposed to be divided between the spouses. That doesn't necessarily mean 50-50. How much each spouse gets depends on the court and on state law, which count such things as the length of the marriage and what was contributed by each (including homemaking services). In general, inheritances and assets owned before marriage stay with the spouse they belong to.

9. *Parents without custody should expect generous child-visitation rights.* Both courts and lawyers have grown more sensitive to the rights of parents who don't intend to divorce their children. Although custody generally goes to the mother, fathers have stronger claims than they used to.

10. *Parents with custody shouldn't have to settle for bare-bones child support.* In court cases, many judges have been stingy when awarding child support. In private agreements, women (who usually seek custody of small children) have sometimes felt forced to accept too little, in return for the father's agreement not to sue for custody himself.

Happily, all states are now required to have guidelines showing what percentage of a parent's income has to go for child support. Both parents' incomes are counted. But the upshot is that middle-income fathers are generally paying more. A mother whose child-support award falls below the guidelines may be able to get it raised. Similarly, a father who has custody may be able to enforce the guidelines against his ex-wife.

If your support is too low, sign up with the child-support enforcement agency in your state. It may be too understaffed to serve anyone but welfare mothers, but many state agencies accept all emergencies that come in the door. If your income is low, the state charges no more than $25 to take your case to court. About one-third of the states may charge more, however, depending on your ability to pay. The state can also help you track down a parent who skipped.

Even privately negotiated child-support payments can be raised, if they're obviously too low. How easy that is depends on state law. But the courts generally won't change an alimony award or property settlement.

Several states will automatically withhold child-support payments (but not alimony) from a parent's paycheck. With some exceptions, this rule goes national starting in 1994. Even now, you can get automatic withholding if the parent is one month in arrears—although, in some states, the process is slow. It's also hard to keep up with a parent who deliberately moves around. If the father wins custody and the mother has a good job, she may be required to pay child support.

Consider cost-of-living adjustments (COLAs) for long-term child-support payments, so that your children's standard of living won't fall. If you don't have a COLA clause in your divorce agreement, ask your state's child-support agency about getting the payments raised to today's guideline levels. It may take a court case, but it's worth it.

How well all these rules work depends on where you live. Some states have terrific child-support procedures and a large enough staff to keep up with all the new cases coming in. They can even help you collect your money by tapping your ex-spouse's state and federal income-tax refunds. But many other states are desultory and understaffed. Still, always try the public child-support office before paying the large sum a lawyer would want.

The government publishes a free *Handbook on Child Support Enforcement,* prepared by the federal Office of Child Support Enforcement. Get it by writing to Handbook, Dept. 628M, Consumer Information Center, Pueblo, CO, 81009.

A super organization that helps women collect their child-support awards is the Association for Children for Enforcement of Support, 723 Phillips Ave., Suite 216, Toledo, OH, 43612 (or call 800-537-7072). ACES will work with you directly or put you in touch with a local chapter. It publishes a booklet called *How to Collect Child Support,* which, at this writing, costs $7.95.

You're most apt to collect your child support if you're on good terms with your ex-spouse and he or she sees the children regularly. In most states, it's still hard to get money from a spouse who's determined to resist.

11. *Reach an agreement on who pays for college.* But even when the father says he'll pay, the mother may still be on the hook. Colleges and universities may base any scholarship aid on both parents' incomes (in-

cluding the incomes of step-parents), regardless of who is formally responsible.

12. *Hire an investigative accountant, if your spouse owns a business.* Wholly owned businesses are notorious for hiding income and assets. One accountant, who specializes in divorce cases, says that underreporting deprives spouses (usually wives) of 20 to 50 percent of their rightful share of property and support. You need someone with a well-developed sense of the absurd to examine your spouse's business tax returns and to press for documents that show more fully what the business earns. (Sorry, but you've nothing to gain by vindictively calling the IRS. If your spouse underreported personal income, and you signed the joint income-tax return and benefited from the tax evasion, you're equally liable for the taxes owed.)

13. *Hire a lawyer who believes in mediation.* He or she is more willing to look for a peaceful solution. That keeps you out of court, holds down your costs, and leaves your relationship reasonably cordial. Special mediation services also exist, to help resolve differences between you and your spouse. When looking for a lawyer, get recommendations from friends who have been divorced for a while and have some perspective on what they went through.

Don't hire a "bomber," who gets his or her kicks by hanging up your spouse by the thumbs. Such tactics lengthen the negotiation, tempt you into dishonorable acts, ruin any hope of an amicable relationship after the divorce, and fatten the lawyers' bills. Don't get a bomber even if your spouse has one; they'll play well-rehearsed war games at your expense. Just be sure that your own lawyer is experienced with divorces. Bombers eat general practitioners and corporate lawyers for lunch.

The same lawyer shouldn't represent you both. In theory, this could work if the split is amicable, both parties support themselves comfortably, you're in perfect agreement about who gets what property, and no children are involved. Even so, most lawyers think it unethical to work for both of you, and would encourage you to get separate representation.

What raises the price of divorce is arguments. The more you quarrel over property; the more you struggle over payments, custody, and visiting rights; the more you delay, prevaricate, and punish each other, the more you'll pay. If you're speaking to each other, try to draft a tentative settlement even before you see your lawyers.

14. *Get good tax advice, if there's a lot of money at stake.* You need to know what's deductible and what's not, and what the after-tax value of

your settlement is. For example, if you accept highly appreciated stock as part of the settlement, you'll pay a lot of taxes when you convert it to cash. So it's not worth as much as you thought it was.

15. *If you work for the federal government, get an attorney familiar with its benefits.* Ex-military, foreign-service, and civil-service spouses qualify for a variety of benefits, depending on how their divorce is structured.

16. *Do it yourself, with help.* In some states, lawyers have published do-it-yourself divorce guides. They work best for working couples who are ending their marriage politely, with no children to consider. But before you make it final, pay a visit to a lawyer, just to be sure that you interpreted the directions correctly and haven't overlooked anything important.

17. *Don't lose your health benefits.* Wives are no longer dropped automatically from their husbands' company health plans, and vice versa. If the company employs at least 20 people, notify the employee-benefits office within 60 days of your legal separation or divorce. You can stay in the ex-spouse's group plan, at your expense, for up to three years. You normally lose the coverage, however, if you remarry and are covered by your new spouse's insurance, or get a job that covers you with another plan. Your old plan has to keep you only if you're ill and the new plan won't cover pre-existing conditions.

18. *Get life insurance on your spouse, for as long as alimony or child-support payments are due.* You need an inexpensive term-insurance policy that runs out when the obligation does. It's probably best if you own the policy and make the premium payments. Your spouse can reimburse you through regular support payments. (If you let your spouse keep the policy, he or she may drop it without telling you, or change the beneficiary. You can always sue his or her estate for the money, but there might not be enough to collect.)

19. *Collect all your Social Security benefits.* That you're divorced doesn't cut you loose. You are generally entitled to benefits on your ex-spouse's account as long as the marriage lasted for at least 10 years. Social Security looks first to your own account, to see how high your personal benefits are. If you'd collect more as an ex-spouse, that's what you'll get. Here's when you can stake a claim:

a. For retirement benefits—(1) You're at least 62 and aren't remarried. (2) Your ex-spouse is also on Social Security. (3) If your spouse is eligible for benefits but not collecting them, you can still collect as long as you've been divorced for at least two years.

b. For survivor's benefits, after your ex-spouse's death—(1) You're 60 or older and aren't remarried. (2) You're any age, unmarried, and caring for the deceased worker's child who is disabled or under 16. In this case, you can collect even if you were married for less than 10 years. (3) You remarried after age 60, but are entitled to a better Social Security benefit from your ex-spouse's account than from the account of your new spouse.

c. For disability benefits—(1) You're at least 50 and unmarried, and your ex-spouse is dead. (2) You're permanently and totally disabled, under Social Security's hard-nosed rules. (3) You remarried, but did so after age 50 and after becoming disabled. In this case, you can still collect from your ex-spouse's account, if that payment is more than you'd get from the account of your new spouse.

What if your ex-spouse remarried? Both you and the new spouse collect exactly the same maximum benefit. Neither of you takes one dime from the other.

20. *Don't take a note from your spouse for money owed*, unless it pays a competitive interest rate and is guaranteed by a performance bond or a lien against property. You need some easy way to collect in case he or she declines to pay.

21. *Don't challenge a premarital (or postmarital) agreement*, unless you can truly show that you were bullied into signing and harassed into keeping silent about it or that, by failing to disclose some significant assets, your spouse led you to a wrong decision. Judges are reluctant to revoke these contracts except for a very good reason. Generally speaking, it does no good to argue that the contract is unfair. Presumably, you knew that when you signed it.

22. *Change your beneficiaries.* As soon as you separate, take your spouse's name off your savings account, brokerage account, retirement accounts, pension plan, and will. Whether to change your life insurance depends on whether you expect the insurance policy to be included as part of the financial settlement.

23. *Do it right the first time.* Except for child support, divorce agreements usually can't be reopened unless you both agree.

2 FINDING THE MONEY

Most people don't come to financial planning until they have some extra money. They start with the question, "How should I invest?"

You should start earlier. The right question is, "How will I get the money that I will then wonder how to invest?" You need a way to acquire cash.

You can win your kitty in a lottery. You can hope to marry well. You can wait for the ground to open before you, and a delicate hand to thrust $100,000 into your waiting wallet. Or you can cull the money from what you earn. Save it or borrow it. You are the source. If you do something you'll have something. If you do nothing . . . (finish the sentence yourself).

The earlier this idea hits you, the richer you can be. Time is as much a money machine as earning power. Funds put away when you're 25 are worth far more than funds put away at 40, which in turn are worth more than funds put away at 55. So don't just sit there. Read.

8
A SPENDING PLAN
THAT WORKS:

How to Take Charge of Your Money—
At Last

If all of us had every dime that we've wasted in
our lives, we'd be a nation of millionaires.

Make yourself a spending plan. Not
for discipline, not for tidiness, not because your mother told you to.
Make it for your own sake. That's the only way to coerce your money
into doing what you really want. I've lived with spending plans and I've
lived without. I come back to them every time I'm in a pinch.

A SPENDING PLAN ALWAYS WORKS. It captures the cash that slips through your
fingers, unnoticed, every day. It discriminates between what you really
want and what you buy because it's there. It rescues you when your
income falls short. It lets you save money painlessly, and that's the truth.

A plan is an active strategy for getting wherever you want to go. It
starts with a general idea: "I want to live better." "I want to get out of
debt." "I want to invest more." "I want to retire early." Then it breaks
up that dream into small, specific, everyday actions that you can accomplish one by one.

Plans always have to be written down. And they need simple measuring posts to show how you're doing. Imaginary plans that you follow in your head won't get you anywhere.

To start, take this test: Write down where your money went last month. Don't do it from memory; use your checkbook for reference.

Compare the result with your take-home pay. Odds are that you can't account for all the money. In fact, there will probably be a substantial gap between what you earned and what you can remember spending . . . money that seems to have gone up in smoke. Some of it did.

Here's another test: Of all the things you bought last month, how many could have been put off for 30 days without doing any harm? And then put off for another 30 days? You probably could have postponed quite a bit. In fact, now that you think of it, some of what you bought may not be worth the debt you're carrying.

Now the final test: How inviolate, really, is your must-spend list? Can you cut your taxes, pay less for insurance, refinance your mortgage to get lower payments, find a cheaper apartment, sell your second car? (Spending $15 on taxis every working day might cost $3,600 a year—a fraction of the price of owning, insuring, gassing, and repairing an automobile. And think of the savings if you took a bus.). If you paid off more debt, you would reduce your interest payments.

I am not advising that you lower your standard of living. Good financial planning starts from where you are and makes things better. On the other hand, neither should you feel locked into your current way of life, no matter how immutable the bills may seem. There are—as a science fiction writer would say—*alternative realities*. And you are going to find them.

Truth in authoring compels me to say that this process used to carry another name. An awful name. *Budgeting*, the dreaded B word, smelling of shortages, self-denial, and regret. A budget seemed to say, "I can't afford the things I want," and on that depressing thought good intentions foundered.

A spending plan, on the other hand, says, "You can get what you want just by figuring out how to do it." It's a positive step that allows for choices and new ideas. It puts you in control.

SEVENTEEN REASONS TO HAVE A SPENDING PLAN

1. To find out what you're spending money on. Few of us know.
2. To extract more money for savings and investments.

3. To make a decision about quitting work, moving, building a house, having a baby.

4. To get out of debt.

5. To show the spouse who doesn't pay the bills where the money goes.

6. To live on your income.

7. To prepare for big expenses like college, a new house, a major vacation, a facelift (it's probably not covered by your Blue Cross!).

8. To retool your life after losing a job, losing a spouse, becoming too sick to work.

9. To keep money from slipping through your fingers.

10. To determine the minimum income you can live on—so you can handle a cut in earnings, erratic paychecks, a divorce, a period of retraining for a different job, early retirement.

11. To know how you'll handle unexpected expenses.

12. To be able to buy what you want.

13. To prepare for harder times.

14. To make the best use of the money you get in better times.

15. To get the whole family pulling in the same direction.

16. To put a tool in your hands that can change your life.

17. To put your new financial plan into action. Which plan? The one you're developing as you read this book.

THREE REASONS NOT TO HAVE A PLAN

1. You're rich enough to buy anything you want and still have plenty of money left over.

2. I forget the other two.

A LIST OF FREE EXCUSES FOR DUCKING THIS JOB

1. *Making a spending plan takes too much time.* (It will take no more than a weekend of thinking, research, and erasing what you just wrote down—followed by a few minutes every day for a month or so. In the beginning, you'll spend an hour or two, once a month, to see how you're doing. After that, it's just as easy as spending money without a plan.)

2. *I won't keep it up.* (But you might. Most people do, once they decide they want better control of their money—because this is the only way to get it. As soon as your plan is up and running, there's not a lot more to do.)

3. *I don't want to live in a straitjacket.* (You won't. Your plan will move and breathe. If it pinches, you can change it. It will always include a provision for buying some of the things you really like, so you won't feel deprived.)

4. *I hate arithmetic.* (So do I. So what?)

5. *None of my friends do it.* (Too bad for them.)

6. *I budget in my head.* (And all your good intentions run out your ears. You're *sure* that you have an extra $55 this month for a mock-turtle sweater. Then you discover that you can't pay the dentist. Besides, I'm not asking you to budget. I'm asking you to plan.)

7. *I'm too tired, too young, too old, too busy, too poor, not poor enough. My husband, wife, daughter, parakeet won't cooperate. It won't work, can't work, would drive me bananas if it really did work. I'm too dumb, too smart, too short, too tall, too fat, and can't give up smoking.* (You can always think of reasons not to take charge of your life. But if you don't mean to change, why did you waste your money by buying this book?)

HOW TO BEGIN

Write down all your cash expenditures every day for a month. And I mean everything. Carry a notebook in your pocket or purse so that no expense will slip away. Start with "Monday, February 8" and go on to "Tuesday, February 9." Day by day by day.

Some things may seem too trivial to bother with. Coffee, newspapers, flowers, an apple. But look at it this way: If you saved $5 every day for a year you'd have $1,825. That would nearly fund your Individual Retirement Account or give you two nice weeks in Maui, watching whales. Small expenses are *not* trivial.

During this month make no effort to change your spending habits. You're simply making a snapshot of how you live now.

Take one weekend to go through your checkbooks and itemized bank card statements for the past six months. Write down the size of your regular monthly bills: utilities, mortgage, car payments, day care. On another sheet, write down your intermittent expenses: clothing, life-insurance payments, birthday presents, car repairs, dentist bills.

Some spending is hard to reconstruct. Maybe you've been throwing out old credit card bills. Maybe you haven't been noting on your checks exactly what the money was for. When your records are bad, it might take two or three months to learn where all the money goes.

Once you've got the information, organize it into categories, showing how much you spend every month. Laundry. Groceries. Drinks. Books. Cosmetics. Gasoline. Bus fare. Credit card debt. Tennis. Haircuts. Restaurants. Children's clothes. Your clothes. Doctors. Real-estate taxes. Movies. The more precise the better. You need a detailed picture as a starting point.

Construct a chart of how you spent your money, month by month, over the past six months. Assume that the walking-around expenses that you recorded in your notebook will always be the same.

Now write down your monthly income, minus federal, state, and local income taxes, Social Security taxes, and any other automatic deductions such as union dues. Include all your income: wages, annuities, pensions, dividends, interest, rents, everything.

Compare your spending with your income, and don't panic if you're in the red. That's what a spending plan will fix.

The snapshot you took may surprise you.

Many people learn that—except for credit card repayments—they are actually spending less than they earn. They are short of money only because they are doing battle with old debt. Once they pay it off, they'll have a substantial sum of money to invest.

Others are astonished at how much they are spending on particular items—health clubs, books, fast-food restaurants, beauty parlors, tools, fishing. You *must* spend money on yourself; otherwise your spending plan will be too disheartening to stick with. But maybe you can pick one thing and cut down on others. Exercise with weights at home, get a library card, make your own hamburgers, give yourself facials, ski cross-country instead of downhill. That frees cash for something else.

It is not unusual to discover that you are better off than you thought. Fear often arises from ignorance. Once you take an organized look at your situation, you might see that your worries have no basis in fact.

On the other hand, if you really are in trouble, you'll learn by how much.

Above all, you'll finally find out where the money goes, because most of us really don't have a clue. With that snapshot as a guide, you are ready to channel some of your spending in new directions.

WHAT DO YOU REALLY WANT?

First, you need to know what you're redirecting your spending *for*. What do you want from your money that you're not getting now?

Maybe you need to be out of debt. Maybe you need college money, for your children or yourself. Maybe you want to build a rainy-day fund or save for a down payment on a house.

Your goal won't always be the same. The important thing right now is to focus on a limited and specific objective that you can achieve.

Write it down at the top of your spending plan. "Goal: Save an extra $100 a month." Or, "Goal: Put an extra $100 a month toward paying off the Visa card." Take that money right off the top of every paycheck. Then rearrange the rest of your spending to fit within the income that's left.

DRAWING YOUR PLAN

The plan (page 146) will look very much like a b- - - -t. But it differs in four ways.

First, you enter your current "Goal" at the top of the page. That *will* be funded every month, before you pay any other bills. Don't even give it a moment's thought. Set the money aside, and then start to juggle. Just having that goal transforms a b- - - -t into a plan.

Second, there's a column called "Current Spending." Here, you write down what you've been spending in every category. This is your benchmark—the money habits you have now, which you want to change.

Third comes your "Spending Plan." Play with your income and expenses and write down where you'd like the money to go.

Fourth comes the payoff—the column called "Actual." Once a month, enter what you actually spent in each category. If you're paying more than you planned for "telephone" or "sports," you may have to strengthen your resolve. On the other hand, maybe your spending plan is unrealistic and should be changed. After several months, you'll arrive at a plan you can live with. Then it becomes a habit.

Some Technical Matters

Start with a six-month plan, to see how it works. One year is too long for someone just learning where the money goes.

Make your categories specific. For example, instead of lumping all your medical expenses together, create separate columns for Doctor, Dentist, Therapist, Medicines, Veterinarian. Instead of "Utilities," write Water, Electricity, Heat, Telephone.

To cut spending, squeeze a little something out of every category rather than slashing just one or two. Above all, don't wipe out all the things that make you the happiest. You need to get some fun from your money, to have the incentive to carry on. Every member of your family also needs a personal playpen.

It helps to enter your spending weekly, so you won't lose track. The categories in the sample Spending Plan are just a suggestion; most plans contain many more.

When a bill is paid quarterly, budget for one-third of it every month. For the first two months, that money stays in your checking account; in the third, you'll have enough for the payment. If you're an irrepressible spender, move the funds into a savings account where you won't notice them. Or subtract one-third of the cost from your checkbook every month, without actually writing a check. If you don't see the money, you won't spend it (I hope). When you balance the checkbook, just add back the funds that were subtracted.

Handle clothing the same way. Budget a certain amount every month and let it build up. Some months you'll exceed your plan but over a year it should even out.

Unexpected expenses, like car repairs or an operation for a sick dog, should be listed in their proper categories so you'll know how much you've spent. But you cannot specifically budget for them. Instead, put some money for these bills into a reserve fund every month. For the size of your reserve fund, see page 147.

You will have some bothersome spending overruns. Don't quit: just try again. Spending plans don't prohibit splurges. They merely show you —graphically—that for every extra purchase, you have to cut spending in another category or go further into debt.

Add up your spending every month to see how you're doing. Juggle the categories; some will be high, others will be low. But it shouldn't take long to work it out. If you overspend in one area in February, you'll have to find a place to compensate in March.

SPENDING PLAN

Month _____, 19____
Total income _____
Special goal _____
Reserve fund _____

Expenses	Current Spending	Spending Plan	Wk. 1	Wk. 2	Actual Wk. 3	Wk. 4	Total
Savings							
Mortgage/rent							
Heat/light/water							
Telephone							
Life insurance							
Health insurance							
Disability insurance							
Homeowner's insurance							
Auto insurance							
Auto loan							
Credit card payments							
Back bills							
School/college							
Child care/support							
Groceries/drinks							
Clothing							
Doctor/dentist							
Veterinarian							
Gasoline							
Bus/subway/taxi							
Restaurants							
Entertainment							
Sports/pastimes							
Books/magazines							
Repairs/upkeep							
Housecleaning							
Personal care							
Laundry							
Contributions							
Furniture							
Birthdays/holidays							
Vacation							
Walking-around money							
TOTALS							

YOUR RESERVE FUND

This has nothing to do with your savings or investments. Nor is it the money that you build up over a couple of months in order to pay your quarterly bills.

The reserve fund is your accident insurance. Use it when the roof leaks, the car needs a valve job, your son breaks his arm in two places, the furnace dies. It is *not* for discretionary spending. If you empty this fund for a cashmere coat or a fishing rod, you'll be cutting a hole in your safety net.

Any money drained from your reserve should be put back as fast as you can earn it. For a while, that becomes your top budget priority. Forget your other savings goals until this money is repaid.

The reserve also shores you up if you lose your job. Typically, the fund should contain three months' living expenses, kept partly in a ready bank account or money market mutual fund, for easy access, and partly in certificates of deposit—see page 168. Enlarge this fund, if your company's medical plan requires you to pay a lot out of pocket.

The self-employed need a larger fund, to guard against the risk of business drying up from time to time. So do people who smell layoffs coming at their companies.

In recent years, reserve funds have fallen out of fashion. "Cash on hand" has meant borrowing on your credit cards or home-equity line of credit. But a lot of credit cards are now borrowed up, and consumer interest payments are no longer tax-deductible. Your home-equity line still offers tax-deductible interest, but the bank may freeze the line if it learns that you're unemployed. Cash is again becoming king.

SPENDING PLANS FOR WORKING COUPLES

Some couples pool their money. A single, unified spending plan is all they need.

Other couples keep their paychecks separate. They might need three plans; one each for husband and wife, to keep track of their personal expenses and set their personal saving and spending goals, and one for shared household expenses, to which each contributes. The shared account should include the reserve fund, on which you both may need to draw.

CAN ANYONE LOVE A DECIMAL POINT?

Some people love keeping records to the penny, and may the God of the Green Eyeshade be with them. Others manage quite nicely by rounding off. Rounding off a lot. A lucky few don't even care if the columns add up as long as they're (probably) not too far wrong.

Keep your accounts however it suits you. The object is mainly to *keep accounts*. You'll learn more from setting up detailed budget categories than you will from struggling over the math.

WAYS TO SHIFT SPENDING

To get more money for something you want, you have to spend less on something else. That's all there is to it. You can climb the highest mountain, consult the wisest wizard, and you'll get the same answer.

You can borrow the money—but then you'll have even less to spend, because there's another loan to repay. That's like having another mouth to feed. Too many mouths, and pretty soon you are really *poor*.

Everyone finds different ways to save. But here are some sure-fire places to look.

Bury your credit cards. Charge nothing. Interest payments will then melt away. (OK, charge *something*, but not much.)

Declare a new-clothes moratorium until you have your present wardrobe paid for.

Quit smoking. You'll save on cigarettes, life insurance, doctor bills, breath sweeteners, and soap to rub off the yellow stains.

Drink wine instead of hard liquor. Cheap wine.

Rent, don't buy, things you rarely use. Or split the cost with a neighbor (even-steven on the snowblower and all repairs).

Buy toilet paper labeled Toilet Paper. Buy peanut butter labeled Peanut Butter. If you hate the generic stuff switch back to the higher-priced brand names, but try the cheap one first.

Shop with a list and stick to it. No impulse purchases, unless . . .

. . . unless there's a terrific sale. Then buy in bulk. You say you can't be bothered saving $5.50 on tuna fish? Do you realize that you need $100 in the bank to *earn* $5.50?

Own an economy car. It runs on economy gas, with economy insurance and economy repairs.

Use up your savings to get out of debt. Only losers pay 18 percent on their credit cards so they can keep on earning 6 percent on their bank accounts.

Never pass up a garage sale. (But pass up most of what's there. It's hard to believe what people buy at garage sales and then chuck into their own garages.)

Don't trust any bills, especially those that are computer-generated. If you take the time to check for errors, you'll find a lot of overcharges.

Stop subscribing to magazines you don't read. That not only saves you money, it saves the space next to your bed where they pile up.

Refinance any high-rate loan. But use home-equity loans to eliminate credit card bills *only* if you're swearing off your credit cards. Otherwise, you'll wind up with two debts where there used to be one.

Serve punch and hors d'oeuvres at parties rather than drinks and dinner. People drink less punch because the cups get sticky.

Learn to love your neighbors. With them, you can pool services like babysitting and transportation. You can even swap skills: You do my taxes, I'll paint your garage.

Track down all local resale shops, discount centers, and factory outlets.

Vacation at off-season rates. The sun is just as hot the week before Memorial Day as the week after.

Sell something that's expensive to keep, like a second car that you don't use regularly to drive to work.

Call your mother in the evening, at cheap rates. Better yet, write, don't call. Or don't write. Maybe she'll call you.

Go to the movies instead of buying a VCR. If you already own a VCR, rent videos instead of going to the movies. Or get a library card and borrow videos.

Maintain your car properly so you can keep it longer.

Eat more meals at home.

Ask your doctor to write prescriptions for generic drugs.

Look for cheaper insurance. You can probably find a company that charges less than you're paying now. Take a larger deductible on your fire and auto coverage. Cancel collision insurance on an old car. You might find that it's not even worth insuring, because the company won't pay much toward its repair.

Make your own gifts. Or perform a personal service instead of purchasing a *thing*.

Look for cheap entertainment. Museums. The zoo. Parks. Picnics. Parades. Friends.

Do your own home repair, car repair, sewing, reupholstering, painting.

Pay cash for gasoline instead of using a credit card. You might save up to 5 cents a gallon at many service stations. And use self-service pumps.

Eat more meatless meals. They're good for you.

Switch to lower-watt bulbs in all but your reading lamps.

Exercise at home instead of at a health club. Or join a "Y."

Find new uses for things instead of throwing them out. Start seedlings in the cut-off bottoms of milk cartons. Twist newspapers into cylinders for kindling. Maintain a useless-objects shelf, for items that might be reclaimed some day. The handier you are, the more money you'll save.

When you think you're at rock bottom, with *all* of the air sucked out of your budget, go back for one more try.

WHEN THERE REALLY IS *NO MONEY*

When you're truly living on a wing and a prayer, it is fruitless to look for meaningful budget cuts. You'll have to increase your income in some way. A second job. A better job. A session of night school, to qualify for a different line of work. A sideline business run from home.

If those routes aren't practical, try for a job with better employee benefits. A company puts money into your pocket by paying most of your doctor bills as surely as it does by giving you a raise.

HOW LONG, OH LORD?

Keep up your monthly budget for as long as it takes to get more from your money. By then, you should know how to do it without always putting pencil to paper.

As your goals change, however, you may need new spending plans to achieve them.

Your first year's aim might be quite modest: "Reduce by half my credit card debt," achieved by doubling payments every month. Having succeeded, you'll get more ambitious: "Carry no debt and build a reserve fund." Then you'll move on to: "Save 10 percent of my income."

Along the way you'll have minigoals, like: "Buy a VCR." "Give more parties." Write them down, allocate money to them, and check them off as you succeed.

Sometimes you force a goal on yourself—for example, by buying a house. Meeting your mortgage payments then becomes your first priority. All the rest of your spending shrinks.

Once you've got a plan that works, there may be no reason for keeping monthly accounts. Start over again, however, if:

· Something changes in your life.

· You begin to feel that you're losing track.

· You notice that you can't meet expenses without putting down a credit card and stretching out payments. That means you're spending more than you earn.

SPECIAL PROBLEMS WITH IRREGULAR INCOMES

Neat monthly spending plans may sound hopeless to the person without a regular paycheck. But you can do it, easily. Start with the premise that your total income is more predictable than when your paychecks will arrive. And budget this way.

Draw a regular, monthly plan based on the smallest monthly income you expect. Whenever a fee comes in, put it in the bank and spend it in strict accordance with your budget. If there's money left over, leave it alone; it might be a while before another check comes in.

Build a reserve fund of about six months' living expenses. Once you have that, you can risk spending any extra money you earn.

If, after a few months, it appears that your income will fall short this year, revise your spending plan downward. If you're doing better than expected, revise it upward. Whenever you dip into your reserves, replace the money before doing any more extra spending.

PLANNING WHEN TAXES AREN'T WITHHELD

People paid by fee, with no taxes withheld, are true heroes if they make it to April 15 without spending any of their tax money. You have to pay estimated taxes every quarter. But it's all too easy to fall behind. If you're too far behind, you'll owe a penalty on top of the tax.

How to solve this problem? Look at last year's tax return to see what percentage of your total income went to taxes. Take that amount off the top of every single check you get. Earmark it for taxes and tuck it into a savings account. Only your *net spendable* income, after taxes, should land in your checking account.

PLANNING FOR A RAISE

Will you gross an extra $2,000 this year? If you spend it all, you'll be worse off than you were before. A $2,000 raise may leave only around $1,200 in the bank, after state and local income and Social Security taxes. Spending the gross puts you into debt—which is why so many people feel poorer and poorer as their incomes rise.

Anyone allergic to saving money should regard a raise as a Main Chance. Just pretend it didn't happen. Keep on living the way you did before and put the extra money in the bank. Or buy one thing and save what's left.

PLANNING WHEN YOU'VE BEEN LAID OFF

At first, you may panic—especially if you've never lost a job before. You're spending every penny you make. How can you live on a nickel less? *This very month,* the bank will foreclose. The creditors will cart off your furniture. You'll join the homeless. Your children will have to live on a grate.

Not so. You have far more financial resilience than you imagine. Here's what to do.

1. Draw up a bare-bones spending plan. Cover the mortgage, car loan, utilities, gasoline, food, insurance, and the expenses of looking for another job. At first, budget only for these. Put all other bills aside.

2. Add up what remains of your regular income: a second paycheck in the family, union benefits, interest from savings, dividends, unemployment insurance. Don't reject unemployment payments. Many white-collar workers are ashamed or afraid of standing in unemployment lines. But times have changed. Whole echelons of middle management are being laid off. Your ex-employer pays taxes to assure that you get some financial support between jobs, and you should take every nickel due you. You'll find your peers in line behind you.

3. Compare your remaining monthly income with your bare-bones spending plan. There will probably be a gap. Write down how much more you're going to need each month.

4. Add up all your lump sums of money: a final paycheck due from your company, severance pay, savings, investments. A portion of this cash reserve can be used each month to fill the gap in your spending plan. *Your goal, at this point, is to find a way to cover your essential bills for at least nine months, and longer if you think your job hunt will be a tough one.* (But don't spend a lump sum from your retirement plan unless absolutely necessary, because of the taxes and penalties you'll owe—page 741.)

5. Try to reduce those expenses that look immutable but might not be. For example, if your child is in day care or college, tell the school about your financial emergency and ask for a moratorium on payments. Promise that all back payments will be made up, with interest, when you get a job. You can almost always make a deal. Take the same approach with any other service that you feel should not be interrupted, like dental procedures or children's music lessons.

6. If you have enough income left over, after covering bare-bones expenses, allocate it to other expenses, like paying the minimum on your credit card bills.

7. *Do not pay what you can't afford to pay!* That sounds obvious, but it's a basic rule of survival that laid-off workers violate all the time.

Make *no* payments on postponable bills, if doing so means that you'll run out of money within a few months. Don't worry about hurting your credit rating. You can repair it later (see page 202). It's far more important to conserve your savings in order to keep the lights on, the telephone working, gas in the car, and food on the table.

You *must*, however, tell your creditors what you're doing. Write each one a letter, explaining that you have been laid off and cannot currently pay your bill. But say that you will, absolutely, resume making payments in full (including interest and late charges) when you get work. Another approach is to say that you will pay $5 or $10 a month as a token of your good faith.

Many creditors will take this deal. If they don't respond (or if only their computers respond, with another bill), telephone for a personal appointment to discuss the debt.

If you don't find work in a couple of months, write or call again. This keeps the creditors informed and reassures them that you're not going to skip.

HOLD TO YOUR POSITION, EVEN IF THEY BLUSTER, THREATEN TO RUIN YOUR CREDIT RATING, OR CLAIM THAT THEY'LL SUE. Keep on explaining your situation, in reasonable language. Say that you're out of work; say that you'll pay eventually; say that you can't pay now, or can only pay $5 a month. Don't cave in, even if your account is turned over to a bill collector. Your number-one priorities are to husband cash, hold your life together, and keep your job search going. When you find a job, and you will, you can work out a repayment plan.

It's tough to write those letters and make those appointments. You'd rather keep your joblessness—and your cashlessness—a secret. But by coming clean, instead of ducking, you stand a better chance of getting your creditors to lay off.

8. If two months pass without a job nibble, talk to the bank that holds your mortgage. It might agree to accept only the interest payments for a few months, letting the principal coast. This will take a personal visit, but it usually works.

9. Try to bring in some extra income. Sign up with a temporary-help agency. Pitch for consulting jobs. Advertise your services in the neighborhood: typing, carpentry, accounting, day care. If your spouse doesn't work, now is the time for him or her to start. Ask your teenagers to pitch in with after-school jobs.

10. How should you handle a lump-sum payout from your company pension or tax-deferred savings plan? Ideally, you'd roll it into an Individual Retirement Account, to avoid current taxes and keep that money building up. But if cash is short, you might not have the luxury of keeping your retirement savings whole. Some of the funds might have to go for current bills.

Fortunately, you don't have to make this decision right away. The law gives you 60 days before the tax-free rollover has to be accomplished. If you find work within that time, fine. You can afford to choose the IRA. If you haven't found work, there are two ways to play it.

The first way is to put all the money in a bank account and use it. You will pay taxes on it, plus a 10 percent penalty for early withdrawal. (The penalty is normally forgiven only if you are totally disabled or have reached age 59½.) This approach makes sense for small sums.

The second way is to put the money into a no-risk IRA that can be tapped easily, like a bank money market account. Withdraw funds only as you need them. You will owe taxes and a penalty on the money you take. But the moment you find work you can stop the withdrawals, leaving the rest of your IRA intact.

11. If you don't find work and see that your money won't last, it's time to rethink your life from the ground up. Look for cheaper housing:

an apartment, or a home far out in the country. Find an area where living costs are lower. Consider jobs at a lower salary. Maybe your child will have to leave college for while, or go for a scholarship at a community college.

Reach these decisions *before* you start borrowing from relatives. My reasoning here is tactical, not moral. Your relatives are normally your ace in the hole, the only people who might help you finance a new start in life. So try to tap them last, not first.

PLANNING FOR INFLATION AND DEFLATION

You can't. The effects are too unpredictable to be built into a spending plan. That's why budgets do best on a six-month cycle; you can look at your actual spending and adjust.

SPENDING AND YOUR FINANCIAL PLAN

A spending plan is the visible evidence of financial planning at work. The other chapters of this book will help you make strategic choices. The spending plan executes them.

9
SAVING MORE MONEY:

*Patented, Painless Ways to Save, and Where
to Save It*

The 1980s worshiped spending. The 1990s will
belong to the saver.

     It seems like only yesterday that savers were dorks. They kept piggy banks. They drove last year's cars. They fished in their change purses for nickels while the superstars flashed credit cards.

Today, values have changed. The new object of veneration is not money on the hoof but money in the bank—and the dorks all have it. The more you save the freer you'll get, because time is on the saver's side. Compound interest floats all boats.

Like most people who make their own money, I started out living paycheck to paycheck. I could cover my bills (most of the time). But I "knew" that I couldn't afford to save, so I didn't bother. Even had I bothered, my small $20 or so a week wouldn't have seemed worth the effort.

Some years (and many lost $20s) later, I learned I was wrong. Anyone can put money aside, at any level of income. You just have to *do* it. Of all of the New Era's new virtues—daily jogging, eating bran, quitting smoking—saving money is the simplest and the least demanding of your time and attention. Savers can lie in a hammock all day eating Mars Bars and still feel good about themselves. As for the value of a tiny $20 a week, take a look at the chart on page 159.

A financial plan is grounded in savings. That's how you get enough money to pay off your debts and accumulate an investment fund.

How much should you save? The answer comes from ancient times. You *tithe*. It was learned generations ago—and is still true—that most people can save up to 10 percent of their incomes *and hardly notice.* I can't tell you why it works, only that it does. Maybe tithing just collects the money that otherwise goes up in smoke (it's 9:00 A.M.; do you know where yesterday's $10 is?). On a $30,000 paycheck, you can save $250 a month, $3,000 a year. On a $40,000 paycheck, shoot for $333 a month, about $4,000 a year. On $60,000, save $500 a month, for $6,000 a year.

I hear you, I hear you. You say you can't do it. Your rent is too high, your bills are too large, your needs are too great, your credit lines are too long. None of those things is actually an impediment, but it will take you a while to see that. So start by saving only 5 percent of your income. Take that money off the top of every paycheck and live on what's left. Once you find that your appetites are not being pinched, go to 7 percent. I predict that you'll be at 10 percent within the year.

If you're already tithing to your savings account, take a moment to feel superior. What's life without a touch of smug?

WHAT ARE YOU SAVING MONEY *FOR?*

A savings account isn't something to hang on the wall and stare at, like a Rembrandt. You're not hoarding. You're preparing to use your money in a different way.

Refer, please, to your Spending Plan (Chapter 8). It says that your current goal is three months' living expenses in the bank. Or $2,000 more in a college account this year. Or $5,000 for long-term investments. Or $1,000 to play the slots in Vegas, where you'll *really* make some money. Tithing, or semitithing, is how you're going to raise your stake.

Here's how to accomplish it.

First, write down how much you're going to save (5 or 10 percent of each paycheck).

Second, write down how long it will take to reach your goal. At $250 a month, you'll have your college account in eight months. You'll have a college account *and* Las Vegas in 12 months. (Tip: It's easier to save $59 a week than $250 a month. The smaller sum sounds more doable, even though it's all the same in the end.)

Third, note each future $250 (or $59) payment on your calendar and check off every one you make. That may sound hokey, but it's a strong motivational tool. Every time you turn to a new week or new month, there's a written reminder to keep up your resolve. Saving money is easier if you see it climb toward a specific end. It's like polishing the car. You feel that you've accomplished something.

Fourth, when you've reached your goal give yourself a little present. Then start the process all over again.

SAVING VERSUS INVESTING

Savings are, by definition, *safe.* You can turn your back and they won't escape. When the market crashes, they're unalarmed. Every time you look, they've earned more interest. You're never going to lose a dime.

Investments, by contrast, put your money at risk. Good investments yield much more than savings over the long run. But you have to put up with occasional losses, too.

SAVINGS WILL NOT MAKE YOU RICH. Only canny investments do that. The role of savings is to keep you from becoming poor. They're your security. Your base. They preserve your purchasing power. With enough savings tucked into your jeans, you can afford to take chances with the rest of your money, and with your life.

THE BEST YEARS OF YOUR LIFE . . .

. . . are when you're young. At least, they're the best years for saving money. They sooner you start, the longer your money has to compound and the better your shot at true financial independence.

Typically, young people turn a deaf ear. "I'm too broke," they say. "I'll save when I'm older."

But later money won't earn you nearly the return that early money pays.

Take a look at the startling chart below, prepared by Professor Emeritus Richard L. D. Morse of Kansas State University, who knows more about savings-account interest than anyone in the country.

The Early Saver deposits $1,000 a year for 10 years, at 8 percent compounded daily. Then she stops. Having put in a total of $10,000, she leaves her stash alone to build.

The Late Saver doesn't darken a bank door for a decade. In the 11th year he gets religion and starts saving $1,000 a year, also at 8 percent. Forty years later, he has put up a total of $40,000. But he hasn't caught up with the Early Saver—*and never will!* He can go on depositing $1,000 a year until the millennium. At 8 percent interest, the Early Saver (although still depositing no more money) will pull further ahead of the Late Saver every year. *

	EARLY SAVER	LATE SAVER
	Depositing $1,000 a year at 8%	*Depositing nothing*
Year 1	$ 1,083	0
Year 5	6,397	0
Year 10	15,939	0
	Depositing nothing, but building at 8%	*Depositing $1,000 a year at 8%*
Year 11	$ 17,267	$ 1,083
Year 15	23,778	6,397
Year 20	35,471	15,939
Year 25	52,914	30,174
Year 30	78,934	51,410
Year 35	117,751	83,088
Year 40	175,656	130,344
Year 45	262,036	200,839
Year 50	390,895	306,000

Source: Richard L. D. Morse

21 PATENTED PAINLESS WAYS TO SAVE . . .

1. Pay yourself first. That's the oldest financial advice in the world, and one of those things you can't improve on. Take a slice of savings off

* At 6.8 percent interest, the Late Saver would catch up to the Early Saver after 63 years. Just in time for the nursing home.

the top of every paycheck, before paying any of your bills. If you pay your bills first and save what's left you'll always be broke, because there is never anything left.

2. Bill yourself first. Keep stamped envelopes, addressed to your bank, in the same drawer as your bills. Send the bank a fixed check every month, as if it were just as pressing as keeping the mortgage current. In point of fact, it is. If you're paid irregularly, send a fixed percentage of every paycheck. American Express's new Membership Savings program will send cardholders a monthly bill that covers the money they want to save.

3. Get someone else to save for you (Part One). Your bank or S&L might transfer a fixed sum of money every month from your checking account into savings or into a mutual fund. Enter each transfer in your checkbook, so you won't accidentally overdraw.

4. Get someone else to save for you (Part Two). You'll never find a better savings machine than your company's payroll deduction plan. A fixed amount of money is taken out of every paycheck, so the cash never hits your checking account. What you don't see, you don't miss—and you don't spend. If the money goes into a 401(k) plan, reserve this for retirement savings (because you can't easily draw the money out—see page 743).

5. Do coupons turn you on? Create your own Christmas Club or Vacation Club. Decide how much money you want 12 months from now, divide it into 12 equal payments, and make "coupons" to remind you to keep up with the monthly deposits. Or make 52 coupons for weekly payments. You could call it a Down Payment Club or a State University Club. Put the funds into a bank money market account or a money market mutual fund.

6. Save all dividends and interest. If you have a mutual fund, arrange for all dividends to be automatically reinvested.

7. Don't spend your next raise. Put the extra money away. The more money you earn, the more of it you should set aside. Toward late middle age, you should be saving 15 to 20 percent of your income, at least.

8. Quit spending your year-end bonus in advance. Save it instead. At the very least, quit spending *more* than your bonus.

9. Save all gifts you get in cash, even small ones. *Nothing* is too small to save.

10. Pay off your mortgage faster, by doubling up on principal pay-

ments every month. You'll build equity sooner, which is a form of saving. You'll also spend much less on interest payments.

11. Quit buying books (except, of course, for this one, which no prudent saver should be without!). Get a library card, instead.

12. Refinance your personal, auto, or other high-interest loans at a lower interest rate, maybe by taking a home-equity loan. Use the money you're saving to pay off loan principal.

13. Don't trade in your car as soon as the loan is paid off. Make repairs, if you have to, and keep it for a year or two longer. Save the money you were spending on monthly car payments.

14. Pay cash for everything. You will spend less, because it's harder to part with cash than to put down a credit card.

15. Take $5 out of your wallet every day and put it in a coffee can. That's $1,825 a year—almost enough to fund an Individual Retirement Account in full.

16. Take a part-time job and save all the income.

17. Let the government withhold extra tax money from your paycheck, and save the refund.

18. Pay off your credit cards, then save the money you're no longer spending on interest charges.

19. Trim your spending by 5 percent, then trim it by another 5 percent.

20. Buy cash-value life insurance. Your payments go partly for life insurance and partly into a savings fund. This is not the best of all possible routes to thrift (see page 272). I suggest it for people who cannot save money any other way.

21. Save early and often. The sooner you put some money away, the longer it has to fatten on compound interest. Saving money *young* is a painless way of saving *more*.

. . . PLUS SEVEN TAX-BLESSED WAYS OF RAISING RETIREMENT MONEY

1. Join the company savings plan. Your contribution may escape current taxes and will accumulate tax deferred. What's more, these plans usually *give away money free*. The company matches your contribution— say, one dollar for every two dollars you put up. That's a 50 percent return on investment, instantly and at no risk. There's no better investment deal in the entire U.S. of A.

2. Join your company's stock-purchase plan. You run the risk that the stock will fall. But over long periods of time your investment should do better than a savings account.

3. Sign up for an Individual Retirement Account, even if it's not tax deductible. Make monthly payments, so you won't have to scramble for money when the deadline for contributions looms.

4. Don't spend the lump-sum distribution you get from your pension plan when you leave the company. Roll it into an Individual Retirement Account, or into your new company's pension plan.

5. If it takes a contribution to join your company's pension plan, make it—even if you're young. If you leave early, you'll get your money back plus everything your money earned. If you last at least 3 to 5 years you'll walk away with company's contributions, too. (With some plans, you have to work 7 years to get the full company contribution.)

6. Start a tax-deferred Keogh plan if you're self-employed or earn self-employment money by moonlighting.

7. Consider a tax-deferred annuity, if it has a good investment record and you'll hold the investment for 15 years (see page 763).

More on this subject in Chapter 28.

WHAT YOUR SAVINGS HAVE TO EARN

Say that inflation is running at around 5 percent. And say that you're earning 8 percent in a savings deposit. What's the effective return on your money, after state and federal taxes? Probably pretty close to zero. You have preserved your purchasing power, but you haven't increased it. If your money is earning 9 percent, you've probably gained a real 1 percent.

I'm not knocking this result. The basic job of a bond or a bank account is to keep you from falling behind. But you won't achieve even this result unless you avoid low-rate deposits.

The table below gives you some guidelines. Find the current inflation rate at the left, then look across to the column showing your federal income-tax bracket. Take the interest rate shown and up it a little, to compensate for state and local taxes. That's the minimum rate that your money needs to earn, to keep the value of your savings from falling behind.

At this rate of inflation	You need to earn this rate of interest to break even in the following tax brackets		
	15%	28%	31%
1%	1.20%	1.39%	1.49%
2%	2.35	2.78	2.90
3%	3.53	4.17	4.35
4%	4.71	5.56	5.80
5%	5.88	6.94	7.25
6%	7.06	8.33	8.70
7%	8.24	9.72	10.14
8%	9.41	11.11	11.59
9%	10.59	12.50	13.04
10%	11.76	13.89	14.49
11%	12.94	15.28	15.94
12%	14.12	16.67	17.39

Source: Goldstein Golub Kessler & Co.

WHERE TO KEEP YOUR SAVINGS

Don't automatically think "bank." That's only one of many choices. To find the right place to keep your savings, start with what you want from your money and work back. You need: (1) at least the "breakeven" yield that you've found above; (2) access to the money when you need it, and not a day sooner. Funds you won't want until next year can be invested differently—and more profitably—from funds you're going to use next week.

For Savings You'll Need Immediately

(And I mean right now. Or a week from Friday. Within three months, at the very most.)

Hold this part of your cash cache to a minimum—because ready money earns less interest than money invested for longer terms. I'd include only:

1. Funds that you know will be spent very soon—like a down payment on a car you'll buy this month.

2. Your permanent floating emergency fund, which can be called on at any time. Don't let this fund get too large. Keeping $10,000 in a passbook account—just in case the house should burn, the world explode, or your hair drop out—is dumb. Into the dailiness of life, alarming emergencies rarely fall. If one does, you can always retrieve your money from wherever you stashed it. A quick-cash fund of one month's salary should be plenty. The rest of your emergency fund can be saved at higher interest rates.

3. Money waiting to be invested in stocks, bonds, or real estate. Here's where your short-term money can be kept.

MONEY MARKET DEPOSIT ACCOUNTS AT BANKS. They're handy, they're easy, they're government insured. You earn a floating interest rate that is loosely tied to the general level of market rates. (And I mean loosely. When other interest rates go up, banks are slow to raise the rate on money market accounts. But they drop rates enthusiastically, when other interest rates go down.) You can take out your money whenever you want, although usually only three withdrawals a month can be made by check. Minimum deposits fall in the area of $500 to $2,500. You'll pay a penalty, if your account drops below the minimum.

Ready access, however, has its price. The interest rate paid on the average money market account rarely meets the breakeven test. Your savings lose value, after counting inflation and taxes. If the bank charges fees, you'll lose even more. The only way to maintain your money's purchasing power is to search out an institution that pays especially high interest rates on money market deposits. (Do it by subscribing to *100 Highest Yields*, page 68.)

PASSBOOK ACCOUNTS. These are even worse than money market accounts for keeping up the value of your savings. Skip them.

TAXABLE MONEY MARKET MUTUAL FUNDS. Money funds offer a much better chance of breaking even. Even after management fees, the average fund pays around 1 to 1.5 percentage points more than the average bank money market account.

Your cash is kept in safe investments that earn taxable interest—the safest being Treasury securities, high-quality bank certificates of deposit, and top-grade commercial paper (short-term loans to creditworthy corporations). They all mature within a brief time—a day, a week, three months.

A money market mutual fund is typically worth one dollar a share, no more, no less. It pays dividends daily, passing along whatever the fund is currently earning. Your minimum investment: usually around $1,000, but sometimes less.

You can write an unlimited number of checks on the fund, generally for a minimum of $250 or $500. A few cash $100 checks—which invites you to use them as interest-paying checking accounts. You pay no penalties for low deposits, although many funds will cash out your shares if your account falls below a certain minimum, like $500 or so.

Money funds don't carry federal deposit insurance. They're *extremely* safe but not *perfectly* safe. There is always that one, dumb (or unlucky) money manager who misses a trick and risks a loss. In 1979, a fund got into trouble by gambling on longer-term investments, like two-year maturities. Interest rates rose and the fund lost some money. Nothing like that has happened since. In 1989 and 1990, some corporations defaulted on their commercial paper—a potential loss to a few money funds. Fortunately, they all belonged to solvent financial-services organizations, which dipped into their own pockets to make investors whole.

Some funds invest only in U.S. government securities. That's practically the same as having deposit insurance. The super-super-safe funds buy Treasuries directly. The merely super-safe invest indirectly, through "repurchase agreements" or "repos."

Repos don't bother me at all. But they do some people, so I'll give you the song and dance about them. If you'll take my word for it that repos are okay, it will save you reading the following paragraph, which is pretty heavy.

Under a repo agreement, the money fund buys Treasuries from a broker, holds them for a short time (usually a day), then sells them back at a slightly higher price. The risk is that the broker might go bankrupt before buying them back. Normally, that shouldn't hurt the fund. As long as it owns the Treasuries, it can easily sell them to someone else. The concern, on the part of professional worriers, is that the broker's creditors might lay claim to the Treasuries, thereby threatening the fund with a loss. That's an event that's pretty remote. It could happen, of course. But of all the things to worry about in this life, I put repos pretty close to the bottom of the list.

You always owe federal income taxes on dividends earned from mutual funds invested in Treasuries. But whether you owe state and local taxes depends on where you live. Two-thirds of the states exempt these dividends from taxation. The rest don't. Or they may tax some kinds of Treasury funds but not others. Ask your fund whether it's taxable in your state. If it's not sure, ask your state's tax office.

Money funds invested entirely in Treasuries yield about half a per-

centage point less than the funds that also buy other kinds of instruments. That's $250 a year, on $5,000. In my opinion, the money funds
with broader investment policies—sponsored by major financial organizations—are safe enough.

Even among similar types of money funds, yields vary. But don't
break your neck hunting for the highest payer. There's always a different
fund at the top of the list, depending on how fast they all respond to
daily changes in interest rates.

I'd use six criteria in choosing a fund.

1. Are its expenses low? You'll usually find the answer in the prospectus, in the table that shows all the fees and expenses. Managers who
charge 0.5 percent of assets or less have a good shot at being top performers. Fees of 1 percent or more usually mark the funds that do the worst.
Some funds with low expense ratios levy separate service charges, like
$2 per check or $5 per telephone transfer. If those fees were figured into
the expense ratio, the fund would show a slightly higher cost. Some
funds are temporarily waiving fees. For now, they flash an especially high
yield. But when the fees start, your yield will drop. In general, large
money funds are more cost-efficient than small ones.

2. Is it handy? The fund's minimum balance and check-writing rules
should fit your purse. It should also have plenty of telephone lines, so
you don't always get a busy signal.

3. Is it linked to a good stock-owning mutual fund? You want to be
able to shift your money into stocks, just by making a telephone call. So
pick your favorite stock fund first. Then take a look at the money fund
that serves it.

4. What's the fund's average maturity—meaning, how long does it
take for its investments to come due? The shorter the term, the less risk
the fund takes. Money funds don't invest for any longer than an average
of 120 days, and usually much less. I like to see 50 or 60 days. The
average maturities for all the funds are printed once a week in *The Wall
Street Journal* and many other newspapers.

5. Does the fund belong to a major financial organization—a mutual
fund group, a large brokerage house, an insurance company? This is your
equivalent of deposit insurance. A large organization will generally pay
for its mistakes rather than saddle its shareholders with losses. An independent money fund might not be able to cover the cost.

6. Does the fund invest only in top-grade securities? If a fund buys
certificates of deposit, it should deal only with the soundest banks. If it

buys commercial paper, it should stick with companies rated "P1" by Moody's rating service or "A" by Standard & Poor's (S&P's very highest rating being "A1"). How do you find out what a money fund buys? Only one way. Read the prospectus.

TAX-EXEMPT MONEY MARKET FUNDS. Some people will do anything to beat Uncle Sam out of a few bucks, even if it costs them money. Take the knee-jerk popularity of the tax-exempt money funds. Half the people in them would probably do better in a taxable fund—but they've never even checked it out.

Look at a tax-free fund only if: (1) you are in the top federal tax bracket (31 percent plus add-ons that can bring it to 33 percent or higher), or (2) you're in the next-highest bracket (28 percent), live in a highly taxed state, and get a fund that's exempt from state and local taxes.

Here's how to figure whether you'll net more money from a tax-exempt fund: Subtract your tax bracket from 1.00. Divide the result into the current yield of the tax-exempt fund you're looking at. The result is your breakeven point. If you can find a taxable fund paying more than the breakeven point, buy it.

For example, say you're in the 28 percent bracket and are considering a tax-free fund yielding 4.7 percent. Subtracting 0.28 from 1.00 gives you 0.72. Dividing that into 4.7 gives you 6.5. A taxable fund paying more than 6.5 percent will yield you more, after federal taxes, than the tax-free fund.

JUNK MONEY MARKET FUNDS. Some funds hike their yields by a few extra tenths of a point by investing in foreign securities or second-grade commercial paper. Some tax-free funds buy "floaters"—long-term bonds that a bank promises to redeem as needed. The extra risk is small—but then, so is the extra return. On $5,000, the difference between 6.5 and 6.9 percent comes to $20 a year. Big deal. If you've got $5 million, that 0.4 percent is worth a tidy $20,000—but short of that, why mess around?

Where can you find a money market mutual fund? All the major mutual-fund groups sell them, and so do stockbrokers. For investment information on no-load (no sales charge) mutual funds, including 130 money funds, get the excellent *Handbook for No-Load Fund Investors*—at this writing, $42 from *The No-Load Fund Investor*, P.O. Box 283, Hastings-on-Hudson, NY, 10706. For a listing of over 1,800 load and no-load mutual funds, including 425 money funds, get *Donoghue's Mutual Funds Almanac*—at this writing, $23, from P.O. Box 540, Holliston, MA, 01746.

For Money You'll Need for Sure in Six Months to Four Years

Here, I count everything from college tuition due next fall to the down payment on the house you hope to buy year after next. You can't risk losing a penny of it, so you can't afford to play around. On the other hand, neither should these funds nap in a low-interest savings account. By investing at a higher interest rate, you'll pile up savings faster.

Most of you will agree with me about six-month money. But four years sounds a lot further away. Why not invest in stocks for growth? Here is my argument against: Stock prices rise and fall. For money you *need*, it's the "fall" you have to worry about. If you have the bad luck to invest just before stocks go into a decline, you'll lose some of your principal. Since the 1930s, it has taken investors an average of four years to get even again, after a major market drop. So that's the time period to be careful about.

CERTIFICATES OF DEPOSIT. With a CD, you put your money in a bank, savings and loan, or credit union for a fixed term. You normally earn a higher interest rate than you would in a money market account.

Some people hate CDs because they feel that their money is "locked up." But it's not. You can break into a certificate anytime you want, before maturity. The worst that can happen is that you'll be charged an interest penalty. Big deal. That's nothing, compared with the interest you lose by keeping too much money in a low-interest passbook or money market account. Besides, no emergency will happen. You *won't* have to interrupt your CD.

Institutions may offer standard terms for CDs, like 6 months, 12 months, or 30 months. Some let you pick whatever term you like. Normally, the longer the term, the more interest you earn. For the many varieties of certificates of deposit, and how to get higher interest through "laddering," see page 67.

U.S. TREASURY SECURITIES. A Treasury security is the fruit of federal deficit spending. When the government spends more money than it collects in taxes, it has to borrow to make up the difference. It borrows from you, by selling you Treasuries. You are actually lending money to Uncle Sam for a fixed period of time, earning interest all the while.

It takes a little more effort to buy a Treasury than a certificate of deposit. Instead of walking into a bank or S&L, you have to visit, or write to, the nearest Federal Reserve Bank (page 178) and: (1) get information about buying Treasuries; (2) read the directions; (3) fill in a form: (4) send in a certified check. The job is not exactly a brain-buster, and there are no charges to pay when you buy from the Fed. Still, I can hear some of you groaning. If this sounds like too much work, a bank or a stockbroker will buy Treasuries for you, for a fee.

What's your reward for becoming a Treasury investor? An instant break on your income taxes. The interest you earn on U.S. Treasury securities—while taxed at the federal level—cannot be taxed by states and cities. So you might earn a higher after-tax return than you'd get from the average certificate of deposit.

The yield on a Treasury security is set through public auction, by the big institutions that put in bids. When you buy directly from the Federal Reserve, you piggyback on what the institutions pay. A phone call to the Fed gets you the most recent auction prices and yields. Which Treasuries to buy depends on when you'll want the money.

TREASURY BILLS mature in three months, six months, or one year. Minimum investment: $10,000, plus $5,000 increments. You send the Fed a certified check. Immediately after the auction you get a "discount" payment back, representing the difference between the face value of the bill and the lower auction price. At maturity, you're paid the face value. Your profit is the difference between the two.

For example, say you send $10,000 for a one-year bill that sells for $9,200. The Treasury sends you $800 back. At maturity, your T-bill pays $10,000, yielding an $800 profit.

There are two ways of measuring your return on investment. The newspaper stories generally highlight the "discount rate," which compares your profit ($800) with the bill's face value ($10,000). By this measure, you've earned about 8 percent.

But forget about the discount rate. It understates what you really earn. After all, you didn't put up the full $10,000. In this example, you invested only $9,200. An $800 return on $9,200 comes to about 8.7 percent. That's called the "coupon equivalent yield"—and is the only true measure of your return. Use it to compare the profit in Treasury bills with what you might get from alternative investments, like bonds and

CDs. You'll find the coupon equivalent yields in the newspaper tables reporting the outcomes of Treasury auctions. Often, they're given in the newspaper stories, too.

T-bills let you play income-tax games. If you buy a security today that matures in the next calendar year, your interest income falls into that year. So you have deferred the tax you owe. Note that your taxable profit is not the discount check that the Treasury sends you right away. It's the profit you make when the bill matures.

TREASURY NOTES mature in 2, 3, 4, 5, 7, or 10 years. Minimum investment: $5,000 for 2- and 3-year notes, plus $5,000 increments; or $1,000 for longer terms, plus $1,000 increments. Different maturities are auctioned at different times—all of which the Fed will be glad to fill you in on. You send in a check for the face amount of the notes you want. After the auction, you will usually get a small payment back—just a few dollars—because the notes sold for a hair less than their actual face value. Only one, true yield is reported (there's no coupon equivalent yield to worry about, as Treasury bills have). Interest is paid on your full investment twice a year.

When choosing Treasury notes, take a maturity that coincides with the date you'll want to use the money. For information on buying Treasuries, see page 177.

TREASURY BONDS have the longest maturities, usually 30 years. Minimum investment: $1,000, with $1,000 increments. They're auctioned in the same way as Treasury notes, with interest payable twice a year. I mention them here only to be orderly. They are *not* a good place for money that you can't afford to lose. The odds are high that you'll sell a 30-year bond before maturity. That will expose you to the hard, cold winds of the open market, where the bond might bring less than you originally paid. Long-term bonds should be thought of as a speculation on interest-rate changes, not as a savings account. For ways to use them, see page 643.

ZERO-COUPON TREASURIES can be good ways to save over four years. Just be sure that the bond will actually mature in that span of time. You may lose money if you have to sell a zero before maturity.

The *coupon* is the interest rate, so *zero coupon* means that no interest is paid currently on these bonds. Instead, you buy at a discount from the bond's face value. Every year, the interest builds up within the bond itself, until it reaches face value at maturity. For example, you might pay $692 (before sales commissions) for a zero that will be worth $1,000 in five years' time. That's an annual compound yield of 7.6 percent.

What's nice about zeros is that they reinvest your interest at the same rate that you're earning on the bond itself. With an 8 percent zero, for example, you earn 8 percent on every interest payment. With other bonds, you're paid in cash and have to reinvest the money yourself. Small payments (if not spent) will probably land in a bank account or money market fund, where they'll generally earn much less than the bond is paying.

What's bad about zeros is that you're taxed every year on the interest that builds up, even though you don't physically receive the money. To avoid the tax, buy a zero in a tax-deferred retirement account. Or give the zero to a child who owes no taxes.

A four-year zero-coupon Treasury is a reasonable bet for your teenager's education fund. Buy one when the child is 14 years old, to cash in when he or she reaches 18. Your money is safe and the earnings should compound at a reasonable rate of interest. (For younger children, don't buy zeros, buy stocks—see page 454.)

Long-term, 20- or 30-year zeros are another story. Like regular long-term Treasury bonds, they are strictly for speculators, not for savers. Zeros are hard to sell at a decent price before maturity, especially in small denominations. If the market turns against you, zeros lose value faster than other bonds do.

Zero-coupon Treasuries are bought through stockbrokers. But some firms clip you for a higher price than you should pay. They trap you by quoting a dollar figure—"only $650 for these bonds"—without telling you what the bonds are priced to yield. That might saddle you with an unfairly low rate of return.

A smart investor buys through a discount broker. Ask for both the dollar price and the *net yield to maturity after sales charges,* which is what the bond pays over its full term.

For Money You Won't Need for Five Years or More

Risk a majority of it in the stock market, real estate, or other growth investments. Otherwise, you'll never get ahead of inflation and taxes.

But you might want to keep even some of your long-term money absolutely safe. For this purpose, two suggestions:

FIVE-YEAR CERTIFICATES OF DEPOSIT OR TREASURY NOTES, CONTINUALLY REINVESTED. They should roughly preserve your purchasing power, provided that you reinvest all of the interest as well as the principal. You're buying for only five years at a time, so you'll probably be able to hold each note until maturity. That's important. You might lose money, if you have to sell before maturity.

You can "ladder" Treasury bills and notes just the way you do certificates of deposit (explained on page 638). But the traditional ladder requires that you buy some shorter-term Treasuries, which are expensive. So I'd suggest a special Treasury ladder, built from the notes that cost only $1,000 each.

Buy a five-year Treasury note this year, another one next year, a third one the year after, and so on for five years. When your first note matures, use the cash if you need it. If not, reinvest the money for another five years. The following year, you have the same choice—use the cash or reinvest it in another five-year note. And so on and so on. You have ready access to some of your money every year without the need to sell a note before maturity. Yet all of your savings are earning interest at the five-year rate instead of the lower one-year rate.

U.S. SAVINGS BONDS. Interest rates now float, on Series EE and Series E bonds. You get 85 per cent of the average yield on regular, five-year Treasury securities, with the rate changing every May 1 and November 1. Bonds purchased today can't earn less than 6 percent, compounded semi-annually, as long as you hold them for at least five years. And they may well earn more than 6 percent, depending on what happens to market rates. For current Savings Bond interest rates, call toll-free 800-US-BONDS.

Obviously, you would earn 15 percent more interest by buying regular five-year Treasuries. For many investors, that's a better choice. But Savings Bonds have some special virtues.

1. You can earn these rates on a very small amount of money. The cheapest bond costs $25.

2. You can tax-defer the interest until the bonds are finally cashed in. So your net return is usually higher than it looks.

3. You receive no money until redemption. So you can't go out and spend the interest. In this respect, Savings Bonds (as well as zero-coupon bonds) force you to save.

4. Parents who buy Savings Bonds after December 31, 1989, and use the money to pay for college tuition, may pay no income tax on the interest they earn (see page 453).

Savings Bonds sell at a 50 percent discount from face value. The

$100 bond costs $50; the $500 bond costs $250. Each year's interest is added to the bond's redemption value. After an initial six-month holding period, you can cash in your bond whenever it suits you. As with other Treasury securities, you owe only federal income taxes on the interest you earn, no state and local income taxes.

Printed on the face of each newly issued bond is the date when that bond will stop earning interest. Here are the final maturity dates for all older bonds: For Series bonds issued earlier than December 1965—exactly 40 years after their issue date. For E and EE bonds and Freedom Shares issued after November 1965—30 years after their issue date. For Series H bonds issued between 1959 and 1979—30 years after their issue date. For Series HH bonds issued since 1980—20 years after their issue date.

SOME ANGLES TO SAVINGS BOND INVESTMENTS:

✓ You'll earn less than 6 percent if you cash in before five years are up. At this writing, the interest rate ranges from 4.16 percent on bonds held just over six months to 5.75 percent on bonds held for four and a half years. On a $200 or $300 investment, that's probably better than you'd net from a passbook savings account, considering the fees that banks impose.

But the picture changes if you can afford a higher-paying money market mutual fund or money market deposit account. They're better than Savings Bonds for short-term investments.

✓ Children who own Savings Bonds, and are in low (or zero) tax brackets, should not defer the taxes due. It's cheaper to report the interest now than to wait until the child grows up. If the child has no tax liability, each year's Savings Bond interest will pass tax free.

To get this tax break, file a return for the child, showing the gain in value of his or her EE bonds (your bank, S&L, or credit union may give you this information, or write to the Bureau of the Public Debt, Parkersburg, WV, 26106). If the child owes no taxes, and continues not to in subsequent years, no more tax returns have to be filed for those particular bonds. If the child does owe taxes, however, you'll have to report the gains each year.

What if your child deferred income taxes in the past and now wants to pay them currently? Taxes will be due, all at once, on all past deferrals for all bonds held.

Keep copies of all the child's tax returns. When the bonds are cashed in, you must be prepared to prove which gains were previously reported. Otherwise, the IRS might conclude that the child owes taxes on all of the profits.

Sometimes, children should defer the tax. Do it when they have enough unearned income to owe the "kiddie tax" (page 89), which is payable in the parent's highest bracket.

What if the child has been paying taxes currently and now wants to defer? Just file Form 3115, Application for Change in Accounting Method, with the child's tax return for the year you want the change to start.

✔ Bonds earn interest from the issue date, which is always the first day of the month. If you buy a bond on the last day of the month, it will be backdated to the first day. For the first two years (after an initial six-month holding period), interest on a Series EE bond is credited on the first day of every month. After that, it is credited every six months from the issue date. You earn more money by cashing in your bond after the issue date rather than just before.

✔ You can redeem just part of a bond, if its face value is at least $50 for Series E bonds, $100 for Series EE, or $1,000 for Series H or HH. For example, a bond worth $1,000, with an accrued value of $700, can be turned in for $700 in cash and a $300 bond. The new bond would have the same issue date as the old one did.

✔ You can tax-defer your gains on Series E and EE bonds by exchanging them for HH bonds. HH bonds pay out taxable interest every six months.

But HH bonds are a lousy deal. For 10 long years, they won't pay more than the guaranteed interest rate on the day they were issued—currently only 6 percent. And you can't expect any better treatment in the second 10 years. Here are two alternatives to HH bonds: (1) Hang on to your E and EE bonds, cashing in 6 percent of them every year. If you have $20,000 in EE bonds, for example, you might cash in $1,200 worth. You get the same 6 percent income that HH bonds would pay—but because it's from EE bonds, only part of the income is taxable. The other part is a return of your own, original capital. What's more, your remaining EE bonds are probably earning a tax-deferred interest rate higher than 6 percent. So by the end of the year, they would be worth more than $20,000. You would then cash in 6 percent of them again. (2) Cash in all your E and EE bonds, pay the tax, and buy a 10-year

Treasury note. This strategy may yield a higher income than HH bonds pay.

✓ Don't hang on to old Savings Bonds that aren't paying interest anymore! Cash them in and get the money. This applies to all E bonds bought between May 1, 1941, and April 30, 1952, that either have reached their final maturity or will reach it by April 1992. Ask older family members whether they have any E bonds stashed away, and check the dates. When an E or EE bond reaches its final maturity, all the unreported interest becomes taxable, unless you exchange it for an HH bond.

✓ If you buy a Savings Bond in your own name, you control it completely. If you name a beneficiary on an EE bond, you can change the beneficiary whenever you want, just by filling in form PD 4000 (available from Federal Reserve Banks, page 178, and from many of the agents who issue Savings Bonds). The rules are different for the older, Series E bonds. With them, the beneficiary has to agree to being removed, by signing form PD 4000.

✓ If you buy a Savings Bond in joint names, both owners have to agree to any changes. But either one of you can cash in the bond—so whoever holds it, controls it. The person whose money bought the bond is called the "principal co-owner." All the income is taxed to him or her, even if the other co-owner redeems the bond and takes the proceeds. If both of you contributed, there is no principal co-owner and taxes are allocated according to what percent each of you paid.

✓ If you buy a bond as a gift for a child, don't name yourself co-owner. If you do, the interest will be taxed to you.

✓ If you give away a Savings Bond, and have it reissued in another's name, you'll owe income taxes currently on the accumulated interest. (Savings Bonds can be reissued only to certain people—husband, wife, other close relatives, and some trusts.) The new owner owes the tax only if the exchange takes place after your death.

✓ What if you buy a bond, and it comes with your name spelled wrong or the wrong date on it? Don't fix it yourself. You cannot redeem a bond that has been altered. Return it to the person who issued it and get the error fixed.

✓ What if you marry and change your name? You don't have to get your Savings Bonds reissued. When you cash them in, just sign the bond with both your maiden name and your married name.

✓ Under the law, you cannot borrow against your Savings Bonds.

✓ If you lose a bond, it's easy to replace—as long as you know its denomination, issue date, serial number, and the name or names in which it was issued.

If you don't keep good records, the Treasury may be able to trace the bond for you—especially if it was issued since January 1974. All those Savings Bonds have Social Security numbers on them. What's lost can be found, if the Treasury knows the Social Security number of the first owner named on the bond.

Older bonds sometimes carry Social Security numbers, too. If not, the Treasury can't hope to trace ownership unless it knows the name on the bond and that person's address when it was bought.

A lost bond can be replaced, at no cost to you, by the Bureau of the Public Debt, Bond Consultant Branch, Parkersburg, WV, 26106. If you're replacing a partly burned or mutilated bond, send Parkersburg the remains. The form used for replacement is PD 1048.

✓ You can buy EE bonds through many banks and S&Ls, Federal Reserve Banks or branches (page 178), the Bureau of the Public Debt (address above), or payroll-deduction plans at work. HH bonds (if you really want them) are available by mail through a Federal Reserve Bank or branch or the Bureau of the Public Debt. If your bank is an issuing agent for Savings Bonds, it will help you fill in the HH-bond purchase form at no fee.

✓ Anyone authorized to sell EE bonds can also cash them in for you (although some redemptions, like those by a guardian or trustee, have to be handled directly by the government). Try to redeem in a place where you're known, like your own bank. If you're not known, you will need documentary identification, like an employee card with your picture on it, and will be limited to redeeming only $1,000 worth of bonds.

✓ Savings Bonds, although issued by the U.S. Treasury, are *not* what investors know as "Treasury securities." Treasuries pay competitive interest rates and can be bought and sold on the open market. Savings Bonds don't, and can't.

✓ For a good, free guide, write for *The Savings Bonds Question and Answer Book*, Office of Public Affairs, U.S. Savings Bonds Division, Department of the Treasury, Washington, DC, 20226.

HOW TO BUY TREASURIES

There's no such thing as a physical Treasury certificate anymore. Your purchase is recorded. You get a statement. But you don't get the thing itself to hold in your hand—because there *is* no "thing itself." A Treasury certificate has become a concept in the mind and a byte in the computer.

You can buy Treasuries through a Federal Reserve Bank or branch, or through a commercial bank or stockbroker. Which one to choose depends on the kind of investor you are.

Savers: Buy Through the Fed

Every penny you earn in yield is yours to keep, because you pay no fees or commissions. All your transactions are handled free. There's almost no paperwork, because everything is accomplished electronically.

Under a system called Treasury Direct, you open an account with the Federal Reserve, which keeps track of all your transactions. Your principal and interest payments are wired directly to your bank account. Securities are held until maturity (to sell any earlier, you have to transfer them out of Treasury Direct). If you're a buyer of Treasury bills (not notes or bonds), you can arrange to reinvest your proceeds automatically.

The Fed will send you a packet of information on how to open a Treasury Direct account. You'll be asked for your bank's nine-digit American Bankers Association Routing Transit Number. That's the number on the bottom of any check or deposit slip.

Speculators: Buy Through Banks or Stockbrokers

Speculators buy and sell long-term Treasuries as interest rates change, in hopes of earning a capital gain. This means selling securities before they mature, and only commercial banks or stockbrokers do that. If you're holding securities in a Treasury Direct account, and want to sell early, you'll have to transfer them into something called a "commercial book-entry system," to make them accessible to brokers.

Banks and brokers let you order by phone (the Treasury requires orders in writing). They'll also lend you money against your securities. Sales commissions: a minimum of $25 to $60 every time you buy or sell.

It makes no sense to use brokers for small orders of short-term securities. On a $10,000 order, the commission might drop your yield by half a percent on a one-year bill and 1 percent on a six-month bill. On larger

---

FEDERAL RESERVE BANKS

600 Atlantic Avenue
Boston, MA, 02106
(617) 973-3000

33 Liberty Street
Federal Reserve Postal Station
New York, NY, 10045
(212) 720-5000

Ten Independence Mall
(P.O. Box 66)
Philadelphia, PA 19105
(215) 574-6000

1455 East Sixth Street
(Box 6387)
Cleveland, OH, 44101
(216) 579-2000

701 East Byrd Street
(Box 27622)
Richmond, VA, 23219
(804) 697-8000

104 Marietta Street, N.W.
Atlanta, GA, 30303
(404) 521-8500

230 South LaSalle Street
(Box 834)
Chicago, IL, 60604
(312) 322-5322

411 Locust Street (Box 442)
St. Louis, MO, 63166
(314) 444-8444

250 Marquette Avenue
Minneapolis, MN, 55480
(612) 340-2345

925 Grand Avenue
Federal Reserve Station
Kansas City, MO, 64198
(816) 881-2000

400 South Akard Street,
   Station K
Dallas, TX, 75222
(214) 651-6111

101 Market Street (Box 7702)
San Francisco, CA, 94105
(415) 974-2000

---

purchases or longer-term securities, however, brokerage fees don't take such a big bite.

SHOULD YOU BUY A MUTUAL FUND THAT INVESTS IN YOUR TREASURIES?

If you're a saver, no.

Savers need a sure thing. You want to earn interest while keeping your capital absolutely safe. Treasuries do that for you—as long as you buy them directly and hold them to maturity.

But buying a mutual fund that invests in Treasuries introduces risk.

Maybe you'll make money; then again, maybe you'll lose it. The value of your mutual fund will rise and fall along with changes in interest rates.

That's okay for speculators who know what they're doing (to find out what you're doing, see Chapter 24). But hard-core savers should stay away. If you don't have the $10,000 for a Treasury bill, and don't want to put your $1,000 into a Treasury note lasting four years or more, put your money into a certificate of deposit.

One other point about mutual funds: They might cost you extra money in taxes.

Individual Treasury securities are exempt from state and local income taxes. But about one-third of the states tax the dividends paid by mutual funds that invest in Treasuries. So find out your state's rules on this—either from the fund itself or from the state tax office. Some states tax some Treasury funds but not others, depending on the kinds of investments they buy.

SAVING MONEY IN A LIFE INSURANCE POLICY

When you buy cash-value life insurance, you buy a kind of savings account that builds up over many years. But there are two fatal drawbacks to this form of savings: (1) Very little money normally accumulates in the early years. (2) To get at your money, you generally have to borrow it, paying interest as you go. I'm all for good insurance, and a cash-value policy may be exactly what you want (page 262). But if savings are your primary interest, look somewhere else.

SAVING VERSUS BORROWING

Here's a question I get a lot: "I need a new car. I have enough money in the bank to pay cash. Should I use that money or take an auto loan instead?"

Two arguments favor the loan. (1) You will be forced to repay the money, whereas no one will grump if you leave a hole in your savings account. (2) You don't want to leave yourself without ready cash.

Cost is the best argument for cash. Borrowing raises the price of the things you buy—even more so, now that the loan interest on consumer purchases isn't tax deductible. Why waste money on interest payments if you can pay cash?

In most cases, I'm for paying cash. Buy what you want, then make regular payments into your savings account to replace the money you took out. As long as you're saving money regularly, you don't have to worry about using it from time to time.

But I'd vote differently if your savings cache came from an inheritance, a life-insurance payoff, or a lottery ticket. Windfall money is almost impossible to replace. In this case, take out a loan to buy the car. Preserve the big money for college tuition or for your old age.

WHEN TO STOP SAVING

When you're young, you have to learn how to save. When you're old, you have to learn how to stop. Many older people live on the edge of poverty because they're afraid to spend the money that they have so carefully put aside.

But past a certain age, it's time to spend your children's inheritance, in order to give yourself the decent retirement you deserve. In Chapter 29, you'll find guidelines on how to spend your money without running out.

10
KICKING THE CREDIT
CARD HABIT:

Learning to Live Without Consumer Debt

———

The new macho for the 1990s is canceling your
credit cards. It says that you have money
enough not to take plastic seriously.

Why do you need a fistful of credit
cards? They're heavy. They make your wallet bulge. They cost money.
You can't remember how much you've charged on them. Now that even
the hoi polloi carry gold cards, prestige lies in flashing a plain-vanilla
Visa, MasterCard, or American Express. For an even bigger thrill, pay
cash.

As a status symbol, the credit card is finished. It's now just a transactions workhorse. Assuming, as I do, that you want to get out of debt
and build some savings, plastic ought to serve a single purpose: convenience. You put it down instead of writing a check or paying cash. At
the end of the month, you pay the bill. The *whole* bill.

Not that you're perfect. Even when your credit is clean, you'll still
stretch the occasional bill over two or three months—maybe at Christ-

mas or after a vacation. But your goal is never to charge any more than you can easily repay. For the 1990s, debt is Out.

HOW TO GET RID OF CONSUMER DEBT

It's so simple that I'm almost embarrassed to mention it.

Don't borrow any more.

That's all there is to it.

Say to yourself, "Today, I am not going to put down a charge card for anything." If you have to buy something, pay cash or write a check.

Tomorrow, say the same thing: "I am not going to put down a charge card for anything. I am not even going to borrow $10 from a friend." Take it slowly, one day at a time. It's like stopping smoking. You'll be nervous at first; you won't see how it's possible to live; you'll suffer relapses and sneak a new debt or two. But every day when you get up in the morning, renew your pledge. To make it easier, *quit using credit cards.*

I hear you saying, "I can't get along without a credit card." Of course you can. You can pay by check. On trips, you can use travelers checks. You may have to show a credit card to rent a car. But when you bring the car back, you can pay the bill by personal check or travelers check (use your card for identification only). If you object that you can't pay by check because you don't have enough money in the bank, you're missing my point. When you don't have the money in the bank, don't buy. If you find that you have to put down plastic, use an American Express card. It's not a credit card. You have to pay your bill in full by the end of the month.

Once you stop using credit cards, three things will happen.

1. You will buy less—and whatever you do buy will probably be a less expensive model or make. Studies have found that people spend more when they pay with plastic, because it doesn't feel like real money. When it *is* real money, you're more sensible.

2. Your total debt will shrink rapidly. You are paying off back bills, you are not adding new ones, and you have extra money (because you're buying less). That surplus cash will reduce your debt faster than you could imagine.

3. You will grow incredibly smug. You're the first on your block to get out of debt. Others will follow, but you'll be the first.

I'm not against credit cards. They're easy to use. They're handy. If your card has a low annual fee and a 25-day, interest-free grace period for paying your bills, you're getting monthly loans for practically nothing. What I'm against is buying more on your credit cards than you can pay for at the end of the month.

Once you've fought your way out of debt you can start using credit cards again—but only for the convenience of not carrying cash. Your days of debt are done. A big expense may sometimes drive you over the limit. A stereo. A llama. A hot-air balloon. Whenever you limp home, back in debt, recite your mantra: "From now on, I'm not going to put down a charge card for anything." Stick with it until you're free again.

WHAT'S THE BEST CREDIT CARD?

It all depends on how you pay.

When you don't carry debt, the Best Credit Card has no annual fee or only a small one—no more than $10. And it offers a 25-day grace period, during which time no interest is charged on the money you owe. That's all. You don't give two hoots what the interest rate is. The bank could charge 30 percent and it wouldn't matter, because you'll never (*almost* never) have to pay it. You are getting your monthly credit virtually free.

Unreconstructed debtors need a different kind of card. For you, the annual fee doesn't matter. Neither does the grace period, since you'll never use it. Your Best Credit Card has the lowest possible interest rate, because you are always rolling over debt.

Many of us have a foot in both camps—sometimes staying ahead, sometimes falling behind. This suggests owning two credit cards: (1) *a convenience card,* with a low fee and a grace period, for bills that you know you can cover at the end of the month. Buy all perishables, like restaurant meals and gasoline, with this card. (2) A *low-interest card,* for purchases that will take months to pay for. Go for an interest rate in the area of 12 to 15 percent. Charge only items that will last a long time—because those are the only ones worth paying interest for.

FINDING A LOW-RATE CREDIT CARD

Super-low-rate credit cards—maybe 12 to 13.5 percent a year—are generally offered by smaller institutions and go only to the very best credit risks. That's someone who: (1) carries a modest amount of debt relative to his or her income; (2) always pays on time; (3) doesn't have a lot of open credit lines; (4) has worked at the same company, and lived in the same place, for a couple of years; (5) had no credit problems in the past; (6) has not applied for any other new credit recently.

The last point—no new credit lately—eliminates a lot of people who think of themselves as good credit risks. Here's why:

Whenever you apply for credit, the lender inquiries about your payment history. That inquiry shows on your credit report. If you have just refinanced your house at one bank and applied for a new credit card at another one, your credit report will show that two lenders asked about you. The report doesn't say whether they accepted you or turned you down; only that they asked.

A low-interest-rate lender doesn't like to see that. He will assume that you are suddenly loading up on credit, for purposes he doesn't care to think about. He'll reject you rather than take the risk

So you need a strategic plan for getting an especially low-rate card. First, let a year go by without applying for any new loans at all. Second, cancel all credit cards that you don't use by writing to the creditor, directing that your card be dropped from its credit file. Get a copy of your credit report to be sure the accounts are actually listed as closed. Then apply for the low-rate card you want.

If you can't land a card at 12 or 13 percent, move to the next level: credit cards at 14 to 17 percent. These should be available at banks or S&Ls right in your own city, and you don't have to be squeaky clean to qualify. Anyone with a decent credit history should be able to get one. Such cards are often issued by smaller lenders who rarely send out mass mailings to attract customers.

Here's another strategy: Take a card with a variable interest rate, which rises and falls as the general level of interest rates changes. It starts out cheaper than the average fixed-rate card. When rates rise you'll pay more (but you can always control your payments by putting fewer purchases on the card). When rates fall, you'll pay less. Overall, you'll probably save money.

Now we come to the cards that charge 18 to 22 percent a year. They take practically everybody who can faintly be called creditworthy. Good credit risks shouldn't bother with these high-rate cards. You can do better. Why do so many people take them anyway? Because they're lazy. It's easier to go to the nearest bank, or to sign an application that you got in the mail, than to hunt around for a cheaper card.

Several organizations publish lists of banks with cheap credit cards.

The names on their lists are all slightly different and many contain errors, but they give you a good idea of what's around: RAM Cardtrak Research & Publishing, P.O. Box 1700 (College Estates), Frederick, MD, 21702—$5 for a combined list of the lower-rate cards, low-annual-fee cards, well-priced premium cards, and secured cards (page 192). You might also try Bankcard Holders of America, 560 Herndon Parkway, Suite 120, Herndon, VA, 22070—$1.50 each, for a list of low-rate cards or a list of cards with no annual fee.

Be warned that the issuers of low-interest-rate cards are picky. They want only the very best credit risks. Many hopefuls apply and few are accepted. So also consider the Credit Card Locator, which covers a wider range of cards—$17 from Consumer Credit-Card Rating Service, P.O. Box 5219, Ocean Park Station, Santa Monica, CA, 90405. It includes some good cards at higher interest rates, which accept more people.

WHY ARE YOU SO POPULAR?

Your mail is full of letters from bankers, begging you to take a new credit card. It's not your good looks that attracts them. It's not even your income. It's your gorgeous pile of debt.

These banks buy lists of names from credit bureaus. They want people who have no more than four or five credit cards already, are carrying debt on most of them, and pay their bills on time. You may be choking on your debts. You may be paying just the minimum on every single card you have. You may be taking cash from one card to pay off another. That doesn't matter. As long as you're not a late payer, these bankers want you. They'll tempt you with credit lines of $1,000 to $5,000 or more, on which they charge 19 or 21 percent.

Spendaholics imagine that as long as the bankers keep offering them credit, they must not be too deeply in debt. They think that the credit machine will flash *tilt* when they have finally gone too far. That's an illusion. Banks that charge high interest rates find it profitable to give cards even to spendaholics and deal with any problems later. A certain percentage of defaults is built right into the interest rate they charge. If you go broke that's your lookout, not theirs.

WHAT'S HAPPENING TO CREDIT CARD PRICES

They're going up. Everyone—both convenience user and permanent debtor—will be paying higher fees.

One surprising reason for it is that more people have been paying off their bills in full. Banks hate this. Their profits lie in the interest they earn on revolving debt. They never met a convenience user they didn't dislike.

But you have to get up early to outfox a banker. Lenders are looking for ways to raise more money even from people who pay off their bills. They are increasing the annual fees. Cutting out grace periods. A few are charging a usage fee of $1 to $2.50 every month. There's even some talk about charging for every transaction or levying special fees on people who *don't* roll over debt.

As cards grow more expensive, convenience users, who don't carry debt, might think about switching to debit cards, instead (page 193).

If you get behind on your minimum monthly payments, you'll really see the fees rain down. There are stiff new fees for late payment, for exceeding your credit limit, and for paying your bank card bill with a rubber check.

If you have a lot of credit cards, save yourself money by canceling all but one or two. And ask yourself whether you really need a premium card, like a gold card.

Gold cards offer higher credit lines, which a cautious spender doesn't need. To get them, you pay maybe $30 to $50, compared with $15 to $25 for a regular card.

Both premium cards and, increasingly, regular cards are loaded with services and gimmicks, which might cost another $20 to $35. Among the extras offered by various cards: extended warranties for certain products purchased with the card; travel rebates if you book through a certain travel agent; frequent-flyer miles; rental-car collision insurance (although you may already have it in your auto policy); baggage insurance; discount catalogue shopping. Maybe you find these enhancements worth it. But maybe not.

HOW TO MAKE SURE YOU CAN PAY ALL YOUR CREDIT CARD BILLS

Every time you charge something, write it on your check register and deduct the money from the balance you show. When the bills come in, you'll already have set aside the funds to pay them.

YOUR CREDIT CARD FACT SHEET

• Visa, MasterCard, Discover, and Optima are revolving-credit cards. You can charge up to a certain limit and carry most of the debt forward from one month to the next.

• Department-store cards work like Visa and MasterCard, but they may have a lower credit limit and a higher interest rate. It usually pays to use your bank card instead of the store's own charge card.

• The combined credit card and telephone calling card sold by AT&T and US Sprint carry high interest rates, so they're not terrific for permanent debtors. But take a look at the AT&T Universal Card if you're a convenience user, a traveler, and a customer of AT&T. On long-distance calls placed through the AT&T network and charged to your credit card (which will generally be calls made from out of town), you get 10 percent off. For 10 percent off on calls placed through MCI, you can use your American Express card, through a program called Connect Plus.

• American Express, Carte Blanche, and Diners Club are travel-and-entertainment (T&E) cards. You generally have to pay off these bills in full every month. In a few cases, credit is allowed. For example, you can stretch out payments on airline tickets charged to American Express.

But do you really need travel-and-entertainment cards? They charge higher annual fees than bank cards do, and bank cards are accepted in more places, even abroad. T&E cards have two advantages: (1) Discipline. You normally have to pay off the entire credit balance every month, so you don't accumulate high interest charges. (2) Big expenses. They're built to handle charges for airplanes, rental cars, hotels, and restaurants, which would eat up the credit lines on the average Visa or MasterCard pretty fast. Still, frequent travelers can use bank cards as long as they have high credit lines. Infrequent travelers don't need a T&E card at all.

• Oil-company cards usually require that you pay each monthly bill in full. But some let you stretch out payments for tires or car repairs.

· The interest rates and charges on Visa and MasterCard are not set by a central organization. Each issuing bank sets its own prices, and costs vary widely. There are wonderful Visa cards and rotten Visa cards, depending on the deal. By contrast, the prices on travel-and-entertainment cards are set centrally. All of the cards from a T&E company cost the same.

· Most cards have fixed interest rates. Those with variable rates start out by charging one or two percentage points less than a comparable fixed-rate card. If interest rates follow the usual cycle of ups and downs, variables will cost less. If high inflation returns, however, holders of variable cards should be prepared to pay off their loans in a hurry. There are no interest-rate caps on most variable-rate credit cards (although most states limit how high consumer-loan rates can rise.)

· Don't be fooled by the grace period on your credit card. It allows for interest-free purchases, as long as you pay your bill within, say, 25 days. But it works only if you paid your previous month's bill in full.

There is no grace period when: (1) you are carrying forward debt from the previous month. Say, for example, that you owe $200 on your card and add $100 in purchases. At the end of the month you pay off the card. You'll be charged interest on the full $300, even though your card has a 25-day grace period. The grace period doesn't operate when there is *any* outstanding debt. (2) You have a cash advance against your card. Interest is always charged on your cash advances from the very first day.

· Some institutions charge an extra 2 percent or so for cash advances, on top of the regular interest rate. Avoid them. Some institutions require that you take a $2,000 cash advance when you sign up for the card, so you start out with a $2,000 debt. Avoid them, too.

· Lenders ask for the lowest possible payment every month. They want you to carry debt on your card, in order to run up your interest costs. But these minimum payments will keep you perpetually under water. Always pay as much as you can.

· Having too many credit cards will prevent you from getting other loans, even if all your payments are up to date. Here's why: Each of your cards has a line of credit that you could borrow against at any time. A lender will ask: Could you carry your debts if you borrowed against every card to the max? If not, you'll be denied another loan. How does a lender know how big your credit lines are? They show on your credit report, at the credit bureau.

• You say that you canceled the credit cards that you don't use? Have you looked to see if the cancellation took? Some lenders keep on reporting you as a cardholder, even after you drop them. There's only one way to tell whether that card has been wiped out of your credit history. Get a copy of your credit report (page 200) and look. If it hasn't been listed as closed (using a designation such as "paid satisfied"), call your former creditor and find out what it takes to get your name off its files.

• You might be offered a bank card through your college, a charity, or your union. My question: Has the group bargained for the best deal for its members, or has it taken the best deal for itself?

Most organizations think "me first." They get perhaps 0.5 percent of whatever you charge on the card, or 25 cents per transaction, or a bounty for everyone who signs up. This might make the card more expensive to use. For you, a credit card makes sense only if it carries a competitive interest rate, a grace period, or no annual fee. If you want to support your college or a charity, give money directly and make it tax-deductible.

• You are not responsible for your spouse's debts that occurred before the marriage, or occurred during the marriage but for purposes unrelated to it. For example, you wouldn't have to pay if your spouse sneaked off to Las Vegas and put the trip on his or her personal credit card. But you're generally responsible for debts incurred during the marriage that are considered "necessaries," or purchases made by one spouse as "agent" for the other. You're also responsible if you co-signed the debt or the credit card (including the credit card used for the Vegas trip).

• Credit card registration services keep a list of all your cards and will notify the issuers if you lose your wallet or change your address. But is this service really worth it? It's cheap and easy to write down all your card numbers (or photocopy your cards) and cancel them yourself.

• If you marry and change your name, change it on your credit cards, too. Always use the same name when you apply for credit, in order to keep your credit history all together.

• Before taking a card, find out how the bank will calculate the interest you'll owe on your credit card debt. The best is the *adjusted balance method*—the interest is applied to the amount you owe, after subtracting the payments you made. Next best (and most widely used) is the *average daily balance method*—which averages the amount of debt you had in your account each day during the month. The worst by a mile is the *previous balance method*—where you're charged interest on the balance in your account at the end of the previous month, with no credit at all for payments made currently.

WHAT MAKES YOU CREDITWORTHY?

Lenders build computer models to define the kinds of borrowers who repay their debts. You're given points for various conditions of your life, like how long you've been on the job and how many years you've been in the workforce. It doesn't matter if you score low on some items, as long as you score high on others. If you accumulate enough points in the computer, you get a credit card.

Each lender skews its credit-scoring system to approve the kinds of customers it wants. But you're the ideal applicant everywhere *if*:

• You have held your job for a while (you probably aren't going to be fired).

• You own your home (owners are less transient than renters).

• You've lived in your home for a while (you can handle the payments).

• You hold just a few credit cards and always pay on time.

• You have reasonable debts and credit lines compared with your income.

• You work in a field considered steady (teachers are more desirable than farm owners, because farms can go bust; doctors are more desirable than lawyers, because lawyers worry less about being sued).

If you're turned down for credit, lenders have to say why. The letter might list several things you scored low on, but none is the deciding factor. If just one of them had been higher, it might have pulled you above the line. Ask to talk to a credit manager personally, for information on how to improve your score. Don't let embarrassment put you off. Would-be borrowers do this all the time.

Sometimes you can get the decision reversed by explaining the circumstances. Did your credit report show two recent inquiries by other lenders? Maybe you were merely refinancing a mortgage at a lower interest rate. Have you lived at your address for only two months? Maybe you just got a new job and a big promotion. That might put you in a different light. Does your credit history show an unpaid bill? Maybe there was a dispute and you didn't file your side of the story with the credit bureau, or the bureau forgot to include your explanation in your credit file, or the creditor didn't pay attention to it. That happens a lot.

If you don't meet the lender's standards today, you might be accepted some time in the future. In the meantime, try another lender. Almost everyone can get credit *somewhere.*

If you've just moved, keep on using the bank cards you have already. This isn't the moment to apply for a card with a lower rate. Don't ask for new credit (except, perhaps, a department store charge) until you have been at your new job and new address for a year.

DON'T APPLY FOR A LOT OF CREDIT AT ONCE. Every time a potential lender pulls your credit history, that "inquiry" shows on your record. Some lenders automatically turn down anyone with two or three inquiries—say, for a mortgage and a credit card—over a short period of time. Apply for just one card and build a good credit history on it. Then apply for your second (following the strategy of owning two different types of cards— page 183). After that, get another card only if it's better than one you already have. And don't keep too many cards.

HOW TO GET YOUR FIRST CREDIT CARD

College students are often solicited for cards. Sometimes, they get them entirely on their own (the lenders assume that if they get into trouble, their parents will bail them out). Or a parent may be asked to co-sign. Assuming that you trust your child, go ahead and co-sign. Credit cards can help kids out of a jam, like a car breakdown on the way home from college. They're accepted in places where a personal check might not be. Furthermore, standards are more lenient for students. It's easier to get a bank card or American Express as an undergraduate than as a new graduate with a poorly paid job.

A card-carrying student is building a solid credit history. After graduation, your child should be able to cancel the co-signed card and start out with one of his or her own. Any debt on the old card is either paid off or transferred to the new one.

Start a checking and savings account at a bank or S&L. After a few months as a good customer, apply for a Visa or MasterCard. If you're turned down, make an appointment with the credit card manager and ask what you have to do to qualify. And do it. *Make sure that the lender reports to a credit bureau* (not all small institutions do). You need more than a credit card; you need a credit history, to give you access to even more loans.

If you've had a steady job and address for a few months, go to a major department store (one that will report your payment history to a credit bureau) and apply for a charge account. At the start, you'll be given a low line of credit but that doesn't matter. Once you prove your reliability, you'll be able to charge more.

What if you're a widow whose credit history and credit cards were all in your late husband's name? To get your own card, start with the bank where you've always done business. Show your income and your assets and make the case (if true) that you always paid the family bills. Make the same case at the stores where you've always charged. You know, of course, that you should have put your husband's credit history into your own name before he died (page 205). But many creditors will extend you that courtesy, even now. Make an appointment, or write a letter, and ask.

If you're turned down by one credit granter, don't assume that you're dead meat. Each lender has its own rules. Another bank, another store, may be willing to take you. *Any time you're turned down, ask specifically what the problem is. You might be able to fix it.*

CREDIT CARDS FOR PEOPLE WHO CAN'T GET CREDIT

Did you once embarrass yourself by not paying your bills? Are you an ex-bankrupt? Have you no credit history? Are you a bartender (bartenders' jobs are considered unstable)?

You need a *secured* card. You make a cash deposit into an interest-paying bank account. In return, the bank gives you a Visa or Master-Card. The card's credit limit may be 50 to 100 percent of the money you've left on deposit. If you deposit $500, for example, you can charge $250 to $500 worth of goods. Typically, you pay 18 to 22 percent interest on unpaid balances. If you make timely payments, you can graduate to a regular credit card in a year's time. If you don't pay on time, your cash deposit can be seized to cover the debt.

Make an appointment to talk to your own bank or credit union about getting a secured card. Many lenders provide them, even when they don't advertise the fact. If it's no go, send $3 to the Bankcard Holders of America (560 Herndon Parkway, Suite 120, Herndon, VA, 22070) for its list of banks that offer secured cards. Not every bank on the BHA list is a good deal. Avoid those that charge $60 to $70 in application fees, besides $35 to $40 in annual fees or extra fees for a cash advance— all on top of a 21 percent interest rate. And avoid lenders who don't report to a credit bureau. You need a credit history, to open the door to other loans.

Three banks with good secured-card programs: (1) Key Federal Savings Bank, Havre de Grace, MD (301-939-0016); First Consumers National Bank, Portland, OR (800-876-1220); American National Bank, Larchmont, NY (914-833-0560).

No secured lender guarantees to take you. American National, for example, sticks with people whose credit records have been clean for the past year. Key Federal turns down about half of the people who apply. You are ineligible if your income is too low to cover your debts, if you're so far in hock that you can't even pay your current bills, or if you're currently in bankruptcy. Secured cards are for *reformed* spendaholics, not for those who are still hitting the plastic.

DON'T ANSWER THE ADS YOU SEE IN NEWSPAPERS, READING "GET A VISA CARD, $25. BAD CREDIT, BANKRUPT—NO PROBLEM." It's *always* a problem. You'll pay $25 and may not get a card, because your credit is too poor even for secured lenders. The people who place these ads may send you an application for Key Federal or a similar bank. But the banks didn't hire them as agents and have no obligation to accept you. If you're turned down, you may find it hard to get your $25 back. Also, don't buy cards that can be used only to purchase goods from a catalogue. Their ads claim that they'll help you reestablish credit. That's blarney. Major credit grantors pay no attention to them. You'll just run up more debts buying catalogue goods.

RETAIL DEBIT CARDS

You'll see a lot more of these in the 1990s. They're the electronic equivalent of a check—for when you want to pay cash instead of using credit.

Your ATM (automated teller machine) card is a debit card. It "debits"—withdraws—money from your bank. It becomes a *retail* debit card when you can also use it to buy goods. When you pay with that card, you are telling the bank to take money directly out of your account and give it to the store.

These cards come in two types.

First, there is the basic ATM card—accepted by a growing number of supermarkets, gas stations, and convenience stores. You slip the card into a terminal. After the clerk adds up your purchases, you punch in your personal identification number (PIN) and zap the payment out of your account. When you use a debit card at certain Exxon and Mobil gas stations, you get the 3- to 5-cent discount given to customers who pay cash.

Second, there is the ATM card with a Visa or MasterCard logo on it. It can be used in any store or restaurant, anywhere in the world, which also takes the credit card. There are no terminals and, for retail use, no PINs. You use the card just the way you would a credit card. In fact, the clerk probably can't tell the difference. Only when the transaction reaches your bank does it register as a debit. Banks that offer this program (and so far, only a limited number do) usually charge an extra $12 to $15 for putting the Visa or MasterCard logo on your ATM card.

You can also get this type of card by opening a cash-management account at some of the major stockbrokerage houses. You would then keep your cash in the broker's money market mutual fund instead of a bank. Whenever you used the debit card, payment would be made from the money fund account.

So far, consumers haven't seen much use for a debit card. If you want to pay cash, you can always use greenbacks or write a check. You can even put down a credit card and pay at the end of the month, before running up any interest charges. But as more people struggle to get their spending under control, the convenience of debiting will grow more apparent.

What a debit card is good for:

1. You're swearing off credit cards but want the convenience of paying with plastic.

2. You don't want to bother carrying your checkbook or hauling out identification to get your check approved.

3. You're married, with a joint checking account. Debit cards eliminate the need to juggle two checkbooks or carry loose checks.

4. You need a fallback when you're short of cash in hand. With a debit card, you don't have to go to the ATM so often.

5. You don't want to run the risk of paying interest on your purchases—as you might, if you paid with a credit card and couldn't cover the full bill at the end of the month.

6. You're learning financial discipline. Debit cards don't let you spend any more money than you have in the bank. (A few debit cards give you access to loans if you overdraw. Resist.)

What about the float? When you write a check, you have a couple of days before it clears, during which time your funds can still earn interest. There is no float at all when you pay by inserting an ATM card into a terminal. However, the ATM cards with VISA or MasterCard logos allow a float ranging from one day to more than a week, depending on how fast the merchants send in their chits for payment. The smaller the merchant, the longer it may take for your debit to clear.

YOUR RIGHTS WHEN YOU PAY . . .

. . . With a Credit Card

Here's what you have to pay if your credit card is stolen and charges are run up: *nothing,* if you reported the loss to the bank before a fraudulent charge occurred. *Only $50,* for charges run up before the theft was reported to the card issuer—and banks often waive even that small fee. *Nothing,* if you still have your card but your number was used fraudulently —for example, in a mail-order transaction.

Here's how to solve a billing error, or withhold payment for defective goods or services, under the Fair Credit Billing Act: Notify the credit card issuer *immediately and in writing* that a problem exists. A phone call won't preserve your rights. The card issuer has to receive your letter within 60 days of the date the statement was mailed.

Give your name and account number, a description of what's wrong (with copies of supporting documents), and the dollar amount in dispute. Keep a copy of the letter. The card issuer has up to 90 days to resolve the problem. In the meantime, you can withhold payment, although any other charges on your bill must be paid as usual. If you turn out to be right, the disputed charge and any finance charges related to it will be taken off your bill. You will be given your money back if you've already paid.

If the card issuer says you're wrong, however, you have three choices.

1. Pay the bill, including any late charges.

2. Don't pay, be reported as delinquent to your credit bureau, and risk being sued by the card issuer. In this case, you should send a statement of your side of the story to the credit bureau, to be included in your file.

3. If the goods are defective, don't pay—and tell the card issuer (whether it's a store card, bank card, or a travel-and entertainment card) that you're holding it responsible. You can do this if the item cost more than $50 and you bought it in your home state or within 100 miles of

your mailing address. (Some states consider telephone and mail-order purchases to have been made in your home state, as long as the company advertised in-state or sent material to you there.)

When you make a defective-goods claim, the card issuer may charge the disputed payment back to the merchant. Or it may sue you. Until the argument is resolved, the issuer cannot close your account or report you as delinquent—although it can state that the payment is in dispute. If you're found to be right, the card issuer will remove the unpaid amount, plus any finance charges, from your account. But it will not restore any part of the disputed payment that has already been paid to the merchant. To get that money, you'll have to deal with the merchant directly.

What if you waited for more than 60 days to tell the card issuer that you received defective merchandise and refuse to pay? You then have to try to settle the problem with the merchant. If you can't, notify the card issuer in writing. If you used a bank or travel-and-entertainment card, you're subject to the rules and limits outlined in point 3 above. If you used the retailer's own card, you can pursue the store for any sum of money, with no geographical limitations.

You can rescind a charge *if:* you're billed for something you didn't buy; you're charged the wrong price; the goods never came; you refused to accept the goods on delivery; or the goods weren't delivered according to your agreement (for example, they were defective).

You can refuse to pay a finance charge *if:* the reason you're late is that the bill went to the wrong address (assuming that you gave the lender the right address at least 20 days before the end of the billing period); you are disputing the bill and you win; or you paid the bill and shouldn't have been charged any interest on it.

Check all bills for the following not uncommon errors:

· You get someone else's bills.

· An item you returned is never credited to your account.

· When the store finds its mistake, it doesn't rescind the interest you were charged.

· You aren't charged for something you bought (that's an honesty test; would you tell?).

· You're charged twice for the same purchase (*now* would you tell?).

· The bill was mailed to your old address and by the time you got it finance charges were due.

· Your bill was mailed too late to reach you before the clock started running on finance charges.

• The item you ordered arrived broken and hasn't been replaced, but the bills (and finance charges) keep coming.

Many credit card bills don't include copies of your receipts. Instead, you get a list of purchases. Sometimes the store might not even be listed, just the store's corporate owner. So keep your own receipts until the bills come in, to make it easier to find mistakes.

. . . With a Debit Card

Here's what you pay if your card is lost or stolen and charges are run up: $50, as long as you report the loss within two or four days, depending on the type of debit system used (check your agreement, to see which time limit applies). If you wait longer, it may cost you up to $500. If you let more than 60 or 90 days pass after getting the bank statement showing the fraudulent charges (again, the time limit depends on your debit agreement), all subsequent losses may be yours. So check those statements! Only in a few states are limits put on how much you can lose.

In a billing dispute, you get exactly the same protection that you would with a credit card. But if the dispute involves shoddy goods, your level of protection depends on which card you have. With a Visa or MasterCard debit card, the bank will help you get your money back from the merchant. With a regular debit card, it won't.

. . . With a Check

If a thief cashes one of your checks, and you sign an affidavit of forgery, the bank will pay. So you're fully protected.

If you regret your purchase, you can ask the bank to stop the check. You'll have to follow up your telephone call with a written stop-check order. If the check slips through anyway, it's the bank's responsibility.

YOUR CREDIT HISTORY

Here's what shows up on a typical credit report:

1. How many charge accounts and bank cards you have and how long you've had them.

2. The date of your last payment.

3. The largest amount that you've ever owed to that particular creditor, or the top that you're allowed to charge.

4. The current amount owed.

5. Whether your payments are up to date.

6. The amount that's past due.

7. The type of loan or account, and its terms.

8. The latest you ever paid on that account, and how many times you've been delinquent.

9. Any special problems with your account—for example, that goods were repossessed or that a bill collector had to be called in.

10. Court actions, such as liens, judgments awarded to creditors, bankruptcies, foreclosures.

11. Your legal relationship to the account—are you jointly responsible? Individually responsible? A co-signer?

12. Past accounts, paid in full but now closed.

13. Whether you've put a statement on the record in a dispute with the lender.

A credit bureau may know what you do for a living but not how much money you make. It doesn't know if you're divorced or have nine kids or drink. It does *not* give you a credit rating. It simply reports your payment history to lenders who are thinking about giving you money. The lenders then make their own judgments about whether to take you on. There is no such thing as a hard and fast credit rating. One lender may love you and give you a huge credit line; another one may turn you down.

Most people have good credit. Mainly, what you need is a steady job with a history of paying bills approximately on time. Your credit won't be ruined if you sometimes pay bills late. You can even go through a rough patch—getting stiff overdue notices—without damaging your basic creditworthiness. It's not smart to apply for new credit at a time when you're behind. But once you've caught up, you'll be back in most lenders' good graces.

Here's what lenders *don't* like to see:

• You already have a lot of credit cards, with large credit lines.

• You had to be chased for payment by a collection agency.

• You were sued for money owed.

• There's a lien on your property.

• A creditor closed one of your accounts.

• You went bankrupt.

• You have been applying for a lot of credit lately. (Maybe you're in trouble? Maybe you're going to charge a lot and go bankrupt?)

How long information stays in your credit file depends partly on the company. Regular data normally stays for seven years, including the history of closed accounts. Most adverse information clings for seven years (and longer, in certain situations—for example, if you apply for $50,000 or more in credit). "Wage earner plans" under the Bankruptcy Code (page 209) may be wiped out after 7 years, but straight bankruptcies will weigh down your record for up to 10 years.

It's not only lenders who look at your credit history. You may be checked out when you apply for life insurance or even for a job.

What Credit Bureaus Don't Know

Most people assume that credit bureaus know all the shabby little secrets of their financial lives. But if you look at your credit report, you'll see things missing. Small shops usually don't report their charge-account customers to credit bureaus. Neither do some small banks, S&Ls, and credit unions. Neither do doctors, most hospitals, and utility companies (although you might be found out if they give your account to a bill collector who reports). Some oil-company cards aren't yet on line. Home-equity lines of credit are generally reported, but first mortgages and traditional second mortgages are coming on line more slowly.

As for your payment history, it may look better than it really is, because some lenders consider payment within 60 days satisfactory and give it the same top rating that other lenders reserve for 30-day payments.

In short, if your credit history errs, it's just as apt to be on the bright side as on the dark one.

Fixing Mistakes in Your Credit Report

Where do credit bureaus get their information? Either from your creditors, who report your payment history on computer tape, or from their connections at courthouses, where lawsuits are tracked. If their informants are wrong, there will be a mistake in your credit report. Mistakes might also be made by the bureau itself. A minor error makes no difference, as long as it doesn't prevent you from getting credit. But you never know what's going to be minor. Take a single, erroneous "slow-pay" report. A lender that charges 21 percent might overlook it; one that charges 12 percent might turn you down. A major mistake, like combining your payment history with that of a deadbeat of the same name, will probably cut you off from credit. You'll be considered a deadbeat, too, during the months—sometimes years—it takes for you to straighten out the mess.

GET A COPY OF YOUR CREDIT HISTORY AND CHECK IT FOR ACCURACY. It might cost any-where from $2 to $15. You fill in a request form, giving your name, Social Security number, present address, previous address, and birthday —information designed to prove you're the person you say you are. Some bureaus will send you your spouse's record; others require his or her express consent. The spouse's record goes to the address shown on the credit file, so you can't spy on a spouse who is living somewhere else.

There are three major credit bureaus: (1) TRW Credit Data, 505 City Parkway West, Orange, CA, 92668; (2) Equifax Credit Information Services, 1600 Peachtree St. N.W., P.O. Box 4081, Atlanta, GA, 30302; (3) Trans Union Corp., Consumer Relations Dept., P.O. Box 119001, Chicago, IL, 60611. Your name might be in all three places; check the Yellow Pages for their local offices. You might also be in the files of smaller local or regional bureaus used by local stores. Any mistake reported to one bureau may be reported to all of them.

IF YOU FIND YOURSELF IN ANY OF THE FOLLOWING FIVE SITUATIONS, IT'S ESPECIALLY IMPORTANT THAT YOU CHECK YOUR CREDIT REPORT AND FIX ANY MISTAKES.

1. You are applying for an important loan, like a mortgage. An inaccurate credit history might keep you from getting it.

Married people should ask for reports listed under their personal names and Social Security numbers. For backup (in case your spouse is co-signing the loan) get your spouse's history. There is no such thing as a joint credit report, covering both of you. Transactions arising from joint accounts are reported twice, once to the husband's account, once to the wife's. (The credit card shows the same number in both reports, so a potential lender won't double-count it.)

2. You are separating from your spouse, and want his or her new transactions off your personal credit record. Write to all your creditors, closing joint accounts and asking for a new account in your name alone (tell your spouse you're doing it, so that he or she can write for a personal card at the same time; it's vindictive to leave a spouse with an invalid card). Three months later, get a copy of your credit report. It should show your joint accounts as closed. If it doesn't, tell the credit bureau— and chase after each separate creditor yourself. Not all joint debts will vanish from your record. Any loans you co-signed, or any unpaid revolv-ing credit that you're both responsible for, will stay on your credit history until the debt is cleared.

3. You've paid off a court judgment against you for money owed.

Your credit report may carry the judgment. You want to be sure that the record shows that the judgment was paid.

4. You've had a dispute with a store and refused to pay a bill. You and the store cannot reach agreement, so you're reported as delinquent. You are entitled to put a 100-word explanation into your credit report. (The credit bureau will help you frame your case succinctly.) The file will summarize your side of the story. If a potential lender wants to know more, it can send for your full explanation. Get the report to be sure that your objection is noted.

5. You have been turned down for credit on the basis of information in a credit report. The lender has to tell you the name and address of the bureau it used. That bureau will send you a free copy of your report (as long as you ask for it within 30 days). You're also entitled to the names of everyone who got the report in the past six months (the past two years, if the report was supplied to a potential employer). You can challenge any item you think wrong.

To Fix Mistakes in the Record:

Note the errors on the copy of the report you get and mail it back to the credit bureau. The bureau has to check the disputed information. If it can't be verified within a reasonable time (around 25 days), it should be deleted.

That's the good news. It's also good news if the mistake originated with the credit bureau, because that's usually pretty easy to fix.

It's bad news, however, if one of your creditors—say, a department store—erred. When the bureau checks with the store, it may merely verify the original mistake. You'll have to persuade the store itself that you don't owe the money, so that your records can be changed at the source. Only then will your name be cleared. To insure that the blot isn't showing up somewhere else, check your report at every credit bureau the store deals with—and ask those bureaus to send fresh reports to the smaller bureaus they sell information to. Sometimes this job is only a headache. Sometimes it is a nightmare.

If any change is made in your credit report, the credit bureau has to send a corrected copy to any creditor who received it in the past six months.

Improving Your Credit History

Here are the only legitimate ways of doing it.

- Start paying all your bills on time.
- Pay off back bills. They don't go away.
- Reduce the monthly payments you owe (including your mortage) to less than 35 percent of your gross monthly income.
- Fix any mistakes on your credit record.
- Cancel any credit cards you're not using. You increase your borrowing power just by getting rid of excess credit lines. (The accounts will not actually be taken off your credit history, but they should be shown as closed.)
- Give the credit bureau an explanation for any black mark, like several bills three months past due two years ago. Detail what happened and point out that these accounts are now up to date. Your explanation becomes part of your file.
- Tell the credit bureau to remove any data older than 7 years and bankruptcies older than 10 years. This should happen automatically, but sometimes credit bureaus slip up.
- Don't waste your time trying to add any good accounts that don't normally report to the credit bureau. Some bureau's won't take them; some will, but charge you two to five dollars. The information isn't useful, because it won't be updated regularly. Potential creditors may reject reports from lenders who don't belong to the credit bureau, for fear that some of those accounts are fraudulent.

IF MANIC OVERSPENDING GOT YOU INTO TROUBLE, A ROTTEN CREDIT HISTORY ACTUALLY DOES YOU A FAVOR. It stops you from getting any deeper into debt. Once you quit borrowing more than you can repay, your credit history will gradually repair itself.

How long that takes depends on why you fell behind in the first place. Lenders are not gentle to the middle-class deadbeat who charges too much, then has to be wrestled to the mat for payment. They look more kindly on people whose money troubles were at least partly beyond their control—unemployment, illness, and divorce being the most acceptable excuses.

Still, those are big black marks on your record. If you've straightened out, and if you're dealing with a local lender to whom you can explain yourself, you might get your credit back in a year or two. But chronic delinquents may not get another bank card for years.

The best time to go broke is when everyone around you is doing the same—as in Texas during the oil crash. During a financial crisis, local lenders may not apply the traditional credit standards; if they did, they'd have hardly any business at all. In this situation, your credit history matters a lot less than your current income and level of debt. As long as you're now out of trouble, you can probably qualify for a loan again.

You can generally get an auto loan with bad credit behind you as long as it's *behind* you. Lenders take the chance because they can repossess if you don't pay. But you might have to put down 50 percent of the price in cash. As for a mortgage, not every bank or mortgage company will take you on, but some may. When you apply, warn the lender that your credit report won't look so hot, and explain why. Talk, talk, talk. Explain, explain, explain. You'll get sick of it, but you'll eventually find a loan. (If you can't bear the pain, hire a lawyer to look for a mortgage for you.)

If you have some cash, you can help your credit report by putting the money in a bank, borrowing against it, and making loan payments on time. I'm not crazy about this idea because it costs you interest you don't really have to pay. But it's a piece of the proof that you've put your bad habits behind you.

One exception to this happy ending is the bankrupt. Lenders like to see people fight their way out of debt. They hate bankruptcies. If you have a steady job and roots in the community you might get short-term credit, like an auto loan after a couple of years. You might even get a secured credit card (page 192). But few lenders will give you open-ended credit or a mortgage loan, lest you go bust again. You'll have to struggle along, without a major source of credit, for 10 long years—which is something the bankruptcy lawyer might not have made absolutely clear.

Don't expect a lender to suggest that you might be borrowing too much. *You* have to decide. Lenders do take a general look at your balance sheet and outstanding credit lines, and turn down people who are obviously overloaded. But the only way they make money is to make more loans. So they'll cheerfully take you right to the brink, and sometimes beyond. They charge a high enough interest rate to cover a certain number of defaults, so going broke is your worry, not theirs.

Credit Repair Firms

Don't give them a nickel. Their ads imply that they can wave a wand over a bad credit history and bring you out smelling like a rose. They can't. If there are errors in your record, you can fix them yourself (page 200). True information cannot legally be removed.

Some credit repairers harass credit bureaus, challenging even items that are correct. Their strategy is to question more than the credit bureau can verify within the time limit, so it will have to expunge the derogatory facts. But credit bureaus are resisting. They don't have to follow up on challenges that are frivolous. In fact, they might not even deal with credit clinics at all. You might pay a clinic from $50 to $2,000 or more and end up with the same lousy credit history you started with.

Incidentally, you can't get rid of a bad credit report by moving. The big bureaus are national. Your record follows you everywhere.

Investigative Reports

When you apply for a big life insurance policy, the insurer wants to know more than whether you pay your bills. It will be curious about whether you've told the truth about where you work, whether you've ever been caught driving drunk, and whether your hobby is sky-diving. So it will turn to one of the bureaus that specializes in gathering personal information. Some employers do the same. You give permission for the investigation when you sign the insurance- or job-application form.

Who is the chief source of information for this type of report? Usually you. The investigator calls you up and asks you some questions. He verifies the information on your application. He may talk to your neighbors or a former employer. The interviewer has to identify himself and his purpose before starting to ask questions. Before answering, write down the interviewer's name and get a place to call to check up on *him*.

These reports are not kept very long because the information goes stale. They may be junked after just 90 days (although they'll stay in storage for six months, in case a consumer requests disclosure). If you're turned down for insurance, or charged more than the basic rate based on information in an investigative report, you have a right to see and challenge it. The bureau can withhold two things from you: (1) the names of the people who gave it the information, and (2) the nature of any medical information that may have been given directly to whoever asked for the report without being copied into the bureau's files.

CREDIT DISCRIMINATION

You can't be denied credit solely on the basis of color, race, religion, sex, age, marital status, national origin, or the fact that you're on welfare. If you *are* turned down for a loan or a bank card, it is probably because:

1. You don't have enough income.
2. You don't have a steady job history.
3. Your debts are too large relative to your income.
4. You don't have a credit history.

Wives and Credit

Many married women apply for credit solely on the basis of their own incomes and think it's discrimination if they're turned down. It's probably not. They simply haven't focused on how large their debts really are.

Take a wife who co-signs a mortgage with her husband. If he skips out, that obligation becomes hers. It would probably overwhelm her resources.

She doesn't think about that debt as long as she's well married, but her creditors do. If she tries to get credit based on her income alone, the lender will set off that mortgage against her paycheck and conclude that she can't carry any more loans. The same would be true for a married man who couldn't meet the mortgage payments were it not for the salary of his wife.

Learning this, some married women wonder how they will ever get credit "in their own names." But they don't understand what that phrase means. You *have* credit in your own name, as long as the accounts you hold jointly with your husband are reported in your name at the credit bureau as well as in his—Joan Smith, not Mrs. John Smith.

That's all there is to it. It doesn't matter whether the loan or the credit card is supported by your income, by both your incomes, or by your husband's income alone. As long as it's reported under your personal name rather than your Mrs., it is your credit.

Married couples usually apply for credit jointly, in order to get the benefit of both incomes. When a married person applies separately, it's usually for a business loan. A bank can ask you for a co-signer, but it can't demand that the co-signer be your spouse. What if your spouse has an interest in the property you're putting up as collateral? The lender can require the spouse to sign a waiver, allowing the property to be seized if you don't pay—but that's different from co-signing the loan itself. As a practical matter, however, your spouse is usually your best co-signer.

If you're widowed or divorced, and your credit cards were granted partly on the strength of your spouse's income, the lender can require you to show that you're still creditworthy. You may have to reapply for credit, showing your current level of income and debt. While you're being rechecked, your credit cannot be revoked—unless you fail to pay your bills. If you're too distraught, at the time of the crisis, to open the mail and write checks, find someone who can do that for you.

Often, widows just keep on using their cards. Nobody finds out and nobody kicks. Obviously, lenders would rather you confessed that you're now single (and some may put a clause in your credit card contract requiring it). But nothing in federal law stops you from keeping mum.

The divorced can't help revealing their status, when they close joint accounts and ask for new cards in their own names. If your payment record has been good, creditors will generally issue you a card without question. But they're entitled to put you through a credit check all over again. The lender must consider alimony as part of your regular income, unless there's evidence that it's not being paid.

On a marital card, a spouse can be either *jointly responsible* for the debt or an *authorized user,* with the other spouse solely responsible for payment. You normally want to be jointly responsible. That's what protects your right to credit. If you're only an authorized user, and are widowed or divorced, the lender can force you to reapply for credit and yank your card if you don't qualify. How do you find out what your status is? The easiest way is to get a copy of your credit report, which will tell you. How do you change your status? Write to the lender and request it.

It's important to understand, however, that the lender doesn't have to make you jointly responsible. The law requires only that the account be reported in each spouse's name. To raise your status, you and your spouse may have to reapply for credit jointly, and you might have to show that you have an income (although usually not).

Any account opened with your spouse since June 1, 1977, will be reported in both your names, whether you're jointly responsible or not. But wives whose accounts were opened earlier may find all the credit reported only in their husband's name. To change that, you have to write to the store or the bank and ask that your name be put on the credit file, too. You'll normally get a form to sign. If it's an "authorized user" form, write back to the card issuer and ask how you can become jointly responsible—although in some cases, you won't want to be.

If your spouse is a deadbeat, his or her bad habits will taint your own creditworthiness, unless you can show that you lead a more responsible life. One way to do this: Get a bank card or store charge in your name (even if a friend or a parent co-signs for it), keep it solely for your own use, and keep the bills up to date. You can show that account as proof of your personal reliability. Similarly, buy a car yourself (or with a co-signer), and make all the payments on it. It will show on your credit history as your own debt. Finally, don't co-sign any of your spouse's loans or credit cards. If circumstances allow it, you should cancel the cards and credit lines that you've co-signed already.

Older People and Credit

Older people often feel that they're being discriminated against. More likely, it's that their clean lifestyle doesn't fit the profile of a good credit risk. Here are several eye-opening cases that were supplied to me by the American Association of Retired Persons.

• Ray G., age 71, retired businessman, was refused a Visa card because of his "limited credit experience." His mistake: When he retired, he paid up everything, dropped all his credit cards, and started living on cash. Six years later, when he wanted a credit card to travel with, he no longer had sufficient credit history.

• Martin K. couldn't get a Discover card because he had too many other cards. That made him sore, because nine of his cards he never used—but how was the lender to know that? If you have accumulated a lot of cards over the years, get rid of all but one or two of them.

• Evelyn L., 75 and widowed, was turned down for a card because she had no credit history. She had always paid cash for everything, a way of life handed down to her by her parents. In old age, she wanted a credit card for catalogue shopping but couldn't get one.

The moral of these stories is to get a card when you're young, working, and laden with debt—the very customer the lenders want. Keep that card for when you retire or are widowed, even if you don't use it. The time may come when you'll want it again, and it's hard to recover your credit once you've given it up.

None of the turndowns above were illegal. They were all based on legitimate credit criteria. But consider the following stories.

• Marjorie W., 68, bought a travel trailer on an installment contract. Later, the dealer called and canceled, because the finance company wouldn't lend more than $6,000 to someone over 65.

· Robert M., 72, was denied a loan because his bank wouldn't lend to anyone over 70.

· Martha P., 71, was rejected by a finance company because she didn't qualify for credit life insurance.

All of these lenders broke the law. You cannot be turned down for credit solely on the basis of age. Nor can a lender set different terms for older people than for younger people in the same situation. A lender is allowed to consider age only if it makes a proven difference to creditworthiness. For example, if a 75-year-old applies for a 30-year mortgage, a bank might legitimately ask about her future cash flow, or request a larger down payment. But the senior can't be turned down, if the loan would be granted to a younger person with the same income and assets.

What can an older person do, if he or she has no credit history? Ask your bank for a card with a low credit limit. Ask a store where you shop for a charge account. It may take a personal visit, but it's worth it. Or get a secured card (page 192).

IF YOU CAN'T PAY YOUR BILLS

Don't hide. Don't cry. Don't shove unopened bills into a drawer. Don't have your cousin tell the bank that you've gone to Sicily for the summer. *That won't help.* Someone will find you—probably a bill collector—and you'll be in more trouble than you were before.

What's your biggest problem when you can't pay your bills? Money, you say. *I* say it's fear. You're sure that everyone will point and sneer. Your son will be kicked out of Boy Scouts. The police will hang you up by your thumbs. *But nothing like that is going to happen.* You're not Jack the Ripper. You don't beat up babies or set fire to cats. All you did wrong was to buy more things than you can pay for right away. That's an error of judgment but not a sin. You will pay eventually, and your errors will be forgiven.

If you can't pay your bills, write a letter to your creditors and tell them so. For a really big bill, like a mortgage, make an appointment to see someone in the credit department. Don't slump in like a bankrupt. Approach the interview like a businessperson with a problem to solve.

To do this you need: (1) a spending plan, showing how much money you need to live on (page 139); (2) a repayment plan, showing how much you can spread among your creditors every month; (3) a specific offer for each creditor—as in, "I will pay you $50 a month and clear up this bill in 10 months."

Each creditor will want more. But if you hold firm—and keep making the payments you've decided on—they will eventually accept the deal. If someone threatens to sue, don't ruin your rehabilitation plan by trying to accommodate him. Keep on talking, keep making your payments, even go to court. No judge will order you to pay more than you can afford, and your creditors know it. Your strengths are three: The lender would rather stretch out payments than repossess, it's cheaper to talk than to hire a debt collector, and the interest you pay is compensation for the delay.

If you can't handle these negotiations yourself, or if you're such a spendaholic that you find yourself hurtling toward bankruptcy, credit counselors can help. Counselors give you moral support. They help you develop a bud--t, er, I mean, a spending plan. They talk to your creditors and get them to accept smaller payments. Their fees are modest: maybe $10 to $50 a month, and zero for clients with low incomes. For the name of a nonprofit counseling agency, ask your city's department of social services; the debt-collection office of your bank, credit union, or a major department store; the National Foundation for Consumer Credit, 8701 Georgia Ave., Silver Spring, MD, 20910; or Family Service America, 11700 West Lake Park Dr., Milwaukee, WI, 53224. The last two organizations have affiliates all over the country, although not all FSA affiliates offer credit counseling. *Don't be afraid to ask for help.* Thousands of people share your problem. Counselors and credit managers have seen it all before and consider it their job to haul you out of the pit.

Do *not* pay a lawyer or firm that offers to straighten out your debts in return for a percentage of what you owe. You can't afford it and it won't work.

If negotiation doesn't solve the problem, consider Chapter 13 of the Bankruptcy Code, formerly known as the "wage-earner plan." It stops your creditors from hounding you and lets you keep your property, while you enter on a formal, court-approved plan to pay at least part of your debts over three to five years.

If even that's too tough, go for Chapter 7, straight bankruptcy. Most of your debts will be canceled, although you may have to give up some of your property to repay creditors. Get good legal advice. It's risky to read a book and try to do it yourself, because you might miss something of advantage to you.

Certain debts normally cannot be discharged, although there are some exceptions to the rules. These debts include recent student loans, child support, alimony, most taxes, loans you didn't mention on your bankruptcy petition, loans granted on the basis of untrue financial statements, and court judgments for certain damages, such as an accident you caused while driving drunk. You also can't get out of consumer loans over $500 owed to a single creditor and incurred for luxury goods and services within 40 days of a bankruptcy filing (that's the "no-last-minute-BMWs" rule); or cash advances for more than $1,000 from an open-ended credit plan taken within 20 days of the filing (the "no-last-minute-Caribbean-vacation" rule).

Chapter 7 bankruptcy is the hardest for lenders to forget. It hangs around on your credit record for a decade.

HOW TO TELL YOU'RE IN TROUBLE

Quit buying on credit if:

1. You can afford to pay only the minimum on your credit cards every month, and even that's a stretch.

2. You have to charge purchases that you used to pay for in cash.

3. You took a debt-consolidation loan and now you're running up fresh debts.

4. You can't save a dime.

5. You look forward to the junk mail, hoping that a new bank will be careless enough to offer you a credit card.

6. You're taking cash advances from one card in order to make payments on another.

7. You can't pay your basic bills on time.

8. You're being dunned.

9. You get turned down for credit.

10. You don't even want some of the things you buy.

11. Your friends can't figure out how you manage to live so well.

12. Without overtime or moonlighting, you'd lose your house, your car, and your kids.

13. You're taking cash advances for daily expenses like food and rent.

14. You borrow $50 from the guy in the next office, until the end of the week. You borrow $500 from your brother.

15. You don't open an envelope that you know contains a bill.

16. When you buy on credit, you always choose the longest time period to repay.

17. You never pay off your credit cards completely.

18. You put off paying by fiddling your creditors—putting the bill for the dentist in the envelope addressed to the doctor and vice versa.

19. You bounce checks.

20. You get scared about money in the middle of the night.

21. You don't dare tell your mother. Or your spouse. Or, sometimes, yourself.

Credit card issuers have developed sophisticated systems for identifying borrowers who are likely to default. They call it "behavior scoring." Here are six of the warning signals that creditors look for:

1. You pay only the bare minimum every month and never more than the minimum.

2. You make partial payments.

3. You started falling behind on your payments soon after opening the account.

4. You have taken the maximum cash advance.

5. Your account balance always grows; you can't ever seem to pay it off.

6. You have periodic bouts of late payment.

If this describes you, your number-one job is to get out of debt. Only then can you start getting rich.

11
WHEN TO HOCK
THE FARM:

All the Best Ways to Borrow Money to Invest

The rich didn't get that way by saving pennies.
That's only what they tell their biographers.
They made their fortunes on borrowed money.

Don't borrow to spend. Occasional debt on a credit card never hurt anybody, but permanent indebtedness to support an implacable spending habit is a staggering waste. A loser's game. At 18 percent interest, you are overpaying for everything, by nearly one-fifth. Why would you want to throw that much money away? You're living rich while growing poor.

But don't be shy about *borrowing* to invest. That's how people get rich. They use OPM—Other People's Money—to build something of value for themselves. Here are the classic steps to wealth: First, shed consumer debt. Second, build assets—through homeownership, saving money, and investing. Third, borrow prudently against some of those assets, to invest for even more net worth.

WHAT IS INVESTMENT DEBT?

Investment debt is money you borrow to acquire an asset that, with luck, might rise in value. For example, when you take out a home mortgage, you hope that your house will go up enough in price to cover the interest and yield a profit (and it probably will, as long as you hold it for five or six years). A college loan is a great investment because it builds your earning power, or the earning power of your children. A loan to start or buy into a business will multiply your money many times, if the business succeeds. A car loan can support your investment program, if you take it in place of raiding cash that is profitably at work. Even a debt-consolidation loan is worthwhile, if it lowers the interest you have to pay.

The critical test of any loan is that the money you borrow not disappear. It should be used in some way to maintain and improve your wealth.

HOW MUCH INVESTMENT DEBT CAN YOU AFFORD?

WHEN YOU BORROW FOR INVESTMENT...

1. *You can afford any debt that will support itself.* Can you rent out a duplex for enough to cover the costs? Can you invest your life-insurance cash values at a higher interest rate than it costs to borrow the money out of the policy? If so, go ahead and do it.

2. *You can afford any debt that you can cover out of your personal earnings.* In general, up to 40 percent of your income can be safely committed to monthly repayments (including mortgage repayments).

When you borrow against your earning power, however, those loans should be used chiefly for *liquid* investments, which are things that can be easily sold. That's your fallback position. If your income drops and you're pressed for cash, you can dump the investment and eliminate the debt.

Mutual funds are liquid. Second homes aren't. When you finance a second home out of earnings, you should either be dead sure of your job or have enough savings to carry the mortgage for a year or so, if your income falls.

3. *You can risk a debt for an illiquid investment, as long as you have a substantial amount of liquid securities or money in the bank.* Say, for example, that you borrow to buy a piece of land that can be subdivided and

sold as separate building lots. Then you lose your job. The land may not be instantly salable. But your lender (that stone-hearted bean counter) seems to think you should keep on making monthly payments. How will you manage? No sweat, as long as you have a lot of cash and stocks to fall back on. If you don't, never finance an investment like this. You'll be playing dice with your solvency.

THE MONEY STORES

When you want a loan, don't put on the sackcloth of a mendicant and approach your banker on bended knee. You are a *customer* in a *money store*. Everyone wants your business, if you're a good credit risk. You can negotiate terms just the way you negotiate a new-car price. Bankers expect borrowers to be choosy and are astounded when they're not.

In any city, the most costly lender may charge anywhere from two to six percentage points more than the cheapest one. A poor credit risk may have to accept those terms; a good one doesn't.

Your search for a loan might start with a credit union, if you can find one to join (page 52). After that, look at S&Ls, then at banks. In general, smaller institutions charge lower rates and fewer fees than large ones. Your own bank might give you an interest-rate discount. But even with the discount, the loan might be more expensive than you'd get at another institution. Think about moving all your accounts to a place where you'll get a better deal.

Make an appointment to see a loan officer, don't just wander in off the street. Innocents wander; smarties prearrange.

Make a list of the things you want to know: annual percentage rate; fees; down payment; repayment schedule. Ask: "Is that the best you can do?" Ask: "Will you cut half a point off the interest rate? Will you lower the points I have to pay up front?" If it's a big personal loan, ask: "Can I borrow at 1 percent over the prime lending rate?" (which is the bank's standard rate for business loans). Or, "Can I borrow at prime?" Then say, "Thanks very much, I'll think it over," and leave.

Repeat the scene with one or two more lenders. If your favorite bank has a higher interest rate than the others, tell it what the competition is doing. If it wants your business, it will come down. You'll get the best rate if you have at least two banks bidding for the loan.

The major finance or consumer-loan companies can be competitive for large home-equity lines. But generally speaking, they charge higher interest rates and higher fees. Use them only if you can't get credit somewhere else. If you already have a finance-company loan, try to pay it off with a lower-rate loan from a credit union or bank.

Finance companies usually want your house as collateral, even on very small loans. A borrower who continually returns to a finance company for small loans will find fee piled on fee, making borrowing hugely expensive.

BORROWING AGAINST YOUR HOUSE

It may sound uncharacteristically wild of me to suggest your home as a source of risk capital. But that is the only source that most of us have. If you think you can profit by borrowing money out of your home to invest somewhere else, it's worth a try. But *only* if you can comfortably carry the larger mortgage; *only* if you're sure of your income; *only* if you've applied the rules of sound investing (Chapter 21); *only* if you expect the investment to appreciate by more than your net interest cost; and *only* if you wouldn't be devastated if the deal flopped.

Generally speaking, people feel more comfortable tapping their homes for real-estate investments than for stocks. For example, you might use the equity in your first home to finance a second one.

But there's nothing wrong with carrying a larger mortgage in order to be invested in stocks, as long as your mortgage interest rate is 10 percent or less. Stocks should earn more than that over the long run. In an emergency, you could always sell the stocks to reduce the loan.

Second Mortgages and Home-Equity Lines

The loan of choice today is a second mortgage. Pretty soon it will be standard issue, like a car loan or blue jeans. Every homeowner will have one, for good or for ill.

It's a child of the tax laws. You can tax deduct the interest on second mortgages up to $100,000 (although the loan can't exceed your home's fair market value). By contrast, you get no tax deduction at all for interest paid on auto loans, student loans, credit card debt, and personal loans. You'll save money, then, by skipping these loans and putting your house in hock, instead.

A traditional second mortgage works just like a first. You borrow a fixed amount of money and pay back over a fixed term, usually 10 to 15 years. The interest rate may be fixed or variable. The cheapest fixed-rate second mortgage is probably a home-improvement loan insured by the Federal Housing Administration and offered by many mortgage banks as well as some commercial banks and S&Ls.

But borrowers have fallen in love with a different kind of second mortgage—the home-equity line of credit. It's a loan tailor-made for our self-service times. Instead of borrowing a fixed amount of money, you arrange for a fixed amount of borrowing power. After that, you can give yourself a loan any time you want. You just write a check (the minimum loan is usually $250 to $500), make a phone call asking that funds be transferred into your checking account, or put down a credit or debit card. You pay interest only on the money that you actually use. The interest rate usually rises and falls, along with the general level of rates.

How fast you repay is often up to you. You can generally choose to: (1) pay interest and a small amount of principal each month. Sometimes the unpaid balance is due in 10 or 15 years. Sometimes there's an indefinite term—effectively, lasting until you sell your house. (2) Pay only the interest, with all of the principal due in a lump sum after 5 to 10 years. (3) Pay substantial amounts each month, to clear up the loan as fast as you can. There are usually no prepayment penalties.

Home-equity lines are offered by banks, S&Ls, credit unions, finance companies, even some large brokerage houses. Credit unions often have the best terms. Finance companies often have the worst.

SHOULD YOU TAKE A HOME-EQUITY LINE OR A TRADITIONAL SECOND MORTGAGE?

A traditional second mortgage is all discipline. Your monthly payments are usually fixed, so you don't have to shiver when interest rates rise. You cannot easily add to the loan—no temptation there. It's a good way to borrow for a single purpose, like redoing the kitchen. It's the right loan for people on limited budgets. And it's a good defensive loan in a shaky marriage. You can insist that every check written against the proceeds carry both your signatures, so you always know where the money is going.

But it's the wrong choice for anyone (in a sound marriage) who will keep going back to borrow more. You pay brand new mortgage costs every time you rewrite this loan for a larger amount.

A home-equity line, by contrast, is all rubber. You open a large line of credit (pledging your house as collateral) and can borrow against it whenever you want. So it's the right loan for meeting a series of needs, like college tuition for the next four years plus kitchen remodeling. If you're married, it takes only one signature to originate a loan, not both. Your interest rate usually rises and falls in line with the general level of rates, so your monthly payments will vary, too. This loan is safest for people with substantial incomes who won't be fazed if the payments go up.

Which is cheaper, a traditional second mortgage or a home-equity loan? That's hard to tell. You cannot compare these loans' annual percentage rates of interest (APR), because they're figured differently.

On the fixed-rate second mortgage, all the financing fees are counted toward the APR. On the home-equity line, by contrast, the APR is figured *without* the upfront points (a point is 1 percent of the loan amount) or loan-origination fees. If they were included, you'd see that home-equity lines cost one to perhaps four percentage points more than you think you are paying.

So even though the published APR on a home-equity line seems cheaper by a point or more, that loan actually might be more expensive than a competing fixed-rate second mortgage.

The only way to compare these loans is by listing all their costs: their interest rates, financing fees (application fees, points, and loan-origination fees), and service fees (for title search, survey, appraisal, legal work, and so on). On home-equity lines, check for annual fees of $25 to $50 and transaction fees for tapping the line.

In general, commercial banks and S&Ls price their fixed-rate second mortgages a little higher than their floating-rate lines of credit. But if interest rates rise, your line of credit will get more expensive. At a mortgage bank, fixed-rate second mortgages may carry lower interest rates, but you'll usually have to pay higher fees.

SHOULD YOU TAKE A HOME-EQUITY LOAN OR AN AUTO LOAN? Unfortunately, you can't compare the annual percentage rates of interest (APR) to see which is better. Upfront fees are figured into the APR for the auto loan but not for the home-equity loan, which makes the latter look a little cheaper than it really is.

The auto loan might be cheaper if: (1) You don't, at present, have a home-equity line. If you open one solely for the auto purchase, you may pay more in fees than the taxes you save. (2) You can use an auto dealer's low-cost promotional loan. Otherwise, the home-equity loan should cost you less, because you can tax deduct the interest.

SHOULD YOU TAKE A HOME-EQUITY LOAN TO PAY OFF YOUR CREDIT CARD DEBT? I can think of two reasons to say yes and four to say no. First, the positives.

At this writing, most credit cards are charging 15 to 22 percent interest. Home equity loans cost substantially less. It's almost always smart to substitute low-cost debt for high-cost debt. You can use the savings to repay all your consumer loans, which frees you for serious investing.

There's normally no tax deduction for credit-card interest. But home-equity interest can be fully deducted on loans up to $100,000.

Now the negatives.

Most credit card debts are paid off in about 15 months. That holds down the interest bill. On home-equity lines, however, loans usually linger much longer. Some people treat them as permanent debt to be paid off when the house is sold. So even with a lower interest rate, a home-equity loan might cost you more.

You might borrow against your home to clean up your credit card debt, then run up your credit cards all over again. That leaves you with two sets of consumer loans instead of one.

With so much home equity at your fingertips, you might shop up a storm. Your home value could vanish in a mad afternoon at the mall.

When you don't repay your credit card debt, the lender duns you and may sue. At worst, this ruins your credit record. But if you don't repay home-equity debt, you are foreclosed. For this reason, you shouldn't pile all your consumer loans onto your house, regardless of the tax advantage. In an emergency, you need some loans that you can duck.

Refinancing non-tax-deductible consumer debt with a home-equity loan is fine *if* you pay it off fast and resist new debt. Otherwise, forget it. To spendaholics, home-equity lines are a doomsday machine.

SHOULD YOU AGREE TO A HOME-EQUITY LINE IF YOUR MARRIAGE IS IN TROUBLE? Absolutely not. And you should freeze any lines you already have. You both sign for the debt, but one spouse could withdraw all the money and spend it. Most of your home equities might vanish. A divorce-court judge ought to tell the spouse who took the money to pay it back, but you can't count on that. The other spouse might have to pay, too.

SHOULD YOU TAKE A HOME-EQUITY LOAN TO MAKE AN INVESTMENT? Yes, if the expected returns from the investment surpass the upfront and continuing costs of the loan, *and* you won't be devastated if the investment flops. Otherwise, no.

How to Use Home-Equity Lines

1. *Don't open a larger credit line than you really need.* You pay closing costs on the entire line, even though you plan to borrow only a small part of the money. Say, for example, that the charge is two points. That's just $400 on a $20,000 line but $1,000 on a $50,000 line. The lender makes it easy for you to take a larger line, by lending you the closing costs. Tell the lender no. If you need substantially more money later, you can probably increase the line for a fee of $100 to $200, although some banks charge more. (To decrease your line, just make the request in writing. At this writing, some lenders offer lines with no points.)

A large credit line has another drawback. On your credit history, the entire line is treated as an outstanding loan, even if you haven't borrowed against it. That huge amount of borrowing power might keep you from getting a new credit card that you particularly want.

2. *Don't overborrow.* The bank will usually lend as much as 70 to 85 percent of the value of your house, minus the amount remaining on your first mortgage. If your income seems too low to carry that large a debt, it will lend less. But many bankers will stretch you right to the edge of your income, if you let them. It's up to you to say, "Enough."

3. *Borrow at a variable interest rate.* Variable loans should be cheaper than fixed-rate loans over any normal interest-rate cycle. You'd pay more only if high inflation returned and stayed. (In that case, however, you could lower your payments by reducing the debt.)

On variable lines, the interest rate usually floats one-half to three percentage points above the prime lending rate or the Treasury-bill rate. (You'll save yourself some money by shopping for a narrow spread.) If interest rates rise, so do your payments—but that's generally not a big deal. On a loan with $15,000 left, a jump from 10 percent interest to 15 percent might add only $44 to your monthly costs, if you're on a 10-year payback schedule. And your payments decline when interest rates fall. Some lenders give you a cheap rate the first year, then raise it later.

Not many lenders offer fixed-rate home-equity lines. Those that do generally fix the rate for only five years or so, and then are free to put it up. Such lines cost about 0.5 percent more at the start than variables do.

4. *Check out the cap.* All agreements signed after December 8, 1987, set a limit on how high your interest rate can rise. A common cap is 5

to 6 percentage points over the rate you started with, but you'll find lenders with both higher and lower ceilings. *If you opened your home-equity line before caps were required, you have no hyperinflation protection.* Ask the lender to add it to your agreement. That's cheaper than opening a new line somewhere else.

Where there's a ceiling there's sometimes a floor. Your rate might not be allowed to drop lower than 10 or 9 percent. But if the general level of rates goes much further down, you can always refinance. Few home-equity lines have prepayment penalties.

5. *Read the fine print.* Lenders choose tiny type for information that they don't care if you overlook. So do yourself a favor: Put on your glasses and read through the loan agreement.

You'll probably learn that your credit line can be reduced or frozen if: (1) you don't pass continuing credit checks, (2) the value of your house goes down, or (3) interest rates have risen above the cap. You'll learn how your interest rate changes, what the fees are, and whether you'll face a single large payment when the loan falls due. On credit lines opened before November 7, 1989, the lender can change all the terms at will—raising fees, changing the way interest rates are calculated, changing the monthly amounts you repay. On credit lines opened since then, however, most of the terms are guaranteed.

When you open a home-equity line of credit, you're supposed to get a government-mandated brochure, telling you what to ask the lender. Get answers to every question raised.

6. *Repay early and often.* Lenders often encourage you to take 10 or 20 years to repay. But stretching out your loans over that long a time is a sucker's game. If you use your credit line to buy a new car every three years, and make only the minimum payments, you could be paying for five cars at once before you're through. That's a lot of money down the drain.

So fit your payment schedule to the purchase. Get rid of a debt-consolidation loan in a year and a half. Clean up an auto loan in three to four years. Don't let a home-improvement loan hang around for more than seven years. Reduce a loan that is carrying a successful investment, so you'll have the equity to make more investments.

7. *Beware the call clause.* Lenders reserve the right to "call," or force you to repay, a home-equity loan that might be in trouble. This could happen if you lose your job and miss some payments, or if you endanger

the bank's interest in the house, perhaps by being unable to keep it in good repair. Exactly what can trigger a call will be outlined in your loan agreement. The moral: Back up your home-equity loans with liquid investments. You should be prepared to make six months of payments, even if you're out of work.

8. *Don't bet against the real-estate market.* If house prices are getting beaten up in your community, stay away from home-equity loans. If you have a big loan, and are forced to move, your entire equity could be eaten up by the loan repayments and the real-estate broker's commission. You'd have little or nothing to put down on another house.

IT'S OKAY TO BORROW AGAINST YOUR HOUSE WHEN:
• You put no consumables, like parties or clothes, on the credit line. Put these on a credit card and pay them off in the same month.
• You use the line to consolidate expensive credit-card debt and repay the loan fast.
• You use it for unavoidable consumer debt, like buying a car, and repay it fast.
• You use it for major investments—education, home improvements, buying property or stocks. The investments should yield more than the cost of the loan.
• You don't run up other loans, in addition to those on your home-equity line.
• You can handle the payments comfortably. If your income drops, you can sell assets to repay the loan.
• You have other stashes of cash, to help make up a down payment on a new house if you move.
• You hate and fear home-equity lines. You worry when you use them. You treat them like time bombs.

IT'S WRONG TO BORROW AGAINST YOUR HOUSE WHEN:
• You love home-equity lines. They're mother's milk. You feel wealthy when you use them.
• You borrow to support your consumer spending habit.
• You will stretch out the loans for many years, letting interest payments dribble out of your bank account.
• You think of the loan as a permanent debt, not to be repaid until you sell your house.
• Your job is shaky.

- You're a spendaholic.
- You're borrowing to make an investment, but have made rotten choices in the past.
- You'd be left with so little equity that, if you sold your house and repaid all the loans, you couldn't afford the down payment on a new house.
- You will need your home equity pretty soon to pay for college.
- You can't repay if your income drops, except by selling the house.
- Home values in your area are going down.

Refinancing Your House

When you refinance, you get a new first mortgage and use the proceeds to pay off the old one. If your house has risen in value, you can take a larger mortgage than you had before and use the extra money for other investments.

If you're going to tap your house for funds, which is the better way to do it: refinance with a larger first mortgage, or take a home-equity line of credit? To decide, compare the following costs and risks.

UPFRONT COSTS. Refinancing probably carries more upfront costs, because they're levied on a larger loan. Fees run in the area of 3 to 6 percent of the mortgage amount, although your own lender may do the job for less. (If you're refinancing only for a lower interest rate, and take little or no extra money out of the house, your own lender may do the job for only $250 to $300.)

INTEREST RATE. The rate will be lower on a refinanced first mortgage, but that doesn't necessarily make it cheaper. Compare the monthly payment on a refinanced loan with the monthly cost of keeping your old mortgage and adding a home-equity loan.

FLEXIBILITY. The home-equity line has it. You borrow periodically rather than in a big lump sum. You pay interest only on the money you actually take. And you can change the size of your monthly repayments, a useful option in months when your income falls short.

INTEREST RATE RISK—meaning how fast and how high your monthly payments could rise, if interest rates go up. Your risk is higher with home-equity lines. Minimum monthly payments change immediately, and rates can run higher, than on first mortgages.

What You Can Tax-Deduct on a Refinancing

1. Deduct interest on any new mortgage loan that equals your old loan plus up to $100,000

2. Deduct interest on any new loan that equals your old loan plus the cost of a home improvement (*if* you are borrowing to finance that home improvement) plus $100,000.

Both of these rules apply to your regular house and to one vacation house. A cabin, a condominium, a mobile home, even a sleep-in boat can count as a house.

Both of these rules are also subject to a cap. You can't deduct mortgage interest on loans higher than $1.1 million, on your regular house and vacation house, combined. If you borrow more, however, and use the extra money to start a business or make investments, the interest may be deductible as business or investment interest. (Mortgages acquired on or before October 13, 1987, are still fully deductible even if they exceed the $1.1 million cap.)

3. Upfront points paid to the lender when you refinance have to be deducted over the life of the loan. You cannot write them all off in the first year.

BORROWING AGAINST YOUR LIFE INSURANCE

This might be your smartest loan. But you won't know for sure until you've determined the real cost of borrowing, which is higher than you might think.

With an insurance loan, you don't take the cash directly from your policy. You borrow *against* your cash values, using them as collateral. All your cash goes on earning interest. But when you borrow, it earns interest at a lower rate than it did before—and that loss of interest increases the cost of your loan. The chart on page 224 shows how to figure the true rate of interest on a policy loan.

Ask your insurance agent to project what will happen to your cash values and death benefit, both with and without the loan. If your outside investment can more than make up for what you're losing in the policy, go ahead and borrow.

The interest doesn't have to be paid out of pocket (although it could be, if you wanted to). Typically, it's compounded and subtracted from your policy's cash value.

· · ·

When you take a loan, the face value of your insurance policy will decline by that amount. If you have a $100,000 policy and borrow $30,000, for example, there's a $70,000 death benefit left. Each year, the cash value will rise by the interest earned on your money, plus your dividends, if any—but decline by the unpaid interest on the loan.

The drop in the death benefit is not necessarily a loss to your heirs.

FIGURING THE TRUE RATE OF INTEREST ON AN INSURANCE POLICY LOAN

The Method	*An Example*
1. Find out the stated loan interest rate. Some old policies charge 4.5 to 6 percent; newer ones usually charge 8 percent or a variable rate that can run even higher.	Your policy loan rate is 8 percent.
2. Find out what rate of interest the insurance company currently pays on your cash values. Typically, you're earning about the same as you would on a Treasury bond.	Your company credits 8.5 percent on cash values.
3. Find out what interest rate the company pays on any cash values you borrow against. It might be as little as 4 to 5.5 percent.	If you borrow $5,000, the insurer credits $5,000 of your cash values with an interest rate of only 5 percent.
4. Subtract the reduced rate of interest from the interest paid when there is no borrowing (point 2 above), to see how much interest you are losing.	You are earning 5 percent on $5,000 in cash values instead of 8.5 percent, a 3.5 percent loss.
5. Your true borrowing cost is the stated rate of loan interest, plus the interest lost on your cash values.	Your $5,000 loan costs 8 percent plus 3.5 percent, 11.5 percent in all.

If you invest that $30,000 in a stock-owning mutual fund that goes up an average of 10 percent a year for 10 years, your heirs might get $147,800—$70,000 from the life insurance and the rest from the growth of your outside investment. That's probably more than they would have had if you'd left the policy alone.

Here's the worst-case result: You take the loan, buy stocks, lose the money in a market crash, then jump out a window. Your survivors would get less than if you had not taken out the loan. Your gamble is that you'll live long enough for your stock investments to come out ahead. Maybe you'll win, maybe you'll lose. Trying to increase your capital by more than a guaranteed interest rate is always a risk. But if you buy stocks for the long term, history is on your side.

If you have a universal-life policy, you can withdraw some of the money you paid into the policy without taking a loan and without paying taxes. You pay a fee (maybe $25 for administration, and often a partial-surrender fee). But you save yourself the loan-interest costs. Be sure to leave enough cash in the policy to assure that it will stay in force for the rest of your life. If you take out too much, the policy may expire before you do. Your insurance agent will tell you where the limits lie. As usual, the policy's death benefit will be reduced by the amount you withdraw.

BORROWING AGAINST CERTIFICATES OF DEPOSIT

The bank will lend you money against your CDs. But do you want that loan at all? Would it be smarter to cancel the CD, pay the early withdrawal penalty, and use cash instead?

To answer this question, use your hand-held calculator and your common sense. Figure out how much interest you would pay on the loan, and how much money you would lose (interest plus penalty) by cashing in the CD. Then . . .

· Take the loan if it costs less than cashing in the CD.

· Take the loan even if it costs a little more. Savings are so hard to accumulate that you shouldn't disturb them for a nickel-and-dime advantage.

· Take the loan if you inherited the money in the CD and would never be able to save such a sum yourself.

· Take the loan if the CD represents your total savings. It's risky to strip yourself entirely of cash.

· Break the CD if the loan costs considerably more *and* you have both the income and the willpower to replace those savings.

· Break the CD if you took a loan and now discover that the payments are killing you.

Loans against CDs aren't as cheap as the banks make them out to be. Say that you borrow at 11 percent, while your CD is earning 8 percent. Your banker might say that you're paying only 3 percent "real." But that's not true. You are paying 11 percent "real." To help clarify this, assume that your CD earns 8 percent and your auto dealer offers you a loan at 10 percent. Would you say you're paying only 2 percent "real"? Probably not. Yet that's the same screwy logic that your banker is using.

The "real" cost of a loan is its stated interest rate. A 10 percent auto-dealer loan will cost you less than an 11 percent bank loan, no matter what your banker says.

BORROWING AGAINST STOCKS, BONDS, AND MUTUAL FUNDS

Loans against securities are called *margin* loans. You usually borrow from a stockbroker, although banks are in this business, too. You can borrow up to 50 percent of the value of listed stocks, certain mutual funds, some over-the-counter stocks, and listed convertible bonds; up to 75 percent of the value of listed corporate bonds; up to 85 percent on municipal bonds; and up to 95 percent on Treasury securities. Your broker sets your borrowing limits.

Margin loans are usually used to buy securities. With just $10,000 cash, you can borrow enough money to buy $20,000 worth of listed stocks or $200,000 worth of U.S. government bonds.

But you can borrow against your securities for other purposes, too. Interest rates run 0.5 to 2.5 percentage points over the broker call rate, which is what banks charge brokers for their money. You don't have to make any loan repayments. The interest compounds in your brokerage account, payable when the securities are sold.

There are two major risks with margin loans.

1. Interest charges and sales commissions can easily eat up the profits on securities held on margin for many months.

2. If your stocks drop too far in price, the broker will ask for more collateral, in the form of cash or securities. That's what's known as a *margin call.* If you don't have the money, some of your securities will be sold to cover the debt. You usually get a margin call if the value of your interest in the securities, net of the debt, shrinks to 30 or 25 percent of the market price.

THOUSANDS OF INVESTORS TAKE MARGIN LOANS WITHOUT REALIZING WHAT THEY'VE DONE. Here's how that happens.

When you get your monthly statement from your broker, it may show, in one corner, your "borrowing power." The broker encourages you to use the money to buy a car or take a vacation. (His firm earns a nice piece of change on these loans.) He forgets to tell you that the loan can be called. Suddenly the market drops. You have to repay part of what you borrowed or lose some of your securities. But you've spent the money and haven't got any spare cash. So you're sold out of some of your stocks.

There goes the retirement money, down the drain.

If you borrow from your broker, don't do it for spending money.

Borrow only to buy more securities, in hopes of increasing your net worth.

Buying on margin can be profitable, *but only if the market moves in your direction, fast.* Assume, for example, that you have $5,000 to spend on a $50 stock. You can buy 100 shares for cash. Or you can buy 200 shares, putting up half the price, borrowing the rest, and pledging the shares as collateral. If the price rises by $5 a share, the cash investor makes $500, or 10 percent on a $5,000 investment. The margin investor makes $1,000, or 20 percent, minus his interest costs. So margin loans can build fortunes faster.

But this gain depends on a fast rise in price. If you hold your position for a year, at a loan rate of 12.5 percent, your profits (in the example above) will be nearly wiped out by interest charges and commissions. For a margin position to work, you need either very large gains or very quick ones.

On the down side, margin loans are poison. Still using the example above, assume that the share price drops by $5. The cash investor loses 10 percent while the margin investor loses 20 percent. If the price drops by $12 a share, the cash investor is merely holding on to a loser. The margin buyer may have to put up more money or be partly sold out.

DO YOU REALLY WANT TO BORROW AGAINST YOUR SECURITIES?

Yes, if you're a proven success as an investor and will use those loans to compound your winnings. *Yes,* if you're able, temperamentally, to sell a losing stock quickly. *Yes,* if you understand the cost of your loan and will balance it carefully against your potential for profit.

No, if you're a new or uncertain investor, because you'll probably go wrong. *No,* if you're a long-term investor rather than a quick trader. *No,* if it wouldn't occur to you to borrow unless your stockbroker suggested it. *No,* if you're borrowing to take a vacation or buy a car—that simply consumes the investments that you are laboring so hard to build. *No,* if you're dabbling in mysterious investments that you only faintly understand. Some of the biggest losses in the Crash of '87 were taken by investors who were borrowing against their stocks to pyramid stock-index options. They didn't have a clue what they were doing. Many wound up losing far more money than they invested.

BORROWING AGAINST YOUR SMILE

Collateral is property you put up to guarantee or *secure* a loan. Stocks, certificates of deposit, automobiles, and real estate can all be used as collateral. The lender will grab them if you don't pay.

An *unsecured* loan is given on the strength of your paycheck and credit history. If you don't pay, the lender can only sue. The interest rate is higher than on secured loans, and the repayment period often shorter.

The commonest unsecured loans are the lines of credit you arrange in connection with your credit card or checking account. The lender gives you the right to borrow up to a certain amount—maybe $1,500 to $15,000—whenever you want. You get the money by writing a check for more than you have in your account, or by slipping your bank card into an automated teller machine.

Your interest rate is the same as, or higher than, the rate on the unpaid balance on your credit card. There may also be a transaction fee. Some banks lend money only in multiples of $50 or $100—so if you write an overdraft for $105 you might find that you've had to borrow $150 or $200. You are rarely pressed to eliminate the debt, beyond a minimum monthly payment. The bank has you just where it wants you: in hock. Use credit card advances or overdraft checking for sudden, small needs. Then clear up this expensive debt as fast as you can.

If you need a larger sum of money for a short period of time—say, to pay your taxes—your bank might give you a three-month loan at a lower rate than you'd pay for overdraft checking. This loan can usually be renewed a couple of times. The warmer your relationship with your banker, and the more accounts you keep there, the easier these loans are to get. That's one reason I recommend a small bank or branch. It's simpler to get to know the people in charge.

If you have a good salary and a high net worth, you might qualify for "personal banking." Someone is assigned to your account and it's his or her job to make you happy. Whatever you need—loans, brokerage services, certificates of deposit, Treasury securities—your personal banker makes it work. Interest rates are negotiable. High-income clients can usually get a better deal than anyone else, because they bring the bank more business.

How much you can borrow unsecured depends on your salary and the value of your assets—savings, investments, real estate. It's not illegal to puff your net worth a bit by taking an optimistic view of the value of your house. But if you borrow more than you can handle, you're the loser in the end.

BORROWING AGAINST YOUR RETIREMENT FUNDS

Here's an idea that people rarely think of. Take a loan against your company thrift plan, 401(k), or profit-sharing plan, if the firm allows it. (For more on these plans, see Chapter 29). Many companies let you use plan money to buy stock-owning mutual funds, so you probably won't need to borrow for this purpose. But you might want to buy real estate or invest in a business.

A loan against a company savings plan does not necessarily deplete your retirement fund. In fact, it can enhance it. Follow me through the transaction and I'll show you how.

1. You borrow the money from the retirement plan and invest it.

2. You pay interest on the loan, say at 12 percent. That interest payment usually goes right into your own retirement account—so you're paying interest to yourself instead of to a bank. If your retirement account was formerly earning 10 percent on the money you borrowed, you have just picked up an extra two percentage points, which will accumulate tax-deferred.

3. The interest you pay on the loan may be deductible on your income taxes if it meets two tests: You borrowed your employer's contributions, not yours, and the money will be used for a deductible purpose. A "deductible purpose" covers loans used toward your small business or to make an investment (page 230).

4. You repay most loans over five years, in regular monthly or quarterly amounts. As I see it, that's a form of forced saving. You can take 10 to 30 years to repay, depending on the plan, if you use the money to buy a principal residence. Loan repayments are usually deducted automatically from your paycheck.

5. Meanwhile, the money you borrowed is (one hopes) prospering in your outside investment.

THIS DEAL MAKES SENSE AS LONG AS:

· You pay a higher interest rate on the loan than your pension was earning on its investments. That way, you are adding assets to your plan.

· You make more on the outside investment than your money was earning in your pension fund.

• Your interest payments are tax deductible. If the interest is not deductible, that money will be taxed twice—once when you earn it and pay it into the plan, and again when you retire and start making withdrawals from your retirement fund.

From a tax point of view, you should not borrow from your retirement funds for a nondeductible purpose. Yet, necessity taking precedence over tax planning, the two most popular reasons for borrowing are nondeductible: to pay college tuition and to make a down payment on a house. (Interest on the down-payment loan is deductible only if you can put up the house as collateral, which most plans don't allow.)

When you borrow for a nondeductible purpose like college tuition, it makes no difference, economically, whether you borrow from your pension plan or from a bank. So be guided by which lender has the better rates and terms. The bank's terms are better if you're borrowing against your house, because the interest on that loan will be tax deductible.

HERE'S HOW MUCH YOU CAN BORROW: (1) Up to 50 percent of the assets in your company savings or profit-sharing plan or $50,000, whichever is smaller. If you borrow any more, it will be treated as a taxable withdrawal. (2) If your plan is worth less than $20,000, you *may* be able to borrow up to $10,000, as long as the loan is adequately secured.

If you leave your job, a few companies let you continue the payments as scheduled. More likely, you'll have to repay your loan or else treat the money as a withdrawal. If it's a withdrawal, you'll owe income taxes on the loan amount. You'll also owe a 10 percent penalty if you're younger than age 59½. So don't borrow against your retirement funds if you expect to leave the company anytime soon.

You'll sometimes need your spouse's agreement to taking a loan from a company plan. The agreement must be in writing and notarized.

With Keogh Plans, you can borrow if you're an employee but not if you own the business or are self-employed. With Individual Retirement Accounts, you cannot borrow at all.

YOUR TAX DEDUCTION ON LOANS FOR INVESTMENT

You're going to hate this. The deduction is so complicated that it makes no sense for me to try to explain it. For the gory details, get a current tax guide. I'll just give you the gist.

If you take out a loan to make an investment, the interest is deductible *to the extent that you have net taxable income from investments* (after deducting your expenses).

Say, for example, that you collect a net of $1,500 in dividends and interest. That allows you to write off $1,500 of the interest you pay on any loans you took to make investments. If you pay more loan interest than you receive in investment income, the extra can be carried forward and deducted in future years.

Answers to Some of Your Tax Questions

What if you borrow money and do two things with the proceeds: buy some stocks and buy a car? The interest on the money used to buy stocks falls under the investment rule—deductible, to the extent that you have net investment income. The interest on the money used to buy the car falls under the rule on consumer loans—not deductible at all. Are you still with me? If not, write your congressperson.

What if you borrow against your house? The interest may be fully deductible as mortgage interest, as long as you stay within the loan limits (page 215). The interest on larger loans can be deducted as investment interest, if you indeed make investments with the money.

What if you borrow to buy tax-exempt municipals? The interest on such loans is never deductible.

What if you borrow to fund an Individual Retirement Account? The interest deduction is kaput.

What if you borrow to buy investment real estate? The interest is deductible against your rents, as well as against income from limited partnerships and other tax-shelter investments (check the tax guides for the "passive activity" rules). If you have a vacation home that you rent out, larger amounts of interest are sometimes deductible (see page 417).

What if you borrow to start or enlarge your own business? All the interest is deductible, as a business expense.

What if you borrow from your company savings plan? You get no j tax deduction for interest on any part of the loan attributable to your own pretax contributions plus the money earned on those amounts—no matter what you use the money for. But you should be okay on the write-off if you borrow for a deductible purpose and take money the company contributed (page 229). So specify that those are the funds you want.

What if you contributed after-tax money to your company plan? You can borrow against it (for a deductible purpose) and get the write-off.

What if you borrow from your company savings plan to buy a principal residence? The interest is deductible only if you put up your house as collateral for the loan. Unfortunately, most company plans won't let you do this, so you lose what ought to have been a mortgage deduction.

What if you're a key employee of the business (generally, owners and officers) and borrow from the company savings plan? You get no interest deduction, no matter what you invest in.

HERE'S HOW TO ASSURE THAT YOU GET YOUR PROPER INTEREST DEDUCTIONS. When you borrow money for more than one purpose, don't put all the loan proceeds in the same bank account. Keep separate checking accounts for personal borrowing (which is nondeductible), business borrowing, and investment borrowing.

Say, for example, that you take a $22,000 bank loan to buy a car, buy a computer for your business, and buy some stock. Put $14,000 for the car into your regular, personal account, $3,000 for the computer into your business account, and $5,000 for the stock into an investment account. That makes it very clear how much interest is deductible on each part of the loan.

DON'T PUT ALL THE LOAN PROCEEDS INTO YOUR PERSONAL CHECKING ACCOUNT. If you do, and wait more than 15 days to buy your business computer or make an investment, some of the loan may be treated as funding your normal living expenses. That will reduce your loan-interest deduction.

I'll stop there. In detail, the rules are even more complicated. It's madness to have to take on the expense of extra bank accounts just to keep track of your tax deductions. Even thinking about it can drive you nuts.

AUTO LOANS

Car dealers love you when cars aren't selling well. On American makes, they'll offer the lowest interest rate on the block—as little as zero to 4 percent on two-year loans. But when dealers are fat, their interest rates rise. Then, the best deal might be a home-equity loan.

Always compare the two types of loans *after tax*. You can deduct the interest on a home-equity loan if you itemize on your tax return. But on auto loans from any other source, there's no write-off at all.

If you don't want to borrow against your house (or don't own a house), look first to a credit union, followed by S&Ls and banks. Some banks give you a discount of up to 1 percent if you keep other accounts there. To compete, some auto dealers cut the rate by 0.5 percent or so, for customers with top credit ratings.

Auto loans come with fixed interest rates or variable rates. Consider a variable only if you can get it for at least one percentage point less than the cheapest fixed-rate loan you can find. You deserve a lower payment for shouldering the risk that rates will rise. A variable loan will be cheaper if interest rates decline, stay level, or rise just a little bit. But these loans have no caps, or high caps, so you'd be hurt if inflation took a sudden jump.

If you do choose a variable loan and interest rates rise, one of two things will happen: (1) Your monthly payments will go up. On a $10,000, four-year, 12 percent loan, an increase to 14 percent would cost you an extra $10 a month. (2) Your payments will stay level but the term of your loan will be extended. Taking the above example and assuming that the rate rose after the first 12 months, you'd owe an extra 1.4 months worth of payments.

Many lenders are adding upfront fees that raise the effective cost of your loan. Compare each loan's annual percentage rate (APR), to see which is cheapest. Rates can vary by three or four percentage points within the same metropolitan area.

When you borrow through a car dealer, you usually need a 10 to 20 percent down payment, which can often be covered by the value of the car you trade in. If you don't have the down payment, try a bank or credit union. Many of them lend 100 percent of the car price, although such a loan may cost you an extra 1 percent interest.

NOW FOR THE NUB OF YOUR DECISION: HOW MANY YEARS WILL YOU CARRY THE LOAN? The longer the term the lower the monthly payment and the easier it is to buy today's expensive cars. Auto-finance companies let you borrow for up to five years. Some banks and auto dealers offer six- or seven-year loans on luxury cars. On a $20,000 loan at 12 percent, you pay $136 less a month by stretching the loan to six years instead of holding it down to four. The downside is that the longer-term loan costs you an extra $2,879 in interest.

To a hardened borrower, interest costs are a yawn. So I'll give long-term borrowers something else to worry about. (What good is a personal-finance book that doesn't give readers something to worry about?)

A LONG-TERM AUTO LOAN MAY PREVENT YOU FROM TRADING IN YOUR CAR AS SOON AS YOU'D LIKE. Why? Because you're "upside down"—the industry's term for owing more than the car is worth.

Most auto loans are upside down in the first year or three. But then they straighten up. Gradually you build equity value. That equity gives you a trade-in allowance when you buy a new car.

But long-term loans may be upside down for four or five years, so there's nothing to trade with. Your car's net value is less than zero.

If you paint yourself into this corner, and want a new car, you have three choices.

1. Find the cash to repay your old loan *and* make a down payment on a new car. Your savings take a hit, but your debts don't balloon.

2. Refinance your remaining loan and borrow even more to buy a new car. That means you'll be carrying two auto loans instead of one.

3. Repair your old car. Keep on driving it until it's paid for. This choice gets my vote every time. If you feel trapped—well, you've now learned something about long-term car loans.

NO CAR SHOULD BE FINANCED OVER MORE YEARS THAN YOU EXPECT TO KEEP IT. If you'll turn it in after four years, get a four-year loan. Even better, get a three-year loan. You'll save on interest payments and drive the last year "free."

You'll need personal discipline to follow this rule if you finance with a home-equity loan. Your banker—no slouch when it comes to collecting interest payments—may let you stretch the loan over 10 or 15 years. But what if you want a new car three years from now? No problem. You just borrow against your home equities again. And then again three years after that. You'd then be paying for your present car plus two old cars you no longer drive. That's a never-ending spiral down. To avoid it, find out what it takes to repay your car loan over three or four years, and repay your home-equity loan at that rate.

If you do take a six-year auto loan, prepare to drive your car for the full term. Keep it tuned up, with the brakes lined and the oil changed. Do what it says in the owner's manual. Make small repairs as they come along. Swallow a big repair if you have to. Your car can run, reliably, for 100,000 miles or more.

Financing a Used Car

A used-car loan costs more than a new-car loan, by a couple of percentage points. That makes a home-equity loan look even better as a financing tool—always assuming that you'll hustle to pay it off. Like a new car, a used car should be financed over the number of years you expect to drive it. If you don't own a house, or have no spare equity in your home, start your search for a car loan with a credit union (see page 52, for information on how you might join one).

Pay Cash or Take Out a Loan?

It's cheaper to pay cash. But many auto dealers (who make money on car loans) have come up with a clever, computerized gimmick to bamboozle customers into thinking that loans are a better deal.

For example, say you have $10,000. You can put it into a certificate of deposit earning 8.5 percent interest or use it toward buying a new car. The dealer may argue that it's smarter to choose the CD and take out a 12 percent auto loan.

Here's how he "proves" it:

· Four-year interest on the auto loan's declining balance: $2,640
· Four-year earnings on the CD: $4,049

By taking the loan, you appear to be $1,409 ahead. Even after taxes in the 28 percent bracket, you're $1,014 to the good, and you still have your CD intact.

There's just one little thing that the dealer overlooked. How will you repay the loan?

If you take the monthly payments out of your savings, you won't earn as much interest as the dealer projected. In fact, your savings will be wiped out before the loan is entirely repaid.

If you make the monthly payments out of earnings, you're giving up money that could have been saved or invested.

So, the smart buyer pays cash. You take the monthly payment, which you're *not* spending on the auto loan, and use it to replenish your savings. At the end of the term, you have your car and more than $10,000 back.

I'd vote for the loan only if: (1) Paying cash for the car would completely strip your savings account. You always need some money on hand, for emergencies. (2) Your fat savings account was a windfall—a gift, an inheritance, a winning lottery ticket—that you'd never be able to replace.

Should You Lease Instead of Buy?

For the poor of pocketbook but rich in taste, auto leasing is hard to beat. You can drive out of a dealer's lot on four of his classiest wheels for a small upfront deposit and lower monthly payments than you'd owe on most auto loans. A lease costs you more in the end. But it's easier on the budget, month by month.

MANY BUYERS SHOULDN'T EVEN LOOK AT A LEASE. *Don't do it* if you'll drive your car for a long time. Loan payments eventually stop; lease payments never do. It's like burying your grandfather in a rented suit. *Don't do it* if you're looking for tax breaks. There aren't any. Business use of your car is deductible whether you lease or own. *Don't do it* if you want to save money over the long term. Leasing costs more than taking an auto loan or paying cash. *Don't do it* if you'll want to trade in the car before the lease is up. Early termination costs are large. *Don't do it* if you expect to move out of the state. Some lenders charge an extra $10 a month for leaving the state. Others make you convert your lease to a loan. (If you're forced to convert, refuse to pay prepayment penalties. The lender will usually go along.)

BUT THINK ABOUT A LEASE IF:

· You have no car to trade in.

· You don't have the cash for a down payment (although some banks now give no-down-payment loans).

· You have the down payment but can put it to work earning more than 15 percent a year. (You can pick up the equivalent of 15 percent just by paying off credit-card debt that is costing that much in interest.)

· You want lower monthly payments.

· You want a more expensive car than you can afford to buy.

· You're trading in your car in the fourth year of a six-year auto loan and owe more than the car is worth. You can't afford to pay off your old loan and make a down payment on a new car, too.

· You love cars and want to drive a new one every two years.

· You make plenty of money and want someone else to worry about keeping your car in good repair. For an extra fee ($25 a month and up), the lessor will do all the maintenance and lend you a car to drive while yours is in the shop.

The leasing formula is pretty simple. You typically pay one or two months' rent up front as a refundable deposit and drive away. On a *closed-end lease*, your basic costs are fixed; at the end of the term, you can turn in your keys and get a new car. Almost all consumer leases are closed-end. On an *open-end lease*, which should cost less per month, your final cost depends on the car's resale value. If it sells for more than the lessor expected, you may get a refund. If it sells for less, you pay the difference (although you normally cannot be charged more than three times the monthly payment).

On both types of leases, you buy your own auto insurance and are responsible for general maintenance. You have to make engine repairs and keep the body in good shape. You'll owe an extra 7 to 12 cents a mile for driving more than 15,000 miles or so. There are also extra charges for excessive wear and tear, like broken power windows and big dents. The lessor decides how much wear is excessive—but he probably won't overreach. If you get sore, he loses your business.

DON'T LEASE THE CAR FOR A LONGER PERIOD THAN YOU EXPECT TO DRIVE IT. Five-year leases are popular because of their low monthly payments. The dealer might even tell you there's no problem breaking the lease early, if you want to switch to a brand new car. But there *is* a problem. You generally face "prepayment" penalties—maybe just $100, but sometimes in the $2,000 range. Worse, your car won't be worth as much as you owe on the leasing contract and you'll have to pay the difference yourself. Sometimes the dealer can roll the debt into your next lease, but not always.

The formula for fixing your early-termination penalty will be printed in your contract, probably in Sanskrit. So here's how to find out exactly what your liability would be: Ask the lease manager what you'd owe at the end of each year if you wanted out, compared with the estimated value of your car at the time. The difference is your total penalty. To avoid it, plan to drive the car for the lease's full term.

If you're charged an excessive early-termination penalty—for example, all the remaining payments due on the lease—hire a lawyer and threaten a counterclaim. Such penalties are probably "unreasonable" under the Consumer Leasing Act, in the opinion of the National Consumer Law Center in Boston. Dealers faced with counterclaims usually settle on terms favorable to the consumer.

What happens if your leased car is stolen or wrecked? That's usually counted as an early termination. Your auto insurance will cover the car's market value. But you pay everything else still owed on the lease.

THREE TIPS FOR GETTING THE CHEAPEST LEASE:
1. When talking with the dealer, first bargain down the price of the car. Then say that you want to finance it on a lease. Consumers who ignore the underlying car price usually wind up with higher monthly payments.

2. If you'll drive more than the standard 15,000 miles usually allowed on a lease, buy excess mileage in advance. For example, you might arrange to drive the car for 25,000 miles. It's usually cheaper than paying for that extra 10,000 miles when you turn the car in.

3. Do business with an independent leasing company rather than an auto dealer. The leasing company tracks new-car leases throughout your area and can find the best prices and terms. You'll find these companies in the Yellow Pages.

HOW TO LOWER YOUR INTEREST CHARGES

1. *Pick the right type of rate.* Variable-rate loans should be cheaper than fixed-rate loans, if you hold for many years. You start out with lower payments, which saves money right there. Payments go up when interest rates do, so you have to be able to afford the increase. But rates generally don't rise for much more than two or three years at a clip. After that they decline and your loan payments shrink.

If deflation lies ahead in the 1990s, a variable-rate loan will be especially cheap. But rising inflation remains a risk. To guard against it, your loan should carry an interest-rate cap, to keep your rate from rising by more than five percentage points.

2. *Pick the right lender.* Credit unions often charge less than S&Ls, which often charge less than banks. Competing lenders may be two or three percentage points apart in rates, which is discoverable only by people who price-shop. You might get a lower rate if you open a certificate of deposit or a checking account with the lending institution.

3. *Pick the right loan.* Home-equity loans cost less than credit card debt (if you repay swiftly). Auto loans cost less than personal loans. Loans backed by a certificate of deposit cost less than unsecured loans. Short-term personal loans, for three or six months, sometimes go for a point or two over the prime lending rate. Tell your banker how much money you want and when you'll pay it back. Then ask how cheaply the deal can be done.

4. *Pick the right annual percentage rate (APR).* Don't look only at the interest rate. Look at the APR, which usually counts upfront fees as well as the interest itself.

5. *Pick the right time period.* The longer the term, the more expensive the loan—because you make so many more payments. If you're doing something constructive with the money, like holding an appreciating

piece of land, never mind the longer term. But on depreciating assets like a car, keep the term as short as possible.

6. *Put on the squeeze.* Many borrowers don't realize that lenders compete. If Bank A will give you an adjustable-rate mortgage at 8.1 percent in the first year, and you tell that to Bank B, dear old Bank B may counter with 7.9 percent. It happens a lot, but only to borrowers who price-shop. If you're borrowing a lot of money, you might get a quarter-point off your interest rate just by asking for it.

7. *Avoid traditional installment loans.* They're often front-end-loaded. You pay more of the interest in the early months than you do in the later ones, which penalizes you if you pay off your loan ahead of time. The better loans charge the same amount of interest every month.

Given two loans with the same annual percentage rate, the one with equal interest payments will cost less over the life of the loan than the one with front-end loading.

How can you tell if you're offered a front-end-loaded loan? Your installment-loan agreement will say that interest is figured by the "Rule of 78s." Retailers may offer only front-loaded loans. But at a bank, you should be able to get a loan with level interest payments, if you ask for it.

8. *Don't buy credit life and disability insurance from the lender.* These policies cover your loan payments if you die, or during any period that you're totally disabled. But they're overpriced, and the disability policy pays only in very limited circumstances. For the same money, you can buy more—and better—coverage from an insurance agent.

If you don't have decent life and disability protection, these limited policies are better than nothing. But I hate to give them even that much credit. Go out and buy yourself the real thing.

The price of credit insurance is usually rolled right into your loan, so you wind up borrowing—and paying interest on—your insurance premiums. It's a costly system, and it often enriches the loan officer personally. At some banks, he or she earns commissions on the sales. It's illegal to require you to buy this insurance as a condition of getting the loan—but it's still done. Here are some tactics to counter the pressure: (1) Tell the loan officer, flat out, that requiring credit insurance breaks the law. (2) Ask the loan officer for a pen and start writing down what you're being told. For example, "You say that without this insurance my loan application may be reconsidered?" The officer may back down. (3) If you're forced to insure, send a letter and a copy of your notes to the bank president. Say that you didn't want the insurance, and ask whether it's the bank's policy to require it. The president may cancel the coverage, to avoid trouble. (4) Turn in the bank to your local consumer agency, which may write a letter on your behalf. (5) Walk away. It's hateful to deal with dishonest bankers.

YOUR PERSONAL FINANCIAL STATEMENT

For a big loan, a bank wants a financial statement and, often, a copy of your income-tax return. What do you earn? What's the value of your house, your other real estate, your savings accounts, your stocks? How much do you owe? Put down everything you can think of, including any bonuses due. How much you can borrow depends a lot on what you're worth.

IF YOU'RE TURNED DOWN FOR CREDIT

Lenders have to say *why* they turned you down. If it's because of something they saw in your credit report, get a copy of the report and check it for errors (page 199). If it's because your credit score is too low (page 190), talk to the lender, in person or by phone, to find out how you might qualify. Don't be embarrassed. Lenders expect to be grilled. A conversation might get you the loan, or show you how to qualify. If one lender won't take you, another one might.

CO-SIGNERS

If your personal credit isn't strong enough to get you a loan, you'll need a *co-signer*—defined as a saint, an idiot, or a parent. A co-signer puts his or her name on the note along with yours, as a guarantee of payment. If you default, he or she will be liable for every nickel of the debt. This is true not only for bank loans but for an apartment lease or any other obligation that's co-signed. The lender won't even bother pursuing you. He'll turn to the co-signer and ask for the money in a lump sum. Your co-signer is your fall guy. Even a saint might turn you down.

DOOMSDAY

What if the world falls apart? Your income drops, your spouse gets fired, you can't pay your bills, your children are crying, and you have to give away the dog. With all these overhanging risks, isn't it dangerous to borrow to invest?

Not if you follow sound principles. First, you make suitable investments (Chapter 21). Second, you construct yourself an escape hatch.

To save yourself if hard times strike, your investments should meet one or more of the following tests.

1. They must be liquid—meaning they can easily be sold to pay off your debt. Mutual funds are liquid. Vacant lots are not.

2. If not liquid, your investments should yield enough income to carry themselves. If you buy a condominium, the rents should cover the mortgage, taxes, monthly maintenance, insurance and other expenses, plus 5 to 10 percent for emergencies. That saves you from having to unload the condo at a give-away price, if your personal earnings drop.

3. Any investment that is not liquid and not yielding enough income should be backstopped by liquid investments. For example, if you buy a rental property that isn't covering its costs, you should have enough money in mutual funds or in the bank to support the property and cover your living expenses for 12 months. If you don't have this much liquidity, don't make such investments. They're too risky for you.

4. The value of your investment shouldn't fall below the size of the debt that's carrying it. If its price declines, put it on the market while you're still ahead. Sell it as soon as you can, and pay off your loan.

Debt isn't a free pass to the high life. Overused, it can bankrupt you. But well used, debt is *the* building block of wealth.

3 YOUR SAFETY NET

Insurance is a protection racket. Everyone hates to pay the price.

But until you are well enough insured, you might as well have no assets at all. Everything you own is a hostage to fortune. Sickness or accident could leave you a pauper.

I know. I hear you. It's never going to happen to you.

The funny thing is, I've never met anyone "it" was going to happen to. So who are all those people in the hospitals, the wheelchairs, the funeral homes? Who are those stunned families staring at smoking ruins? Visitors from Mars?

A classic story for personal-finance reporters is the interview with some unfortunate souls who found out what "it" really feels like. They deliver a lecture that might be generically entitled, "What You Should Do Right Now So You Won't End Up a Wreck Like Me."

Here is that lecture.

12
THE MONEY ON
YOUR LIFE:

What Kind of Life Insurance?
How Much Is Enough?

———

Life insurance is full of more angles than a
hardware store. Maybe that's why grieving
widows are handed small checks when they
could have been handed large ones.

Here is the single most important
thing to know about life insurance. *It is not for you!* It's for the people
you'll leave behind. You pay for it; they use it. Wear that principle like
an amulet, to ward off nonsense. If you're not leaving anyone behind—
and don't want to leave a special bequest to a charity—you don't need
life insurance.

The second rule is to *keep it simple.* Life insurance can be numbingly
complicated. Clients often turn off their brains and surrender their judgment to the very agent or planner who brought on their coma in the first
place. Clean and easy policies are the surest. Fancy tax-dodging deals
make money for the agent but may not reliably do the job you want.

The third rule: *Be a cheapskate.* If you want to show off your spending power, do it in a way that counts—like, say, 10 carats. Buy the lowest-cost life insurance policy you can find.

For most people, the coverage that best fills the bill is plain vanilla *term insurance.* It's cheap and simple, with nothing in it for you but the knowledge that you've done the right thing. Term insurance pays off if you die prematurely. That's all. No gimmicks, no tax games, no investment values. Just a check—and a large one—paid to the people who depend on you.

All other forms of coverage—known generally as *cash value insurance* —contain a savings or investment element that raises your out-of-pocket outlay. One of these policies might be a reasonable place to invest some of your long-term money *if* you can afford all the coverage you need. Most of us can't. In any event, whether to invest through life insurance is an entirely separate decision from whether to have death protection at all and if so, how much.

WHO NEEDS LIFE INSURANCE?

1. *You're young, single, with no dependents.* Forget life insurance. Buy disability coverage (page 331), and add to your investments instead.

Ignore an insurance agent who advises you to buy cash-value coverage because premiums are lower for the young. If you don't need insurance, you'd be wasting your money. It's like buying a tennis racket just in case, ten years from now, you might want to learn the game.

Besides, insurance premiums rise so slowly that waiting doesn't matter much. If you buy a $100,000 term policy at age 40 instead of 30, you might pay an extra $27 that year. Big deal. A cash-value policy might cost you an extra $550 or so. If you don't buy life insurance right now, and bank the money you don't spend, those accumulated savings will more than cover the higher premiums you might pay in the future, if you should ever need a policy.

One other argument says, "Buy now just in case you develop a dread disease and become uninsurable." You might just as easily marry a zillionaire and not need life insurance at all. The odds of either are very small. One exception: You might want to buy cash-value coverage if you're at risk of getting AIDS. Many insurers let you withdraw part of your policy's face value if you become terminally ill; alternatively, you can usually sell the policy for 50 to 70 percent of face value (see page 284). So for you, insurance is like a big savings account.

2. *You're older and single, with no dependents.* Maybe you never mar-

ried. Maybe you're a widow whose children have left home. You need no insurance. If you do have coverage, investigate what it's earning (page 274) and ask yourself whether you'd rather have ready money than cash building up inside an insurance policy. Your beneficiaries might prefer that you keep the policy. But if you need more income to live on, cancel it and put the cash value, if any, into savings or investments.

3. *You're single, with dependents.* What happens to those dependents if you die? If you're a divorced mother, and the children would go to their father, you may not need life insurance—assuming that the father can afford to take care of them. If he can't, keep the policy for the children's education and support (your lawyer, financial planner, or insurance agent can help you make sure that the money goes to the kids, not to your ex, perhaps by leaving the proceeds in trust for them). Keep the policy, too, if the children will go to one of your relatives. They shouldn't arrive like beggars, cup in hand. You may also need life insurance if you're supporting an elderly parent.

4. *You're a DINK—a double-income couple with no kids.* You might not need insurance. Each spouse could be self-supporting if the other died. Buy coverage only to keep the other from sinking to an unacceptable standard of living.

5. *You're an OINK—a one-income couple with no kids.* The working spouse probably needs life insurance, if you want to preserve the standard of living of the spouse at home.

6. *You're married, with young children.* You need insurance, a lot of it. Those kids have to be raised and educated, and it's not cheap. But you probably need the coverage only until they're on their own. Then this portion of your insurance can be canceled.

6a. *You had kids at an older age.* You need insurance, just as a young parent does, and it will have to last into your sixties or seventies. For full protection, term insurance may still be your best bet. Take special pains to find an inexpensive policy (page 257), checking the premiums both for your present age and for later ages. You might also compare term rates with the cost of insurance inside a universal life policy (page 265), to make sure that term is really better.

7. *You're a wife who doesn't work.* Insurance on your life is generally misguided. You have no income that has to be replaced. You'll be more secure if your husband spends the money on extra savings and investments, instead. *If* you have small children, and *if* your husband couldn't afford day care and housecleaning services at your death, and *if* he couldn't afford your funeral, and *if* there's enough insurance on your

husband's life to cover you and the kids in full (which hardly ever happens, especially in families that couldn't afford day care), *maybe* you might want to think about a policy of your own. Otherwise, forget it. (Ditto for a husband who is supported by his wife.)

8. *You're retired.* You need insurance only if your spouse couldn't live on the Social Security, pension, and savings you'll leave behind. If your spouse dies, cancel the insurance. Keep it only if you have plenty of money to live on and want to leave a bigger estate for a charity or your kids.

9. *You're a kid.* Insurance on a child is a waste of money. What secures a child's future is life insurance on the parents and the child's own college-savings fund. Some parents are persuaded to save for college in a cash-value, kid-insurance policy. But the cost of the needless life insurance greatly slashes the return on investment. For a far larger college fund, put money into a growth mutual fund, instead.

9a. *You're a college student.* I can think of only one reason to have life insurance: You plan to repay your parents for the money they're spending on your education. Otherwise, coverage is a waste of money.

10. *You own a business.* Either you or the company will doubtless need a policy on your life. For sole owners, the impetus may be to cover the debts they signed personally or to pay estate taxes. (You may want a trust to own the policy, to hold down taxes by keeping the proceeds out of your estate). A co-owner may want to be able to buy his or her partner's share of the business, if the partner dies or becomes disabled. Talk to your lawyer about a buy/sell agreement, funded by life and disability insurance. Don't leave your spouse and kids to a partner's tender mercies, no matter how friendly you are now. The business might never make a cash distribution or declare a dividend, and your family wouldn't get a dime.

11. *You're filthy rich.* Life insurance can help pay your estate taxes. On the other hand, you're rich enough so that taxes can be paid out of your investments. On the third hand, your investments may be illiquid (real estate, a small business)—so your estate will need the insurance for ready cash. Take your pick. To keep the insurance proceeds out of your estate (lest they raise your taxes even more), put the policy into an irrevocable trust.

12. *Your job is covered by Social Security.* You automatically have "free" insurance that covers an older spouse, a spouse caring for young children, your children, even parents you support—see page 295.

HOW MUCH INSURANCE?

If you need it at all, you probably need plenty—almost certainly more than you have now. And you can afford it. Low-cost term insurance can be slipped into almost any spending plan.

In fact, buying it is the easy part. The hard part is knowing how much to buy.

I've seen rules of thumb about how much life insurance you need: three times income, five times income, ten times income, depending on how heavy the thumb. None of them is accurate, because so much depends on how old you are, whether you have children, what your spouse earns, and how much money you've saved.

If you want to play it fast and loose, the National Insurance Consumer Organization (NICO) recommends seven times income, for a family with two or more small children. That sum includes any group insurance you get at work. When only one parent works, he or she should carry all the coverage. When both parents work, split the coverage proportionately. If the wife earns 40 percent of the family income, she should carry 40 percent of the coverage, leaving the remaining 60 percent to the husband. NICO assumes that, if a parent dies, the policy's proceeds will be invested conservatively, and that the surviving family will spend both income and principal.

On the next page is another quick fix—one that takes a little calculating. It calls for a different amount of insurance than NICO does, for two reasons: (1) It addresses your needs more specifically, and (2) it assumes that you leave your current nest egg intact, spending only the income. Over time, however, you can dip into that nest egg to offset inflation.

The trouble with these quick solutions is that they may be wide of the mark. You might buy too much insurance for your particular needs —and why pay one nickel more than you have to? Or you might buy too little, leaving your family at risk.

For a true fix on your insurance needs, turn to the Appendix, page 844, for The Best Insurance Planner You Will Ever Find. You will be following a system used by the top professionals in the field of financial planning. In no other place have I seen this sophisticated calculation broken down into orderly steps for individuals.

So take advantage of it. You're aiming for just enough coverage to fill the gap between your family's expenses and their other sources of

THE QUICK-FIX INSURANCE PLANNER

	Your money	My example
1. Your family's annual cost of living	$ _____	$55,000
2. Your family's annual income from:		
• Social Security *	$ _____	$10,800
• Spouse's earnings	$ _____	$20,000
• Other (except income from investments)	$ _____	0
TOTAL	$ _____	$30,800
3. Your family's investment income:		
• Your capital, from page 30	$ _____	$100,000
• Multiply by what your capital can earn pretax: 6%? 8%? 10%?	× _____	8%
RESULT: Your family's annual income from savings	$ _____	$8,000
4. Your family's annual budget gap: The totals in steps 2 and 3 subtracted from line 1	$ _____	$16,200
5. To fill that budget gap:		
• Turn to the table on page 901, to estimate your spouse's life expectancy.	_____ years	45
• Turn to the table on page 789,† and find the column that shows what you think your money can earn (the same percentage you used in step 3, above).	_____ %	8%
• Looking down that column, find your spouse's life expectancy or something close to it. Look across to the left to see what percent of capital your spouse can withdraw annually to make the money last a lifetime.‡	_____ %	4%
• Divide line 4 by the percent your spouse will withdraw annually.		
RESULT: The additional money needed for living expenses	$ _____	$405,000
6. College fund for the children (page 425)	$ _____	$70,000
7. TOTAL LIFE INSURANCE NEEDED	$ _____	$475,000

* For two small children. This drops to zero when the children pass age 18 or 19.

† Assuming a 4 percent inflation rate. For other inflation rates, see page 894.

‡ If your spouse's exact life expectancy doesn't appear, you might estimate a withdrawal rate. Using my example, if the money will earn 8 percent and your spouse has a 45-year life expectancy, he or she should withdraw the capital at a rate of 3.9 percent annually. That dictates $490,000 in life insurance rather than the $475,000 shown.

income—no more, no less. Getting the right answer takes a little work, but that's why God made yellow pads.

THE GREAT DEBATE: TERM INSURANCE VERSUS CASH-VALUE COVERAGE

TERM INSURANCE is pure protection, like fire insurance or auto insurance. Its sole function is to pay your family if you die. You get far more coverage for your money than you do from cash-value insurance—so it's the right kind of policy for anyone with an average income and family responsibilities.

The cost of term coverage rises gradually as you age. Once you reach your middle to late sixties, you probably won't want to carry this policy any more. With any luck, you will not need it. Your savings, pension, and Social Security will support any remaining dependents if you die.

CASH-VALUE INSURANCE comes in two parts: (1) an insurance policy and (2) a savings or investment account. You pay a large premium, compared with the premium for term insurance. Most of the extra money goes into savings, which build up tax-deferred.

If you die, the company uses those savings to pay part of your death benefit. As the years go by, your mounting savings normally cover more and more of the policy's face value, leaving the insurer responsible for less and less.

Because the company's risk declines (and because it can draw on the money it earns by investing your cash values), it doesn't have to raise your rates as you get older. You pay more at the start for a cash-value policy than you'd pay for term. But the premiums generally stay level for life. These are the only policies that most people can afford to carry into their seventies and eighties, if it turns out that they'll need insurance that long.

The cash tucked into your policy is always yours to use. You can borrow against it, just as you'd borrow against a bank certificate of deposit. The loan is subtracted from the policy's proceeds if you die. If you cancel the policy, you can put the cash value (net of surrender charges) into your pocket.

Because of the higher premiums on cash-value coverage, wage-earners usually can't buy as much of it as they need. That's why term coverage is usually the better choice; you can afford so much more of it. Furthermore, by the time you're old, the purchasing power of a cash-value policy will have shrunk greatly, so it's not necessarily the long-term boon that it seems now.

But higher-income people, who can afford plenty of insurance coverage, might consider certain cash-value policies as a long-term investment (see page 272).

ALL ABOUT TERM INSURANCE

For total family protection, the term-ites are right. To get the large amount of insurance you probably need, pure term coverage is the only answer.

How Much Cheaper Is Term Insurance?

Picking only from lower-cost companies, the table below shows dramatically how much more coverage you get for your money with term insurance. I've priced a $100,000 policy for a nonsmoking male. The term premiums rise every year; those for cash-value policies can stay level for life. But in terms of what's affordable at any given age, term insurance wins hands down.

YEARLY PREMIUMS FOR A $100,000 POLICY

Age	Term Insurance	Universal-Life Insurance*	Whole-Life Insurance*
30	$136	$ 590	$ 875
35	140	746	1,095
40	163	950	1,391
45	205	1,217	1,776
50	320	1,583	2,311
55	440	2,078	3,038
60	610	2,741	4,717
65	980	3,665	5,376

* For a full discussion of cash-value policies, including universal-life and whole-life, see page 262.
Source: National Insurance Consumer Organization.

Employee Term Insurance

This is often the best deal in town. A certain amount of life insurance is usually free. You may be able to buy even more at your own expense. But check its price against the list on page 258. Occasionally, employee group insurance costs more than policies on the outside, especially if you're young.

If you leave your job, you can generally convert your group-term coverage to an individual cash-value policy. But the price is high. Don't do it unless you're too sick to qualify for coverage elsewhere.

Any life insurance you get as an employee or retiree generally can be reduced or eliminated by the company. Benefits are not guaranteed. It's reasonable to expect a payoff, but don't stake your spouse's future on it. By the time retirement comes, you should have enough savings, pension income, and Social Security so that the proceeds from a company-paid life-insurance policy will be frosting on the cake.

Other Group Term Coverage

Apply a sniff test to group coverage offered by trade groups, professional associations, alumni associations, and fraternal orders. Sometimes it's terrific; sometimes it's not. Professional associations often slant their coverage toward younger people—offering them much better rates, relatively speaking, than older people get. If you're middle-aged, in good health, and don't smoke, you should be able to find a cheaper policy elsewhere. Check the rates you're offered against the table on page 258.

Usually, the insurance company reserves the right to ask you to pass a physical exam—but not always. Where there's no exam, the premiums are higher than on policies that reject the sick. A no-exam policy may be a bargain for the ill but not for the healthy.

Group-term insurance may not be convertible into individual cash-value coverage (page 256), which is a drawback. Cash-value coverage is sometimes needed by people who discovered that they'll need life insurance into late old age. If you buy nonconvertible group term as part of your family protection plan, include some individual convertible term, as well.

Individual Term Insurance Policies

Plain vanilla term insurance is good, reliable, and cheap. You can afford to buy your dependents a huge benefit, as a hedge against your death. Term policies require higher out-of-pocket payments as you get older. When you reach your late sixties, you will probably want to cancel out. But your policy will have done its job, if it protected your spouse and young children when they needed it.

Life-insurance agents are perfectly willing to sell term insurance, if you insist. But they'll generally press you to buy cash-value coverage, too. They've been taught that cash-value insurance is better. What's more, they earn higher commissions by selling it. Some agents may push the high-cost policy even though it leaves your family poorly protected. Here are some answers to their silky arguments against term insurance.

WHAT TO THINK WHEN THE LIFE-INSURANCE AGENT SAYS . . .

"Term premiums are wasted because you have nothing to show for them in the end." Wrong. You've had years of protection out of your policy, and that's what you paid for. Would you say that your fire insurance premiums are wasted just because your house didn't burn down?

"Term is like renting. Whole-life is like buying." True. And some things it's smarter to rent, like life insurance.

"Term·insurance is an illusion. Hardly anybody collects on it." Hardly anyone collects on fire insurance, either. Term insurance is *meant* to be canceled when the need for protection no longer exists. When you think about "collecting" on your own life insurance, you are thinking "What's in it for me?"—and that's the thought that leads you wrong.

"You will need permanent life insurance eventually, so you might as well buy it now." Any life insurance policy, including term insurance, is "permanent," if it lasts until you die. If the agent means, "You will always need life insurance until you die of old age," the answer is "nonsense." An insurance policy replaces earnings if you die prematurely. When you retire, you have no paycheck to replace. You'll be living on your pension, your savings, and Social Security—all of which can continue to pay your spouse after you die.

You will need insurance well into old age only if: (1) You plan to work until you drop *and* you expect that your spouse or children will always be dependent on that income. (2) You don't expect to leave your spouse enough income to live on, from your pension, savings, and Social Security. (3) You make a lot of money, maybe in your own business, and will need insurance to cover the death taxes. (4) You want to leave extra money to your children or a charity. (For a discussion of using life insurance to replace a pension, see page 798.)

"You should start converting your term insurance into a permanent policy, so you'll never be without protection." Same answer as above.

"You will need insurance in middle age to protect your family. Term insurance is too expensive then." If you use one of the price-quote services

on page 259, you can find low-cost term insurance even when you're 60 to 70.

"Cash-value policies force you to save for old age." Here again, the agent is getting you to wonder "What's in it for me?" By putting yourself first, you put your spouse and children last. The rule is: protection first, savings later. If you can afford all the term insurance you need and still have some money left over, *then* think about whether you want to use a life-insurance policy as a piggy bank.

"I can sell you paid-up insurance so—at age 60—you'll have a permanent policy with no more premuims due." Big deal. This kind of coverage costs you larger-than-usual premiums in the early years. You are prepaying for something you may not need in the first place.

"Buy term, but also take a small cash-value policy just in case you'll need it in old age." And what will that "valuable" policy be worth when you're old? At 4 percent inflation, a $50,000 death benefit bought today will have a purchasing power of about $15,000 in 30 years. That won't keep the wolf from the door. Even with policies whose death benefit is projected to rise in the future, the increase might not be rapid enough to keep up with inflation. A surer approach is to buy more term insurance as you go along and build up your savings and investments. If you eventually decide that you do need cash-value coverage, you can always pick it up in middle age by converting some of your term insurance. When you reach age 45, a $100,000 policy might cost $100 a month.

"Since you can afford all the insurance you need, think about using a cash-value policy for tax-sheltered savings or to build a larger estate." This is the only legitimate argument. And it's legit only for a cash-value policy with low costs and a genuinely competitive return (page 273).

When You Buy Term Insurance . . .

MAKE IT RENEWABLE. The policy should be renewable automatically, regardless of your health. For most term insurance, renewal comes annually. Your price will rise, but not by much. A $100,000 policy might cost a nonsmoking woman four dollars more at age 36 than at 35.

Some term policies go for 5 or 10 years at the same premium, before renewal. They cost a little more to start, but in some cases may be cheaper over the whole period. So take a look.

MAKE IT RENEWABLE FOR AS LONG AS YOU MIGHT NEED IT. Some policies can't be renewed after 10 or 15 years—which usually makes them especially cheap. They're good for, say, a widowed mother, insuring herself until her child gets out of college. But if you have a dependent spouse, you'll want a policy that's renewable until you're 70.

MAKE IT CONVERTIBLE. Your term policy should be convertible into cash-value coverage, at standard rates and without a health exam, right up to age 65. That assures your opportunity to continue your policy into old age, even if your health deteriorates. Your agent may constantly encourage you to convert when you're young. Don't do it unless there's a very good reason. What might be a reason? (1) You plan to go on working well into old age, and someone (a spouse, a teenager) will depend on those earnings. (2) You have a disabled child and want to leave plenty of money for his or her care. (3) You got rich, and want money to pay the estate taxes. If you do decide that you need a cash-value policy, don't automatically convert the term policy you have. If you're insurable, you might find less expensive coverage through another company. Your fifties are good years for making the switch.

MAKE IT A NONSMOKER POLICY. Save money. Quit smoking. Nonsmokers live longer than smokers (Tobacco Institute: call New York Life), and pay as much as 40 to 60 percent less for their life insurance. You're a nonsmoker if you've avoided the weed for at least one or two years.

LOOK FOR GUARANTEED PREMIUMS. Some policies guarantee your premiums for up to 10 years or so. Others offer "low current premiums," but reserve the right to raise them later to a specified maximum. Many companies that have the right to raise your premiums may not do so—but it's a risk. If two policies are priced about the same and one guarantees low premiums for many more years, take it.

TELL THE WHOLE TRUTH. Don't misspeak on your application, or let the insurance agent misspeak for you. If you don't answer all of the health questions honestly and in full (including whether you smoke cigarettes), and die during the first two or three years you hold the policy, the company may cancel your coverage posthumously. If that happens, your beneficiaries will get back all the premiums you paid but will lose the large lump sum they needed. Insurers can test your honesty with a medical exam or by checking your medical history with the Medical Information Bureau (page 316).

Will the Real "Low-Cost" Term Policy Please Stand Up?

Some policies are cheap in the early years but get more expensive (relative to other term policies) when you've held them a while. Other policies cost more at first but relatively less by the 10th or 15th year. Which type to buy?

1. Pick the first kind, if you'll want insurance only for five years or so.

2. Pick the first kind, if you'll shop for a new insurance company every five years. When its rates get too high, you can hop to a lower-cost insurer. (But if you've become uninsurable—a remote possibility—you'll be locked into the policy you have.)

3. Pick the second kind, if you want to keep the policy for more than five years.

How to Find Cheap Term Insurance

There are three ways of doing it. The first way doesn't work. But it's the one recommended in all the consumer handbooks, so I'll tell you about it anyway.

THE FIRST WAY. Ask the salesperson for the policy's "interest-adjusted net payment index" number. That's an index that looks not only at the average annual premiums you pay but also at any projected dividends, assuming that the money is reinvested at 5 percent. The calculation is standardized. In general, the lower the number, the better the buy.

But how low is low? A single index number doesn't tell you anything. You have to compare it with the index numbers of a lot of other term policies for people your age, and few people do that. Furthermore, interest-adjusted indexes can be—and are—manipulated by insurance companies to make some policies look better than they really are. Finally, the agent may stack the sales pitch, by showing you policies with worse index numbers and falsely implying that his policy is tops.

If you have a long list of the interest-adjusted index numbers for similar policies written for someone of your age, those at the top of the list are probably better than those at the bottom. But that's about all you can say. I consider the interest-adjusted index practically useless.

THE SECOND WAY. This has the virtue of being simple and straightforward. Go by the judgment of the National Insurance Consumer Organization (NICO). In early 1991, it set out the following *maximum* rates that consumers ought to pay for annual renewable term insurance. If your coverage costs more, it's too expensive. You can probably find lower rates than these, however, by checking the insurance-quote services (page 259).

THE MOST YOU SHOULD PAY FOR TERM INSURANCE

Nonsmokers			Smokers		
	Annual premium*			Annual premium*	
Age	Male	Female	Age	Male	Female
18–30	$ .76	$ .68	18–30	$ 1.05	$ 1.01
31	.76	.69	31	1.10	1.05
32	.77	.70	32	1.15	1.10
33	.78	.71	33	1.21	1.15
34	.79	.72	34	1.28	1.20
35	.80	.74	35	1.35	1.25
36	.84	.78	36	1.45	1.31
37	.88	.82	37	1.56	1.38
38	.92	.86	38	1.68	1.45
39	.97	.90	39	1.81	1.52
40	1.03	.95	40	1.95	1.60
41	1.09	1.00	41	2.12	1.73
42	1.17	1.05	42	2.30	1.89
43	1.25	1.10	43	2.50	2.05
44	1.34	1.15	44	2.72	2.22
45	1.45	1.20	45	2.95	2.40
46	1.59	1.29	46	3.22	2.59
47	1.74	1.41	47	3.52	2.79
48	1.91	1.53	48	3.85	3.01
49	2.10	1.66	49	4.21	3.23
50	2.30	1.76	50	4.60	3.50
51	2.49	1.90	51	4.97	3.79
52	2.70	2.06	52	5.38	4.10
53	2.96	2.22	53	5.82	4.44
54	3.40	2.40	54	6.29	4.80
55	3.40	2.60	55	6.80	5.20
56	3.66	2.79	56	7.31	5.58
57	3.94	3.00	57	7.87	5.99
58	4.23	3.22	58	8.46	6.43
59	4.55	3.46	59	9.10	6.90
60	4.90	3.70	60	9.80	7.40
61	5.43	3.98	61	10.83	7.95
62	6.02	4.28	62	11.98	8.54
63	6.67	4.60	63	13.25	9.18
64	7.40	4.93	64	14.65	9.86
65	8.20	5.30	65	16.20	10.60

* Per $1,000 of coverage, per year.
Source: National Insurance Consumer Organization.

Notes to the table:
• The table shows the premium rate per $1,000 of coverage. If you're buying a $100,000 policy, multiply the cost by 100 and add $60 (for the insurer's fixed policy expenses) to see the most that you should pay.
• Policies smaller than $100,000 cost a little more. Policies written for $500,000 and up cost a little less.
• Nonsmoker rates are for preferred health risks.
• The relative rates for smokers keep rising, as insurers see how fast the smokers are popping off.
• Rates and companies may have changed by the time you read this. For an update, check the latest NICO guide: Taking the Bite Out of Insurance. For buying information, see page 275.

THE THIRD WAY. Ask a computerized price-quote service to find cheap term insurance for you. Your age and health status is run through a data bank. Out comes a list of up to six low-cost policies to consider. Their prices will probably be even lower than the benchmarks shown on page 258. I found my own low-cost term policy through these services, and wouldn't dream of shopping any other way. Every five years, run yourself through the computers again. If you stay in good health, you probably will be able to find something cheaper.

One price-quote company sells information only: Insurance Information, Inc., of Hyannis, Massachusetts (800-472-5800). For $50, it will send you the names of the five insurers (out of 200 to 300 it monitors) that offer the lowest term rates for someone in your circumstances. It gives you a cost index, averaged over three and five years. Your $50 will be refunded if you don't find a policy more than $50 cheaper than the one you have now.

Insurance Information sells no insurance. You merely get the names and phone numbers of the companies. When you call a company, you will be directed to a local insurance agent. Because the printout shows only five years of prices, you can't tell if these policies are slated to get more expensive than competing policies in future years. But the agent will run out the projected prices for you.

The other price-quote services are offered by insurance agents. If you like what you see, the agent will buy the policy for you and earn the commission. But there's no obligation to buy through the quote service and no salesperson will call.

SELECTQUOTE of San Francisco (800-343-1985). You're shown the 5-, 10-, 15-, and 20-year net payment indexes (page 257), which gives you a good idea of what a low index number is—subject to all the caveats above.

INSURANCEQUOTE of Chandler, Arizona (800-972-1104). You get policy prices and descriptions but not net payment indexes, unless you call and ask for them.

TERMQUOTE of Dayton, Ohio (800-444-TERM). You're sent the particulars on up to six policies. Net payment indexes are supplied on request.

Warning: The price quotes are accompanied by brief descriptions of the insurance policies. But they don't explain very much. Call the quote service and ask for details. Many of the recommended policies are "re-entry" or "revertible" term (see below). The computer shows only the premiums you'll pay if you keep your health. If you fall ill and no longer qualify for the special re-entry rate, renewal costs will probably be higher than for the standard policies on the list.

Re-Entry Term

Some term policies regularly reevaluate your health—say, after three years, five years, eight years, and so on. If you pass the health exam, you'll get a discount from the standard rate. That's called "re-entry" or "revertible" term. It's the perfect policy for anyone who can see into the future and knows that he or she will always be in perfect health.

But if your crystal ball is as dim as mine, these policies are a gambler's game. If you can't pass the health exam, you could be stuck with higher prices than you'd have paid on a regular policy. Compare the re-entry rates for good health and bad with the premiums shown on page 258. If the re-entry rate is spectacularly low, and the bad-health rate only moderately high, the policy is worth the risk. Otherwise not.

Savings Bank Insurance

You can buy term life insurance at many savings banks in:
- Massachusetts—up to $250,000.
- Connecticut—up to $200,000 at banks that offer a group policy to customers, plus another $100,000 in an individual policy.
- New York—up to $350,000 at banks with group policies.

You qualify if you live or work in the state. Check the price against the table on page 258. New York's rates start low but rise rapidly. Massachusetts' unisex rates (where men and women pay the same) are not so good for women but at least are competitive with other rates in the state. Connecticut's rates are often not competitive.

Mortgage-Life Insurance

Do you want to leave your survivors a house free and clear? If so, insure yourself for the principal due on the mortgage. There are two ways to go.

1. Buy "mortgage-life" insurance from the lender. It's a term policy whose cost can be bundled right into your monthly mortgage payment. If you die, the proceeds pay off your loan.

Sound good so far? Now watch me trash it. Mortgage-life locks your survivors into using the proceeds of the policy to pay off the mortgage. Maybe they'd rather use the money for something else. Worse, this coverage can be shockingly expensive. Mortgage-life is worth consider-ing only for smokers and people in poor health who can't get life insur-ance elsewhere at standard rates. (And even then, compare prices before settling for the lender's policy.)

2. The better choice is to buy regular term insurance through a price-quote service or a life-insurance agent. It should cost much less than the lender's policy. You can either buy "level term," which pays the same no matter when you die, or "decreasing term," whose face value declines along with your mortgage. The proceeds of this policy go to your survivors, not to the lender. Your survivors decide what to do with the money. Maybe they'd rather keep on making monthly mortgage payments and use the money for savings or investments.

Credit-Life Insurance

Like mortgage insurance, it's offered by a lender. And it's overpriced in most states, especially for younger people and those in good health.

Credit-life may be offered in tandem with a car loan, a personal loan, an installment loan, or a home-equity line of credit. You *do not* have to buy the insurance in order to get the loan. It's against the law to pressure you into taking a policy, although lenders may try; they make a lot of money selling credit life. If you want all your debts paid off at your death, skip these high-priced bits of credit insurance and buy more renewable term insurance instead.

I make one exception. If you're so sick that you're uninsurable, try for all the credit-life insurance you can get. There is often no health test to pass. Credit-life is sometimes available even to people on their death-beds.

Although legal, buying deathbed insurance is clearly an abuse of the system. In some states, credit-life insurers can now refuse to pay if you die within six months of the policy's start-up date, from an illness that was treated or diagnosed in the six months before you bought the policy. Other insurers have started to collect medical information from people taking out policies larger than $20,000 to $25,000. Payment can be denied if you hide your true physical condition and die within less than two years.

Miscellaneous Insurance

Keep a note in your life-insurance file if you qualify for any of the following payments, so that your survivors will know to collect.

1. Credit unions sometimes provide a small amount of free insurance —on the order of $4,000 in coverage for a $2,000 account.

2. If you charge a travel ticket to a credit card, it may generate $100,000 or more of free life insurance. You might be covered for accidental death and dismemberment, whether you travel by plane, train, bus, or ship. Ditto, if your accident occurs in an airline terminal, or while traveling on public transportation to and from the terminal.

3. If you belong to the American Automobile Association, your membership fee may include a small amount of life insurance, if you die in an auto accident.

4. You might have bought some credit-life insurance when you took out a loan. I don't recommend it (page 261). But if you do buy, note it in your file so the money won't be wasted.

ALL ABOUT CASH-VALUE INSURANCE

Cash-value insurance has two appeals.

First, you can hold its premiums level. So the policy stays affordable (or reasonably so) right into old age. You'll need to keep your coverage in old age when: (1) you expect to be working into late old age, and have a spouse or handicapped child who depends on your income; (2) your pension provides no cost-of-living increases, and your savings aren't large enough to protect your spouse against rising costs; (3) your estate will owe death taxes, and you want them paid out of life-insurance proceeds. Term policies grow impossibly expensive in late old age, if, indeed, you can buy them at all.

The second reason for buying cash-value insurance is the tax-deferred investment it provides. In old age, you can either borrow against that money or surrender the policy and pocket the proceeds.

Here's the big question: Do you *want* to put your investment funds into cash-value life insurance? Are the returns high enough? Or should you buy only term insurance and invest your money somewhere else?

This used to be a no-brainer: Buy cheap term insurance and invest elsewhere. And you still should, if your separate investment account is tax deductible and tax deferred. Term insurance plus a deductible Individual Retirement Account (page 752) or company 401(k) plan (page 743) will beat cash-value policies that make comparable investments.

But *some* modern policies, from *some* companies, for *some* people, can be good investments, if you play them right. I repeat that you must be able to afford enough insurance to protect your family, which usually means term coverage. But provided that that necessity is seen to, certain cash-value policies can be interesting.

Two important points: (1) You must choose carefully. Many of the advertised yields are deceptive. Your cash values may be earning far less than you think. (2) If interest rates fall—and they well might—your policy won't build the value you expected.

There are five kinds of cash-value policies: traditional whole-life, interest-sensitive whole-life, mixed whole-life and term, universal-life, and variable-life. Here's the scoop on all of them.

Traditional Whole-Life Insurance

Call these policies "no surprises." You pay a fixed premium every year. You earn interest on your cash values. Your beneficiaries get a fixed benefit if you die.

What percentage return will you earn on the money you invest in a whole-life policy? Beats me. The insurance company does not reveal how much of each premium goes to cover the cost of insurance and overhead expenses. So you can't tell what you're earning on the rest of your funds. Neither, for that matter, can the life insurance agent.

The agent may assume a return (a handsome one, naturally). He or she can crank it through a computer and produce a beauty of a policy illustration. But these illustrations are often deceptive. A policy claiming an 11 percent return might actually be earning a net of only 4 percent —"we have plenty of examples of this sort," reports insurance professor Harold Skipper of Georgia State University.

By the same token, agents opposed to whole-life insurance use counterdeceptions of their own. Joseph Belth of Indiana University, in his book, *Life Insurance: A Consumer's Handbook,* tells about a policy whose insurance portion was said—by a deceptive agent—to be overpriced at $173.60 when the true cost was more like $8.93.

Deception is possible in insurance sales because you cannot easily determine the yield yourself. Still, you don't have to swallow whatever the agent dishes out. Get an independent opinion of the policy's investment value from the National Insurance Consumer Organization. (For details on this excellent service, see page 274). A good policy will earn as much as a quality corporate bond, tax deferred. You're guaranteed a minimum yield, usually in the area of 4 to 6 percent.

WHO MIGHT BUY. Whole-life policies are for insurance investors who want plain vanilla coverage. You pay your money, get a death benefit, and earn tax-deferred interest at something close to a market rate. Period. The policy takes you into old age for the same premium you started out with. The cash value gives you an extra source of retirement money if you need it. Or, if you want to quit paying premiums, you can use the cash value to buy a smaller "paid up" policy, on which no more premiums are due.

Interest-Sensitive Whole-Life Insurance

These newer whole-life policies compete with universal-life insurance (below). You are promised a current market interest rate on your cash values, and that rate is disclosed. If all goes well, the cash values may grow faster than they do in traditional whole-life insurance. And your annual premiums are usually lower (although not always).

Premiums tend to be fixed. Some interest-sensitive policies, however, may quote you a range—say, $1,000 a year but no higher than $1,200. You pay a penalty if you surrender the policy before a certain number of years have passed. That penalty greatly reduces the return on your investment.

Beware of two deceptions sometimes practiced on buyers of interest-sensitive whole-life. First, the insurer can raise the effective cost of your policy without your realizing it! The company merely raises the "mortality" charge subtracted from your premium, which will slow the rise in your cash value. On paper, you are still earning top market interest rates; in practice, the insurer is draining some of that money away. Second, you are probably not earning as much interest on your savings as you think. You were probably quoted a gross rate of interest, before expenses were deducted. Your net rate of interest may be much smaller. For details, see page 269.

WHO MIGHT BUY? Interest-sensitive policies suit buyers who hope for a higher return on their money than they'd get from traditional whole-life, and who want to know what gross rate of interest their cash values earn. They also like the fixed premiums, as opposed to the flexible premiums of universal-life. Interest-sensitive policies might be cheaper than universal ones, because they're easier to administer.

Mixed Whole-Life and Term

These policies might be 60 percent whole-life and 40 percent term, although this division won't be immediately obvious to you. Dividends are used to buy additional whole-life coverage, which gradually replaces the term insurance. You pay lower premiums than for regular whole life, and earn lower cash values in the earlier years.

WHO MIGHT BUY. People who will need life insurance into old age and are searching for an especially low fixed premium. A mixed policy might be exactly the answer. Unfortunately, there aren't very many of them around. One source: Northwestern Mutual Life in Milwaukee.

Universal-Life Insurance

Call these policies "mix 'n' match." You decide how much to pay into them every year, subject to specified minimums and maximums. The insurance company will recommend a "target" premium. That's what you have to pay—under the company's current assumptions—to keep the policy in force to age 100. But you're always free to pay less or more. You can vary the size of your premiums. You can add extra money this month, then skip three months. The choice of what to pay and how much to accumulate is yours. In any month that you don't pay enough to cover the price of your coverage, the extra sum needed will be subtracted from your cash values.

You can also choose how large a death benefit you want your premium to buy. With Option A, you get a level death benefit and greater cash values. With Option B, you get a rising death benefit and lower cash values. You might start with Option B when your family is young and later switch to Option A—because buying a rising death benefit gets pretty expensive at later ages. With either A or B, you can vary the policy's face amount, but to get an increase, you may have to pass a medical exam.

You can take money out of a universal-life policy without treating the transaction as a loan. There's generally a $25 withdrawal fee. (Ask the insurance company whether any part of the withdrawal is taxable. The answer depends on actuarial calculations.) There may be surrender charges if you drop the policy before 7 to 20 years have passed.

Unlike most traditional whole-life insurance, universal policies disclose the yield that you're earning on your policy's cash values. Interest rates are normally guaranteed for a year at a time. Once a year, you get a statement showing how much interest you earned, how much was withdrawn from your policy to cover expenses and the cost of insurance, and how much your savings fund increased.

There are two problems with universal life.

PROBLEM ONE. The advertised yield tells you next to nothing! You may earn high interest on your life-insurance savings. But at the same time, the insurer may be charging a large sum for insurance and expenses. A policy with a lower interest rate and lower expenses might actually build higher cash values over the long run.

You will also be docked if you cancel the policy. The surrender charges in the early years can slash your return to a number too low to mention in polite company. ("Oh, c'mon, say it," urges insurance analyst Glenn Daily, who read this chapter in manuscript form. "You can lose 100 percent of the money you put up.")

One more point: Those illustrated interest rates are not guaranteed. Actual rates will be lower, or higher, than the insurance company projects. Typically, rates change every year. You are guaranteed only the company's minimum rate—perhaps 4 to 6 percent.

Never compare the iffy advertised interest rates on life-insurance savings with the guaranteed interest rates on bonds or bank accounts. They don't compute. You can't even compare one insurer's interest rates with another, because the companies subtract different amounts from your cash values to cover their costs. If you're thinking about buying a universal-life policy (or any other form of cash-value insurance) write to the National Insurance Consumer Organization (page 274) for an analysis of what the policy might really earn.

PROBLEM TWO. You can kid yourself that your universal policy is providing you with enough savings and insurance when it's really not.

When interest rates fall, your cash values will not build up as fast as expected. But the insurer may let you coast along in ignorance. You might keep on paying the same old premium, even though it no longer covers the full cost of insuring you. The shortfall is taken out of your cash value.

Some insurance agents and insurance companies tell you what's happening, but others don't. If the cash in your policy runs down, you won't have the retirement savings—to withdraw or to borrow against—that you expected. Your investment plan will have come a cropper. In the worst case, a retiree might be forced to put up substantially more money if he or she wanted to keep the insurance in force.

ANYONE WITH A UNIVERSAL POLICY SHOULD:

· Pay at least the minimum target premium into the plan. If you can't afford the target premium, you probably won't be able to keep the policy over the long run. In that case, you'd be better off choosing term insurance.

• Check with your insurance agent when interest rates fall, to see if you ought to raise your premiums.

• If you find that you're way behind on your cash-value goals, send the policy statements to NICO for analysis. Don't add more money unless you know that you're earning a decent return. If you're not, reduce or cancel the coverage. Buy term insurance or a truly competitive universal-life policy instead.

Some people invest extra money in their universal-life insurance, for the tax-deferred return. This introduces a new complication. Too large an investment will turn your policy into something called a "modified endowment contract." Loans and withdrawals against modified endowments create taxable income plus a 10 percent penalty if you're under age 59½ and not disabled. Ask your insurance agent how much you can safely invest without running into tax complications.

WHO MIGHT BUY. Look at universal-life if you want the flexibility of deciding how much money to invest. You can add more funds to the policy, or skip several months of premium payments, depending on your circumstances. But keep an eye on the cash value, to be sure it's large enough to keep the policy in force into your old age.

Variable-Life Insurance

A variable-life policy ties your death benefit and cash values to the investment performance of stocks, bonds, or money market securities. With *straight* variable-life, you pay a fixed annual premium. With *universal* variable-life—the kind most commonly sold—you can vary the premiums.

The death benefit can rise, if your investments perform well. If your investments perform badly, here's what will happen: (1) With most universal variable policies, you might have to increase your premiums to keep the policy in force. (2) With most straight variable-life policies, the death benefit generally will not fall below the policy's face value, so your survivors are protected. (But beware the few policies that let your coverage expire if your investments do poorly.)

Neither type of policy guarantees your cash values. In a good market, they'll rise; in a bad one, they could drop.

Over 20 or 30 years, you assume, the value of your policy has nowhere to go but up. But how far up? Not nearly as much as you might imagine. What's more, the internal charges levied against variable-life policies tend to be higher than on other forms of cash-value coverage, because of all the investment and administrative expenses. Result: You pay more for your life insurance, in return for the right to gamble on a higher payoff. Not a great offer, in my opinion.

SOME LITTLE-KNOWN FACTS ABOUT VARIABLE-LIFE:

1. Your death benefit doesn't necessarily rise when the market does —a fact many buyers don't understand. With some policies, you have to net an average gain of 4 or 4.5 percent a year just to hold your coverage even. That means 4 or 4.5 percent after all charges for insurance, brokerage fees, management fees on the investments, and so on. So the gross has to be higher still. Any time your net yield falls below 4 or 4.5 percent, that money has to be made up before the death benefit can rise. On policies that don't require a 4 or 4.5 percent floor, you still have to cover all expenses before the cash values and death benefits go up.

2. With straight variable-life, death benefits fall much faster than they rise. On one policy I reviewed, an 0.75 percent return in the fifth year lowered the death benefit by 5.2 percent. So your risks on the downside are greater than your opportunities on the upside.

3. Loans reduce your investment return. As long as you carry a loan against your policy, an equal amount of your cash values will be credited with a low 4 or 5 percent interest rate. That holds down your long-term rate of return and defeats the very purpose of variable-life. If you take this kind of policy, don't borrow against it.

4. You can't compare the advertised returns on variable-life with returns from other investment vehicles. When the stock fund in your variable-life policy rises 15 percent, you earn that money only on part of your investment—after sales charges, fees, premium taxes, the cost of insurance protection, risk charges, and administrative expenses have been taken out. The rate of return on your entire deposit will be lower than 15 percent.

HOW TO INVEST WITH VARIABLE-LIFE. Here's the truth: Low- and medium-yield investments are a waste of money.

Your policy might offer you a money market mutual fund. But that fund's low yield has virtually no chance of raising your death benefit.

Your policy might offer you a bond fund. But that yields about the same as you'd get from a regular life-insurance policy. You'd be paying the extra cost of variable-life for nothing.

If you're going to gamble on variable-life, go all the way. Put your money into a pure stock fund and leave it there. Don't even bother with an asset-allocation fund, which switches your money from one type of investment to another. If you don't want to hold stocks for the long term, don't buy variable-life insurance.

WHO MIGHT BUY. A gambler. Because of a variable policy's high costs, you need superior stock market returns, over a long holding period, for this policy to do better than other forms of cash-value insurance. If you plan to hold for 20 years or so, you have a shot.

A SIMPLE WAY THROUGH THE REST OF THIS CHAPTER

Skip directly to page 273, where you'll find the names of two fine, high-value, low-cost insurance policies. You can buy them yourself, by telephone. They're blue chips. What else do you really need to know?

Between this page and that you'll find a lot of detail about why it's so hard to analyze an insurance proposal and how an insurance agent can lead you down the garden path.

Take my word for it: A lay person can't tell a good proposal from a bad. You'll simplify your life by choosing one of the two policies known to be good.

CAN YOU TRUST COMPUTER-GENERATED LIFE INSURANCE PROPOSALS?

No. Not for a minute. They're pure GIGO—"garbage in, garbage out."

Computer-printed illustrations look so authoritative that they're hard to resist. Their neat rows of columns pretend to show what your cash-value policy will be worth 20 years or more into the future. But many illustrations are shamelessly manipulated, to make the policy look less expensive than it really is.

Their sins are impossible for a layman to spot. The projection might:

• Lower your apparent cost by assuming longer average lifespans in the future.

• Raise your projected cash values, by assuming that you'll hold the policy for 10 or 15 years and will therefore earn an interest or premium bonus.

· Assume that the bonuses are guaranteed, when in fact they're not.

· Tout a guaranteed bonus, without telling you that the rate to which the bonus is linked may drop.

· Throw in some extra money in years 5, 10, 15, and 20. Buyers often use those years for comparison shopping. The years between, however, may be undernourished.

· Dazzle you with a high interest rate on your cash values, then take it away by charging a high price for the underlying insurance.

· Assume that dividends will rise in the future, when in fact they might not.

The printouts also assume that today's level of dividends and interest rates will last forever—when, in fact, they generally last a year or less. Your *guaranteed* return is generally only 4 to 6 percent. But that's not a good measure, either, because you will doubtless earn more than the guarantee.

SO FORGET 20-YEAR GIGO PROJECTIONS. DON'T BOTHER TRYING TO UNDERSTAND THEM. THEY'RE COLUMNS OF NUMBERS DESIGNED TO CONFUSE YOU. THROW THEM OUT!
You won't get much more help from the interest-adjusted cost indexes, which were once believed to be the ultimate answer to life insurance cost comparisons. The "net payment index" ranks a policy by its average annual premiums and projected dividends, assuming that the money is reinvested at 5 percent. The "surrender-cost index" ranks policies according to how well you do when you cash them in. Given the 20-year index numbers of a long list of policies, those with the lowest numbers should be better than those with the highest, if held for 20 years.

But that's about the best you can say. Those in the middle are a question mark, and those ranked right next to each other may or may not be in the proper order. Some other complaints: (1) The system is biased against lower-premium, lower-dividend policies, which may in fact be among the best. (2) The policy illustrations on which the index numbers were based may have been pure GIGO, which also slants the results. (3) You know nothing at all about a company's other insurance policies, which weren't on the interest-adjusted list. They may rank well below the policies that were publicized.

So treat the cost indexes as being of only marginal value. Pay more attention to:

HOW MUCH OF YOUR PREMIUM IS RETURNED IN CASH VALUES AND DIVIDENDS IN THE FIRST THREE YEARS? Almost all of the money that you pay in premiums should go toward building up cash values. Hardly anything should be taken out for sales and marketing expenses. If you surrender the policy, even in the very first year, you should get back almost as much as you paid (page 282).

EXACTLY WHAT IS GUARANTEED—WHAT PREMIUM, WHAT CASH VALUE, WHAT DEATH BENE-FIT? I'm not suggesting that you buy a policy based on its guarantees. But you need to know what part of your policy is rock solid and what can change. Some projections that appear to be guaranteed aren't. Ask about each portion of the policy: dividends, cash values, face values, and the number of years you have to pay premiums.

WHERE IN THE POLICY ARE YOUR GUARANTEES WRITTEN DOWN? The insurance agent may promise more than the policy does.

HOW LONG DO YOU HAVE TO HOLD THE POLICY TO GET HIGH RETURNS? Some policies appear more competitive after 20 years than after only 5 years. Consider such a policy only if you're absolutely sure that you'll hold it for the full 20-year span.

The sad truth is that performance data on insurance companies are not rigorous, not comprehensive, and not reliable. So keep your suspicions on the boil. New York–based insurance analyst Glenn Daily, who studies his field with a clearer eye than most, guesses that at least half of all the insurance companies in America could claim to be among the top-performing 5 percent, through a clever selection of measuring rods.

WHAT YOU SHOULD KNOW ABOUT SALES COMMISSIONS

A traditional, "loaded" product deducts sales commissions from the premiums you pay. There may also be overrides for office and training expenses, fringe benefits for agents, and other marketing costs. These loads run from a low of 30 percent to more than 100 percent of your first-year premium, and diminishing percentages of the premiums you pay in subsequent years. The cost comes out of your cash values, which may be zero in the first year and low for several years thereafter.

With a "back-end load" or surrender charge, you pay no overt sales fee when you buy. Some insurance agents go so far as to tell you that these policies are "free." They are not. The selling agent is paid an upfront commission by the insurance company. That expense is recovered by building higher costs into your policy, or crediting you with less interest. Also, you'll pay a surrender charge if you cancel the policy within, say, the first 15 or 20 years. So you are locked in. Still, surrender-charge policies may yield higher cash values than policies with front-end loads.

"Low-load" policies don't pay the agent his or her standard fee. Some selling expenses are built into the policy, but they're uncommonly low. Cash values build much faster than they do with back-end-load products. The two policies recommended by the National Insurance Consumer Organization fall into this category (next page). So do the products sold by financial planners who charge fees for their services rather than collect sales commissions.

SOME INSURANCE COMPANIES OFFER POLICIES THAT ARE VIRTUALLY THE SAME EXCEPT FOR THE SALES COMMISSION. The agent can take a high commission (giving you lower cash values) or a low commission (giving you higher cash values). You normally won't know that he or she has the choice. Always ask the agent whether you can get the same policy, at the same premium, but with higher cash values. You might luck out.

Here are the ingredients of a low-cost policy: (1) The premiums are low. (2) The cash values are high in the policy's early years, compared with the premiums you've paid. (3) The cash surrender values are almost as high as, or equal to, the cash values, right from the start. So if you quit the policy, you get virtually all of your money out.

SHOULD YOU INVEST IN CASH-VALUE INSURANCE?

CONSIDER IT, IF . . .

1. You have used up all the tax-deductible, tax-deferred savings available to you. Company 401(k) plans, pension annuities, deferred compensation, and deductible Individual Retirement Accounts are better deals than cash-value insurance. If your IRA is not tax deductible, however, the insurance may be better.

2. You don't expect to need the savings in your life-insurance policy for a long time—at least 10 years and often more. (Large numbers of whole-life policies are canceled earlier, which makes most of them money losers. Two exceptions are listed below.)

3. You can afford all the insurance protection that your family needs.

4. You are content to earn annual tax-deferred returns similar to those paid by quality corporate bonds or longer-term certificates of deposit. If you gamble on higher returns by buying stock-owning variable-

life, you must be prepared to hold for the 15 to 20 years that it might take for this strategy to work.

5. You discover a policy that's reasonably priced, pays good rates on your savings, and offers high cash values right from the start. That means a policy with unusually low sales expenses.

HOW DO YOU FIND SUCH A PARAGON OF A POLICY? THERE ARE TWO WAYS.
THE FIRST WAY.

Call USAA Life in San Antonio, Texas (800-531-8000) or VEST Insurance Marketing Corporation in Houston (800-552-3553).

That's the recommendation of the National Insurance Consumer Organization (NICO). Both companies offer a universal-life insurance policy that NICO thinks is a good investment. Both sell nationally, by telephone or mail, rather than through a network of insurance agents. Niether charges you the usual sales commission that takes so much out of a regular policy. Neither levies a surrender charge. If you cancel the policy in the first couple of years, you should get most or all of your money back.

USAA sells its own policies. Its rates are generally better for younger people than for older ones.

VEST sells a policy issued by Ameritas Life Insurance Corporation in Lincoln, Nebraska. Its rates are competitive at any age. This policy is also available, without upfront sales commission, through a handful of regional brokers and financial planners. To find them, call Ameritas at 800-255-9678.

Best bet: Ask both Ameritas and USAA for a universal-life proposal, showing the same death benefit and the same premium. The policy with the better cash surrender value is the better deal.

A few other companies may not charge the usual sales commission —for example, Lincoln Benefit Life. But its low-load policies are generally available only through fee-only financial planners (page 833). Lincoln Benefit's own insurance agents can sell low-load policies if they want to. But on the whole, they stick to products with the normal commission.

Warning: Ameritas also sells full-commission products through insurance agents. Those policies are more expensive because of the sales load you pay. For the low-priced product, you have to call VEST or Ameritas's 800 telephone number.

Another warning: A life-insurance agent may show you a competing policy that appears to build better cash values than Ameritas's or USAA's. But remember GIGO (page 269)! The illustration is probably full of gimmicks that you'll never be able to find. You can't be sure that other policies will really do better until 20 years have elapsed. And meanwhile, you'll have paid a big sales commission.

THE SECOND WAY.
Write to the National Insurance Consumer Organization.

NICO is the only place I know where you can get an unbiased analysis of cash-value life insurance. It evaluates any proposal you get from an insurance agent, as well as the current worth of your present policy.

The basis for the judgment is simple: You're told the interest rate that you would need from a competing investment for your cash values to earn more outside the insurance policy than in it. You may also get a handwritten note from NICO director Jim Hunt, giving his opinion of your policy and suggesting a better choice.

At this writing, you pay $30 for the first analysis and $20 for each additional analysis asked for in the same letter. Send a stamped, self-addressed envelope to: National Insurance Consumer Organization, 121 N. Payne St., Alexandria, VA, 22314. If you join NICO for $100, Jim Hunt will help you search for a good insurance policy by giving you personal direction by phone.

Consult NICO when you're considering a new whole-life, universal-life, or variable-life policy, or when you're thinking about replacing a policy you already have. *But don't send the insurance policy iself.* Send only the following information.

FOR A NEW POLICY. Send the computerized proposal you got from the life-insurance agent. It should show your age, sex, smoking status, the policy's face amount, annual premium, and the projected cash values, year by year, for at least 20 years. Send a proposal without any riders, or with the cost of the riders shown separately.

FOR A POLICY YOU ALREADY OWN. Send an "in-force ledger statement" (your agent can get it for you). It shows the policy values for the next several years, based on current mortality charges and interest rates. The cost of any riders should be shown separately. If they're not, send NICO a copy of the page of your insurance policy that specifies the riders' price. NICO can also work with the original proposal or with the original Statement of Policy Cost and Benefit Information, if the policy is quite new.

NICO publishes a first-class guide to buying both term and cash-value policies, called *Taking the Bite Out of Insurance: How to Save Money on Life Insurance*. At this writing, it's $13.95.

An Investment Q&A

Question: What's a better retirement-savings strategy, good cash-value insurance or term insurance plus an interest-paying tax-deferred annuity (page 763)? *Answer:* Good cash-value insurance. Both investments give you insurance and tax-deferred savings. But when your earnings are withdrawn from the annuity, they will be taxed, whereas you can borrow earnings from the life-insurance policy untaxed. No taxes are ever due on the insurance policy, if you keep it until you die.

Question: What's a better long-term investment, good cash-value insurance that pays a tax-deferred rate of interest each year or term insurance plus a no-load (no sales charge) mutual fund invested in stocks? *Answer:* Probably term insurance plus a mutual fund, assuming that you pick a good fund. Over long holding periods—10 to 15 years and more—stocks outdo fixed-rate investments. You get some tax deferral from mutual funds, too, simply by not selling them.

Question: What's a better investment, variable-life insurance invested solely in stocks or term insurance plus a no-load mutual fund? *Answer:* In both the short and medium term, term insurance plus a mutual fund. The heavy costs of a variable-life policy drag down its yield. In the long term (15 to 20 years), the variable-life insurance has a shot at doing better, because of the tax deferral. But it's a gamble. The higher your income-tax rate, the more attractive the variable-life-insurance option.

Question: What's a better 10-year investment, good cash-value insurance or term insurance plus a 10-year bond or certificate of deposit? *Answer:* Compared with the average policy, term insurance plus the bond or CD. Over short holding periods, the expenses built into a cash-value insurance policy lower its return. Over longer periods, however, good cash-value insurance should be better, because the return is tax-deferred. *Exception:* A "low-load" universal policy, with minimal sales fees, should beat term insurance plus a CD even at the shorter 10-year period. Two such: USAA and the Ameritas policy (page 273).

Question: What's the better investment, good cash-value insurance or term insurance plus a tax-deductible Individual Retirement Account? *Answer:* Term plus the IRA. Ditto for term insurance plus tax-deductible 401(k)s. Life insurance tax-defers the earnings in the policy but you can't deduct the money you spend on the policy itself.

SINGLE-PREMIUM LIFE: A GREAT INVESTMENT FOR SOME PEOPLE

You are exactly the right person for a single-premium cash-value life policy if you (1) are over age 59½, (2) are well fixed financially, (3) want to leave even more money to your beneficiaries, but (4) want an out just in case you should need extra cash. If you nodded your way through all four points, read on.

With these policies, you put up a lump sum of money—as little as $5,000 but more often $20,000 to $50,000. You get insurance for life (with no further payments due), plus a substantial pool of cash values, the amount depending on your company and your age.

With a regular single-premium policy, either whole-life or universal-life, your cash values earn interest at a rate fixed by the insurance company, usually changing once a year. That rate ought to compete with longer-term bank certificates of deposit. (But don't go by the gross rate you're quoted. Ask the agent to get you the net rate, after the company deducts its expenses and mortality charges. One USAA policy offered at 9 percent interest netted down to a yearly rate of return of 7.8 percent after 10 years.)

With a variable single-premium policy, you pick your own investments—choosing from stocks, bonds, and money market funds. The variable policies carry extra costs. To take just one example, a 12 percent annual yield on a variable Merrill Lynch Prime Plan dropped to 9.5 percent over 20 years, because of all the fees. So your investments have to do unusually well to make variable policies pay (page 268).

If you bought a single-premium policy before June 21, 1988, congratulations. You can use your investment profits without paying any taxes on them, just by borrowing against the cash value. (But if you ever cancel the policy, taxes may fall due.)

The deal's not as sweet for newer single-premium policies, also known as "modified endowment contracts." On policies issued since June 21, 1988, any loans, up to the amount of money that the policy has earned, are now treated as taxable income. So are the withdrawals from a universal policy. If you are under age 59½, and not disabled, you also pay a 10 percent penalty on the earnings you borrow or withdraw.

Still, these are perfectly good investments for people who don't expect to borrow against them or withdraw any funds. The cash in the policy grows tax deferred, and the rising cash value can increase the death benefit. (Death benefits rise much faster in some policies than in others, so compare.) If it turns out that you have to withdraw some money and pay a tax, so what? You are probably still leaving more for your heirs than if that money had stayed in a certificate of deposit.

WARNING: Some companies are trying to recreate the old-style single-premium life policy by combining it with an annuity. You pay a single premium. Part of your money goes for life insurance, the rest goes into the annuity. Over the next six years, the annuity pays your life-insurance premiums. After that, you have a paid-up policy. You can borrow against it any time you want, with no taxes due, because you didn't pay for it all at once. The drawbacks: (1) You owe taxes on the annuity interest every year, (2) you get a small death benefit relative to the money you invested, and (3) the government may rain on your parade at any time. This policy attracts people who will waste their money on practically anything, if they see a tax angle to it.

RIDERS TO YOUR POLICY

A rider is an extra policy benefit that you pay for separately. Here are the most common ones.

WAIVER OF PREMIUM—pays your insurance premiums if you're totally disabled before a certain age, usually 65. It's a worthwhile backup to a separate disability-income policy (page 331), although not a substitute for it. Ask what the company means by "disabled." For the first few years, you're probably covered if you can't work at your regular occupation. After that, the waiver may continue only if you can't handle any sort of suitable work.

ACCIDENTAL DEATH BENEFIT—pays off in the unlikely case that you die in an accident. People buy it like a lottery ticket, but it's not worth the price. (Neither is the travel insurance you buy in airports or buy through credit card companies.)

COST OF LIVING—raises your death benefit annually in tandem with the

Consumer Price Index, without your having to take a health exam. You pay both for the right to buy the extra insurance and for the insurance itself. In NICO's opinion, the rider costs too much. Still, if you can afford the luxury, it's a small hedge against the remote risk of becoming uninsurable.

GUARANTEED INSURABILITY—lets you buy more insurance, at standard rates, without taking a health exam. You have to buy certain amounts at certain ages; if you skip a buying opportunity, you don't get it back. This rider is generally available only to people under 40, and usually with cash-value policies (not term insurance). It becomes valuable only if (1) your health gets so bad that you can't buy normal coverage *and* (2) you think you might need substantially larger amounts of life insurance. NICO advises you to forget the guaranteed-insurability option. If you'll need more coverage, buy it now, in the form of extra term insurance. But anyone with a health risk in the family should certainly give this option a look.

TERM-INSURANCE POLICIES—attached as riders to a cash-value policy. Some riders are expensive, others aren't. Check their rates against the term prices on page 258.

DIVIDENDS OR NOT?

For any buyer of cash-value insurance, dividend-paying policies have traditionally been the better buy. Their premiums are typically higher than those charged by companies that pay no dividends. But the dividend is a form of profit sharing. After dividends, your policy costs less.

Lately, however, nondividend-policies have also been sharing profits with policyholders, through premium reductions or extra interest credited to the cash values. As a result, the difference between these two types of policies isn't as clear as it was in the past.

So . . .

Choose nondividend-paying policies for term insurance. They usually carry the lowest price. Besides, any dividends on term policies are usually small.

Choose the cash-value policy that gives the best value for your age, whether dividend-paying or not. All things being equal, the dividend policy might have an edge. But it doesn't make much difference any more.

·   ·   ·

FIVE WAYS OF HANDLING INSURANCE-POLICY DIVIDENDS:

1. Take the money in cash. (It's not taxed, unless you have a modified-endowment policy or the dividends exceed the premiums you've paid.)

2. Use the dividends to reduce your annual premium.

3. Leave the dividends with the insurance company to earn interest. The interest will be taxable, just as bank interest is, and you can withdraw the money at any time. Your survivors get the dividends and interest as well as the policy's death benefit.

4. Buy small, "paid-up" additions to your cash-value policy (you cannot get them with term insurance.) There's no medical exam, so this is an especially good choice for people in poor health. It's also smart for people who will need more insurance, because you don't pay sales commissions. The coverage lasts for life, and gives you some inflation protection.

5. Buy extra term insurance, good for one year. Only a few companies offer this option, but it can be a valuable one, if the rates are low.

PAYING PREMIUMS

It's cheapest to pay premiums annually or through monthly payments drawn automatically from your bank account. You can also pay semi-annually, quarterly, or monthly by check—each one costing a bit more.

You pay into universal-life policies any time you want. If you skip some payments, the insurance charges will be taken out of your cash values.

THE GRACE PERIOD

Insurers continue to cover you for 31 days after the date the premium was due. If you die during this period, your survivors get the full payoff, minus the missing premium.

INCONTESTABILITY

Once you've held a life-insurance policy for two years, it's generally impregnable. Your survivors get the payoff, even if you made minor misstatements on your application.

If you misstated your age, the payout will be adjusted to reflect how old you really were. Tell your beneficiaries where to find proof of your age, in case a mistake is made on your death certificate.

There is an exception for fraud. The company can refuse to pay if you blatantly and deliberately lied on your application, and if the insurer is prepared to prove it by going to court. In that case, your survivors' claims may be denied.

SUICIDE

Your survivors get no payoff if you kill yourself within one or two years after taking out the policy (the exact time limit depends on the company and state law). The insurer merely pays your premiums back, sometimes with interest. But after that, you can swallow poison or jump out a window and your survivors will collect in full. Aren't you glad you asked?

PAID-UP POLICIES

Premium payments normally last until your 100th birthday. But you can arrange for the policy to be "paid up" (meaning fully paid for) over a shorter period. For example, you might want it paid up by the time you're 65, or paid up in 10 years. The sooner you want the policy paid for, the higher the premiums will be. Your contract guarantees that you'll be done with all payments after a fixed period of time.

Much iffier is the policy known as *vanishing premium*. You think you'll stop paying at, say, age 65. But that depends on the policy's dividends, expenses, and mortality charges. None of these items is guaranteed. If dividends fall (and they very well might), you'll have to pay premiums for a longer time than you expected. *Ask about this! The agent doesn't always tell you!*

POLICY LOANS

You can borrow from the insurance company, using as collateral the cash value of your insurance policy. If you die without repaying the loan, the loan proceeds and all the compounded interest are deducted from the death benefit. So your survivors get less.

Life-insurance loans are said to be cheap, cheap, cheap. Older policies may charge 4.5 to 6 percent interest. Newer ones charge 8 percent, or a variable rate linked to market conditions. *But all these loans are more expensive than you think!* Here's why.

The insurance company pays interest on all your cash values every year, even if you have a loan outstanding. But it pays less on the cash that you borrowed against. Say, for example, that you have $20,000 in the policy and borrow $5,000 at 8 percent interest. At the end of the year, the company may credit $15,000 of your cash values with 8.5 interest, but the remaining $5,000 may be credited with only 5 percent interest. So your true cost of borrowing comes to 11.5 percent—the 8 percent stated loan interest plus the 3.5 percent that wasn't credited to your cash values. Ask about this, any time you take a loan.

What about a "zero percent" loan? The insurer pays, say, 8 percent on your cash value and charges 8 percent for your loan—so it's a wash, right? Wrong. Don't kid yourself. Bottom line, you've paid a real 8 percent, because you'd have *earned* 8 percent if you hadn't borrowed.

With a variable-life policy, the cash you borrowed against is transferred to a low-interest account. That might prevent the death benefit from going up (page 268).

With a universal policy, it may be cheaper to withdraw money from the cash value than to borrow against it—especially if you expect to keep the loan for a long time. You can probably withdraw a substantial amount before incurring any income taxes (but check with your agent). One problem: Taking out cash might erode your policy from within. Be sure that you're keeping enough money there to prevent your premiums from going up.

If you have a policy with a low, 5 or 6 percent borrowing rate, and choose not to borrow against it, it's probably costing you money. Many companies pay lower dividends on these policies, whether you have a loan or not. Solve the problem in one of two ways.

1. Find out if the company will raise your dividends if you'll accept

a higher interest rate on loans. If you don't plan to borrow, it doesn't matter what the loan rate is.

2. If you can't get higher dividends, borrow every nickel you can from the policy and invest it for a higher return. Or throw in the towel and switch companies.

Here are the rules on tax deducting the interest you pay on life insurance loans.

• If you don't pay the interest out of pocket, but simply let it compound inside the policy: It's not tax deductible.

• If you pay the interest out of pocket and use the loan for college or consumer purchases: It's not deductible.

• If you pay the interest and use the proceeds to make other investments: You can deduct the interest to the extent that you have net income from investments.

• If you pay the interest and use the money in your business: It's probably deductible in full, but check with your accountant.

If you have a modified endowment contract, your loan (as well as any withdrawals) creates taxable income, up to the amount that the policy has earned. You'll also pay a 10 percent penalty, unless you're over age 59½ or disabled.

QUITTING

If you cancel a cash-value policy, you'll get some money back. There are three things you can do with it.

1. Put the cash in your pocket. You'll owe income taxes on any gains (page 292).

2. Buy a smaller, paid-up insurance policy. It will sit there for life, without your putting any more money in (although inflation will erode its purchasing power).

3. Convert the policy to term insurance. You'll be covered for as long as the money lasts. The price of this "extended term" option is usually high, so choose it only if you're ill and think you won't outlive the benefit. Otherwise, buy a new policy from another company.

COLLECTING

When cashing in a policy, or collecting its death benefit, there are usually five ways of taking the money. Don't lock your beneficiary into any one of these options in advance. You can't predict which one will work out the best.

1. *A lump sum.* This is best for small payments, for money you will need to live on, or for people who want to invest the proceeds themselves.

2. *Interest only.* You park the money until you decide what to do with it. The principal is invested with the insurance company; you receive regular interest payments. Parking makes sense only if the insurance company pays as well as a bank and if you can take the principal any time you want.

3. *Installment payments.* The insurance company pays you in regular installments of interest and principal. You can arrange for a fixed amount per month or for payments over a fixed period of time. You want a competitive rate of interest and the right to change the size of the payments when it suits you.

4. *An annuity.* This method of payment guarantees you (or you plus a spouse or partner) a fixed and guaranteed monthly income for life. You can also arrange for payments to go to a beneficiary if you die before a certain number of years have elapsed (typically 10). But inflation will eat up fixed payments that last for much more than 10 years. So you wouldn't want the bulk of your money in an annuity, unless you're, say, over 75. Nor would you choose an annuity if you're in poor health, because you might not live long enough to collect very much.

Before converting your insurance proceeds into an annuity with the same company, check what other insurers are offering. Some companies pay much more per month than others (page 803). You might raise your income by taking your payout in a lump sum and buying an annuity from someone else.

If you buy from the same company that carried the life-insurance policy, ask if you're getting "settlement-option" rates. They should be better than regular annuity rates. And make sure that your monthly payment is fully guaranteed. Some companies guarantee only a minimum payment, with the rest of your income linked to the size of the company's dividend.

5. *The deal du jour.* Most quality companies will offer beneficiaries a particularly low-cost deal on any one of the options above, or on a combination of options. These deals vary with corporate policy and market conditions.

SECOND-TO-DIE INSURANCE

These policies are for well-to-do married couples (often, joint owners of a business) who want extra cash to cover the death tax. No tax is generally due when the first spouse dies, because the second spouse inherits. It's when the second spouse dies that Uncle Sam takes his cut.

Enter second-to-die insurance. It insures both lives but pays off only at the second death. The premium is lower than if you bought separate policies, one for each. Still, separate policies may be the better choice. The surviving spouse may need money immediately. Or the surviving spouse might want to invest the life-insurance proceeds, for a much larger payoff in the long run.

If you do decide on a second-to-die policy, it should probably be paid into an irrevocable trust, so as not to be taxed in your estate. The trust buys assets from the estate; that gives the estate the cash it needs to pay the tax. Don't rely on an insurance agent to structure this arrangement for you. See a tax attorney who specializes in estate planning.

Before buying, check what will happen to your insurance if interest rates fall. You may have to pay higher premiums than you expected, or pay over a longer period of time.

Also, look at your options if you get divorced or if tax laws change. You should be able to split the entire policy into separate coverage for each of you, without having to pass a health exam. There should be no fee for the split, and no sales commissions on the new policies.

INSURANCE ALIVE

It's a pity that the only way to collect on your life insurance is to die. Such a pity that the industry dreamed up a product that pays off while you're still alive.

With a "living benefits" policy, you can withdraw some of the face value if you're struck by one of half a dozen dread diseases (stroke, terminal cancer, Alzheimer's, heart attack, kidney failure) or dread operations (cardiac bypass, organ transplant). Other policies pay if you're diagnosed as having only 6 to 12 months to live. Yet others supply monthly benefits if you enter a nursing home for the rest of your life.

Living benefits are available only with cash-value policies, not with term insurance. They are packaged as part of the policies themselves or sold separately as a rider. Some policies charge 5 to 15 percent more than regular whole-life. Or you might pay the regular premium, plus an extra charge if you take early payouts.

Who might be interested? (1) Those at risk for AIDS. (2) The middle-aged who worry about serious illnesses. A nursing-home rider may actually be cheaper than buying separate nursing-home insurance—but check the provisions to be sure of getting top coverage (page 326).

It's important to note that living benefits are strictly a luxury, for people who have money to spare. Here's why.

You need a larger-than-normal policy. The benefits have to be large enough to cover your potential withdrawal and still leave enough for your survivors. If you can't afford the extra insurance, stay away from living-benefits life.

You need a good disability-income policy before even considering this coverage. Disability insurance covers all illnesses, not just a few.

If you don't need life insurance (because you have no dependents), or don't need cash-value insurance (because you will only need a policy for a few years, until your children are grown), you don't need living-benefits life. Never pay for unnecessary coverage just to get an incidental benefit that would be nice to have. One exception: Those at risk of getting AIDS. A handful of companies buy the policies of the terminally ill, paying 50 to 70 percent of face value. So a substantial life-insurance policy can provide you with money when you need it most.

RATING YOU FOR RISK

You don't smoke? Good news. You will live longer, and you will get a break on your insurance rates (page 258).

At some insurance companies, nonsmokers are further divided into preferred and nonpreferred risks. Preferred nonsmokers pay the least. If you're paying the standard nonsmoker rate, you may not be getting the lowest price.

Expect to pay more if you've recently had cancer or a heart attack, have other serious health problems, or go skydiving on weekends. You're what the industry calls a "rated" risk. People with AIDS, or the HIV antibodies that announce the likelihood of developing AIDS, will find it almost impossible to get life insurance at all.

Companies normally do blood and urine tests on people applying for at least $100,000 worth of life insurance, and sometimes for policies as small as $50,000. Besides disease, they look for hard drugs, for liver damage that can reveal a problem drinker, and for nicotine in the blood of people claiming not to smoke. If your condition is suspect, they may order more tests.

HERE'S WHAT TO DO IF YOU'RE A RATED RISK.

1. Don't meekly accept a higher premium on an individual policy. Shop around. One company might quote a high price to a person with high blood pressure. Another—believing that the condition is under control—might give that same person a standard rate.

2. Don't work with the captive insurance agent of a single company. He or she will rarely get you the best price. Go to an independent agent. In fact, go to two. They typically work with different companies. If each of them knows that someone else is bidding for the business, they'll both work a little harder for you.

3. Look for trade or professional groups you can join. There's usually a medical questionnaire, but your rate may be lower than you'd get on an individual policy.

4. Try to buy extra coverage through your employer.

5. If your health has improved, shop around again for coverage. A person who had a stroke five years ago, with no further symptoms or recurrence, might get a new policy at a standard rate. The same might be true five years after a heart attack, or after being cured of certain types of cancer.

6. If you can't get normal coverage, even at a higher price, look at "guaranteed-acceptance" insurance that signs up all comers. These are not great policies. They're expensive, and your beneficiary runs a high risk of never collecting a dime. But if you're interested, and your state allows their sale, the policies fall into two main classes.

NO QUESTIONS ASKED. You can usually buy up to $25,000 in coverage, just by signing a check. But you have to live for a while to collect in full. Some policies merely repay your premium (plus interest) if you die in the first two years. Others pay graded benefits: 10 to 30 percent of the death benefit if you die in the first year, 25 to 60 percent in the second year, and full payment from the third or fourth year on.

SOME QUESTIONS ASKED. You can get up to $100,000 of coverage if you don't have AIDS and worked full time for the past six months. But again, you're paid graded benefits. Full coverage doesn't take effect until you've lasted three years.

7. In many states, you can still buy credit-life insurance even on your deathbed. You might, for example, buy a car on credit and insure

the loan. When you die, the insurance company will pay. But credit-life policies are growing more restrictive—so don't buy one without checking all the limitations on payment (page 261).

WOMEN AND RISK

On average, women live longer than men, so they normally get lower life-insurance rates. But how much lower? Some companies arbitrarily charge the male rate minus three years. That's okay for younger women, but not for women age 50 and up. Where companies have developed separate female mortality tables, older women pay roughly the same as men who are five or six years younger.

Montana and Massachusetts are special cases. They have "unisex" rules that average women's rates with men's. In those states, women pay more. Woman can buy cheaper policies out of state, but only from insurance companies not licensed to do business in their states. Buying from such companies diminishes your consumer protection.

SHOULD YOU SWITCH POLICIES?

This is one of the hottest arguments in life insurance today. When you switch policies, you pay the sales commission and other expenses all over again. That's good for the insurance agent but bad for you, unless you get a better deal. In general, five types of switching are going on.

SWITCH ONE. You have a small cash-value policy and trade it in for a larger amount of term insurance. This makes sense for a family that shouldn't have bought cash-value insurance in the first place. You need more coverage and term is the only way to get it. But a switch isn't the only solution. If your cash-value policy is yielding a high return, it might be better to keep it and buy a big term-insurance policy on the side.

(Watch out for the A. L. Williams group, now known as Primerica Financial Services, which specializes in Switch Ones. Its term insurance, from the Massachusetts Indemnity and Life Insurance Company [MILICO], is usually packaged with a mutual fund. MILICO's 20-year term policies are not cheap, no matter what its agents say to the contrary. You can find lower-cost coverage through the insurance-quote services on page 259. Furthermore, the Primerica agents may present a misleading comparison between your present cash-value policy and the MILICO plan—principally by leaving out all your dividends, so your present policy appears to be worth much less than is really the case. Ask NICO what return you're getting on your policy before cashing it in for a MILICO plan—see page 274.)

SWITCH TWO. You have a term-insurance policy and find another one with a much lower premium. This is a no-brainer. Switch. In fact, you should check term-insurance rates every five years or so, to find cheaper coverage. Companies with low rates for young people may not be the best for the middle-aged.

SWITCH THREE. You have an older whole-life policy, and your agent suggests that you switch to a newer one or to universal-life. This may make sense, especially if your old policy pays no dividends. The newer ones charge lower premiums and build cash values faster.

The downside is that you'll pay another sales commission. The cost comes out of your cash value, so you'll lose some money on the switch. Your new policy has to do *much* better than your old one did, just to raise your cash value to the amount you had before.

Consider replacing:

· Nondividend-paying policies that are at least 7 to 10 years old. They probably aren't paying high enough interest rates.

· Some older dividend policies. Long-time policyholders may be earning a much lower rate of interest than new buyers get. The better policies have updated their dividends, however, to give their older customers a better shake.

· Small policies. It might be cheaper to consolidate them into one large policy.

· Certain paid-up policies, especially if they pay no dividends. They may contain enough cash to buy a new paid-up policy for the same face value, with some money left over for an outside investment.

SWITCH FOUR. You have been paying your premiums with money borrowed against your policy's cash values. That's not smart anymore, now that the tax deduction for loan-interest payments has been phased out. What should you do with that old policy, which is costing you interest every year?

1. You can die. Not recommended.

2. You can start paying premiums out of pocket, and use each year's dividends to reduce your loan. This makes sense if your policy pays high interest rates on your cash value.

3. You can cancel the policy and start all over again with pure term

insurance. You'd owe income taxes on the difference between the policy's cash value (including all the money you borrowed against it) and the amount you put into it.

4. You can switch. Swap to another policy in the same company, or in a different company. Some insurers have even created a special "exchange policy" to bail you out. It might offer the same face value but a lower cash value and lower loan. Or you might wind up with less insurance and a lower cash value, but no loan at all. *If you're healthy, avoid exchange policies that don't require a medical exam.* Such policies cost more than you ought to be paying.

As of this writing, the Internal Revenue Service hasn't said whether a swap that reduces your loan is taxable. Most insurers are gambling that it won't be. Before you buy, ask if the IRS has ruled. If not, and this risk worries you, carry over your loan to the new policy and start using your higher dividends to pay it off.

SWITCH FIVE. Your insurer is in trouble and you want out. You'll lose some of your cash values, but may save your coverage overall.

ABOVE ALL, APPROACH WITH CAUTION ANY COMPARISON SHOWN YOU BY AGENTS WHO WANT YOU TO SWITCH. There are a dozen ways to mislead you and lay persons can't possibly spot the lie. Every day, unprincipled agents churn the assets in somebody's insurance policy, in order to earn a sales commission. Too many Americans are innocently turning in good policies that they ought to keep.

NEVER SWITCH POLICIES WITHOUT MAKING THE FOLLOWING TWO CHECKS.

• Talk to the agent who sold you your present policy (or someone from the same company). He or she may show you how to get more mileage from coverage you have now, and at a better price. For example, you might:

1. Get a higher dividend on an old policy, by agreeing to give up a 5 or 6 percent policy loan rate.

2. Take advantage of a low loan rate by borrowing against the policy and reinvesting the money in a higher-paying certificate of deposit or mutual fund. This improves your total yield. The loan interest should be tax deductible (page 282).

3. Switch to a paid-up status. You'll get a smaller policy on which no more premiums are due. But it may pay a higher yield on cash values than you'd get from a policy that you started new.

4. If you're strapped for cash, lower your out-of-pocket cost by borrowing against the cash values to pay your premiums.

· Get a copy of the agent's proposed switcheroo and a copy of the in-force ledger statement for your present policy. If the two policies have similar premiums and face amounts, compare their annual increase in cash values, to see which seems best. Or send the statements to the National Insurance Consumer Organization for analysis (page 274). NICO will tell you whether a switch makes sense—and if so, might suggest a better company to switch to.

DEALING WITH A LIFE INSURANCE AGENT

This subject makes my heart sink. Yes, there are many splendid life-insurance agents in the United States. Yes, they can do wonderful work for you. Yes, agents with a Chartered Life Underwriter (CLU) designation usually know more about insurance than agents without.

It's just that when I interview agents (including CLUs) about policies, I often run into problems. Some agents don't know a lot about their policies and bluff. Some agents have been trained to mislead and are too thick to know it. Some agents know it and don't care. Some agents say they'll shop the market for you and don't. Some agents resist new information and ideas. Some agents assume that everyone needs to buy something, which often isn't true. Some agents mean well but are sincerely and honestly wrong. Some agents have blind spots. Some agents will say anything to close a sale. (Sales commissions run from about 50 percent to more than 100 percent of your first premium, plus substantial percentages of your renewal premiums, and maybe a bonus trip to Hawaii.)

On the other hand, some agents search out good policies, go to bat for you with the company, understand what they're selling, have smart ideas, don't press you to buy, supply you with information, admit to what they don't know, and research your questions to find the right answers.

I don't know how one finds a smart, straightforward insurance agent. You ask around. You listen to proposals. You ask the agent questions—about which companies he or she represents, how he or she investigates them for soundness, what kinds of policies he or she likes, and why. You think about whether the answers ring true. You carry a lighted lamp against the dark.

The best defense is always a good offense. Don't buy solely on an agent's say-so. Read the brochure that comes with the agent's proposal and get an explanation for everything that puzzles you.

Even then, don't close the deal solely on the strength of what you see in the brochure, because it won't tell you the whole story. Get a sample policy and read it. If the agent won't give you one, find another agent. (You could wait to read your policy until the agent delivers it. If you don't like it, you have 10 days to cancel and get your money back. But at that point you're probably committed. It's better to do your reading in advance.)

Deciphering some policies is like cracking code. But plow through the paragraphs, putting questions marks on sections you don't understand. Don't worry about wasting the agent's time—you're paying the commission and are entitled. Study all the conditions and exclusions. Ask how the policy's projected cash values were arrived at. Ask whether any gimmicks were used (page 269). If anything bothers you, bail out.

For comparison, get a universal-life proposal from both USAA and Ameritas (page 273). Ask your agent if—using the same premium and death benefit *and a no-gimmicks illustration*—he or she can produce better coverage and cash values. Check it out with NICO, to be sure that no gimmicks were actually used.

Keep all your correspondence with the insurance agent, all the sales literature, and all the policy illustrations. You may need them, if the policy goes sour.

Many financial planners also sell life insurance. All the caveats about insurance agents apply to planners, too. For more on planners, see page 828.

CELEBRITY INSURANCE

Dick Van Dyke, say it isn't so. Gavin MacLeod, how could you?

You've seen them all over cable TV, promoting "low-cost life insurance" to older people—duping healthy seniors into buying a policy that, for them, is a waste of money. The insurance might cost around five dollars a month, regardless of your health. But that money doesn't buy a lot of coverage—perhaps $500 for a 65-year-old, and less as you get older. At age 70, your coverage might drop to only $350. By age 71, you'd have paid a total of $360, for coverage worth only $350. After that, every month you keep that foolish policy, you're losing money.

It gets worse. If you die of natural causes during the first two years, these policies won't pay a dime. You're covered only if you die in an accident.

So don't go near celebrity policies. The stars who promote them ought to be ashamed. The only people who should remotely consider this coverage are the sick, who need to leave more money to their dependents, who can't get other coverage, expect to live for two years, but expect to die in three or four years. That's almost nobody.

MAIL ORDER INSURANCE

If you get an unasked-for solicitation in the mail, selling *any* kind of insurance, toss it. Mail-order policies are the creeps of the crop—including those offered by big-name insurers and through banks or credit card companies.

Typically, mail-order policies are overpriced for the amount of coverage they offer. Typically, the benefits are minor—and may even overlap coverage you already have. Typically, they're stuffed with exclusions. Mail-order insurance tends to give you only the illusion of protection.

There are a few exceptions to my general grumpiness about mail order. You might welcome an insurance mailer put out by a trade or professional group you've joined. Some excellent companies, like USAA, also do business by mail—but they respond to a call from a customer rather than blanket the country with solicitations.

As a general rule, don't buy. Here are the phrases to beware of: "Group Insurance!" "Low Cost!" "Cash Benefits!" "Valuable Protection!" "Can't Be Turned Down!" "Costs Just Pennies a Day!" Cruelly misleading, every word.

INSURANCE AND TAXES

Here's everything you didn't want to know about the taxes due on your life insurance.

The interest paid on your cash values accumulates in the policy tax deferred. That's a plus for people in high tax brackets, less exciting for people in low ones.

Insurance-policy dividends are not taxed until they exceed the policy's premiums. Until then, they're treated as a return of the money you paid in.

You pay no taxes on money borrowed against traditional policies. If you actually withdraw some cash—as you might with universal policies—some taxes may be due. Ask your agent about it.

Single-premium policies issued after June 20, 1988, as well as other policies that allow a fast cash buildup, are a special case. They're known as "modified endowment policies." If you own one, you owe income taxes on loans you take against the policy, up to the amount that the policy has earned. Ditto for any money received when pledging your policy as collateral. You owe a further 10 percent penalty on loans or withdrawals made before age 59½ (unless you're totally disabled; in that case, you owe taxes but no penalty).

If you die owning a life insurance policy, the proceeds go into your taxable estate. But there is no federal death tax if you're worth less than $600,000; if your estate is going to your spouse; or if, before you died, you gave the policy to someone else, like your children or a trust (but the proceeds will be taxed to your estate if you die within three years of making the gift). State inheritance taxes may be due on estates worth less than $600,000.

Your beneficiaries receive the proceeds of the policy income-tax free.

If you cash in the policy, you'll be taxed on the extent to which the cash value exceeds all the premiums you paid, minus any dividends not used to buy more insurance. This is one clear advantage that cash-value insurance has over term insurance plus outside savings. The money you earn on your cash values is tax sheltered by the premiums you pay. *But don't let the tax break blind you to high costs and commissions.*

STICK WITH SUPER-SAFE COMPANIES

Buying insurance is an act of faith. When you die—in 30 or 40 or 50 years—you expect some young kid, not yet born, to be there at the computer, sending your family a check.

So far, that's been a good bet. But in recent years, the number of insurance companies with financial problems has been going up.

What would happen if your life insurance company failed?

• Your policies might be bought by another company. Your payout would be safe. But your premiums could rise, and your cash values might not accumulate as fast as they did before.

• If no one buys your policy, you might be protected by an industry-supported guaranty fund that steps in to pay if the insurer can't. At this writing, all but three states (Colorado, Louisiana, and New Jersey) and the District of Columbia have them. But large policies aren't covered.

States typically cap payments on an individual policy at $100,000 for cash values or annuities, $300,000 for death benefits, and $300,000 for all claims combined. In a truly major bankruptcy, however, these funds don't work. They are simply not fat enough. Instead, major companies in the industry try to arrange a bailout. In the meantime, your cash values will probably be frozen and some claims may not be paid.

· If your state has no guaranty fund, and your policy isn't bought, you're up the creek—as happened a few years ago to a group of older policyholders in Tennessee, before its fund began. They had purchased insurance when they were young; during their lifetimes, they paid for the coverage in full. But in their old age, their insurer failed.

When that happens, claims might eventually be paid, out of the assets of the bankrupt company. But all the certainty drains away. Besides, by the time the mess is straightened out you might be dead.

· Even if your company doesn't fail, a weak balance sheet could mean lower dividends and skimpier cash values in the years ahead. Cash-value investors might not get the returns they expected. Term-policy buyers might have to pay more for their coverage.

So buy only from a company with high quality ratings: AAA from Standard & Poor or Duff & Phelps, Aaa from Moody's, and A-plus from A. M. Best. For the finest roundup anywhere of both safe and questionable life, health, and property-insurance companies, send $10 for the September 1990 issue of the newsletter *The Insurance Forum*, P.O. Box 245, Ellettsville, IN, 47429. It lists all the companies given top marks by the various ratings agencies—A. M. Best, Moody's, Standard & Poor's, and Duff & Phelps; all the companies whose A. M. Best ratings declined from 1989 to 1990; and all the companies showing abnormal financial ratios, which might be under surveillance by the state insurance commissioners.

If your company slips in the ratings and doesn't recover, think about switching. Baldwin-United's insurance companies, major sellers of annuities, failed in 1983 with an A. M. Best rating of A. Since then, A. M. Best has been reviewing insurer's financial data more often.

Here's the real shocker: *You generally have no control over which company ultimately owns your insurance policy or annuity.* You might shop diligently for an A-plus insurer. But in most states, that company can transfer your policy to any other insurance company it wants, without your permission. Some policyholders have been transferred to companies that ultimately failed. They are suing for damages.

If you get a letter saying that your policy is being transferred, check the new company's safety rating. If it's not up to snuff, refuse, write a letter to your company saying, "I won't go." Then call your state's insurance commission and complain that you're being transferred against your will. The commission may arrange for you to stay with the company you first chose. If not, transfer your business to a better company through a tax-free exchange. Your new company will tell you how to do that.

WHEN ALL IS SAID AND DONE, HOW WOULD I BUY LIFE INSURANCE?

I'd stick with low-cost term insurance, expecting to cancel it when I retire or when my kids are grown and my spouse is self-supporting. I'd buy it through a telephone-quote service.

I'd build up investments somewhere else—in no-load stock-owning mutual funds, Treasury securities, retirement funds, and real estate—to guarantee my security.

I'd check my "free" insurance (page 777). Social Security pays an income to: (1) surviving spouses age 60 and up and disabled spouses 50 and up who have not remarried (a spouse who remarries a Social Security recipient can still collect on the first spouse's account if it pays more); (2) unremarried surviving spouses caring for the worker's child who is under 16 or was disabled before age 22; (3) unmarried dependent children under 18, or under 19 if still in secondary school; (4) parents 62 and older who got at least half their support from the worker who died. There's also a lump-sum death benefit of $255.

If I got a proposal from a life-insurance agent, I'd ask the National Insurance Consumer Organization (NICO) to evaluate it.

If I wanted to accumulate some money in a cash-value policy, or needed lifetime coverage for personal, business or estate-tax reasons, I'd go with USAA Life, Ameritas, or another policy NICO suggested.

If I had some employee coverage, a small cash-value policy, and a family, I would hastily buy more term insurance to protect them.

If I owned an old cash-value policy, especially one that paid no dividends, I'd have it evaluated by NICO, to see if I should switch.

I'd buy insurance only from a company rated A-plus by A. M. Best for the past 10 years.

I'd pay the premiums on my term life insurance policy even in hard times. I owe it to the people who depend on me.

13

TO YOUR
GOOD HEALTH:

*Avoiding a Heart Attack
over Medical Bills*

___

You're paying more and getting less. That's the
story of our times.

When it comes to decent medical
coverage, Americans are cleanly divided into "haves" and "have nots."
The "haves" work for companies that pick up most employee medical
costs. The "have nots" have to cover their own.

As neatly as dominoes, the "have nots" are divided, too. They can
either afford comprehensive coverage or they can't. Anyone who can't
should at least try to insure against major illnesses. There's almost no
tolerance left in the medical system for charity patients.

No matter who pays, your insurer either allows you to choose your
own doctor and plan of treatment, or it doesn't. If not, you will need
permission for surgery and certain other forms of care. If you ignore these
rules, you won't be reimbursed in full.

IF YOU WORK FOR A BIG COMPANY . . .

You're a lucky duck. Your insurance is probably the best that America has to offer, and in most cases you qualify without passing a medical exam. Still, group-health insurance is being pared away at the edges, to counter soaring costs.

READ ALL THE BORING MEMOS THAT COME FROM YOUR COMPANY'S EMPLOYEE BENEFITS OFFICE! They announce new procedures. If you don't follow all the rules, your medical bills might not get paid. Increasingly, you have to:

• Pay $150 or more for every person in the family (up to a $300 ceiling), before the company plan kicks in.

• Pay 10 or 20 percent of your hospital bills, up to a ceiling of $2,000.

• Pay a larger percentage of the health-insurance premium that applies to your dependents.

• Choose a doctor from a list approved by the insurance company. These doctors have agreed to treat you at a lower price. You're always free to see someone else, but the company won't pay that bill. (Some companies still pay for outside doctors, but at a reduced rate.)

• Get permission from the insurer to enter the hospital for nonemergency treatment. The insurer has rules on how long you can stay for any procedure. If you overstay, without permission, your company won't pay.

• Undergo certain operations, like tonsillectomies and cataract removal, in a clinic or doctor's office, not a hospital. If you insist on a hospital, your company won't pay the whole bill.

• Join a health maintenance organization (HMO—see page 306). Some employee plans will pay part of the bill for doctors outside the HMO network; others won't pay a dime.

IF BOTH HUSBAND AND WIFE HAVE EMPLOYEE PLANS, and you don't have children, you each may pay little or nothing for your own health insurance. Your costs start to rise, however, when you have dependents to take care of.

Family benefits typically cost you 10 to 30 percent of the annual premium, with the employer picking up the rest. Here's how to decide whether to pay for one family plan or two.

1. Normally, you'd pay only for the better plan, after comparing them point by point. The other spouse would take no family benefits. (Memo to the other spouse: Find out how to reclaim those benefits, in case you're divorced or your spouse dies.)

2. You might pay for both plans, if the premiums are low and your

children (and spouse) can be covered by both simultaneously. The bills not paid by one spouse's plan—including the deductible—are picked up by the other plan. The children's bills generally go first to the plan of the spouse whose birthday falls earlier in the year. Any unpaid expenses are then submitted to the second plan. If your employer doesn't follow the birthday rule, here's another idea: One spouse could choose an HMO while the other takes a traditional plan. The HMO offers more services; the traditional plan offers more choice. You could treat your child through one or the other, depending on the illness.

3. You're in clover if one spouse has a "cafeteria plan." That lets you pick what you want from a long list of employee benefits. One of you might choose family health insurance, while the other takes extra savings or child care, if the employer offers them.

If your company plan has a lifetime top of $250,000, you're underinsured. A few insurers sell high-limit "major medical" policies, to cover devastating illnesses up to $500,000 or even $1 million, with a deductible of $25,000 or so. This type of insurance may not cost very much and buys a lot of peace of mind. Alternatively, petition your company to raise its maximum.

IF YOU WORK FOR A SMALL COMPANY . . .

You may not have coverage at all. If you do, it probably won't be as comprehensive as big companies offer. To qualify, both you and your dependents will have to fill in a health questionnaire. The insurer may decide to accept you, accept most of you (excluding certain preexisting medical conditions, temporarily or permanently), accept some of you (you, but not your diabetic child), or reject you entirely. In the last case, your employer might buy you a separate policy, if you're insurable at all.

Rates often rise rapidly on small-company health policies. After a few years, your present plan might cost more than your company can afford. Responsible employers switch to a new insurer that will cover every employee, even those with medical problems. But sometimes, the sick get dropped during the switch. Or your company may decide that it can't afford health insurance, period, and cancel out. In that case, you might be given a chance to convert your group policy into individual coverage. But some states allow insurers to drop you flat.

Small-company coverage is scandalously insecure. In general, you're safest if your company carries (and doesn't cancel) Blue Cross/Blue Shield or an HMO, and at the greatest risk if you're in a Multiple Employer Welfare Association, many of which have collapsed.

LEAVING YOUR COMPANY

IF YOU LEAVE YOUR JOB, AND DON'T COME UNDER A NEW GROUP-HEALTH PLAN, YOU CAN PROBABLY KEEP YOUR OLD PLAN AT YOUR EXPENSE. This rule applies at almost all companies that employ 20 or more people. You're allowed up to 18 months of group coverage if you quit, are laid off, have your hours reduced to less than part time, even if you're fired—as long as it's not for "gross misconduct." You pay the group-health premium, plus up to 2 percent. If you leave your job because you're totally disabled, you can keep the group plan for up to 29 months, but might be charged as much as 50 percent extra.

Large company or small, you may be able to convert your group plan to individual insurance without a medical exam. But conversion policies are hugely expensive and don't offer much in the way of benefits. Convert only if you or a family member is so ill that you can't get coverage somewhere else.

If you die and leave a spouse in poor health, that spouse might also have the right to convert to an individual plan.

IF YOU'RE BUYING YOUR OWN INSURANCE . . .

My condolences. Good health insurance does not exist at a bargain price—especially when you have a family. And in recent years, insurers have hired Abominable No-Men to choose the health risks they'll insure. Some day, the tragedy of the uninsured and underinsured will surely spark a political revolt.

You must make every sacrifice to buy health insurance. I've heard too many stories about families wiped out by a breadwinner's cancer, a newborn's deformity, a paralyzing automobile accident. *Buy personal health insurance coverage while you're still healthy!* If you wait until you're sick, you'll pay much more for a policy—if you can get one at all.

The Best Buys and the Cheapest Ways In

✓ *Buy group insurance.* Many organizations offer health insurance to members: professional groups, trade groups, even political-action and social-responsibility groups. Group coverage generally costs less than individual coverage—but not always. Compare both the price and the benefits with what you can get from Blue Cross/Blue Shield or other private policies.

You'll probably have to answer some health questions, both for yourself and for your dependents. Anyone with AIDS or certain other serious illnesses will usually be turned down.

Other problems—like a bad back—might not be covered for a year, or might be excluded from the policy entirely. If you neglect to mention an illness, and it crops up during the one- or two-year period when the insurer has the right to contest your claim, those particular bills might not be covered. Your policy might even be canceled and your premiums refunded.

Avoid a policy that won't cover the very illness you're the most likely to get. Shop other group and individual plans. Accept the exclusion only if there's no alternative.

There are some drawbacks to group insurance.

First, your policy can be canceled right out from under you, on very short notice. This is happening more frequently, as medical costs rise and group policies grow less profitable. Sometimes the group finds another insurer, but sometimes it doesn't. Sometimes the new insurer picks up everyone covered under the old policy, but sometimes it doesn't. Individual policies, by contrast, normally aren't canceled.

Second, the price of group insurance may climb steeply from year to year. State regulators don't review rate increases in advance, as they do for individual coverage.

Third, group policies often have low maximum benefits. To top up your coverage, you might want to add a major-medical policy, with a $25,000 deductible and up to $1 million in lifetime protection.

Be suspicious of pitches for group policies that arrive, unsolicited, in the mail. They sound terrific up front, but are often riddled with unfair exclusions.

✓ *Look for unisex rates,* if you're a woman. Women generally pay more for their coverage than men. But some groups charge men and women the same.

✓ *Create your own group insurance.* If you're self-employed or a business owner, you can generally buy at group rates. But ask whether you're pooled with thousands of others. If not, your renewal rates may leap. For more stable costs, try Blue Cross/ Blue Shield or an HMO.

If you have an employee who's in poor health, some states let the insurer exclude him or her from the plan. Other states require that the whole group either be accepted or rejected (but the stricken employee can withdraw "voluntarily"). If the employee is insurable, consider buying him an individual policy and covering everyone else as a group.

Don't jump at a policy just because it's low-priced. Some insurers lure you with first-year bargain rates, then sock you with huge increases. You can always switch to another insurer as long as your workers stay in the pink of health. But if someone comes down sick, and won't be accepted by another plan, you might find yourself locked into a policy that you can't afford. Have a long chat with the agent about how the company does its pricing and what you can expect in the future.

✓ *Join a health maintenance organization (HMO)* (look for a listing in the Yellow Pages of your telephone book). HMOs generally cost less than traditional insurers. If they charge the same they should offer more benefits. But even HMOs are not the bargain they used to be, especially for the self-employed and small-business groups.

✓ *Check out Blue Cross/Blue Shield.* The first covers hospital bills, the second covers doctor bills. They're often cheaper than other private insurance companies—but not always. Where their price is lower, their coverage sometimes isn't as good. Get a price quote and list of benefits from the Blues, then ask an insurance agent if he or she can beat it. The Blues generally charge everyone of the same age and sex, in the same geographical area, the same price. So they're bargains for the unhealthy, but may be poorer buys for the thoroughly well.

✓ *Check out a preferred-provider organization (PPO).* These are available from some Blue Cross/Blue Shield plans and other insurance companies. You pay less for the coverage. But you're restricted to doctors who've joined the plan and the specialists they refer you to.

✓ *Get a "managed care" or "utilization review" policy.* They're available from a few health insurance companies and as riders to some of the Blue Cross/Blue Shield plans. Some Blues even build them right into their basic coverage.

With utilization review, you're subject to the rules that run many employee-group plans: mandatory second opinions, permission before undergoing nonemergency surgery, limits on hospital stays. For your trouble, you pay a lower premium. If you violate the terms of your managed-care plan, like getting elective surgery without permission, your insurer might pay only 50 percent of the usual insured amount.

Talk to at least two insurance agents about individual coverage. Some carry the lower-priced managed-care policies while others don't.

✓ *Take a health exam, if you can pass it.* Policies that refuse poor health risks are cheaper than policies that take all comers. Most insurers routinely do blood tests, for AIDS and other illnesses, and urine tests to check for drugs.

✓ *Take a big deductible.* A "deductible" is the amount you pay before your insurance policy takes over. The more small bills you cover yourself, the less your health insurance costs. At Time Insurance Company in Milwaukee, a policy with a $1,000 deductible might be 23 percent cheaper than one with only a $100 deductible.

Send all medical bills to your insurer, even though they're below the deductible. Your coverage will click in as soon as your bills exceed the limit. The deductible should be levied only once a year, and—on a family policy—only on the first two or three of you.

✓ *Share the cost with the insurer.* A policy that pays only 80 percent of certain hospital and doctor bills costs less than one that pays 100 percent. Typically, you'd pay 20 percent up to a ceiling, like $2,500. After that, the policy would pay in full. Policies without ceilings leave you vulnerable to huge bills.

✓ *Take a "service benefit."* Under this method of payment, your insurance covers a fixed percentage of each bill you present. The alternative is an "indemnity benefit," which pays a fixed sum toward each bill. "We pay 90 percent of the cost of a semiprivate room" is a service benefit. "We pay $200 a day when you're in the hospital" is an indemnity benefit.

Service benefits cost more because they cover more. Indemnity payments don't do nearly as much. If you can't afford a service benefit, however, an indemnity policy with a high daily hospital payment is your next best bet.

✓ *Take a "waiver of premium."* It's like an insurance policy. If a disabling accident or injury keeps you out of work, the waiver lets you quit paying health-insurance premiums while retaining your policy. Without the waiver, you might not be able to afford health insurance at the very time when you need it most.

✓ *Get a policy that's "guaranteed renewable."* This prevents the company from canceling your individual policy, or raising your premiums, just because your health goes bad. You need this protection! Don't accept any policy without it. At age 65, your coverage should be automatically convertible into a policy that fills the gaps in Medicare, again without having to pass a health exam.

Your premiums will go up every year, in line with your increasing age and the general rise in medical costs. But these price hikes will apply to all of the company's policies, not just to yours. Still, your coverage isn't 100 percent safe. Your company might decide to cancel an entire category of policies, yours included. In that case, however, many states require that you be offered replacement coverage without taking a health exam.

✓ *Tag along with your ex-company's plan.* Employee group-health insurance is a real bargain. If your company employs at least 20 people, and you leave your job for almost any reason, you can keep this insurance, at your expense, for up to 18 months (and up to 29 months if you're disabled.) Don't miss the deadline for getting this coverage! Your company has to send you a notice of eligibility, after which you have 60 days to sign up. The coverage ends as soon as you become eligible for another group plan or for Medicare.

✓ *Buy short-term coverage.* If you leave your job without health insurance, and don't move into a new employee plan, you're dangerously at risk. A sudden illness could wipe you out. So ask an insurance agent to find you a short-term health policy, with coverage up to six months. Many Blue Cross/Blue Shield plans also have short-term policies. Better yet, buy one of the Blues' regular policies, pay by the quarter, and keep the coverage for exactly as long as you want.

✓ *Watch for the introduction of bare-bones policies.* At this writing, they're generally not available. State laws prevent companies from offering individual-health policies with limited coverage. But the industry is working on ways to provide them. Better a well-designed, stripped-down policy that you can afford than none at all.

✓ *Talk to your parents.* Young people in low-paying jobs have a hard time paying their rent, let alone their health insurance. Feeling immortal, they often go without. Parents shouldn't let that happen. If your child got hurt, you would pay if you could—so buying your kid a health insurance policy protects your own financial plan.

✓ *Give blood.* When you donate blood to a blood bank, you're entitled to draw on it for yourself (and sometimes for a family member) at little or no cost.

✓ *Pay by the month.* The price may be just a tad higher than if you paid annually, but the size of each bite is a lot more manageable. Monthly payment plans are almost always set up to work automatically. Your bank deducts the premium from your checking account and sends the money to your insurer.

✓ *Ask about Medicaid.* States pay the medical bills for people with very low incomes.

The Money Words

The annual price you pay for the plan as a whole is called a *premium.* It's based on your age and sex, the number of people covered by your policy, the extent of your coverage, and where you live. Employee plans usually charge you a premium only when you add family members.

The *deductible* is the portion of the medical bill that you pay out of pocket each year, before the insurance coverage kicks in. Typically, it's $150 per person, up to a cap of $300 or $400 for the entire family.

Co-insurance is your share of any doctor or hospital bill. For example, you might pay 20 percent while the plan picks up 80 percent. There is usually a cap on your co-insurance—say, $1,000 per person per year or $2,500 in all—after which the policy picks up all of the covered bills.

Uninsured bills are those not covered: perhaps physical exams, well-baby checkups, and routine dental bills.

Health maintenance organizations charge only an annual premium, and sometimes a small extra cost for each office visit. There are normally no deductibles or co-insurance.

What Your Policy Should Cover

Don't ever assume that "everything is covered." It isn't. Inexpensive policies don't pay much at all, no matter what the advertising says. In general, here's what you should get from a comprehensive health insurance plan.

• *The full cost of basic hospital services* (minus your deductible and co-insurance). This includes a semiprivate room, board, emergency room, nurses, medicines, X-rays, and lab tests. If you take a private room, the extra cost is all yours.

• *The full cost of surgery,* including anesthesia and outpatient surgery.

Some policies, however, pay only a specified amount for each type of surgical procedure. Ask your doctor if he or she will accept that amount as the full fee.

• *Good coverage for children.* They should stay on your policy up to age 19, if they're not full-time students, and age 23 or 25, if they are. At some companies, even older children can be covered at your expense (page 318). Find out what happens if the child goes to school part-time or drops out for a year. Notify your insurer in writing if you're responsible for children who live elsewhere—for example, children who live with a former spouse.

• *Care for an infant from the moment it is born.* Some policies exclude neonatal ailments—a disgrace, but it's done. You generally have to notify the insurer of the new arrival within 30 days of birth for the child to continue to be covered under your family benefits.

• *Coverage for stepchildren and foster children,* if you're responsible for their support.

• *Most doctor bills,* in full or in part.

• *Part of the bill for convalescing in a nursing home,* after you've been in the hospital.

• *Part of the cost of prescription drugs.*

• *Part of the bill for home-health care* that is ordered by your doctor.

• *Part of the treatment for mental problems, drug abuse, and alcohol abuse,* although some plans are cutting this coverage back.

• *Most of the cost of incidental expenses:* private-duty nursing, physical therapy, oxygen, pacemakers and other medical devices, and so on.

• *Part of the cost of dental surgery.*

• *Elephant medical bills.* Many policies stop at $250,000. But that's insufficient, in these days of heart transplants and miracle rescues of premature infants. A maximum of $500,000 or even $1 million doesn't cost much more, because so few bills ever run that high.

• *Preexisting conditions.* A "preexisting condition" is a problem that was diagnosed or treated—or was manifestly obvious—any time from six months to three years before you bought the policy. Check this point, so you'll know exactly. The shorter the period, the better the policy. Big-company health plans usually start covering preexisting conditions within three months. But individual plans, or group plans offered by small companies or associations, may not pay these bills until a year has passed. Some plans wait two years—not a good choice. A few wait until you've passed one full year without needing treatment for that condition at all, which is a really rotten exclusion. A growing number of policies won't cover preexisting conditions at all—another reason why it's so important to get health insurance while you're still in good shape.

• *Continuing coverage for the family after the breadwinner's death.*

THE BARE-BONES POLICIES THAT INSURERS HOPE TO DEVELOP WOULDN'T COVER ALL THESE EXPENSES. They'd pay fixed benefits toward hospital and surgical bills, and leave out the frills like private-duty nursing, prescription drugs, and mental health. It won't be the Cadillac coverage that Americans have grown used to. But maybe we can't afford Cadillacs anymore.

Maternity Benefits

Some states require that all policies include maternity benefits. But where there's a choice, you might decide to pass them by. Maternity coverage usually carries a high deductible and might add 40 to 60 percent to your policy's price. It often pays to handle the maternity bill yourself. If you do buy the benefits, and have your baby less than a year later, your expenses may not be covered at all.

You do need insurance for complications of pregnancy, including Caesarian sections. But that's normally included in your basic policy, even if you don't buy maternity coverage. Ask about it.

HMOs: LOVE 'EM OR LEAVE 'EM

Health Maintenance Organizations (HMOs) offer total care. You (or your employer) pay regular premiums plus a small charge per office visit. In return, all your health needs are attended to. You're even covered for physical exams and other odds and ends that traditional health insurers won't touch. There are never any claim forms to fill in. On paper, you get more coverage per premium dollar than from any other insurance plan. I say "on paper" because HMOs, on principle, give less treatment than you'd get from a traditional medical practice.

Members usually have to see a doctor employed by the organization. Some HMOs are like giant clinics, with doctors, nurses, and therapists on staff. A variant—the Individual Practice Association (IPA)—signs up doctors who practice in their own offices. If you don't like your doctor, you can generally switch to another within the group.

The doctor you pick controls your treatment. He or she decides whether you see a specialist or enter a hospital. If you doubt the diagnosis, you can see a doctor outside the HMO. Normally, your insurance won't cover such a visit. A growing number of HMOs, however, are picking up 75 to 80 percent of an outside doctor's bill—something to ask about before you join.

What if you're traveling and get sick? The HMO covers emergency services out of town. But it won't cover doctor visits that aren't emergencies. If you winter in Florida but summer in New Hampshire, a Florida HMO is not for you.

HMOs save you money by practicing an abstemious sort of medicine —fewer diagnostic tests, fewer visits to specialists, fewer stays in the hospital. Maybe HMOs undertreat. But maybe traditional doctors overtreat. That's something you'll have to decide. Studies show that, in general, HMO patients do no better and no worse than anyone else.

But if you're seriously—and expensively—ill, you should take note of certain conflicts of interest.

· In an HMO, the doctors may get bonuses based on how much money they save.

· In an IPA, a doctor is usually paid a fixed income per patient, no matter how much it costs to treat.

· A pool of money may be set aside for lab tests and other treatments, with the doctors getting part of any money left in the pool at the end of the year.

A patient whose problem can't be diagnosed without a lot of costly tests, who is chronically ill, or whose illness is expensive, will reduce the doctor's personal income. Each doctor intends to do the best for each patient. Still, the system builds in incentives to skimp.

Thousands of people are happy with their HMOs, and just as loyal to them as others are to their family doctors. But experienced HMO patients say they have to be more aggressive in making appointments, seeking explanations, and pursuing treatment than patients in a traditional practice. Some HMO members occasionally visit an outside doctor at their own expense, in order to get a second opinion or a more timely appointment.

If you're under 65, and your HMO doesn't make you happy, you can switch to regular health insurance. You're locked in only if you work for a company that keeps an HMO as its sole health-insurance plan.

HMOs When You're 65 or Older

Some HMOs sign up with Medicare to cover all of your medical costs. Financially, it's a good deal. For the same price that you'd pay for a Medigap policy (page 324), or less, you get Medicare, plus Medigap, and often additional coverage that normal insurance doesn't offer, things like free annual physicals, free eyeglasses, and cut-rate prices on prescription drugs. There's absolutely no paperwork. The Medicare portion of your HMO cost is paid automatically by the government. (A few HMOs offer a "high-option" plan that includes extra services and costs more.)

To profit, you have to live in the vicinity full time. If you join a Medicare HMO in Texas but spend four months a year in Maine, none of your Maine doctor bills will be covered—either by Medicare or by the HMO. Medicare pays for non-HMO care only if you are *temporarily* out of town and urgently need to see a doctor.

Thousands of older people are grateful for their money-saving Medicare HMOs and are entirely satisfied with the treatment they provide. They're an especially good deal for middle-income people who can't afford a lot of medical bills. But there are three risks to be aware of.

1. Newer HMOs sometimes find that they cannot cover all their expenses on the money that Medicare pays them. So they drop their Medicare contracts. You're notified at least 60 days in advance, your Medicare coverage continues, and you purchase another Medigap policy. If you're ill, the HMO is required to find you a policy that covers your existing conditions, or else cover those conditions itself. Still, it's a hassle that the elderly could do without.

2. If your HMO fails or loses its Medicare contract (as some have), you might find yourself pressed for some doctor or hospital bills that it left unpaid. Legally, the HMO is responsible. But hospitals and medical professionals aren't happy with patients whose insurers owe them money. To minimize this risk, sign up only with a large HMO that has a good mix of patients of all ages and has been with Medicare for several years.

3. If you hate your HMO doctors, or think you're not getting the treatment you need, you can't just switch to a doctor somewhere else. You are locked into a Medicare HMO for up to a month at a time. If you go to an outside doctor, neither Medicare nor the HMO will pay the bill. You have to cover it yourself. If that outside doctor sends you to a hospital, you also have to pay the hospital bill. You have the right to appeal the HMO's decision not to cover a particular medical treatment

(your HMO will tell you the rules). But while you appeal, the bills pile up.

To leave a Medicare HMO, you have to give it written notice. You're officially out on the first day of the following month. But it may take a month or more for Medicare's computers to catch up with your move. If, during that time, you see another doctor, Medicare might refuse to pay, in the mistaken belief that you're still an HMO member.

Eventually, your records will be straightened out and all back bills paid. But in the meantime you may pop a blood vessel. Don't sign up with a Medicare HMO without talking to a lot of its clients who are your age, to make sure that they're really happy there.

BE AWARE THAT A SMALL NUMBER OF MEDICARE HMOs ARE THE NEXT WORST THINGS TO SCAMS. They unleash high-pressure salespeople onto the elderly. Patients sign up without understanding the rules. Specifically, they don't understand the lock-in provision that requires them to see only HMO doctors. After one or two visits to the HMO, they may return to their regular doctors. When the bills come in, both Medicare and the HMO will refuse to pay, leaving the patient feeling angry, frightened, and betrayed.

If you think that you (or your elderly parents) were deceived by an HMO salesperson, complain to your local Social Security office. If you signed up for the HMO but never truly used its services, and can show that you didn't understand the lock-in provision, the government might decide that you were never actually a member. In that case, your back medical bills will all be paid, just as if you had never signed up. This process is called "retroactive disenrollment."

GOOD MEDICARE HMOs CAN SAVE YOU MONEY AND GIVE YOU GOOD CARE. But never sign up on the word of a telephone or door-to-door salesperson, or through a newspaper ad. Visit the HMO, get its brochures, and ask for a line-by-line explanation of how everything works. For detailed advice, get *Choosing an HMO: An Evaluation Checklist* free from Fulfillment, American Association of Retired Persons, 1909 K St. N.W., Washington, DC, 20049.

WAYS TO SAVE MONEY ON MEDICAL COSTS

Here's the number one secret to saving money: Abandon the notion that better doctors charge higher fees. Sometimes they do. But a doctor's fees also reflect the office rent, the philosophy of treatment, and the number of kids he or she has in college. Individual practitioners generally charge both the most and the least. Group practitioners tend to monitor one another's bills to keep one doctor from getting out of line.

Some tested cost-cutters to try:

• For a doctor, start with quality, then test for price. If possible, get recommendations from friends who are doctors or nurses. Then call those doctors' offices and ask what they charge for an office visit, a physical exam, and a chest X-ray—and go to the cheaper ones first.

• Ask the doctor which hospitals he or she uses, then call those hospitals and ask what they charge for room, meals, and use of the operating room. Some are much more expensive than others, without delivering better care. A few high-cost hospitals "buy" their patients, by paying doctors to send you there. Tell your doctor you want the lower-cost cure.

• Explain to your doctor how much of each bill you pay yourself and that you're trying to hold costs down. Doctors pay more attention to expense when they know that you're spending your own money. Or they might refer you to a doctor who charges less. If you plead poverty, the doctor may ask you to prove it by bringing in your income-tax return.

• Hold diagnostic tests to a minimum. Have your old X-rays sent to a new doctor or dentist; that should save you the cost, and the risk, of being X-rayed again. "More" is not "better."

• Get advice by telephone, from the doctor or the nurse. It saves the cost of an office visit.

• If you're on Medicare, look for a doctor who "accepts assignment." Such a doctor charges no more than Medicare's "reasonable" fee, whatever it may be. You still pay your deductible and your 20 percent share of the doctor bill. But you don't have to pay any excess charges. How do you find such a doctor? You ask a friend, a doctor or nurse, a hospital, or a nursing home. You ask the insurance company that administers Medicare locally; it's required to publish a list. At least one copy of that list should be in your local Social Security office.

If your individual health insurance policy pays fixed amounts for medical services (as many Blue Shield plans do), ask if the doctor will treat you for whatever the insurer pays.

• Medicare patients facing surgery should find out in advance whether every member of the surgical team accepts assignment. It's not uncommon for the anesthesiologist to refuse it. But because you rarely meet him or her until you're heading for the operating room, you don't have a chance to negotiate price. So ask your surgeon about his or her whole team. If the anesthesiologist declines assignment, make a stink and see what happens.

• If you need a specialist, go to one who's "board certified," by a board of experts recognized by the American Medical Association. These doctors have specifically met the medical standards of the field. Better-qualified doctors save you money in the long run, through superior diagnoses and treatment.

• Check your insurance coverage, before undergoing elective surgery. Your plan might not pay unless you get a second opinion. If you have any doubts about your condition, get a second opinion anyway.

• Get itemized bills—from both doctors and hospitals—so you know exactly what you're paying for. Hospitals are notorious for billing you for treatments that you didn't use. They list their services in code so that you won't notice.

Go over the easy parts of the bill yourself. Were you actually in the hospital that day? Did you really use the services you were billed for? Sometimes you can knock off some money right there. Then, just for the sport, visit the billing office and ask the hospital to itemize the huge lump sum for "pharmacy" or "miscellaneous." You'll be surprised at what turns up—or rather, at what doesn't turn up. Don't pay for anything that can't be accounted for.

Hospital overcharges are so endemic that some employers pay their workers a bounty for catching them.

• If there's a 24-hour emergency clinic in your area, check its prices. It's generally cheaper than a hospital emergency room. A visit to your doctor—if you can reach him or her—should be cheaper than either.

• Take your own aspirin, sleeping pills, and other routine medication to the hospital. Hospitals may charge three dollars or more a pill for dispensing these drugs themselves.

• Question any drug your doctor orders. Ask for a full list of possible side effects. Buy a copy of the *Physician's Desk Reference* or a similar book listing drug side effects, for your home medical library, and check out all the drugs yourself. Many medicines can do you harm as well as good.

• Argue over preadmission tests. The hospital may do more than is really needed. Get your doctor to go to bat for you.

• If you have a choice, don't enter a hospital on weekends. Don't enter for procedures that can be done in a clinic or for presurgical or diagnostic tests. Nowadays, most company plans won't even pay for such overnight stays.

· Make a living will, to avoid the extraordinary cost of futile treatments when you are terminally ill (page 118).

· Compare drug prices at several pharmacies. You'll find wide differences. The American Association of Retired Persons in Washington, D.C., runs a mail-order pharmacy, where prices are generally low. Health maintenance organizations may also run their own low-cost pharmacies.

· Ask your doctor to prescribe generic rather than brand-name drugs. Good generics are just as effective and cost less.

· Try store-brand, over-the-counter drugs. They're cheaper than brand-name remedies and often just as effective.

· Check yourself regularly for breast cancer.

· Learn how to take care of your illnesses yourself, and follow your doctor's directions to the letter. A large percentage of the people readmitted to a hospital soon after being discharged come back only because they didn't follow doctor's orders.

· Don't rush to the doctor every time you feel sick. A lot of illnesses go away by themselves.

· Lose weight. Quit smoking. Drink less. Eat right. Wear seat belts. Exercise. There is no doctor bill so cheap as the one that no one has to pay.

DON'T WASTE YOUR MONEY ON . . .

ONE-DISEASE INSURANCE, like coverage specifically for cancer or heart attacks. The odds are strongly against your lucking into the specific disease you insured against. You need coverage for everything. Once you've bought it, you don't need special heart or cancer insurance.

ACCIDENT INSURANCE. It pays medical bills that result from an accident, not an illness. But why would you think that your biggest risk in life is falling off a ladder or being hit by a truck? Only 4.5 percent of deaths are accidental. When such deaths occur, they often give rise to a lawsuit —which is "insurance" enough. You need a policy that covers accident *and* sickness equally.

TV-ADVERTISED INSURANCE, hawked by celebrities. These policies usually accept all comers, but have long waiting periods before they'll cover any illness that you had when you signed up. You have only the illusion of being well insured. The celebrities ought to be run off the air.

MAIL-ORDER POLICIES that arrive in your mailbox unsolicited. They generally have long waiting periods before you're covered for ailments you already have. If you enter the hospital, it might be three days before benefits start. You could be in and out without collecting a cent. These policies come cheap not because they're bargains but because they insure you for so little. "Group" mail-order policies may be just as bad as individual ones.

STUDENT POLICIES. Your prep school or college student is probably covered by your own policy. If not, see how much the student policy covers. You might want something more comprehensive.

INDEMNITY POLICIES that offer low fixed payments for every day you're in the hospital. The average hospital stay is about seven days. The average cost is over $500 a day, or $3,500 for a seven-day stay. If your policy pays $50 a day, you're insured for an average of only $350. Spend the insurance premium on something better, like lamb chops for two. If you buy an indemnity policy, go for one with high daily payments.

DOUBLE COVERAGE. An insurance agent might urge you to add a cancer policy or hospital indemnity to the health insurance you already have. The appeal: "This gives you an extra payment when you need it." Or, "This fills the gaps that your other policy doesn't cover." You might better say that it fills the gaps in the insurance agent's personal income. The best way to get extra money is to build up your own personal savings. Cheap hit-or-miss policies are always a waste.

WHAT IF YOU GET A NASTY DISEASE AND ARE UNINSURED?

You've got problems. As far as private insurers are concerned, you might as well be dead. You can't even count on getting employee-group insurance, if you work for a small company. Insurers are increasingly rejecting individual workers (or their dependents) who represent a high risk.

The moral is: Don't wait to buy health insurance. Get it now, while you know you can. Here are your health-insurance choices if you don't qualify for regular coverage.

· Call Blue Cross/Blue Shield or an HMO. They often have open-enrollment periods, when they take all comers—even AIDS patients—at standard rates. But you're subject to the rule on preexisting conditions, which may deny coverage for your particular illness for one to two years.

• Some group-health plans will accept anyone, regardless of health. One such is the American Association of Retired Persons in Washington, D.C., which has an all-comers Medigap policy.

• Get a job with a big company that has a good group policy. You're covered as long as you can work. When you leave, you can often continue the group plan for up to 18 months at your expense (page 303). After that, you may be allowed to convert to an individual policy without passing a health exam (although that policy will be expensive). State and federal laws generally prohibit certain employers from refusing you a job, or firing you, if you're handicapped. That might include workers whose only crime is to run up the company's health-insurance bill. But that's not an easy case to prove.

• Your spouse might try for a job at a company with a good group policy. Many big companies accept new employees and their dependents without requiring a medical questionnaire. Smaller companies, by contrast, may require medical information before extending group coverage. If they find that you're sick, you may be excluded from the plan.

• Work with an independent insurance agent. You might get lucky. Some insurers are more liberal than others about accepting certain kinds of health risks. You'll be charged a higher-than-normal premium. But better to pay extra for comprehensive insurance than to settle for a policy that covers all diseases except the one you're most likely to get.

• Reconsider those mail-order policies, if that's the only coverage you qualify for. Look for a plan where the waiting period for covering preexisting illnesses doesn't exceed two years, benefits are reasonable, and you're entitled to payments from the first day you enter the hospital. *Still, policies hawked by TV celebrities are almost never worth their price.*

• If your state has a health-insurance pool for the uninsurable, check it out. Your premiums might be up to 50 percent higher than normal, and the deductible might run as much as $2,000. But at least you're protected from catastrophic costs. At this writing, pools have been approved in 20 states. They're up and running in Connecticut, Florida, Illinois, Indiana, Iowa, Maine, Minnesota, Montana, Nebraska, New Mexico, North Dakota, Oregon, South Carolina, Tennessee, Texas,

Washington, and Wisconsin. California, Georgia, and Utah are just getting started. Pools in some other states are pending.

• The healthy dependents of an unhealthy worker can buy their own insurance, through many associations, Blue Cross/Blue Shield, or another private insurance company.

• *Don't lie on your insurance application.* The company might find you out by checking with the Medical Information Bureau (page 316). If it learns that you failed to mention a health problem, it will probably turn you down. If it writes the policy and catches your "error" before two or three years are up (depending on your state), it may legally deny any claims arising from that preexisting illness. It may even cancel your entire policy, returning the premiums you paid. If your omission is so blatant and deliberate as to constitute fraud, the company can refuse payment even after two or three years have passed, although to enforce its decision it would have to be prepared to take you to court.

THE TRAP OF POST-CLAIMS UNDERWRITING

To "underwrite" means to evaluate you as a health risk. Some insurance companies don't pay a lot of attention to your state of health when you apply for coverage. But if you fall ill during the first two or three years, watch out. They'll go over your application with a magnifying glass, looking for reasons to reject your claim.

They may deny payment—or revoke your entire policy—if any statement on your application turns out to be anything less than 100 percent true. Even if you told them the truth, they might nit-pick the way you phrased it.

If the company is being unfair or unreasonable, the state insurance department should help you collect on your claim. But you'll be hung out to dry if your application wasn't forthright. To protect yourself:

• Answer every question honestly and in full. Put down everything. Don't listen to an insurance agent who says, "No one needs to know that." Remember, those medical facts may already be on file at the Medical Information Bureau.

• Make sure the insurance agent records your answers properly on the application form. Some agents put "no" where they should put "yes," so that the company will accept you. If your claim is rejected later, it's no skin off the agent's nose. He may claim that the error was yours.

· When you get your health-insurance policy, a copy of your application form should be attached. Double-check it for accuracy. If you find a mistake, notify the company in writing. If the company says you're okay, get its answer in writing. What's "okay" now may not be when you file a claim.

· Be wary of companies that issue health-insurance policies on the quick. It's a sign that they do their investigating later. You're better off with a company that requires a health exam and a statement from your doctor.

YOU'RE KIDDING YOURSELF IF YOU GET HEALTH INSURANCE UNDER FALSE PRETENSES. When you file a claim, you'll find that the policy isn't worth the paper it's written on.

YOUR MEDICAL HISTORY

Few people have ever heard of the Medical Information Bureau. But if you've applied for individual health, life, or disability insurance, the company may have checked with MIB before it wrote the policy.

MIB exists, first, to catch people who falsify their insurance applications. If one insurer learns that you've had a heart attack, that information goes to MIB. Should you then approach another insurer and fail to mention your heart attack, a check with MIB will tell the tale.

But MIB has another function that even the truthful have to beware of. Say, for example, that you take a medical exam and the insurance-company doctor thinks there's something odd about your electrocardiogram. It will be sent to MIB. The insurer may ultimately accept you at preferred rates, because lots of EKGs have little squiggles that mean nothing. But you now have something "suspicious" on your record that you don't know anything about.

If you apply for coverage with another company, it may check with MIB, decide that for its purposes your EKG doesn't look good enough, and refuse to accept you at preferred rates. You're supposed to be told if you're turned down for something seen on your MIB file—but the insurance agent might forget. You have to know about MIB, and ask for your file, to find out what the problem is.

Files are kept on 11 to 12 million people. MIB reports on specific illnesses, pertinent X-rays and lab tests, suicide attempts, occupational poisoning, overweight and underweight, a family history of certain diseases, drug addiction or alcoholism if confirmed by the applicant or a medical source, and anything an insurance company considers medically suspicious. There's a nonmedical category, noting reckless driving records, hazardous sports, amateur flying, and applications for much more life insurance than seems warranted. Disability insurers can use MIB to find out if you're carrying policies that you didn't mention on your application.

You can get a free copy of your nonmedical file from the Medical Information Bureau at P.O. Box 105, Essex Station, Boston, MA, 02112 (or call 617-426-3660). The medical information will be sent to any medical professional you designate (doctor, nurse, dentist, even pharmacist), who will discuss it with you. You're entitled to correct any information in the record, or add anything that will explain it.

SPOUSES AND CHILDREN WITHOUT THEIR OWN MEDICAL COVERAGE

Everything here applies equally to men. But this is overwhelmingly a women's issue.

If you are covered under your husband's employee-group plan, you risk losing your health insurance if he separates from the company plan or separates from you. That can happen if he dies, if you divorce or separate legally, or if he goes onto Medicare. You can buy your own policy, as an individual or through an association, but it may be expensive. If you're in poor health, you might not find coverage at any price.

For some wives, safety nets exist. But it all depends on where your husband works and what kind of policy he has.

IF YOUR SPOUSE'S COMPANY EMPLOYS 20 PEOPLE OR MORE: You're usually allowed to stay in the employee plan for up to three years, at your expense. You're charged the group premium plus 2 percent. The price may be higher than you'd like. But you'll probably get more coverage per dollar than individual policies offer.

To stay in the group, you must: (1) make sure that your husband's company notifies the insurer about your eligibility. Notification has to be made within 30 days from the day your husband dies or goes onto Medicare, or within 60 days of your divorce or legal separation. Call the company yourself, if you think that your husband might not. (2) Watch for a letter from the insurance company, asking if you want to continue. You have 60 days to say yes. If you miss any of these deadlines, you're dropped from the plan without right of appeal.

Your grown children can stay in the group for up to three years after they get too old for formal family coverage. To keep them enrolled, alert the plan within 60 days of each child's cut-off age.

All this coverage ends as soon as you (or the child) qualify for another group plan—for example, if you get a job with employee benefits. But if you have an illness that the new plan won't cover right away, your old plan will keep on paying the bills.

If your three years runs out and your health is poor, you may be allowed to convert to individual coverage without a health exam. That policy won't come cheap, and its benefits will be limited. But if you can't get any other coverage, it's a jewel beyond price.

IF YOUR SPOUSE'S COMPANY EMPLOYS FEWER THAN 20 PEOPLE: You're up the creek. No law requires the group plan to keep you on, and it probably won't. You might be able to convert to individual coverage, but at high rates. You're better off shopping for coverage somewhere else.

IF YOUR FAMILY CARRIES ITS OWN INDIVIDUAL COVERAGE: You can keep the policy, if your husband dies. In fact, your premiums will go down, because the policy is now carrying one less person. Many new widows don't realize this and keep on paying for health insurance at the old rate. As soon as you tell the insurer about the death, however, any overpayments should be refunded. Also, ask for a lower premium as soon as your children leave school and are no longer covered under your policy.

If your husband pays for the policy and you divorce or legally separate, you lose your benefits. The children can still come under his plan, as long as he agrees to it. Coverage for you might be part of the separation agreement. Otherwise, you'll have to buy your own.

FILE FAST, FAST, FAST

Don't let medical bills linger in a desk drawer. Insurers require prompt filing. If you dally too long—say, a year or more—the bill may be refused. The outside limit for making a claim will be spelled out in your policy. (Still, a persistent claimant with a good excuse might have a bill accepted, even past the deadline.)

MEDICARE

Welcome to the world of 65-year-olds. When you reach that robust age, you're eligible for Medicare.

You qualify for coverage if you've met the work requirement for Social Security benefits. That's a majority of us.

You also qualify if you can claim benefits on the account of someone who has met the work requirement. That covers most of the rest of us. This group includes spouses, unmarried ex-spouses whose marriages lasted at least 10 years, widows and widowers, and parents who got half their support from a Social-Security-eligible child who has died or become disabled.

You can go on Medicare earlier than age 65 if you've been receiving Social Security disability payments for two years, or if you have lost the use of your kidneys.

MEDICARE INSURANCE COMES IN TWO PARTS.

Part A covers hospital bills and bills for skilled nursing homes, hospice care, and a certain amount of home-health care. You have already paid for this coverage in your Social Security taxes, so you're entitled to it automatically at age 65.

Part B is optional. It covers doctor bills, outpatient surgery, emergency-room treatment for patients not admitted to the hosptial, X-rays, laboratory tests, certain medical supplies, certain prescription drugs, and other costs. If you want Part B, you have to pay extra.

When you register for Medicare Part A at age 65, you're asked if you also want Part B. Here's how to decide.

YOU WILL NEED PART B IF . . .

• *You are moving from an employee plan to a retiree group plan that is still subsidized by your employer.* Your health benefits stay pretty much the same. But after you reach age 65, your company plan pays only the bills that Medicare doesn't. So you need Part B. Some companies pay the Part B premium for you.

• *You have individual (or family) health insurance.* At age 65, these plans turn into Medigap policies, which pay only certain bills that Medicare doesn't. You have to register for Part B and pay the premium yourself.

• *You're covered under your spouse's retiree or private Medigap plan,* and you're 65 and up. You typically get the same coverage as your spouse, so will need Part B.

• *You have no other health insurance.* You depend entirely on Medicare to pay your covered medical bills. If you're at the official poverty level, your state Medicaid program will pay the Part B premium for you.

· *You're totally disabled,* and have been on a company disability plan. Some companies supplement the coverage you get from Parts A and B.

· *Although you're 65, you are still working, for a company that employs fewer than 20 people.* You will usually be taken off the group-health plan (if there is one) and put onto Medicare. Any additional benefits you get depend on how generous your company is. It might pay your Part B premium; it might provide a complete, supplemental Medigap plan; it might offer nothing.

CONSIDER TAKING ONLY PART A IF...

· *You are still working, for a company that employs 20 people or more, and you have a good health plan.* Under the law, you must be continued in the group plan with no reduction in benefits. Your medical bills are insured by the company, just as they were before you turned 65. So there's generally no point in paying for Part B.

But don't fail to sign up for Part A! It doesn't cost you anything and gives you extra coverage. Any hospital expenses not paid by the company's insurance (including deductibles and co-payments) can be submitted to Medicare—an ace in the hole that younger employees don't have. You are subject to the usual Medicare deductibles. But after that, the government picks up any eligible bills that your health plan doesn't.

If you do sign up for Part B, it, too, will pay covered expenses that your company plan doesn't. But Part B is worth the money only if the company plan is so awful that you really need supplemental insurance.

· *You are still working, for a company that employs fewer than 20 people, but you're part of a multiemployer plan.* All the employers might have agreed to keep their workers on group insurance, regardless of their age. This puts you in the same situation as the big-company employee, described above. Sign up for Part A, but in most cases Part B won't be worth the expense.

WHAT IF YOU'RE 65 AND READY TO RETIRE, BUT YOUR SPOUSE STILL WORKS AND YOU HAVE BEEN COVERED BY YOUR SPOUSE'S PLAN? Ask your spouse's employee-benefits office about your status.

In a company with fewer than 20 employees, you will probably have to go on Medicare. Still, the company plan might pick up some of the bills that Medicare doesn't.

In a larger company, your spouse's plan is primarily responsible for your bills. You'd join Medicare Part A, but only as a backup for the bills the company doesn't pay (see above). You usually wouldn't bother with Part B.

If you *enter* the spouse's plan at age 65, there may be a medical exam and a waiting period for covering preexisting conditions. In that case, you'd want both Parts A and B.

If you have health insurance under your own retiree plan, *and* your working spouse has health insurance, you can be in both plans. But that spousal coverage usually isn't worth paying for. Medicare and your own plan will most likely cover enough of your bills.

Furthermore, there's a risk, when you wind up with multiple insurers: No one wants to be the first to pay, especially if your bills are large. Your plans' "coordination of benefits" clauses, which specify who pays first, may be contradictory. Result: delay, hassle, and heartburn until everything gets straightened out.

Both Medicare and the Health Insurance Association of America recommend that, in these tangled cases, the spouse's insurer pay first, followed by Medicare for what's left of the eligible bills, followed by the retiree plan, if any bills are still outstanding.

WHAT IF YOUR SPOUSE IS ABOUT TO RETIRE, YOU HAVE NO EMPLOYEE PLAN OF YOUR OWN, AND YOU'RE NOT YET ELIGIBLE FOR MEDICARE? There are several ways that you might be insured:

1. Your spouse's retiree plan. It might cover you fully, as a dependent.

2. Your spouse's employee group-health plan. You may be eligible for up to three years of coverage at your expense—provided that you notify the plan in time (page 317).

3. A conversion policy. Your spouse's old group policy may be convertible into an individual plan for you alone. But it's expensive. You'd buy it only if you couldn't find a cheaper plan somewhere else.

4. The privately purchased family plan that you've had until now. It can be retooled to provide full coverage for you alone, and perhaps Medicare-supplement insurance for your spouse.

5. A new individual policy that you buy for yourself.

If you retired early, or are receiving Social Security disability benefits, you'll be enrolled in Medicare automatically when you reach 65.

You get a notice when coverage starts. If you don't want Part B, just check a box on the notice and send it back.

If you're 65 and about to retire, sign up for Medicare when you apply for Social Security. Do it during the three months before your 65th birthday. You'll then be covered from the month of your birthday on. If you sign up in your birthday month, your Part B coverage starts the first day of the following month.

If you're 65 and still working, sign up for Part A (and Part B, if you want it) during the three months before your 65th birthday, and no later than your birthday month.

Don't miss those sign-up dates! If you do, and get sick, here's what happens: (1) You're okay on your Part A bills. They're always covered retroactively for the past six months. (2) There will be a gap in your Part B insurance.

If you sign up for Part B during the three months after you turn 65, there's a two-month waiting period before you're covered. Any bills incurred during that period will not be paid.

If you let three months pass after turning 65, without signing up for Part B, you won't have another chance to join until the next general enrollment period—January 1 through March 31 of each year, with coverage beginning on July 1. Your premium will be 10 percent higher for each 12-month period when you could have been enrolled but weren't.

The rules are different for someone who kept on working past age 65 and remained in his or her employer plan. You pay no late-enrollment penalties, as long as you join Part B within seven months after you retire. If you join in the actual month you retire, you are covered as of that month. If you join during the following six months, you are covered from the first day of the month after the month you enroll.

Any 65-year-old, working or retired, can sign up for Part A of Medicare at any time, without penalty. If someone forgets to enroll and enters a hospital, the patient or his representative normally fills out a statement of intent to claim Medicare benefits. That's considered an application for Medicare, and the bills will be covered (although a formal application must be made eventually). If no intent form is signed at the hospital and the patient dies, Medicare won't pay.

WHAT MEDICARE DOESN'T PAY

· I won't list here all the benefits Medicare provides. The government publishes dandy free booklets on the subject, which you can get from your Social Security office.

It's more important that you understand all the *gaps* in your government insurance.

1. Medicare charges you a deductible when you enter the hospital, and part of the bill if you stay more than 60 days.

2. Medicare covers 80 percent of all reasonable doctor bills, after an annual deductible. But deep in that sentence lie two expensive loopholes. First, you're left with 20 percent of each reasonable bill. Second, Medicare keeps a list of all the charges it calls "reasonable." For example: If you submit a bill from your doctor for $350 and the computer says that procedure should cost only $300, Medicare pays 80 percent of $300. That's only $240; you pay the remaining $110.

Some doctors charge no more than Medicare's maximum payment. That's called "accepting assignment." How do you find such a paragon? Ask your doctor. Ask your friends. Ask a hospital or nursing home. Ask the insurance company, which administers Medicare locally. Or call the local Social Security Office, which should have a list.

WARNING: When you go to the hospital for surgery, you may think that you've controlled your costs because your doctor accepts assignment. But the doctor in the X-ray department or the anesthesiologist may not accept it—which you won't realize until you get their bills. For these doctors, you're a captive patient; they don't have to compete for your business by charging a "Medicare-reasonable" price. To me, the whole arrangement smacks of monopoly profits. The hospitals should not allow it. Your own doctor should not allow it. You should be able to assemble an entire team that accepts Medicare assignment.

3. Medicare pays for "appropriate" treatment that is "medically necessary." If your doctor keeps you in the hospital one day longer than Medicare thinks appropriate, it won't cover that extra day. It might also deny payment for treatment that it doesn't think you need.

You can, and should, appeal a decision that goes against you. Information on how to do it, and the deadlines for filing, are enclosed with the form denying the claim. Don't let anyone discourage you, including personnel at the Social Security office. Thousands of people win their cases.

If your doctor anticipates a problem with the board that decides how long you should be hospitalized, he or she should present your case before you're even admitted.

4. Medicare covers a certain amount of skilled nursing care. But it does not cover custodial care—feeding, bathing, dressing—for people who simply can't take care of themselves. For that, you need long term care insurance (page 326).

5. Medicare normally does not cover routine physical, eye, or hearing exams, glasses, hearing aids, private-duty nurses, medical bills you incur while traveling abroad, most immunizations, dentures, routine dental and foot care, orthopedic shoes, homemaker services, and most prescription drugs. Some of these can be covered by a Medigap policy or a Medicare HMO (page 308).

ONE OF THE KINDEST THINGS THAT CHILDREN CAN DO FOR THEIR ELDERLY PARENTS IS TO SEE THAT ALL THE MEDICARE BILLS ARE REIMBURSED PROPERLY. You should also appeal all bad Medicare decisions and get the money your parent is owed. Patients have rights under Medicare. Be sure they're exercised.

Plugging the Medigap

How will you cover the expenses that Medicare doesn't? Many lucky retirees are covered by company insurance, at low or no cost. Low-income people are insured by the government, through Medicaid. Everyone else needs a "Medigap" policy that fills in the holes in Medicare.

When shopping for a policy, look for one that is automatically renewable; covers preexisting conditions after three or six months (no longer); pays from the first day you enter the hospital; and pays the percentage of each reasonable bill that Medicare doesn't, rather than a flat number of dollars toward each bill.

Basic policies cover the deductibles and the co-insurance, like the 20 percent of each doctor bill that you have to pay. For a higher price, you can insure against part or all of the surplus portion of the doctor's bill, the price of very long-term hospital stays (beyond 150 days), longer stays in a skilled nursing home, and outpatient prescription drugs. Of these extras, the surplus doctor-bill coverage is probably the most valuable, but only if your doctor chooses not to take Medicare assignment. Least valuable: the prescription-drug coverage, which might wind up costing about the same as the drugs themselves.

When policy shopping, compare the price of (1) turning your present employee-group plan into an individual Medigap plan; (2) a Blue Cross/

Blue Shield plan; (3) a plan from the American Association of Retired Persons in Washington, D.C.; and (4) a plan proposed by your insurance agent, which might be tops for healthy retirees. If you have health problems, however, call the AARP, which takes all comers at the same price. So do many of the Blues, at certain sign-up periods.

Under a Medigap reform law, generally effective in August 1992, you have the following protections: (1) The insurance companies must sell standard policies, so that you can easily compare them. (2) Agents can't sell you a second Medigap policy unless you drop the first. (3) You can't be sold Medigap coverage if you're on Medicaid, which already pays your bills. (4) At age 65, you have six months to buy a policy, at standard rates, without passing a health exam.

Whatever you do, buy from a company rated A-plus by the insurance rating service, A. M. Best. Don't buy from companies whose literature leads you to think they're connected with Medicare or Social Security. The government does not sell Medigap insurance.

Games Some Sleazy Agents Play

They claim to be from Medicare, when they're not.

They scare you into thinking that your next illness will wipe you out. It won't. Medicare covers almost all big doctor and hospital bills.

They tell you your present Medigap policy is awful, just so they can switch you to a new one or add another one to it.

They claim that their policy will cover you for things it won't (read the policy and see).

They don't report your recent illnesses when they fill out your insurance application. That gets you a policy at a good price—but you're not really covered. When you file a claim, the insurer can refuse to pay, on the ground that you failed to disclose your true state of health.

They want cash or a check made out to them. If you do that, you'll never see that money again.

They sell you a string of dread-disease policies or indemnity policies that pay $50 or $100 a day when you're in the hospital. But when you have Medigap or Medicaid, this stuff is unnecessary.

You should buy a *single, comprehensive Medigap policy* that covers everything. The agents who push the other junk on you belong in jail.

Retiree Health Insurance

When you retire, your company may buy you a Medigap plan.

But your free (or low-cost) coverage may not last in its present form. Early retirements, longer lifespans, and soaring medical costs are making retiree health insurance far more costly than companies ever expected.

A company cannot cancel a benefit that was solemnly promised, except in a bankruptcy or corporate takeover. But today's retiree plans come with a "maybe not" clause—as in, "I'm paying all your medical bills today, but maybe not tomorrow."

Check the booklet that describes your benefits. If it clearly states that the company has the right to make changes, your health insurance is not guaranteed. Most likely, you'll be asked to pay more of the cost. Your only consolation is that, even at a higher price, you have a much better deal than people who have no company plan at all.

LONG-TERM CARE

This is what's generally known as nursing-home coverage. You go to a home not for therapy or medical treatment (which may be covered under Medicare), but because you no longer can manage alone, or because your spouse or your children can't handle your physical problems any more.

Nursing-home policies are changing rapidly, with better coverage showing up every year. If you're under 60 and in good health, it makes sense to wait before buying. You'll pay a higher price at later ages, but the insurance will be much improved. Get a policy in middle age only if it's offered by your employer. In group plans, premiums are a real bargain —around 30 percent less than you'd pay in the individual market.

By age 65, long-term care insurance starts to make sense for people with money. If you wait much longer, the expense is too high.

Why do I limit this insurance to people "with money"? Because if you have no money, or very little, Medicaid will pay your way. Nursing-home coverage is only for people who would otherwise have to spend their own savings, and would rather not. Buy it if you want to be sure that your spouse's standard of living won't fall because of your nursing-home expenses, or if you want to leave a large inheritance for your children, with nothing deducted for nursing-home costs.

If you have no spouse, and your children are well provided for, forget the insurance. Spend your own money. Medical care is one of the contingencies that you spent a lifetime saving *for*.

Read any policy carefully before signing up—and I mean the actual policy, not the sales literature. Some literature waffles; some salespeople misspeak. Here's what you want to see in a long-term care policy, in black and white:

1. Your right to enter custodial nursing care directly from your own home, without being in a hospital or skilled nursing facility first. (A "skilled" facility treats you for medical problems, reimbursable by Medicare.)

2. Your right to payment regardless of whether you're getting "skilled," "intermediate," or "custodial" care, or the order in which you might have received these different types of treatment. Some companies manipulate words like "intermediate," in order to deny honest claims.

3. The chance to buy inflation coverage, so that your policy payout will rise along with nursing-home costs. Today's policies might pay $60 a day, but what will that buy 20 years from now? Sweet nothing.

4. A clear, written statement that you're covered for Alzheimer's disease and other confusions of the brain. Some policies exclude mental disorders.

5. A minimal wait—no more than six months—before you're covered for illnesses you had when the policy was written. Some policies pay with no waiting period at all.

6. Home health care, without having to be in a hospital first.

7. Noncancellable coverage—meaning that you get to keep your policy, at its present cost, for life. Many policies are merely "guaranteed renewable"—which sounds safer than is actually the case. The "guarantee" means only that the company can't drop your particular policy, or raise your price, if you make a lot of claims. But it can cancel, or raise prices, on all of the policies in your category.

NEWER POLICIES TEND TO BE GENEROUS. OLDER ONES MAY NOT OFFER ALL THE BENEFITS LISTED ABOVE. If you have an older policy, ask your company if you can upgrade to something better. Otherwise, you might find that your nursing-home claim can easily be denied.

GETTING PAID

The vast majority of insurance claims are faithfully paid. But then there's that unhappy 10 percent.

Some of those cases smell like fraud—so it's right for insurers to resist. But many others are honest claims with a bit of a problem at the edge. Maybe there's the technical question of whether the insurance applies. Maybe there's evidence that can be read as fraud even when it's not. Maybe the company wants to improve its profits by toughing out every marginal case.

In denying your claim, an insurance company has little to lose. You might give up and go away. Or the settlement might take a couple of years, during which time the company keeps the money. Complain to the state insurance department before going to court. The state might settle your problem, at no cost to you.

DON'T LET YOUR INSURER GET AWAY WITH REFUSING AN HONEST CLAIM. The law is on your side if (1) the language of the policy is unclear, or (2) the terms of the policy could reasonably lead you to think you were covered. Nor will the law let you be stripped of your coverage on a technicality, like missing the date for filing the claim.

The tragedy is that, while you're arguing, a family member lies desperately ill with no one at hand to pay the bills. Without guaranteed payment, hospitals, doctors, and therapists may be reluctant to rally around.

No one can predict when an insurer might turn tough. But here are some precautions to take.

• Get a "true copy" of your insurance coverage. Your agent might have given you only a certificate of insurance with a vague description of what you bought. (If you're covered by group insurance, the booklet that explains the benefits is effectively your copy. You can't be ruled by fine print in a master contract that you've never seen.)

• Read the true copy. Get an explanation for every single little thing that you don't understand. That's one of the services that insurance agents are paid for, so spend as much time as you need. Put notes in the margin, to remind yourself of what the agent said (he or she may misstate, which could be important evidence in an administrative hearing run by the state insurance department, or in court). Pay special attention to the stated exclusions. But be aware of unstated exclusions. For example, the policy may cover treatment in a "skilled nursing facility." By inference, this means no coverage in other types of nursing homes.

• Ask the company (or your employee benefits office) for its definition of a "dependent." Are your 18-year-old children covered automatically, or will you have to prove that they haven't become independent adults?

• If your claim is denied, get a written explanation for why the company turned you down. Check the reasons against the language in your policy. If the language can be read in another way, complain to the state insurance department. You may have a case.

• Talk to your insurance agent or company benefits officer. Either one might help you get your denial reconsidered.

• Write to the person who heads the insurer's claims department (call the company to get the name). That sometimes stirs someone to take another look at your case. If it doesn't, write to the company president, with a copy to the state insurance department. Complain, complain, complain. Nothing will happen if you don't.

• Keep complete records—of your claim, the medical bills, and all the communications you have with the insurer. Keep copies of letters. Note the date and purpose of telephone calls, and follow up those calls with a short letter. This strengthens your hand if you have to sue. It might show bad faith on the company's part.

• Above all, be prepared to fight, for minor claims as well as major ones. You paid for the insurance. Don't settle for less than is truly due.

If the company processing Medicare claims unfairly refuses to pay a bill, take your complaint to the local Medicare office. If you're not satisfied with the decision and the amount in dispute is $100 or more, you can ask for a hearing. If you still lose, you can appeal the decision. It takes time, but a lot of money has been recovered this way. While you're at it, write to your congressperson. A congressional office might follow up on your complaint as part of its constituent services. Also, check the Yellow Pages under "Senior Citizens." You may find an organization that helps older people with problems like these.

CODA

Turn over every stone, every shingle, to get some kind of health insurance. It should top your list of necessities, after food, clothing, and shelter. Insure against major illnesses—by taking big deductibles—even if you can't afford coverage for everyday care. No one wants a charity case. City hospitals for the poor are swamped, while suburban hospitals may not admit you for anything but emergency care unless you have an insurance card.

In financial terms, "going bare"—that is, without health insurance —endangers your personal solvency. A single bad illness could take all you have.

Of greater importance is that uninsured people often can't get any treatment at all. So going bare endangers your life.

14
DISABILITY—THE BIG BLACK HOLE:

The Risk That Everyone Forgets

___

You insure your house, your car, even your old
couches and chairs. But you forget your single
biggest asset—your earning power.

You plot. You plan. You save. You
invest. Then you fall off a roof (or your spouse does), wind up in a
wheelchair, and your entire financial plan falls apart. You go through
your savings like a buzz saw. Your comfortable standard of living goes
down the drain.

All because you forgot to insure your earning power, which is your
most valuable single asset. If you're sick, you have health insurance. If
you die, your family can cash in your life insurance policy. But disability
falls between the cracks. You're alive—in a bed or a wheelchair—and
have no money coming in. Perversely, the brilliant advances in medicine
have made disability more common. Diseases that used to kill you are
now more likely to leave you chronically impaired.

Are you just about ready to skip this chapter because you already have a policy? Not so fast! When did you buy it? If you got it ten years ago, it doesn't come close to replacing the income you have today.

For single people, up-to-date disability insurance is a must. You have no spouse to support you if you can't work. Anyone at risk of getting AIDS should buy right now, before the damning antibodies show up in the blood, making you uninsurable. If you're carrying life insurance, and have no dependents, drop it and buy disability coverage instead. If you have dependents, consider "living benefits" life insurance (page 284), which lets you draw on the face value in the final months of a terminal illness.

For married people, the need for a disability policy depends on the importance of your income. If you're immobile or in a coma, could your spouse support the family comfortably? If so, you don't need insurance. If not, you need it badly. In many two-paycheck families, husband and wife should each carry a policy. ("Housewife disability" policies appeared briefly a few years ago, but seem to have vanished. The benefits were small and the price high.)

THE PRICE

It's no secret why so many people "forget" disability: It's expensive. A good policy might cost $500 to more than $1,500 a year, depending on your age and circumstances. Prices have been rising, because of:

- More drug abuse among the executive classes.
- More mental-health claims due to stress.
- Claims filed for illnesses that didn't used to keep people out of work —on the theory, "I paid premiums, so I'm entitled to my money back."
- Larger numbers of laid-back workers, who are in no hurry to return to work.
- More pregnancy claims, the fruits of the baby boom's baby boom-let.
- Miracle medical cures, which leave you alive but unable to work.
- Policy fraud, by people who overinsure themselves, then discover "bad backs."
- Jogging and exercise machines. They're good for your heart but can lead to arthritis and musculo-skeletal problems. (That's right, health nuts. You just can't win.)

How much you pay for an individual policy depends on your age, your health, the policy you choose, whether you smoke, the job you hold, and—sometimes—your sex. A few companies charge women more than men because they make more disability claims. Others charge men and women the same. Any woman buying coverage should make sure that she's getting a unisex rate. Otherwise, she'll be paying much more than necessary.

BUT HERE'S THE GOOD NEWS. SOME ADVENTUROUS COMPANIES ARE BRINGING OUT A LINE OF MORE AFFORDABLE POLICIES.

They're called *annually renewable disability income* (ARDI) policies and work much like term life insurance. The price starts low and increases a little every year. By contrast, a traditional policy charges more at the time you buy but fixes that price for the policy's entire term.

ARDI is being snapped up by younger professionals and business people who, in the past, may have felt that they couldn't afford disability coverage. Depending on your age, you can cut 25 to 50 percent off the initial cost.

Your gamble is that, as the price of the policy rises, so will your income. That's a pretty good bet. ARDI's modest extra cost each year shouldn't be a strain. In early middle age, however, you'll probably want to convert to fixed-price coverage, because ARDI starts getting pretty expensive. At around age 55, take a look at the fixed-price policy offered by USAA in San Antonio, Texas (800-531-8000), which pretty much beats the ARDI competition.

ARDI was pioneered as a separate policy by General American Life in St. Louis and at this writing is offered by a handful of other companies —Ohio National in Cincinnati, National Life of Vermont in Montpelier, the Guardian Life and Equitable Life in New York. The latter two tend to be somewhat higher-priced. If you run a small company or a professional practice, you might also consider ARDI for your group-health plan.

Another place to look for affordable disability insurance is a group policy offered through a trade or professional association. But always compare both the price and the benefits with individual policies, especially ARDI coverage and fixed-price policies from USAA. Some groups cost more. Some of the groups that cost less offer poorer benefits.

A third possibility is an insurance company with *step rates*—lower rates in the first few years, when your earnings are low, and higher rates later. (But the steps may be big; ARDI raises the price just a little every year and is, to my mind, a better choice.)

If you're not in good health, your insurance is going to cost you extra

—even your ARDI, if you can buy it. Here's where there's no substitute for an energetic and independent insurance agent. Some companies do much better than others for so-called "rated risks." Your agent should shop your case around, to find the best deal.

The nature of your job determines how much you pay for disability insurance. The greater your occupational risk (based on claims filed with the insurer), the higher your cost or the sparser your benefits.

The lowest prices attach to clean-hands jobs like lawyer or business executive. The accident risk is low and, when disabled, people in these lines of work are usually eager to get back to the office.

Clerical workers, by contrast, often can't get affordable coverage because, when disabled, they may not be strongly motivated to return to work. Blue-collar workers also have a strike against them, both for motivational reasons and because of the risk of industrial accidents. A few insurers, however, do offer limited coverage to people in skilled blue-collar jobs. Generally, these policies start paying when the disability has lasted for six months, and continue benefits for a maximum of 2, 5, or 10 years.

When you shop for a policy, ask your insurance agent how your job has been classified. If it's not in the top class, ask the agent to try a couple more companies. Different insurers rank jobs differently. If you can wiggle into the top class, you'll save yourself a lot of money.

Here's a general look at how insurers rate the riskiness of the work you do. People in Class 5 jobs pay the least for their disability coverage. People in Class 1 jobs pay the most. Almost all private disability insurance is sold to Classes 5 and 4. They also get the most favorable definitions of disability, and the best options.

CLASS 5. Selected professionals, including accountants, architects, college professors, dentists, physicians, attorneys, and pharmacists.

CLASS 4. Other professionals, technicians, and office workers.

CLASS 3. White-collar and selected blue-collar workers, including supervisors, skilled clerical and technical workers, real estate agents, and teachers.

CLASS 2. Semiskilled and unskilled blue-collar workers, including manual workers, barbers, unskilled clerical workers, and sales clerks.

CLASS 1. Others in less insurable work, including carpenters, bricklayers, baggage handlers, porters, and skycraper ironworkers.

YOUR "FREE" COVERAGE

If you can't afford private insurance, you're not left entirely on your own. Almost every worker has a source of at least some disability pay.

THERE'S WORKER'S COMPENSATION, for work-related injuries. Disability payments vary widely, according to state law. The maximum is 66.6 percent of your predisability gross wages, or 80 percent of your take-home pay, up to a specified ceiling. Employers buy worker's comp for their employees; the self-employed have to buy their own.

THERE'S THE COMPANY OR UNION HEALTH PLAN, which may provide sick pay for three to six months. A growing number of plans include long-term disability benefits. Generally, the company pays the premiums, although sometimes the employees do. If you're offered such a plan, don't fail to buy it. It's the cheapest coverage you're going to find. But check out its limits. Often, the disability benefit is reduced by certain other payments you get, including Social Security and your company's retirement benefit.

But—to the surprise of most employees—company-paid plans are rarely enough. If you become disabled, they might pay 40 to 60 percent of your income, but that's before taxes. After tax, you'd net much less. You need an additional policy to bring your after-tax coverage up to 65 or 70 percent.

There's one more good reason to own an additional policy: You may lose your company coverage if you leave your job. That outside policy, together with an option that lets you buy more disability insurance without passing a health exam, guarantees that you'll always have coverage, no matter what happens.

THERE'S SOCIAL SECURITY, if you worked long enough to be eligible for coverage or are eligible on your spouse's account. But you have to be so pulverized, physically or mentally, that you cannot work in any substantial job (there's a limited exception for the blind). Your checks don't start until you've been disabled for five consecutive months. Furthermore, your disability has to be expected to last for at least a year or to lead to your death.

Social Security applies these rules strictly, sometimes too strictly. You may have to appeal (ideally, with the help of a lawyer) to collect the benefit truly due you. More than two-thirds of those who apply for benefits are turned down, generally because they're judged fit for some kind of work. If you carry a private disability policy, the insurance company may pay the legal costs of challenging a Social Security turndown. Anything you get from Social Security usually reduces the monthly amount that the private insurer has to pay.

To find out what Social Security might pay for you and your dependents, see page 777. Beneficiaries get annual cost-of-living increases, which protects their purchasing power. After 24 months on Social Security disability, you qualify for Medicare.

THERE'S VETERANS' INSURANCE. You're generally covered if your ailment traces to something that happened while you were on active duty with the armed forces. Low-income veterans who are totally disabled, and who served during periods designated as "wartime," can get benefits even for disabilities that are not service-related.

THERE ARE DISABILITY FUNDS IN SEVERAL STATES, including California, Hawaii, New Jersey, New York, and Rhode Island, plus Puerto Rico. They pay sickness benefits, for a limited number of weeks, to people disabled off the job.

HOW MUCH MORE INSURANCE DO YOU NEED?

You need enough disability insurance to feel safe. As a general rule, that means enough to bring you up to a decent standard of living even if you couldn't work. Your purchase is stated in monthly dollar amounts. For example, you might buy a policy paying $1,500 a month or $2,500 a month.

To get a handle on how much is enough, go back to page 33. That's where you figured how much money you'd have in the kitty if you didn't work. (What? You skipped that calculation? This proves my point about needing insurance: You never know when you'll get caught.)

Estimate how much income your kitty might throw off. Add that to your other sources of income, like spouse's earnings, company-paid disability benefits, and Social Security. If that's not enough to pay your bills, fill the gap with a disability policy.

Insurers won't knowingly sell you enough insurance to replace your entire income. That destroys your incentive to work. Instead, a policy will cover a percentage of your income, depending on how much you earn. High-income people might be able to replace only 30 to 55 percent of their earnings with insurance benefits (some companies sell you more coverage than others). Middle-income people might get 60 to 80 percent.

What happens if you go for 100 percent coverage, by buying a second policy without telling the insurer about the first one? You'd have to lie on your insurance application. That opens you to the risk of having the second policy canceled if the company investigates your claim. Besides, 100 percent coverage isn't worth its price. Better to put the extra money into savings and investments.

Once your policy has been in effect for two years (three years in some states, including California), the insurer normally can't deny payment based on errors of fact in your application. If you put down the wrong age, however, payments will be adjusted to match your real age. If your misstatements are so blatant, so deliberate, so costly to the insurance company that it decides to accuse you of fraud, payment can be denied even if the two- or three-year period has passed. But the insurer has to be prepared to carry its case to court.

In general, disability policies are bought by people in their thirties and forties, to protect against illnesses that might strike in their fifties and sixties. The younger you are, the less you pay for the insurance. If you buy new coverage after age 60, the maximum period for collecting benefits usually can't exceed two years.

Younger people should add to their coverage as their income rises. The price of each addition depends on your age at the time. You don't have to buy from the same insurance company. If you find one with a better rate, use it. A health check is required for each addition, unless you bought a rider letting you forgo it (page 343).

Forget the credit disability policies that may be tacked to auto loans, personal loans, and mortgages. They cover your monthly loan payments if you're totally disabled. But they're expensive, relative to the tiny benefits they pay. Apply the money instead to a straight disability policy that will help you cover all your expenses.

From a disability-income standpoint, your most vulnerable moment may come when you change jobs. You'll probably lose any disability coverage you had with your old employer. And your new company may not add you to its disability plan until you've been there for a year or two. That's another reason to own a private policy on the side.

If you're self-employed and work at home, disability coverage is hard to get. The insurer cannot easily tell exactly when you're working and when you're not. You need an aggressive insurance agent, to be sure that every stone is turned.

POLICY FEATURES: WHAT YOU NEED, WHAT YOU DON'T

Disability policies vary a lot in their details, which makes it hard to compare them exactly. Each company may define its terms a little differently than I have here. Still, this gives you the gist of what you're looking for.

• **"NONCANCELLABLE."** Look for that magic word on the front of your policy. It guarantees your right to renew your policy every year for as long as it lasts. The company cannot change the benefits or raise the price. With a policy that is merely "guaranteed renewable," the insurer is allowed to raise the price on the category of policies that includes yours.

If you buy disability coverage through an association, you generally have no continuity rights at all. The policy can be canceled at will by the association or the insurer, or its premiums raised.

Keep track of your policy's renewal date! It's not unknown for a company to forget to send the bill. If you don't pay your premium on time, for whatever reason, your policy will expire. To avoid any slip-ups, you can usually have the premium deducted automatically from your checking account each month. You'll pay only slightly more than you would for an annual premium.

It is rare, but not unknown, for a company to "neglect" to send renewals to certain policyholders, who might have accounted for a lot of claims. This practice, known in some states as *starring,* is illegal. If you think it has happened to you, complain to the state insurance department.

• **BENEFITS AND COVERAGE GOOD TO AGE 65.** Policies that pay benefits for just a year or two are relatively inexpensive and might sound like a good bet. Only around 10 percent of disabilities last longer than a year. But what if you're one of the unlucky 10 percent? You and your family need protection against the very worst that can happen, which means a steady disability income to age 65. At that point, your benefits would stop.

You'd pick up Social Security retirement pay (if you're not already on Social Security disability) and maybe a pension.

You can also buy a policy that pays benefits for life, if you're disabled anytime up to age 65. But the price is much higher. Lifetime benefits are strictly a luxury buy, for a person with a high current income who isn't saving very much of it. In real life, many people cancel their disability policies earlier than age 65. They may retire early. Or they may accumulate enough net worth to guarantee an income even if they couldn't work, which means they don't need disability coverage.

Depending on your occupation, you might not be able to get coverage to age 65. In that case, take the longest period you can get or that you can afford.

Don't keep your disability policy after you retire. It's a total waste of money. Your policy won't pay unless you're forced by a disability to leave a paying job.

If you're still working after age 65, and not receiving disability benefits, you might be able to continue your coverage to age 70 or 75 but at a high price. It's probably not worth it.

• **MAXIMUM COVERAGE.** Don't save money by buying less disability income than you actually need. The policy either supports you when you can't work or it doesn't—and if it doesn't, your financial plan isn't worth a tinker's damn.

Generally, insurers put your maximum coverage at around 40 to 80 percent of your current earnings. (For the average person, they don't count other sources of income, such as interest and capital gains). The more you make, the lower the percentage they'll cover. A person earning $30,000 a year should be able to buy 75 percent coverage ($1,875 a month). But a person earning $200,000 may be able to buy only 55 percent coverage ($9,166 a month). Some companies offer higher maximums, so ask your insurance agent to shop around.

If you have a lot of income from interest, dividends, and capital gains, you won't be able to buy as much disability insurance. The rules on this point vary from company to company. Some might restrict your coverage if your unearned income reaches $1,500 to $5,000 a month; others, if your unearned income exceeds 20 percent of your earnings. The wildly rich can't buy disability insurance at all. They don't need it. They'll live on their capital if they can't work.

What if you can't afford maximum coverage all the way to age 65? Insurers recommend that you buy the top benefit for as many years as you can afford.

  • **THE RIGHT DEFINITION OF "DISABILITY."** The most expensive policies cover you if you can't perform the major duties of *your own occupation*. A surgeon is disabled if he or she loses a finger. You would receive a full disability check even if you took up another line of work. "Own occ" coverage is generally limited to professionals and others with well-paid, clearly defined jobs.

But is such a high-cost policy a wise use of your insurance dollar? I don't think so. You want to protect your income, not your occupation. There's no point spending extra money on "own occ."

Instead, take a look at a less-expensive *income replacement* policy, offered by just a few insurers. It doesn't cover your job at all. It looks only at how much you're earning. If you're totally disabled, you get your full insured benefit. If you can work at your own job part-time, or can handle a lower-paying job for which you are reasonably suited, your policy pays the percentage difference between your lower earnings and your insured benefit. For example, say that you're earning 60 percent of what you did before. Your policy will pay 40 percent of your disability benefit. So whatever happens, you can rely on having the insured portion of your income fully protected.

Not many companies sell income-replacement policies, because buyers are so mesmerized by the notion of "own occ." But it's worth exploring. One company in this business: USAA in San Antonio, Texas.

Your third choice is a mixed definition of disability. For the first two to eight years, depending on the policy, you're disabled if you can't work in your own occupation. After that, you're disabled only if you can't work at any job that *reasonably fits your education, experience, and training.* If the nine-fingered surgeon can teach medicine, he'd no longer be disabled. His checks would stop, whether or not he actually found a teaching job. A medical exam determines whether you're still disabled under this broader definition.

For some jobs, "reasonable occ" is the only coverage offered. But it's perfectly serviceable. In most cases, if you can't work in your own profession you can't work in any job—in which case, "reasonable occ" coverage pays the same disability benefits as "own occ," and for a lower price.

Different insurers offer different kinds of benefits for people in different occupations. It's a boutique business. Policies are tailor made. Ask at least two independent insurance agents to make you a proposal.

• RESIDUAL BENEFITS. These provide income replacement to people who choose an "own occ" definition of disability, then recover the ability to work in their own jobs *part-time*. Without residual benefits, your disability payments would stop, because you're back to work in your own occupation. With residual benefits, the part-time nature of your income is acknowledged.

You are paid a percentage of what you were insured for, depending on how much you can earn. Say, for example, that your policy carried a maximum benefit of $3,000 a month. If, after a stroke, you can work part-time earning half your previous income, you'd get half your disability benefit, or $1,500.

Residual benefits should also click in if you're capable of working at your old job part-time but choose to take another job instead. Check this point. Some policies fail to cover it—meaning that you'd be forced back to your old job part-time, like it or not. You're generally considered partially disabled if, because of your health, you lose at least 20 percent of your former income.

Many insurers require a period of total disability before residual benefits can be paid. Others cover you right from the start. You can collect "resid" for the policy's full term.

Normally, you cannot coast on your "own occ" coverage if you're capable of going back to your own job part-time. The insurer will insist that you do so, on pain of losing benefits.

But some companies leave the back-to-work decision up to you— and if you get residual benefits, working usually pays. Say, for example, that after a skiing accident, a surgeon can stay on his feet only for short operations. But he's able to earn 50 percent of his old salary. Fifty percent of his old pay plus 50 percent of his insured benefit usually add up to more than he'd get in total disability pay.

Who needs residual benefits? Usually the self-employed, like doctors and other professionals, whose income depends on the amount of time they work.

Corporate executives should think twice. Would you get your full salary, even if you returned to work for a shorter day? If so, drop residual benefits. (Some insurers package them right into their basic policies;

others sell "resid" separately.) On the other hand, maybe you'd have to leave your job and find something less taxing but still in your own occupation. In that case, residual benefits would help.

Some less-expensive policies make fixed-dollar payments for partial disability—for example, $1,000 a month, regardless of what you can earn. You're entitled to benefits if you can't perform one or more of the major duties of your occupation or can't work full-time. But these payments usually stop after 6 or 12 months.

• **A LONG WAITING (OR ELIMINATION) PERIOD.** Don't arrange for payments to start the first day you're disabled, or even after the first month. Early coverage costs too much. A three- or six-month waiting period makes more sense. A 180-day wait might cut your insurance premium by 30 percent.

You should coordinate your coverage with any temporary sick pay that you'd get from your employer. If the company pays you for six months, your private policy should pick up from there. Or coordinate your policy with the amount of cash you keep in your emergency fund. If you usually have three months' salary on hand, your disability policy should start in the fourth month.

• **REHABILITATION PAYMENTS.** Your policy should pay for a rehabilitation program, in order to get you back to work. It may also help you train for a new job. But it won't finance any rehabilitation if it's clear that you'll never be able to work again.

• **TRANSITION BENEFITS.** Disability income normally stops when you return to work full-time. But what if you go back too soon and find that you haven't the stamina to earn as much money as you did before? Your policy should take up the slack. It should also resume paying benefits if a relapse puts you back in bed.

• **NONSMOKER DISCOUNT.** Not all companies offer this. If you don't smoke, look for a policy that rewards you for it.

• **PRESUMPTIVE DISABILITY.** You are presumed to be totally disabled if you lose the use of any two limbs, eyesight, speech, or hearing. Full payment is due, even if you find a way to go back to work.

• • •

• **WAIVER OF PREMIUM.** When you become disabled, you no longer have to pay for your disability coverage. This waiver is a smart buy.

• **INTEGRATED WITH SOCIAL SECURITY AND OTHER PLANS.** Some policies automatically reduce your payment if you collect any disability income from Social Security, worker's compensation, military benefits, or a state disability fund. This provision lowers the price you pay.

Other policies take the reverse tack. They assume that, if you're totally disabled, you'll qualify for Social Security. You can buy a rider that will pay you extra income if Social Security turns you down. Given Social Security's gimlet eyes, that's a rider you'll want to have.

• **A COMPETITIVE PRICE.** Costs vary widely from company to company. So consult at least two different insurance agents, to widen the choice of policies you'll be offered. Mutual insurance companies may charge higher premiums, but they usually pay dividends, which could make their policies cheaper in the long run.

For level-premium coverage, the National Insurance Consumer Organization suggests that you use as a benchmark a policy from the USAA Life Insurance Company (800-531-8000) in San Antonio, Texas. Get a price quote and a list of benefits. Then ask insurance agents to try to find you something better. If they can't, go with USAA. It has no insurance agents and pays no sales commissions. You deal with the company yourself, by phone or mail. USAA writes life and disability coverage for the general public (only its auto and homeowner's policies are restricted to present or former military officers and their dependents).

If you don't want, or can't afford, level-premium coverage, get a quote on annually renewable insurance from a couple of the companies offering it (page 333).

THE EXTRAS

Insurers offer a lot of riders that raise the price of your basic policy. Some are worth it. Most aren't.

• **FUTURE-PURCHASE OPTION.** Worth considering, but only if the price is reasonable. It lets you add coverage, even if you become uninsurable. And incidentally, you don't have to be sick to be uninsurable. A company might reject you if you've had a mild heart attack or been diagnosed as prediabetic.

The right to buy more insurance without a health exam may cost 5 to 20 percent of the policy price, depending on your age and the company. Each time you exercise this option, you'll pay the premiums for your age at the time.

If you take this rider, use it. Add to your policy on a regular basis. A future-purchase option generally expires sometime between age 46 and 52—so don't fail to update your policy in that final year.

If you don't choose this option, and stay in good health, you can still increase your disability insurance as your income rises. But you'll have to pass a medical exam.

· **INFLATION PROTECTION.** Many policies have a small amount of inflation protection built in. Your insured amount might rise by 5 percent a year for the next five years. Or your insured amount might be linked to the Consumer Price Index. But once you become disabled and start getting benefits, your payments are fixed.

To index your actual payments, you generally have to buy a cost-of-living rider. This rider guarantees that, once you're disabled, your payments will increase every year. You might choose a fixed annual raise, like 4 percent or 7.5 percent. Price: around 20 to 45 percent of the basic premium. For more precise inflation protection, link your payment to the Consumer Price Index. Price: perhaps 16 to 40 percent of the basic premium. Not cheap, but worth the cost if you can afford it. A fixed disability payment could be chewed up by inflation in just a few years.

In looking at what you can afford, spend your money first on the maximum monthly benefit. Then add the future-purchase option, which contains an element of inflation protection. Last, add the cost-of-living rider.

· **PREMIUM REFUND.** After 5 or 10 years, you get some or all of your premium back, if you've made no claims. Or you get a multiple of your premium back, minus your claims. This option costs an extra 50 percent or more—definitely not worth it. Put the extra money in the bank.

· **HOSPITAL INCOME.** You get a certain number of dollars per day while you're in the hospital. Forget it. Hospital bills are covered under your health insurance.

• • •

• **ACCIDENTAL DEATH AND DISMEMBERMENT.** This unnecessary rider hitches a bit of life insurance to your coverage. But it pays only if you die (or lose a limb) in an accident. *No* accident policies are worth what you pay for them.

PREEXISTING CONDITIONS

When you fill out your application, you have to disclose all the illnesses you've had in the past. The insurance company will either (1) cover them at the policy's regular price; (2) charge you a higher price; (3) restrict your benefit; (4) refuse to cover a particular ailment; or (5) refuse to cover you at all. If any restriction is applied to the ailments covered, ask your insurance agent to talk to more companies—or try a different insurance agent. Some insurers will accept more risks than others. You don't want to be uninsured, or underinsured, for the illness most likely to disable you, if you can possibly avoid it.

Don't lie about your illnesses. The insurer will check your health history through the Medical Information Bureau (page 316). It may also check your medical history with your doctor. If you've had your policy for two years (three, in some states), you're fully covered, even if you made misstatements on your application form. But if a disability strikes in less than two (or three) years, your claim can be denied and the policy rescinded.

INCOME TAXES

You pay no tax on disability income from policies that you buy with your own after-tax money. Most worker's compensation isn't taxable. Nor is income from state disability funds (unless the payments are in lieu of unemployment pay). But income from employer-paid plans is fully taxed. Up to half of your Social Security disability income can also be taxed, depending on how much other income you have.

DON'T LEAVE HOME WITHOUT IT

If you have to work for a living, and have no disability insurance, you effectively have no financial plan. Everything you own is held hostage to your continuing ability to get up in the morning and catch a bus. That's no way to live. Buy as much income-replacement coverage as you need or can get. Fit it into your budget the way you do any other necessity, and go on with your life.

15
THE DRIVING
DREAM:

The Search for the Cheapest Auto Insurance

———

If you hold your car for four years or so, and
have a teenage driver, it can cost you more to
insure it than it did to buy it.

Auto insurance is a toll bridge, over
which every honest driver has to pass. Policies cost the most in cities
and suburbs. That's where most of the cars are, and, as night follows
day, most of the accidents. But even in the wide-open countryside, the
price of insurance is going up.

Rates are rising for a lot of reasons.

Today's cars are getting complex and expensive to repair.

Streets are getting more congested, so people bump into each other
more often.

In some cities—Boston, especially—theft is endemic. In others,
fraud seems unstoppable—with Los Angeles its capital city.

Medical costs are out of sight.

There's more litigation and higher settlements in injury cases.

Badly designed no-fault laws encourage litigation rather than discourage it.

More buyers have been choosing small cars and sports cars, which generate more collision and injury claims than big cars.

By law, insurance companies are allowed to exchange price information, so they may not compete as much as they should.

In some states, inept regulation has forced even good drivers into assigned-risk pools, where they're charged extra for their coverage. The whole crazy system needs reform.

There are ways to reduce your insurance costs, about which more below. But how you insure against an auto accident—and what you yourself can expect to recover—depend on where you live.

FAULT VERSUS NO-FAULT

IF YOU LIVE IN A "FAULT" STATE, and are hurt in an auto accident that is the other driver's fault, you collect from his or her insurance company. That presumes that the other driver *has* insurance, which may not be the case. Many of the country's most reckless road hogs don't bother with coverage, even in states that supposedly require it.

If you luck out, and the other guy does have insurance, the policy might be too small to cover all of your injuries.

You can sue for a larger amount. But it won't do you any good, unless the driver is rich enough to pay. Moral: Make very sure that you're hit only by a millionaire.

If you caused the accident, you'll probably collect nothing from your auto insurance for your own injuries. If you're partly at fault, state law dictates to what extent your policy pays.

The "fault" system does produce occasionally huge judgments. You can sue not only for medical costs and the wages you lost while out of work, but also for "pain and suffering," which is often where the big money lies. But it's a lottery. You collect only (a) if the other guy has enough insurance and personal assets to cover a judgment and (b) if the accident was his fault. Many injured people get much less than they deserve, or nothing at all.

IF YOU LIVE IN A "NO-FAULT" STATE, and are hurt in an auto accident, your own insurance company pays auto-medical bills and lost wages up to a certain ceiling. You collect the money even if the accident was entirely your fault. (But if no-fault sharply limits how much it will pay for each medical service, as it does in New York, you may have trouble finding a good doctor to treat you, especially if your injuries are serious.)

If your injuries are bad enough, you can also go to court and try for a pain-and-suffering award. There, the "fault" rules apply: You don't collect unless you can prove that the other driver was at fault.

IN EITHER TYPE OF STATE, your insurer will investigate the case, handle the settlement negotiations, defend you in a lawsuit, and pay any judgment against you up to the limit of your policy. If the judgment is larger, you have to cover the excess amount yourself.

WHAT KIND OF COVERAGE DO YOU NEED?

Liability for Bodily Injury

ABSOLUTELY ESSENTIAL. It protects you if you're sued for injuring someone in an accident, including pedestrians and passengers riding in your car. The policy pays the victim's medical costs, loss of earnings, and pain and suffering. You're also protected if someone is injured by a family member driving your car, a friend who is driving your car with permission, or a family member who is driving someone else's car with permission.

How much liability coverage should you carry? That depends on how you look at it. I offer three angles of vision.

1. *Protect your assets.* That means buying enough insurance to cover the highest judgment you might reasonably be called upon to pay. If you don't own much besides your car, you'd buy only the minimum that your state requires—maybe $10,000 for every person injured, up to a cap of $20,000 for the whole accident. You could be sued for more but it's unlikely, because there's no chance you could pay. By contrast, a homeowner might want to insure for $100,000 for each person injured, with a maximum of $300,000 per accident—or even a straight $300,000 per accident. The wealthy might want $500,000 to $1 million worth of coverage or more. The richer you are, the more protection you need. Count it money well spent.

2. *Protect yourself.* If you're hurt by a driver who's uninsured (or underinsured), you can be covered by your own policy. But you can't collect any more than you bought to protect the other guy. A $10,000 cap for him means a $10,000 cap for you, too. If that's not enough, buy more.

3. *Protect the injured.* Drivers have a social and moral obligation to everyone else on the road. If you damage a life you should pay for it. That means buying a substantial insurance policy even if you don't have a lot of assets to protect. Higher liability limits may not even cost very much.

Liability for Property Damage

USEFUL, BUT NOT IN LARGE AMOUNTS. This pays for damage to someone else's property, usually the car but sometimes a store front or gasoline pump. You need at least enough to cover the fair market value of the average car—say $15,000, or $60,000 if you worry about hitting a new Mercedes.

Medical Payments

NOT MUCH NEEDED IN FAULT STATES. This coverage picks up the medical (and funeral) bills of anyone injured in your car, without regard to who caused the accident. It covers your family if they're hurt as pedestrians or while riding in another vehicle, including a taxi or a bus. It covers an elderly friend who stumbles while getting into your parked car and breaks her hip.

But it offers less protection than meets the eye. Your health insurance already covers your medical bills. If your auto insurance pays only the bills not covered by health insurance, any payout may be small. People injured in your car may also have health insurance; if they want more money, they'll sue for it. For these reasons, many people skip medical-payments insurance, or buy $2,000 per person just to plug the deductible in a health-insurance policy. If your health insurance is skimpy, beef up that policy, not this one.

IN NO-FAULT STATES, MEDICAL PAYMENTS ARE TUCKED INTO YOUR BASIC AUTO-INSURANCE POLICY.

Personal-Injury Protection

REQUIRED, IN NO-FAULT STATES. You're covered for: (a) your own medical bills up to a stated limit; (b) part of your lost wages; (c) funeral expenses; (d) in some states, replacement services—for example, a baby-sitter hired while a mother is in the hospital.

How much you ultimately collect depends on your state. There may be no ceiling, or one as low as $1,000. There may be a low ceiling on each doctor bill. You can usually fall back on your health insurance, if no-fault doesn't pay enough of each bill—but that depends on your state.

New York, for one, requires that medical bills under $50,000 be paid only through your no-fault auto policy. Furthermore, it puts sharp limits on what doctors and therapists can charge.

To lower the cost of your personal-injury protection (PIP), see if your medical bills and lost wages can be paid primarily by your regular health and disability insurance. If so, you can then buy less PIP. It becomes a backup system, for expenses otherwise unpaid. (Your auto insurance agent may forget to mention this possibility, because anything that lowers your price lowers his or her sales commission.)

Collision

ESSENTIAL FOR NEW CARS; USEFUL AS LONG AS A CAR HAS SUFFICIENT VALUE. This portion of your policy covers repairs to your own car after an accident, no matter who caused it. If the car is totalled, and was financed, you need the insurance to repay the loan.

The price of collision insurance depends on the size of the deductible. That's the amount you pay toward each repair before the insurance policy kicks in. Deductibles range from $100 to $1,000. The higher the number the less your insurance costs. If the accident wasn't your fault, your insurer may arrange for the deductible to be paid by the other driver's policy.

Collision insurance is generally written to cover the car's fair market value—defined as its book value (as determined by standard tables), minus the cost of making repairs, minus a charge for unusually high mileage. The insurer won't pay a penny more. So drop the coverage on cars so old or so dented that their value is nominal. What's nominal? Any loss that leaves you philosophical instead of sore. Probably, that means something under $1,500.

Comprehensive

ESSENTIAL FOR NEW CARS; USEFUL EVEN FOR OLDER ONES. This pays for random damage to your car from fire, flood, vandalism, hail, pets chewing the upholstery, and the odd stone thrown up on the highway. It also covers theft, and perhaps the use of a rental car after a theft. (Removable tape decks, CB radios, and other expensive equipment might be covered by your homeowner's policy, or by a special rider to that policy.) Deductibles range from $50 to $500; the higher the deductible, the cheaper your insurance. Windshields may be insurable separately, with no deductible.

Comprehensive insurance covers the car's fair market value, which generally declines with time. Many drivers keep their comprehensive even after dropping collision, because comprehensive tends to be cheaper. Still, the insurer won't pay anything more than the car is worth.

Uninsured and Underinsured Motorist

REQUIRED, IN MANY STATES. OTHERWISE, YOUR CALL. This coverage pays the cost of your own injuries if you're hit by (1) an uninsured driver who's at fault, (2) an at-fault driver whose small insurance policy won't cover all your damages, or (3) a hit-and-run. It also covers lost wages. In some states, you might even be reimbursed for damage to your car.

Why bother with uninsured-motorist coverage (you might ask), if your life, health, and disability policies already protect your family, cover your injuries, and pay you an income? One reason might be that uninsured motorist insurance covers more. If you didn't cause the accident, or were clipped by a hit-and-run driver, you may be able to collect a sum for pain and suffering. That could help with other expenses, like support systems if you become disabled. Another reason might be that, due to the nature of your work, you can't get good disability insurance.

If you want this coverage, don't skimp. Many states (but not all) let you buy as much to protect yourself as you buy to protect the other guy. In no-fault states, your uninsured-motorist coverage clicks in if you're injured badly enough to sue. You can collect from this policy on top of your no-fault, personal-injury protection.

But if you're satisfied that your life, health, and disability insurance is top-flight, uninsured motorist coverage is a waste. You'd be better off adding to your regular disability policy, which covers you at all times, not just when you're driving a car. Skip this coverage, too, if you live in a state with a good no-fault law, like Michigan. There, no-fault benefits are generous and it's hard to sue for pain and suffering. So uninsured-motorist insurance doesn't add much.

Towing and Service/Rental Car Reimbursement

A TOSS-IN. If you have an accident or your car breaks down, you're covered for the cost of towing and the labor charges for repairs. The price: $5 or so a year. For another $20 to $30, you might get $15 to $20 a day to rent a car while yours is being repaired. Small stuff like this you can take or leave. If you belong to an auto club, leave it; these benefits probably duplicate what you have already.

Umbrella Insurance

WORTHWHILE, IF YOU'RE RICH. An umbrella policy covers liability judgments that exceed the limits of your auto and homeowner's policies. Typically, you have to carry $300,000 worth of liability on your basic policies. After that, you can insure for up to $1 million or more. Umbrella insurance is generally priced according to the number of cars you own. Expect costs to range from $75 to $200 or more a year. Some companies tuck a $1 million liability option right into your auto and homeowner's policies.

Umbrella coverage may defend you not only against claims of damage or personal injury, but also against libel (unless you're a professional writer or broadcaster), slander, false arrest, invasion of privacy, and similar charges that spoil your day.

MORE WAYS TO SAVE MONEY ON AUTO INSURANCE

• *Compare prices.* Here lies your single biggest shot at saving money. In any city, some insurers charge up to 50 percent more than others and their customers may not even realize it.

Insurers don't price-advertise, so it takes some work to find a policy that's low-cost. No single company always has the best rates. Each one prices differently, in different places, for different kinds of customers.

The National Insurance Consumer Organization recommends that you start with a quote from State Farm (which sells through agents) and GEICO (sellng by mail from Washington, D.C.; call 800-841-3000). Both companies tend to be in the lower price range. Present or former military officers, including their spouses, widows, and widowers, should try USAA in San Antonio, Texas (800-531-8080).* Their grown children can insure with a USAA subsidiary, which charges somewhat higher rates.

With these prices in hand, ask an independent insurance agent if he or she can do any better for you. Often, the agent can turn up an even lower rate.

When you find a company that's substantially cheaper, switch. But

---

* For auto insurance, USAA accepts commissioned or warrant officers and their families from all of the uniformed services, including the Coast Guard, the National Oceanic and Atmospheric Administration, the Public Health Service and the U.S. Information Agency; also, foreign service officers of the U.S. State Department, Special Agents of the FBI and Treasury, and officer candidates.

if you've been with your company for many years, don't leave just for penny-ante savings. Long-term policyholders sometimes get special treatment. For example, your insurer might be less likely to raise your premium after an accident. If you do switch, don't let your old policy run out until the new one is in force.

· *Find out if your state has an auto-insurance buyer's guide.* A few consumer-minded insurance commissioners publish price guides, showing what the various auto-insurance companies charge. It's a true public service—something all states should do, since they have all the rates on file. To see if your state has a buyer's guide, call the insurance commissioner's office in the state capital.

· *Don't buy your collision and comprehensive coverage from the lender who finances your car, or any insurer he or she recommends.* That's going to be high-cost insurance. Count on it.

· *Buy a car that's cheap to repair.* Your insurance agent can tell you which cars are money-eaters and which aren't. By this measure, a Ford Escort might cost $400 less to insure than a Cadillac Eldorado.

· *Raise the deductible on your collision insurance, from $250 to $500.* You pay less for the policy if you eat the smaller bills yourself.

· *Drop collision insurance on an older car.* You may be paying more for coverage than the car is worth. If you get into an accident, the insurer won't pay any more than the car's fair market value. To determine that value, ask your auto dealer for an appraisal. The value is generally calculated as the car's book value if it were in pristine condition, minus the cost of making repairs, minus a charge for unusually high mileage.

· *Earn a discount, by insuring all your cars with the same company, and by buying your homeowner's or tenant's insurance there, too.* But shop first for the cheapest insurer. Even with a discount, high-priced policies are no bargain.

There may be additional discounts for young drivers who take driver education; teetotalers; nonsmokers; graduates of defensive-driving courses; senior citizens; students with good grades; families whose teen-age drivers go to school more than 100 miles away (so they can't get at the car!); cars parked in a garage or off the street; low-mileage cars; drivers who car pool; cars with airbags or seatbelts that wrap around you automatically; cars with four-wheel, antilock braking systems; and cars with antitheft devices.

· *Describe exactly how your car is used.* A car driven for pleasure costs less to insure than a car used for everyday commuting.

• *Tell your insurance company or agent about any changes that could lower your rate.* For example, you should pay less when: (1) the young driver in your family graduates from college and leaves home; (2) you retire and stop using your car for commuting; (3) you start car pooling, or move closer to your place of work; (4) you install an antitheft device; (5) you move from the city to the country; (6) you divorce, and your spouse (who has all the speeding tickets) stops using your car.

• *Pay the premium all at once, if you can afford it.* It costs more to pay in monthly or quarterly installments. (But the smaller monthly payments are often easier to handle.)

• *Share your car with your teenager (if you can stand it).* When teens have their own cars, or drive your car more than half of the time, they're "principal drivers" and cost more to insure. They cost less when they're "occasional drivers," using your car less than half the time.

• *Drive safely.* Your rates go up if your record shows convictions for drunk driving, "chargeable accidents" (meaning they're at least partly your fault), or several speeding tickets.

• *Reform.* If your bad driving record landed you in a high-risk pool, or tags you with a higher rate at your insurance company, work at keeping your record squeaky clean. After a year or so, you might qualify for coverage at a lower rate. One insurer that specializes in high-risk drivers: the Progressive Corporation, Mayfield Heights, Ohio.

• *Make all valid claims.* Drivers often don't make small claims on their companies, for fear of driving up their insurance rates. But the claim might not affect your price at all. For example, you're normally not held responsible for certain types of physical damage, like a windshield broken by flying gravel; accidents caused by animals; accidents that aren't your fault; and claims below a certain limit, like $300 or $600, even if you were at fault. Ask your company for a detailed statement, in writing, of what claims make your rates go up. That should ease your mind about reporting other kinds of claims.

• *Move.* Low insurance rates give you yet one more reason to avoid big, crowded cities. You can save $1,000 or more by living in a small city, a suburb, or the country.

BUY QUALITY

Not all insurance companies survive. Some go broke, sending their policyholders scrambling. The industry supports state insurance-guaranty funds, to make sure that the claims of all policyholders will eventually be paid. But a truly large bankruptcy might test the funds' soundness.

So why tempt fate? Buy from a company rated A-plus for financial solvency by the A. M. Best rating service.

One more thing: When your policy arrives, check it for accuracy. A number of policies come through with mistakes: wrong amounts of coverage, a child left off the list of drivers, a discount forgotten. If you don't catch the error, you won't have the coverage you expected.

WHAT TO DO IF YOU HAVE AN ACCIDENT

Keep this list in the glove compartment, just in case.

1. Attend to any injuries. Have someone call an ambulance and the police.

2. Move your car to a safer place, if it can be driven, in order to prevent further damage. Warn oncoming traffic away from the wreck.

3. Get the other driver's name, address, phone number, license number, vehicle registration number, and insurance company, and give him yours. Look at his or her license, to see if there are any restrictions he or she wasn't observing (wearing eyeglasses, for example). If the car is registered to someone else, get that person's name and address.

4. Get the names and addresses of witnesses, and their statements of what they saw. This is especially important if you think you weren't at fault. If they won't talk, get the license numbers of their cars. Get the names and badge numbers of the police who arrive on the scene.

5. If you think the other driver was drinking, insist that you both take a breath test.

6. Jot down your recollection of how the accident happened, including the speed you were traveling at. Note weather conditions, time of day, and any hazardous conditions. Describe the area, writing down exactly where you're located. Fresh impressions are compelling in court.

7. Don't sign anything. Don't admit guilt, or shared guilt. Don't say that your insurance will cover everything. Don't say how much insurance you have.

8. Ask the police whether you should report the accident yourself, and if so, how and where.

9. Call your insurance agent and tell him or her what happened. Summarize the evidence you have. Don't rely on the other driver's promise to pay; that might not last long. Report even small accidents, if someone was injured. That injury might turn out to be serious. You risk losing coverage if you don't report promptly.

10. If you or any of your passengers were injured in any way, even bruised, see a doctor.

11. Cooperate with your insurance company, on filling in forms and making reports. But don't make a quick, final settlement, with your own company or with the other driver's. Injuries that don't seem serious at first may worsen with time.

12. If you're struck by a hit-and-run driver, tell the police within 24 hours. If you don't, you might lose your insurance coverage.

13. Keep records of all expenses connected with the accident, such as the cost of renting a car until yours is fixed. In a no-fault state, your company might pay. In a fault state, the other person's company should reimburse you, if the accident was his or her fault.

14. If the accident was serious, talk to a lawyer about what happened, to get a handle on your rights and what your damages might be.

WHEN TO SEE A LAWYER

The following claims will be paid immediately, without a lawyer's intercession: *in no-fault states,* your own medical bills and lost earnings, and those of everyone in the car with you; *in fault states,* only the medical bills that are paid through your own health insurer, or through the medical-payments coverage you carry on your auto insurance; *in both kinds of states,* car repairs, if you carry collision insurance.

You will need a lawyer: *in no-fault states,* when the injuries are serious enough to warrant going into court; *in fault states,* when the accident was serious. You need an evaluation of the settlement proposed by the insurance company.

The insurance company will defend you if you're sued. But if you bring the lawsuit, you'll need a lawyer of your own. He or she should have long experience in trying personal-injury cases. At a first meeting (which might be free, or might cost a flat fee), the lawyer will advise you whether the case is worth pursuing. Sometimes it is, sometimes it isn't. If you go ahead, you typically pay the lawyer nothing if you lose and a fixed percentage (usually one-third, plus expenses), if you win. If the insurance company has already made you an offer, a lawyer might be persuaded to take one-third to one-half of anything extra he or she can get.

· · ·

Collision claims are usually negotiated between you and your company, without legal intercession. A good insurance company inspects the car, tells you to get an estimate of what it will cost to repair, and promptly pays its share of the bill. No muss, no fuss.

And then there's the other kind of insurer: a foot-dragger, a corner-cutter. Don't blindly sign a piece of paper accepting the insurer's estimate as the full cost of the repair. Get a second opinion from your own mechanic. If you're forced to take your car to the insurer's repair shop, don't sign a release until your mechanic has looked at the work. If more work is needed and the claims adjuster balks, invoke the arbitration clause contained in many auto-insurance contracts. When it's all over, find a better insurance company.

If your car is totalled or stolen, the insurer is supposed to pay fair market value. If the offer is too low, get signed statements from auto dealers in your area, attesting to your car's actual value. With those statements in hand, make a pitch for more. You never get what you don't ask for.

If you think you're being taken, go on the offensive. Complain to your insurance agent, the state insurance commissioner (copy to the president of the insurance company), and your local consumer office. Ask a lawyer to write a letter on your behalf to the insurance company's president. Tell your insurance agent that you're pulling all of your policies—auto and homeowner's—out of the company. Sometimes, pressure works.

If the accident was the other person's fault, your company will go after his or her insurer and collect your property-damage claim in full. In that case, you're owed a refund for the deductible you paid. Don't forget to ask for it.

FITTING YOUR COVERAGE INTO YOUR FINANCIAL PLAN

Spend your money on high liability coverage, so that any reparations you owe will be paid by the insurance company, not by you personally. Good auto insurance protects your personal assets just as surely as a good investment plan.

16
FIRE! THEFT! WIND! FLOOD!

Protecting Your Home and Everything in It

Without enough insurance, you're betting your
savings that nothing bad will happen. I'd rather
bet a few extra bucks that something might.

■ have a friend whose house burned
down. Luckily, he'd updated his fire-insurance policy just a few months
before. Unluckily, he'd made the mistake of pegging his coverage to the
resale value of his house. He figured that—for insurance purposes—his
house was worth what he could sell it for, minus an estimate for the
price of the land and the cost of the foundation, which wouldn't burn.

That's a mistake a lot of people make. The resale value of your house
is almost always less than the cost of rebuilding it from the foundation
up—and rebuilding a house is what fire insurance is all about. My
friend's policy turned out to be too small. His error cost him plenty.

Homeowner or tenant, you're living in a dream world if your property isn't fully protected. It doesn't matter that you've drawn a nice
financial plan. It doesn't matter that you're saving money and living
smart. One pretty day you might come home from work and see nothing

but fire engines and flames. In a few shocking hours your house is gone. And so are your savings, if you don't have enough homeowner's or tenant's insurance to make good the loss. You'll have to start building up capital all over again.

Some people deliberately play the odds. It's rare for a house to be destroyed completely, so they limit their coverage to only 80 percent of the cost. *But a financial plan is only as sound as its backup systems.* When you insure your home for something less than 100 percent, you are holding your savings hostage to luck. If your coverage slips below 80 percent of replacement cost, which it easily might, even your lesser losses won't be fully insured (page 362).

WHAT TYPE OF INSURANCE TO BUY

Each insurance company has a slightly different policy. But they all follow the same broad outline.

HO-1, FORM 1, OR "BASIC FORM," is the cheapest. It covers no more than 11 or 12 risks, leaving out such common accidents as burst pipes, falling tree limbs, and sudden leaks from an air-conditioning system. Don't settle for HO-1 if you can avoid it. Knowing its flaws, many companies have quit offering it. Some policies cut you down to 8 or 9 risks, perhaps leaving out vandalism, glass breakage, and theft. That's usually for a remote or one-season cottage that is uninhabited for months at a time. Buy it only if it's the best you can get.

HO-2, FORM 2, OR "BROAD FORM," costs a little more. It covers 17 to 19 risks to your house and personal property, ranging from fire, wind, and living in the path of the Mount St. Helens volcano, to burst pipes and a short-circuited electrical system.

HO-3, FORM 3, OR "SPECIAL FORM," is better yet. On your personal property (like clothes and furniture), it covers loss or damage from the same risks named in HO-2. On the house itself, however, you're protected from all risks except a few that are specifically excluded, like earthquakes, sewer backups, floods, and wars. Some companies offer similar coverage for specified personal property.

HO-4, OR FORM 4, for renters or owners of cooperative apartments, covers 17 or 18 risks to your personal property, just like the better homeowner's policies. An HO-6 policy covers personal property as well as structural damage to alterations that owners of condominiums and cooperative apartments made themselves. A few insurance companies offer top-of-the-line, "all-risks" coverage to renters and coop and condo owners.

Some renters and condo owners think they're covered by the insurance held by their landlord or owners' association. Not so. You need separate protection for your personal property, for any part of the structure that is your personal responsibility, for any improvements you make to your own apartment or unit, and for your liability to anyone who is injured in your home.

If you've made a lot of renovations, take a look at how much you're covered for. Normally, only 10 percent of your policy's face value can be used to make repairs on your own additions or alterations. You might want to boost this part of your coverage.

HO-8 IS A SPECIAL POLICY FOR UNIQUE OLDER HOMES, like fine Victorians or true Colonials. They'd cost far more to replace than their current market value. In some cases, they cannot be replaced at all. So in many states, your coverage is based on the market value instead of the rebuilding cost. A few states require insurers to pay the replacement cost less depreciation, if that comes to more than the market value. (Depreciation is the loss in value attributed to age.) But they don't have to pay the full replacement cost. If an antique banister burns you'll get a new banister, but not one of intricately carved oak.

Your unique house is covered only against the 11 risks commonly used for HO-1 policies. That leaves out burst pipes and faulty wiring, which older homes are especially subject to. You can't even get replacement-cost coverage for personal property or for lesser losses, like a kitchen fire. Nor can you usually insure your personal property for more than 50 percent of the policy's face value. HO-8, in short, is mediocre —but sometimes the best that you can get.

INFLATION PROTECTION costs extra, but it keeps your coverage from lagging far behind the actual cost of rebuilding your home. The face value of your policy is raised automatically by a fixed percentage every three months, or by the annual increase in local construction costs. But there's no guarantee that this rider will always keep you fully insured. If it doesn't, the extra cost comes out of your pocket.

GUARANTEED REPLACEMENT-COST COVERAGE IS THE CADILLAC POLICY. Buy it if you can. If your house is damaged, the insurer will pay to repair or replace it in virtually every detail, even if the cost exceeds the policy's face value. If you built the house yourself, the insurer may even pay for supervision by the same architect you had before, and the same interior designer who helped you pick out the tile and other built-in items.

You have to insure for 100 percent of the expected reconstruction cost, minus the cost of the foundation and underground pipes. Every year, the face value (and the price) of your policy rises automatically, in line with the increase in local building costs. If you improve your house in some way, you have to notify the insurer so that that extra value can be covered, too.

From time to time, the insurer may make an on-the-spot evaluation. Don't accept a big increase that you think is unjustified. You're not required to pay for anything more than what it would cost to rebuild today. If you think the insurer is overvaluing your property, take your case to your insurance agent or get a counterappraisal of your own.

HOW MUCH INSURANCE DO YOU NEED?

More than you think.

For all of your losses to be covered in full, you must be insured for the house's full replacement cost. You can't go by market value, which includes the land as well as the house. You need to know what it would cost to rebuild from the foundation up.

You'll get the best answer from a builder or appraiser. Otherwise, go by your insurance agent's rules of thumb. Leave out the cost of the basement and foundation walls, as well as underground pipes and drains. They rarely need replacing. But include the cost of everything above ground, including a detached garage.

"Guaranteed replacement-cost" coverage keeps you fully insured for the right amount. Second best is automatic inflation protection. Third best is to use your insurance company's worksheet every time your policy comes up for renewal to figure out how much more insurance you need to buy. *You'll probably have to increase your coverage even if housing values fall.* No matter how bad the real-estate market, building costs generally go up.

What happens if you're insured for less than replacement cost? That depends on how much less.

IF YOU'RE COVERED FOR 80 PERCENT OR MORE OF REPLACEMENT COST, your insured losses are paid in full, up to the limits of your policy. Say, for example, that your home's replacement cost is $100,000 and you're insured for

$80,000. If a fire in the kitchen costs you $5,000, the whole bill is paid (less a deductible). If the house burns to the ground, you collect $80,000. (A few companies require 90 percent coverage before smaller losses will be paid in full.)

IF YOU'RE COVERED FOR LESS THAN 80 PERCENT, you will not collect in full on any loss, even a small one. On a kitchen fire that costs $5,000 to fix, you might get $4,000 or less. The exact amount will depend on the age of the house and the payment formula used.

Some homeowners gamble that the worst won't happen and don't insure for 100 percent. I think that's nuts, but maybe you know more about the future than I do. At the very least, keep your policy at 85 percent of replacement cost. That assures full coverage for anything but a catastrophic loss and avoids philosophical discussions with your insurer over whether your coverage met the critical 80 percent test.

If you're totally burned out, you can build a different kind of house. But unless you have replacement-cost coverage, the insurer won't pay more than the policy limit. If that's not enough to rebuild, too bad.

WHAT'S COVERED, WHAT ISN'T

Policies differ. So do state laws governing what has to be covered. But here's a general look at what your policy might include.

• Garages, sheds, driveways, fences, and other detached structures.

• For homeowners, trees, shrubs, and plants worth up to 5 percent of the policy's face value, with a maximum of $500 per item. For renters or condo owners, it's 10 percent.

• The contents of a house—covered for 50 percent of the policy's face value. Some insurers have raised that limit to 75 percent. You're insured for losses both at home and away from home, including things stolen from your bank safe deposit box.

• Reasonable living expenses if you have to move out of your house while it's being repaired. Ditto if the authorities move you out of your house because of direct damage to a neighbor's house by a peril that your policy insures against. For example, your company would pay your hotel bill if the police or fire department prevented you from going home because your neighbor's house was on fire. This coverage is sometimes limited to 20 percent of your policy's face value.

• Lost rent if you rent out part of your house and those quarters become uninhabitable because of a fire or other insured damage. But you don't get the full amount. The insurer deducts the rental-business expenses that you normally would have incurred.

· Removing debris from your property.

· Up to $500 if your town doesn't have a fire department and you contract with the firefighters of another town to pay a fee if they make a house call.

· "Medical payments coverage," for the minor medical bills of visitors or employees hurt on your property or injured by your family or pets away from home. If your dog bites the window-washer, you can send your insurer his doctor bill. Typically, you're insured for up to $1,000. For a few bucks more, you can raise that to $5,000.

· Up to $500 worth of damage that you accidentally do to the property of others, and another $500 or $1,000 for losses from forgery, counterfeit money, credit card theft, or theft by a computer whiz who lifts money electronically out of your account.

· Theft or damage to the personal property of a guest or a domestic employee.

· Up to $1,000 for a loss to your condo or coop building, if your owners' association assesses you for it.

DIFFERENT POLICIES HAVE DIFFERENT EXCEPTIONS. BUT IN GENERAL, HERE'S WHAT MIGHT BE RULED OUT.

· A separate structure on the property that's used for business or rented out.

· Losses due to a power failure from a source outside your home.

· Water damage, including floods, tides, sewer backups, and seepage from ground water. But you're covered if accidental damage to the roof lets in the rain, and from the havoc wrought by firefighters' hoses.

· Losses from neglect—for example, property that's stolen because you walked away from a partly burned home without boarding up the windows.

· Damage you deliberately do yourself.

· Earthquake, except by special rider.

· Ice or snow damage to awnings, fences, patios, and swimming pools.

· Vandalism to houses left vacant for more than 30 days.

· Frozen or burst pipes in a house you've left unoccupied, without maintaining the heat or draining the pipes.

· Damage from settling or cracking.

- War.
- Normal wear and tear.
- Damage done by birds, rodents, insects, or your own pets (although the policy will pay if a porch collapses due to hidden insect damage).
- Smoke damage from nearby factories or agricultural smudging.
- Claims on policies obtained by misrepresentation or fraud. So don't lie if you're asked whether your dog bites.
- A continuous leak from the plumbing, heating, or air-conditioning system (you're covered only for sudden leaks).
- Nuclear explosion—although if you're nuked, the exclusions in your homeowner's policy will be the least of your troubles.

COVERING YOUR PERSONAL PROPERTY

Standard coverage is the cheapest. But it looks better on paper than it is in fact. Go for more comprehensive coverage, if you can afford it.

Standard Coverage

Your clothes, furniture, and other personal effects are normally insured for up to half the face value of your homeowner's policy. A few companies insure them for 75 percent. With a $200,000 policy, then, you get $100,000 to $150,000 worth of personal-property protection. You can usually raise that ceiling by paying an extra premium. Your property is covered when it's in your home, when it's temporarily out of your home, or when it's with one of your children at college.

If you're a renter, or own a condominium or cooperative apartment, you insure for the full value of your personal property.

Standard Reimbursement

It's not terrific. Your couch may have cost $700—but that was five years ago, before it was clawed by your cat and used as a trampoline by your kids. Your insurance covers only its current market (or flea-market) value, which—as priced by standard formulas—might be $400. The additional cost of a new couch comes out of your pocket.

Almost everything new loses value over the years: furniture, clothing, electronics, cameras, broadloom. Your insurer will repair the damaged item or reimburse you for its current value, whichever is less. But you won't get the money you need to buy something new.

Antiques, on the other hand, should go up in value as the years go by. Your basic insurance will generally cover their current appraised value, even though it's higher than when the policy was new. But you'll have to prove your claim—with a proof of purchase, a new appraisal, a picture, and other details about the items. The insurer can also decide to repair an item rather than replace it.

Replacement-Cost Coverage

If you can afford it, this is the kind of insurance to have. It gives you the money you need to start over from scratch. For example, when your $700 couch goes up in flames, you might collect $900, because that's what it costs to buy a couch of similar quality, new. The insurance company will also make repairs, if the item can be restored to its original condition.

Only replacement-cost coverage can restock your closets, rooms, and china cabinets after a major wipeout. Good insurance companies pay the full retail price. The only articles not covered are those that are obsolete and in storage (your old Schwinn bicycle) and articles not in working condition (the broken TV set in the back bedroom).

Before buying the insurance, check the following cheapskate games that some companies play: (1) The policy might pay no more than four times the "actual cash value" of any item. Actual cash value means the replacement cost minus depreciation. This formula lowers your recovery on very old furniture. (2) The policy might reimburse you only for what it would have cost the insurance company to replace a particular item. That might be wholesale rather than retail. Don't be nickeled and dimed like this. Find a better insurer. Replacement-cost coverage, from a good company, is far, far better than standard reimbursement. Well worth its higher price.

Standard Limits on Valuables

In standard policies, insurers pay a fixed, maximum price for certain items, no matter how large your total coverage is. The limits: $2,500 for the theft of silverware, goldware, pewterware, and gold and silver plate; $200 for all bullion coins, rare coins, cash, and gold, silver, or platinum bars; $1,000 for all securities, deeds, manuscripts (which might include rare books), tickets, letters of credit, accounts, evidence of money owed you, and stamps; $1,000 for boats and their trailers, furnishings, equipment, and motors; $1,000 for other trailers; $1,000 for grave markers;

$2,000 for guns; $2,500 for business property on the premises; $250 for business property away from the premises (such as a laptop computer stolen at an airport); and $1,500 for the theft of jewelry, watches, gems, and furs. That does not, incidentally, mean $1,500 for your jewelry, another $1,500 for your watches, and so on. It's a flat $1,500 for the entire class of items.

These limits apply to valuables in your bank safe deposit box as well as to property kept at home. To raise your coverage, see below.

Blanket Coverage

For a small extra payment, you can raise the limit on most of the categories listed above. For example, you might want to cover $10,000 worth of jewelry with a $2,500 limit per item. If something is stolen, you'd report the loss, substantiate its value, and collect. No proofs of ownership are required in advance, but you'll need them if you make a claim. So keep sales slips and take pictures of your valuables, just in case.

Scheduled Coverage

Particular items of special value should be individually insured. Have each one appraised and listed separately: sterling silver flatware, $5,000; mink coat, $6,000; Hope Diamond, $7 zillion. If any scheduled item is stolen, damaged, or lost, the insurer pays its scheduled value, with no deductible. But there may be no coverage for accidental breakage, unless you pay extra.

Other valuables, such as antiques, collectors items, fine china, guns, musical instruments, or golfing equipment, don't have to be scheduled to be fully covered. You can insure them for their actual cash value (including any appreciation in value) right along with your other personal property.

HERE ARE THE ADVANTAGES OF SCHEDULING YOUR VALUABLES.

1. They're covered if they merely disappear. If they're not scheduled, there has to be a likelihood of theft.

2. They're protected against practically all forms of damage, not just the 18 listed in your regular policy. This includes accidental wine or ink stains on an Oriental rug.

3. If they're included in your basic policy, they might push the value of your personal possessions above the policy's maximum limit. It's often cheaper to schedule a few items than to raise the ceiling on your total coverage.

4. You won't have to haggle with the insurer over whether you really owned the items and what they were worth.

HERE ARE THE DISADVANTAGES OF SCHEDULING:

1. It costs extra money.

2. You're covered for no more than the exact amount of the appraisal. If your Picasso lithograph was listed at $2,500 that's what you'll get—even if the appraisal is old and the lithograph is worth $4,000 today. Had it not been scheduled, you'd have gotten its current market value, minus the deductible.

3. You may wind up paying for insurance that you don't really have. Say, for example, that you scheduled your mink for $5,000. It's now three years old and worth only $3,500. If it's stolen, you'll normally get only $3,500, even though it's insured for more. Solution: Buy replacement-cost coverage for scheduled items. You'll then be paid the full value that they were insured for.

All scheduled items should be reappraised regularly, so they won't be underinsured. But the special items that you don't schedule need to be appraised only once, and their pictures taken. If they're damaged, their value can be updated, based on the work that was done before.

Count the Risks

You're insured only against the specific risks listed in the contract—as few as 9, as many as 18. You can also buy "all-risks" coverage, which actually should be called "almost all risks." It leaves out things like floods, war, and wear and tear. But only all-risks coverage protects you against paint dropped on the carpet or wine stains on your pink velvet loveseat. Ask your company about cigarette burns. Some cover them under the "fire" clause in your basic policy; others pay only if you buy all-risk insurance. Also ask about breakage: What's covered, what isn't?

If a guest damages your property, his or her policy might pay, under the property-damage clause or the liability clause.

What May Not Be Covered

Policies vary on this point, but here are some likely examples:

• Pets.

• Damage done to your property by pets (although if your neighbor's dog knocks over your Ming vase, the neighbor's policy might pay).

• Aircraft.

• Boats, except in very limited circumstances.

• Most motorized vehicles and the equipment, radios, or tape decks in them (unless they're parked on your property). But you're usually covered for off-road vehicles that service the premises, like lawnmowers, or that assist the handicapped, like motorized wheelchairs.

• The property in a room you rent regularly to someone not in your family.

• Records and data pertaining to your business.

• Theft of materials from a house under construction.

• Items that disappear, without the likelihood of theft.

• Breakage, unless it's vandalism.

• Loss of a gem from its setting.

• Marring.

• Wear and tear.

• Your roommate's property. Each of you needs a policy of your own.

Ask about any special items in your home. A computer. A satellite dish antenna. A wine cellar. A coin collection. Ask about family members. Does the policy cover your mother who lives with you? Clarify your coverage *before* any damage is done.

When You Don't Replace

What if a spare camera is stolen from your house and you don't want to buy another one? At the very least, you'll be paid its current, flea-market value (replacement cost minus depreciation). If you carry replacement-cost coverage, you may get the full replacement value only if it's not substantially higher than the market value or not over $1,000. Some companies, however, pay straight replacement value, whether you buy a new camera or not.

When Your Lost or Stolen Property Is Found

You can give it to the insurer and keep the money. Or you can keep the property and give back the money. Your choice.

UPPER-CRUST COVERAGE

Some policies are specifically aimed at the well-to-do. You get replacement-cost coverage on both your house and its contents. You get protection against "all risks." In addition, there might be:

• Higher payments for valuable items. For example, jewelry and furs may be covered up to $5,000, silverware up to $10,000, and guns up to $5,000.

· Coverage for a power outage in your neighborhood.

· Coverage for food lost when your freezer thawed.

· A bit of liability coverage for a small, part-time business run out of your house. The policy might also pay toward replacing data lost in an accident to your personal computer.

· Coverage for damage from the backing up of a sewer or drain—not included in the average policy.

· Higher limits on your coverage for personal liability.

· Recompense, up to $500, for the cost of changing the locks when your keys are stolen.

· The additional cost of rebuilding a damaged or burned-out portion of your house to meet the standards of a new building code.

· Reimbursement for items not obviously stolen but simply missing.

· Homeowner's, auto, and umbrella insurance, bundled together for a single package price.

You can get much (but not all) of this upper-crust coverage by increasing the limits on your regular policy or by buying riders. Which choice to make depends on what you need. Ask the insurance agent to make a list of all the extras in the higher-cost policy. Cross off the ones that aren't essential. When you've pared down the list, find out what it would cost to add those extras to a standard policy. There's no point buying more insurance than necessary.

Even with upper-crust coverage, you may have to schedule valuable items like silverware, jewelry, and furs.

LIABILITY INSURANCE

This is your "banana-peel" coverage. You're protected if someone—not a family member—slips on your banana peel, breaks a leg, and sues. You're covered for injuries on your premises. Your family members (and pets) are also covered for their actions (or bites) away from home. Some states require that you carry worker's compensation, to cover domestics, painters, gardeners, and other full-time or occasional employees. You're also covered for property damage—for example, if the wind blows a branch off your oak tree and drops it on your neighbor's car. It doesn't matter that you told her not to park her car there. It was your oak.

Only *unintentional* damage and injuries are covered, unless the perpetrator is under 13. So you can't slash your neighbor's tires in a driveway dispute and expect your insurer to replace them. But it will pay in full if your small daughter hits your neighbor in the eye with a rock.

What if that same daughter, at 14, vents her emotions by deliberately setting fire to your neighbor's porch? The property damage won't be covered. But injury to your neighbor might. Your lawyer (you'll need one!) will argue that, although she meant to scorch the porch, your daughter didn't intend to send anyone to the hospital for smoke inhalation, so the injury was unintentional. Right now, some policies pay if a court holds a parent financially responsible for children's evil deeds. Other policies don't.

If your dog bites the United Parcel Service driver, your insurance pays. If the dog lunches next on the driver for Federal Express, it pays again. But at that point the insurer may cancel your policy, refuse to renew it, or try to exclude the dog (I say "try to" because it's not clear that such an exclusion would stand up in court). In some states, courts can levy extra, "punitive" damages after a second bite—your punishment for keeping a dangerous dog unleashed. Those extra damages might not be covered by your insurance. After a dog bite, find out what your liability could be, if the sweet pooch should ever get loose again.

Your basic policy probably includes $100,000 of liability coverage. That's not much, especially if you own a swimming pool. For a small additional fee, you can have $300,000 of coverage or even $500,000. Some companies take you up to $1 million.

Alternatively, you can buy "umbrella insurance," which covers losses in excess of the limits on both your homeowner's and auto policies. You're required to carry certain minimums on your basic policies, maybe $300,000. After that, the umbrella goes up. The ceiling can be $5 million or more. The insurance might also cover your liability if you're charged with invasion of privacy, false arrest, libel, or slander.

NOT COVERED MIGHT BE:

• Employees and clients, if you run a business from home. Ditto if you run a child-care service. For these risks, you need separate business or day-care insurance.

• Aircraft.

• Injuries from most boats and motor vehicles (they have to be insured separately). But off-road vehicles like golf carts and dirt bikes might be covered. Ditto small boats, or boats parked in your yard.

• Claims by one family member against another.

· Damage to your own property.

· Any disease that someone catches from you.

· Damage done by a leaking waterbed to an apartment you rent, unless you cover the bed with a special rider.

If you're sued, your insurance company not only handles the damages, it covers all the legal costs of reaching a settlement or going to court.

FLOOD INSURANCE

YOUR POLICY PROBABLY DOESN'T INSURE YOU AGAINST FLOODS. In fact, there's usually not much protection against water damage of any sort. If flooding is a risk, and your community has met federal flood-prevention standards, you can insure yourself through the government's National Flood Insurance Program. For information, call 800-638-6620.

EARTHQUAKE INSURANCE

Insurance companies may sell earthquake insurance as a separate policy or as a rider to your homeowner's policy. In California, the minimum deductible is commonly 10 percent of the insured value. With a $300,000 policy, you would have to sustain more than $30,000 worth of damage before you'd collect. In other states, the minimum deductible may be 2 or 5 percent. The smaller the deductible you choose, the higher the price.

Prices are lowest for policies on wood-frame houses, which can sway with a quake and aren't too expensive to build. On brick or stone houses, Californians pay perhaps five times more (prices are much lower in other states). Best advice: Find out if you live anywhere near a geological "fault" (there are some in states other than California), and if so, get coverage.

What's the very best earthquake insurance?

Move to Dallas, where the earth doesn't move.

THE INVENTORY

Make a day of it—maybe a rainy Saturday in March. Lay in plenty of film. Plenty of diet soda. Plenty of chocolate bars to keep up your energy. Photograph everything in your house. Open every drawer, every cabinet, every closet, and take pictures from a close enough range to show all the contents. Make overall views of your rooms and what's in them. Take closeups of special items like good china, Waterford crystal, and antiques. Don't ignore the cellar and attic. When it stops raining, take pictures of the outside of your house—the landscaping, driveway, sidewalks, tool shed, pool.

When the pictures come back, describe the items briefly on the back. Put down the model number and price of the more costly items, and when you bought them.

If you have a video camera, use it instead. Talk about each item as you show it, recording the model and price on tape.

The inventory is your guarantee that you'll collect all the protection you paid for. With it, you can make a full list of all of your losses. Insurers will generally accept a list you reconstruct from memory. But you'll never recall every item, and all those little things add up. Pictures also show the quality of your furniture, and prove that your modest home really did contain an antique Oriental rug.

Keep the inventory—along with sales slips for the more expensive items and any appraisals or descriptive material about them—in your safe deposit box. You'd be chagrined if these records burned in the same fire that destroyed everything else.

Tot up the rough value of everything you own. It's probably double what you thought. When buying insurance most people focus only on their few expensive pieces of furniture. But what drives up the price of refurnishing a house is the pencils and potholders, jackets and mittens, baseballs and houseplants. Your family's clothing alone may be worth $8,000 or more.

APPRAISALS

All special items should be separately described and appraised—furs, good jewelry, antiques, paintings, Oriental carpets, rare books, special collections, and so on. Take pictures of them in relation to things in your home, to prove they were there. To find an appraiser, ask your insurer, ask a local jeweler and a furrier, or look in the Yellow Pages. Keep the pictures and appraisals in your safe deposit box.

The first appraisal is the most expensive, because everything has to be written up. After that, you can coast. The only appraisals that have to be updated regularly are those for the jewelry, silver, furs, and other items that are separately scheduled (see page 367). Leave everything else alone. When something is stolen or damaged, you just take in the description, the picture, and the original appraisal. The appraiser will update the value for you.

The only reason to reappraise everything is to run a check on whether you have enough personal-property insurance to cover all of your possessions.

WAYS TO SAVE MONEY ON HOMEOWNER'S AND TENANT'S INSURANCE

1. *Find a low-cost company by calling several agents and comparing prices.* Some charge much more than others for the same coverage. Prices vary depending on where you live, so the same company may not be the cheapest everywhere. Start with a price quote from State Farm or Allstate, then ask an insurance agent if he or she can beat it. If you belong to the family of a present or former military officer, call USAA in San Antonio, Texas (800-531-8080). * Grown children of officers can insure with a USAA subsidiary that charges somewhat more. State Farm and USAA are known for providing good service. Another high-rated company is Amica Mutual in Providence, Rhode Island (800-242-6422), which does business through its own branch offices rather than through insurance agents. It's cost isn't the lowest, but customer satisfaction is high.

2. *Buy your auto, homeowner's, and umbrella policies from the same company.* You may get a package deal.

3. *Install deadbolt locks, smoke detectors, a fire extinguisher, and burglar alarms.* You get a discount if your house is protected.

4. *Pay annually.* It's cheaper than paying semiannually or quarterly.

5. *Raise the deductible.* The standard deductible is $250—meaning that you pay the first $250 of any claim. The price of your policy goes down if you take a $500 or $1,000 deductible, but the savings may be

---

* For homeowner's insurance, USAA accepts commissioned or warrant officers and their families from all of the uniformed services, including the Coast Guard, the National Oceanic and Atmospheric Administration, the Public Health Service, and the U.S. Information Agency; also, foreign service officers of the U.S. State Department, Special Agents of the FBI and Treasury, and officer candidates.

only $50 or so. Ask yourself whether such a small price cut is worth the risk.

6. *Quit smoking.* Many insurers give nonsmokers lower rates.

7. *Buy replacement-cost coverage.* This costs more up front but may save you a bundle if you have a loss. Too many homeowners forget to increase their coverage every year, or don't increase it by enough. Replacement-cost coverage spares you the risk of being underinsured.

8. *Retire.* Many companies charge retirees less, because they're more likely to be home during the day.

9. *Call your state insurance department.* A few states help you price shop, by publishing booklets that compare what various companies charge.

10. *Buy a recently built house.* Discounts are often available for insurance on houses up to seven years old.

11. *Don't overinsure!* You might be paying for more coverage than you can use. Check it out, if you bought your house within the past few years and put only a small amount of money down. The lender typically requires you to buy enough homeowner's insurance to cover your mortgage. But the mortgage may have paid for part of the land as well as the house. So you're uselessly insuring your yard against fire and theft. Get an appraisal of the value of the house versus the value of the land, and a letter from your insurance agent confirming that the company won't pay any more than the value of the house. That should convince the lender to let you reduce your coverage.

WILL YOUR PRICE GO UP?

Make every claim you can on your homeowner's insurance. Multiple claims don't raise your rates. But if you have too many fires or thefts, your insurer might conclude that you're careless (or a cheater) and cancel your coverage. Ask your agent about your company's rule on this point.

THE PUBLIC ADJUSTER

As you're standing in the street, staring at the smoking ruins of your house, someone may shove a card into your hand. It's a public adjuster. He or she helps you evaluate your losses and bird dogs your insurance claim. The fee: 10 to 15 percent of what you recover.

Some people figure it's worth the price, to have the adjuster chase after proofs of value and handle all the paperwork needed to process a claim. But you shouldn't need an adjuster to get a fair settlement.

Your insurer or agent will give you advice on filing the claim. In the normal course, you'll be paid in full, without having to hire a consultant. If you don't agree with your insurer's appraisal, you can get one of your own and demand a referee. If you do decide to turn to a public adjuster, base the fee on the additional amount of money you ultimately get, beyond what you were originally offered.

A LIFE WITH CRIME

If insurers think that your neighborhood is too risky, they might not write coverage there. People who can't get normal homeowner's or tenant's coverage have two options.

FEDERAL CRIME INSURANCE—government-subsidized policies against robbery and burglary, available to people in high-crime areas who protect their property with deadbolt locks and other security devices. For information, ask an insurance agent or call 800-638-8780.

FAIR ACCESS TO INSURANCE REQUIREMENTS (FAIR) PLANS—private, and expensive, insurance policies, available in about half the states. Ask your insurance agent about them.

WHAT TO DO AFTER A LOSS

1. After a fire or theft, board up the broken windows in your home, so that the remaining property can't be stolen. Your insurer will pay for it.

2. After a theft, notify the police. Or notify the credit card or ATM card company.

3. Call your insurance agent.

4. Make a list of everything you lost, approximately when you bought it, and what you paid for it (or smugly produce the inventory you made in advance). The insurer will help you estimate current cash value.

5. Keep a list of all your expenses.

6. Get estimates for repairs.

7. Don't sign any contract to work with a public adjuster until you've first tried working with your insurance company.

8. If anyone is injured, don't take the blame without first calling your insurance company.

BUY THE BEST

Some homeowner's insurance companies have gone broke, and more will in the future. All the states have property/casualty guaranty funds to assure that policyholders don't get stuck. But the maximum recovery may be only $100,000 to $300,000, which might not be enough to cover your house. Save yourself the grief. Buy only from an insurer rated A-plus for financial solvency by A. M. Best.

TRUST NO ONE

When you get an insurance policy—any policy—double-check it to see that you got what your ordered. Large numbers of policies come through with mistakes: wrong amounts, wrong endorsements, wrong type of coverage. When you put in a claim and find you're not covered, it's too late to argue.

Once upon a time, a big wind flattened the flimsy homes made of sticks and straw that had been ruining the neighborhood. The gentry moved in and property values went up. The third little pig—with the house of brick—grew fat and prospered. Those were the days when everyone knew that houses mattered.

Nowadays it isn't so clear. House prices are high. Mortgage payments are stiff. In many parts of the country, property values are flat to down. For this (we ask ourselves), we're cleaning the gutters, painting the shutters, paying the taxes, and feeling broke? Why not rent a house and let the landlord worry?

But Americans won't, and never will. For all the huffing and puffing of the doubters, a home of our own is still the rock on which our hopes are built. Price appreciation aside (and most houses will appreciate, eventually), homeownership is a state of mind. It's your piece of the earth. It's where a family's toes grow roots. It's where the flowers are yours, not God's.

17

A HOUSE IS A
SECURITY BLANKET:

Yes, Doubters, It Still Pays to Own

Ignore the doomsters who advise you to rent,
not buy. They're moving investments around
on a chessboard. You're living a life.

Homeownership is your only hope of living "free" when you retire. Rent goes on forever. Mortgage payments eventually come to a stop.

A house may not be your best investment in the decade ahead. If the 1980s taught us anything it's that real estate doesn't always go up. Over the long run, the value of homes should follow the inflation rate. But over the time that you own your particular house, its value might rise or fall or stall. You can't predict.

But there are reasons other than profit for owning a home. Mortgage payments force you to save, while rental payments don't. You get tax deductions, and can tax-shelter your capital gains. You're landlord-free. You know the deep contentment of holding a spot of ground that others can enter by invitation only. You won't lose your lease. You can renovate to suit. Your mortgage payments build a pool of usable funds that you might not otherwise have saved. A house is collateral for a loan. House payments often cost less than rent, after tax. Above all, you can look forward to the day when—finally—you'll live mortgage-free.

27 WAYS OF BUYING YOUR FIRST HOME

1. *Save money for a down payment.* People are doing it every day. No video toys. No dinners out. A cheaper apartment than you really could afford. A night job. The average first-home buyer accumulates a down payment in about two and a half years—even when housing prices are going up.

2. *Borrow the down payment from your company profit-sharing, 401(k), or thrift plan,* if your firm allows it. For the details on taking this loan, see page 228.

3. *Withdraw the down payment from your company profit-sharing, 401(k), or thrift plan,* if your firm allows it. For details on cash withdrawals, as opposed to loans, see page 745. But this tack costs you income taxes, not to mention a 10 percent penalty if you're under age 59½. Loans are better than withdrawals, as long as you can carry the payments.

4. *Move.* If you can't afford a house near Washington, D.C., or Los Angeles, think about Wisconsin or Tennessee. Think it when you're young and looking for your first job, because that's often the place where you'll buy your first house.

5. *Commute.* The farther into the country you're willing to go, the cheaper the houses.

6. *Renovate.* If you can stand living with plaster and sawdust for a year or two, and are handy with tools, you can buy a wreck cheap and fix it up.

7. *Get lucky.* Some communities hold lotteries for affordable houses and townhouses. Some let you rent city-owned housing, and apply your rent money to a down payment. Some let you buy with no money down, or lend you a down payment. Some offer subsidized mortgages. You need a modest income (up to $20,000; sometimes up to $40,000) to apply. To find out if your state or city has any homeownership programs going, call your local housing agency or ask a real-estate agent.

8. *Get a mortgage backed by the Federal Housing Administration or the Department of Veterans Affairs.* They're given chiefly by local mortgage banks, as well as some commercial banks and S&Ls. With the FHA, you

can put down as little as 3 percent on a property appraised at $50,000 or less, under 5 percent on higher-valued properties, and 10 percent on newly built homes. With VA loans, there's often no down payment at all, although your lender may require one. You qualify for a VA loan if you're a member of the armed forces or certain other agencies or organizations, a veteran, or the unmarried spouse of a veteran who died from a service-connected illness or accident or who is missing in action.

FHA loans are only for houses that are modestly priced for their geographic area; so, effectively, are VA loans. Both carry slightly lower interest rates than conventional loans. With both, you owe insurance fees and loan-origination fees. FHA buyers pay points up front; points on VA loans are paid by the seller, although their cost may be included in the price of the house. The formulas that establish the loan ceilings pretty much reserve them for people of average or below-average means.

Some FHA lenders want to deal only with middle-class buyers. So they try to drive the lower-income people away. They do it by charging excessive fees on small mortgages—say, 4 or 5 percentage points on a $40,000 loan. (Anyone offered such a rotten deal should indeed shop the Yellow Pages for another lender.) Some banks establish minimum sizes on their FHA loans, which is illegal and should be reported to an FHA office.

One warning about mortgages with low down payments: If you resell within just two or three years, and pay a real-estate broker's commission, the money that's left may not be enough to repay what you owe the bank. So if you put almost no money down, try to make larger monthly payments to beef up your equity.

9. *Visit the Mommy-and-Daddy Bank.* Many children nowadays rely on their parents to lend or give them their first down payment. A parent who's a gambler might even co-sign your mortgage loan.

10. *Lower your consumer debt.* The less debt you have the larger the mortgage you can get. Mortgage debt helps improve your balance sheet; consumer debt doesn't.

11. *Buy private mortgage insurance through the lender.* With it, you're generally allowed to put down only 10 percent of the house price, and sometimes less. Without it, you normally need 20 percent. Typical price of private mortgage insurance: anywhere from 0.3 to 1 percent up front, plus a small charge each year. But private insurance isn't granted to everyone. You have to be creditworthy, and real-estate prices in your

neighborhood must be stable to rising. Once your equity reaches 20 to 25 percent, you may be able to cancel the insurance; ask your lender about it.

12. *Borrow part of the payment from your bank.* Take a loan against the credit line on your bank credit card, or write a check against your overdraft checking. This choice should be desperation only, to wrap up a deal; the money is expensive and lenders don't want a loan to supply the down payment. You might use these funds to cover your final closing costs.

13. *Sell your stocks and mutual funds.* You're not losing money if you put the proceeds into a down payment, you're just transferring your funds from one pocket to another.

14. *Make a deal with the seller.* The longer the seller has had the house on the market, the more willing he'll be to bend your way. Maybe he'll lower the price by enough to cover your closing costs. Maybe he'll let you pay part of the down payment over time. Monthly payments can be scheduled as if the loan were for 30 years, with the whole sum falling due in just one to three years. As a guarantee that you'll really pay, you give the seller a second mortgage as collateral. Right at the start of your house search, tell the real-estate broker that you need this kind of deal.

15. *Buy from a builder in a new development.* Builders often sell on especially affordable terms.

16. *Lease with an option to buy.* You generally pay a nonrefundable fee (perhaps $3,000 to $10,000 or more) for the right to buy the house in one to three years at a stated price. Then you move in as tenant, paying more than the normal rent. Part of each monthly payment, plus the upfront fee, is credited toward your down payment. Sometimes the buying price is set by formula rather than stated as a fixed amount. (With lease options, practically everything is negotiable.) When it comes time to buy, you have to get your own mortgage for the remaining money owed. To find a lease option, ask a real-estate agent, look for lease-option ads in the newspaper, or look at the classifieds under "Rentals." People renting out houses would sometimes rather sell. If you can't get a mortgage when the time comes to buy, and the option price is less than the house's fair market value, advertise the option for sale. That recoups at least some of your costs. Otherwise, the option will expire and you'll lose your money. Before doing a lease option, ask a lender whether you really have a shot at a mortgage. Also, show the documents to a lawyer.

17. *Buy a foreclosed house.* The Federal Housing Administration,

Department of Veterans Affairs, and Federal National Mortgage Association (Fannie Mae) will take low down payments on the homes they hold, and they offer reasonable prices and mortgage terms. On foreclosed homes held by banks or S&Ls, higher down payments are charged. For information on finding these houses, see pages 398–99. Many foreclosed homes need serious repairs, especially those belonging to the FHA and VA. Some are in neighborhoods you wouldn't touch, but others are terrific buys.

18. *Work nights and save the money.*

19. *Don't take a vacation.* Save the money instead.

20. *Do an equity-sharing deal with a relative or an independent investor.* There are many ways of tailoring this arrangement. But typically, the investor puts up most or all of the down payment and you handle the monthly payments. You and the investor divide any profits from the house's appreciation. For details, see page 406.

21. *Find a shared-appreciation loan.* These aren't around much nowadays. But they'll return if house prices once again start moving sharply up. You get a below-market interest rate, which reduces your monthly payments. In return, you give the lender 30 to 50 percent of the house's gain in value—due in a fixed number of years. To pay the bank, you either have to sell the house or refinance it. You may owe extra interest if the price of the house doesn't rise as much as expected.

22. *Buy a house with a couple of friends.* Not recommended. As your lives change, you'll each want to do something different with the property. You might fight. It could be hard to get your money out.

23. *Do a buydown.* The seller might put up $3,000 or so, to reduce your mortgage payments for one to three years. That lets you qualify for the loan. The downside is that the $3,000 will be added to the price of the house, and you'll pay more interest over the life of the loan. Many builders do buydowns to get the houses in their developments sold.

24. *Get a job with a company that helps its employees buy houses.* Some pay closing costs, or buy down the mortgage rate for a few years, or make low-interest loans to help you meet the down payment.

25. *Buy an older house.* It might cost 15 to 25 percent less than a newly built house, for the same floor space. So the down payment will be lower.

26. *Assume a mortgage.* When a seller has a low-rate mortgage, see if you can take it over. Usually, the lender will require that you pass a credit check and pay today's interest rate, but you'll save on closing

costs. Occasionally, you run into a mortgage that's assumable at the original, low rate, or at a discount from current rates.

When you assume a mortgage, you owe the seller the difference between the house price and the value of the old mortgage. If you can't raise the money, ask the seller to let you make monthly payments. (Urgent memo to seller: Be sure that the lender releases you from liability on the mortgage. Otherwise, you're responsible if the person who assumed it defaults.)

27. *Buy a condominium—an apartment or a townhouse.* They're cheaper than comparable free-standing homes. But they don't gain in value as much as a house (if they gain at all). And they're harder to sell when you want to trade up. For more on condos, see page 408.

Don't buy a mobile home unless you expect to keep it. Mobile homes generally lose value, so you're not building equity toward something bigger.

HOW LARGE A MORTGAGE CAN YOU AFFORD?

First house or fifth, here's what a lender classically wants to see.

• No more than 28 percent of your gross monthly income spent on housing expenses—principal, interest, insurance, and taxes. "Income" is the regular income you've had for at least a year, the bonuses and overtime that you've had for two years, or the alimony or child support that will last at least three years.

Lenders let you creep over this limit if you have a good credit history, offer a big down payment, already spend more than 28 percent of your income on housing expenses, or have liquid assets (like bank certificates of deposit) equal to three months' mortgage payments. Acceptable housing debt might rise to 30 percent, 32 percent, or even more. On the other hand, lenders will discount your gross income if you're self-employed. They'll go by what's left of your earnings after deducting business expenses.

• Total debt (mortgage and consumer debt) not exceeding 36 percent of your gross monthly income. Count as consumer debt any bills with at least 10 payments left. You might be restricted to 33 percent if you're putting less than 10 percent down. But again, people with good credit histories who have been carrying higher debt can probably go over these limits. VA loans may be available to people whose debts reach 41 percent of their gross monthly income.

• Scratch all these limits for high-cost housing areas such as California. There, you can qualify for a mortgage with housing expenses exceeding 40 percent of your income, as long as your job seems stable and your character sound.

A TECHNICAL PHRASE YOU CAN'T IGNORE

NEGATIVE AMORTIZATION. Negative "am," as it's called for short, is a high-tech, death-defying, money-eating system for owing *more* money every time you make a monthly mortgage payment. "Amortization" is the payment schedule by which you reduce a loan to zero. "Negative" amortization means that, instead of going down, your loan goes up.

You run into negative am whenever your monthly payments aren't large enough to cover all the interest due. As an example, say that you're paying $1,100 a month on a floating-rate mortgage whose rates go up. Your interest payment alone is now $1,175, but you keep paying $1,100. The bank adds that missing $75 to your loan principal, so you now owe more than you did last month. Your debt will compound because you're paying interest on interest. This happens principally with graduated-payment mortgages (page 388) and with adjustable-rate mortgages whose payments stay level for set periods while interest rates are going up.

POSITIVE AMORTIZATION is the opposite. Every time you make a payment, your debt goes down. If you're making fixed monthly payments on a floating-rate loan, and interest rates decline, your payment is now a little higher than necessary. That extra money reduces the loan principal.

From time to time, the lender will adjust your monthly payment, to account for all the positive and negative changes in your loan balance. But I have no evidence that your extra principal payments in the good years wipe out the effect of rising debt in the bad years.

Don't take a loan with negative amortization. When you sell your house, you might find that you owe even more than you originally borrowed.

FINDING THE RIGHT MORTGAGE

It used to be so easy. A 30-year loan. A fixed interest rate. Sign here.

Now you have dozens of choices—different rates, different terms, different fees. Here's the menu.

Adjustable-Rate Mortgages (ARMs)

In a normal world, I like these best. The interest rate and monthly payment change periodically with the general level of rates. Over a whole interest-rate cycle (where rates rise and then fall), ARMs should cost less than fixed-rate loans. They start out two or three percentage points cheaper, which gives you a big advantage right there. Any rise in payments should be temporary (although "temporary" means anywhere from two to perhaps four years). After that, your payments should drop again. Still, an ARM is a bet that inflation won't explode again. If interest rates rise for many years, it will be more expensive than a fixed-rate loan.

GET AN ARM IF: (1) You need the lower monthly payment in the first year, to buy the house you want; (2) you can handle higher payments when they come; (3) you won't panic when payments rise, because you have faith that they'll fall again; (4) you expect to own the house for only three or four years (short-term owners should go for the cheapest ARM they can find); (5) you have plenty of money, or plenty of confidence that your income will rise.

Fixed-Rate Mortgages

These loans offer personal security. You make fixed monthly payments for the term of the loan, no matter how high inflation goes. If interest rates fall, just refinance at a lower rate, although you may pay points and closing costs all over again. Fixed-rate mortgages make the most economic sense when they're priced within one percentage point of an ARM's *regular* interest rate (not its discount "teaser" rate, which may be offered in the ARM's first year). Fixed rates look particularly good when they come within nodding distance of 9 percent.

GET A FIXED-RATE LOAN IF: (1) The payments don't stop you from buying the house you want; (2) you can't count on your income going up, so you want to lock in your mortgage payments at their present level; (3) the thought of rising mortgage payments scares you stiff; (4) you think mortgage rates are unusually low; (5) you're near retirement and will be living on a modest income; (6) you couldn't afford your house if your mortgage payment rose.

Graduated-Payment Mortgages

You start out with lower payments than it normally takes to amortize the loan—lower even than you'd get on an ARM. In those first years, your payment is too small to cover all the interest due, so you suffer negative amortization (page 387). That means that your loan gets larger instead of smaller. Over a 5- to 10-year schedule, however, monthly payments gradually rise to cover principal as well as interest. You wind up paying more than you would have for a regular loan. Most GPMs have fixed interest rates, so you know what your payments are going to be. A few have adjustable rates, which makes them unpredictable. I don't like GPMs in principle, because of the negative amortization. I especially don't like adjustable-rate GPMs. Their changing payments defeat the whole purpose of locking in a price.

CONSIDER A FIXED-RATE GPM IF: (1) You need a rock-bottom monthly payment in the early years; (2) you want to lock in your future payments; (3) you'll own the house long enough to overcome any negative amortization (page 387); (4) you're sure that your income will rise by enough to cover all the higher payments; (5) there's no prepayment penalty, and you're free to refinance at a lower rate.

Renegotiable Mortgages

These are 20- or 30-year loans, at a fixed interest rate, which are called in for renegotiation every 2 years, or 5, or 10. At that point, the loan is rewritten at whatever interest rate is then current. The lender usually isn't required to renew the loan. If your credit has weakened, you can be told to pay up—which would force you to sell the house or find a mortgage somewhere else.

CONSIDER A RENEGOTIABLE LOAN IF: (1) You're getting a good interest rate and have no doubt that your credit will stay good; (2) you expect to sell before the loan comes up for renegotiation. Otherwise, an ARM makes more sense, because the full term of your loan is guaranteed.

Balloons

Balloon mortgages allow low, fixed payments for a short time, maybe one to seven years. After that, the entire loan falls due. Most commercial lenders promise to refinance the balloon when it pops. But to qualify, your payments can't have been any more than 30 days late over the past year; the property must be free of liens; and mortgage rates can't have risen more than 5 percentage points. Otherwise, refinancing isn't a sure thing. Most private loans by sellers are balloons, and without a refinancing guarantee.

GET A BALLOON IF: (1) You're an executive who expects to be transferred before the balloon falls due. (2) You're a first-time homebuyer who will trade up in a few years. (3) You are dead sure you can refinance the balloon. If you can't, you might lose the house.

ALL ABOUT ARMS

Take this checklist with you when you go to the bank.

✓ *What is the interest rate linked to?* The two most popular indexes are (1) one-year Treasury bills and (2) the cost of funds for S&Ls in the 11th District, which covers California, Arizona, and Nevada. Treasury-bill rates change faster, so your payments bounce around more. The cost-of-funds index changes slowly so your payments are more stable. But the very sluggishness of the cost-of-funds index means that it may still be going up when rates in general are coming down. Over a whole interest-rate cycle, a mortgage linked to Treasuries should cost less.

✓ *What is the spread between the stated mortgage-interest rate and the underlying index?* One lender might be two and a half points over the Treasury-bill index; another might be three points over. Between two lenders using the identical index, look for the narrower spread.

✓ *How often does the interest rate change?* Annual changes are the most common, although adjustments may be made as often as monthly or as rarely as every three to five years. Generally speaking, the more frequent the adjustment, the cheaper the mortgage over an entire interest-rate cycle (including both rising and falling rates). But if you're going to own the house for no more than three years, you might want an ARM that locks in your rate for that period of time.

✓ *How often does the monthly payment change?* You want it to change every time the interest rate does. Some lenders change the interest rate monthly but adjust your payments only once a year. That's a bad idea. When the interest rate rises but payments don't, you risk negative amortization, which increases the size of your loan. Better to change both the rate and the payment every six months or every year.

✓ *How many points will I have to pay?* One point is one percentage point of the loan amount—for example, $2,000 on a $200,000 loan. These charges are normally due when the loan is closed.

✓ *What are the caps?* You want limits on how much you'll have to pay if interest rates go leaping up. Some ARMs cap your monthly payments, letting them rise no more than 7.5 percent a year. But if interest rates rise faster, you'll wind up with negative amortization and a larger loan. So don't accept a payment cap. The risk isn't worth it. Instead, look for caps on how high the interest rate can rise, with no negative amortization. The best loans won't let rates rise by more than two percentage points a year, with a lifetime increase no greater than five percentage points above the rate you started with.

✓ *What happens next year?* You may have started with a "teaser" rate, maybe one to three percentage points less than the ARM would have cost without the first-year discount. In the second year, your rate will rise to its normal level (subject to the annual cap, if the loan has one). So your monthly payment will probably go up, even if interest rates decline. Be sure that higher payment won't be a problem.

✓ *How bad can it get?* Look at the largest monthly payment the loan might require. If that dismays you, get a fixed-rate loan or shop for an ARM with a lower lifetime cap.

✓ *What happened in the past?* Ask the lender to show you what would have happened to a mortgage payment the size of yours over the past ten years. If its gyrations seem too great, get a fixed-rate loan.

✓ *Is there negative amortization?* Loans with negative am occasionally allow your monthly payments to slip below the total amount of interest due. The unpaid interest is added to the loan balance. So your loan goes up instead of down. Not recommended. you'll find plenty of ARMs without this catch.

✓ *Can I convert?* Some ARMs carry the right to switch to a fixed-rate mortgage after a certain number of months or years, without paying closing costs all over again. Lenders vary as to how they charge for this privilege. Some add an extra eighth or quarter of a point to your interest rate. Some charge slightly more from the second year on. Some tack an extra eighth or quarter of a point to the fixed-rate loan you convert to. Some don't charge at all. At conversion, you might pay as little as $250 or as much as one point plus $250. Convertible ARMs are good buys if they cost no more than regular ARMs. If there's a charge, compare it with the cost of a regular ARM plus the price of refinancing it.

✓ *How do I check the rate?* If I had one dollar for every mistake a lender made when it adjusted an ARM payment, I'd be an instant millionaire. The bank may pick the wrong index, or pick the wrong date, or round the interest rate up when it should have been rounded down. When you take out an ARM, ask the lender to explain exactly when the rate will be adjusted, how it's done, and how you can track the index that your loan is linked to. Verify the rate whenever it changes, or whenever a change looks too big, or whenever your payment rises when interest rates in general have been going down. If you don't want to do the arithmetic yourself, you can have the accuracy of your payment checked by Loantech, Inc., P.O. Box 3635, Gaithersburg, MD, 20878; or LoanChek, Ltd., 7770 Regents Rd., #113, Suite 301, San Diego, CA, 92122. Both services charge $49 and both verify only principal and interest. Your monthly payments may also cover real-estate taxes and homeowner's insurance. Ask your lender how to check those.

FINDING THE RIGHT MORTGAGE LENDER

Mortgage banks are usually the cheapest. Their main business is making mortgages—especially those backed by the Federal Housing Administration or Department of Veterans Affairs.

Credit unions are your next-best bet.

Then try savings and loan associations.

Then try commercial banks.

A good real-estate broker knows the cheapest mortgages in your area. A few have computers that show them a range of loans at a glance. (But take care. Some brokers establish computer links with lenders, and earn fees for sending them your application. Those lenders may charge higher rates than you'd find elsewhere.) Another source of information: the services that survey the rates of the major mortgage lenders in various states and cities. Try HSH Associates, 1200 Rte. 23, Butler, NJ, 07405 (phone 800-873-2837 or 201-838-3330), at this writing, $20 for one weekly survey, either on paper or on computer disc; and Gary S. Meyers & Associates, 308 W. Erie St., Suite 300, Chicago, IL, 60610 (phone 312-642-9000), at this writing, $20 for one week's survey. Call first, to see if your area is covered.

IN THE SAME TOWN, ONE LENDER MIGHT CHARGE TWO OR THREE PERCENTAGE POINTS LESS THAN ANOTHER! So don't just drop into any old bank and ask for a loan. Over 10 years of payments, the difference between 10 and 12 percent interest on a $100,000, 30-year, fixed-rate mortgage is $18,125. The difference in payments comes to about $151 a month. That's a saving worth taking some trouble to find.

MORE MORTGAGE FACTS

• The formal mortgage application fee is sometimes stiff. You don't want to pay it fruitlessly. So *prequalify* yourself for a loan, to find out exactly how much you can borrow. A lender can tell you, just by looking at your income, your assets, and all of your debts. With this knowledge, you know how expensive a house you can afford to consider.

· To make the mortgage, a lender might charge you one to three points. A point is 1 percent of the loan amount. On a $75,000 mortgage, one point comes to $750, three points to $2,250. The larger your mortgage, the more willing the lender will be to lower the points, in order to get your business. So negotiate.

· Even with a small mortgage, you can lower the points by accepting a higher interest rate. What's your best choice? Take fewer points if you'll live in the house for four years or less. If you'll live there longer, accept extra points in order to get a lower mortgage rate. Some lenders will bundle the cost of points right into your mortgage loan. That saves you money up front but costs you big bucks in extra interest payments.

· Some lenders offer no-point loans. They cost you one-quarter to one-half point more than loans with points.

· To compare the cost of fixed-rate loans, look at the annual percentage rate (APR). The APR includes points and certain other financing charges, and is always higher than the stated rate. Unfortunately, this comparison isn't much use for adjustable-rate loans, because their APRs are good only until the rate changes.

· Look for a loan without a prepayment penalty. Lenders shouldn't charge borrowers extra just for paying off their mortgages ahead of time.

· It might take 30 to 90 days to close your mortgage. During that time, interest rates may change. A "floating" loan commitment provides the interest rate and number of points that are current on the day your loan is closed. A "lock-in" guarantees the rate and points available when you first apply. Use a floating commitment if rates seem to be falling; choose a lock-in (there's usually a fee) if rates seem to be rising.

Some lenders protect you against higher rates while allowing you any lower rates that come along. But get the lock-in in writing and read the fine print. It might be void if certain things happen—for example, if the rate on VA loans goes up.

The fee for the lock-in may be credited toward the mortgage-origination fee. You'll forfeit the fee, however, if you walk away from the deal. Lock-ins expire after a set period of time. So keep on the phone with the lender to make sure that the mortgage closes on time.

If you want to close on a new house before selling your old one, your lender may give you a "bridge loan" to cover the cost. Due in six months or a year, in a lump sum, it's a gamble for sure.

• A few lenders make quickie, "low-documentation" loans, to buyers who can put down 25 to 30 percent of the house price. There's only a cursory check of your income and employment. The lender closes your mortgage within 14 to 30 days. You need a blue-chip credit history and may be charged an extra one-half to three-quarters of a point in interest. *Question:* If you're so blue-chip, why would you voluntarily accept a higher mortgage rate? You might if you're self-employed and your tax returns don't show how flush with cash you really are. Or if your income varies a lot. Or if your debts are too high for a normal loan.

• Mortgages occasionally contain "calls." With a call, a lender can order you to repay or refinance the loan at any time. Watch out for this clause, especially in an ARM with a low lifetime interest-rate cap. If interest rates get over the cap, the mortgage agreement might allow the lender to call in the loan—forcing you to refinance at a higher cost. Fixed-rate loans may also contain a call clause, to save the lender if interest rates jump. *Never sign a contract with a call provision. The day may come when you'll regret it. Deeply regret it.*

• Some lenders offer "rate-reduction" mortgages. Takers start out with a fixed-rate, 30-year loan. If interest rates drop by anywhere from one and a quarter to two percentage points, during the loan's first one to five years, you have the one-time right to lower your own interest rate to match. However, you might pay a conversion fee of $250 to $500. You might also pay one-eighth of a point more interest for the loan itself. (Personally, I prefer an ARM that gives you the right to convert to a fixed-rate loan—see page 391. It's cheaper.)

• When you take a mortgage, you'll usually be offered tie-in insurance—life insurance, disability insurance, even unemployment insurance. If you die, become disabled, or lose your job, your mortgage payments will be made for you. Don't buy. The lender's life and disability policies are much more expensive than those bought through regular insurance agents. The disability coverage may be sharply limited. Unemployment insurance—also expensive—is particularly ephemeral. You're probably covered only if you're fired without cause (not if you're temporarily laid off, on strike, pregnant, disabled, or forced to retire early), and only if you qualify for unemployment benefits in your state. Even then, payments rarely last for more than a year. If you lose your job a couple of times, your policy might not be renewed.

• Your monthly payment to the lender usually includes the cost of your homeowner's insurance and real-estate tax. Those funds go into an escrow account, from which the bank pays the premiums and taxes when they come due. You might earn 5 percent on these accounts, if state law requires it. More likely, you'll earn exactly nothing.

Some lenders require that you keep an extra-high cushion in this account, forcing you to let a lot of money lie fallow. You should: (1) Ask the bank if you can pay your own taxes and insurance. This won't be allowed if the lender intends to sell your mortgage to an investor. But it's often done with very large loans that the lender keeps. (2) Ask that the escrow account pay a higher interest rate—rarely granted, but you'll never know if you don't ask. (3) Learn how to decode your annual escrow statement, to be sure that excess funds aren't building up. By law, the lender's cushion shouldn't be more than an extra two months' worth of payments. (4) If you find an extra two-month cushion, ask for it back. Some lenders say yes.

• Read all the loan disclosures. Question everything you don't understand. Don't rely only on the banker or real-estate agent to tell you how your mortgage works. Federal regulations require enough disclosure to make a mortgage foolproof—but nothing can make it dam-foolproof, if you will not read what you are signing.

LARGE DOWN PAYMENT OR SMALL?

If you have a choice, is it better to sock a lot of money into your home and take a small mortgage? Or should you take a large mortgage and invest the extra cash somewhere else? Different borrowers will reach different conclusions. Here are the issues to consider.

HOW MUCH WILL YOU EARN ON YOUR SEPARATE INVESTMENT? To be profitable, it has to yield more than the interest you're paying on the mortgage.

HOW MUCH DO YOU CARE ABOUT LOW MONTHLY PAYMENTS? If you care a lot, go for the largest down payment you can muster. The more cash that you put into the house, the smaller the loan you'll have to take and the less you'll have to pay each month. Buyers close to retirement usually put a lot of money down. Younger buyers usually don't.

HOW MUCH DO YOU CARE ABOUT A LOW-COST MORTGAGE? The bigger your down payment, the less your lender is likely to charge. You'll pay fewer points, and may even get a lower rate of interest.

HOW LIQUID ARE YOU? Everyone needs ready money. Don't make an extra-large down payment if doing so strips you of most of your cash. In theory, you can access the cash in your house just by taking a home-equity line of credit. But in practice, the lender can freeze that line if home values fall or your income goes down.

HOW SECURE IS YOUR JOB? If insecure, keep more cash in the bank. You can't rely on a home-equity line of credit as a fail-safe source of cash. If the bank ever heard you were out of work, your credit line might be frozen, and with it your ability to pay your bills.

Some accountants argue that, for tax reasons, you should take the largest first mortgage you can. With the leftover cash, you would then (1) make investments, at yields higher than your mortgage rate, or (2) pay cash for expensive consumer purchases, rather than acquire consumer debt. Your mortgage interest is tax deductible while consumer interest isn't.

That's good advice for people with high salaries, steady investment programs, and an inclination to avoid consumer debt. But if you're a spendaholic, or close to retirement, tax-deductible borrowing power matters much less than hanging on to your savings or reducing your monthly mortgage payments. For you, large down payments make more sense.

SHORT TERM OR LONG?

The traditional loan runs for 30 years. Young people usually choose this term, because the monthly payments are low. But it's expensive. You repay more than three times the amount you borrow over the mortgage's full term.

If you love punishment, some lenders even offer 40-year mortgages —where you repay more than four times the amount you borrow. Super-long terms aren't worth their price. You don't save enough on the monthly payment to compensate you for the ultimate cost. On a $100,000 loan, for example, choosing to repay over 40 years rather than 30 years reduces your monthly payment by only $28. And your equity grows much more slowly.

Among the middle aged, buyers are tumbling to 15-year loans, and sometimes even shorter terms. Monthly payments are higher, but these loans build equity faster and cut way down on your interest debt. You repay less than double the amount you borrow. With short-term mortgages, you can own your home free and clear by the time you retire.*

Biweekly mortgages also help you pay in a hurry. You amortize your loan over 30 years, to keep payments down. But instead of paying once a month, you make half a monthly payment every two weeks. This results in one extra monthly payment per year. In roughly 18 to 21 years you'll be free of mortgage debt, and at absolutely no pain. Biweekly payments are normally deducted automatically from your bank account.

With a growing-equity mortgage (GEM), monthly payments rise by a fixed amount each year. Each higher payment is applied directly to principal, to reduce the term of your loan. But your payment schedule is set in stone. You can't pull back if your income falls. You might also have to pay a higher rate of interest than you would for a regular loan. GEMs are good discipline. But personally, I'd rather have a conventional mortgage and accelerate it at my convenience.

ANY TIME YOU WANT, YOU CAN SPEED UP THE PAYMENTS ON YOUR PRESENT MORTGAGE. Ask the lender how to handle it (and make sure there won't be a prepayment penalty). Normally, you just send in a check for a larger amount than is actually due. Include a note, saying that the extra money should be used to reduce the loan principal. *Every extra dollar put into your mortgage may save you around three dollars in the future.* It also adds to your equity and shortens the term of the loan. (But just because you've prepaid some money, you don't have the right to skip a month. You still owe the basic monthly payment, no matter how far ahead of schedule you are.)

Here's how the different terms compare for a $100,000 loan:

	Monthly Payment*	Total repaid*
40-year loan	$ 849	$407,520
30-year loan	877	316,080
30-year biweekly	878†	237,605
15-year loan	1,075	193,500

* At 10 percent interest.
† Every four weeks. Loan repaid in 20 years, 10 months.
Source: Mortgage Bankers Association.

* Here's another idea for ensuring that you'll own your home free and clear in retirement. Look at how much you'll have left on your mortgage in the year you'll retire. Buy a zero-coupon bond (page 661) that matures in that year and delivers enough cash to pay off the mortgage.

IS IT WORTH YOUR WHILE TO PAY OFF YOUR MORTGAGE FASTER?

Often, yes. Faster payments will:

• Force you to save. Otherwise, that money might be frittered away.

• Build up your equity faster. By the time your children are 18, there should be enough money in your home to help cover their college tuition.

• Put you in a better position to trade up to a larger house. When you sell, you'll have more money in hand to put toward your next down payment.

• Insure that you'll own your own house by the time you retire.

• Save a small fortune in interest payments, even after taxes.

• Get you a lower interest rate. The rate on a 15-year loan may be a quarter- or half-point lower than the rate on a 30-year loan.

But it doesn't make sense to quick-pay your mortgage if:

• You're carrying a lot of 15 to 20 percent credit-card debt. You get a 15 to 20 percent return on your money just by paying it off. Do so, before accelerating mortgage payments.

• You can invest the money at a higher percentage return than you're paying in loan interest, *and* you really will do it.

• You'll live in the house for only three or four years. You still save some interest costs with accelerated payments. But with short-term residence, the amount is too small to notice.

Some small-time promoters are offering to accelerate your mortgage for you. You authorize them to withdraw the monthly mortgage payments from your bank account, along with a fee for their services. They pass your payments along to your lender. But what's the point? You can accelerate your own mortgage for free. These useless companies justify themselves by saying that you're too lazy, too careless, too undisciplined, or too stupid to do it. But you're not. Save your money and give these folks the wave.

BUYING A FORECLOSED HOUSE

Some get-rich-quick shows on late-night cable TV make you think you can buy a foreclosed home for no money down. That is almost never true. The financial institution that took back the house will want you to put up some purchase money.

Banks and S&Ls often ask for a standard down payment, which is their insurance against getting the property back again. Even higher down payments may be required if you're borrowing to buy a low-priced house that the bank doesn't own. Occasionally, you can make no-cash deals with the Federal Housing Administration or Department of Veterans Affairs, but they usually want some money, too.

Where you might get a break is the interest rate. The institution that holds the mortgage might cut your rate for the first year or two and even cover the closing costs. In deals like these, everything is negotiable.

Many real-estate brokers handle foreclosed properties for banks and government agencies, so ask about them. Your other options:

• By following the foreclosure sales, get the name of the officer at the bank who's handling a specific house you're interested in. Call him or her and offer at least 10 percent below market value (investors, as opposed to home-buyers, would want 20 percent off). You have to know local real-estate values. The bank won't give you any hints.

• Write for a list of the local foreclosed properties owned by the Federal National Mortgage Association. Address: Fannie Mae Properties, P.O. Box 13165, Baltimore, MD, 21203. Ask for its free booklet, "How to Buy a Foreclosed Home."

• Call 800-RTC-3006 in Dallas, to ask for a list of the local foreclosed properties held by the Resolution Trust Corporation, which is cleaning up the hundreds of failed S&Ls. You can ask for single-family homes, duplexes, mobile homes, apartment houses, land, or commercial properties. The RTC wants you to find your own mortgage. If you can't, however, you may be able to borrow 85 percent of the cost from the RTC.

To buy a house at the foreclosure sale itself, watch the newspaper for auction ads. They'll be published on the days when real-estate advertising is the heaviest. Properties put in foreclosure by the Federal Housing Administration or Department of Veterans Affairs should be listed there, along with their addresses. Information on foreclosure sales for private lenders, however, may be carried in obscure legal newspapers. Ask at the courthouse where you can find this information.

Before going to the auction, drive by the properties that interest you. When a bank holds the mortgage, the people being foreclosed upon are usually still in the house. You can ask permission to look inside but may be turned down. So you'll have no idea what damage, if any, the owners have done. Some properties are in super condition, others have been trashed. Properties repossessed by the FHA and VA will usually be empty but boarded up. Sometimes a real-estate broker will let you in for a "flashlight inspection" (there won't be power in the house). In cold climates, in winter, the pipes may have burst—but you won't know it.

Run a title search on the properties, to see what liens and judgments exist. You can find out the size of the lien that threw the house into foreclosure, but you can't tell for sure how big all the others are. The original lien amounts will be listed, but not the interest accrued, any further payments due, or attorney's fees. These hidden costs will all be yours if you buy the house. Ditto the repair costs, so ask a contractor to estimate the price of fixing any visible damage. Ask a real-estate broker to estimate the house's market value. You need all this information in order to decide how much to bid.

Finally, find out exactly what the bidding procedures are, whether there's a minimum bid, how large a cashier's check you will need, and to whom it should be payable.

Can you buy a bargain in foreclosure? Yes, if you've done your homework and know how much the house is worth. In the normal course of business, discounts to home buyers run in the area of 5 to 10 percent, although you might luck into 15 percent off. Professional investors wait for properties selling at discounts of 20 percent or more.

When you buy at a sale, however, the former owner may have the right to reclaim the property within a short period of time. Or he may sell that right to an investor. Investors are attracted to houses that sell for less than market value. You might get your money back plus interest but lose the house you thought you'd bought. In short, finding a home through foreclosed-property sales can be complicated. You have to know what you're getting into.

Some hardy buyers deal directly with the owner, before the property goes to auction. Doing so carries extra risks. If your seller declares bankruptcy, the creditors may try to get the house sale set aside. If the seller refuses to move, you have to evict. On the other hand, you'll generally get an attractive price. You might also be able to assume the mortgage and make the down payment in installments.

AT THE MORTGAGE CLOSING

Bring money. The lender is required to mail you a good-faith estimate of all the closing costs within three business days of receiving your mortgage application. Before the closing, your lawyer or real-estate bro-ker should give you the exact figures. Expect to pay anywhere from 2 to 7 percent of the loan amount—for title search, title insurance, survey, appraisal, credit check, loan-origination fees, processing fees, legal fees, recording fees, homeowner's insurance, mortgage insurance, taxes, and points. These are big bucks—perhaps $7,000 on a $100,000 home. Many first-time buyers who can make the down payment don't have the extra money they need for closing costs.

When looking for a lender, compare closing costs as well as interest rates. Some banks and S&Ls extract much less from you than others.

WRITING IT OFF

All interest is deductible on mortgage loans up to $1 million and on home-equity loans up to $100,000. Those two loans can be bundled into a single tax-deductible first mortgage for $1.1 million. Mortgages ac-quired on or before October 13, 1987, are still fully deductible even if they exceed the $1.1 million cap.

You can spread your deductible loan over two homes (one of which is your personal residence), but not over three or more.

The mortgage has to be secured by the property. If you borrow against your stocks in order to build your dream house, you lose the mortgage interest deduction.

To prove that you have a deductible mortgage, you have to borrow the money within 90 days of paying for the house. If you miss the deadline, tough luck.

If you build a house, the interest on your home-construction loan is normally deductible for two years from the time you first break ground. The loan also must be secured by the property. You have to get your permanent mortgage within 90 days of the finishing date.

You can deduct upfront points on a loan taken to buy or improve your principal home. But points paid for the mortgage on your vacation home have to be written off over the life of the loan.

Any profit you make when you sell your principal residence can be rolled, untaxed, into a new house, as long as: (1) you build or buy the new house, and occupy it, within two years before or after selling the old one and (2) the new house costs at least as much as you sold the old one for. If you buy a cheaper house, part or all of your capital gain will be taxed.

If you're 55 or older, up to $125,000 of your accumulated capital gains can be excluded from tax. But you get this tax break only once, whether you're single or a couple. If a widow marries a man who has already taken his tax break, and then sells her house, she doesn't get a tax break of her own. Solution: Sell the house before getting married. For more on the age-55 exclusion, see page 814.

IT'S 9:00 P.M. DO YOU KNOW WHERE YOUR MORTGAGE IS?

Probably not. The days are long gone when your banker kept your mortgage in his vault.

Nowadays, banks sell most of their mortgages to private investors. You still might mail your monthly payment to the bank you borrowed from. But the bank only "services" your mortgage by processing your check, paying your real-estate taxes and homeowner's insurance, and sending the investor the rest of the money. For this, the bank collects a fee. It also answers any questions and handles problems that arise.

That is, if you're lucky. Your bank might also have sold the right to service your mortgage. In that case, you'll be mailing your checks to a different company. You're supposed to receive its name, address, and phone number; the name of a contact person there; and instructions on how to make out your checks.

Switching servicers sometimes scrambles your escrow account, which holds the money used to pay your taxes and insurance. There might be a delay in transferring the money. The new servicer might miss a payment. It might discover that your old lender wasn't escrowing enough money, which means that you'll have to make higher payments. If the servicer gets behind on your payments, your tax district will charge late fees and you might even lose your homeowner's insurance.

Ultimately, it's your responsibility to see that this doesn't happen. Check the copies you get of your tax and insurance bills. If they're not being paid on time, or if you're charged penalties, complain to the mortgage servicer, loud and clear. It's the servicer's job to clean up the mess. If you made timely payments, but the servicer missed the deadline for paying your taxes, the servicer owes the penalties, not you.

Warning: All this switching of accounts has created an opening for crooks. You may get a letter, announcing that a new company is now handling your mortgage and telling you where to send your next check.

The crook cashes it and vanishes before you learn it was a fraud. When you get such a letter, double-check with your lender to make sure that the right to service your mortgage has indeed been sold.

WHEN TO REFINANCE

Mortgage rates are a moving target. When they skid, anyone who wants to refinance should hit the phone immediately. If you dally, rates may jump again.

You refinance a mortgage when you take a new loan and use the proceeds to pay off the old one. Here's when to consider it.

• Any fixed-rate mortgage should be up for refinancing when the interest on a new fixed-rate loan falls one and a half to two percentage points below the rate you pay now.

• An adjustable-rate mortgage might be switched to a fixed-rate loan when you think that fixed rates are attractively low.

• An adjustable-rate mortgage might be exchanged for another ARM, if the new ARM offers a particularly low first-year interest rate. That could save you two or three percentage points this year and lower the cap on how high your rate can ultimately rise.

Compare the total dollar cost of refinancing with how much you save in monthly interest payments. You should recoup all of your costs within two to three years. Don't refinance if you plan to sell your house within that time.

You can usually recast your present mortgage—for perhaps $250 to $300—without going through a full-scale refinancing. So visit your original lender before shopping terms in other places. For your tax deductions on a refinancing, see page 222.

When you trade mortgages, you can: (1) keep the same size mortgage and mortgage term but lower your monthly payment; (2) keep the same size mortgage and monthly payment but shorten the mortgage term; or (3) take a larger mortgage and use the extra cash for other purposes. For more information on how to take money out of your home, see page 215.

Your income, liabilities, and net worth will get much closer scrutiny if you want a larger mortgage than if you simply refinance the loan you now have.

GET YOUR FHA REFUND

If your mortgage is insured by the Federal Housing Administration, and you borrowed the money since September 1983, a refund should eventually come your way. You were charged a premium, upfront, for 30 years worth of FHA mortgage insurance. If you repay your loan ahead of time, without default, you're entitled to some of that premium back.

To be sure that you can collect your money, see that your lender tells the FHA when the loan is paid off. The FHA will send a refund-claim form to the address on the mortgage, so don't fail to give the Post Office your forwarding address. If you don't get the claim form within 60 days, write to the Department of Housing and Urban Development, P.O. Box 44372, Washington, D.C. 20026, and inquire. Or call HUD at 703-235-8117. That's a special telephone number set up to handle refund inquiries.

Note: You get no refund if your mortgage was assumed by the buyer. Instead, the refund will go to the buyer when he or she pays off the loan. So check on the amount of the refund owed you and collect it from the buyer at the time you sell. It should be included in the sales contract as a credit due you.

For years, the FHA has also had a refund program for mortgages taken out prior to September 1983. At present, no money is being paid, although it might be in the future. This program is known as "distributive shares." It keeps track of the projected expenses connected with each group of mortgage loans (segregated by year and term), compared with the insurance premiums paid. If expenses (including foreclosures) are low, extra money is said to be in that year's pool. The money, in theory, should be refunded to borrowers on a pro rata basis, when each mortgage is repaid.

Distributive shares were put on hold in November 1990, when a new audit found the FHA to be financially unsound. The government plans to restore these refunds when the FHA is stronger, which will take many years. Nevertheless, when you pay off a loan keep a note of your FHA case number (it's on the canceled mortgage), just in case it helps you get a refund some time in the future.

A REAL-ESTATE BROKER IS NOT YOUR FRIEND

That is, the broker is not your friend if you're the buyer. The broker works for the seller, because the seller pays the sales commission. I'll say it again, in a louder voice: *The real-estate broker has the seller's interests at heart.*

It doesn't seem that way to buyers, because brokers work so hard at finding the house you want. They listen sympathetically to your life's story. They drive out with you in all weathers to check houses that have just come on the market. You tell them everything—how much money you have, the top dollar you're willing to spend, how soon you're going to be forced to move, and how passionately you want that little Cape Cod with the roses climbing on the fence.

But a real-estate broker works for the seller. The higher the price, the happier the seller and the more money the broker earns. The more you blab, the more ammunition you hand the other side. "They're offering $150,000," a broker might tell the seller, "but they'll go up another $10,000." "Fine," says the seller, "go for it." And you fork over the other $10,000.

So . . . play it cool with the broker. Say you won't go a penny over your budget. Say that it doesn't matter if you lose the pretty Cape Cod because there are other houses around. Say that you're making your very best offer and won't come up. Keep your top price to yourself.

Some buyers hire their own real-estate broker, to look for a house and to represent them in negotiations with the seller—a practice known as "buyer brokering." The local board of realtors can tell you who's in that business. Buyer's brokers typically charge flat fees or a percentage— often 3 percent—of the buying price. They'll check a house for defects more carefully than a seller's broker would, and try harder to get you a lower price.

If you're using a seller's broker, don't feel you have to stick with just one. If your first broker isn't producing anything, visit someone else at a different firm. If you're buying into a real-estate development, the developer's broker will definitely not be on your side. Call some of the neighbors to ask how well their houses have stood up.

BUY A FRIEND; HIRE A LAWYER

Whether you're a buyer or a seller, your lawyer works—or should work—exclusively for you. He or she checks all the clauses in the contracts, deleting some, adding others, for your protection. There's no such thing as a standard real-estate contract. Everything is negotiable and may favor one side or the other.

Don't use the lender's attorney, or the attorney for the seller. Don't leave your contract in the hands of the real-estate broker. Hire your own, local lawyer who knows local procedures and whose only obligation is to look after your interests. The real-estate broker can give you some names. Call two or three lawyers and ask for the price. That usually gets you a lower quote.

EQUITY SHARING

Once upon a time, it took only one income to buy a house. Then it took two. Now, in the highest-cost parts of the country, it takes two incomes plus an investor who puts in the down payment.

This arrangement is called equity sharing. There are many ways of cutting the deal. But typically, the investor puts up most or all of the down payment and gets the tax deductions available to business properties (interest, taxes, depreciation). The occupant covers any remaining down payment plus points and closing costs, lives in the house, pays for the utilities, and handles minor repairs.

The occupant also makes the mortgage payments. For tax purposes, the portion of each mortgage payment that covers the investor's share of the loan is treated as if it were rent paid by the occupant to the investor. That rental income is sheltered with tax deductions (obviously, you need a tax lawyer to set up this deal properly). Both the investor's and the occupant's names go on the deed.

After a specified period of time—usually three to five years—the occupant has to refinance the house and buy out the investor. Or the house is sold and the profits split. A typical split is 50-50—which may be fair if the occupant put nothing down. But if the occupant helped with the down payment, he or she deserves a large piece. The deal succeeds if housing prices rise by enough to give the investor a decent return and to give the occupant enough money to possess a home of his own.

The classic application of equity sharing is between parent and adult child. The parents make the down payment, earning (they hope) a nice return on their investment when the child eventually buys them out. If you haven't got a monied parent or other relative, you might find an investor who is willing to take a flyer. A few employers (mostly in California) are developing equity-sharing pools to help their employees buy homes of their own.

If you have to take back a mortgage in order to sell your house, you might make equity sharing part of the deal. Offer your buyer a low-rate second mortgage; in return, take part of the appreciation after three years.

Where equity-sharing isn't well established, investors can be hard to find. Bank loans are also scarce. If banks and S&Ls lend at all, they may tack an extra half-point onto the mortgage interest rate, especially if the occupant doesn't put any money down.

If equity sharing interests you, as occupant or as investor, here are the answers to some of the questions you will have.

WHERE WILL YOU FIND AN INVESTOR? Turn first to family and friends. If that fails, ask your real-estate agent. Some agents invest themselves, or keep names of people who want to invest. Also, check the real-estate pages of newspapers for ads from professional equity investors. Professionals can usually act quickly, which is what you need when you find a house that you want to bid on. But check out their fees before signing on.

AS AN OCCUPANT, WHAT ARE YOUR RISKS? If housing prices fall, stay flat, or rise by only a small amount, you won't accumulate enough equity in your house to buy out the investor when the term is up. The house will be sold, and you still won't be able to finance a home entirely on your own. On the other hand, if housing prices leap hugely and your salary doesn't, you might not earn enough to command the big mortgage you'd need to buy out your partner's share.

Before getting into a deal, ask an accountant to make some projections for you. Find out what would happen, under the terms of the agreement, if house prices stayed flat or fell, if they rose at their current rate, and if they rose at some other rate that seemed reasonable. How much equity would accumulate? How much of it would be yours? How much would your income have to rise to get the mortgage you'd need to take over the house? If you plan to sell the house, how much equity would you have to walk away with in order to buy a house of your own?

AS AN INVESTOR, WHAT ARE YOUR RISKS? If housing prices go nowhere, so does your investment. If the deal works out, however, you usually get a rich return and without the headaches of being a landlord. For true success, you need stable occupants. If they get divorced or lose their jobs, you might have to take over the mortgage payments. A tenant who doesn't pay the rent can be evicted, but you can't so easily dispose of a nonperforming co-owner, especially if that person gets a good lawyer. To minimize this risk, invest in an equity-sharing pool that owns a piece of several houses.

If your co-owner leaves town, you'll have a tough time taking full possession of the property. For at least a whisper of protection, ask your partner to put up part of the down payment—say, 5 percent.

If you need money before the contract ends, you're probably stuck. The occupant may not be able to buy you out. If he or she does, you'll have to accept a discount price.

One final point: The mortgage debt will show on your credit record. This might prevent you from getting other loans.

THE GREAT CONDO QUESTION

Condominiums and townhouses are homes attached to one another. You own a unit but share common areas—such as lobbies, a central heating system, and landscaping—with your neighbors. Co-operative apartments are similar, except that you own shares in the building as a whole, with a right to lease a certain unit. Monthly maintenance fees are levied on each owner, to keep the common areas in good repair. You're also assessed for special expenses, such as replacing an elevator.

Condos and townhouses have two big advantages: They cost less than comparable free-standing houses and they require less personal upkeep. For example, if you're in a condo and the roof starts to leak, you don't have to call the roofer or nail up the shingles yourself, you only have to help pay for repairs. For the young, condominiums are often a first step into the housing market. For the old, they're a comfortable step back from the burden of caring for a house.

But check these drawbacks, before you opt for condo or co-op living.

• Condominiums typically rise less in value than free-standing houses and fall much faster when market conditions are poor. You're far more likely to lose money on a condo than on a house. Young people ready to trade up may find that they've built little or no equity.

• Not all lenders give home-equity loans on condos.

· The condo owners might be suing the builder for shoddy construction and other sins. Check this out before you buy. Also ask if any special assessments are in the wind, for improvements or major repairs.

· A large proportion of units in the condo (say, 25 or 30 percent) may be owned by investors rather than residents. If investors can't find enough tenants, or earn enough rent, they might not pay their maintenance fees. That could force the building down to a bare-bones budget —reducing services, deferring maintenance, and cutting the value of your unit. There may also be special assessments on the other unit holders, to cover the bills.

· Townhouse developments have long lists of "don'ts": Don't paint your front door red, don't plant bushes by your front walk, don't put a dish antenna behind your unit, don't use an outdoor clothesline, don't keep a large dog, don't, don't, don't, don't. These rules will be enforced by neighborhood posses who want to keep the grounds looking uniformly attractive. If you like red doors and dish antennas, don't move in.

· Buildings converting to condo or co-op ownership may have hidden flaws. If the present owner of your apartment building proposes that you buy it, the tenants should hire their own lawyer and engineer. You need to know exactly what's wrong with the building (will it need a new roof? new wiring? at how much per tenant?); what it will cost to run the building well; what taxes you'll pay after conversion; and how good the deed is. Will you own the land under the building or only the building itself? If someone else owns the land, what's to prevent him or her from jacking up the rent or, worse, not renewing the lease? Your lawyer will also negotiate with the building's present owner to get a good price. An insider's price is usually low. But it's no bargain if the building needs serious repairs or the units aren't easy to resell. Unless you feel certain that the unit is a sound investment, try to stay there as a renter and let the new owners handle the headaches. Or bail out.

· Each condominium development or co-op building is governed by a board of owners. Your property values depend on how well the board members do their job. Do they enforce collections from people who don't pay their maintenance fees on time? Are they unafraid to levy higher assessments for essential maintenance, like a new boiler? Can they settle disagreements about what amenities the building should invest in? Will they see that the building is always kept in good repair? Under an ineffectual board, a condominium can fall apart.

· If an owner doesn't pay his or her maintenance fee, the condo board generally has the right to foreclose. But even then, the condo may not get the money it's owed. The proceeds of the foreclosure sale go first to satisfy tax liens and second to repay the first mortgage. Only then can the condo collect, and there may not be enough money left—especially on units that are fairly new or where condo values have declined. The remaining owners may be assessed to cover the default.

• Buyers of co-operative apartments run similar risks. You're on the line for the building's entire mortgage, tax bill, and upkeep. If your neighbors don't pay their share, you may have to kick in. However, co-ops can often evict an owner who doesn't pay and sell the unit on the open market. The co-op then takes any money it's owed; the former owner gets whatever is left. To minimize defaults, co-op boards don't let you sell your apartment at will. The buyer first has to be checked for financial responsibility. If the board finds reason to object, you lose the sale.

IF YOU WANT TO BUY A CONDO OR CO-OP, HERE'S THE BEST WAY TO MAKE MONEY ON THE DEAL.
Find a building whose units are almost entirely occupied by owners rather than by renters. These buildings are almost always better maintained. Beware the building where the sponsor couldn't get enough tenants to buy their own apartments.

Buy a two-bedroom condo rather than a studio. The larger units hold their value better, because there are more potential buyers.

Buy a well-kept, well-run older condo rather than a new one. Its price will be lower and you don't risk the new-condo problems: careless construction, unfinished amenities, and higher taxes and maintenance fees than the salespeople said. The owners' association will be functioning smoothly. There should be a sizable reserve for unexpected repairs.

Find a unit with amenities appropriate to the people who might buy from you—good schools and a playground for young families; social spaces and bus service for older people.

Don't buy where vast numbers of new condos are going up. Most buyers will choose the new ones. Sellers won't be able to move unless they drastically cut the price.

Don't buy without reading all the condo documents (murky as they are), to be sure that you understand—and can live with—the bylaws, the budget, and the rules.

• When checking the budget, look for a sizable reserve for repairs. If there isn't one, take a walk. It shows that the building is poorly run. Ditto if there's no reserve for legal expenses to collect the maintenance fees from any owners who default. Ask about the delinquency rate: What percentage of owners aren't paying their bills? What is the board doing about it? A sound building assumes a certain percentage of deadbeats and budgets for it. If the budget assumes that everyone will pay, you're going to get a nasty surprise. On principle, you should avoid a building with a lot of defaults, or where more than 25 or 30 percent of the units are owned by outside investors. Investors default at a much higher rate than owner-occupants—and when others don't pay, you'll have to pick up the slack.

THE STRATEGIC RENTER

In some circumstances, it's definitely smarter to rent than to buy.

Maybe you have a rent-controlled apartment that's unbelievably cheap. With the money you save, you might be able to buy a second home.

Maybe you expect to move in a year or two. You'd doubtless lose money on a house if you bought and sold in that short period of time.

Maybe you're young and single and want to be ready to change your life in a moment. Or you're newly divorced and haven't yet decided what you'll do next.

Maybe you see house prices slipping in your area and hope to buy more cheaply if you wait a year.

Maybe you think house prices are going to crash and don't want to be invested in one. That's one gamble I wouldn't make. Prices will fluctuate; you can't count on increases every year. But I'd bet that the long-term trend is up. Even slow growth is a windfall when your equity is low. For example, take a $100,000 house that gains $3,000 in value, which is 3 percent. If you bought that house on $15,000 down, you've just made 20 percent on your money. On a $10,000 down payment, you've made 30 percent. For some estimates of the investment value of buying versus renting, see the Appendix, page 868.

On paper, there's nothing wrong with putting your down payment money into something other than a house—as long as you really do it, and faithfully add to your investments every month. But to equal what you get from a paid-up house, you'll have to build a large enough fund to cover your rent from the day you retire until the end of your life. I don't see many pots that large. Whoever first said that a house was a security blanket wasn't kidding.

18

A SECOND HOME
FOR FUN AND PROFIT:

The House That Doesn't Cost You Anything
(Much)

——

Imagine a house that helps pay for itself. While
you're sitting in the sun, it's making money and
lifting the mortgage off your back.

As luck would have it, I'm writing
this chapter in my second home. My husband and I have had a string of
them. We've built them, rented them out, sold at a profit, and built
again. We've made some money and had a lot of fun. A vacation house
that comes close to carrying itself is a dream property. It's always on tap
for your own weeks off and the renters help you pay the bills.

But you shouldn't think of a house like this as a true investment. It's
more like owning a pleasure palace at a discount price. You'll almost
never get enough rent to cover your expenses or make annual profits. A
portion of the cost is going to have to come out of your pocket every
year. If property values rise by enough, the house might make money
after all. But to measure up as a "good" investment, the sale price has to
be large enough to cover your annual losses plus interest and deliver a

compounded double-digit profit for each year you held. That's a tall order, not often achieved.

Back when we built our vacation houses, the profit hurdle wasn't so high. We broke even on rentals after tax and made good money on capital gains. We got out of the game the first year we found that our costs, after tax, would exceed our rents. It's a bad business when you *must* get huge capital gains to bail you out. The one house we kept (and still put up for rent) isn't quite at breakeven. From an investment point of view, we'd do better with our money in a tax-exempt bond. But it's not much fun vacationing in a tax-exempt bond. It has a lousy view of the sea.

So even when a vacation house is a poor investment, it can make enough money so that, when added to your personal enjoyment, you feel that you're coming out ahead. In this regard, renters are wonderful. They help you carry a house that you otherwise might not be able to afford.

TO BUY A HOUSE THAT YOU PLAN TO RENT...

• Buy an existing house. If it has a rental history, so much the better. You'll know what your net costs are likely to be. If you fix up the house, you can raise the rent and perhaps rent for a longer season than the previous owner did.

• Buy a condominium. Older condos are usually cheaper than new ones, and often just as nice. Ask a real-estate broker to show you some places. If you refurnish, you might be able to raise the rent. (But condos are harder to resell than free-standing homes, and generally don't rise nearly as much in value. Better to view yours principally as a vacation home, with renters providing a little income on the side.)

• Buy a piece of land and pay for it as fast as you can. Once the property is yours, put a house on it. You can get a mortgage for 75 to 80 percent of the combined value of the house and land. That's usually enough money to build the house and furnish it.

Your rental success depends on the right answers to these questions:

1. *Is the house or condo in a known vacation spot that's easy to get to?* For a steady supply of renters, buy where vacationers already come. You need an infrastructure—advertising, rental agents, house cleaners, and service people who make quick repairs. Your home shouldn't be much more than half a day's drive from a major population center. The house-

rental trade leans heavily toward families. You'll have extra rentals if you'll allow them to bring their dogs. (I do, and have never had any damage.)

2. *Is the house and property something special?* Land on a lake or an ocean costs more than land elsewhere. But houses on water rent for a premium and rent for more weeks each season than equally good houses without a view. That extra income helps you cover the higher price. Property on water also rises faster in value (provided, of course, that beach erosion doesn't sweep it away). In ski areas, houses with picture-perfect views of the mountains do better than houses overlooking the road. Condominiums with classy amenities (pool, health club, beach) do better than those with no pool and a drive to the beach. But condos with no pools are cheaper, so check the demand for lower-priced rentals. If demand is strong, you can buy a modest place and still attract enough business to cover a comfortable piece of your cost. Regardless of price range, look for something a little special—a garden, a good layout, quiet woods in back. To bring in extra renters, you need an edge.

3. *Is the house or condo well furnished?* Today's affluent renters won't put up with early Salvation Army furniture, lumpy mattresses, and camp-fire kitchens. They want comfort and will pay for it. So set up a conve-nient house, with modern appliances, good chairs and beds, plenty of lamps and, for summer homes, air-conditioning—in the bedrooms, if nowhere else. Keep the pillows and shower curtains fresh, the grime out of the bathroom, and the screens in good repair. Your renters will repay you by returning year after year. You'll also get a steady trade from rental agents, who like houses that clients don't complain about.

4. *Do you have a good rental agent?* If you do only one or two rentals a summer, maybe you can find the tenants yourself. But to rent more often, you'll need an agent. Look for one who's well located on the main road, handles rentals full time, advertises widely, and is well known in the community. An agent keeps your house as full as its location and condition allow, collects the rents, sends you the checks, cleans up between tenants, and makes small repairs. The commission: typically 15 to 25 percent of the rent.

5. *Can you rent for enough to cover most of your cash costs?* Ideally, the rents cover everything—mortgages, taxes, insurance, utilities, re-pairs. In practice, however, you usually have to finance part of the house yourself. So the question becomes: How much can you afford to pay each year, and can you count on the rentals to cover the rest?

If you *must* have extra income to maintain the house, don't take the salesperson's word that "rentals are no problem." Check the history of the property, or properties just like it. Build in a safety margin. Could you carry the house if it rented only half as much as you expected? How long could you carry it if damage occurred and you couldn't rent it for a while? (Disregard these rules if profits don't matter. Some owners are happy with any rentals that offset the cost of carrying their homes.)

YOU'RE AT RISK IF YOU . . .

. . . Buy a piece of land in a vacation development where few tourists come. You might love the spot yourself. But don't expect to rent the house much or sell it easily.

. . . Buy a house that's remote. Neither renters nor buyers will beat a path to your door.

. . . Buy a small, dreary house, even in a strong tourist town. Renters will avoid you, except when everything else is full. So will real-estate agents, because their clients would complain. You won't even attract many tenants by dropping your rent. No vacationer wants to be stuck in a dingy living room, with grumpy kids, when it rains.

. . . Buy land or a condominium from a developer who is constantly putting new properties on the market. As long as he's in business, he'll hog all the buyers who come to visit. It won't be easy to find someone to sell to. If the development has no rental history, you don't know what income you're likely to get.

. . . Buy a house in a spot that's overrun with For Sale signs. You may get the place at a bargain price, which is great for your personal use, but it probably won't be an easy sale if you want out.

. . . Respond to a postcard that offers "free gifts" for sitting through a sales pitch. In the enthusiasm of the moment, you might sign up for a property that you don't really want and can't resell. Salespeople often exaggerate investment potential. More than likely, you'll lose money. You might not be able to resell at any price.

FINANCING A SECOND HOME

Get a local lender. Your bank at home won't lend money on real estate that's out of town. Loans on second homes are usually more expensive than those on first homes. Expect a higher interest rate and extra points. You might also have to put more money down.

Developers often offer their own financing, for the land or homes they have for sale. You put a small sum of money down and pay the rest over 7 to 10 years.

BUYING INSURANCE

When you rent out your house regularly, insurance costs more. In remote places, theft and vandalism coverage might not be available at all. Go to the company that insures your primary home; it should pick up your second home at a discount. Keep your liability coverage high, in case a renter is injured and sues. Don't let hazards linger—repair the front steps, replace the bad lamp cord, stick nonskid pads on the shower floor.

THE TAX GOD LOVES SECOND HOMEOWNERS, TOO

Almost all of the rules that apply to your first home apply equally to your second (page 401). You can deduct mortgage interest, property taxes, and casualty losses. You lose your interest deductions only for houses number three and up—unless they're purely business properties, in which case they operate under different rules.

BUT THE TAX GOD HAS DOUBTS ABOUT PEOPLE WHO TAKE RENTERS

When you rent your house or condo to others, what's deductible depends on your income and how much you use the house yourself. Here are the general rules.

YOUR RENTAL HOME IS TREATED AS A PERSONAL RESIDENCE if you use it more than 14 days a year or more than 10 percent as much time as you rent it, whichever is greater. Days you visit the home to make repairs and attend to your rental business are not counted as personal use. On the other hand, if you rent to a friend at something less than the going rate, that *is* personal use.

All your expenses are allocated between business and personal use. If the house is rented 40 percent of the time, then 40 percent of the overhead—interest, taxes, utilities, repairs, maintenance, rental costs —is a business expense. When preparing your income taxes, you would normally:

1. Figure the portion of interest and taxes that applies to your personal use and deduct it along with your other itemized deductions.

2. Report the rental income on Schedule E. Deduct from it, first, the portion of interest and taxes that apply to the rental use of the property. After that, you can deduct other expenses—but only to the limit of your remaining rental income. (The Internal Revenue Service and the Tax Court disagree on how to allocate interest and taxes to rental use, with the Tax Court endorsing a more favorable approach. If you go with the Tax Court, you risk a challenge to your return—so which course to take depends on your stomach for a fight. For specifics, read a tax guide or see an accountant.)

3. If any business expenses remain, they may not be deducted against the rest of your income. Only your rental income can be sheltered.

Keep track of those business expenses that you can't deduct, including depreciation. They're subtracted from your profits when the house is sold, which reduces the tax on your capital gain.

There's a twist to the rules if you rent for fewer than 15 days. You don't report that income on your tax return and you don't deduct any rental expenses.

YOUR RENTAL HOME IS TREATED AS A BUSINESS PROPERTY if your own use amounts to no more than 14 days or 10 percent as much time as you rent it, whichever is less. You allocate expenses to personal or business use, just as you would if it were a personal residence. You cannot deduct the mortgage interest for the short time that covers your personal use; only business interest is deductible. But if the property operates at a loss (and it probably does, especially when depreciation is counted), *you may be able to turn the house into a tax shelter.*

With a shelter, you can deduct your losses from your regular earnings as well as from your rental income. Full deductions are allowed for up to $25,000 of business losses, including depreciation, *if* your adjusted gross income (not counting income and losses from other tax shelters) doesn't exceed $100,000 and you actively participate in the property's management. If your income exceeds $100,000, that $25,000 deduction for business losses starts to phase out. You lose it entirely when your income tops $150,000.

In short, a vacation home is still a super shelter for most middle- and upper-middle-income people, as long as they operate it as a business property (which means not using it much themselves). But there's normally no shelter there for higher-income people. When your income exceeds $150,000, you can write off your losses only against your (1) rental income or (2) any income you're getting from other tax-shelter investments. Any unused losses on business properties can be deducted from your profits when you sell.

IS IT BETTER TO TREAT YOUR SECOND HOME AS A PERSONAL RESIDENCE OR AS A BUSINESS PROPERTY? If you have a choice, the answer isn't easy. It depends, among other things, on the size of your interest payments, the amount of your rental income, and how much you earn from other sources. In general, however, you're better off with a personal residence unless you're within the income range (under $150,000) that qualifies for that extra $25,000 in deductible expenses.

ALL ABOUT TIMESHARES

If you can't afford a house, and you can't afford a condominium, maybe you can afford a piece of a condominium.

That's a timeshare. You generally buy the right to vacation in the same unit, for the same week, every year. If you buy a "floater," you can be put into any unit of the size you contracted for.

The most desirable timeshares are in spiffy resort areas—on the beach, by a golf course, near Disney World. You can buy for cash or on terms. You have to make regular maintenance payments to keep the property clean and in good repair. The promoter may find you a tenant anytime you can't use your regular week (you pay a rental commission of 25 to 50 percent). Or you can swap—using someone else's unit in a different resort, in return for letting a stranger make use of yours.

THE ADVANTAGES:

1. A timeshare is a cheap vacation, especially for a family.

2. You see some of the same friends around the swimming pool every year.

3. You can swap for a timeshare in other parts of the country, or elsewhere in the world, and get a unit of about the same quality as yours.

THE DISADVANTAGES:

1. Unless you buy a good timeshare—a desirable place, a desirable unit, a desirable week—you might not be able to make a good swap. You'll be confined, every year, to the unit you have or to a place of inferior quality. If you own an off-season week, you generally can't swap for a week at a better time of year.

2. If you get tired of your timeshare, you will find it hard—maybe impossible—to sell. Almost all the new buyers are culled by developers, not by individuals with units to resell. If you do sell, it will usually be at a price substantially less than you paid. Some timeshares are clubs that don't even permit resales.

In short, this deal is easy to get into and hard to get out of. Monthly maintenance fees continue for as long as the unit is yours.

How do you get out of a timeshare that you haven't been able to sell? You probably can't if you're only a year or two into the deal. If you quit paying, you'll be sued. If you've paid for the unit, or almost paid, and decide to walk, you might not be sued for any remaining money due or for the unpaid maintenance costs. But the default will probably show up on your credit history.

INSTEAD OF BUYING A TIMESHARE, CONSIDER RENTING A UNIT IN A TIMESHARE BUILDING. You can get a gorgeous place at far less than the weekly cost of a hotel or motel. Timeshares offer one to three bedrooms, a kitchen, a living room, perhaps a swimming pool, and easy access to all the local entertainments. You could rent every year when the children are small. When they're older and scorn a family vacation, you'll be free to go anywhere you want, without making monthly timeshare payments. You can also rent condominiums that aren't used as timeshares. Condo resorts are usually top-of-the-line.

Your travel agent can find you a condo or timeshare rental. Or write for a free list of rental agents, for any vacation area that interests you. The lists are compiled by the Resort Property Owners Association (RPOA), P.O. Box 2395, Northbrook, IL, 60062.

You can also rent a timeshare directly from the developer of the resort—often at a discount price. But in return, you'll have to sit through a 90-minute sales pitch aimed at getting you to buy. The salesperson will probably tell you that a timeshare is a terrific investment (it's not) and easy to resell at a profit (not true). Buy only if you know that you'll want to vacation in this resort, or others like it, for many years into the future.

IF YOU STILL WANT TO OWN A TIMESHARE, DON'T BUY FROM THE DEVELOPER. BUY FROM ONE OF THE THOUSANDS OF PEOPLE TRYING TO RESELL. Resales are available through local real-estate agents (free lists of agents are available from the RPOA, at the above address). You might get a splendid unit at 50 percent or more off the developer's price.

Before signing any timeshare contract, read through all the clauses and decipher the rules. What are the monthly maintenance fees? How often do they rise? What special expenses can be assessed? What do you actually own? Can you sell to someone else (assuming you can find a buyer) or are resales prohibited? Do you get the same unit every year? If you're offered a "bonus week," when can you take it? What happens if one of your fellow owners doesn't pay his or her share of the costs? Who manages the property? (You want an independent company that's in the hospitality business, not a subsidiary of the developer.) What if someone is injured in your unit? What if the developer doesn't finish the project, leaving you without some of the promised amenities? How is the property owners' association run, and what are its rules? What kind of unit can you expect on an exchange?

Don't buy from a resort that lures prospects with "free gifts." Or from salespeople who imply that you're making a good investment. Or if you're told that "today only" there's a discount price. Or without taking home the sales contract and other ownership documents, to read and consider quietly.

Stick with a nationally known company, of good reputation, whose resorts you have visited and liked, and whose salespeople don't hustle you.

FITTING A SECOND HOME INTO YOUR FINANCIAL PLAN

Like a first home, a second home does double duty. It's a place to live and has elements of an investment. It forces you to save and usually gives you more borrowing power. It costs you money as long as you own it, but you hope to sell for more than you paid. On the downside, you've made a costly purchase that probably can't be sold in a hurry. You may lose money if your resort suffers a real-estate slump.

When you own two homes, you need the protection of cash in the bank to pay the mortgages just in case your income stops. If you've tapped all your cash to buy the house, make it your top priority to build up that reservoir again.

5 PAYING FOR COLLEGE

A friend and I were celebrating over lunch. He had just written his last tuition check. My husband and I had the end in sight.

"It's funny," my friend said. "For years, I was terrorized by the unimaginable price of college. The cost projections were appalling. How was I ever going to pay? I saved some money but not enough. When my daughter started filling out applications, I lived every day with a stone cold fear.

"Then I borrowed some money through one of those college-payment plans and suddenly it was over. And it wasn't so bad.

"I suppose," he went on, "that if I hadn't been scared into saving some money, I couldn't have done it. But in the end, I lived."

I recount this story just to remind you that almost every child who wants to go to college gets there. And when your children graduate, life resumes.

19

TUITION,

ROOM, AND BOARD:

The Matterhorn of Personal Finance

Paying for college is a peak experience. No
one who has stood in those chill winds ever
forgets them.

College is worth it. Write that tuition check and repeat after me: College is worth it. Tomorrow's best jobs will all take smarts. Regardless of what you pay for a college degree, you —or your child—will earn it back in spades.

The burden is heavy. But it shouldn't get very much worse in the twenty-first century than it is right now.

Parents pale when they see college-cost projections. *But as the price of a degree goes up, so will your income and assets.* Relatively speaking, the average college should cost you just about the same in the year 2001 as in 1991—especially the state colleges and universities. The price of highly selective private colleges may continue to rise faster than disposable incomes. But those schools will eventually be forced to moderate their tuition increases and create more innovative payment plans.

You *will* find a way to pay for college. Everyone does. If you don't save, you'll have to borrow. But you'll make it.

HOW MUCH? HOW MUCH?

That depends on the school you choose. Most state colleges and universities are not unreasonably priced, especially for in-state students. Private colleges cost much more. Highly selective private colleges are practically off the charts. But the top-dollar schools also have the biggest financial-aid budgets. So don't assume that you can't afford the freight.

The table on page 425 tells you what to expect, assuming that total costs rise by 7 percent annually. The projections include tuition, fees, room, board, books, supplies, transportation, and personal expenses. Many state schools charge considerably less than what's shown here. The best-known private colleges cost much more—in fact, they're already closing in on $90,000 for four years of education.

Don't brush off these figures as out of this world. Similar projections made a decade ago greatly underestimated how high costs would rise, especially for the best private schools.

The good news is that a $45,000 salary will rise to $119,000 in 20 years, assuming 5 percent wage inflation. You'll earn even more if you're promoted to higher-level jobs. So you will, some way, find the money to pay—if not for a private school then for a top public university.

PRICE, QUALITY, AND PRESTIGE

Here's a tale for our times. It's about two private colleges, Dim Bulb U and Wise Guy Tech. Both were down in the dumps because enrollment had fallen off. How could they attract more students?

Dim Bulb U cut its price, to make its degree more affordable. The kids stopped coming, and its reputation sagged. Wise Guy Tech jacked up its price to Ivy League levels, and students banged down the doors to get in. It added more services, and its prestige ballooned.

This story is true. Only the names have been changed to protect the guilty. Parents tend to equate price with quality. In the competition for students, schools have found it pays to charge more. That's one of the reasons that private institutions cost so much (not to mention their fundamental expenses, like the price competition for good faculty and continuing investment in program improvements.) High prices bring in

GET OUT THE SMELLING SALTS, MA,
SHE'S ABOUT TO MENTION WHAT COLLEGE WILL COST

The year your child starts school	Four years at a public college*	Four years at a private college
1991	$ 33,219	$ 63,384
1992	35,545	67,820
1993	38,033	72,568
1994	40,695	77,648
1995	43,544	83,083
1996	46,592	88,899
1997	49,853	95,122
1998	53,343	101,780
1999	57,077	108,905
2000	61,072	116,528
2001	65,347	124,685
2002	69,922	133,413
2003	74,816	142,752
2004	80,053	152,745
2005	85,657	163,437
2006	91,653	174,877
2007	98,069	187,119
2008	104,934	200,217
2009	112,279	214,232
2010	120,139	229,228

* In-state residents only. Out-of-staters—add $3,073 to the cost for 1991 and multiply by 7 percent annually until you reach your matriculation year. Sources: The College Board; T. Rowe Price.

extra money from well-to-do students, which can be spent, Robin-Hood style, supporting students who can't pay.

Do you want to play this game? If so, keep on writing out those checks. If not:

• Consider a high-priced private college only if it truly has a national reputation that lives up to its cost, if you can get a lot of student aid, or if you have a specific, personal reason for valuing that school's environment.

• Apply to several lower-priced private colleges. Many of them do a splendid job, especially for the average student. Check out a wide range of schools, to see what each offers in student aid.

• Take a good, long look at state colleges and universities. Many of them offer a top education at half the price. Better a first-rate public school than a second-rate private one.

As the price gap between public and private schools widens, more and more students are streaming into the public universities. The private colleges are being forced to lower their rate of tuition increases and raise large sums of money to provide more student aid.

HOW MUCH OF THE PRICE WILL YOU HAVE TO PAY?

ALL OF IT, probably, if you now make $60,000 to $70,000 and up.
PART OF IT, if you make $30,000 or $40,000.
ONLY A SLIVER, if you earn under $15,000 or $20,000.

These are such bald generalizations that you ought to chase me out of town. The amount of aid you actually get also depends on such things as the size of your family, the age of the parents, the cost of the school, and the avoirdupois of your savings account. A student judged able to pay in full for good old State U might qualify for a grant in the Ivy League. Still, those income ranges give you a general feel for the landscape.

Upper-middle-class parents, just barely getting by on $70,000 a year, feel broke. They haven't got the money for the pricey private school they want. So they assume that the school will come to their rescue with a reasonable grant.

Forget it. You're telling your sad tale to a financial-aid officer who may be earning only $35,000. From that perspective, you don't look broke. In fact, you look like a high-liver who saw college coming 18 years ago and didn't bother to save enough money. Why should the school pull your chestnuts out of the fire? You might get a loan, but don't look for much free money. Aid officers save their sympathy, and their funds, for promising kids whose families earn less.

College aid is based on a standard calculation of "need," which all schools define in about the same way. Conceptually, it works roughly like this:

1. Add up all your family income and assets.
2. Subtract the money you need to live on, plus a savings allowance (as determined by a standard "need analysis" mandated by the federal government and used by all schools).
3. The remaining money has to be spent for college. That's your expected "parental contribution."
4. Look up the total price of the school that your child wants.
5. Subtract your parental contribution.

6. Subtract the money your child is expected to pay, out of his or her income and savings.

7. The remainder is your "financial need." It's the difference between what you and your child are expected to pay and the college's total cost.

8. The college that accepts your child fills as much of your need as it can with student grants and loans.

On paper, that approach sounds reasonable. The college tries to make up the difference between what it charges and what you can afford to pay. If your family contribution is determined to be $5,000, and the school costs $8,000, you might get $3,000 in aid. If your family contribution is $5,000 and the school costs $15,000, you could get $10,000 in aid. Your family contribution remains the same, no matter which institution you choose. So the pricier the school, the better your chance of getting help.

But the joker lies in the calculation's second line: the amount of money you need to live on. No one cares about your actual bills. Instead, your income and assets are judged by a standard formula developed by the federal government. It assesses your need by playing a game of "let's pretend."

Let's pretend, it says, that you live on a near-poverty budget (the standard low-income budget compiled annually by the U.S. Department of Labor). That's your official living allowance. Anyone with that size income is presumed to be too broke to pay for a college education. But anyone above that line is expected to make a contribution. If your actual living expenses are higher than the low-income budget allows, tough luck. You can't expect the college to make up for the fact that you're living higher on the hog.

When the low-income budget is subtracted from your earnings, there appears to be lots of money left over. No matter that most of that money goes for locked-in expenses like mortgage payments and real-estate taxes. The standard formula pretends that you really are living a bare-bones life. So it concludes that you have much more money to spend on college than, from your point of view, is actually the case.

Most middle- and upper-middle-income families will be shocked by the amount that the colleges expect them to pay. That's why you should start saving now. It will protect you from a lot of borrowing later. Even lower-income families will be pressed for as much as they can possibly come up with.

THE BOTTOM LINE

The table below shows how much an average family was expected to contribute toward college in 1991–92. Here's how to use it.

· Look for your 1990 pretax income on the left. (In any year, how much you're expected to pay for college generally depends on your earnings for the *previous* year.)

· Read across to the column that best represents your 1990 net worth: the value of your savings, investments, home equities, other real estate, farm, and family business, minus your mortgage and other debts.

· You'll see there what a college might expect you to pay toward one year of school. If that figure fully covers the cost of the school that your child will attend, you can't expect any student aid. If that figure falls short, at least some aid should come your way.

· When you have more than one child in college, your parental contribution is divided among them, making each of them eligible for more aid. For example, if you have to pay $5,000 for one child, your expected contribution will be only $2,500 for each of two.

· For years after 1991–92, guesstimate your contribution this way: Find your base contribution for 1991–92, then multiply that number by the subsequent growth in the consumer price index.

· On top of the parental contribution shown here, a contribution is expected from student earnings: $700 for the first year of school and $900 for each subsequent year.

YOUR PARENTAL CONTRIBUTION
(WHAT YOU MIGHT PAY FOR ONE YEAR OF COLLEGE*)

1990 income	Net family assets (in 1990)					
	$20,000	$40,000	$60,000	$80,000	$100,000	$120,000
$20,000	$ 41	$ 370	$ 898	$ 1,426	$ 1,960	$ 2,575
$30,000	1,648	1,896	2,498	3,210	4,057	5,068
$40,000	3,679	3,951	4,943	6,071	7,199	8,327
$50,000	6,509	6,836	7,964	9,092	10,220	11,348
$60,000	9,470	9,798	10,926	12,054	13,182	14,310
$70,000	12,478	12,806	13,934	15,062	16,190	17,318

*In 1991–92. Source: The College Board.

The table above will not exactly fit your circumstances. It's for families in the following circumstances: two parents live at home, only one parent works, the older parent is 45, there are no unusual expenses, one of two children is in college, and they use the standard deduction on their income-tax form. You will pay a little less than this table suggests if both parents work, if a parent is older than 45, if you have more than two children, or if you itemize on your tax return. You'll pay a little more if you're a one-child family. But it doesn't matter that this table doesn't hit your contribution on the button. You get the general idea.

HOW WILL YOU PAY?

You have five sources of funds.

SAVINGS AND INVESTMENTS. This is by far the cheapest source of money. When you save in advance, you cover part of the tuition with money you earn from interest, dividends, and capital gains. For the tremendous boost you get from starting early on college savings, see the table on page 159.

CURRENT INCOME. Spending current income reduces your standard of living for as long as the college bills last. But at least it's over when it's over.

LOANS. This is the most costly source of funds, because loan-interest payments hang around your neck for years. Young college graduates can probably handle the payments. They get low-interest loans and can look forward to a lifetime of rising incomes. Parents aren't so lucky. Loans mortgage their future, at a time when they may not have much working time left.

WORK. The "work-study" program is open to middle-income kids as well as the poor. It lets students earn some of their tuition by taking a job. Some schools provide jobs for any student who wants one.

GRANTS. Free money goes to students in the greatest need. But hardly anyone gets a totally free ride. Most needy students get an aid package made up of low-interest loans and a work-study job, as well as a grant.

FIVE STEPS TO COLLEGE AID

STEP ONE. Get a financial-aid form from your college or high school guidance office, fill it in, and mail it to the government-designated aid-processing center as soon as possible after January 1. The center analyzes your financial capability to determine what you can afford to pay.

Don't drag your feet. Most colleges have early deadlines, like February. Pell Grants (the government's leading grant program, page 436) and government-subsidized student loans (page 440) are always available to qualified students, no matter when you ask for them. But if you apply late, the money in the other programs may be used up. A trough that was full in February may be empty by April. You want to get your nose in first.

The form has the same, grim feel as an income-tax return.

First you put down all your taxable and nontaxable income, major medical expenses, and any tuition you're paying for other children. Next you add up certain assets—bank account, home equity, other real estate, investments, farm, and family business.

Then the student weighs in with his or her own income and assets. If the student is married, the spouse has to report, too.

That's for federal programs. Many colleges have an additional form that digs deeper. You may have to disclose the funds you carry in insurance policies, salary-deferral plans, pension plans, and tax-deferred annuities.

Leave no questions blank, unless the form specifically tells you to. If something doesn't apply to you, write 0 (zero) where the answer should go. Otherwise, the people who process the forms will have to check back with you, which holds up your paperwork.

Try to do your tax return early, so you'll know exactly how much you earned. A completed tax return also simplifies the job of filling in the financial-aid form, because many of the questions are keyed to lines on the 1040 or 1040A. (You don't actually have to file your tax return early, if you don't want to; just fill it in and use the data to help you apply for college aid.)

If the W-2 form from your employer is late, don't wait for it. Make a close estimate of your income, so that you can mail the financial-aid form on time. You can send the college your exact earnings later. You may be asked for your tax return, as verification.

The aid form asks if you want this information sent to the government agencies that make Pell Grants or give out state aid. Say yes. You have nothing to lose. Applying for a Pell is a prerequisite to being considered for a subsidized student loan and many college grants. (You have to apply separately for student loans, however, and sometimes for state aid, too.)

Keep a copy of the financial-aid form, just in case the original gets lost. You don't want to have to suffer through filling it out again. If you need help completing the form—and thousands of families do—ask for it at your high school guidance office or college financial-aid office.

STEP TWO. Watch the mail. You should get an acknowledgment from the aid-processing center within three to six weeks. If you don't, call the Federal Student Aid Information Center (301-722-9200), and ask what's happening to your application.

After the aid processor crunches you through its computers, it will send its findings to state student-aid agencies and to the colleges you've specified. You'll get a form containing a preliminary estimate of how much you'll be expected to pay. You'll also get a Student Aid Report (SAR), saying whether you qualify for a Pell Grant. Check the data for accuracy, to make sure that the processor didn't make a mistake about your income or family size. Return the form to the processor only if there's an error or if you want the financial report sent to some colleges that weren't originally on your list.

STEP THREE. If you qualify for a Pell Grant, send a copy of the SAR to the colleges you're interested in. They should already have received the analysis of your ability to pay.

Then wait to hear. The college's own office of financial aid establishes a budget for each student, depending on whether he or she is single, married, living in a dorm, living in an apartment, living at home, and so on. From that budget is subtracted the money that parents and student are expected to pay. Any gap between the student's budget and your total family contribution is called "financial need."

A few schools fill this need for every student they accept. If you're $4,000 short that year, that's what you'll get, in a combination of grants, loans, and student jobs.

Most schools give full aid to some applicants while leaving others hanging. A student with a $4,000 need may be offered only $3,000 worth of help. If you can raise the missing $1,000, fine. Otherwise, ta-ta.

Many schools offer aid to super-bright kids who could actually afford to pay their own way. For information on no-need scholarships, see page 439.

STEP FOUR. Accept, reject, or negotiate. If you qualify for aid, your package will reflect how badly the school wants you. The greater its interest, the more you'll be offered in free grants. Students further down the list will be offered smaller grants and larger loans.

Telephone the school if the aid package is too small and you think that something has been overlooked. Maybe a parent died suddenly. Maybe another school has offered a larger grant and you're hoping that your first-choice school will match it. Any change that raises your grant and lowers your loan puts money in your pocket. Usually, however, the package stands. It always stands if your only complaint is, "I can't afford it." No one can afford it.

STEP FIVE. Return to "Go." Every year, you have to suffer through this process all over again. Your eligibility for aid may change. The mix of loans and grants may change. Often, the colleges engage in a form of "bait and switch": They give larger grants to freshmen to get them aboard, then gradually replace those grants with loans. This policy also reflects the fact that upperclassmen and college graduates are better loan risks than freshmen.

FOR PARENTS ONLY

WHAT IF YOU'RE FIGHTING WITH YOUR KID AND REFUSE TO PAY FOR COLLEGE OR FILL IN A FINANCIAL-AID FORM? The child is usually stuck. In almost all cases, the college won't award any aid without financial information from the parents.

WHAT IF YOU'RE A DIVORCED SINGLE PARENT? If the child lives with you, he or she can apply for a Pell Grant based on your income alone. But for the programs they administer, about half of the colleges will want to see the other parent's income, too. Private colleges, in particular, are apt to ask. If the other parent won't cooperate, the child might not qualify for much.

WHAT IF YOU'RE A STEPPARENT? Your income is counted right along with that of the blood parent.

WHAT IF YOU DON'T WANT YOUR CHILDREN TO KNOW HOW MUCH YOU EARN? You could fill in the form privately and simply tell your child to sign. But the Student Aid Report, showing all the financial data, comes back to the child. I suppose you could hang around the mailbox and intercept it, but your secret probably can't be kept.

WHAT IF YOU DON'T WANT TO SHOW ANYONE YOUR TAX RETURNS? You may have no option. The college might insist on seeing tax returns, as a condition of granting aid.

FOR INDEPENDENT STUDENTS

If you're an independent student, you can apply for aid based on your own income rather than on that of your parents. The sons and daughters of the middle classes often try to "go independent," because that usually qualifies them for more help. By contrast, students from low-income families might get more help if they file as dependents rather than as independent.

You are generally considered independent if you'll be 24 by December 31 of the year the grant will be awarded. This is true even if you're living at home on your parents' dole and even if you're taken as a dependent on their income-tax return. (When you're living at home, however, some schools may still decide to count family income as part of your financial resources. This won't affect your eligibility for a federal Pell Grant, but will make it harder to qualify for aid controlled directly by the college.)

If you're under 24, you're independent if:

· You're an orphan or ward of the court.

· You're a veteran.

· You're married or a graduate student, and won't be claimed as a dependent on your parents' tax return in the year the grant is awarded.

· You have dependent children.

· You're an unmarried undergraduate; you weren't claimed by your parents as a tax dependent for the two years before the year you're asking for the grant; and in each of those two years you earned at least $4,000.

· You're declared independent by a financial-aid officer, because of special circumstances.

Independent students can generally get Pell Grants, if their income is low enough. But you won't necessarily qualify for other programs. The colleges can continue to expect parental contributions, and often do.

WHERE THE LOOPHOLES ARE

You can manipulate the financial-aid form in your favor. Of two families with exactly the same income and assets, one child may qualify for more assistance simply because the parents used all the available loopholes. It's unfair, but not illegal. Still, I'd discourage you from trying it because—counting all the costs—the game usually isn't worth the candle.

Here's what you might try, and the drawbacks.

1. *Reduce the size of your reported assets.* You can do this (without lying) because the standard financial-aid form asks about some assets but not others. You have to disclose your bank accounts, stocks, bonds, mutual funds, real estate, and home equity—but not the money saved

in tax-deferred annuities, life insurance policies, and retirement plans, such as 401(k)s, Keogh plans, and Individual Retirement Accounts (only your current year's IRA or Keogh contribution is counted). If you took $20,000 out of the bank and invested it in a tax-deferred annuity, you would suddenly look $20,000 "poorer." That might qualify you for an extra $1,120 in aid.

But—Many schools have their own questionnaires that ask about these hidden assets. So you might have bought that tax-deferred annuity for nothing. Even if the school doesn't ask, you can't be sure that it will grant you the extra aid. Worst of all, by buying annuities or insurance policies, you have put your cash out of easy reach. If you need this money to help pay the tuition, you'll owe taxes and maybe penalties on the withdrawals.

2. *Low-ball the value of your house.* The aid form asks what you paid for your house and what it's worth now. It's expected to have risen in value by a certain amount, based on a national housing index. Parents may report that their house just matches the average, even if it did better.

But—You don't know exactly what the housing index calls for. Some colleges use regional indexes, rather than the national one. If you guess too low, you will unleash some embarrassing questions. Anyone caught cheating may hurt his child's chance of admission.

3. *Avoid taking capital gains, from the year before college starts until your child's last year in school.* Your realized gains are reported as income, which the college will tap more heavily than it taps the value of unsold investments.

But—What if you felt that some of your stocks were overpriced, but failed to sell lest it affect your student aid? If stock prices slump, and you need the money for tuition, you'll have to sell at a lower price.

4. *Take strategic loans.* Say you need $15,000 to buy a new car. Don't go for a regular auto loan. Instead, borrow against your home. Reducing your home equity reduces your reported assets, making you look $15,000 poorer. You can also reduce your assets by buying the car for cash.

But—Cutting $15,000 off your assets makes a negligible difference to your eligibility for student aid. You might pick up only $840 (and there's a risk that you might get nothing extra at all). Even if your aid package was $840 heavier, the extra money might come in the form of a student loan that has to be repaid. If you need a car anyway, borrowing against home equity is often the cheapest way of financing it. But don't run up unnecessary loans just to add a few hundred dollars in student aid.

5. *Save college money in your own name, not in your child's.* Almost all of a child's savings are expected to be spent for four years of education, whereas only part of a parent's are. Assume, for example, that you put aside $18,000 for tuition. If it's in your daughter's bank account, the college will take $6,300 in the first year, or 35 percent. But if it's in your bank account, the college will take about $1,008, or 5.6 percent. This holds down the money you're forced to spend and may qualify your child for more student aid.

But—This helps only those families who are likely to get aid in the first place. If you're over the income limit, it's smarter to keep at least some assets in the child's name, because the child will pay lower taxes on the earnings (page 89).

6. *Attend college part-time.* If a parent enrolls in college, the amount he or she is expected to contribute to the child's education may be cut in half. A $6,000 contribution, for example, could be reduced to only $3,000. That might qualify your child for additional aid. The money you save can help finance your own course of study.

But—The aid officer isn't required to follow this formula. Your child may get only a negligible increase in student aid, leaving you saddled with two expensive tuition bills. Private colleges, in particular, may be hard on you, because they're dispensing their own funds. Public universities, which are dishing out taxpayer dollars, pay less attention.

7. *Manipulate your small-business income.* Farmers and small-business owners have a lot of holes for hiding income in.

But—Many colleges have special small-business forms, asking about dividends and assets. Financial-aid officers are pretty skeptical of claims that a family business isn't throwing off a living wage.

8. *Hire an accountant or financial planner to carry out all these dodges.* To answer this takes five *buts.*

But—It costs money to play asset games. You pay a fee to the accountant or planner, then pay a sales commission for the life insurance that he or she may recommend. Your expenses could easily exceed what you pick up in aid.

But—You lose ready access to some of your money, which you may need for college bills in the end. For example, there's a 10 percent penalty for any funds withdrawn from a tax-deferred annuity before age 59½. It's especially dumb to hide a child's assets in an annuity, although some planners have suggested it.

But—There's no guarantee that your efforts will yield any extra aid at all. As you can see by the chart on page 428, the size of your college-aid package is driven more by the level of your income than by the size of your net assets.

But—You may ruin your child's chances of getting any financial aid at all. "Every family has one opportunity to tell the complete truth," one aid officer told me. "If I catch anything, I put that application at the bottom of the heap and look at it again only if I have any money left." By contrast, aid officers can be tremendous advocates for students whose families play it straight.

But—Manipulating your assets is unfair to the spirit of the whole student-aid system. Whether to do so is more than a financial issue. It's a conscience call.

GRANT ME A GRANT

A grant is the college subsidy of choice. It's free money. You don't work for it, and no one wants it back.

• For undergraduates, the largest single source of grants is Uncle Sugar—most of whose money is reserved for the poor. At this writing, the government's Pell Grants run to a maximum of $2,400 for the lowest-income undergraduates (although Congress is considering an increase). The size declines as family income rises. If your family earns $25,000, a Pell might not offer more than $300 or $400.

Apply for a Pell even if you know you don't qualify (all it takes is checking a box on the standard financial-aid form). It's a prerequisite for getting a government-subsidized student loan or a college grant. Pells are generally available to full-time or half-time students at accredited academic, technical, or vocational institutions (this even includes certain correspondence courses).

You get especially favorable treatment from the Pell program if you are: (1) a "displaced homemaker" (a woman who stayed out of the workforce to raise her kids, lost her husband by death or divorce, and needs some training to find a good job), or (2) a "dislocated worker" (someone who was fired or laid off because a factory closed, or a self-employed person out of a job because the local economy is in the pits).

· The U.S. government's Supplemental Educational Opportunity Grants (SEOGs) are dispensed through college-aid offices, to especially low-income people who have no hope of raising other funds. Awards run from $100 to as much as $4,000, with the biggest ones going to the truly poor. Like Pells, SEOGs go only to undergraduates.

· The federal work-study program isn't exactly free money, because you have to take an approved job. But you don't have to pay anything back. Work-study, administered by the college-aid office, is often open to middle-income students as well as the poor, and graduate students as well as undergraduates. You work until you've earned your full award— say, $1,000—then the job is over. To earn more money, you'll have to find a different job.

· The states make awards, mostly to state residents going to in-state schools (although some states offer reciprocity to each other's students). A few awards are based entirely on merit. Most target financial need. For information, talk to your high school guidance office or college financial-aid office.

· Colleges make need-based grants, in the form of tuition discounts. Instead of charging you the full $9,000, they may settle for only $7,000. One warning: You'll get the most aid in your freshman year. Once you're committed, most schools will start shaving your grant, giving you a little less money every year.

· Special grants often go to scholars, musicians, and other students with unusual talents, even when they have no financial need (page 439). In athletics, colleges need tennis and lacrosse players just as much as they need footballers. And you don't have to be a superstar. Better-than-average is often enough. For a sports scholarship, sell yourself (by letter and in person) to the coach as well as to the financial-aid office.

· You can sometimes give yourself a grant equivalent by:

✓ Taking advanced-placement courses in high school. If the college gives you credit for them (always check this point before applying), you might get through school in six or seven semesters rather than the traditional eight. That saves you a bundle.

✓ Going to a junior college for two years, at a low price, then transferring to a full-term college for your last two years. Just be sure that all your course credits are transferrable, so that you won't have to stay an extra semester at the second school.

✓ Living more cheaply off campus than on. Or living at home for a couple of years.

✓ Taking courses in the summer, for credits that can be applied to your degree. Enough of these courses might save you a whole semester.

· Computerized college scholarship services offer to tap you into a running river of private scholarships, many of them (they claim) unused. That's baloney, to begin with. Most "unused" grants are those available to corporate employees, which you couldn't qualify for anyway.

You pay these services maybe $65 to $100 and get back a printout supposedly tailored to your personal profile. For most students, it's money down the drain. Many of the scholarships will not actually apply to you. Many will be too small to make much difference ($100 to $500). Many you knew about anyway (like Pell Grants). Many are available only for specific colleges that you might not want to attend. *Even if you find a substantial award, it may not reduce the amount your family is expected to contribute toward your college education* (see below)! You're better off putting your time into researching colleges with good grant and loan programs.

The Delusion of Private Scholarships

You see it every year: Thousands of students competing for the hundreds of private scholarships offered by foundations, clubs, corporations, and civic groups. The kids do science projects, enter debates, write essays on "America, My Home." They turn the pages of huge directories of scholarships, or send $65 to a computer outfit to find scholarships for them. Some awards are based on merit; most take financial need into consideration.

Let's say you win one. Everyone cheers. There's a formal presentation and you get your picture in the newspaper.

Then what?

Your college may effectively take your scholarship away. One common way of doing so is to reduce your college grant, dollar for dollar, by any scholarship you win on the outside.

Say, for example, that your college costs $12,500, of which you're expected to pay $7,000 yourself, leaving a $5,500 gap. To plug that gap, the college offers a $3,000 grant and a $2,500 loan. You then win a $1,000 Mother's Club scholarship. Result: The college takes $1,000 out of your grant, giving you only $2,000. The kindly Mothers saved the college some money, not you.

The colleges say it isn't their fault. Under the standard federal rules for awarding aid, all your sources of income have to be taken into consideration—and an outside scholarship is a source of income.

So why bother writing essays? I see three possibilities:

1. If you don't qualify for college aid. A merit award would indeed reduce the amount that you have to pay yourself.

2. If your college has admitted you, but has not given you all the aid you need. In that case, it *might* let you keep any scholarship you capture privately.

3. If the college is giving you both a grant and a loan. The aid officer *might* reduce your loan by the amount of your outside scholarship, rather than your grant. So when you graduate, you'll be less in debt.

Money for Rich Kids

Not all grants are based on financial need. Certain highly desired students can also find aid, even if they come from well-to-do families.

"No-need" scholarships are offered by colleges that want to upgrade the quality of their student bodies. They're buying brains, just as the Big Ten colleges buy quarterbacks.

You needn't be a genius to qualify. At some schools, money is available to any student with a B average, a spot in the top third of his or her high school class, and above-average scores on one of the college testing programs (that generally means more than 900 total on the Scholastic Aptitude Test or an 18.7 composite on the American College Testing program). The better schools look for B-plus or A averages, SATs exceeding 1250, or ACT scores over 27.

Certain colleges also make no-need awards to students with special skills, like acting or music. And, of course, there are always athletic scholarships—with more offered to girls than used to be the case.

For a rundown of what's available at about 1,200 schools, send for *The A's and B's of Academic Scholarships,* at this writing $6.50 from Octameron Associates, P.O. Box 2748, Alexandria, VA, 22301. Some are tiny grants, maybe $200 or $300. But others run to $1,000 or more.

You won't find the nation's most prestigious colleges on the list, because they attract all the talent they can handle. But the second-rank schools are begging for brains. Some states also grant no-need awards to students attending in-state schools.

Be sure to ask if the award is renewable. Some schools pay you to come but don't pay you to stay. Also, look for schools that have special honors programs, so your brains won't go to waste.

Scholarships and Taxes

Grants for tuition, books, fees, supplies, and equipment are still tax free for students working toward a degree. But any money you get for room and board has to be reported as taxable income. Ditto for grants or tuition reductions given in return for teaching or other services.

LEND ME A LOAN

The cheapest loans go directly to students, courtesy of the state and federal governments. Students can borrow without collateral, co-signers, or credit histories.

Loans for parents carry higher interest rates, and you have to pass a credit check.

On none of these loans is the interest tax deductible. But where rates are truly low, or the repayment terms attractive, that may not matter.

Here are your choices.

• One of the best deals going is a federally subsidized Perkins Loan, at only 5 percent interest. But you can't apply for it on your own. It's awarded by the college, to lower-income students, as part of a package of financial aid. At this writing, you can borrow up to $4,500 for a vocational program; $4,500 for your first two years of college; $9,000 for all four years; and a total of $18,000 for both undergraduate and graduate school. The government pays the interest while you're in school. Repayments start nine months after you've finished school and can be stretched over 10 years or more.

• Next best is the plain old "student loan" (known officially as the Stafford student loan). The government pays the interest while you're in school. When you leave, you normally repay at 8 percent interest during the first four years and 10 percent interest thereafter. * Repayment

---

* The government is experimenting with "income-contingent" loans. Under a small pilot program, you pay market interest rates (not the low rates charged for regular student loans). But the size of your monthly repayments depends on the size of your paycheck. Payments can't exceed 5 percent of income for low earners, rising to 12 percent for high earners. Income-contingent loans make sense for students who will enter low-paid professions. But students aiming for higher incomes are better off with a standard Stafford loan.

period: 5 to 10 years. Stafford loans can be had from some banks, S&Ls, credit unions, and state loan-guarantee agencies. If you don't know where to ask for one, your college will. You can use them for trade schools as well as academic studies—although lenders won't provide money for trade schools whose students have high loan-default rates.

To get a student loan, you have to show financial need. Your college financial-aid office does the "need" calculation for you. Here's how it runs:

Start with the cost of the college you'll attend	$_____
Subtract the student and parent's expected contribution to college (page 428)	$_____
Subtract your grants and other forms of student aid	$_____
The remainder is your financial need	$_____

Stafford loans can be used toward that remaining need. At expensive schools, even students with above-average incomes will probably qualify. Freshmen and sophomores can borrow up to $2,625 a year; juniors, seniors, and fifth-year undergraduates, up to $4,000 a year, with a cap of $17,250 on undergraduate loans. Graduate students can get up to $7,500 a year, with a $54,750 cap on their total loans. The minimum loan is $500.

Apply for a student loan as soon as your college has accepted you. You can borrow either in your home state or in the state where you're going to school. Check lenders in both places; some charge higher fees than others. There's a 5 percent loan-origination fee, plus an insurance fee of up to 3 percent.

• The feds maintain one more program for people who can't get attractive loans anywhere else. It's got two names: Parent Loans to Undergraduate Students (PLUS), for loans made to parents, and Supplemental Loans for Students (SLS), for loans to graduate students and independent undergraduates. You don't have to prove financial need or put up collateral, although parents may have to pass a credit check.

The interest rate floats at 3.25 points over the rate for one-year Treasury bills, with a 12 percent cap. Loan limits: up to $4,000 a year per student, to a maximum of $20,000. Loan term: 5 to 10 years. Fee: up to 3 percent, to cover the cost of loan defaults.

You can choose when to start making monthly repayments: within 60 days after you borrow the money or after the student finally leaves school. If you defer repayment, the interest accumulates and your loan gets larger.

PLUS/SLS loans are harder to find than regular student loans, although your college should know which local banks, S&Ls, and credit unions are in the program. A few colleges are starting to take applications for these loans themselves. Or call 800-333-INFO, to find some lenders' names. Students have to apply for a Pell Grant and a Stafford student loan before being considered for an SLS.

· Some states offer terrific loans at low interest rates. Out-of-state students might even quality.

· State college-loan agencies cut special deals with students who want to be teachers. If, after two years of clapping erasers, you decide that you can't stand the little darlings one moment longer, you can switch to another field without penalty.

· If you're training for one of the health professions, Uncle Sugar really rolls out the cart. You'll find loans for doctors, nurses, dentists, optometrists, public health officers, podiatrists, veterinarians, pharmacists, physical therapists, and others. Any medical or professional school will have a full list.

· The college may offer you a loan of its own, at low or no interest. Or it may send you the brochures of one or more commercial lenders who offer a variety of installment plans.

· Here are five commercial-loan sources that let you defer repaying principal for four years while the student is in school: (1) The Education Resources Institute, 330 Stuart St., Boston, MA, 02116, and the Professional Education Plan (PEP, for graduate students) at the same address; (2) ConSern, 205 Van Buren, Herndon, VA, 22070; (3) The Alliance Education Loan Program, Bank of Boston, P.O. Box 1296, Boston, MA, 02104; (4) The New England Education Loan Marketing Corporation (Nellie Mae), 50 Braintree Hill Park, Braintree, MA, 02184; (5) ExtraCredit, from CollegeCredit Service Center, P.O. Box 1330, Merrifield, VA, 22116.

All these programs, except PEP, require that you pay interest currently, even though you've deferred repaying principal. PEP lets you defer interest payments, too. The Nellie Mae loan can be secured with a home mortgage, which may make the interest tax deductible. If your company, large or small, joins ConSern through the U.S. Chamber of Commerce, employees can get loans for half a point less in interest.

Get the brochures from all the programs and compare the cost with what you'd pay for a PLUS/SLS loan. The commercial plans lend more money than you can get through PLUS/SLS, but their variable interest rates can go higher than 12 percent. They also require that you pass a credit check.

· Homeowners should probably borrow against their home equities (page 215). The interest on these loans is tax deductible on loans up to $100,000. Interest is not deductible on personal loans, student loans, or education loans against pension plans.

· Your college may send you brochures for one or more commercial tuition plans. These plans convert the twice-a-year lump-sum payments required by many schools into 12 equal monthly installments. There may also be 5- or 10-year payment plans at variable interest rates (not tax deductible). Tuition plans generally include life and disability insurance. If you die or become totally disabled, all the rest of your child's college bills will be paid in full. A leader in the field is Knight Tuition Payment Plans, 855 Boylston St., Boston, MA, 02116.

· As an alternative to Knight-type plans, consider this: Pay the college bill with a home-equity loan, which, unlike other loans, is tax deductible. Buy more term life insurance to guarantee your child's education if you die, and pray that you won't become disabled. (If you do become disabled, your child will qualify for much more student aid.)

· If you have some savings but not enough, consider the Security Educational Loan Program, offered by the United States Trust Company in association with the College Financing Foundation, 625 Mount Auburn St., Cambridge, MA, 02138. You deposit your savings in a 6 percent savings account. The bank gives you a credit line worth up to two and a half times your deposit, for four years of college. You borrow only the money you need each semester; interest is charged, at 9.85 percent, only on the balance outstanding. The program is structured so that the interest you earn on your savings can be used to pay all of the charges on the loan. You repay the principal over six years, eight months. After that, your original savings deposit is returned. The deadline for deposits is July 1 for the fall semester and November 1 for the spring semester.

The Collegeaire plan (P.O. Box 88370, Atlanta, GA, 30356) is similar, except that your savings don't earn enough to cover all your loan interest. The Citizen's Bank of Dallas, GA, pays 5.25 percent on your deposit; the credit line costs 11.9 percent, with seven years to repay.

Should You Borrow from Your Company Savings Plan?

Don't borrow from your plan to pay tuition if you can possibly avoid it. It makes no sense to tap retirement savings for loans whose interest isn't tax deductible (see page 228), and student loans are definitely not. Borrow against your house, instead. If you don't have that option, however, your retirement plan is a source to consider. Borrow if the plan gives you better terms than you'd get from a commercial student-loan program (page 442) or from a bank.

Who Should Borrow, Parent or Student?

Where there's a choice, I vote for the student. Students' debts aren't nearly as unmanageable as most people think. Two studies in California found that less than 5 percent of the college seniors who borrow will actually wind up in trouble. Average indebtedness remains low relative to starting salaries. As the salaries of college graduates rise, student loans get easier to repay. Defaults are high among low-income students who attend trade schools, but generally not among the graduates of community colleges and four-year institutions.

When parents take on debt (as they usually must), repayment typically takes 8 to 10 years. That takes them right to the edge of retirement and beyond, reducing their nest egg and permanently lowering their standard of living in old age. I know that no sacrifice is too great etcetera etcetera. But the plain fact is that the young people are better placed than the old to eliminate debt and still build a comfortable future for themselves.

Besides, it's the students who gain the most from the education. So why shouldn't they shoulder more of the price?

Uncle Sam Has Got You Where He Wants You

Around the time of the Vietnam draft resistance, Congress passed a tricky little law. No male born after January 1, 1960, can get a federally subsidized, student loan unless he registers for the draft. No one is now being drafted, but that's entirely beside the point. If you won't play with Uncle Sam, he won't play with you. Aid forms are computer-matched against selective service lists to catch artful dodgers.

You are supposed to register at age 18, and no later than age 25. Many an older protester who now wants to go to graduate school finds he can't get a Pell Grant or student loan because he never got a draft card. So sell out, give in, and sign up. Registrants in their early twenties aren't being prosecuted. Government loans may be the only ones you can get, because they require no collateral.

Strategic Repayment

When you take college loans, go for those that defer principal payments until your student is out of school. These include government-subsidized student loans, PLUS loans, and some of the commercial loans (page 442). You generally cannot tax-deduct any interest you pay. But that hardly matters because the payments are so low. With subsidized loans, the government pays all the interest while the student is in school.

When it's time to repay, don't hustle to get rid of a Perkins loan, which carries a low, 5 percent interest rate. Ditto a Stafford student loan, as long as you're paying only 8 percent. But when the Stafford jumps to 10 percent, reconsider. You might find it cheaper to pay it off with the proceeds of a home-equity loan whose interest charges are tax deductible. Ditto the PLUS/SLS loans, which could be costing you 12 percent.

This strategy saves money, however, only if you repay your home-equity loan over the same 5- to 10-year period that the student loan would have lasted. If you take a lot longer, the home-equity loan may cost more in the end.

Some lenders offer graduated-repayment loans. Repayments start low, when your income is presumably at its lowest, and increase with time. Stick with the original loan as long as your payments stay small. When they rise, consider refinancing with a home-equity loan or a consolidation loan.

Loan Consolidation: Yes or No?

If you're oppressed by your student-loan payments, there's a way out. As long as you're out of school, owe $5,000 or more, and your payments are up to date, you can consolidate your debt.

Consolidation reduces your monthly payments, by stretching out your loan for another 10 to 25 years. The interest rate equals the weighted average of all of the loans you put into the pot or 9 percent, whichever is greater. There are no other fees. Some lenders start your payments low and gradually increase them, on the assumption that your income will be rising, too.

Ask your own lender whether it offers this deal. If not, write to the Student Loan Marketing Association, 1050 Thomas Jefferson St. N.W., Washington, DC, 20007, or the New England Education Loan Marketing Corporation, 50 Braintree Hill Park, Braintree, MA, 02184. You don't have to put up any collateral or even pass a credit check. Their consolidation loans are granted on your signature alone.

DON'T CONSOLIDATE UNLESS YOU'RE DESPERATE. Consolidation means many extra years of nondeductible interest payments, often at a higher interest rate than you're paying now. You might still be paying off the cost of your own education when it's time for your children to enter school.

When Loans Are Forgiven

A government loan doesn't necessarily have to be repaid, or repaid on time. *Depending on the loan, your payments will be deferred if you:*
- Teach in a place that the government defines as short of teachers.
- Join the Armed Forces, Public Health Service, or National Oceanic and Atmospheric Administration.
- Join the Peace Corps, ACTION, VISTA, or a similar program.
- Cannot find a job, but are actively looking for work.
- Have to serve an internship to qualify for your profession.
- Are temporarily disabled.
- Have to care for a dependent who's temporarily disabled.
- Return to school.
- Take a parental leave from work.
- Have small children and are a working mother entering (or reentering) the work force at a low wage.
- Borrowed money as a parent, for your child's education, and are now in school yourself.
- Are ill or have personal problems. The lender may agree to let you stop paying for a while, or make smaller payments.

YOUR LOAN CAN BE CANCELED IF YOU:
- Die.
- Become totally and permanently disabled.
- Go bankrupt (although in some cases your student loan may not be discharged in bankruptcy).
- Enlist in the Army, the Army National Guard, or the Army Reserve. If you sign up for certain kinds of work, like the infantry, part of your loan will be forgiven for each year you serve.
- Are a Perkins-loan holder and teach low-income or handicapped

students, serve in the Armed Forces in an "area of hostilities," serve in the Peace Corps, or join VISTA. Part of your loan is forgiven for each year you serve.

Never Default!

If you do . . .

. . . You can't get a Pell Grant or other federal student aid.

. . . A collection agent may pursue you.

. . . Your delinquency may show up on your credit report.

. . . If you work for the federal government, the payments may be withheld from your salary.

. . . Your income-tax refunds may be held back. If you file jointly, so might your spouse's.

. . . Your college may refuse to send out your transcripts.

. . . There will be less money in the Perkins loan fund, depriving some other student of help.

. . . You'll be a dirty rat.

ADULT STUDENTS

Adults can apply to all the same programs that kid students do. But Catch-22 in the college handbook may stop you from getting a lot of aid. Because you're a grownup, you probably have been holding a job. Because of your job, you may earn too much to qualify for very much help. You'll point out, of course, that your earnings will decline when you enter school. That won't help you with a Pell Grant (unless you're a displaced homemaker or dislocated worker—page 436). But colleges may take your projected drop in income into consideration when awarding other forms of aid.

RAISING MONEY FOR GRADUATE SCHOOL

As a parent, you're financially exhausted. Child One is through college; Child Two will be finished in two years. Retirement is within sight.

Then Child One says she wants to go to graduate school. No boxer could deliver a harder punch.

Most parents assume that their financial obligations stop with the undergraduate degree. If the kid wants more education, that's his or her responsibility.

But try telling that to a university. Most of them look at parental income before granting any financial aid. Parents of graduate students aren't squeezed as hard as the parents of undergraduates. Still, your expected contribution may be high. If you won't help pay, your child might not be able to go.

How much aid is available depends on what your child will study. In medicine, law, and other well-paid professions, middle-class students are expected to pay their own way. Borrow it or earn it, but don't look to the grad school for much of a grant.

Advanced science degrees, on the other hand, are heavily funded by scholarships and research assistantships, which are often awarded on merit, not need. The social sciences offer administrative assistantships, like being a counselor. The arts may give teaching assistantships. Write for *A Selected List of Fellowship Opportunities and Aids to Advanced Education*, free from the Publications Office, National Science Foundation, 1800 G St. N.W., Washington, DC, 20550 (it includes opportunities in the humanities as well as the sciences).

When hunting for a grant, talk to the head of the academic department you want to join, as well as to the student-aid office. Also, take a look at cooperative education (see below).

What if the student still comes up short? The grad schools aren't entirely flint-hearted. Some don't pursue the parents of students who have been self-supporting for three years. Some let stepparents off the hook. Every family should talk to the financial-aid office, to see if there's any wiggle room.

THE JOB CONNECTION

Sometimes your job can lead to a grant. Some employers will help pay for college courses. Some let you alternate between work and school. In the Army, you can march for your money. Whatever the deal, you get an education at a fraction of the cost that other students pay. Here's what's out there.

Cooperative Education

A co-op student gets a job related to his or her field of study. Your salary pays a significant share of your college costs—an average of $7,000 a year. Schedules vary. You might alternate semesters, one in school, one at work. You might attend classes in the morning and work in the afternoon. It may take five years to win a baccalaureate degree. Co-op programs are also offered by two-year community colleges and some graduate schools. Around 250,000 students participate.

For the free *Cooperative Education Undergraduate Program Directory,* write to the National Commission for Cooperative Education, 360 Huntington Ave., Boston, MA, 02115. There's a separate list for graduate education, although it's not very current.

For a roundup of the co-op jobs offered by federal agencies, write for *Earn and Learn,* $4.25 (at this writing) from Octameron Associates, P.O. Box 2748, Alexandria, VA, 22301. More than 16,000 federal jobs are available, through participating schools.

Junior Fellowships

Do you have financial need? Does your family income not exceed about $35,000 (or sometimes a little more)? Do you think you might like to work for the federal government? Will you be attending an accredited two- or four-year school? Uncle Sam's Junior Fellowship program can give you a job during every break in your academic calendar, all year long. When you graduate, you'll generally be offered a permanent slot (although you are not required to take it).

The time to apply for a Junior Fellowship is during your senior year of high school. You have to be nominated by your school, so be sure that the high school guidance office knows about the program. Openings are available in federal agencies all over the country. For more information, ask at the recruiting office for any federal agency in your city (look for one under U.S. government in the phone book; also, look to see if there's a U.S. Office of Personnel Management), or write to the Office of Personnel Management, Assistant Director for Recruiting and Employment, 1900 E St. N.W., Room 6355, Washington, DC, 20415.

At this writing, the government has no separate brochure about its Junior Fellowships but says it's working on one. A majority of the jobs are related to the following seven fields: accounting, the biological sciences, business administration, computer science, engineering, mathematics, and the physical sciences.

The Military Budget

Military scholarships are harder to come by, now that the size of the nation's armies will apparently be reduced. But at least some new officers have to be trained, so college money is still on tap. To win a two- to five-year scholarship from the Reserve Officers Training Corps (ROTC), you need high grades and, usually, a tilt toward math, science, or engineering. But smaller grants exist, including a salary for your third and fourth year with an on-campus ROTC program (but not for your first and second ROTC year).

If you enlist, grants are available for taking courses at local colleges on your own time. You can also allocate $1,200 of your military pay toward a college fund. If you do, and stay in the service for two full years, the Department of Veterans Affairs will pay $250 a month for up to three years of full-time study ($9,000). A three-year hitch is worth $300 a month (up to $10,800). Your particular branch of service may add even more, if you enlist in certain lines of work, like the infantry.

Reserve enlistments are especially attractive. For a six-year commitment, you can get an education grant worth $140 a month for up to three years ($5,040), forgiveness of part of your student loan, and drill pay besides. Of course, you might also have to fight.

The spouses and children of veterans may qualify for special benefits if the vet died or was permanently or totally disabled because of his service duties, is missing in action, or was a prisoner of war for more than 90 days. Children can apply if their parent served in a war and has since died of other causes. Awards are generally based on need. A few grants and loans are available to bright, needy children of any active or retired serviceman or woman. To qualify, the children have to be high school graduates or between 18 and 26.

For a thorough guide to military scholarships, get *Need a Lift?*, $2 from the American Legion, National Emblem Sales, P.O. Box 1050, Indianapolis, IN, 46206. This booklet also covers co-operative education, some private scholarships, and the main sources of state and federal funds.

The Company Perk

Some companies pay part or all of the price of courses at local undergraduate institutions or training schools. The big question is, will you be taxed on the value of the company contribution? The answer is no, if the course is designed to improve your performance in your present job. But Congress has been going back and forth on any courses you're taking to get an undergraduate or graduate degree, to prepare yourself for a better job, or just for the fun of it. At this writing, you pay no taxes on tuition aid, for these studies, either, up to $5,250. But check with your employee-benefits department for the latest information.

FOR MORE INFORMATION ON RAISING MONEY FOR COLLEGE*

Get the government's excellent free booklet on its own student-aid programs—*The Student Guide: Financial Aid from the U.S. Department of Education.* Call, toll free, 800-333-4636. At that same number, someone will answer any questions you have on federal aid.

Send $6.50 to Octameron Associates, P.O. Box 2748, Alexandria, VA, 22301, for *Don't Miss Out,* a sound, strategic guide to finding and qualifying for student aid. Octameron publishes many other booklets on specific kinds of aid. *College Check Mate* ($7.50), for example, lists the discounts, loans, and flexible payment plans that various colleges offer.

For $19.95, get Peterson's *College Money Handbook,* available through bookstores. It lists 1,700 institutions, their expenses, the amount of aid on tap, the no-need awards you can apply for, money-saving options (like accelerated degrees, ROTC, co-op education, guaranteed tuition plans, and off-campus living), and athletic scholarships. A helpful chart gives parents a general idea of what they'll be expected to contribute to their children's education.

Try The College Board's *College Cost Book,* available through bookstores or for $16.90 from College Board Publications, Box 886, New York, NY, 10101. This general guide to college aid gives you worksheets showing what's on the financial-aid forms, the costs of more than 3,100 colleges, universities, and proprietary schools and the kinds of grants they offer, lists of schools with tuition waivers or special tuition-payment plans, as well as a table showing how much parents should expect to pay.

WHAT'S YOUR BEST SHOT AT GETTING COLLEGE AID?

For low-income kids, the money is there—although even these families will be pressed to their limit for contributions.

---

* By the time you read this, prices may be up.

1. Check out schools with no-need scholarships.

2. Apply to schools where your academic record puts you in the top 25 percent of the applicant pool.

3. Do not miss any deadlines for college-aid applications, which may be as early as February 1.

4. Tell the school you'd like a work-study job.

5. Check all the financial data about your family when you get the aid form back from the processor, to be sure that nothing was entered wrong.

6. Work the loopholes that make sense (page 433).

7. Go for co-operative education.

8. Go to a school in your home state.

9. Ask the student-aid officer to base your grant on your projected income rather than on last year's earnings. This is critical to students whose earnings will drop—for example, adults who give up jobs to return to school. The standard formula might rule you ineligible unless you raise the issue personally.

Grants are nice when you can get them. But, bottom line, you won't get through school without a lot of savings and loans.

20
THE BEST COLLEGE INVESTMENT PLANS:

How to Beat the College Inflation Rate

If you play it too safe with your college funds,
you'll never raise the money you need.

Most parents blanch when I talk about putting money into stocks. "They're too risky." "The market might fall." "I need something safe."

So you buy a nice, reliable Series EE Savings Bond for your two-year-old and earn 6 to 7 percent a year. You don't lose your money. But you may lose purchasing power, which amounts to the same thing. If the cost of college rises by 7 to 9 percent, your EE bonds will cover an ever-smaller share of the tuition bill. Meanwhile, well-chosen stock-owning mutual funds will probably earn 10 to 12 percent annually, on money invested for at least a decade. For stock buyers, college gets *cheaper*, because their investments rise faster than tuitions do.

In some years, stocks drop. On rare occasions, the market has gone nowhere for a decade, so it's not wrong to hedge by owning a few bonds. But the odds strongly favor stock-market investments. Over the long term, nothing beats them for growth.

A STRATEGY FOR COLLEGE INVESTING

What to buy depends on how old your children are. When you're young, make it stocks. If the market drops, you can afford to wait for prices to jump up again. When your children are older, however, their college money should be kept in investments that are absolutely safe.

For Children Zero to 12

Save money regularly. The sooner you start the less college will cost you, because you'll be paying part of the bill with money that your money earned. To appreciate the astonishing value of early savings, take a look at the chart on page 159.

Put your savings into stock-owning mutual funds with good records (page 583). Don't try to buy and sell as market conditions change; too often, you'll guess wrong. Just faithfully put your money away, month after month, in good times and bad, and reinvest the dividends. Don't worry if the market falls. It will rise again. Over 10 years or so, your stocks should far outpace certificates of deposit, Series EE Savings Bonds, zero-coupon Treasuries, or any of the other popular college-saving deals.

Many parents are tempted by zero-coupon bonds, which guarantee a fixed sum of money at maturity (page 661). But the yield on a zero, after tax, probably won't keep up with the rise in the cost of college. If by some miracle it does, you will just about break even. Your money won't grow. For this reason, zeros don't interest me as a core investment for young children. However, you might put 10 percent of your money into zeros, as a hedge against the rare occasions when stocks are flat for an entire decade.

For Children 12 to 14

Over these years, deposit your new savings into safe havens: Series EE Bonds, long-term certificates of deposit, and zero-coupon Treasuries that will mature when your child starts school. What's more, start methodically moving some of your money out of stocks. By the time your child reaches 14, half your college savings should be earning interest in secure investments. These funds may lose some purchasing power, after taxes and inflation. But that's a small worry, compared with the risk that stock prices will drop and not recover by the time that college bills are due. This hoard of safe money guarantees your child's freshman and sophomore years.

Keep the other half of your money in stocks, for your child's junior and senior years. Over five-year periods, stock investors have a 64 percent chance of earning at least 10 percent a year, compared with only a 6 percent chance of losing money, according to data developed by Ibbotson Associates. Those odds are worth taking.

When Your Child Reaches 14

If any of your child's *freshman-year* money is still in stocks, take it out. The market beats everything in the long run, but in the short run it can kill you. Since World War II, it has taken stock investors an average of four years * to get even after a market fall—so that's the time period for playing it safe. The market might not fall, but you can't take the risk. If you own a long-term bond mutual fund, or any other investment that puts your principal at risk, sell it, too.

Put every penny of your freshman-year money into safe investments *that will mature shortly before the start of the college term.* For the fall semester, that's July or August, four years from now. Consider certificates of deposit. Consider shorter-term Treasury securities (including zero-coupon bonds), whose interest is taxed at the federal level but not by states or cities. For any money available five years before college starts, consider Series EE Savings Bonds, whose interest earnings may not be taxed at all (page 463). You have to hold Savings Bonds for five years in order to get the full interest rate.

The next year, when the child is 15, get all your sophomore-year money out of the market and stored somewhere safe. When the child is 16, take out the junior-year money. At age 17, take out the senior-year money. Your timing on these removals may vary a bit, because you won't want to sell if the market is down. But over these critical four or five years, move your money gradually out of harm's way.

Additional investments made in these years should also go into safety-first instruments, not into mutual funds.

While the child is in college, don't fool around. Always keep the money absolutely safe. The college may give you a price break if you can pay four years' tuition in advance.

---

* Since World War II, the longest it has taken investors to get even was 10 years, from 1973 to 1983. The shortest time: one year. After the Great Crash of 1929, it took investors 14 long years to get even—a reminder that the worst does happen. For this data, thank you Tony Tabell of Delafield, Harvey, Tabell, Inc.

If You Don't Start Saving Until Your Child is 13 or 14

You've missed the safest part of your personal stock-market curve. To buy stocks now is too great a risk. Keep your capital safe, with Series EE bonds, Treasuries, or certificates of deposit.

Parents who start saving *very* late may have to borrow so much money for college that they can't afford to retire at age 65. Ditto for divorced men who remarry and start second families, and women who have children in their late thirties or early forties.

WHAT IF YOU CAN'T SAVE AS MUCH AS YOU NEED?

Save less. Try to acquire half the money you're going to need and borrow the rest when your child is in school.

Start with a small amount each month, and raise it every time your income goes up. Or tell your child from an early age that he or she will have to contribute part of the cost.

Aim for a state college or university, even if you yourself went to a private school. Many state schools are terrific. Private colleges offer more student aid—but they'll leave you with huge debts if you haven't saved much money yourself.

HOW TO SAVE FOR COLLEGE AND RETIREMENT AT THE SAME TIME

Here's a surprising answer to a question you might think unanswerable. *Don't* specifically save for college. Instead:

1. Buy a house. Build equity by adding extra dollars to your payment every month, to pay down the mortgage as quickly as possible. You are creating a savings pool, with money that you otherwise might have spent.

2. Set up a tax-deferred retirement savings plan, like a Keogh or a company 401(k) (Chapter 29). Sock every penny into it you can. Retirement plans are wonderful ways to save, because your contributions are pre-tax. In company plans, your employer usually matches part of your contribution—which is *free money*, not to be missed! What's more, the accumulated value of retirement plans is not counted as personal

wealth on the standard college financial-aid application, which might help you qualify for a student loan or grant.

3. Set up a separate college savings account *only* if you have money to spare, after fully funding your Keogh, 401(k), 403(b) annuity, or tax-deductible Individual Retirement Account. College savings accounts use after-tax dollars, which aren't nearly as valuable as the pre-tax dollars that go into retirement plans.

4. When your child goes to college, quit adding to your retirement savings plan. Set that money aside for your personal future. Don't borrow against it; leave it alone to grow.

5. The money that you were saving out of your salary for retirement now goes for tuition, as do any funds saved outside your pension plan.

6. Borrow against your house. The interest is tax deductible whereas interest on student loans is not. (In Texas, however, where second mortgages aren't allowed, fund your pension plan fully, pay the *minimum* on your mortgage, and start a college savings account.)

7. When your children are through college, use the income that formerly went for tuition to pay off your home-equity loan.

8. All during the financially tight college years, your retirement fund will continue to accumulate even though you can't afford fresh contributions. As soon as possible, however, resume putting money into your plan, in order to collect those matching funds from your employer.

WHAT CAN GO WRONG? You might not accumulate enough home equity to support a sizable loan. Or your income might not be large enough to qualify you for the big loan you need. So you'd have to turn to student or parent loans, whose interest payments are not tax deductible.

WHAT ELSE CAN GO WRONG? You might have to retire early and couldn't afford to take on college debt. That's why, if you have the money, you should fund for college and retirement at the same time. The "retirement first" strategy is for people who can't afford both.

ANYTHING ELSE? Sure. Your house might drop in value. Instead of making money (and creating borrowing power) from the extra mortgage payments, you'd come out behind. The decision to prepay a mortgage is obviously an investment-judgment call. If the value of homes in your neighborhood is declining, it's smarter to put that extra money into other investments.

Still, the value of your house doesn't have to rise by very much to make prepayment a smart move. Say, for example, that you paid

$150,000 for your house and put $30,000 down. Next year, your house is worth $154,500—up $4,500. That's a modest 3 percent gain on the value of your house, but a 15 percent gain on your $30,000 investment. On balance, prepayment pays.

IF YOU HAVE A SEPARATE COLLEGE FUND, WHO SHOULD OWN IT?

Keep the savings (or part of them) in your child's name, if you don't expect to qualify for student aid. Kids get a tax break on their income from savings. So the money is worth more in their account than in yours, as long as you don't run afoul of the kiddie tax (page 89).

But if you expect to collect college aid, keep the savings in your own account. The college-aid formula counts only 5.6 percent of a parent's savings, when deciding how much the family should pay (page 435). But it counts 35 percent of the child's savings. If you own the savings, you'll pay a little more in income taxes, but should be rewarded with extra college aid.

THE DOWNSIDE TO GIVING THE FUNDS TO YOUR CHILD:

1. You probably can't get that money back, if you should need it.

2. A dependent child with unearned income over $500 has to pay taxes on the money.

3. The child gets the money at age 18 (21 in some states), even if immature.

4. Having unearned income requires a child to pay a bit more in tax on his or her earned income.

5. Unearned income over $1,000 is taxed at the parent's rate until the child is 14.

THE DOWNSIDE TO KEEPING THE MONEY YOURSELF:

1. You pay income taxes on the earnings, at a higher rate than your child would.

2. You might not get student aid after all, because your income rose too high.

3. If you get extra aid, it might not be enough to compensate for the extra taxes you paid over the years.

4. The money is part of your estate, which is subject to federal taxes for amounts over $600,000.

So go figure.

Some planners recommend a "minority trust" as a way around the kiddie tax. It's for children under 14 who have a lot of money in their names. But the costs associated with setting up and managing the trust may wipe out any tax advantage.

If you buy Series EE Savings Bonds for college, you should own them yourself. That's the only way of getting the tax break, as long as your income isn't too high to qualify.

SIX SMART INVESTMENT MOVES

You'll find the scoop on the following investments in other parts of this book. Here, just a word about how to use them for college savings.

1. *Stocks*—the best buy when the children are small. Make regular monthly or quarterly contributions to stock-owning mutual funds, in good markets and bad. Choose a fund without sales charges and with a good performance record (page 510). If you and your broker want to chase the "next Xerox," do it with your play money, not with your college fund.

As college approaches, don't sell the shares yourself. Give them to your child and let the child sell them. Then the gain will be taxed in the child's lower bracket. You can give your child up to $10,000 a year gift-tax free ($20,000, if the gift is made jointly with your spouse).

2. *Home equities*—accelerate your mortgage payments, so as to build equity faster. You'll then have more tax-deductible borrowing power, when the time comes for a college loan. Prepaying mortgages makes sense as long as your house is rising at least modestly in price (page 398). Your house is also your hedge against a high-inflation economy. Under those conditions, stocks may go nowhere for several years—but you hope that the value of real estate would rise.

3. *Company retirement plans*—fund them right to the limit, even to the exclusion of other forms of long-term saving. They're your guarantee of a comfortable old age, despite the squeeze that college puts you through. If need be, you can usually borrow against company plans.

4. *Certificates of deposit*—worthwhile during that one- to four-year period before tuition is due, when you have to keep your money safe.

5. *Series EE Savings Bonds*—better than certificates of deposit if you've headed for safety five years before tuition is due, because of the tax-deferral and possible tax exemption—page 463. (You have to hold savings bonds for at least five years in order to get the full rate of interest).

6. *Bonds*—over ten-year holding periods, there is a *tiny* risk that stocks won't yield their usual gains. For that reason, consider putting 10 percent of your college savings into zero-coupon bonds that will mature when college starts. They are your hedge against a bad economy that pulls inflation, corporate profits, and the stock market down.

Zeros can also be good, safe investments for the four or five years before matriculation. For all the details on these bonds, see pages 170–71 and 661. Here's how to use them for college investing:

Buy bonds that will mature just before college-matriculation day. This is the best advice on zeros that you'll ever get! Too many fond grandparents buy their grandchildren 20 or 30-year zeros that will have to be sold before maturity. An early sale exposes your money to market risk. If interest rates rise, the value of your zeros will plunge and you can kiss part of your savings goodbye. Also, small amounts of zeros don't fetch a good price—another reason not to sell in advance.

That advice is so good that I'll give it again, a little more strongly: Buy *only* those bonds that will mature shortly before college begins. Stagger your maturities, so that a zero bond falls due in each of the four years that your child will be in school.

Go for newly issued zeros, not the older zeros up for resale on the secondary markets. You don't get such good prices on the secondary markets, and the tax complications of buying older zeros are disheartening (page 662).

Buy zero Treasuries, not zero tax exempts, for the following reasons: (1) If you're looking for a new-issue, five-year maturity, you're more likely to find it in a Treasury than in a tax-exempt municipal bond. (2) If you have to sell before maturity, Treasuries fetch better prices. (3) If you're buying long-term zeros, most Treasuries cannot be called away from you before maturity, whereas a municipal might be called after just 10 years.

Federal taxes are owed on Treasury-bond interest, but not state and local taxes. Income on zeros held in the child's name will be taxed at a lower rate, if the child doesn't have much other unearned income or if the child is 14 or older (page 89).

Two mutual fund groups—Benham Target in Mountain View, California, and Scudder in Boston—offer taxable, zero-coupon mutual funds whose bonds mature in specific years. But they subtract an annual management fee, so long-term holders will do better buying individual bonds.

Use mutual funds only if you want to invest small amounts, such as $100 a month.

THE RISKS IN SOME OTHER COLLEGE INVESTMENTS

Some parents are just too scared to buy stocks for young children. They feel safer with bonds and real estate. If you go that route, here's what you're up against.

1. *Long-term (20-year) bond mutual funds*—almost as risky as stocks. You'll make some money when interest rates fall but lose some money when interest rates rise (for more on bonds, see Chapter 25). If rates stay roughly level, your after-tax return will probably not keep up with the rising cost of college. If you do buy bond funds, start selling them when your child reaches 14, for the very same reason that other parents are selling stocks: the risk.

2. *Straight long-term Treasuries, maturing when college begins*—your principal is safe but your interest, after tax, will probably not keep up with the rise in college tuitions. So your Treasuries will gradually lose purchasing power. If high inflation resumes, these investments are sunk.

3. *Short-term bond funds*—not worth a look. Their yields are lower than the yields on long- and intermediate-term funds, and they don't keep ahead of college inflation, after tax. Short-term funds aren't even good for the four years before your child starts school, because their share prices fluctuate. In those years, you need an investment that's perfectly safe.

4. *Real estate*—some families invest in a one- or two-family home and rent it out, as a way of building savings for college. In the year before the child matriculates, they plan to sell the house, put the equity into the bank, and draw on the money as tuition bills come due.

But rental houses are often mediocre deals. The rent is probably too low to cover all your expenses. So it may cost you money to run the property every year, even after tax. To make up these losses and earn a profit, you'd need substantial annual appreciation, and gains like that can't be guaranteed. For what it takes to succeed with a rental property, see page 716.

Financial planners love to talk about buying a house in the town where your child decides to go to college, renting rooms to students to cover part of the mortgage, and paying the child a deductible salary to manage the building. That's neat on paper, but not too many of us have junior real-estate moguls sprawled on our living-room floors.

HOW ABOUT LIFE INSURANCE?

Here's the pitch you'll get from an insurance agent: "Save for college in a universal-life-insurance policy. The cash in the policy builds up tax deferred. At college time, you can withdraw, tax free, a sum equal to the premiums you paid. You can also borrow against the cash value. Regular premium payments are a disciplined way of building tax-deferred savings, and there's money for college if you die."

But how large a savings pot do you build? Not enough to be interesting. After you pay the insurance premium and the sales commission, there's not much left for your cash account, especially in the early years. Insurance policies typically don't start accumulating serious money until after the 15th year. That doesn't help a parent whose daughter will matriculate 10 or 12 years from now. Furthermore, the gross interest rate that the company advertises may be much higher than the net rate that is actually credited to your cash values (page 266). An advertised 8.5 percent may net down to only 5 percent, after expenses.

At bottom, the very design of insurance policies conflicts with the goal of college savings. Insurers try to maximize death benefits rather than cash values—but cash is what suffering parents need the most.

If you do need more life insurance, as well as college savings, here's a simple alternative: Buy cheap term insurance (to be canceled after the children leave college) and devote the rest of your money to growth investments.

What about variable-universal-life insurance, whose cash values can be invested in stocks? Forget it, for college savings. Variable-life policies carry heavy administrative fees. To overcome these costs, you need high returns on your stock investments (page 267) over a long period of time —at least 10 years. But college savers ought to drop out of stocks in the four or five years before college begins—which may curtail your investment too soon. Worse, in order to get the safety you'd need in those final years, the cash values in your variable-life policy would have to be switched into money market mutual funds. But money funds don't yield enough to justify the insurance policy's high costs.

In short, don't bother. Variable-life insurance is no solution to the need for growth investing.

WHATEVER YOU DO, RESIST BUYING A LIFE-INSURANCE POLICY ON A CHILD IN ORDER TO BUILD COLLEGE FUNDS. It's a total waste of money. A good part of each payment goes for life insurance, which the child doesn't need. If you deposited $1,200 a year ($100 a month) into an insurance policy for a five-year-old, with a gross yield of 8.8 percent, you might have $23,000 in cash when the child reached 18. That same money invested in Series EE Savings Bonds at only 7 percent would yield $26,000, and might be tax exempt (below). A 10 percent mutual fund would pay much more.

If you already own a life-insurance policy on a child, cancel it. Put the proceeds into a better investment.

PLANS DESIGNED FOR COLLEGE SAVINGS

In terms of potential total return, none of these special college-savings plans are as good as plain old stock-owning mutual funds, held for the long term. But each has an interesting gimmick—especially for nervous savers who don't mind if they fall behind college inflation as long as they don't risk any principal.

Series EE Savings Bonds

Series EE bonds are hung like a Christmas tree with income-tax breaks. For all buyers, the interest can be tax deferred until the savings bonds are redeemed. For some buyers, that interest is partly or entirely tax free. You escape all taxes if you meet *all* of the following conditions:

• You bought the EE bond any time from 1990 on. The tax break doesn't apply to bonds bought before that date.

• At the time of the purchase, you were at least 24 years old.

• The bond is owned in your name or co-owned with your spouse. It cannot be carried in your child's name or co-owned with your child.

• You redeem the EE bond to cover college fees and tuition for yourself, your spouse, or your child (but not your grandchild. If grandparents want to help, they should give money to the parents and let the parents buy the EE bond).

• You meet an income test, in the year that the bonds are redeemed.

The base year for this test was 1990. Back then, EE-bond interest passed tax free for married couples with gross incomes (adjusted by various factors) below $60,000 and singles with incomes below $40,000.

Above those levels, taxes were gradually phased in. The tax break vanished entirely for couples with incomes of $90,000 or more and singles with $55,000 or more.

Each year, those income levels rise with inflation, so most Americans will qualify for at least a partial exemption. But if your income rises faster than inflation (as it does for many managers or for people who get regular promotions), you may find yourself—at college time—eligible only for a negligible tax break.

WARNING: Even if your income doesn't appear to exceed the ceiling, your tax break may be smaller than you expect! Here's why.

In the year you redeem an EE bond, your reported income is enlarged by the EE-bond interest you just collected. And the higher your reported income, the harder it is to get the full tax break.

Say, for example, that you're a single parent with an income of $39,000 in 1990 dollars. You pick up another $4,000 by cashing in some EE bonds. Your total income is now $43,000—putting you $3,000 over the limit for collecting EE-bond interest entirely tax free. Part of your interest will be tax exempt but not all of it.

WHAT TO DO: Buy EE bonds in relatively small denominations, so you won't have to redeem in higher amounts than you actually need. That helps keep extra taxes to a minimum.

EE bonds carry a variable interest rate, so you have some protection if rates rise. That's a clear advantage over tax-exempt Baccalaureate Bonds (below), whose rates are fixed. If interest rates decline, you'll earn a minimum of 6 percent if you hold the bonds for at least five years. For more on EE bonds, see page 172.

Baccalaureate Bonds

These are tax-exempt zero-coupon bonds, sold by a few states expressly for college savings. You invest a small amount of money and it grows to a fixed sum by the time your child matriculates. Your state might add a tiny kicker to the yield—worth maybe $100 to $400—if your child chooses an in-state school.

Whenever Baccalaureate Bonds are issued, small savers line up to buy them. But that's often a mistake. If you'll probably qualify for a full tax break on Series EE bonds, compare the yields on EEs with the yields on Baccalaureates and buy the one that pays the most. Lean toward Baccalaureates, however, if you think that your income will be too high to use the tax exemption on Series EEs.

EE bonds give you inflation protection through their variable interest rates, which Baccalaureates don't. On the other hand, Baccalaureates will yield more if interest rates gradually trend down.

If you do buy a Baccalaureate Bond, be sure it matures when you're going to need the money. If you have to sell early, you may take a loss.

State Prepaid Tuition Plans

At this writing, seven states—Alabama, Alaska, Florida, Michigan, New Mexico, Ohio, and Wyoming—have active college-savings plans, with others on the way. Parents put up a certain amount of money, depending on the child's age. The state guarantees that this sum will cover tuition and fees, or a certain number of course hours, when the child is ready to go to school. Between now and then, tuition might rise 50 percent, 100 percent, 5 zillion percent. No matter. Your initial payment will cover the bill. Some prepaid plans include room or board.

This price guarantee applies only to a public college within the state. If the child wants a private college or an out-of-state school, or doesn't go to college at all, the parents will get their principal back. But how much interest they'll be paid depends on the state. Check on this before you invest. Also find out if your state lets you change your mind and withdraw the money.

Should you buy into these state plans?

Yes, if you're pretty sure that your child will be attending a state school, *and* if you think that you otherwise won't accumulate enough for college, *and* if you buy for cash, without borrowing any money.

But *no,* if you think that your child will go to a private school or a school out of state.* And *no,* if you're a savvy investor—because that same money invested in stock-owning mutual funds, for 10 years or more, should cover tuition with something left over for all the other college costs. And *maybe not* if you have to borrow money to participate. The deal isn't worth it if you'll pay more in loan interest than the average increase in college costs (now running around 7 to 8 percent). A loan might indeed make sense, however, if you use a tax-deductible home-equity line of credit.

---

* One exception is Michigan. If your child goes to a private or out-of-state college, Michigan will pay you the current price of the average state college, so your funds will still have kept up with college inflation.

College Prepaid Tuition Plans

Some colleges invite alumni and others to register their young children and prepay for four years of school—either tuition only, or tuition, room, and board. For a relatively small sum of money now, you guarantee that the giant bill of the future will always be considered fully paid. Furthermore, you all but guarantee that the school will accept your child, since it won't want to lose both the money and your good will. But what if your babe grows up and doesn't like your school? I see quarrels in my crystal ball. Your child may be forced to sit through one year of the college you chose before you can get the rest of your money out. I say, don't ask for trouble. Pass this idea by.

Some prepayment plans cover several colleges, letting you choose any one of the group. But if your child wants a school out of the group, you'll probably find that your money has earned only a small investment return. Pass this idea by, too.

Many colleges offer not to raise your costs for four years running, if —when your child matriculates—you pay four years' tuition in advance. This is an interesting proposition. If your investments are earning 7 percent after tax, and college inflation is 8 percent, prepayment is going to save you some money. It might even make sense to borrow the money to pay in advance, especially if you will need loans in any event. To borrow a four-year sum all at once, check (1) your home-equity credit line; (2) the borrowing plans offered by the school; and (3) the New England Education Loan Marketing Corporation (Nellie Mae), 50 Braintree Hill Park, Braintree, MA, 02184. *Tip:* Find out how much money you'll get back from the school if your child drops out.

Some dreamers are working on a universal prepayment plan that all the major colleges and universities would join. You would prepay without picking any particular school. Your money would be managed like a college endowment fund, presumably earning more than you could on your own. The tuition guarantee would eventually be applied to any college your child chose. *That,* if it ever comes off, would be a plan worth looking at.

Bank Prepaid Tuition Plans

The granddaddy is the CollegeSure certificate of deposit, created by the College Savings Bank at 5 Vaughn Dr., Princeton, NJ, 08540. Other banks are licensing it under different names. Here's how it works:

You deposit a lump sum into a federally insured CD, or start making regular installment payments. You put in more money than college costs today. By investing that excess money, the bank can guarantee that your account will grow by enough to match the average private-college inflation rate.

You choose whether to save the entire amount you need or only a part. If you buy a full unit, it's guaranteed to pay one year's future charges at the average private school—tuition, fees, room, and board. There's no tax advantage. You owe income taxes each year on the interest earned, so keep at least part of this CD in the child's name, to make use of his or her lower tax bracket. You'll pay stiff penalties for withdrawing the deposit before the child is of college age.

Is this a good buy? Its yields are modest. A tax-deferred Series EE bond may serve you better, even if you don't get a full tax exemption on the interest.

CollegeSure's chief appeal is its guarantee. If college inflation runs higher than it is today, this CD should meet it, while fixed-rate investments would fall behind. (The variable-rate EE bond, however, should also keep up.)

A few other banks have competing programs. For example, the Maine Savings Bank in Portland will show you how much you have to deposit each month to cover the cost of the college you want. When costs rise, the bank recomputes the payments, so you'll know that you're always meeting the school's inflation rate. Once a year, you can withdraw part or all of the money penalty free.

BUM INVESTMENTS FOR COLLEGE

1. Tax-deferred annuities. There's a 10 percent tax penalty if you withdraw money before you reach age 59½. You may also owe withdrawal penalties to the insurance company.

2. Any bonds, including zero-coupon bonds, that will have to be sold before maturity. You risk taking a beating on the price.

3. Life-insurance policies on children.

4. Life-insurance policies on adults, because of their slow cash buildups.

5. Money market mutual funds, because the after-tax return is so low.

6. Limited partnerships that invest in oil, real estate, and so on. You haven't a clue what they'll pay, when they'll pay, or *if* they'll pay.

7. Lottery tickets.

8. Unit trusts (page 680). You periodically get small payments that have to be reinvested, usually at a low interest rate. You might lose some of your capital if you have to sell before maturity.

9. Index options, gold coins, options on oil futures, penny stocks, new issues, retail bank bonds that are uninsured, football games, racehorses. Well, maybe not racehorses. I knew a horse once named Rutland Road . . .

LET'S HEAR IT FOR GRANDPARENTS!

A grandparent can pay any amount at all for college, with no gift-tax consequences, as long as the money goes directly to the school and is used to help cover tuition and fees.

A grandparent (and anyone else, for that matter) can also make a tax-free gift of up to $10,000 a year to each child. Gifts to kids are generally made through state Uniform Gifts (or Transfers) to Minors Acts (page 90).

ARE YOU A SUCKER TO SAVE?

No, you're not. It's a myth among struggling college savers that they may be making a mistake. The more you save, they say, the greater your assets, so the less you'll get in college aid. The aid formulas penalize savers and reward spendthrifts.

There is some truth to that statement, but not much.

It's true that the greater your assets, the less student aid you'll get. But the size of your student-aid package is based mostly on income. Your assets don't make a whole lot of difference. Furthermore, every aid package contains loans. By saving less, you wind up having to borrow more.

Spendthrift, low-asset families might pick up an extra $1,000 in grants and student loans. And then what are they going to do? They'll still owe a huge sum of money, and they won't have the savings to cover it. They'll be up to their necklaces in debts.

Truly, savers win the day.

THE BEST-GUESS COLLEGE PLANNER (SHORT FORM)

How much should you be saving for college? Here's a down-and-dirty way of estimating what to put away each month.

But use this quick calculation only if: (1) You have no other college savings. (2) You are comfortable with targeting the average college cost, rather than the cost of a particular school. (3) You are willing to assume that college expenses will rise by 7 percent annually. (4) You are willing to guess that your investments will earn 8 percent after tax (which probably means that you're buying stock-owning mutual funds, for the long term). Otherwise, skip to the Best-Guess College Planner (Long Form) on page 870 of the Appendix. That allows for more options in figuring out how much to save.

In truth, I'd rather have everyone go to the Long Form, because it gives you a better answer. The Short Form (and most conventional college planners) advises you to save a fixed sum of money—for example, $500 a month. But that's unrealistic. Right now, $500 a month might be more than you can afford. Ten years from now, it might be pocket change.

The Long Form, by contrast, works out what *portion* of your income you should be saving every year. If you settle on a fixed percentage—such as 5 percent a year—your college contributions can start low and rise as your salary does.

But for Short Form addicts, here's the easiest way, courtesy of the mutual-fund company T. Rowe Price.

Short Form

1. Add up the number of years from now that your child will start school. Count the current year. A 10-year-old will matriculate in nine years—this year plus eight years more.

Number of years until school starts: _____

2. Enter the average four-year cost of the type of college that your child will attend. See the table on page 425 and decide between a private and a public school.

*College cost: $*_____

3. Look down the left-hand column, below, to the number of years before college starts. Read across to the proper column. That's how much you have to save each month to meet the average college cost.

Years to College	Monthly Investment	
	Public	Private
1	$2,651	$5,057
2	1,362	2,598
3	932	1,778
4	717	1,369
5	589	1,123
6	503	960
7	442	843
8	396	755
9	360	687
10	332	633
11	308	588
12	289	551
13	272	520
14	258	493
15	246	469
16	235	449
17	226	430
18	217	414
19	210	400
20	203	387

CONQUERING YOUR FEAR OF FLYING

When savings are hard to come by, it can be terrifying to put them into stocks. Who will forget the stunning Crash of 1987? Who can feel safe from another crash? Who can deny that a long and devastating bear market, lasting a couple of years or more, can cut the value of stocks in half?

On the other hand, if you don't buy stocks for the long term, your college fund may lose purchasing power rather than gain it.

So . . . take a look at the 10-year performance of stocks on page 478. It should comfort you. Take a look at the lists of mutual funds with good records starting on page 583, get their prospectuses, and choose a couple.

With 10 years or more to invest, the courageous will go heavily into stocks. But the timid don't have to copy them. Try putting just half of your money into stocks—perhaps of buying some mutual fund shares every month. *Once you've started, don't pay any attention to stock market reports! Don't panic if the averages fall!* Just keep on investing, through thick and thin, over 10 years or more. Stow the other half of your money in Series EE bonds or similar under-the-mattress safeholes.

You'll be okay.

When college finally starts, I'll wager that your stocks have won the day.

6 UNDER-STANDING INVESTING

There is a secret to investing that cuts a path directly to the profits that you're looking for. The secret is simplicity. The more elementary your investment style, the more confident you can be of making money in the long run.

This insight isn't easy for investors to accept. Wall Street resembles nothing so much as an Oriental souk, whose subtle vendors bow and beckon, urging this purchase and that. The goods are colorful and varied. The more intricate an investment package, the greater its aura of success. But in fact, it's stuffed with risks you're unaware of. This glittering merchandise almost always profits the vendors more than you.

And you don't need it! You can rack up a superb lifetime investment record with just two or three good stock-owning mutual funds, maybe a bond fund, and some Treasury securities or tax exempts. That's all you really need to know. Investing is easy, if you buy the simple things and buy them well.

21

DRAWING UP
YOUR BATTLE PLAN:

Which Kinds of Investments Serve You Best?

———

When you start, the jigsaw puzzle that's your
personal money lies in dozens of pieces, all
jumbled up. When you finish, the picture will
be clear.

For investment success, you need a concept, a framework on which to hang all the thoughts and suggestions that are constantly coming your way. Should you buy this mutual fund or that one? How do you choose between stocks and bonds? Which risks make sense and which don't?

There are logical answers to these questions, but only if you start with a good, long-term investment plan. Once you've drawn that plan, the mysteries of money will become more clear. You will see exactly the kinds of investments you ought to be making. Just as crucial, you'll know which investments to avoid.

Your plan will not make you rich tomorrow. You're not betting the farm on the pipe dream of a quick return. Instead, you're using your common sense to map a strategy for building wealth.

YOU CAN ONLY GET POOR QUICKLY; GETTING RICH IS SLOW

I would write a get-rich-quick book if I could. Everyone (me in-cluded) dreams of learning how to beat Wall Street in three easy lessons and with no risk. But the investment schemes behind such books are usually a ticket to the poorhouse.

There are no easy ways to beat Wall Street! That's not even an intelligent goal. Thoughtful investors buy the kinds of investments that will yield the combination of safety, income, and growth they need. At the end of the road, they will look back and see that they did well.

FIRST PRINCIPLES OF INVESTING

Before you draw up your own battle plan, you need to know what has worked in the past. These are the lessons that history teaches:

1. For building capital long term, buy stocks. You are taking hardly any risk. Over 10-year periods, stocks have almost always outperformed bonds and have left simple bank accounts in the dust.

2. Buy stock-owning mutual funds, not stocks themselves. Good mutual funds give you full-time, professional money management, which you normally cannot do yourself. The managers diversify your investments and balance your risks. Picking stocks individually is a fascinating game, but for the dedicated hobbyist only.

3. Diversify. Although stocks win the race in the long-term, you and I live in the short term. That means we need buffers—investments that give our capital some protection in a year when the economy falls apart and stocks decline. So think "portfolio"—your portfolio being every investment, savings account, and retirement account you own. Stocks for growth; money market mutual funds for ready savings; bonds and dividend-paying stocks for steady compounding of interest; your home as an inflation hedge.

4. Keep it simple. Plain vanilla stocks and bonds will do the job. All the other stuff—options on futures, commodities, limited partnerships —usually leave you wiser but poorer.

5. Have the courage to hold your mutual funds for the long term. Successful investors check the charts showing long-term stock market action (up, down, up, up) and believe them. When the occasional downturn occurs, they roll into a fetal position until the market comes back.*

6. *Ignore market timing.* Market timers try to sell when the stock market nears its peak and buy again when stocks bottom out. As if they knew. This game isn't worth the candle, because you are so often wrong. On a percentage basis, stocks rise much more often than they fall. So the odds are on the side of the people who stay invested all the time (Your protection against temporary declines is diversification—having some of your money invested somewhere else.)

7. *Invest regularly.* Put a fixed sum of money into mutual funds at regular intervals—maybe once a month. Don't worry about "bad" markets. They are good buys for long-term investors, because stock prices are so low.

8. *Reinvest your dividends.* If I do no more than make you appreciate dividends, this chapter will have done its job. An investor who put $100 into the Standard & Poor's 500-stock average on the last day of 1925, held until June 30, 1990—and spent all the dividends—would have earned $2,806. If that investor reinvested all dividends, he or she would have had $55,091!† Compounding interest and dividends is the investment world's strongest, surest force.

9. *Stick to your investment strategy.* One year you'll make money. One year you'll lose money. But time is always on your side. Don't let impulse investing or sudden market changes shake you out of your long-term plan.

10. *Have patience, patience, patience, patience.* The urge for quick returns hurls you into lunatic investments—the financial equivalent of lottery tickets, with just about the same odds. A successful investor hitches a ride on private industry's long-term growth.

HOW RISKY ARE STOCKS, REALLY?

Having made such a strong pitch for buying stocks, I can hear the echoes coming back—"Yeah, but what about the '87 Crash? What about the '89 Crashette? What about all the other times that stocks have fallen (maybe even as you read!)?"

Well, what about it? Those drops are temporary. No one knows

---

* A *bull* market rises. A *bear* market falls.
† Thank you Ibbotson Associates, Chicago.

what stocks will do tomorrow, but the evidence is clear as to how they'll perform over 10 or 20 years. They will almost certainly go up. A lot.

The table below shows your odds of making money over various holding periods—1 year, 5 years, 10 years, and 20 years. Three facts stand out:

1. In any 1-year period, stocks are dicey. You get the biggest gains, if you hit them right. But you also risk the biggest losses.

2. Over 5-year holding periods, your chance of loss is small. Over 10-year periods, it is negligible.

3. The longer you hold stocks, the stronger the likelihood that you'll earn compound annual returns in the area of 10 to 20 percent (but it's much closer to 10 percent than 20 percent).

YOUR ODDS OF MAKING MONEY IN STOCKS

Holding period	Your chance of earning*			Your chance of losing
	0–10%	10–20%	Over 20%	
1 year	19%	19%	38%	24%
5 years	30	40	24	6
10 years	29	54	16	1
20 years	22	70	8	0†

* Compounded annually.
† Slightly more than zero, but not close to 1 percent. Computed in May 1990 by Chicago's Ibbotson Associates. All dividends reinvested.

ONE FURTHER FACT THAT EVERY INVESTOR SHOULD KNOW: Over long periods of time, stocks have outperformed inflation by roughly 7 percent annually. That's a far better average real return than you'll get from any other financial investment.

Yes, But . . .

What about Murphy's Law, which says that if anything can go wrong it will? Or Quinn's Law, which says that Murphy was an optimist? In this century, stocks have had two especially bad patches.

First, they were trounced by bonds during the early, and deflationary, 1930s. (The reincarnated among us will remember that bonds also rolled over stocks during the deeply deflationary 1870s.)

Second, in the inflationary 1970s, stocks finished just a whisker behind both corporate bonds and Treasury bills. Stocks hate super-high inflation just as they hate severe deflation.

Those, then, are your outside chances of coming in second-best with stocks. In every other decade, stocks finished first, and by a mile. They can do just fine during modest inflation, as long as inflation isn't accelerating over 4 percent. And they're just as happy during modest deflations (although you have to go back to the nineteenth century for proof). That's why smart investors emphasize stocks, with a prudent diversification into bonds just in case.

HOW TO LIMIT ALL YOUR RISKS

Some investors stay out of stocks, in order to keep their money "safe." But they don't know what "safety" really means. Bonds and bank accounts carry hazards that you haven't even thought about. A fixed-income investment can eat up your future just as surely as if you had fed it to sharks. You have to understand your whole range of risks, in order to make good investment decisions.

Of all risks, the most familiar is *market risk*—the risk of losing money in a bad investment.

Adjust for this by (1) diversifying your investments, so that a single loss (even though temporary) doesn't leave a hole in your wealth, (2) buying only the boring old standbys like diversified mutual funds, and (3) skipping the dizzy new ideas that only a stockbroker could love. If you can't resist "diz," give yourself a small mad-money fund to play with. I'll wager that your boring investments come out ahead.

Everyone also endures *economic risk*—the hit you take when the economy turns down.

Adjust for this risk by staying out of the speculative investments that really get bashed in a recession: junk bonds, new issues, limited partnerships whose units can't be sold. Some of these investments may soar in good times, but they also expose you to extra-large losses.

Less understood is *inflation risk*—the risk of losing the purchasing power of your capital.

This is the monster that eats up fixed-income investors. After inflation and taxes, a certificate of deposit, a zero-coupon bond, or a Treasury security yield almost nothing. You might preserve the purchasing power of the cash you deposited, but your money doesn't really grow. After years and years of investing, you come out with a pittance in real terms.

Adjust for inflation risk by (1) not keeping large, permanent sums of cash in money market mutual funds and similar short-term investments, (2) avoiding an all-bond portfolio, even in retirement, and (3) putting

at least some of your money into stocks for real growth. Here's how well
(or how poorly) all the common investments survive inflation.

AVERAGE COMPOUND RETURNS AFTER INFLATION, 1926–89*

U.S. Treasury bills: 0.5%
Long-term government bonds: 1.4%
Intermediate-term government bonds: 1.8%
Common stocks: 7.0%
Small-company stocks: 8.9%

---

*Inflation for the period, 3.1 percent. Dividends reinvested but not adjusted for income taxes.
Source: Ibbotson Associates, Chicago.

The consistency of long-term common-stock yields over inflation is
nothing short of astonishing. Consider the following measurements by
Jack W. Wilson and Charles P. Jones, North Carolina State University,
and Richard Sylla of New York University: From 1926 to 1989, stockholders earned 6.65 percent annually, after inflation. (The result for the
1926–89 period is a tiny bit different from Ibbotson's, above, because of
a different methodology.) From 1871 to 1925, they earned 6.63 percent
—almost exactly the same. So no matter what's happening to your stocks
today, it is reasonable to expect that, 10 or 15 years from now, you'll
show a 6 to 7 percent real return over inflation, whatever that may be.

Bond investors face *interest-rate risk*—the risk that interest rates will
rise. When that happens, the value of your bonds (or bond mutual funds)
falls, and you lose money. Furthermore, the income you're earning may
no longer beat inflation and taxes.

Adjust for interest-rate risk by owning short- to medium-term bonds
(maturing in maybe 2 to 10 years). When rates rise, these bonds don't
fall as much in price as 20- or 30-year bonds do.

Investors in short-term instruments, such as money market mutual
funds and one-year certificates of deposit, face *reinvestment risk*. Say, for
example, that you have to choose between two deposits—a one-year CD
at 10 percent and a five-year CD at 9.2 percent. You decide on the
higher rate. But when that CD matures, one-year rates may be down to
7.5 percent. The higher, 9.2 percent rate that you spurned last year is
no longer available. You'd have made more money by going for the five-
year CD originally.

Adjust for reinvestment risk by "laddering" your fixed-income investments. For example, you might own CDs or bonds maturing in 1
year, 2 years, 3 years, 4 years, 5 years, all the way up to 10 years. Every

year a CD or bond matures. If interest rates rise, you can re-invest the proceeds of that bond at a higher rate. If interest-rates fall, you'll still be getting high interest income from your longer-term investments. For more on laddering see page 638.

If you hold a "callable" bond, you also face reinvestment risk (a bond is callable if the issuer can call it in before maturity). Take a 30-year tax-free municipal that's supposed to pay 11 percent interest for another 20 years. If interest rates fall, the municipality will call in the bond after 5 or 10 years, and you can kiss your high income good-bye. Adjust for this risk by buying only noncallable Treasury bonds.

Then there's *liquidity risk.* A "liquid" investment can be sold immediately, at market price, if you suddenly find that you need the money. An "illiquid" investment can't be. Not all of your investments have to be liquid. But enough of them do to assure you quick cash if you ever need it. So what's liquid?

• A money market mutual fund is liquid. You can get your cash at any time. A certificate of deposit is relatively liquid, but not perfectly so. You can always get the money, but it may cost you an early-withdrawal penalty.

• Mutual-fund shares are normally liquid. You can sell at any time, at current market value. Occasionally, however, a fund's liquidity may be impaired. If scads of investors all want out at the same time—as has happened during panics in the junk-bond and municipal-bond markets —selling pressure can push down the market price. The fund also has the right to suspend telephone redemptions or delay mailing your check for up to seven days.

• Individual stocks are liquid, as long as they trade on the major stock exchanges. Small stocks sold over the counter (page 595), however, may cost you a lot if you have to sell.

• Gold bullion coins are liquid, anywhere in the world.

• Retirement accounts are superficially liquid, in that you can usually cash them in. But I count them illiquid because of the tax cost and penalties of breaking into them too soon.

• Small amounts of tax-exempt bonds are often illiquid. No one wants to buy them except at a discount.

• Precious gems are similarly illiquid. They're salable but the dealer may not offer you anything close to what you think they're worth.

• Real estate is generally illiquid. It can take months to sell, and even then you might have to mark down the property's price.

• Your own business is illiquid.

• Units in most limited partnerships are so illiquid that there may be no market for them at all.

Adjust for liquidity risk by balancing illiquid assets with liquid ones. Anytime you buy something, ask: What happens if I want to sell? Can I get my money fast? Can I sell at market price without taking a discount or paying a penalty? If not, how long might I have to wait for my money? You should have enough liquid assets to carry you for a year, even if no other money were coming in.

The final risk is one almost no one thinks of. It's *holding-period risk* —the chance that you'll have to sell an investment at a time when it's worth less than you paid.

Say, for example, that you've been saving money for a down payment on a house and are keeping it all in a stock-owning mutual fund. Two months before you'll close on the house, the stock market drops. You lose 25 percent of your down payment, can't buy the house, and your marriage breaks up. That's holding-period risk.

Or say that you bought a 30-year zero-coupon bond (page 661) for your child's college education. When college begins, the bond still has 15 years to run. You have to sell it to pay the tuition—but the market is down, no one wants a single bond, and you're stuck. That, too, is holding-period risk.

I like stocks if the holding period will last for at least 4 or 5 years. I love stocks for holding periods of 10 years or more. But I hate and fear stocks for shorter periods, because you cannot count on getting your capital out.

I fear 30-year bonds for any purpose but sheer speculation on falling interest rates (page 643). I hate any bonds that will mature well past the date when I know that I'm going to need the money.

To adjust for holding-period risk, match your investments to how soon you're going to want the funds.

• Cash you'll need within one to four years belongs in a safe place. Two possibilities: money-market mutual funds and shorter-term Treasury bills (page 164). Both preserve your capital while offering some inflation protection. (On money funds, your inflation protection is the fact that interest rates can rise. On three- or six-month Treasuries, you can roll over your investment at a higher rate.)

• Funds you won't need for four years or more should be invested for income and growth.

THE RIGHT SHOE FOR THE RIGHT FOOT

As you cannot escape taking *some* kind of risk, the next thing to ask is whether your current range of risks supports or undermines your purpose. Here's a general guide.

Use safe savings, with no market risk, for:
A cash reserve equal to three months' take-home pay.
Accumulating a down payment on a house.
Saving for a big vacation.
Protecting college tuition that's due within four years.
Protecting capital when you've lost your job.
A parking place for money waiting to be invested elsewhere.
Preserving any sum that you dare not put at the slightest risk.

Use stocks for:
Accumulating college tuition while your child is young.
Building a retirement fund.
Generating an income out of dividends and capital gains.

Use medium-term bonds for:
Adding to your income (from interest earnings).
Adding some price stability to a stock portfolio.
A deflation hedge.

Use long-term bonds for:
Speculating on falling interest rates.
A deflation hedge.

Use investment real estate for:
Building retirement savings over 10 years or more.
An inflation hedge.

To find out if you've matched your own major goals to the right investments, fill in the table on the following page.

First, list all the savings and investments, both inside and outside your retirement plan. Divide them into short-term and long-term. Then list your short- and long-term goals. Note that "growth" isn't a goal, it's a strategy. "Early retirement" or "college tuition" are goals.

The table may show a mishmash of investments, acquired without thinking what goals they should serve. Your down-payment savings may erroneously be in a bond fund; your retirement savings may be in money markets. Later chapters will help you straighten all this out.

DO YOUR CURRENT INVESTMENTS MATCH YOUR GOALS?

Your shorter-term * savings	Your shorter-term goals	Appropriate investments
$_____	$_____	Money market mutual funds
_____	_____	Certificates of deposit
_____	_____	Treasury bills and notes
_____	_____	

Your longer-term investments	Your longer-term goals	Appropriate investments
$_____	$_____	Principally, stock mutual funds
_____	_____	Individual bonds or bond mutual funds
_____	_____	Individual stocks
_____	_____	Real estate

---

* Maturing in four years or less.

SHOOTING CRAPS

"But where's the fun?" you ask. "Where are the kicks, the highs, the joys of the chase? I want to have some sport with my money!"

And why not? So do I. Over the years, I have fallen in love with one oil well (dry), one new venture (bankrupt), one glamour stock (down 80 percent, which is when I learned about stop-loss orders), and one of the worst mutual funds in history. I did make some money on some of my flyers (including that mutual fund, which I dumped before it took me too far down). But that's not the point. What matters is that I was gambling with play money, not with the bulk of my assets. My basic holdings were, and are, in a suitable range of sober investments for my old age.

I want you to get all the pleasure you can from the money you've earned. If that means rolling dice in a Wall Street crap game, so be it. Just don't throw around your kid's college-tuition account or the life-insurance proceeds meant to see you through widowhood. Fund your serious needs seriously. If there's anything left over, do whatever you want with it.

ASSET ALLOCATION: HOW TO DO IT, WHY IT WORKS

So far, we've been matching appropriate investments and levels of risk with a whole range of personal objectives, short term and long.

Now it's time to consider pure long-term investing, like parlaying your savings into enough to live on when you retire. Here, other kinds of matching schemes come into play. You are asking the question: What return do I need from my long-term investments? How much risk am I willing to swallow in order to get it?

Enter the concept of "asset allocation." To explain it, let me start with a tale of two investors, as told by Marshall Blume, professor of finance at the Wharton School in Philadelphia.

Fighter Jock puts $100 into stocks in August 1929, just before the Great Crash. Measured by the Dow Jones Industrial Average, it takes him 16 years to get his money back.

Savvy Sal also has $100, but she puts $50 into stocks and $50 into bonds and maintains that 50-50 split. When her bonds are worth more than 50 percent of her capital, she sells some and buys stocks. When her stocks are worth more, she sells some and buys bonds. She does this every month (Blume is measuring by the market averages here), always seeking to keep half of her money in each investment. In just six years, she recovers her original stake.

Notice what Sal did *not* do.

She did not sell all her stocks at the bottom and give up the market for ever and ever.

She did not try to guess when the market would rise or fall again. She just followed her investment formula.

She did not let herself be swayed by the news of the day. Instead, she invested for the long term.

She did not fail. She beat Fighter Jock, who bought stocks and held them. And she beat the investors who fled the market and put their money in the bank.

Sal practiced asset allocation—which, simply put, means dividing your money among stocks, bonds, cash, and other kinds of investments and keeping it there. People don't pay a lot of attention to asset allocation. *But it's the key decision that determines investment success,* not how smart (or dumb) you are at picking stocks or mutual funds.

"But wait," you say, "Sal was just lucky. What would have happened had stocks bounced right back after 1929?"

In that case, Fighter Jock would have done somewhat better. But from time to time, he'd have taken a big loss.

Sal would also have taken occasional losses on her stocks, as well as her bonds. But because she owned both, her total portfolio of investments would never have dropped as far as Jock's. Her long-term results would still have been fine, without as much fear along the way.

But the fact remains that stocks didn't bounce back after 1929. And Sal was positioned to handle that risk.

TIME OUT FOR THEORY

Even if you know that you're supposed to diversify your investments, maybe you don't know why.

A lot of study has established four things;

1. Different types of investments tend to move in different cycles. Some may go up while others go down. Some go in the same direction, but not at the same time or at the same speed. Some move by larger percentages than others. Owning different types of investments protects you from big losses and can improve your returns. *Something* you own is usually going up (or at least not going down). You are less exposed to risk.

2. *When* you buy isn't nearly as important as *what types of assets* you buy and how much you own of them. You can be all wrong on your market timing and still do well if you are properly diversified.

3. "Market timing" (which means buying before the market goes up and selling before the market goes down, ha-ha) is extraordinarily hard to do. The average investor won't guess right often enough to beat the investor who buys and holds. Most professional investors don't do much better. The Forecaster's Hall of Fame is an empty room.

4. Almost no one—including investment professionals—can "beat the market" over the long term. It's a waste of time to set that kind of standard for yourself.

These findings lead to the conclusion that you shouldn't break your head trying to predict what will happen to stocks, interest rates, or the economy. Don't seek truth in the financial press. Don't consult gurus. Don't be stampeded into the market, or out of it.

Instead, focus on what you're investing for (page 484). Then split your money among the investments most likely to achieve that goal. And stick with them. Amen.

WHO'S ON FIRST?

This table shows the compound annual returns, on various assets, for 15 five-year periods. Each period's top performer is checked. Only a mix of investments would have minimized losses while maximizing gains.

Period	U.S common stocks*	Long-term corporate bonds†	Long-term gov't bonds	Intermed. gov't bonds	U.S. Treasury Bills	Inflation
1971–75	3.2%	6.0%	6.2%	√6.4%	5.8%	6.9‡
1972–76	4.9	√7.4	6.8	7.2	5.9	7.2
1973–77	0.2	6.3	5.5	√6.4	6.2	7.9‡
1974–78	4.3	6.0	5.5	√6.2	√6.2	7.9‡
1975–79	√14.8	5.8	4.3	5.9	7.0	8.2
1976–80	√14.0	2.4	1.7	5.1	7.8	9.2
1977–81	8.1	−1.2	−1.1	4.4	√9.7	10.1‡
1978–82	√14.1	5.8	6.0	9.6	10.8	9.5
1979–83	√17.3	6.8	6.4	10.4	11.1	8.4
1980–84	√14.8	11.1	9.8	12.5	11.0	6.5
1981–85	14.7	√17.8	16.8	15.8	10.3	4.9
1982–86	19.9	√22.4	21.6	17.0	8.6	3.3
1983–87	√16.5	13.8	13.0	11.8	7.6	3.4
1984–88	√15.4	15.1	15.0	11.5	7.1	3.5
1985–89	√20.4	15.0	15.4	11.4	6.8	3.7

* The performance is for all stocks. But in each five-year period from 1973–77 to 1981–85, smaller-company stocks—not shown on this table—greatly outperformed stocks in general.
† High quality.
‡ Inflation beat all the investment averages.
Source: Ibbotson Associates, Chicago.

HOW TO MIX 'N' MATCH

To minimize risk, you need a mix of assets that rise and fall at different times or at different speeds. In the real world, no investments counter each other quite that neatly. Nor do they maintain their relationships consistently. For example, long-term bonds are behaving more like stocks than they used to. In general, however, *here's how the various assets move in relation to each other:*

· Stocks behave differently from Treasury bills.

· Long-term bonds behave differently from short-term bonds.

· Gold stocks behave differently from other stocks.

· Foreign stocks and bonds behave differently from U.S. stocks and bonds over the long term, although not necessarily over the short term.

· Real estate often behaves differently from stocks and bonds, although in specific regions of the country they can all behave alike.

Here's how to choose which assets to own:

· For unanticipated inflation, you want real estate, gold, or money market mutual funds.

· For anticipated (but moderate) inflation and economic growth, you want U.S. and foreign stocks. You also want stocks during periods when price increases are gradually slowing down (disinflation); and perhaps even when prices are falling somewhat (deflation), depending on what the economy does.

· For economic slowdowns and severe deflation, you want high-quality, non-callable long-term bonds—which means Treasuries.

· To stabilize the value of a portfolio, you want cash equivalents (money market mutual funds, short-term Treasuries) and short- to medium-term bonds.

· To prevent weight gain, hair loss, acne, and wrinkles—and to confront an unknown future—you want a stake in all of these investments. The exact mix, however, has to be matched to your personal needs.

· To keep it simple, you want to own many of these investments through mutual funds.

You have *not* diversified if you own ten different stocks or three stock-owning mutual funds. Those are all stocks. Nor have you diversified if you buy a bond fund, a Ginnie Mae fund, and some certificates of deposit. Those, too, are much alike.

At minimum, you need a mix of U.S. stocks, medium-term bonds, and cash equivalents, like short-term Treasury bills or money market mutual funds. An investor with more money will add foreign stocks, maybe foreign bonds, and gold. Real estate also belongs in the pot. Beyond your own house, consider real-estate investment trusts or owning another piece of property.

HERE ARE THREE CLASSIC PORTFOLIOS, RANKED BY MARKET RISK:

• *Low risk*—20 percent stocks, 30 percent medium-term bonds, 50 percent cash equivalents (such as money market mutual funds).

• *Medium risk*—50 percent stocks, 30 percent five-year bonds, 10 percent long-term bonds, 10 percent cash equivalents.

• *High risk*—100 percent stocks.

Take these classics as baselines. Play them against your personal goals to create your own portfolio mix.

Tip toward lower risks if your earnings are low, you carry huge debts, you're in poor health, you don't know much about investing, you're naturally cautious, or you'll need that money within three or four years.

Tip toward higher risks if you earn a lot, have a high net worth, are an experienced investor, are young, or won't need the money for many years.

JUST TO MAKE IT A LITTLE HARDER: Selecting an appropriate level of risk means more than choosing among stocks, bonds, and money market funds. Within any class of investment, some types of securities carry more risk than others.

Say, for example, that you just sold your house and put the proceeds of the sale into a money market mutual fund. These funds carry only a whisper of risk. But one invested entirely in Treasuries is "safer" than one that buys lower-rated commercial paper (page 166).

Or say that you're buying stocks to help fund a college education for your kids. A conservative investment would be a mutual fund that buys blue-chip, dividend-paying companies. An aggressive choice would be a fund that buys the stocks of small companies.

So you really have two decisions to make: (1) What mix of investments best suit your needs? (2) Within each investment class, how much risk do you want to take?

SOME SAMPLE INDIVIDUAL PORTFOLIOS

Here, I've produced some battle plans. They match risk with objectives and make some asset allocations for long-term investing. *These are examples—not gospel!* Every investor is a little bit different as to wealth, health, income, expectations, needs, and financial responsibilities. Every investment advisor will have different ideas about how portfolios should be constructed. Every time period is different, as to interest rates, economic growth, and tax laws—all of which influence portfolio choices. I mean only to show what it means to take a "total portfolio" approach. (You'll find a full discussion of the investments mentioned below in other chapters in this section. If all your retirement investments are in tax-deferred company plans, see page 492.)

A Young Single Person

1. Cash reserve—three months' take-home pay in a money market fund. More, if you're also saving for a down payment on a house.

2. Retirement fund—70 percent in U.S. stock-index and growth-stock mutual funds, 20 percent in foreign stocks, 10 percent in intermediate-term bonds.

A Young Married Couple with Small Children

1. Cash reserve—three months' take-home pay in a money market fund.

2. Inflation hedge—a house and the common stocks in your college and retirement funds.

3. College fund—90 percent in U.S. stock-index and growth-stock mutual funds, 10 percent in zero-coupon bonds.

4. Retirement fund—70 percent in U.S. index and growth-stock funds, 15 percent in foreign stock funds, 15 percent in intermediate-term bonds.

5. Deflation hedge—the zeros and the bonds in your tax-deferred retirement fund, as long as they're noncallable Treasury bonds.

A Middle-Aged Couple with Small Children

1. Cash reserve—three months' take-home pay in a money market fund.

2. Inflation hedge—a house, maybe a vacation house, and the common stocks in your college and retirement funds. Consider gold only if you're wealthy enough to afford that level of worry (page 694).

3. College fund—90 percent in U.S. stock-index and growth-stock funds, 10 percent in zero-coupon bonds.

4. Retirement fund—30 percent in U.S. stock-index or growth-stock funds, 25 percent in growth-and-income or equity-income funds, 15 percent in foreign stock funds, 30 percent in intermediate-term bonds.

5. Deflation hedge—the zeros and the bonds in your tax-deferred retirement fund, as long as they're noncallable Treasury bonds.

A Middle-Aged Couple with Children in College

1. Cash reserve—a paid-up credit card. (All your cash is in the hands of the college bursar! Your only emergency money is your credit line.)

2. Inflation hedge—a house, maybe a vacation house, and the stocks in your retirement fund, Consider gold only if you're wealthy enough to afford that level of worry (page 694).

3. College fund—in Treasuries or bank CDs timed to mature when semesters begin.

4. Retirement fund—25 percent in U.S. stock-index and growth-stock funds, 30 percent in growth-and-income or equity-income funds, 15 percent in foreign stock funds, 30 percent in intermediate-term bonds.

A Young Retiree (55 to 65)

1. Cash reserve—six month's living expenses, in a money market mutual fund.

2. Inflation hedge—a house, a summer house, your common stocks, and any gold you got worried enough to accumulate.

3. Retirement fund—50 percent in U.S. stock-index and growth-and-income or equity-income funds, 15 percent in foreign stock funds, 35 percent in laddered intermediate- and shorter-term bonds (page 638) or divided between intermediate- and shorter-term bond funds.

4. Deflation hedge—your bonds are noncallable Treasury bonds.

An Older Retiree (65 to 75)

1. Cash reserve—one year's living expenses in a money market fund.

2. Inflation hedge—a house, maybe a vacation house, common stocks, and any gold you got worried enough to accumulate.

3. Retirement fund—50 percent in U.S. equity-income or growth-and-income mutual funds, 10 percent in foreign stock funds, 40 percent

in a "laddered" bond portfolio (page 638) or divided between intermediate- and shorter-term bonds.

4. Deflation hedge—your bonds are noncallable Treasuries.

An Even Older Retiree (75 and up)

1. Cash reserve—one year's living expenses in a money market fund and a firm determination to spend your principal as well as your income, if that's what it takes to live comfortably.

2. Inflation hedge—a house and common stocks. You've sold your vacation house and gold, and reinvested the proceeds for income and growth. Why growth? Because you could easily live for another 20 years.

3. Retirement fund—30 percent in U.S. equity-income and growth-and-income mutual funds (see page 495; don't fall for an all-bond portfolio, it carries too much risk), 70 percent in a "laddered" bond portfolio (page 638) or divided between intermediate- and shorter-term bond funds.

4. Deflation hedge—your bonds are noncallable Treasuries.

WHAT IF ALL YOUR RETIREMENT MONEY IS IN COMPANY PLANS THAT DON'T ALLOW THE INVESTMENT CHOICES SUGGESTED IN THE SAMPLE PORTFOLIOS? Your plan should at least have a stock fund and a fixed-income fund. Given these choices, younger people should put every nickel into stocks. It doesn't matter that you might leave the company in five years; you can roll that money into an Individual Retirement Account and continue to keep it invested in stocks. In early middle age (say, ages 40 to 50), you might want 70 percent of your money in stocks. After age 50, your stock allocation might drop to 60 percent. These are examples, not gospel—but they indicate a direction.

DON'T MAKE THE MISTAKE OF DIVERSIFYING YOUR RETIREMENT SAVINGS SEPARATELY FROM YOUR OTHER SAVINGS! Conceptually, you possess a single sum of money, some of it in the retirement fund, some of it not. Your diversification plan should be tailored to that sum of money as a whole. The investments outside your retirement plan can fill in the pieces that the plan doesn't offer.

For example, the retirement plan might restrict your stock investments to U.S. mutual funds. So diversify into a foreign-stock fund with your outside money. Alternatively, allocate higher investment risks to your pension plan (because you won't touch that money for 20 years or more) and choose lower risks for some of the savings you keep outside the plan (because that's Junior's college money that you'll need in five years).

You get the idea. Count *all* of your money, when deciding whether you're properly diversified.

A FIXED MIX VERSUS A FLEXIBLE MIX

Within the church of asset allocation, two theologies are at war.

One says: Fix your portfolio at whatever mix of assets is right for you and stay there until circumstances change (which is my view).

The other says: Keep changing the amount you hold of each asset, to focus on whichever market you think is the strongest.

With a *fixed mix*, you might own, say, 55 percent U.S. stocks, 15 percent foreign stocks, 25 percent bonds, 5 percent cash. Once a year, you'd "rebalance" your portfolio. That means bringing everything back to the percentages that you started with.

To do that, you'd add up the value of all your investments. If your U.S. stocks were now worth, say, 60 percent of your portfolio, you would sell enough to bring the percentage back to 55 percent. The money you got from selling the stocks would go into an asset that had underperformed. If bonds, for example, had dwindled to only 20 percent of your portfolio, you'd buy enough of them to bring the bond segment back up to 25 percent.

Rebalancing forces you to take profits out of assets whose prices have gone up and reinvest that money in assets that are cheap. Miracle of miracles, you are selling high and buying low, just like the market magicians say you should (the average investor buys high and sells low, then wonders why he or she loses money). Rebalancing also saves you from blundering into too much risk. It keeps the percentage of stocks and bonds in your portfolio at a predetermined level.

With a *flexible mix*, you might decide that U.S. stocks willl make up, say, 30 to 70 percent of your portfolio. When times look good, you'll put in 70 percent; when you get real worried, you cut back to 30 percent.

In other words, you try to time the market. And not just one market but perhaps four or five of them, depending on how diverse your portfolio is. To me, this is a gambler's game. It adds greatly to your chance of losing money.

AS A PRACTICAL MATTER, ANY SORT OF ASSET ALLOCATION WORKS BEST WITH NO-LOAD (NO SALES CHARGE) MUTUAL FUNDS. It costs too much to adjust your mix by constantly buying and selling load funds or individual stocks and bonds.

YOUR REWARD, AT LAST

The table on the next page takes much of the guesswork out of allocating assets between stocks and bonds. It helps you decide how much risk you are willing to tolerate in order to earn a desirable return. The measurements cover 1947–89, and were provided by money manager Wesley McCain of Towneley Capital Management in New York. My thanks for permission to reprint.

Here's how to use the table.

Read down the column headed "Your average return." That shows the average long-term return you can expect if you hold the indicated mix of U.S. stocks and long-term bonds.

When you see a return that your wallet says you want—say, 11.8 percent—read across to the last column. There, you'll see the largest percentage loss that that mix of investments is likely to take in a single year. You'll recover that loss in later years, but you must be prepared to suffer through it.

If that loss looks too scary, read on down the column until you find a one-year loss that seems tolerable. Then look over to the first column to see what mix of stocks and bonds you've chosen and what your average return would be. If that return looks too low, rethink the size of the one-year loss that you're willing to risk (remembering that these losses are temporary).

That's investing, in a nutshell. You are looking for the highest possible return commensurate with the risk you're willing to take.

The middle column, by the way, is strictly for fun. It shows the luck you're likely to have in your best year. But it shouldn't enter into your investment decision. Long-term investors won't earn the single highest return, they will earn the *average* return.

THE RISK/REWARD TABLE CARRIES SOME HOME TRUTHS.

To minimize risk, don't choose an all-bond portfolio. Combining bonds with some stocks reduces your risk and improves your return. For proof, compare the all-bond portfolio with the portfolio that contains 80 percent bonds and 20 percent stocks. The mixed portfolio has a better average return and, in its worst year, didn't suffer as big a loss. Moral: Bonds are riskier than you think.

For the greatest growth over the long term, choose all stocks—at least, for that portion of your money available for long-term investment. Stocks show 'he highest risk of loss in a single year but the biggest average gain over

FINDING YOUR CENTER: RISK VERSUS REWARD

If you own	Your average return *	The single largest one-year gain	The single largest one-year loss
100% stocks† No bonds	13.5%	52.6%	−26.5%
90% stocks 10% bonds‡	12.7	48.1	−23.4
80% stocks 20% bonds	11.8	43.5	−20.3
70% stocks 30% bonds	11.0	39.0	−17.2
60% stocks 40% bonds	10.1	34.4	−14.1
50% stocks 50% bonds	9.3	31.6	−11.1
40% stocks 60% bonds	8.4	32.8	−8.0
30% stocks 70% bonds	7.6	34.7	−6.1
20% stocks 80% bonds	6.7	36.6	−5.8
10% stocks 90% bonds	5.9	38.5	−5.9
No stocks 100% bonds	5.0	40.4	−9.2

* From 1947 through 1989, compounded annually, dividends reinvested.
† Measured by Standard & Poor's 500.
‡ Long-term U.S. government bonds.
Sources: Towneley Capital Management, New York; Standard & Poor's Corporation; Ibbotson Associates; Crandall, Pierce and Company.

time. Moral: If you truly mean to leave the money alone for 20 or 30 years—as a younger person might, with a retirement fund—don't bother looking beyond stock-owning mutual funds. (Circumstances sometimes require you to plunder your retirement fund, however. Whether to diversify against that risk with some short-term bonds is strictly your call.)

If you want solid growth but with some protection against market drops, choose a mix of stocks and bonds. Younger people should tip toward higher returns, because they have time for their stocks to recover from any drop. For the young, I'd suggest a stocks-to-bonds ratio of 90/10 to 70/30. Middle-aged people and even young retirees should look at 60/40 or 50/50 splits. Much older retirees might move to 30/70 or 20/80 allocations of stocks to bonds, but never to an all-bond portfolio. Stocks cushion you against inflation, which is critical when you don't have a salary to fall back on. Moral: Good investing isn't dumb luck. Success comes to those who use their heads.

HOW TO GET MONEY TO INVEST

It's no mystery.
Save money.
Buy shares in a mutual fund every month.
Month after month after month after month.
After month.
If that doesn't work, inherit.

HOW TO HANDLE INVESTMENTS AFTER . . .

MARRIAGE. If you have two paychecks, and agree on an investment approach, pool your money into a joint portfolio. Or keep two portfolios with similar kinds of investments.

If you don't agree, set up separate portfolios, shaped to the risks that each of you wants to take. Draw up an overall mix for your mutual assets. Then dole out the higher risks to the more adventuresome partner, and the lower risks to the other. (But even the spouse with the lower risks should own some stock. Why get stuck with the poorer yields, if you divorce?)

If you both work in the same industry and have been buying your company's stock (maybe because you get a special deal on the price), you are overexposed to that industry's risk. Periodically, sell some company stock and diversify into something else.

If you both have employee retirement-savings plans, coordinate your investments. See what each company's plan has to offer, then decide where each of you should direct his or her money. Together, your retirement investments should reflect the mix of stock and fixed-interest vehicles that you find appropriate as a couple.

A NEW BABY. Keep up with your retirement investing (Chapter 29). Any separate college fund should be in stock-owning mutual funds.

AN INHERITANCE. Don't keep a stock just because Mommy loved it or because its price is up (or down). Maybe Mommy was holding a rotten stock. Maybe it yields income when you need growth. Maybe you know almost nothing about the company and don't want to know. Keep only those assets that fit your own investment plan. Everything else should be replaced.

A DIVORCE. Investments made jointly aren't necessarily right for singles. So rethink your portfolio from the ground up. You may have to live on some of the money that you took from the marriage, which means keeping a much larger cash reserve.

A NEW JOB. If you get a lump-sum payout from your former company's pension plan, roll it into an Individual Retirement Account or into the pension plan of your new employer. You can divvy up the money among the same types of investments that you had before, and your nest egg remains tax deferred.

UNEMPLOYMENT. Roll a lump-sum payout from your pension plan into an Individual Retirement Account, in order to preserve its tax-deferred status. Invest the IRA in a money market mutual fund or money market deposit account at a bank. Draw on this cash only as a last resort. Withdrawals will cost you income taxes plus a 10 percent penalty if you're under age 59½ (for a way of avoiding the penalty, see page 759).

If you have stock-market investments, convert them (or part of them) into money market mutual funds. This preserves your capital. You may need to draw on this money and can't run the risk that the market might fall. When you get a job, you can go back into stocks again.

Live on your cash reserve (you have one, right? Worth three months' take-home pay?) and your other savings. If you don't find a job right away and your money runs low, make IRA withdrawals as needed.

RETIREMENT. Don't shift all your money into bonds and money market funds. You will probably live another 20 or 30 years and, during that time, inflation will decimate fixed income. You need a substantial stake in stocks, in order to grow enough capital for your later years.

A WINDFALL. Maybe it's a lottery ticket. Maybe a big royalty check. Maybe the proceeds of selling your house. First, put the money in a bank or money market mutual fund while you think about what to do. Second, clear up your obligations, like paying off debts or setting up a college fund. Third, see an accountant, to find out what's taxed. Finally, study up on investments. Don't talk to a stockbroker or financial planner until you already have a good idea of what you want. Salespeople can mislead the uninformed.

If your windfall is from a lump-sum pension distribution, don't lay a finger on the money until you've talked to an accountant. How much money you'll wind up with will depend on the tax choice you make (page 793).

BE AN AVERAGING INVESTOR

You already know that you ought to invest part of every paycheck— for the good of your soul, for your future, and because your mother told you so.

But regular monthly investing has an even better rationale. It can make you more money than periodic lump-sum investing, because you follow a system known as dollar-cost averaging. Here's how it works.

Say that you put $150 into a stock-owning mutual fund every month. When stock prices rise, your $150 buys fewer shares. When stock prices fall, your $150 buys more shares. In a see-sawing market, dollar-cost averaging lowers your average cost per share. So it builds in a higher profit.

As an example, assume that over five months your $150 goes into a mutual fund whose price each month is $10, $9, $5, $8, and $10 per share. The average price per share over those five months was $8.40. But because you bought more at $5 than you did at $10, your average cost per share is only $7.86. So you bought the fund cheap.

You get the same result on the upside. Say that the fund's monthly prices are $10, $11, $15, $12, $10. The average price comes to $11.60. The cost per share to the dollar-averaging buyer: $11.35.

Dollar-cost averaging disciplines you to keep on investing when prices are down. And it keeps you from plunging too heavily when prices are high. Reinvesting all dividends automatically is a form of dollar-cost averaging.

There are times when this technique may be second best.

If the market is on a roll, you might have made more money by investing a lump sum all at once. Just look at the second example above: You could have had all your shares at $10. But how would you have known? No little birds fly into windows, whistling tomorrow's prices. A cautious investor will dollar-average even a lump sum—say, at the rate of $500 a month.

Dollar-cost averaging is better done with diversified mutual funds than with individual stocks. The broad market always recovers, but certain stocks might not. If you choose a rotten stock, buying more shares on the way down would be throwing good money after bad.

MEMO TO THE NERVOUS

Maybe you quake more easily than others. You know in your heart that stocks are the best investment in the long run, but the thought of owning them scares you stiff.

Obviously, I'd like to change your mind. So try this: Put just a little money into a diversified, stock-owning mutual fund—maybe 20 percent of your savings. Pick a simple fund (page 512), and invest a modest sum every month for the next 12 months. Then forget about it. Pretend it isn't there. Take a look five years from now and see what you've got. The result ought to make you feel pretty good, good enough to put even more money in stocks. If I can divert even a small portion of your long-term retirement savings into the stock market this book will have helped.

But you have to promise to leave that investment alone. If you'll panic and sell the first time stocks drop, forget it. You don't belong in the market just yet. But do keep on reading, to learn more about how it works. *Willingness to accept stock-market risk isn't necessarily a function of your personality. It may be a function of your knowledge.* The more you learn, the more you'll come to understand that long-term stockholdings aren't as risky as you thought.

MEMO TO THE NERVELESS

Some investors are fearless. They're not happy unless they're buying options on futures and borrowing against their house to do it. A reader once asked me what I thought about investing his son's college fund in a single junk bond. I said, "not much." And he said, "but mutual funds are no fun." For him and his kin, this book will have helped if they speculate wildly only with part of their money (preferably a small part).

I'm not asking you to give up your habit. But for your family's sake, balance your high-wire act with a few investments that are reliably dull.

Learning not to take stupid risks is equally a function of knowledge and experience. With luck, you'll learn your lesson while you still have some money left.

THE OUTLOOK

Breathtaking bull markets, like the one that ran from 1978 to 1987, are rare. Stocks will continue to move higher, with dips and pauses every now and then. But gains in this decade should take on a far more normal look—maybe 9 to 10 percent annually, down from the '80s' thrilling pace of 17.5 percent. But the market works its will in any number of ways. So let me suggest some possibilities and how to handle them.

WE MIGHT HAVE A SIDEWAYS MARKET FOR A WHILE—with stocks rising and falling but not making much of a net advance. Dollar-cost averaging does well in a crab-walking market. So does a "fixed-mix" portfolio (page 493), because you're taking profits on any rise and reinvesting in assets that are underpriced. Buy-and-hold isn't much of a thrill. Long-term holders have to look past the sideways years, to the next true market rise.

OUR HOPES MIGHT BE BRIEFLY INTERRUPTED BY A TERRIBLE MARKET—with stocks and bonds both falling, real estate wobbling, and interest rates spiking up. That's why money you'll need within four years should always be kept in safe investments like certificates of deposit, Treasury bills and notes, or money market mutual funds.

Nothing truly prepares you for the hot, nasty breath of the bear, other than the certain knowledge that this too will pass—probably in no more than a year or two. Your portfolio is defended if you own some bear hedges: noncallable Treasury bonds and notes, some shorter-term bond funds, maybe gold-stock mutual funds, and, of course, cash. But keep on buying stocks. You are locking them up at bargain prices. That will earn you good money when the market turns around.

WE MIGHT HAVE A DEFLATIONARY 1930s MARKET—the market of your deepest dread. I'm hard put to make a case for it. But as long as you own cash and Treasury bonds, they'd be your safety nets. Incidentally, there were two bull markets in stocks during the 1930s, for anyone who had the money to play. (Really. Check it out.)

WE MIGHT HAVE AN INFLATIONARY DEPRESSION—with prices spiralling up but business down. Your defense would be gold stocks, money market mutual funds invested in Treasuries, and foreign-currency bank accounts that hedge against a dollar collapse.

WE MIGHT WIND UP WITH A NIFTY '90s —with interest rates down and stocks and bonds pushing higher, both in America and abroad. This case rests on continued international growth, control of inflation, increased savings by the baby-boom generation, expanded world trade, no serious shortages of energy long term, and the continuing spread of the free market faith.

This is not just my favorite forecast, it is also the most likely one. Long term, the world has always gotten richer and stocks have always trended up. On a percentage basis, history says that you might as well invest for success.

WHAT MAKES A GOOD INVESTOR?

To handle money well, you need a certain resilience of spirit. Peter Lynch, former manager of the Fidelity Magellan Fund, one of the most extraordinary mutual funds in history, looks for these qualities:

Patience

Humility

Detachment

Persistence

Flexibility

Comon sense

Self-reliance

Open-mindedness

A tolerance for pain

Ability to admit mistakes

Ability to do your own research

Ability to ignore a general panic

Ability to make decisions on incomplete information

Ability to ignore gut feelings because gut feelings are usually wrong.

22

HOW TO PICK
A MUTUAL FUND:

Every Investor's Bedrock Buy

———

I love mutual funds because they're so easy as
well as so smart. Anyone can learn enough to
buy a good one. What other investment can
make that claim?

There are two ways of investing: *directly*, by buying your own securities from a stockbroker, and *indirectly*, by buying shares in a mutual fund.

I'm for mutual funds, especially for stock investments. Bonds are a little trickier—sometimes bond funds are better, sometimes it's better to buy individual bonds (page 622). But for long-term growth, a stock fund will serve you better than any other financial investment.

MUTUAL FUNDS DEFINED

A mutual fund is a *vehicle*. It takes in money from many different investors. The fund's manager invests that money in specified types of securities. You'll find stock funds, bond funds, money market funds, gold funds, real-estate funds—literally, something for everyone. There are even good funds for people who don't want to bother picking funds (page 512).

NINE REASONS TO LOVE MUTUAL FUNDS

1. You get full-time money management, from the person (or committee) who runs the fund. Believe me, you don't get that from stockbrokers. A broker's job is to sell stuff. They don't have the time to worry about the overall shape of your portfolio.

2. You can pick exactly the level of risk you want to take (page 504). By contrast, when you buy your own stocks, you generally have no idea how risky your total investment position is.

3. You diversify. You share in the fortunes of a large number of securities rather than owning just a few.

4. You can check a fund's past performance record.

5. You can buy and hold for the long term. There's no need to switch from one stock to another as market conditions change. Your mutual-fund manager does that for you.

6. You don't have to spend a lot of time doing stock research and following market conditions.

7. You avoid all the costly risks of falling into the hands of a bad broker—churning, bad recommendations, high sales commissions, and so on (page 565).

8. You can automatically reinvest your dividends and capital gains. Steady compounding doubles and redoubles the returns that you would get from stocks alone.

9. Mutual funds are easy to understand. You can pick good funds yourself, without having to pay for advice.

BUT WHAT ABOUT THE BIG KILLINGS THAT ARE MADE IN STOCKS?

What about them? Your neighbor who buys stocks would be lucky if he made a killing one time out of 30. Meanwhile, his losers and his mediocrities (which he doesn't mention) accumulate. Counting losers as well as winners, I'll bet that he doesn't do nearly as well as the average mutual fund—especially if he doesn't reinvest all his dividends and capital gains.

There are arguments for buying stocks directly (page 593). But I'd buy mutual funds first. And even if I played around with stocks, I'd use funds for my central holdings.

OPEN-END MUTUAL FUNDS

These are the traditional mutual funds that we all know and love. A manager runs a pool of money that belongs to many different investors. You can add your money to the pool, or cash out of it, anytime you want. That's why the fund is called "open-end."

Your shares are priced at their *net asset value (NAV)*. That's the average market value of all the fund's securities, minus costs, divided by the number of shares outstanding. Share prices rise or fall every day, reflecting what happens to the fund's investments.

You receive a pro rata share of the dividends, as well as any net profits from the sale of securities. This income can be taken in cash or reinvested automatically in more fund shares. Payouts are called *distributions,* and may be paid monthly, quarterly, or annually. (Fixed-income funds may declare distributions daily, even though they pay out on monthly or quarterly schedules.)

Open-end funds have prospectuses, usually updated annually, that tell you how the fund invests. The fund's managers also send their shareholders quarterly, semiannual, and annual reports.

UP THE LADDER OF RISK

Here's a summary of the kinds of open-end funds available, what they invest in, and why you might buy them. You'll probably want a money fund (for safety), a medium-term bond fund (for stability), and one or two stock funds (for growth).

I have noted here each fund's objective. For an opinion on the plausibility of that objective, as well as more details on how the funds work, see Chapters 24 and 25.

For the all-time simplest way of picking a mutual fund, without even reading the rest of this chapter, see page 512.

Type of Fund	Risk Level	Investments*	Objective
Money market	Low	Commercial paper, certificates of deposit, Treasuries, etc.	Keep capital safe; earn current short-term interest rates.
Tax-exempt money market	Low	Very short-term municipals.	Keep capital safe; earn current short-term, tax-exempt interest rates.
International money market	Mid–low	Foreign CDs, governments, and other short-term paper.	Hope for higher returns than on regular U.S. money markets; reap gains when the dollar falls and losses when it rises.
Short-term bond, taxable or tax-exempt	Mid–low	Government, corporate, or tax-exempt bonds, 1- to 5-year maturities.	Keep capital fairly safe; earn a slightly higher taxable or tax-exempt income than money markets pay; small risk of loss.
Intermediate-term bond, taxable, or tax-exempt	Mid–low	Government, corporate, or tax-exempt bonds, 5- to 10-year maturities.	Earn a higher taxable or tax-exempt income than on shorter-term bonds; accept more gains and losses of principal; go for solid total returns long term.
Long-term taxable bond	Middle	Government or corporate bonds, 15- to 30-year maturities.	Earn high current income, speculate on declines in interest rates; accept the risk of higher losses in hopes of getting higher total returns.
Long-term tax-exempt bond	Middle	Tax-exempt municipals, 15- to 30-year maturities.	Earn high tax-exempt income, in return for more risk of loss if bonds are sold before maturity; generally not used to speculate on falling interest rates.

Type of Fund	Risk Level	Investments*	Objective
Ginnie Mae	Middle	Securities backed by a pool of government-insured home mortgages; uncertain maturities, usually not more than 12 years.	Earn good income; get a periodic return of capital; accept risk of market loss if interest rates rise.
Global bond	Middle	Bonds of U.S. and foreign companies and countries.	Go for high bond income; win gains when the dollar falls but risk losses when the dollar rises.
International bond	Middle	Bonds of foreign companies and countries.	Go for high bond income; greater gains when the dollar falls, but greater losses when it rises.
Mixed income	Middle	Part dividend-paying stocks, part bonds, part money markets.	Emphasize income, but earn less than pure bond funds pay; get a little growth from stocks in return for accepting modest risk of loss.
Income	Middle	Emphasis on bonds and dividend-paying stocks.	Emphasize income, but get a little more growth than mixed-income funds offer; limited losses when the stock market falls.
Balanced	Middle	Part stocks, part bonds and preferred stocks.	Earn reasonable income; get reasonable growth; limited losses when market falls.
Zero-coupon bond	Mid–high	Discount bonds paying no current interest.	Accrue high bond income; dividends reinvested at the same rate paid by the bond itself; a lucrative speculation on falling interest rates, but big losses when rates rise. Safe if held to maturity.

Type of Fund	Risk Level	Investments*	Objective
Equity income	Mid–high	Stocks that pay high dividends, like blue chips and utilities.	Earn modest income; get good growth; risk of average loss when the stock market falls.
Growth and income	Mid–high	Stocks that pay high dividends and also show good growth.	A little more growth and a little less income than equity-income funds pay; average risk of loss when the market falls.
Asset alllocation (fixed portfolio)	Mid–high	A mix of assets: cash, stocks, bonds, foreign stocks, gold, etc.	Seek good growth and limited losses in any market.
Asset allocation (flexible portfolio)	Mid–high	A constantly changing portfolio, trying to emphasize the best markets at the time.	Seek good growth and limited losses in any market.
Option income	Mid–high	Stocks, with call options (page 688) written against them.	Seek higher income yields than on most stock funds; accept subpar returns in rising markets; hope for limited losses in falling markets.
Convertible	Mid–high	Preferred stocks and bonds, convertible into common stocks.	Earn higher yields than on common stocks but less than on bonds; hope for limited losses; less growth than in pure stock funds.
Fund of funds	Mid–high	Shares of other mutual funds.	Earn average stock-market gains and losses; big risk of paying too much in management fees.
Index	Mid–high	Stocks that represent a specific market as a whole	Earn average stock-market gains and accept average losses for that particular market.
Conscience	Higher	Stocks in "moral" companies—no nuclear, no pollution, no tobacco, etc.	Earn average growth; bigger risk of subpar gains and higher losses because of the limits on investment.

Type of Fund	Risk Level	Investments*	Objective
High-yield bond, taxable or tax-free	Higher	Low- and unrated (junk) bonds; municipals or corporates.	Super-high income return overcoming (one hopes) the high risk of bond defaults and declines in market value.
Global equity	Higher	Stocks of U.S. and foreign companies.	Earn worldwide capital gains; risk of larger losses when markets fall.
Growth	Higher	Stocks whose earnings usually rise fast	Earn above-average market returns; accept larger losses when the market falls.
International equity	Higher	Stocks of foreign companies.	Earn international capital gains; bigger gains when the dollar falls; bigger losses when it rises.
Asset allocation (globally flexible)	High	A constantly changing portfolio, focusing on several U.S. and international markets.	Seek good growth and limited losses in any national or international market; a big risk that the dollar will go against you or that the manager will bet wrong.
Real estate	High	Stocks in real-estate companies.	An inflation hedge; risk of big losses when this industry falters.
Sector	High	Stocks of one particular industry	For market timers, who hope to catch an industry's rising trend, then sell before stocks decline; not for investors who buy and hold; big risk of loss.
Aggressive growth (capital appreciation)	High	Shooting for the moon, with high-growth stocks, options, etc.	Earn above-average gains at the risk of above-average losses; minimal dividend income.

Type of Fund	Risk Level	Investments*	Objective
Small-company growth	High	Stocks in the smaller companies traded on stock exchanges or over the counter.	Achieve superior long-term gains; risk that high gains will be followed by periods of slower gains; above-average risk of loss; minimal dividend income.
Gold and precious metals	High	Stocks of gold and precious-metal mines.	A hedge against war, monetary turmoil, and usually, unexpected inflation; gold stocks often go up when other stocks fall; big risk of loss.

* Some funds in these categories invest differently, but this is the general expectation.

WHAT KINDS OF FUNDS ARE RIGHT FOR YOU?

Take a look at page 484, where you listed your objectives. Below, consider the risks you're prepared to take and match those objectives with suitable types of mutual funds.

Say, for example, that your objective is "college education." If your child is 3 years old, you can afford to invest 100 percent of your money in higher-risk funds—say, growth funds. If your child is 8, you might put 60 percent of your money in growth funds and 40 percent into lower-risk equity-income funds. If your child is 13, you might keep 65 percent of the money in an equity-income fund and switch 35 percent into a money market mutual fund or Series EE bonds. You get the idea.

Objective	% at higher risk	% at lower risk*	Types of funds
	%	%	
	%	%	
	%	%	
	%	%	
	%	%	
	%	%	

* If you want to take no risk of capital loss, the only suitable mutual funds are the money markets. But with money funds, you are certain to lose purchasing power, after inflation and after taxes.

RESEARCHING THE MUTUAL FUNDS

1. Decide how to allocate your assets (above).

2. Look for funds that meet these objectives. Some good sources: *Forbes* magazine's annual September issue of mutual fund performance, *Business Week*'s annual February issue, and *Kiplinger's Personal Finance Magazine*'s annual September issue. *Money* magazine reports at various times. They all list long-term fund performance, according to various measures. You can find back issues in your library. I'm especially fond of *Forbes*, because it gives you a quick fix on how well each fund does in up and down markets. From all these sources, cull a list of the funds that interest you the most—two or three in each category.

Some libraries own, or can borrow, *Weisenberger's Investment Companies Service*, which lists the objectives, investments, and performances of hundreds of funds. A particularly useful book is *The Handbook for No-Load Fund Investors*, at this writing $45 from the *No-Load Fund Investor*, P.O. Box 283, Hastings-on-Hudson, NY, 10706. It's a primer on mutual-fund investing, as well as a guide to fund objectives, performance, and investor services.

3. Check the minimum investment. A few funds have no minimums. A majority want $500 to $3,000. A handful require $25,000 and up. High-minimum funds aren't entirely closed to low-budget investors. They often take $2,000 Individual Retirement Accounts. Alternatively, you can invest small amounts through certain discount brokerage houses (page 530). Once you've become a shareholder, funds might accept additional investments of as little as $100.

4. Go for funds without sales charges—front load, back load, or hidden load (page 514). Sometimes it's worth paying a low upfront sales charge for truly superior performance—for example, the Fidelity Magellan Fund in the 1980s. But all things being equal, you'll do better in no-load funds, because none of your money goes for sales expenses. For a list of no-load fund families, see page 531.

5. Diversify within each category. For growth, consider at least two of the following: U.S. funds, foreign funds, capital-appreciation funds, small-company funds, and equity-income funds. For bond income, look at short-term and intermediate-term funds.

6. Lean toward funds that have weathered recessions and bear markets, with good results. As a practical matter, that means limiting your list to funds that started no later than 1980.

7. If you want an aggressive growth fund: Consider size. How much in assets does the fund have under management? Generally speaking, giant, multi-billion-dollar funds don't rise as fast as smaller ones. That's because big funds tilt their investing toward major companies, while the stocks of the faster-growing smaller companies tend to fall to the smaller funds. Growth funds often stop taking new investors when they reach a certain size, and start a clone with the same investment objective. Under $250 million in assets is a nice cut-off point. But this size rule applies only to growth funds. Income funds and conservative equity funds with blue-chip portfolios can accumulate zillions without harm.

8. Another thing about growth funds: Consider how well the fund is known. The best performers have lots of new money coming in. That frees the manager to buy new stocks without first selling the ones he has. Funds attract new money when their hot performance puts them near the top of the charts, when they're getting good publicity, and when they belong to a fund group that markets heavily.

9. One more tip on aggressive growth funds: In rising markets, the odds are two out of three that this year's winners will be next year's winners. So when picking your fund, hunt among the top performers. In bear markets, however, aggressive growth funds tend to perform the worst.

10. Check the long-term and short-term performance for each fund that interests you. A solid 10-year record (more above-average than below-average years) shows that the fund has good genes. Impressive results for the past year or two tell you that its current managers know what they're doing and may even be on a roll.

11. Call or write to the funds to get the sales literature and the prospectuses, *and read them* (page 512). Prospectuses explain your investment and, nowadays, are refreshingly clear. If you really don't understand them, ask for explanations. If you don't understand the explanations, you aren't yet ready to invest.

12. Buy the funds you like the best, and start a performance sheet (page 877). Put down how much money you invested and the number of shares you bought. Reinvest all the income from the fund, provided that you don't need it to live on. At each reporting period, put down the number of shares you have and what they're worth (to find out their value, multiply the number of shares you own by the net asset value, which is reported daily by the fund or in the newspaper).

13. Don't sell just because the market falls. You're supposed to be

in this game for the long term. But you shouldn't stick with a loser, either. If your fund does worse than other funds of its type for two years running, start the search for another fund. You'll find average performance data, by fund type, once a quarter in *Barron's* magazine, as well as in the other magazines catering to individual investors.

FOR PEOPLE WHO THINK THAT FUND PICKING IS TOO HARD

Take the easy way out. You can:

1. Buy an index fund, which copies the movement of the market as a whole. There are bond index funds and stock index funds, so all you need to know is whether you want capital preservation or growth. The granddaddy of index funds is the Vanguard Group in Valley Forge, Pennsylvania (800-662-2739). To read more about index funds, see page 588.

2. Buy a Spectrum Fund from T. Rowe Price in Baltimore, Maryland (800-638-5660). It is actually two funds, one invested for income, one invested for growth. All you have to do is decide which kind of investor you are. The fund spreads your money over a variety of T. Rowe Price funds that suit your category. You get plenty of diversification without having to think about it twice.

FOR PEOPLE WHO LOVE TO PICK MUTUAL FUNDS

For a splendid analysis of hundreds of funds—stock and bond, domestic and foreign, take a $55 three-month trial subscription to *Mutual Fund Values*, 53 West Jackson Blvd., Suite 460, Chicago, IL, 60604. It's published by Morningstar, Inc., which tracks fund performance. MFV explains each fund's current investment approach, rates the outlook for the securities it owns, and makes buy and sell recommendations. A full year's subscription is $395.

VETTING THE PROSPECTUS

Read the prospectus before you buy! The sales literature is helpful, but the prospectus dishes all the dirt. Most fund prospectuses are written in plain English (if yours isn't, dump the fund; if it can't write clearly, it can't think clearly). Underline. Make margin notes. Ask the fund to explain anything that you don't understand (there are kindly operators at the end of toll-free 800 lines, to help). Keep the prospectus permanently on file. It includes information you're going to need about how to manage your fund investment.

Here's what the prospectus will tell you.

The Fund's Objectives

Read the objectives with great attention. What you see is (usually) what you get. I remember a guy who was horrified by the losses he took in the junk-bond crash of 1989. It had never dawned on him, poor soul, that that's what his high-yield bond fund invested in. I suppose I ought to have felt sorry for him, but I didn't.

As you study the objectives, think about your personal needs. Can you ride with this fund's level of risk? Do you share its attitude toward the relative importance of income, safety, and capital gains? Is this fund manager trying to time the market? Or is he or she a "value investor," who focuses on relatively low-priced shares? Or maybe a "growth" investor, screening for companies whose earnings are rising rapidly?

Different strokes suit different folks. To say, "I want a fund that goes up," is to show that you still have a lot to learn about investing. Over time, virtually all mutual funds go up. What's important is *how* the fund tries to make its profits. The manager should tell you precisely what he or she is aiming for.

Some prospectuses speak for more than one fund. They carry an umbrella name but offer several investment portfolios. If you buy the Vanguard International Equity Index Fund, for example, you can choose the European Portfolio or the Pacific Portfolio, each of which is a separate fund. Don't mix them up. Make sure you sign up for the investment you want.

What the Fund Invests In

This section should tell you exactly how the fund will meet its goals. What will it buy? Just as important, what won't it buy? Does it ban risky moves like borrowing money to buy stocks or speculating in foreign currencies? Or will it take those chances, in hopes of producing a higher yield?

To help you understand its investments, the fund may include little primers on such things as how the bond markets work and what options are.

Special Risks

In the front of the prospectus, READ ANY SENTENCES SET IN CAPITAL LETTERS. That's usually a red alert. Maybe the fund is buying especially risky securities. Maybe its expenses are unusually high. Or whatever. A SENTENCE IN CAPITAL LETTERS MEANS TROUBLE!

What the Fees Are

Mysteriously, most investors don't kick about fees, so many of the funds are cheerfully raising their take. This lowers your yield. If a fund earns 12 percent in the stock market, the net to investors might be anywhere from 11.5 to 9.5 percent, depending on what the manager charges. A difference of 1 or 2 percentage points may not sound like much, but—compounded over many years—it adds up to big money.

You'll find all the charges in the fee table at the front of the prospectus. They might include:

A FRONT-END LOAD—an upfront commission for the salesperson, which can be as high as 8.5 percent. That's $85 for every $1,000 you put up, leaving only $915 to put in the market. Your investment will have to rise by 9.3 percent just for you to break even. "Mid-load" funds charge 5 to 6 percent. "Low-load" funds charge 3 percent or less.

If you make a substantial investment (say, more than $10,000), the commission goes down, maybe to 7.5 percent. With larger investments, the percentage drops even more. If you're going to put up a lot of money, but in stages, see if you can file a "letter of intent," giving you a right to the lower commission right from the start.

Who should pay a full sales load? Absolutely no one. Commissions are the price of advice, and you don't need it. You're smart enough to pick a good fund yourself. In fact, you'll probably pick a better fund than a salesperson would. Brokers may steer you toward funds pushed by their firms, or funds that pay good commissions, even if they're not top performers.

A LOAD ON REINVESTED DIVIDENDS—a charge of maybe 4 percent or more every time you use your dividends to buy more fund shares. This is petty theft. I wouldn't buy a fund that picks your pocket this way. You should be able to reinvest at no cost at all.

A CONTINGENT DEFERRED SALES LOAD—an "exit fee," charged if you sell within five or six years. Many salespeople claim that these funds are "no-loads," because they deduct no sales charge up front. But the broker always gets paid. One way the sponsor covers the broker's commission is to "trap" you in the fund by charging you a fee if you want to sell.

Contingent deferred sales charges might be as high as 6 percent if you pull out of the fund in the first year. The second year you'd pay 5 percent, and so on. Six years would have to pass before you could sell your shares without penalty.

Some funds assess the exit fee against your original investment—for example, 3 percent of the amount you put up. Others assess it against whatever the fund is currently worth, so you'd pay on anything you took out. Any "no-load" sold by a stockbroker or financial planner probably carries this exit fee. Look for it in the prospectus.

A 12b-1 FEE—another hidden sales load. Many funds that charge no commissions up front will take 1 percent or more from fund assets every year. That money goes for brokers' commissions and other marketing expenses. A few 12b-1 fees decline after five or six years. But they're usually charged for as long as you hold the fund.

Over long holding periods, 12b-1s will be even more expensive than an upfront sales load. Over short holding periods, however, 12b-1s might be cheaper—although they're usually combined with contingent deferred sales loads. (If these funds don't get you coming, they get you going.)

Some funds levy small 12b-1 charges, maybe 0.25 percent. That's not so bad. Some funds have "defensive" 12b-1 plans, established for contingency use. I consider them clean, as long as the fee isn't being charged.

At this writing, the industry is talking about putting sharp limits on 12b-1s. Keep your fingers crossed.

REDEMPTION FEES—exit fees of 1 or 2 percent, charged whenever you sell, regardless of how long you've held the fund. Their purpose is to discourage people from trading in and out. These funds want long-term holders or none at all.

EXCHANGE FEES—levied by most fund families when you sell one fund in order to buy another. They run between $5 and $25.

MANAGEMENT FEES—charged by every mutual fund, to compensate the people who choose the securities and manage the fund. Some new funds waive the management fee during the first couple of years. That improves their reported yield and makes the fund look low cost. New money market funds, in particular, have been using this tactic, in order to put themselves at the top of the charts. As long as they're free, they're a good deal—but eventually, fees will be imposed.

OTHER FEES—shareholder accounting, franchise tax, startup fees, account maintenance fees, you name it, someone is charging it.

TOTAL FUND OPERATING EXPENSES—all the expenses charged each year (excluding upfront loads), expressed as a percentage of total assets and known as the *expense ratio*. This ratio is the critical number. All the other things being equal, lower-cost funds (which have lower ratios) will outperform the higher-cost funds.

In 1989, according to *Forbes* magazine, the average stock-owning (equity) fund charged an average of 1.55 percent. On the higher end were the global and international funds, because of the extra cost of investing abroad and the funds specializing in smaller stocks, because of the higher expense of over-the-counter trading. On the lower end were the no-load funds, with a median expense ratio of only 1.16 percent. Some splendid funds charged less than 0.8 percent and a handful (mostly from the well-known no-load Vanguard Group in Valley Forge, Pennsylvania), less than 0.5 percent.

The average bond fund charged 1.08 percent. Once again, the no-loads were cheaper; their median stood at 0.8 percent. A handful—again from Vanguard—charge under 0.4 percent. High fees weigh especially heavily on bond funds, because these funds yield lower returns than stocks.

What's an extra 0.5 percent charge, you might say? On a $10,000 investment, over 20 years, it could be several thousand dollars.

HYPOTHETICAL COSTS IN DOLLARS AND CENTS—a table (or paragraph) in the prospectus tells what you might pay over four different time periods for every $1,000 invested, assuming a modest annual gain in the fund of 5 percent. In 1989, the 10-year cost for the median no-load fund was $122, compared with $220 for load funds, according to the *No-Load Fund Investor*.

If you're buying a load fund, sorting out costs is a little more subtle. Front-end sales charges hurt short-term investors, but aren't quite so bad if you hold for 10 years or more. Shorter-term investors may do better with deferred loads and 12b-1 charges. But neither type of fund is as cheap as a true no-load.

MOST PUBLISHED PERFORMANCE DATA MAKE LOAD FUNDS LOOK BETTER THAN THEY REALLY ARE. That's because the measuring services, like *Forbes,* compute performance without deducting the upfront sales charge.

For example, take a load fund yielding 16.78 this year, versus a no-load yielding 12.99. You might assume that the load fund is better. But after paying an upfront sales charge of 5.75 percent, load-fund investors netted only 10.01 percent—less than the no-load would have paid. Even after five years of similar performance, the no-load is likely to be slightly ahead. You have to hold longer than five years for a consistently superior load fund to outperform a lesser-yielding no-load.

YOUR BEST BUY IS ALWAYS A TOP PERFORMING, TRUE NO-LOAD FUND. It charges no upfront sales load, no deferred load, and no 12b-1. You buy it directly from the fund company itself, without a salesperson's help. For the names and phone numbers of 33 no-load fund groups, see page 531.

The Portfolio Turnover Rate

This tells you how fast the fund manager buys and sells. On average, the turnover rate for stock funds is 87 percent, which means that 87 percent of the average value of the portfolio is changed in a single year.

The higher the turnover rate, the higher the stockbrokerage costs. Rapidly traded funds need better returns to compensate for these extra expenses. Sometimes they get it, sometimes they don't. In general, low-turnover funds yield more, over time, than the fast traders—although some of the very best performers have a high trading ratio.

The Financial Results

The financial tables show the fund's dollars-and-cents results per share, for up to the past 10 years. But frankly, this table is pretty useless. If a fund distributes 87 cents a share, is that good or bad? High for a fund of this type, or low? Who knows?

By the time you read this, better disclosure may be on the way (page 519). Until then, here's what the key lines on the financial table mean.

"NET INVESTMENT INCOME (LOSS)"—shows what the fund is earning in interest and dividends, after expenses. Income funds will show larger dividends; aggressive growth funds, smaller ones.

"DIVIDENDS FROM NET INVESTMENT INCOME"—shows how much fund income is paid out to shareholders. Under current law, you have to receive at least 98 percent.

"NET REALIZED AND UNREALIZED GAINS (LOSSES)"—shows how the securities are performing. Aggressive growth funds may show larger capital gains; income funds, smaller ones.

"DISTRIBUTIONS FROM REALIZED CAPITAL GAINS"—shows how much of the profits are being paid out. Again, a fund has to distribute at least 98 percent of its net capital gains (after deducting losses).

"NET INCREASE (DECREASE) IN NET ASSET VALUE"—shows the change in the value of fund shares, after distributions.

"NET ASSET VALUE AT END OF YEAR"—shows the value of your fund shares at year end. Don't use the change in this number to figure your total gain or loss, because it doesn't include the distributions you got. *Your annual total return—the one figure that matters the most—is just not there!*

What's the Bottom Line?

At this writing, there is no bottom line. A rotten fund doesn't have to tell you exactly how it did, in percentage terms, from one calendar year to the next. Nothing leaps out at you from the financial tables to say THIS IS A LOUSY FUND—which is the single thing you really need to know. Naturally, that's also the single thing that the industry's many mediocre funds have been fighting like tigers to keep you from finding out.

Because of this lacuna, losing funds can pretend to be winners with no one the wiser. Take, for example, the Oppenheimer Special Fund. It once advertised a fabulous average annual return of 21.5 percent. Impressed, I asked management for year-by-year results. Turns out that the fund was misleading investors. It had earned a terrific 39 percent annually in its early years, but lately had been losing money at the annual rate of 4 percent. All its recent investors were in the red.

Some funds (the good guys) voluntarily list their annual percentage gain or loss, if not in the prospectus then in the annual report. But many other funds don't

Always ask for it before you invest. You want the *annual percentage return* (which combines all distributions with the annual change in net asset value) for each of the past 20 calendar years. The report should say, for example, 1987, down 5 percent; 1988, up 8 percent; 1989, up 10 percent. Just that simple. Ask for the same data on the pooled funds run by banks for their trust customers. Some bank funds are world beaters, others are investments from Hell.

HOW DO YOU EVALUATE THOSE RETURNS? You compare them with the returns of other mutual funds that have the same or similar investment objectives (see page 257), which is the best possible measure. The funds should also provide you with standard annual benchmarks. A stock fund should compare itself with a stock-market index, like the Standard & Poor's 500-stock average, over the same period. A bond fund should compare itself with a bond index

In 1989, the Securities and Exchange Commission, which regulates investment companies, proposed that annual percentage total returns be added to the prospectus, along with a benchmark for comparison. Then all the funds would have to tell. What a great idea! Why has it taken the SEC so long?

Maybe, by the time you read this, you'll have that critical information in hand.

The Name of the Manager

Most funds are led by individual money managers. A minority are managed by committee or under strict rules that limit a manager's freedom to act.

At this writing, the prospectus doesn't have to tell you who makes decisions for the fund or how long the current manager has held the reins. Obviously, that's material information and the SEC has proposed (at last) that it be disclosed. Many funds publish the names voluntarily; the rest ought to tell you if you ask.

So ask. You want to know whether a fund's terrific record was run up by the guy who is still on the job or by a guy who left last week.

THE STATEMENT OF ADDITIONAL INFORMATION (SAI)

The SAI is really Part B of the prospectus, free for the asking from any mutual fund. But it's not sent automatically; you have to ask for it. The SAI reveals a lot more financial data, as well as the compensation of the fund's directors and officers. If you're a numbers person, you'll find it good reading. But the average investor needn't bother.

THE PROPAGANDA

With the prospectus comes sales literature. It shows you "the mountain"—the amount by which your investment would have grown had you been in the fund for many years. Most funds have a mountain, unless they're brand new or have dreadful records. But each mountain shows a different time period, so you can't compare one fund's performance with another's. Nor can you easily spot a year when the fund declined in value. In short, the mountain is there to impress, not inform.

Still, the propaganda can tell you a lot about the fund's investment objectives and how securities are chosen.

THE FUND'S REGULAR REPORTS

Read every communication from your fund's manager. He or she should explain, in plain English, exactly what's going on with your fund —why it's doing better than the market averages, or why not, and what the manager sees ahead. This normally isn't boilerplate; it's serious stuff. All funds have to report semiannually; some report quarterly, too.

These reports include the financial statement, for numbers mavens who understand them. And they show what securities the fund held on the reporting date. Most shareholders shouldn't bother trying to analyze those securities. It's not a job for amateurs. Besides, many of those stocks will have been sold before the report even got in the mail.

HOW DISTRIBUTIONS WORK

A "distribution" is money paid out by a mutual fund to its investors. An *income distribution* (known as a dividend) comes from the interest and dividends earned on a fund's securities. A *capital-gains distribution* is the net profit realized by selling securities that rose in price (after subtracting any losses). Common-stock funds generally make distributions once a year.

There's a critical link between your fund's market price (net asset value) and its capital-gains distribution. Smart buyers keep their eye on it, so as not to lose money.

Say, for example, that a fund's capital-gains distribution is $2 a share. On the day before the distribution, the fund sells for $10. Right afterward, it will sell for $8—reflecting the fact that $2 was handed out to shareholders. Investors still have $10 in value, but only $8 remains part of the fund's net asset value. The other $2 is in your pocket (although you may have used it to buy more fund shares). That $2 is taxable dividend income.

That's where the question of strategic buying comes in. Before making an investment, check the fund's capital-gains distribution date (usually in December). If you buy the fund at $10 and immediately get $2 back, you've been handed a $2 taxable gain with no effective gain on your investment. The best time to buy a fund that makes annual distributions is right after the distribution date.

Stock-and-bond funds often make distributions quarterly. Bond funds may declare dividends daily and pay them monthly. Money market mutual funds credit interest daily.

The distribution date doesn't matter, however, if you own your fund in a tax-deferred retirement plan.

THERE ARE THREE WAYS OF HANDLING DISTRIBUTIONS:

1. Reinvest everything in more fund shares (the right option, for anyone trying to lay a nest egg).

2. Reinvest enough of the distribution to preserve your capital's purchasing power (the right option for people who need income but will be living on their capital for many years).

3. Receive everything in cash (the right option for anyone eating up their nest egg—usually in late old age.)

AUTOMATIC MONTHLY INVESTMENTS

If I had my investment life to live over again, here's what I'd do: From the very first day I got a steady paycheck, I'd put money away regularly. Almost any mutual fund will arrange it. You sign the papers; the papers go to your bank; your bank takes a fixed sum per month out of your checking or savings account and sends it to the fund. There's usually a small fee for each transfer—more, if the money is moved by wire; less, if you use a pre-authorized check. Some funds let you start a monthly investment plan with as little as $100, plus additions of only $25 a month.

I sure wish I'd done it. I got smart too late.

BUYING ON A CONTRACTUAL PLAN

Although I love steady monthly investing, "contractual" plans are something else. They chew up your capital because they charge so much.

As a contractual buyer you agree to put, say, $100 a month into a mutual fund for the next 10 or 15 years. What you don't realize is that half of your first year's contribution goes to the salesperson who signed you up—so you start your investment life with a 50 percent loss. You also have to give up another 5.75 to 8.5 percent of each subsequent contribution. Plus there are service charges. You can quit at any time, but after 18 months you cannot recover any of the sales charges.

The fund you invest in might have a spectacular investment record. But you won't earn nearly that amount because of all the fees you pay. Needless to say, the salesperson forgets to mention that little fact. The sales literature lingers lovingly on the terrific pre-fee results but not on the shareholders' mediocre net return.

By all means contribute monthly to a mutual fund. But arrange it yourself, not through a salesperson's contractual plan. The plan is a waste of your hard-earned money.

MUTUAL FUNDS AND RETIREMENT PLANS

Almost all funds accept Individual Retirement Accounts and Keogh plans. You can transfer money from one retirement account to another without paying any taxes on it. Your mutual fund will tell you how. But taxes may be due when you take money out of a regular mutual-fund account and put it into a retirement account. Your shares are first sold (for a taxable gain or loss) and then reinvested in the retirement account.

MANAGING YOUR ACCOUNT BY PHONE

Many funds (including almost all the major groups) accept telephoned instructions. Once you've made the arrangements, you'll be able to sell shares (up to a certain amount) or switch from one fund to another just by picking up the phone. When you sell by phone, you get the very next price that the fund computes—usually its price at the end of that day.

Normally, the money is mailed (or wired) right away to your home address or a pre-designated bank. But the fund has the right to put off sending the money for up to seven days (as it might, in a market panic).

For security reasons, you can't use the phone to change your address or change the bank the money is wired to. Changes have to be made by mail, over a signature guarantee.

An alternative way of selling fund shares: Switch by telephone into a money market fund. Then write a check against the fund.

MANAGING YOUR ACCOUNT BY MAIL

Don't just write a letter asking the fund to cash some of your shares. First, look in the prospectus (you kept it, of course) to see what the drill is. Maybe a simple letter will do. On the other hand, maybe the procedure is more complicated. Writing that letter may delay things.

There are two ways of redeeming fund shares or switching from one fund to another.

ON YOUR SIGNATURE ONLY—offered by many funds (but not all of them), even if you hold the account with another person. Signature redemptions are good for sums up to a certain limit, with a $25,000 ceiling. (At this writing, the fund industry is thinking about taking the ceiling higher.)

WITH A SIGNATURE GUARANTEE—which means taking each buy or sell order to a bank, stock-exchange member, credit union, or S&L, where someone can guarantee that the signature is yours. On joint accounts, you'll need guarantees for both signatures. (Having your signature notarized isn't enough. Notaries merely check your identity and attest to the fact that they saw you sign it. Guarantors insure that you're the person you claim to be. If you're not, the guarantor makes good the loss.)

Some funds require signature guarantees for all transactions. Some funds let you choose between guarantees and plain signatures. Some funds call for plain signatures on all checks up to a certain limit—usually $5,000 to $25,000—as long as they're payable to the account holder and going to the address of record or to a pre-designated bank. Otherwise, signature guarantees are needed.

Normally, money market funds accept one-signature checks, up to the maximum set by the fund. It is possible, however, to set up the account so that two signatures will be required.

The signature-only option is the easiest and, for most people, sufficiently safe. If someone forges your name, the fund (or its transfer agent) bears the responsibility. If the fund sends a check to your address, and someone forges your signature and cashes it, the responsibility shifts to the bank that took the check.

If you want to keep a single joint owner from making withdrawals from the account, go for two-signature accounts with the added protection of a signature guarantee.

WHAT IF YOU AND YOUR SPOUSE HOLD A FUND JOINTLY, AND ONE OF YOU DECIDES TO SPLIT? OR YOU FEAR THAT THE OTHER WILL SPLIT? Notify the fund, by certified letter, that both signatures will be required to withdraw or transfer any money. This order can be entered by either spouse. If you can prove that the fund made an error in letting your spouse withdraw the money, the fund has to make good.

WHAT IF YOUR SPOUSE FORGES YOUR NAME, GETS THE JOINT CHECK, FORGES YOUR SIGNATURE ON THE CHECK, AND CASHES IT? Your bank is responsible for restoring your half of the money. But you'll have to prove your signature was forged (not easy, given the ease with which many husbands and wives sign each other's names). Your best defense is to notify the bank that you won't be signing any joint checks.

CHECK-A-MONTH WITHDRAWAL PLANS

These are wonderful plans. People who live off their capital should make more use of them. You invest your nest egg for growth in a conservative stock-owning mutual fund, maybe an income fund, a growth-and-income fund, or an equity-income fund. Every month (or every quarter), your fund sends you a check. The check can be paid to you or to someone else. You can stop the checks, or change the amount, anytime you want. Not all funds offer withdrawal plans, but the majority do.

Your income is not paid out of the fund's distributions, all of which are reinvested. Instead, enough of your shares are cashed in every month to give you the income you require. If your check exceeds what the fund earned that month, your withdrawal will reduce your principal.

To start the plan, you usually need at least $10,000 invested, although some funds set up plans for as little as $5,000. There's a minimum check amount and a small fee per check. Withdrawals might be made in one of three ways.

1. You can receive a fixed number of dollars—say $250 a month. More shares will have to be sold when the market dips, and fewer when the market rises.

2. You can receive the proceeds from the sale of a fixed number of shares—say 20 shares a month. You'll get less money when the market dips and more when it rises.

3. You can sometimes receive a fixed percentage of your fund investment—say, monthly checks paid at the rate of 6 percent of capital a year. You'll get less money and sell fewer shares on market dips, and get more money when the market rises.

Withdrawal plans, handy as they are, add to your miseries at tax time, because calculating capital gains is such a pain (page 534). You might find it easier to make a lump-sum withdrawal for the year, put the cash in a bank or money market fund, and make your monthly withdrawals from there.

SHOULD YOU SWITCH-HIT?

This is a game played by market timers. They buy, say, a stock fund that's part of a no-load fund family. When they think stocks are going to fall, they switch out of that fund (by telephone) and into a money market fund. When the market starts looking a little better, they switch back to stocks. Usually there is no switching fee, but some funds charge five dollars or so. Don't switch into and out of a fund with a sales charge, because you will pay it anew every time you buy.

You can switch among funds from different no-load families by trading through discount brokers who offer this service (page 530). The broker earns a small commission on each trade.

As a long-term strategy, however, fund switching is a lousy idea, for several reasons.

First, because few investors can time the market well.

Second, because every time you sell your shares you realize your capital gains. Those gains become taxable—which leaves you with less money to reinvest. If you had left your fund alone, you'd have deferred that tax for years.

Third, because the fund-switching newsletters that crow about their performance don't take taxes into account. So you don't know how well they've done for investors in real life.

Some funds limit the number of switches you can make. Some won't accept switches from subscribers to market-timing newsletters, who swing so much capital in and out that they disrupt the fund's operations. A few won't accept telephone switches at all.

WALTZING THE SECTORS

Sector funds specialize in the stocks of a single industry. There are housing funds, utility funds, energy funds, health-care funds, technology funds, financial-services funds, and many more.

Personally, I think that buying these funds is nuts, because they don't follow the market as a whole. Energy stocks may zoom one year and then collapse, while the action switches to housing stocks. What makes you think you'll be smart enough to hop out of oil and into construction companies at just the right time? If you bought the energy stocks because they just went up, their next move will probably be to plateau or decline. Either way, you won't make money. Someone else's sector will be making money.

Profits aside, sector funds are wrong conceptually. The reason to buy a mutual fund is to diversify over the economy as a whole. A sector fund carries most of the risks of being invested in just one stock.

If you insist on waltzing the sectors, don't think for a moment about holding your fund for the long term. Sector funds reward switchers, not stayers. You have to two-step from fund to fund, hoping to make money and get out quick. The best buys are generally among the sectors that, for the moment, are in the pits. *Bonne chance.*

WHY BE A GROUPIE?

Big mutual-fund groups, known as families, dominate the investment world—brand names like Dreyfus, Fidelity, Vanguard, and T. Rowe Price. They offer a long menu of funds, from the most conservative to the most aggressive. The smaller groups, like Twentieth Century, Dodge & Cox, Evergreen, and Janus, offer a smaller selection, but still a variety of risks.

THERE'S ONLY ONE REASON FOR INSISTING ON A GROUP: You're a market timer, who will sell one fund and buy another as conditions change. In that case, make sure that your group will take telephone switches (not all do), and charge no (or very low) fees when you switch. There should be no sales charges for buying a new fund, and no exit fees for leaving an old one.

Groups matter not at all to the investor who will buy and hold. Just go for the fund that looks the best—in a group or not. For your convenience, some independent funds have forged links with other sponsors' money market funds. You can switch from one to another by telephone.

BUYING A NEWLY ISSUED FUND

Why would you bother? A new fund is a risk. In the early months, the new fund's cash-on-hand may actually drag performance down.

Just about half of the new open-end growth funds (49 percent) do better than average in their first full calendar year; the other half are subpar. Among bond funds, only 45 percent excel in their first year, and among income funds, only 42 percent, according to data gathered by the *No-Load Fund Investor.*

I can see a couple of potential advantages to a new stock fund. It usually starts small, so its winning picks will have more impact than they would on a bigger fund. And it might have a steady flow of cash, which helps a good manager with a lot of bright ideas.

Still, performance is a question mark. Unless you have a strong reason to bet on a particular manager, go with a fund whose record is spread out for all to see. Or wait a few months for the new fund to settle down, and then buy in.

FOLLOWING THE PRICE OF YOUR FUND

There's a telephone number you can call to get your fund's net asset value. Or your newspaper may run a fund-performance chart.

The first column in a newspaper chart shows the net asset value (NAV), also known as the "bid" price. That's what you get when you sell the fund.

The next column shows the "asked" or "offer" price. That's the price you pay when you buy. When the asked price is higher than the NAV, the difference is the upfront sales charge.

The third column shows the change in NAV—how much the value of the fund rose or fell that day. But remember that these changes are only part of the story. To know how well your investment is doing, you also have to count the distributions—which is easy, if you're using your distributions to buy new shares. Just count up the number of shares you have now, multiply by the net asset value, and compare the result with your initial investment. That shows your percentage gain.

Very small funds—with fewer than 1,000 shareholders or less than $25 million in assets—aren't included in the mutual-fund performance tables distributed by the National Association of Securities Dealers. Some newspapers publish the results only of the largest funds.

JUDGING HOW WELL YOUR FUND IS DOING

The best way of checking your fund's performance is to compare it with other funds of the same type. One easy way: Once every three months, get *Barron's* magazine's quarterly roundup of mutual-fund performance. Besides reporting on individual funds, it publishes a table called "Averages by Group," which is calculated by Lipper Analytical Services. Compare your fund's performance with the average to see if you're doing better or worse.

The second-best way of checking fund performance is to compare its annual performance with that of a major market index. An index shows the average performance of a certain type of security. There are bond indexes and stock indexes; you need one that reflects the kinds of investments made by your fund. For the comparison, get your fund's annual performance *without* dividends reinvested, because that's how market indexes are generally reported. Here are the indexes you might want to look at.

STANDARD & POOR'S 500 STOCK INDEX—500 industrial stocks, where the larger companies (with the most shares outstanding) count for more than the smaller ones. Use this as a measure of how well a blue-chip mutual fund ought to perform.

THE DOW JONES INDUSTRIAL AVERAGE—30 blue-chip stocks, with the higher-priced stocks counting more than the lower-priced ones. The Dow is fine for judging daily stock-market activity, but it's not as good a standard as the S&P for mutual funds.

THE VALUE LINE COMPOSITE INDEX—more than 1,600 stocks, treated equally, regardless of size. It tells you how the smaller, more speculative stocks are doing, which makes it a useful benchmark for aggressive growth funds.

THE RUSSELL 2000—covering the 2,000 stocks next in size to the 1,000 largest stocks, as measured by the share price times the number of shares outstanding. This is a good measure of what institutional investors sedately call "secondary stocks," as opposed to the tumbleweeds on the over-the-counter markets. Use it as a benchmark for the smaller company funds.

THE MORGAN STANLEY CAPITAL INTERNATIONAL EUROPE, AUSTRALIA, FAR EAST INDEX—more than 1,000 international stocks. This index, known as the EAFE, can be used as a benchmark for funds invested in foreign stocks.

SALOMON BROTHERS NON-U.S. DOLLAR WORLD BOND INDEX—covering government bonds in nine currencies. The index is published in several different maturities and is a good benchmark for mutual funds invested in foreign bonds. Global bond funds, which include U.S. bond investments, might use Salomon's World Bond Index, or something similar.

SHEARSON LEHMAN BROTHERS GOVERNMENT/CORPORATE BOND INDEX—covering investment-grade bonds. It's one of the standard indexes for measuring the performance of U.S. bond funds.

There's one big problem with standard indexes. They show only the movements of the securities themselves, without subtracting the transaction costs that individual investors have to pay. That's why it's better to compare your fund with the average performance of its group.

BUYING FUNDS FROM A SALES REP

Why would you do it? You're perfectly capable of choosing a mutual fund yourself. This isn't brain surgery, nor are you looking for one fund in a million. Dozens of funds will serve your purposes perfectly well.

Stockbrokers and financial planners pick funds for people who don't want to make the choice themselves. They earn their sales commission by saving you the time and sparing you the responsibility.

But here's the surprise: You can't count on getting as good a fund from a broker or planner as you would have picked yourself. That's because sales reps have other fish to fry.

1. Some load funds pay higher sales commissions than others, so those are the ones that many reps will recommend.

2. Some fund sponsors offer trips and prizes to brokers who sell enough of their products. By buying the GeeWhiz Fund, you're helping your broker win a Hawaiian vacation.

3. Your broker may imply that he or she is earning no sales commission because the mutual fund is "no load." That suggestion is "no truth." The broker is paid, out of 12b-1 fees and contingent deferred sales loads (page 514). Look for them in the prospectus. I wouldn't buy a ticket to Heaven from a sales rep who deceived me about sales commissions, or "couldn't" give me the fund prospectus before closing the sale.

There is always a sales commission when you deal with a stockbroker, with the exception, perhaps, of buying a money market fund. There is always a sales commission when you deal with a financial planner, unless the planner specifically says that he or she accepts only fees (page 833). Any broker or planner who tries to palm off a fund with a hidden load as a no-load is dishonest. You do business with such a person at your own risk.

BUYING FUNDS THROUGH A DISCOUNT BROKER

You can buy no-loads from the fund itself, paying absolutely no sales commission. This is the best and cheapest way of buying. You can also buy many no-load funds through about one-third of the discount stockbrokers (page 546), who charge a modest transaction fee. Why would you buy a no-load fund through a discount broker?

1. You want to switch out of one fund group and into another without going through all the paperwork. The broker can accomplish it. You may pay the regular commission on the sale but only a nominal $10 or so on the new purchase.

2. You want to buy the fund on margin—that is, with borrowed money (page 225).

3. You want to cut down on the paper you see. All of your mutual-fund transactions will be reported on a single monthly statement.

4. You want shares in a fund that requires a $25,000 minimum investment, and you have only $5,000. The broker can still get you in.

Among the discount brokers with a big no-load mutual-fund trade: Charles Schwab, headquartered in San Francisco (800-526-8600), and Jack White, headquartered in San Diego (800-233-3411).

Still, if it were me, I'd buy directly from the fund itself. Why pay even a modest fee if you don't have to?

COMPANY-RUN FUNDS

A few major companies have created mutual funds for their employees—among them General Electric, American Airlines, and Owens-Illinois. Depending on the fund, you can invest as little as $100 at a time or 1 percent of salary, through a payroll deduction plan.

If you're not a regular investor, grab these plans. Buy them just because they're there. When it comes to long-term investing, something is better than nothing.

If you're a more experienced investor, however, give these funds the same fish-eye that you would any other fund. Some of them are terrific; others are extracting high fees for mediocre performance. If your company's fund doesn't measure up, take your money somewhere else.

HOW SAFE IS YOUR FUND?

A mutual fund can't go broke, like a mismanaged savings and loan. It's hard to loot, because the securities are always held by a third-party custodian, usually a bank. You can lose money in a bad market; you can be charged outrageous fees; your investment can be returned in the form of securities rather than cash. But no one ever puts a lock on the door and walks away.

A fund cannot suspend redemptions, except during some general emergency that closes the stock exchanges. Your sell order is always priced on the day it comes in. The fund cannot delay mailing your check for more than seven days.

When a fund becomes unprofitable to run, it is generally bought by a larger fund. If no one wants it, the securities will be liquidated and the proceeds distributed to investors.

THE TRUE NO-LOADS

More than 500 stock and bond mutual funds can be described as true no-loads. They charge no sales commissions and no exit fees and have no active 12b-1 plans.

Below is a list of the major no-load fund groups in 1990, with their telephone numbers. For an updated list, send $1 to the *No-Load Fund Investor*, P.O. Box 283, Hastings-on-Hudson, NY, 10706.

American Association of Retired Persons, *
Washington, D.C.   800-253-AARP
Babson, Kansas City, Missouri   800-422-2766
Benham, Mountain View, California   800-472-3389
CGM, Boston   800-345-4048
Columbia, Portland, Oregon   800-547-1707
Counsellors, New York City   800-888-6878
Dodge & Cox, San Francisco   415-981-1710
Evergreen, Purchase, New York   800-235-0064
GIT, Arlington, Virginia   800-336-3063
Harbor, Toledo, Ohio   800-422-1050
IAI, Minneapolis   612-371-2884

* Sells Scudder funds

Ivy, Hingham, Massachusetts	800-235-3322
Janus, Denver	800-525-3713
Lindner, St. Louis	314-727-5305
Mutual Series, Short Hills, New Jersey	800-448-3863
Neuberger & Berman, New York City	800-877-9700
Newton, Milwaukee	800-242-7229
Nicholas, Milwaukee	414-272-6133
Northeast, Boston	800-225-6704
T. Rowe Price, Baltimore	800-638-5660
Rushmore, Bethesda, Maryland	800-343-3355
SAFECO, Seattle	800-426-6730
Scudder, Boston	800-225-2470
SIT New Beginning, Minneapolis	800-332-5580
SteinRoe, Chicago	800-338-2550
Stratton, Plymouth Meeting, Pennsylvania	800-634-5726
Twentieth Century, Kansas City, Missouri	800-345-2021
Unified, Indianapolis	800-862-7283
United Services, San Antonio	800-873-8637
USAA, San Antonio	800-531-8181
Value Line, New York City	800-223-0818
Vanguard, Valley Forge, Pennsylvania	800-662-7447
WPG, New York City*	800-223-3332

The following groups have some pure no-load funds and some loaded or 12b-1 funds.

Boston Co., Boston	800-343-6324
Dreyfus, Garden City, New York	800-645-6561
Fidelity, Boston	800-544-8888
Lexington, Saddle Brook, New Jersey	800-526-0056

For a useful directory of more than 100 true no-load mutual funds, send $2 to the 100% No-Load Mutual Fund Council, 1501 Broadway, Suite 312, New York, NY, 10036. For each member fund, the directory lists the address, phone number, size, age, investment objectives, minimum investment, and shareholder services.

Two other guides to mutual funds:

1. *Investor's Guide to Low Cost Mutual Funds*, $5 at this writing,

* In New York, 212-908-9582

from the Mutual Fund Education Alliance, 1900 Erie St., Suite 120, Kansas City, MO, 64116. It contains information on more than 275 member no-load and low-load funds, divided by investment objective.

2. *Guide to Mutual Funds*, $5 at this writing, from Guide, Investment Company Institute, P.O. Box 66140, Washington, DC, 20035. It covers more than 2,900 load and no-load funds, also listed by investment objectives.

WHEN TO SELL A MUTUAL FUND

Maybe you want to hold your fund for the long term. But events could change your mind. Consider selling when:

A TOP-PERFORMING MANAGER LEAVES THE FUND. A superstar is a hard act to follow. Sometimes a superb replacement is on hand, but sometimes not. So let your eye stray. You can be a long-term stock investor without being married to a particular mutual fund.

YOUR FUND LAGS THE AVERAGE PERFORMANCE OF ITS GROUP FOR TWO STRAIGHT YEARS. No sense sticking with a mediocrity. To discover its relative performance, see page 527. If you learn that the average equity-income fund rose by 11.5 percent, but yours is up only 8 percent, you should ask the fund why. If the answer doesn't sound convincing look for an equity-income fund with a better long-term record.

YOUR FUND TAKES A DIVE WHEN THE REST OF THE MARKET IS GOING UP. In this case, don't stick around for two years. Your fund is telling you good-bye. Other shareholders may sell, too—and the loss of their money will make it even harder for the fund to reinvest in better ideas.

YOU THINK A BEAR MARKET IS UPON YOU, AND YOU'RE TRYING TO CATCH MARKET CYCLES. Market timers tend to choose aggressive growth funds, which shine in good markets and die in bad ones. Anticipating a bad one, you sell. Of course, you might be wrong about where stocks are heading—but that's the risk of laying these bets.

YOU WANT TO TAKE THE EDGE OFF A LOSS. If you lost money in a mutual fund, take advantage of it. Sell the traitor fund, deduct the eligible loss on your tax return, and buy a better fund of the same type. Don't change your objectives, just your vehicle. You will have improved your investment position while letting Uncle Sam ease the sting of losing money.

HOW YOUR FUND IS (GULP) TAXED

Every April 15, I wish I had never heard of mutual funds. Figuring the income tax on gains is a pain in the neck—especially if you don't keep orderly records. So (read my lips) keep orderly records. You'll hate yourself if you toss all your statements into a file and don't sort them out until tax time comes. Here are the rules.

REPORTING DIVIDENDS AND CAPITAL-GAINS. This is the easy part. In January, your fund will tell you how much you got last year (on a 1099-DIV form—one copy to you, one copy to the IRS). You simply enter that income on your tax return. You owe taxes on the income even if it was automatically reinvested in new fund shares. If the fund sends you any other tax information, read it gratefully. Tax-exempt bond funds should alert you to which of their dividends are taxable in your state, and which are not.

REPORTING CAPITAL GAINS AND LOSSES. This is the hard part. You owe taxes when you make a profit by selling fund shares for more than they cost. And you have deductible losses when you sell shares for less than they cost. The big question is: What is your cost? The cost of each share is what you paid for it (including commission, if it's a load fund). Every time you put money in the fund, you are buying new shares at a new price.

When you reinvest dividends or capital-gains distributions, you are buying new shares at the market price on the day of the reinvestment. Your regular, monthly statement will tell you what price you paid.

As time goes by, you will collect a huge pile of shares, acquired at a wide variety of costs. When you sell a share, then, which share have you sold? Which cost do you use, when figuring your gain or loss?

There are two ways to figure it—a (ha ha) simpler way, known as Average Basis and a (truly) complicated way, known as Cost Basis. Why would you choose the complicated way? Because you're a masochist and because you might want to defer some taxes.

Tax Records: The (Ha Ha) Simpler Way

First, you need a Mutual Fund Notebook. Across the top of the page, enter the headings you see on the facing table, titled *Tax Records: Average Basis*. Start a separate page for each fund. Every time you get a statement from one of your funds, showing purchases and sales (including purchases from the automatic reinvestment of dividends and capital gains), enter the information in your Notebook.

WHENEVER YOU SELL, FIGURE YOUR AVERAGE COST PER SHARE. To do that:

1. Add up the cost of all the shares you have ever bought, including reinvested dividends and capital-gains distributions. On the table below, that's the "Cumulative Cost Basis"—of which you should keep a running tally. (As you will find out later, this is your tax cost, not always your actual cost.)

2. Divide by the number of shares you own. On the table, get this number by adding up what you've entered in the "Number of Shares" column.

3. The result is the "Average Cost per Share." Always keep a tally of the cumulative cost of your shares and how many you own, so you won't have to go back to the beginning every time you sell.

4. Compare the average cost with the sale price. In the table, the average cost is $18.69 and and the sale price is $19.90. So there's a $1.21 capital gain per share.

That's the end of the easy part. From now on, it's no more Mr. Nice Guy.

To prepare yourself for figuring your *next* capital gain or loss, you

TAX RECORDS: AVERAGE BASIS

Date	Kind of transaction	Amount	Number of shares	Price per share	Cumulative cost basis	Average cost per share*
12/31/89	New investment†	$10,000.00	535.3	$18.68	$10,000.00	—
1/20/90	Dividend reinvested	267.87	15.1	17.74	10,267.87	—
1/20/90	Capital-gains distribution reinvested	6,455.92	25.7	17.74	10,723.79	—
3/31/90	New investment	1,000.00	51.3	19.48	11,723.79	—
TOTAL			627.4		11,723.79	$18.69
6/12/90	Sale of shares*	$ 2,500.00	(125.6)‡	$19.90	($2,347.46)§	—
NEW TOTAL			501.8		$9,376.33	$18.69

CAPITAL GAIN PER SHARE: $1.21 (selling price of $19.90 minus the average cost of $18.69).

TOTAL TAXABLE CAPITAL GAIN: $151.98 (the $1.21 capital gain per share times 1.25 shares sold).

* No need to figure the average cost until you sell some shares.
† Including sales charge and exit fee, if any.
‡ Figures in parentheses are reductions.
§ This is your tax cost. For an explanation, see page 536. Not all the numbers match exactly, because of rounding.
Source: T. Rowe Price.

have to determine your new cumulative cost. To do that, you calculate the *tax basis* of the transaction—which is the number of shares you sold multiplied by your *average cost*. On the table, you would multiply 125.6 (number of shares) by $18.69 a share (average cost), to get a tax cost of $2,347.46. Subtracting that from your previous cumulative cost gives you $9,376.33. For tax purposes, that is your new cumulative cost. (Note that none of this has anything to do with the actual money you received for your shares, but that's life in the tax trench.)

You have to specify on your tax return that you're cost averaging. Once you start with this system, you have to continue it for that particular fund. You can't change your cost-reporting method without permission from the IRS.

You also have to specify that you're using either the "single-category method," which means averaging all of your shares together, or the "double-category method," which means averaging all the short-term shares (held for a year or less) and separately averaging all the long-term shares (held for more than a year). In most cases, it's not worth the bother—and saves you no money—to go to the effort of separate categories. Investors generally specify a single category, and move on.

At the end of the year, you'll have the full record to use for preparing your income tax.

Tax Records: The (Truly) Complicated Way

Why would you want to keep more complicated records? Because they let you control the size of any capital gains you take. Normally, you will want to reduce the gain, in order to minimize your current tax.

So get a Mutual Fund Notebook and across the top put the headings you see on the facing table titled *Tax Records: Cost Basis*. Enter all purchases, just as you did on the previous table—including the shares you bought when your dividends and capital gains were reinvested.

Before every sale (it must be before), decide exactly which shares you want to sell and specify them in a dated letter to the mutual fund. Using the example given on the facing page, you might write "Redeem 50 of the March 31, 1990, shares that I purchased at a cost of $19.48 per share." Keep a copy of the letter.

Assume you sell those 50 shares for $19.90. If you sell them against an average cost of $18.69, your gain is $1.21 a share. But if you sell the specific shares you bought on March 31 at $19.48, your gain is only 42 cents a share. So you pay less tax. If you sell the shares you bought on April 31 at $20.03, shown on the table below, you'll have a deductible loss of 13 cents a share, even though the fund has been profitable for you overall.

The complicated method of tax reporting is terrific for deferring your tax. But the bookkeeping is horrendous. You have to keep track, perpetually, of which shares you own and which ones you've sold. In the example below, you sold 50 of the shares bought on March 31. To adjust your records, you would cross off the 51.3 shares bought on that date, subtract the 50 you sold, and indicate that you still have 1.3 of those particular March shares left.

TAX RECORDS: COST BASIS

Date	Kind of transaction	Purchase price	Sale price	Number of shares	Cost basis	Per share gain (loss)	Total taxable gain (loss)
12/31/89	Investment *	$18.68	N/A†	535.3	$10,000.00	N/A	N/A
1/20/90	Dividend reinvested	17.74	N/A	15.1	267.87	N/A	N/A
1/20/90	Capital-gains distribution reinvested	17.74	N/A	25.7	455.92	N/A	N/A
3/31/90	Investment *	19.48	N/A	51.3	1,000.00	N/A	N/A
4/31/90	Investment *	20.03	N/A	49.9	1,000.00	N/A	N/A
6/12/90	Sale of shares bought * on 3/31/90	19.48	$19.90	(50.0)‡	($974.00)§	$0.42	$21
TOTAL				627.3	11,749.79		

At this point, go back and cross off the shares you bought on 3/31/90. Subtract the number of shares you sold, and make the following note of what remains:

6/12/90	Remaining shares purchased on 3/31/90	19.48	N/A	1.3	25.32§	N/A	N/A

* Including sales load and exit fee, if any.
† Not applicable.
‡ Figures in parentheses are reductions.
§ This is the tax-cost basis of what you've sold; see the explanation under "*Important,*" above. Not all numbers match because of rounding.
Source: T. Rowe Price.

Important: To get the proper Cost Basis when you sell shares, you multiply the number of shares sold by the price you paid for them. In the example on page 537, you'd multiply the 50 shares sold by the $19.48 you originally paid. To get the Cost Basis of the remaining shares, you'd multiply 1.3 shares by $19.48.

If you didn't designate which shares to sell, you have to assume that the fund sold the shares you held the longest. Use their cost in figuring your gain or loss. In the table, you'd have sold 50 of the shares you bought on 12/31/89.

In any year when you sell shares, your fund will send you a 1099-B form for tax purposes. This form shows the *total* amount you received for your shares. It does not indicate your net gain or loss. Don't accidentally pay taxes on the whole 1099-B amount! Figure out your profit or loss.

Keep all of your statements and transaction records. At tax time, mutual funds are swamped with requests for duplicates, from shareholders who need them to compute their tax. For a small fee, you can usually get duplicate records for five to seven years back. But why get caught in the crush? Set up a file for original records and keep them.

Don't bother asking your mutual fund to help you figure your income tax. The funds are no dopes. They won't do your accounting for you. For the IRS's official word on how mutual-fund holders should handle their taxes, call 800-424-3676 for IRS Publication 564, Mutual Fund Distributions. It's free.

IF YOU OWN AN INTERNATIONAL FUND OR A U.S. FUND THAT ALSO BUYS FOREIGN SECURITIES, you face the same tax rules that govern any other mutual fund. But then the IRS kicks you again.

The year-end statement from the fund will show your share of any foreign taxes paid. You're entitled to either a tax credit or an itemized deduction for that amount. The credit is worth more, but trust me: Trying to figure it out is an exercise in anguish. Take the tax deduction instead.

CLOSED-END MUTUAL FUNDS

A closed-end mutual fund raises money only once. It sells a fixed number of shares and invests the proceeds. The fund is then listed on a stock exchange or on NASDAQ (the National Association of Securities Dealers Automated Quotations system), just like any other public company. If you want to own shares, you buy them through a stockbroker, paying regular brokerage commissions.

The prospectus normally comes out only once, when the fund is first offered to the public. After that, buyers get regular shareholder reports.

Closed-end funds buy practically everything. But they're especially popular for bonds and international investments. Most of the single-country funds—like the Germany Fund and the Spain Fund—are closed-ends.

WHAT A CLOSED-END FUND IS WORTH

Closed-end funds have two relevant measures of value: (1) the current net asset value (NAV) of all the securities in the portfolio, and (2) the market value of the fund's own shares.

Typically, closed-end funds sell at something less than net asset value—known as a *discount*. Take, for example, the Skyrocket Fund, owner of securities worth $10 a share. You can probably buy it for $9 a share, a discount of 10 percent.

Sometimes, however, investors fall in love with a particular closed-end fund and bid up its price to something more than net asset value—known as a *premium*. If you bought the Skyrocket Fund at $11, it would be selling at a 10 percent premium.

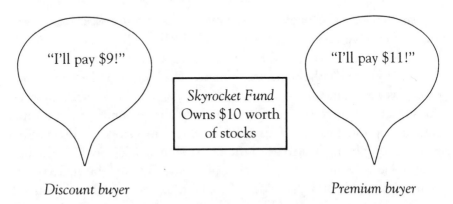

Discount buyer   Premium buyer

Premiums rarely last. When a fund sells for more than its net asset value, it is usually way overpriced. It's almost a certainty that the price will drop.

HERE'S HOW TO PLAY THE CLOSED-ENDS

First, consider the outlook for the fund's basic investments. Do you see a reason for the price of its stocks or bonds to rise?

Second, study the price history of the fund. How low does the discount tend to drop below the fund's net asset value, and what happens then? With the Skyrocket Fund, for example, you might find that every time the discount falls to the 15 percent range, it bounces back—usually to as little as 5 percent under the fund's net asset value.

Long-term investors establish these ranges for several closed-end funds that interest them. One way to do this: Copy two years' worth of premiums and discounts from back issues of *Barron's* magazine, which should be in your public library. When a fund's discount drops into a buy range, buy and hold for long-term appreciation.

But buying and holding isn't typical of closed-end investors. More likely, they trade. They buy when the discount is deep enough—usually, 10 to 15 percent or more. When the discount shrinks to maybe 5 percent, they sell. They buy back when the discount widens again.

Not all deeply discounted funds are good buys. The fund might have bought into a lot of chancy or illiquid enterprises, the expenses may be unusually high, or the funds' past performance unusually low. All these possibilities should be researched. The fund may deserve its low price.

WITH CLOSED-END BOND FUNDS, YOU REALLY HAVE TO KEEP YOUR WITS ABOUT YOU. These funds often give bond investors especially high yields. Sometimes that's legitimate; a fund's yield will rise if its price goes to a discount.

But sometimes the yields are phony. The fund may be paying out capital as well as income—which gives you a bigger check but diminishes the size of your investment. Or the yield might be coming from capital gains or option income. This flim-flam hurts investors in three ways. First, you are being misled as to the fund's actual yield. Second, the net asset value is being eroded, which will eventually hurt the share price. Third, when part of the "dividend" comes from sources other than bond interest, that payment is unlikely to hold. Eventually, the dividend will be cut and the share price will slide. So check on the source of the dividend payments—*before* you invest.

WITH CLOSED-END FUNDS, YOU HAVE THREE WAYS OF MAKING MONEY.
1. The value of its securities can rise. Example: The Skyrocket

Fund, with a net asset value of $10 a share, goes to $12 a share, because the stocks it owns went up in price. You bought it at a 10 percent discount ($9) and, in the market, that discount still holds. Your shares are now worth $10.80 (the new $12 price less 10 percent). Both the net asset value and the share price have risen 20 percent.

2. The discount can shrink. Example: The Skyrocket Fund stays at $10 a share, but investors get interested in its prospects and bid the price up from a 10 percent discount to a 5 percent discount. The $9 price rises to $9.50. The net asset value went nowhere, but investors gained 5.5 percent. Sometimes, a discount even rises to a premium. Occasionally, a closed-end fund switches to open-end, which eliminates the discount.

3. The value of the securities can rise *and* the discount can shrink —the best of all possible worlds. Example: The $10 Skyrocket Fund goes to a $12 net asset value, and the discount shrinks from 10 percent to 5 percent. You bought at $9; now the shares are worth $11.40 (the $12 net asset value minus 5 percent). The net asset value rose 20 percent, but your share value rose 26.6 percent.

NEEDLESS TO SAY, THERE ARE ALSO THREE WAYS OF LOSING MONEY. The net asset value can drop, the discount can deepen (or a premium can drop to a discount), or both of those things can happen at once. The last is the worst of all possible worlds.

You could lose money even when the net asset value is going up. Take the Skyrocket Fund again, with a NAV of $10. You buy it at $12, a 20 percent premium. Stock prices rise, so the NAV goes up to $11. But speculators bail out, and the premium drops to a 10 percent discount. The shares are now worth only $9.90 (the $11 NAV minus 10 percent). So the NAV rose by 10 percent, but investors lost 17.5 percent.

That happens! Especially with funds selling at big premiums. So smarties avoid premiums. And they know the discounts at which a closed-end fund usually trades. Special factors sometimes keep funds at premiums for years, but those prices are almost never worth paying.

A few closed-end funds guarantee you a 10 percent payout each year. It's a gimmick to try to keep the discount from getting too deep. But it doesn't necessarily work and can erode your investment—because, if the fund doesn't earn that much money, your annual payment will come partly out of principal. So don't bother with a gimmick fund. There are plenty of other fish in the sea.

CLOSED-ENDS ARE FOR . . .

1. Anyone who loves stock-market action, because a closed-end fund is a type of stock. You analyze the fund just as you would an individual company and speculate on its price.

2. Any mutual-fund investor interested in betting on a specific foreign country. Single-country open-end mutual funds generally don't exist.

3. Bond investors who find high yields among funds selling at a discount. With this caveat: You have to investigate the yield to find out whether it's for real (page 540).

BUYING A NEW CLOSED-END FUND

There's one simple rule for buying newly issued closed-end funds. Don't. Ever. Never ever.

The offering price of a closed-end fund includes the cost of the offering as well as the commissions paid to the brokers who sell the shares. Buyers pay perhaps 8 percent over the fund's net asset value. The syndicate supports the price while all the shares are being distributed. Then they let it go.

The selling brokers always claim that *this* time, *this* fund will stay at a premium price—which is what persuades their customers to buy. But the price almost always drops. Moral: Buying a closed-end fund on the opening is usually buying into a loss. If you like the fund, wait for it to go to a discount. If it doesn't, forget it and buy something else.

HOW TO BUY A CLOSED-END

Decide on the closed-end you want. Then call a discount stockbroker (page 546), so you'll pay a low commission.

Regular stockbrokers almost never recommend closed-ends, except for new issues that pay them fat commissions. If you ask such a broker to buy you an existing closed-end, he or she may suggest an open-end load fund or unit trust (page 680) instead. The broker will summon "good reasons" for the switch, but only one reason really matters: Brokers earn much higher commissions from load funds and unit trusts. So don't accept a switch. Insist on the closed-end that you asked for.

FOLLOWING YOUR CLOSED-END

The funds' net asset values, share prices, and latest discounts or premiums are reported every Monday in *The Wall Street Journal,* in the financial pages of some other newspapers, and in *Barron's* financial magazine. A leading newsletter in the field is *The Investor's Guide to Closed-End Funds,* P.O. Box 161465, Miami, FL, 33116. Price at this writing: $60 for a two-month trial subscription or $325 a year.

A FINAL SUGGESTION

Here's a strategy for people who crave both wealth and action from their mutual-fund investments.

1. Base your long-term growth investments in open-end mutual funds. Make your selections and (barring poor performance) leave the money there for years. Don't switch in and out in hopes of outguessing the market, because you usually won't. Open-end stock funds may be boring, but eventually they can make you rich.

2. Use closed-end funds to satisfy your urge to play. Buy at deep discounts, sell at narrow discounts, and have a ball. Your trading might not earn you as much as your long-term holdings. But I'll bet that you'll do a lot better than if you tried to trade individual stocks.

23

WORKING WITH A
STOCKBROKER:

Where It Helps and Where It Hurts

—

A stockbroker can make you or—quite literally
—break you. The less you know about
investing, the more breakable you are.

What do you need a stockbroker for?
Only if you want to buy individual stocks, bonds, and other securities.
You place an order with a broker; the broker executes it for you. This is
not like investing in no-load mutual funds, which you can do entirely by
yourself. Stockbrokers are the gatekeepers to the wider market.

Besides handling your orders, a broker may recommend that you buy
specific securities—and here's where things start getting dicey. A conscientious broker should propose common-sense, long-term investments,
tailored to your personal goals and financial position. A less scrupulous
broker will ask "What's the commish?" (meaning "How big is the sales
commission?"), before hitting the phones to call his clients. He pushes
the riskier products that pay him more—yet he may tell you there's no
risk at all.

You can make a lot of money without ever having a stockbroker's name in your Rolodex. Do it by sticking with no-load mutual funds and Treasury securities, which you can buy without any help. But if you do want other investments, the right broker is critical. Much of your success may depend on his or her competence and honesty, as well as how professionally you deal with the relationship.

FIRST, YOU HAVE TO DECIDE WHAT KIND OF A BROKERAGE FIRM YOU NEED. They come in three types.

The most common is the traditional, *full-service broker.* Some are huge, national firms—known as *wirehouses*—like Merrill Lynch, PaineWebber, Dean Witter, and Shearson Lehman Brothers. They offer every service and sell every financial product possible. Or you might prefer a *regional firm* that has special expertise in the stocks of its geographical area—firms like Alex. Brown & Sons in Baltimore, Robert W. Baird in Milwaukee, Piper, Jaffray & Hopwood in Minneapolis, and Sutro & Co. in San Francisco.

The only reason to choose a full-service broker—be it a wirehouse or a regional firm—is for investment advice. Your broker will call you with buying and selling ideas, send you the firm's securities research, handle your orders, keep up with the news about the companies you've bought, schmooze with you about the market, explain what's happening to your stock price (or try to), and help you make investment decisions. For this, you generally pay the full sales commission. Some firms also nickel and dime you with extra charges, like $50 to $60 a year if your account isn't very active.

If you pick your own stocks, however, you don't need a full-service firm. Instead, give your business to a *discount broker.* Discounters generally provide no stock research and offer no investment advice. Their principal job is to execute your orders to buy and sell. For this, they charge lower commissions than a full-service broker does.

Discounters come in two varieties—which one might call "business class" and "coach." In the business class are the Big Three: Charles Schwab & Co., headquartered in San Francisco; Fidelity Investments in Boston; and Quick & Reilly in New York City, all with offices around the country. In terms of the products and services they offer, they are practically indistinguishable from full-service brokers, with one main difference: They don't advise you on which stocks to buy.

Back in coach are the *deep discounters*—beloved of all dedicated stock traders and serious long-term investors. They may offer a limited number of useful investor services. But they're principally bare-bones order-takers. Some even require that the money or securities be in their hands before they'll execute your trade.

HERE'S HOW THE PRICES OF THESE THREE TYPES OF BROKERS COMPARE.

1. The Big Three charge around 55 percent less than the full-service firms (although on some trades they may be only 20 to 30 percent cheaper). You'll get the same savings from banks that offer discount brokerage services.

2. The deep discounters—true bargain shops—charge an average of 73 percent below the full-service firms and 41 percent less than the Big Three, according to a 1990 survey by Mercer, Inc., which reports on the discount brokerage firms.

HERE'S HOW TO DECIDE WHICH TYPE OF BROKER TO USE.

Call a deep discounter for executing one-time trades—for example, if you want to sell all the securities you inherited.

Call a deep discounter all the time if the major service you want from your broker is a low transaction price.

Call one of the Big Three if you're attracted by a special customer service, such as placing your orders via home computer.

Call a full-service broker if you want access to the firm's stock-research department. An experienced investor might keep two accounts; one with a deep discounter for executing his or her own ideas, one with a full-service broker as a resource for other ideas.

Don't call a stockbroker at all if you don't know anything about picking stocks or other investments. Instead, keep your money in a bank, read about no-load mutual funds (Chapter 22), and then buy a fund of your own. Naive investors risk losing a lot of money if they fall into the hands of a manipulative salesperson. Deal with a stockbroker only if you know enough to judge the value of his or her advice.

COMPARISON SHOPPING THE DISCOUNT FIRMS

Each discounter has a different pricing schedule. Some are cheaper for large-volume trades, others are cheaper for trades in high dollar amounts. Fee schedules vary for listed stocks, bonds, options, and other securities. All charge a minimum commission, generally in the area of $30 to $35.

To find the 30 cheapest firms for 25 typical trades, send for Mark Coler's *Discount Brokerage Survey,* Investor's Edition, $29.95 if you cite this book, from Mercer, Inc., 80 Fifth Ave., Suite 800, New York, NY,

10011. The survey includes the names and addresses of 85 discount brokers, as well as price comparisons for more than 115 banks that have discount-brokerage arms. The broker you pick, incidentally, doesn't have to be in your home town. You can handle all your business by phone, fax, and mail.

The table below shows you how much money you can save.

WHAT A STOCKBROKER CHARGES FOR BUYING YOU:			
	100 shares at $30 a share	500 shares at $30 a share	1,000 shares at $30 a share
Typical full-commission broker	$75	$160	$525
The Big Three			
Charles Schwab	49	81	151
Fidelity Investments	48	80.75	150.75
Quick & Reilly	35	57.63	119.98
K. Aufhauser, New York City	22.99	35	74.99
Bidwell & Co., Portland, Oregon	28	45	92.50
Brown & Co., Boston	32	45	95
Pacific Brokerage Services, Los Angeles	25	42	78
York Securities, New York City	35	45	75

Note: Transactions costs, special discounts, and account restrictions may apply.
Source: *Discount Brokerage Survey*, 1990.

CHOOSING A DISCOUNTER

Take a look at the kinds of trades you make: what securities you buy, how often, and how much. Think about the services you want: Will you keep your securities at the brokerage firm? Do you buy on margin? Call some of the firms that interest you and get their brochures. Then call again, and ask the following questions:

1. What securities does the firm trade? Most handle stocks, corporate bonds, and options. Some also trade U.S. Treasury securities, tax-free bonds, and stock-index futures. About one-third trade mutual funds, generally the no-loads (page 530).

2. What commissions are charged for the kinds of trades you usually make?

3. Are there special discounts for large trades? One firm, New York–based Muriel Siebert & Co.—offers individuals who trade thousands of shares the same rock-bottom commissions that institutions get.

4. Must you do a minimum number of trades per year in order to maintain an account? (Even if the answer is yes, the firm will usually take a one-time order—for example, when you're selling inherited securities.)

5. Does the money (or the securities) have to be in your account before the broker will accept an order to buy or sell? Or can you settle within five business days?

6. If you're a steady trader, will the discounters keep custody of your securities? If there's cash in your brokerage account, will it be swept into a money market account to earn interest?

7. Can you place orders by personal computer, if you use one to manage your finances?

8. Is there an asset-management account?

THE ASSET-MANAGEMENT ACCOUNT

Most full-service brokers, some discounters, some large banks, a few insurance companies, and even a few mutual funds offer asset-management accounts. Regular investors love them. These accounts gather up most of your financial transactions and report them to you on a single statement.

You open this account with a minimum deposit of anywhere from $5,000 at Schwab to $25,000 at Fidelity, in cash and securities. The cash usually goes into a money market mutual fund, either taxable or tax exempt.

Different firms offer different ranges of services, but in general, you can use this account as:

• A ready-savings account, paying money market interest rates. Any interest or dividends earned on your investments and any proceeds from the sale of securities are automatically swept into this account—sometimes weekly, sometimes daily—where they will immediately start earning more interest.

• An interest-paying checking account. You can write checks against the cash or securities you hold. You might even be able to pay a merchant by debit card (page 193).

• A source of instant loans, accessed by a credit card.

• A central record keeper. Once a month, you get a statement summarizing all your transactions: purchases and sales of securities, interest and dividends earned, purchases made by check or credit card against your account, and the current value of all your investments. At year-end, you get a cumulative statement for tax purposes. Some asset-management accounts let you code the checks you write, so you can sort them instantly into deductible and nondeductible expenses.

Basic, annual fees run from zero (at Schwab) to $100 at some big banks and brokerage houses. You might also find two tiers of service, one less expensive than the other.

THESE ACCOUNTS DO CARRY ONE PARTICULAR RISK, FOR INVESTORS WHO DON'T UNDERSTAND HOW THEY WORK. At brokerage firms, asset-management accounts are also "margin accounts." That means you can borrow against your securities—generally up to 50 percent against the value of your stocks, convertible bonds, and certain mutual funds; 70 percent against corporate bonds; and 85 to 95 percent against your Treasuries, depending on the broker. You pay a variable rate of interest.

The amount you can borrow is usually featured right at the top of your monthly statement. You obtain the money by writing a check or by putting down your credit card and not repaying the balance in full. The line of credit may be larger than you could get at a prudent bank.

But what happens if you borrow against your securities and then the stock or bond market falls? You'll get a "margin call," asking you to put up more cash. If you can't, some of your securities will be sold out from under you and the money used to repay the debt.

In short, these are not like bank loans—something borrowers may not understand. Margin loans might be called in for payment at any time.

Do not borrow against your securities for consumer purchases. When that happens, you dissipate the net worth you are struggling to build. Borrow against securities only to make other investments—and then, *very* carefully. (For more on margin loans, see page 225.)

HOW TO LEARN ABOUT STOCKS AND BONDS

READ. Three good, classic books on securities analysis are *The Intelligent Investor,* by Benjamin Graham (Harper & Row); *The Battle for Investment Survival,* by Gerald M. Loeb (Fraser Publishing Co.); and *Stock Market Primer,* by Claude N. Rosenberg, Jr. (Warner Books). For a fascinating peek at the mind of a brilliant stock-picker at work, try *One Up on Wall Street* (Penguin), by Peter Lynch, former manager of the Fidelity Magellan Fund. Prowl your library and bookstore for others.

SUBSCRIBE. At minimum, you need *The Wall Street Journal, Barron's, Business Week,* and *Forbes. Kiplinger's Personal Finance Magazine* and *Money* magazine also offer tips to individual investors. Serious students should invest in the weekly *Value Line Investment Survey* ($525, 711 Third Ave., New York, NY, 10017), a guide to public companies, their financial data, and the outlook for their stocks.

JOIN. Try The American Association of Individual Investors (625 North Michigan Ave., Suite 1900, Chicago, IL, 60611). For $49 a year, members get a monthly journal along with other investment information and access to seminars on better investing and financial planning. Or subscribe to AAII's *Computerized Investing* ($60), a bimonthly publication on how to manage your investments by computer. If you join AAII *and* subscribe to *Computerized Investing,* you pay a total of only $79.

Try The National Association of Investment Clubs (1515 East Eleven Mile Rd., Royal Oak, MI, 48067). An individual membership costs $32 a year and includes a subscription to the association's magazine. You can also ask for a manual on how to set up an investment club. Learning in a group is more fun and often more effective than learning on your own.

STUDY. Some schools and colleges offer adult-education courses. But take the time to sit in on a lecture before signing up. You don't want to "study" with a stockbroker whose "courses" are thinly disguised pitches for his or her services. Look for a course taught by a finance professor who has no conflicts of interest.

EXPERIMENT. Set up a "learning account," and use it to buy stocks. Try out the ideas that you've read about in books and magazines. See how it feels to make money and, more important, to lose it. Find out how well you make decisions under conditions of uncertainty. You can't learn on paper. You have to put real money at risk.

THE FULL-SERVICE BROKER

Stockbrokers (or "financial consultants," as they're calling themselves these days) are salespeople. Period. They don't do financial planning, although some may claim to. They're not trained as investment advisors. They don't analyze stocks. Their job is to sell financial products.

Even if they yearn to be serious students of the stock market, they haven't the time. Within three years of joining a major firm, a stockbroker is generally expected to handle $10 million to $30 million a year in buy-and-sell transactions, according to the authors of a useful book called *Winning with Your Stockbroker* (Dearborn Financial Publishing). To do that, they must bring in $40,000 to $120,000 in trades every working day. And to do *that*, they have to spend every minute on the telephone, pitching their current customers and bringing in new ones.

Stockbrokers sincerely want you to do well. Good brokers will think about your long-term objectives and look specifically for investments to match.

But their primary focus is sales commissions. That's what wins them awards and vice-presidencies. When a broker asks a colleague, "How are you doing?" he's not asking "Have your recommendations made money?" All he wants to know is, "How much have you sold and what commissions have you racked up?" The more high-commission products a broker can induce you to buy, the more the broker earns—for himself and for his firm.

The firm, incidentally, is a hard taskmaster. It demands certain levels of commission income. It may circulate each broker's "production" throughout the office to keep up the pressure for higher sales. It lets brokers go if they don't bring in enough accounts or squeeze enough commission income out of the accounts they have.

SO HOW DO YOU FIND A GOOD STOCKBROKER?

I have emphasized the conflicts of interest so that you'll know what you're up against. It's important to know that, kindly and lovely as a broker may be, deep down he or she is not your friend.

HERE'S HOW TO SHOP FOR A FULL-SERVICE BROKER.

1. Gather recommendations from associates whose investment objectives are similar to yours.

2. Call the office managers of the brokerage houses that interest you. Say that you're looking for an *experienced* stockbroker, who entered the business not later than 1980. (That guarantees that he or she will have seen at least one bad market and should have a feel for how to live with another.) Give a brief summary of your resources and your investment objectives and ask for a recommendation. Tell the manager that you want a "good fit," not just the "broker-of-the-day." (The B-O-T-D is the one in line for the next walk-in customer. Often, it's a new broker, or one of the office's less successful brokers.)

3. Stick with firms that belong to the New York Stock Exchange and have been in business for at least 15 years. Firms born of the Great Bull Market may not have staying power. Firms that specialize in issues not listed on the NYSE may be manipulating penny stocks (page 679).

4. Call the brokers on your list, explain that you're looking for someone to help with your investments, and make appointments to interview them by telephone. During the interview, ask how long they've been in business, what colleges they went to and when they graduated, where and when they earned their professional credentials, what other brokerage firms they've worked for, and why they left. Ask what kinds of investments they know the best and which ones they're weak on. Ask what most of their clients buy. An income investor belongs with someone who buys a lot of bonds; a speculator needs a broker who loves new issues and hot stocks. A broker may claim that he's good at everything, but that's not possible. Brokers generally recommend the types of investment that, in their hearts, they like the best.

Tell the brokers about yourself, how much money you'll invest, and what your financial circumstances are. Ask what general kinds of investments they'd suggest for someone like you. Take notes. If you feel that a broker is talking nonsense, or not taking you seriously, or not connecting with your needs, or showing off, or sounding impatient, cross him or her off your list. Also cross off any kids—first, because they still believe the stuff they learned in training school about the virtues of all the firm's financial products, and second, because you don't want a neophyte learning his or her lessons on your money. Kids on the fast track, with a big mortgage, a new Jaguar, and total faith in what they're selling, may push you toward risky investments that pay high commissions. Kids on the slow track may be so afraid of risky investments that they won't invest enough of your money for growth.

5. Ask each broker for the names of three satisfied customers with whom they have worked for at least three years. The broker may say, "That's confidential." You say, "Please get their permission to give out their names." Don't accept excuses or be intimidated by a broker who says that he or she doesn't give referrals. A broker who can't produce happy clients for you to call may not have any. When you talk to the clients, check what the broker has told you against their personal experience. Ask what they think the broker has done for them.

6. Check up on the brokers you're interested in! Check on their college degrees and whether they told the truth about their professional

credentials. Call your state securities office to find out how long they've been registered as stockbrokers, what firms they've worked for, and whether any of their customers filed complaints against them (page 554). All this checking may sound obsessive, but it isn't. You'd be astonished by how many lies are told, even by brokers at famous firms. Here's a story from ex-stockbroker Mary Calhoun of Watertown, Massachusetts, who now acts as an expert witness for customers with claims against their brokers. She says that when she first started, a Merrill Lynch superbroker advised her, "Mary, never tell anyone you've been in business less than seven years!" If you find that a broker has misled you in any way, cross that name off.

7. Once you've finished with the phone work, pare down your list to two or three finalists. Set up personal interviews to see how you like them one-on-one. Also, answer all the questions that the broker is likely to have about you. Discuss how you might best work together. Consider opening accounts with two brokers, not just one. A broker might give a client slightly better prices on, say, bonds, if he knows that he has competition. Also, ask whether the broker offers discounts on sales commissions. Many do if your orders are large enough—especially on ideas that you came up with yourself and that the broker did no work on.

8. If you like to pick some of your own stocks, ask the broker how much help he or she is prepared to give. Some won't give any. They'll send you information on the companies you own, and funnel you research reports from the firm's own analysts. But the rest of their time is reserved for finding customers and taking orders. On the other hand, some brokers will send basic information even on stocks not covered by their firm's research. You might get *Value Line* assessments of the stocks you're interested in, tear sheets on the companies from Standard & Poor's, quarterly and annual reports, the 10K financial disclosure statements that the companies file every year with the Securities and Exchange Commission, and other data that's easy for a brokerage firm to obtain. Spend some time talking to the broker about this, if getting stock information is important to you.

9. Don't be in a rush to find a broker. You've nothing to lose by keeping your money in the bank or a money market mutual fund—even if the market is going up. Stocks, it is said, are like buses. If you miss one, there will be another one by in just a few minutes, and it will be going the same way.

. . .

TO REPLACE A BROKER YOU ALREADY HAVE, GO THROUGH THE SAME PROCESS. Maybe you're uncomfortable with the advice you're getting but not with the firm. In that case, tell the broker—politely—that the relationship isn't working. Then call the office manager and ask to work with someone else. Your original broker shouldn't take offense; this sort of thing happens all the time.

Alternatively, you might want to move to another firm entirely. How you make the switch depends on who's holding your securities. If you hold them yourself, you simply tell the old broker bye-bye and start dealing with your new one. If your securities are at your old firm, fill in an account-transfer form that your new broker will give you. That lets the new broker retrieve your securities while leaving you free to sell them, even though they haven't yet left the old firm's hands. Don't ask the old firm to ship the securities directly to you. That might take weeks of "misunderstandings," arguments, and tears.

COLD CALLS

The phone rings at dinnertime. "Hello, I'm from Famous Brokers, Inc. You've heard of us, of course." Or (a secretary's voice), "Please hold the phone for Mr. von Patter, our vice-president."

You're getting a cold call. A stockbroker has your number and is hoping to hook you before you hang up. "Would you be interested in a rare opportunity? No? How about something medium-rare? You should buy now. This market is ready to move."

Hang up. Say no thanks and good-bye. Don't even wait to hear the spiel. The paragraphs above tell you how to find a stockbroker. Don't settle for one who picked your number from a pack of cards.

DISHING THE DIRT ON YOUR BROKER

Never start an association with a stockbroker and a brokerage house without first checking up on them. Do it even if you're dealing with a well-known firm. Big firms hire hyenas, just as small firms do. A hyena who's a "big producer" (producing huge sales commissions) may be welcome almost everywhere, even though he eventually wipes his customers out.

You can learn a tremendous amount about your broker—at no cost

—by tapping into the computerized Central Registration Depository (CRD), jointly owned by the state divisions of securities regulation and the National Association of Securities Dealers.

The CRD contains the broker's history for the past 10 years—what firms he or she worked for, the reason for leaving, and any years of self-employment or unemployment. It reveals any black marks on the record —gambling convictions, crimes involving money and securities, fraud, bankruptcies, unsatisfied judgments, arbitration awards of $5,000 or more (and smaller amounts, if the original claim was for at least $10,000), and violations of the rules of various regulatory bodies and exchanges. Similar information is recorded about the brokerage firm and its principals (although, at this writing, no arbitration awards against firms are reported). These forms have to be updated any time there's new information—for example, an arbitration decision against the broker, a new complaint, or a change of employment.

TO GET ALL THIS INFORMATION, JUST CALL YOUR STATE SECURITIES OFFICE. For the phone number, ask the information operator in your state capital or call the North American Securities Administrators Association (202-737-0900). Tell the person in your state office that you're planning to open a brokerage account and want background both on the broker and on the firm. Most states give out information by phone and will follow up with copies of the full CRD reports. Other states require a written request. (Don't bother calling the NASD. It costs money, and the NASD—ever protective of the industry—discloses only a fraction of what's on file.)

Most people ask only for the disciplinary record (if any). But you should also get the broker's personal and employment history, as well as the disciplinary record against the firm. Here's what you're looking for.

• Has the broker hopped around from one brokerage house to another? Maybe he churns his way through a book of customers and then starts over somewhere else. Or maybe he works for penny-stock firms that ruin their customers, go out of business, and open up again under another name (page 679).

• Did the broker leave his last firm right after an arbitration award or disciplinary hearing against him? That's not a good sign.

• Is the broker enmeshed in personal troubles—judgments, bankruptcies, lawsuits? At best, they will distract him from his job. At worst, he'll feel pressed to sell the highest-commission products, in order to dig himself out of his hole.

• How long has he or she been practicing? Rookie brokers may fudge on this point. You want someone who has been through both bull and bear markets and has some perspective.

• What kinds of firms has the broker worked for? You'll probably recognize the big national or regional names. But if you see a lot of firms you never heard of, ask your state securities office about them. They may be penny-stock firms.

• What is the firm's disciplinary record? Even minor violations, if there are a lot of them, suggest that the firm isn't paying attention to how its brokers handle accounts. Or it might be a firm that churns a lot of penny stocks.

• What is the broker's disciplinary record? The vast majority of brokers don't have one. You want to be sure that your broker is of that company.

YOUR BASIC BROKERAGE ACCOUNT

When you open an account, a full-service broker willl ask for your full financial profile: savings, investments, liabilities, net worth, investment goals. Don't mislead the broker. He or she needs good information in order to give you good advice. He'll run a credit check on you (and on your spouse, if you live in a community-property state).

Check the form for accuracy and insist on a copy. You might include a simple statement of your objectives, such as "I want to keep my money safe and earn some income. I'd like some growth, but I don't want to take much risk." Or, "My long-term objective is to compound my money at an annual average of 10 percent. I am willing to take prudent risks, but not highly speculative ones." Ask the broker to initial the statement. No offense should be taken, as long as you're friendly and businesslike. The suitability of the broker's recommendations will be measured against your objectives and the financial profile you present.

If you're making a small purchase or sale, a discount broker may ask only for your name, address, and credit references. But if larger trades will go through your account, the discounter may want the same net-worth information that full-service brokers gather.

A *cash account* is for customers who don't want to get fancy. You plan to buy stocks or bonds and pay in cash by the settlement date (usually within five business days of making the trade). When you sell, you return your securities to the broker by the settlement date and receive you money. That's all. Cash-account agreements often preserve your ability to sue, if you think your broker did you wrong. (Some agreements, however, require arbitration—page 570.)

A *margin account* is for people who expect to borrow money from their stockbrokers in order to buy securities. Margin accounts also let you sell short (page 605) and trade a wider variety of securities, like options. Don't sign a margin-account agreement unless you really intend to borrow or invest exotically. Once you have the account, you may be talked into margin buying even though you didn't mean to. Margin agreements may also compel you to take complaints to arbitration rather than to court. If you start with a cash account and subsequently open a margin account, you may find that the latter's arbitration clause embraces the cash account as well.

You may be able to scratch the compulsory arbitration clause, if you're offering the broker a big account. Not that you'll actually want to sue, but it's always nice to have the option. Customers who are obviously interviewing several brokers (page 551) may have a better shot at getting this break than customers who aren't. Some discount brokers and regional firms drop compulsory arbitration as a way of attracting clients.

A *discretionary account* lets the broker buy and sell without getting your permission. That's an open invitation for him or her to earn extra commissions, by stepping up trading in your account. Don't give a broker discretion! Consider it only if you'll be out of the country for a while—and even then, leave your broker only with discretion to sell, not to buy.

A *joint account*—say for husband and wife—allows each of you, separately, to give the stockbroker buy and sell directions. Any check issued from the account, however, will be cut in both your names. If you're into a marital slugfest, your lawyer should notify your broker that any withdrawals from your asset-management account *must* have both signatures on the check. Find out what other steps should be taken to protect your half of the investments.

Disclosure statements, signed when you open a new account, outline all the risks you face—with options, commodities, penny stocks, and any other securities tradable through your account. Read everything. Get explanations for anything you don't understand. If you later complain that you were led down the garden path, the broker will whip out this statement to argue that you knew exactly what you were doing. (But even though you signed the statement, you can still pursue a legitimate claim. You can say that you didn't understand the dangers in a particular investment or that the investment was too risky for someone in your circumstances—page 566.)

A *confirmation slip* shows each buy and sell order—the security, the price, and the broker's commission. Sometimes the commission reads "zero," when in fact the broker has been paid (page 562). Brokers are paid for selling you everything except money market mutual funds.

You have placed an *unsolicited order* when you pick a stock and ask your broker to buy it for you. An order is *solicited* when the broker calls you to recommend the stock. Object immediately if a solicited order is erroneously marked "unsolicited" on your confirmation slip. Ask, in writing, for a correction. When a broker suggests a risky stock, he may try to slip it by as "unsolicited," to give himself some cover if the stock goes bad. A 72-year-old widow might have a good case against a broker who led her into penny gold-mining stocks—but not if the broker can convince the arbitrators that the investment was entirely the widow's idea.

When you do a lot of buying and selling, you might want to keep your securities with your brokerage firm. The shares will be registered in the firm's own name, known as its *street name*. Its records, however, will show that those shares are yours. The companies whose stocks you own will send the broker all your shareholder mail—dividend checks, proxies, annual reports, tender offers. The broker sends the mail on to you. Occasionally, however, you can arrange to receive your quarterly and annual reports from the company directly.

If you trade rarely you may prefer to hold the securities personally. They'll be registered in your own name; the dividend checks and other company mail will come right to you. Keep the securities in a safe deposit box. When you sell, just follow the broker's instructions for signing the securities and mailing them back.

YOU MAY NOT BE ABLE TO HOLD YOUR SECURITIES PERSONALLY, EVEN IF YOU'D LIKE TO. Engraved stock and bond certificates are going the way of the passenger pigeon. Instead, your purchase may be registered by computer in a system known as "book entry." Already, all Treasuries and many municipal bonds are issued only in book-entry form. Your confirmation slip is your proof of ownership—so guard it carefully, just in case your broker's computers go haywire.

And don't suspect your broker of secretly holding on to your Treasury securities. Take my word for it; they no longer exist in paper form.

ONE RISK TO HOLDING SECURITIES PERSONALLY IS THAT YOU MIGHT LOSE THEM, and lost securities can be expensive to replace. Why the high price? Because of the insurance that the issuer has to buy, as proof against the possibility that you, or someone else, might find the securities and cash them in. It's especially costly to lose "bearer bonds," whose coupons anyone can clip.

Replacement takes several weeks to several months. If a lost certificate turns up within a year, however, you might get some of your money back. Fast, free replacements are possible only if newly bought securities, mailed to you, never arrived.

Be sure that your brokerage-house account is covered by the Securities Investor Protection Corporation (SIPC). If a firm fails and can't make all of its customers whole, SIPC steps in. It protects securities accounts worth up to $500,000 (including up to $100,000 in cash). Many brokerage houses buy private insurance that covers even larger amounts.

After a failure, all accounts are usually moved to another firm within a day or two. There's hardly any break in your trading. If some of your securities are missing, because of the firm's tangled record-keeping, SIPC may replace them for you. In that case, you still get all gains or losses in market value since the day the firm closed. If buying replacements is impractical, however, SIPC cashes you out for the value of your securities on the day of the failure.

SALES COMMISSIONS: THE GHOST IN THE CLOSET

Now you have a good broker (you hope). You have a brokerage account and you're starting to trade.

But no matter how well intended your broker, the two of you have no fundamental community of interest. His or her earnings derive not from your investment success but from how often, and how much, you buy and sell. An ethical broker tries to earn commissions without shoving too much down your throat. By contrast, a callous broker may urge you to:

• Trade stocks, instead of holding them for the long term. Shortly after selling you shares in GrandSlam, Inc., your broker may advise that "It's time to take profits." That's two commissions—one for selling GrandSlam and one for buying you another stock. Of course, the broker might be right; maybe you should be taking profits. On the other hand, the broker may be advising other customers to *buy* GrandSlam.

• Buy stocks on margin (page 225). That's risky for you but can raise your broker's commission by 100 percent.

• Buy into investment ideas that require frequent trades, like stock-index options (page 688). The odds of your losing money are high, but your broker can make a fortune.

• Buy certain stocks, bonds, partnerships, or other investments that will particularly profit the firm. To move this merchandise, brokers may be offered higher commissions, bonuses, or points toward a Caribbean vacation. So they hit the phones and call you up. The "analysts" who produce research reports may also get bonuses if you buy the stocks they recommend.

• Buy high-commission products. Instead of selling you plain-vanilla stocks, brokers might push "packaged" products—loaded mutual funds, unit trusts, limited partnerships, and annuities. You'll rarely hear them suggest Treasury securities, because the commission is so low.

But, you say, how can stockbrokers not be preoccupied with how well their customers do? They need satisfied clients, in order to build the business. Yes and no. Obviously, it's nice to have long-term relationships, which many careful brokers cultivate. But when you drop a stockbroker, where do you go? To another stockbroker, natch. And the broker you just left gets some other broker's unhappy customer. So it's just one big shuffle. There are always new suckers—er, customers—coming along.

I should add that a broker needn't be venal or self-interested to burn up your money. He might just be dumb. Here's the comment of a broker who lost an Oklahoma farm couple $200,000 by selling their municipal bonds and putting the money into options trading. "Hey, I'm sorry," he said. "I didn't know what I was doing."

Here's a test for any new broker that you're considering, suggested by former stockbroker Mary Calhoun. Tell the broker that you want to buy a $10,000 Treasury bill (brokerage commission: $50). If he or she says, "Sure," you've probably got a straight shooter. But if the response is, "Why don't you buy our Federal Securities Trust, it's even better," then say good-bye. The broker was trying to switch you to an investment that paid a commission of $300 to $490. The trust is better only for the broker, not for you.

COMMISSIONS UNVEILED

Ever wonder why so many apparently blameless investors wind up buying so much awful stuff? It's the commission structure, which is gravely skewed. Salespeople earn the most by selling you the riskiest investments, or investments whose returns will be hurt by all the expenses loaded onto them.

Graphic proof of what brokers are actively urged to sell lies exposed on the table below. Imagine that you walk into a brokerage firm with $10,000 to invest. That money may generate sales commissions of as little as zero and as much as $1,000, depending on what the broker recommends—and another zero to $1,000 when you sell. Here's the broker's "ladder of temptation":

WHAT A BROKER CAN EARN BY INVESTING $10,000 OF YOUR MONEY

If the broker chooses	The brokerage firm will earn
A limited partnership	$600 to $1,000-plus
An options program	$400 to $1,000-plus *
A loaded † new-issue mutual fund	$600 to $1,000
A loaded † existing mutual fund	$400 to $850
Annuities and life insurance	$400 to $600
Stock bought on margin ‡	$400 to $600
New-issue common stock	$300 to $600
Long-term bonds	$100 to $600
A unit investment trust	$300 to $490
Unmargined stocks on the NYSE §	$200 to $300
Short-term bonds	$50 to $150
U.S. government securities	$50
Bank certificates of deposit	$25 to $50
A no-load mutual fund	nothing

* Options trade often, so these high commissions are paid over and over.
† Front- or rear-end load.
‡ "Margin" means bought with money borrowed from the brokerage house.
§ New York Stock Exchange.
Source: Mary Calhoun.

THESE LOPSIDED COMMISSIONS EXPLAIN A LOT OF THINGS. For example, why might a broker urge you to buy a brand-new mutual fund, with no track record, when you can choose among hundreds of good, seasoned funds already on the market? Answer: He earns a bonus by selling the new one.

And why might a financial planner offer a limited partnership to an older person who says, "I want safety and income," even though partnerships can be high-risk? Answer: she earns more that way.

And why isn't your broker urging you to save state and local income taxes by buying Treasury securities? I don't have to bother writing that answer down.

Your broker almost always earns a commission on anything that he or she sells. So don't be misled if the confirmation slip (confirming your buy or sell order) shows that the broker earned "zero." In many transactions, the compensation to the broker isn't disclosed. This could happen when you buy: (1) new-issue stocks and bonds, where the commission is paid by the issuing company; (2) older bonds bought out of the company's own inventory; and (3) mutual funds that carry 12b-1 fees and exit fees (page 514) instead of an upfront sales charge. The broker earns more on these "zero-commission" sales than he would have by selling you seasoned stocks or mutual funds.

THE RESEARCH DEPARTMENT

Okay, so the broker is driven by commissions. But what about the Famous Brokerage Firm's research department? These workaholics slave night and day over financial reports and computer screens to dope out what's happening to the companies they follow. They know a good buy from a bad one.

But, but, but. The analysts have their necessities, too.

They're an arm of the selling organization. They, too, might earn bonuses or commissions if customers buy the stocks they recommend. They might get special bonuses if their stocks rise in price. They might even be tempted to try to push a stock up, by picking a smaller company and issuing an especially strong recommendation to buy.

They may be held hostage to their firm's investment-banking clients. If, say, their firm is preparing to sell a bond issue for an airline company, the analyst may be pressured to issue a favorable report.

Their best ideas go to the big institutions first. By the time you hear, those institutions may be ready to sell. That's the public's job. To buy up the stocks that the big boys have already wrung the juice from.

Some analysts are afraid to issue negative reports. If they do, their sources in that company might dry up, which could hurt their careers. Or the company might try to harm their reputations, or worse.

Take Marvin Roffman, formerly of the regional brokerage firm Janney Montgomery Scott, in Philadelphia. He once said, in a voice above a whisper, that Donald Trump's casino, the Taj Mahal, wouldn't earn enough money to cover its debt. Trump threatened to sue, and the firm ordered Roffman to recant. When he didn't, he was fired. Janney Montgomery couldn't have cared less that Roffman was telling the public the truth.

In a 1990 survey of leading analysts, done by *Institutional Investor* magazine, 61 percent said they'd been pressured to pull their punches at least once in their careers. And 39 percent did indeed tone down their opinion in their written reports, which go to little guys like you and me. However, they hinted at their true opinions over the phone to major clients.

Here's a quick guide to analysts' recommendations: *Strong buy*—accumulate the stock. *Buy*—the stock isn't collapsing yet, but watch it. *Hold*—sell, as fast as you can. *Sell*—the company failed last week.

You think I'm being cynical? Not cynical enough, by half.

NINE WAYS TO KEEP YOUR BROKER FLYING RIGHT

1. Talk to the broker about your investment goals and how best to balance income, growth, and risk. Set down your conclusions in a letter, ask the broker to initial it, and keep a copy. Those are his or her marching orders. If your letter says, "Prudent growth investments for my nephew's college education 10 years from now," and your broker puts you into stock-index options, you have proof that the investment wasn't suitable. Don't be afraid to present this letter. A good broker finds it helpful to know what your expectations are.

2. Read every word of the account agreement before signing it and get explanations for everything you don't understand. Refuse a margin account if you don't plan to buy on borrowed money. No point being tempted.

3. Confirm every verbal buy or sell order in writing so there's no mistake (and keep a copy). Your letter should include your understanding of the investment's goals. If the broker has told you that this oil-well deal is "safe, for someone who needs income," repeat that promise in your letter. If the hole comes up dry, the letter could help you win an arbitration case. (Remember: A broker, when challenged, will usually say that he or she explained all the risks and you understood them. Your letter shows exactly what you thought you were buying.)

4. Any time a broker recommends an investment, ask: Why are you suggesting this? How does it meet the goals I outlined? How long has

this investment been going up in price? How high are you guessing the price will go, and why? How high is the price/earnings ratio, compared with this stock's historical range (page 599)? What research and financial data can you send me? On a scale of one to ten, how would you rate the market risk? How much do you earn by selling me this? What can go wrong? (There is no investment that can't go wrong.)

Don't decide right then. Get the research material and think about it for a day or two. Never tumble when a broker says, "It's now or never." First, that's rarely true. Second, if it is, say never. Smart investors never buy sight unseen. On the other hand, don't take a week to decide. By then the price may be higher than you ought to pay.

5. Check every slip that confirms a trade. Mistakes are sometimes made in writing up orders. The broker might put down the wrong stock symbol, or write "buy" instead of "sell." If you don't catch the error right away (and didn't confirm your order in writing), the broker may claim that there was no error—and it could be hard for you to prove otherwise.

When you call your broker about a mistake, follow up with a letter. If the error isn't straightened out, call the firm's office manager and ask why. Send the manager a copy of the letter you wrote to the broker. Any broker who is slow to correct a "mistake" may be covering something up.

6. Call (and write) immediately if an investment pitched as "safe" starts to go down or if you suddenly, and unexpectedly, take a loss that you can't afford. The broker might have misrepresented the purchase. But to prove yourself an investor wronged, you must react pronto. Don't dally to see if the price will rise. Too tardy a complaint makes it look as if you're sore only because the speculation failed.

7. Keep written notes of every conversation with your broker, date them, and put them in a file. *This is the best advice on this page!* If the broker ever claims that you gave permission for a trade when you didn't, or argues, falsely, that he or she fully explained a risky investment, your notes will prove otherwise. Arbitrators give a lot of weight to contemporaneous notes, faithfully kept.

Incidentally, let the broker know that you're taking notes—as in, "Just a minute, I'm writing this down." Stockbrokers tend to highlight the promise in any investment and glide over the risks—which might happen less often if they know that their comments are on the record.

8. Keep all paperwork: your new-account agreement, confirmations of trades, monthly statements, copies of the letters you write to your

broker, notes of conversations, literature about your investments. You never know what will help you win an arbitration award.

9. Keep track of the fees and commissions you pay. They're on each confirmation slip, but the brokerage firms (being no dopes) don't normally aggregate them on your monthly statements. Only your broker has the tally—and should send it to you if you ask.

TO FLY RIGHT YOURSELF . . .

. . . Stick to your investment program. By saying yes to what fits and no to what doesn't, you blaze a clear trail for your broker to follow.

. . . Take responsibility for understanding everything you buy. If, after two explanations, you still don't get it, skip it.

. . . Don't whine, or complain, or chew over opportunities lost or opportunities foregone. Let the market bury its dead. This is always the first day of the rest of your investing life.

. . . Don't deceive your broker about the size of your assets, where they're invested, and what other brokerage accounts you keep. A good broker will make better recommendations if he or she knows the whole picture.

. . . Take your losses like a man—er, person. After the crash of 1987, hundreds of speculators tried to walk away from the legitimate debts they owed to their brokers, forcing the brokers to go to court or to arbitration to try to collect.

. . . Don't let greed override the facts. You know in your heart that no investment is risk free. You know in your gut that no one can guarantee an extra-high return. So don't succumb to fantasies.

WHEN BROKERS ARE LIABLE FOR YOUR LOSSES

When you lose money with a broker, you can sometimes force the brokerage firm to give it back. For you to collect, however, the broker has to have handled your money in a way that's specifically illegal (stupidity is not a recompensable offense). Here's a list of the cardinal sins.

1. *Churning.* Securities are constantly bought and sold for your account, solely to generate sales commissions. Sometimes, so much money is siphoned off that it's almost impossible for you to come out ahead. There's no specific rule on how much trading is too much. What's fair in a speculator's account might be illegal in the account of an elderly

widow. To find out what your own broker is doing, average the monthly value of your account over the past 12 months and divide it into the fees and commissions you paid. The result is the percentage return you have to earn just to cover your costs. If you need a return greater than 10 percent (which is the stock market's average long-term return), it's quite likely that you're being churned.

2. *Unsuitable investments.* The broker buys securities that contravene your stated goals or are too risky for someone in your position. Say, for example, that you tell the broker that all you have in the world is $50,000, and that you need it to live on. The broker says, "Sure," and puts you into a real-estate partnership. That investment is totally unsuitable. If you take any losses, the broker should be liable. It makes no difference that you approved the purchase. The broker should never have recommended it in the first place. It may also be unsuitable for a broker to concentrate all of your money in one or two stocks, or to talk you into buying on margin, or even to buy you an aggressive growth stock if you're an elderly widow in desperate need of income.

3. *Unauthorized trading.* The broker buys and sells without your prior permission. This happens more often than you might think and is one strong reason for keeping notes of your conversations. A broker may claim you gave permission when you didn't.

4. *Misrepresentation.* A broker lies about an investment, conceals pertinent information, or plays down known risks. For example, say that your latest monthly statement shows a drop in the value of your account. Your broker might say, falsely, "That's wrong, you're making money. It's just that some of your options profits aren't posted yet." Or, when pitching a real-estate partnership, the broker might tell you, "This is not a risky investment. Real estate is safe, solid, and secure," Similarly, you might be twisted illegally into buying certain stocks. Take the broker who whispers that Red, Inc., is about to merge, and recommends that you load up on it. He neglects to mention that the Justice Department is opposing the takeover. When you read about that in the newspapers, he says that he has a friend at Justice and hears that the government will drop its case. None of that is true. The deal blows apart and your stock heads south. If you can prove any concealments or lies (ideally, from those notes you keep of your conversations with your broker), you should be able to recover your loss.

5. *Overleverage.* A broker induces you to borrow more against your securities than is consistent with your investment goals. Some brokers

may not have fully disclosed the risk of buying securities on margin, or taken the time to see if you really understood. If you didn't grasp the fact that a margin call could cost you some of your stocks, maybe you have a case.

6. *Falsification of documents.* A broker notes on your new-account form or options agreement that you're richer than you really are. This can happen with brokers who peddle high-risk investments, such as options and penny stocks. To trade options, the firm might require you to have a net worth of $100,000, not counting your house. If you're worth less, the broker might put down $100,000 anyway, and later claim that you supplied the false amount. Never sign a brokerage agreement that contains false numbers, or that contains blanks that a broker can fill in later.

7. *Theft.* A broker actually lifts money from your account. For example, your statement might say that your brokerage firm sent you $3,000 from your asset-management account, but it never arrived. Or last month you owned 500 shares of AT&T and now you own only 400 and don't know why. Someone is stealing. A good brokerage firm will always restore these losses. But first you have to notice them. Untold millions of dollars are probably lost each year by people who don't read their brokerage-house statements or don't understand what they read. (Children of elderly parents, take note.)

8. *Unregistered securities.* You can recover your losses if your broker sells a stock, a partnership, or any other security not registered for sale in your state. These are usually over-the-counter stocks selling for less than five dollars a share.

The deadliest sin is incompetence. But it's normally nothing you can collect on. If your broker simply offered muddled advice, and you took it, you'll have to pay. It's not illegal to be dumb.

HOW TO GET ACTION ON YOUR COMPLAINT

ACT IMMEDIATELY. Call your broker the moment anything feels wrong. If you let a problem linger, your complaint may lose its credibility. It might appear that you're angry only because the investment failed.

DON'T YELL. Ask the broker for an explanation and take notes. Ask for his explanation in writing. Tell him exactly how you want the problem corrected ("sell that stock and restore my money"). Send him a letter stating why the investment was unsuitable and reiterating your view of what should be done. If you don't get a written explanation from the broker, it's likely that his verbal excuse won't wash.

FOLLOW UP. If two weeks pass, nothing has changed, and the written explanation hasn't arrived, write a short, polite letter to the head of the brokerage office (call the office and ask for the person's name). Include a copy of the letter you sent to your broker and copies of records that prove your point. These might include monthly account statements, order confirmations, notes to your broker, and the written investment objectives that your broker started out with. State the rule that you think has been violated ("An unsuitable investment for someone in my position. . ." "Misled me as to the risks in options . . ."). Ask for a specific remedy ("Restore my purchase price of $12,000 plus interest lost since 11/13/90 . . ." "Mark on the statement that this trade was solicited, not unsolicited . . ."). Make it clear that you are prepared to take this case further.

If another two weeks pass and still nothing happens, repeat the entire exercise with the president of the brokerage house.

The regrettable truth is that letter writing almost never works. I advise it only because *sometimes* the firm responds favorably, which would save you a lot of trouble. If it rejects your complaint in writing, the letter might support your complaint that the firm doesn't properly supervise its brokers. Some letters falsely state that if you go to arbitration and lose, you'll be liable for the broker's enormous legal fees. That just doesn't happen. The firm is trying to scare you off and should be called on it. Proof of attempted intimidation might win you extra damages from an arbitration panel.

CALL THE COPS. If you get a letter from the firm's lawyer, saying that you're wrong, the broker is right, and your claim is denied, don't fold your tent. Write a letter to the consumer-protection office of your state's division of securities. Enclose copies of your letters to the broker, and copies of the records that prove your claim. Sometimes, your state's enforcers can solve your problem, usually within a few weeks. To get the telephone number of your state securities office, call the North American Securities Administrators Association in Washington, D.C. (202-737-0900). Call the state, too, if the broker simply fails to respond.

(Incidentally, it's rarely effective to write to the Securities and Exchange Commission in Washington, D.C., except to get a letter on the record. An SEC official will refer your complaint back to the offending brokerage house or mutual fund, and you know what that usually means.

No satisfaction at all. Every now and then an SEC letter stirs a little action, but your state enforcers are generally much better.)

BRINGING UP THE BIG GUNS

When a broker does you wrong, and the state securities office can't help, you normally go to arbitration. Either you signed a brokerage-house agreement that requires it, or you deliberately choose to artibrate because it's faster, cheaper, and easier than going to court.

In arbitration, you don't need a lawyer by your side. You need only a clear and well-organized story, any relevant witnesses, and whatever documents support your case.

When a lot of money is at stake, however, spend a couple of hours getting legal advice. Call your state Bar Association and ask for a lawyer who concentrates on securities law or arbitration. Or ask your own lawyer to find you a specialist. A lawyer who doesn't know the field may be worse than no counsel at all.

Make an appointment to discuss your case (for free or for a modest fee). The lawyer will point out the legal issues and tell you whether your case appears strong or weak.

You might want the lawyer to represent you (usually for one-quarter to one-third of your recovery, and nothing if you lose). If the claim is for $25,000 or less, however, the lawyer may tell you it's not worth his time. Another approach is to consult with the lawyer occasionally while you're preparing your case, at the cost of a flat hourly fee.

Experienced lawyers can spot complaints that you didn't even know you had. For example, you might be claiming that the investment was unsuitable, without noticing that the broker was also churning your account. Or you might not think to ask for the brokerage firm's research reports on the stock you bought; instead of following the firm's opinion, the broker might have gone off on his or her own. Good preparation— a lawyer's specialty—is critical. Once your "paper case" is firmly in hand, you can go to the hearing and speak for yourself.

A lawsuit might be possible, depending on the nature of your brokerage agreement. But it's not worth the time and expense unless big bucks are at stake. The types of cases that normally go to court nowadays involve hundreds of thousands of claimants that the brokerage firms don't want to meet in arbitration, one at a time. They'd rather roll them up into a single class-action suit.

HOW TO WIN IN ARBITRATION

When you go to *binding arbitration,* you lay your case before a panel and abide by the result. It's quicker and easier than going to court (although still slow by any standard of justice). The average investor would probably choose arbitration over a lawsuit even if the brokerage firm didn't require it. If you have a big-money claim, however, compulsory arbitration might put a lid on your award—at least, that's what the brokerage firms hope.

Here's how to give yourself the best shot.

CHOOSE THE BEST ARBITRATION PANEL. Arbitration is run by the various securities and commodities exchanges, as well as by the independent American Arbitration Association. Try for an AAA panel; it has a somewhat better record for siding with investors. Perhaps for this reason, your broker may refuse to appear there. (An important New York court decision in 1990 allows customers in any state to choose the AAA if [1] their brokerage agreements are governed by New York law, as many are, and [2] those agreements allow disputes to be settled "in accordance with the rules then in effect" at the New York and American stock exchanges. The rules at the American Stock Exchange may get you to the AAA. It is possible, however, that brokers will rewrite their standard agreements, specifically limiting you to an industry-run panel. At this writing, just a few major brokerage firms are experimenting with allowing certain cases to go before the AAA, if the customers ask for it.)

Of the panels assembled by the securities industry, those run by the National Association of Securities Dealers are generally thought to be the fairest. New York Stock Exchange (NYSE) panels are second best. However, this order of choice varies from city to city, which is why an experienced lawyer's advice can be so helpful. In some cities, the NYSE seems to be okay. In New York City, however, its panels are widely believed to lean toward the industry rather than customer. As the person bringing the complaint, you can choose which of the industry panels to use.

The AAA is more expensive. You pay 3 percent on claims up to $25,000, with a $300 minimum fee. Prices climb from there. A $50,000 claim would cost $1,250. But you may feel that the price is worth it, in view of the fact that the arbitrators are more independent of the securities industry.

Industry panels charge much less. You might pay $30 if you're asking for $1,000 or less; up to $650 for claims in the $50,000 to $100,000 range; and a maximum of $1,800 for claims topping $5 million. If the dispute is settled before the hearing, most or all of the fee will be returned to you. It might also be returned after the hearing, if the panel decides in your favor and thinks that the broker should bear your costs.

Industry panels can and do render fair and impartial judgments, so don't be afraid to use them. Sometimes, they bend over backward to make trusting, but unsophisticated, investors whole. Still, the AAA has a stronger pro-investor record, overall.

SELECT IMPARTIAL ARBITRATORS. For AAA hearings, both sides get the names of 15 arbitrators, along with information on their professional backgrounds. You can reject some of them, if you have a good reason for doing so; the rest are ranked in your order of choice. A panel of three is then assembled.

For securities-industry hearings, you get the names and backgrounds of three arbitrators who have been chosen for the case. You can also ask to see what awards they have made in previous arbitrations (this information is available back to May 1989). Search their records for anything that might worry you. You're allowed to remove any arbitrator who, you have good reason to believe, cannot be impartial. You can remove one arbitrator for no reason at all. Typically, cases are heard by three arbitrators—two from the general public, one from the industry. Selecting arbitrators is another area where consulting a lawyer might help.

At the AAA, incidentally, you cannot get information on how arbitrators decided previous cases they heard. So you're working with less information. On the other hand, you have more names to choose from. If privacy matters to you, AAA awards aren't made public while NYSE and NASD awards are.

GATHER THE INFORMATION YOU NEED TO PROVE YOUR CASE. Here's where your case may be won or lost. Arbitrators hear plenty of cases in which it's the broker's word against the customer's, and they'll often side with the customer. But a little evidence would help.

You should be home free if you kept a running record of your dealings with a broker: for example, the written statement of investment objectives you gave him (and he initialed) when you opened your account; contemporaneous notes of all your conversations, including what the broker told you about each investment; and copies of all of your written instructions.

You need the complete history of your account: all order confirmations, monthly and annual statements, and the new-account agreement showing your financial situation. If you've misplaced any of these documents, ask the brokerage firm to supply them.

Ask for the firm's research on the securities in dispute. Did your broker misrepresent them? Ask for any information it distributed to brokers that described the investment and how to sell it.

Ask for the broker's personnel file, to see what evaluations have been made of his or her performance. Ask for copies of any other complaints against the broker. Get the broker's CRD file (page 554), which will disclose any prior disciplinary actions.

Also ask for the firm's compliance manual. From that, you'll learn whether your broker violated any of the firm's own rules. Do the rules say, "Don't concentrate a client's money in just one or two securities"? Do they say, "Recommend only the stocks that we do research reports on"? If your broker strayed off the reservation, your case is half proved. The manual will also instruct the office manager on how brokers should be supervised—instructions that, in your case, were probably not followed.

The brokerage firm is required to meet your reasonable requests for information. If it resists (and it often does), ask for help from your arbitrator. Schedule a prehearing conference and ask that the firm be ordered to cooperate. Insist on getting the documents by a specified date, so you'll have time to study them. Sometimes documents are produced, quite literally, at the hearing-room door. If you think that the hearing will take two days instead of one, discuss that at a prehearing conference, too. Otherwise, your two days of hearings might be scheduled weeks or months apart. Insist that they run consecutively. Appeal up through the line if the arbitrating body's staff attorney refuses your request.

You will also have to supply data to your brokerage firm—for example, personal financial information and your investment history with any other firm. The broker will be trying to prove that you are a sophisticated investor who knew exactly what you were doing. (However, if, before you met this broker, you kept most of your money in certificates of deposit, that's evidence in your favor, not in his.)

LINE UP WITNESSES. Maybe you know other customers whom the broker similarly misled. Maybe you have another broker who can testify that you always asked only for conservative investments. Maybe someone at work heard you discussing the investment with your broker, and heard you repeat the broker's claim that there was "no risk." You may be able to bring an affidavit from a witness who couldn't appear.

If you want to call the firm's office manager or compliance officer as a witness, and the firm refuses, ask your arbitrator to order it. You might want to ask these officers what they were doing while your broker sold you—a grandmother living on her capital—an oil-and-gas limited partnership. The firm's compliance manual doubtless says that they shouldn't have let such a sale stand. Unfortunately, these witnesses still might not appear. You don't have as many rights in arbitration proceedings as you have in court.

TRY TO SETTLE THE CASE. Now that arbitration awards are being made public, some firms are more willing to settle cases in advance. The stronger your evidence, the more likely they are to make a deal—so accumulate your "paper case" before talking settlement. Your minimum demand should be all your money back, plus interest from the day that the ill-advised investment was made.

In your dealings with the brokerage house, don't shout, don't weep, don't accuse, don't tremble. Lay out your demands in a businesslike way and stick to them.

ASK FOR HEARINGS IN A CONVENIENT PLACE. Hearings should be held in a large city near where you live. Ordinary cases should take a day, maybe two. But complicated cases may stretch over several months—making them almost as troublesome as a lawsuit to pursue.

If your damages come to $10,000 or less, you can ask for simplified arbitration, which doesn't require you to appear in person. You can send a written claim plus statements from witnesses and supporting proof, and wait for a decision. (But being there in person, wearing all your innocence on your sleeve, can help your case.)

ORGANIZE YOUR STORY IN ADVANCE AND PRACTICE TELLING IT. Arbitrators are accustomed to hearing clients present their own cases and will do their best to help you along. You can help them by telling the story in an orderly way and organizing it around the specific points of law that you think the broker violated. Be as clear and forceful as you possibly can.

Typically, each side makes a brief opening statement. Then you present evidence and witnesses. The brokerage firm (which will always have a lawyer) will do the same. Each side will cross-examine the other. The arbitrators question both of you and listen to your final statements.

In general, investors complain that their broker soft-soaped them into thinking that a risky investment was safe, or didn't act on their orders to sell an investment that subsequently declined. The broker replies that the customer knew exactly what he or she was doing and is sore only because the investment failed. The wealthier you are, and the better established in your profession, the tougher it is to argue that you're a Wall Street innocent, even when you are. That's why notes of your conversations with your broker can be so important. They establish what the broker told you at the time.

About six weeks after the hearing ends, you get a decision in the mail. Arbitrators go by what they think is fair, not just by legal precedents. You usually cannot appeal.

PUT A LAWYER ON THE CASE FULL-TIME IF THE CLAIM IS FOR IMPORTANT MONEY. The broker will most definitely bring in a lawyer against you, and the higher the stakes, the tougher the fight.

In cases of flagrant abuse, arbitration panels are starting to award more punitive damages. These are assessed when the broker's behavior is so outrageous that conscience recoils from merely requiring that he or she give the money back.

In 1990, an Oklahoma City arbitration panel brought in arbitration's first RICO (racketeering) award in a case of securities fraud—$1.1 million, against Shearson Lehman Brothers. RICO cases cost an offender triple damages.

You will definitely need a lawyer to represent you if you're going for punitive damages or a RICO award. Lawyers say that the risk presented by these huge claims is encouraging more brokerage firms to settle cases before arbitration.

FOR MORE INFORMATION . . .

The arbitration forums publish consumer guides, explaining exactly how to pursue a claim. For information, write to the Director of Arbitration at:

· The American Arbitration Association, 140 West 51st St., New York, NY, 10020.

· The National Association of Securities Dealers, 33 Whitehall St., New York, 10004.

· The New York Stock Exchange, 11 Wall St., New York, NY, 10005.

· The National Futures Association (for complaints against commodity brokers), 200 West Madison St., Suite 1600, Chicago, IL, 60606. Almost any customer with a modest income and few assets who has been fast-talked into buying options on futures has a good chance of winning. These investments are simply too risky for people like you.

TRUTH BREAKS OUT

A couple of years ago I got a letter from a stockbroker that made a strong impression on me. I had written some newspaper columns that criticized certain shoddy sales practices, and mail from furious brokers was raining down on me. But this letter was different.

I have been employed as a broker for the past 15 years. Most of those years have been with a major (brokerage) house. I must admit that at first your columns angered me as much as anyone who has ever had their lucrative employment threatened by an "outsider." But upon reflection, I am convinced you are right. . . .

The first thing a securities salesman learns is to gain the confidence of his customer. This enables the salesman to more easily sell the customer the products that pay the salesman the highest commission. All securities firms have different commission schedules for different investment products. Most firms will respond that their brokers are free to sell their customers any investment product they wish. But in practice, the broker-salesman is "encouraged" to sell the product most profitable to the firm and do it often. All securities firms also have formulas that indicate how often customer's money should turn over, and these are considered minimums. . . .

When I first entered the business, our firm had a broker who can truly be considered a "customer's man." He had the most clients, and the most money of his clients under his control, that I had ever heard of to that point. The firm's management took the view that he was not producing enough commis-

sions. *The broker said that we were in the middle of a bear market (this was 1974), and he was not going to squander his client's money to produce commissions for the firm. The firm finally pressured the broker so much that he resigned.*

We younger, hungrier brokers fell upon his book of clients like a pack of hungry wolves, and tried everything to keep that book and generate commissions. But I don't think we kept a single one. . . .

I don't want you to conclude from what I have written that I am like that broker—far from it. I, too, have fallen prey to the siren's song of wealth and glamour that has been and is Wall Street. I have overtraded customer accounts, and bought for them "investments" that made more sense for me than them. I guess I wrote (to you) as a catharsis, and to clear my head and that of my colleagues of the siren's song.

The letter was signed "Anonymous Vice-President, Investments, Major Investment Firm," with an invitation to write if I wanted the writer to disclose his name. How tragic to feel that your whole life has been built upon a fraud.

NO-BROKER BUYING: DIVIDEND REINVESTMENT PLANS

More than 1,000 U.S. companies let you buy additional shares without going through a stockbroker. You do it by reinvesting dividends directly in new shares. It's a great deal, when you can get it. Automatic reinvestment keeps those dividends from being frittered away. Consider this example, given by *Money* magazine: In 1985, you could have bought 100 shares of AT&T for $1,950 with a yield, at that time, of 6.2 percent. Had you taken your dividends in cash and spent the money, your shares would have been worth $4,550 five years later. But if you automatically reinvested the dividends, your investment would have grown to 124 shares worth $5,624.

Many dividend reinvestment plans also let you invest cash, ranging from as little as $10 a month to as much as $5,000 a quarter, depending on the company. You generally buy at the current market price—although some firms sell their shares at a small discount, usually around 5 percent. (The amount of the discount is considered taxable income in the year you buy.) You pay little or nothing, either to buy or to sell. But you usually can't sell quickly; it might take four weeks or longer to get your money.

For the names of these companies, and the details of their plans, write for the *Directory of Companies Offering Dividend Reinvestment Plans,* $28.95 at this writing, from Evergreen Enterprises, P.O. Box 763, Laurel, MD, 20725. For a straight list of companies, with no information on each plan, send $2 to Standard & Poor's, Direct Marketing, 25 Broadway, New York, NY, 10004.

Warning: It can be the very devil to figure out your income taxes when you want to sell. Every dividend payment bought you shares, or fractions of shares, at a different price. Your company should have a list of which shares you bought when, if you didn't keep the record. But it's going to be a challenge to figure out your capital gains.

FINDING GOLD IN OLD STOCKS AND BONDS

Maybe you own some mystery securities—stocks or bonds you inherited, or bought years ago, whose prices aren't listed in the newspaper. Some of those companies have expired. But others may be alive and earning profits, maybe as divisions of larger companies. Or they simply may be too small to make your newspaper's daily stock listings. Here's how to find out if your securities have any value.

• Call the information operator in the city where you last knew the corporation to be. It may still be operating at the same old stand. When you get the telephone number, call the company and ask for its share price.

• Write to the company at its last known address, or look for the address in your library. One source: Dun & Bradstreet's *Million Dollar Directory,* which lists 160,000 U.S. corporations with a tangible net worth of more than $500,000. If you find the address, write to the treasurer, who will know what your securities are worth.

• Ask your stockbroker, if you have one. He or she might find the company in the *National Stock Summary,* in the *Pink Sheets,* which list thousands of small companies whose names aren't included in the stock quotations in the newspapers, or in some other reference book.

• Send photocopies of the certificates to R. M. Smythe & Co., 26 Broadway, Suite 271, New York, NY, 10004, with a self-addressed, stamped envelope. Smythe will find out whether each security has value or should be written off as a loss on your income-tax return. The search takes two to three weeks. Cost: $50 for each company.

Don't throw out old stock or bond certificates unless you learn that the company formally went out of business. Even moribund firms are sometimes brought to life again.

INVESTMENT NEWSLETTERS

To add to your knowledge of investing, try subscribing to a range of newsletters. You can buy almost any view on the market that appeals to you. There are market-timing letters. Growth-stock letters. Psychic-advisory letters. Mutual-fund letters. Bond letters. Insider-buying letters. Asset-allocation letters. Technical-analysis letters. Precious-metal letters. Morning-in-America letters. End-of-the-world letters. Letters that channel the spirit of Bernard Baruch. For just $150, anyone can register with the Securities and Exchange Commission as an investment advisor and present himself as a market guru. To publish a newsletter, you don't even have to be registered.

Because of their quirky unevenness, newsletters aren't for stock market innocents. You have to be able to tell the sound from the wacky, the smart from the ordinary. Some are promoted with spurious claims. You might laugh off a writer who claims "874 percent on your money in eight months!" But what about one who claims 35 percent? Is that true or false?

For anyone who already knows something about securities, and wants some fresh sources of ideas, interesting letters make useful reading. Here's how to find some.

1. Buy the first-class *Hulbert Guide to Financial Newsletters* (at this writing, $24.95, from the Hulbert Financial Digest, 316 Commerce St., Alexandria, VA, 22314). Hulbert reviews more than 100 newsletters, compares their performance with the standard market averages, assesses the level of risk they'd expose you to, and—especially welcome—ranks them for clarity. No point reading a newsletter that keeps you guessing.

You want a letter with good five-year performance, whose advice doesn't require daily phone calls to a hot line, and whose risk level you can tolerate.

The average investor cannot make useful comparisons between the published performance results of two different newsletters. They'll cover different time periods, the figures are unaudited, and you don't know how the data were massaged. That's why Hulbert's performance data are so valuable. They're stated in a uniform way for all letters, so that their records *can* be compared. Hulbert also deducts brokerage commissions, which gives a more realistic picture of what a market letter really can do for you.

2. Once you've made some tentative picks from Hulbert's guide, write to the Select Information Exchange, 2315 Broadway, New York, NY, 10024 for its free catalogue, which describes newsletters in all fields. One recent offer: Short trial subscriptions to 20 different letters for $11.95.

INVESTMENT ADVISORS

If you have a large sum of money to invest, *maybe* you'll want a personal investment advisor. Some advisors handle as little as $50,000 or $100,000. But the best people usually set minimums of $1 million and up.

For the smaller accounts, a personal advisor is a vanity play. Why would you need one? Some of this country's best investment brains run no-load mutual funds and charge you maybe 1 percent of assets per year. An advisor probably won't do any better and may cost you 2 or 3 percent, including commissions and custodial fees. What's more, you'll get that manager's standard stock or bond portfolio, which isn't much different from being in a fund. I'd guess that a no-load mutual fund—with its lower fees—will net you more than most advisors can deliver. To me, mutual funds make sense even for people with $1 million or $2 million to invest.

But one of the badges of prosperity is a personal advisor who will meet with you, take your calls, and make you feel more privileged than the hoi polloi in mutual funds. As I said, a vanity play.

A private advisor makes economic sense only if you meet the $1 million minimum and:

• You face a lot of family complications and need a good mind to lead your money through the minefields.

• You have no time whatsoever to think about money management and don't want to.

• You don't feel sure enough of yourself to pick some good mutual funds (although, after reading Chapter 22, I don't know why not!).

• You have a truly large pot of money, like $10 million and up, and want to consult someone continuously about how it should be deployed.

Most investment advisors are acquired through personal recommendations. A free directory of the larger independent advisory firms (but not those associated with broker-dealers or firms that have only one principal) can be had from the Investment Counsel Association of America (20 Exchange Place, New York, NY, 10005). But don't even ask for the directory unless you have at least $1 million. Only five of the 150 advisors that ICA lists accept accounts smaller than that.

A few consultants specialize in finding investment advisors for you. One such: Michael Stolper, Stolper & Co, 525 B St., Suite 630, San Diego, CA, 92101. His minimum fee is $3,000, but it often runs higher. Stolper's managers also want minimum accounts in the $1 million range.

The majority of middle-monied people who seek personal attention head for bank trust departments. Some are mediocre. Others have excellent investment records. To tell which is which, compare the performance of the bank's own pooled funds with standard stock or bond indexes (which is data that the bank should provide). Also, see how well the bank's funds stand up to the average mutual fund, whose performance you can find quarterly in *Barron's* magazine. Check the bank's fees and don't accept its trust documents without having an estate-planning lawyer of your own review them. Your biggest question: Is there any impediment to quitting this deal if I don't like the results? Stay away from a bank that tries to lock you in, or locks in your heirs. The bank should *always* be earning the right to keep your money.

WRAP ACCOUNTS

One day your stockbroker may make a suggestion: Instead of picking stocks and paying sales commissions, why not sign up for a wrap account. With a wrap, both you and the broker quit trying to manage your money. Instead, you jointly pick an investment advisor who will do the job for you. Minimum size for a wrap account is generally $100,000, although some brokers take $50,000. You should get prudent, professional diversification to meet a specified level of risk—which is more than your broker can accomplish.

You pay a flat fee—on stock portfolios, generally 3 percent of assets up to $500,000, and less for larger sums; on bond portfolios, around 1.25 percent on the first $500,000. You don't pay sales commissions on trades, and there should be no markups on any securities bought out of your broker's inventory. The manager provides quarterly performance reports, showing just how well your account is doing compared with standard indexes. At big brokerage firms, you can tap into money managers who normally have minimums of $1 million and up. Regional houses may simply help you find appropriate managers who already offer $100,000 minimums.

In theory, I hate wrap accounts, because the fee is too high. For a mere 1 percent, you could have your $100,000 managed by some of the best brains in the country, who run the top no-load mutual funds. Or, if you want to wear a personal investment advisor like a badge, you could hire one directly, for a total cost, including custodial fees and commissions, of maybe 1.5 percent.

But in practice, a lot of people do stick with their brokerage firms, and for them wrap accounts are a better way. The fee might even be a bargain, if it stops the broker from selling them high-commission products or overtrading their accounts. In any event, wraps end the broker's conflict of interest. His income grows only if your assets do. If your manager stumbles, it costs you nothing extra to switch.

A FINAL WORD

Who really needs a stockbroker? To me, the conventional answer is all wrong.

You're advised to find a broker if you're a new investor, if you're inexperienced, or if you need a lot of help in reaching your investment decisions. Yet these are the very people least able to tell a good broker from a bad one, and the most susceptible to bad advice.

I'd say: If you're a new or inexperienced investor, *don't look for a stockbroker at all!* You can't afford the learning experience. Choose a no-load mutual fund and relax. Only a savvy investor can pick what's choice from a broker's patter and blow off the rest.

There ought to be an admissions test for opening a brokerage account, kind of like SAT tests for college admissions. If you don't score above "innocent" on the Verbal and Math, a kindly investor-protection angel would tell you that a stockbroker isn't for you.

24

YOUR TICKET TO
THE FUTURE:

Stocks—The Growth Investment

Over the long term, stocks beat the tar out of other financial investments. If you haven't yet noticed my preference for stock-owning mutual funds, you've been using this book as a doorstop.

You need two main things from your investments, and stocks offer both. (1) *Real growth*—so that after inflation and taxes you will have more money than you started with. Over the long term, stocks run about 7 percentage points over the inflation rate. By contrast, long-term Treasury bonds run only 1.8 percentage points over, so that after taxes bonds fall behind. (2) *Income*—in case you need to live off your capital. Stocks pay dividends. If you're in a stock-owning mutual fund, that fund will send you a check every month for whatever sum you like (page 524).

WHAT MAKES STOCK PRICES RISE?

Plain old supply and demand. Prices rise when more people want to buy a stock than want to sell it. That happens when:

1. Investors believe that the company's earnings will improve—because of a strong economy, a new product, improved management, and so on.

2. The market in general is moving up, creating enthusiasm for all kinds of shares.

3. Interest rates just dropped, which makes stocks more attractive relative to bonds. (However, if it's early in what turns out to be a long recession, stock prices and interest rates might fall together for a while. In this business there are no guarantees.)

4. There's a takeover offer, or the hope of one.

The reverse of these conditions leads more people to sell stocks than buy them, which makes prices fall.

For all my enthusiasm about stocks, I'm not looking for a repeat of the 1980s. Those were stunning years; stocks gained a compounded 17.5 percent annually. But we have never had two such decades back to back. Super returns are more likely to be followed by average or subnormal returns.

In the 1980s, the smaller companies fell behind the larger ones—but that's typical in a decade when the market does exceptionally well. In quieter decades, the action lies with smaller stocks. If the historical pattern holds, that should make them a buy for the 1990s. Smaller companies have returned 12 percent compounded annually over the long term, while the larger companies have returned only 10 percent.

There are two ways of buying into stocks. You can pick individual issues or you can buy mutual funds.

BUYING STOCK-OWNING MUTUAL FUNDS

Maybe you think that mutual funds are a little dull.

In a way, they are. You can make a lot of money just by buying them and forgetting them. Rightly used, mutual funds have almost no entertainment value.

That's exactly why I like them. For thrills, I go to the racetrack. For my retirement, I buy mutual funds.

Even if you love the blood sport of buying individual stocks, use mutual funds for your core holdings (if you need to be reminded of why this is such a good idea, see page 503).

You might start with an index fund (page 588). Alternatively, start with two funds—one that's adventurous (buying growth stocks or small-company stocks) and one that's more conservative (a growth-and-income fund or equity-income fund, both of which buy dividend-paying stocks).

Another approach is to give some of your money to a "value" manager, who seeks out-of-favor stocks that are selling at low prices and some to a "growth" manager, who picks stocks whose earnings appear to be accelerating.

As your savings increase, add a fund that's invested in foreign stocks.

In the next few pages, I've listed the main types of mutual funds, what they do, and who they're best for. You'll also find the names of some good no-load funds in each category, chosen in 1990 by the San Francisco money-management firm of Brouwer & Janachowski, Inc. * Obviously, no stock-fund recommendations last forever. But those listed below all have seasoned managers and excellent records. Their current performance is at least worth a look. (For where they're located, see page 588.)

Brouwer & Janachowski paid particular attention to how well each fund held up during bad markets. If you can do reasonably well when stock prices rise and minimize losses when prices fall, you should get superior performance over time.

1. AGGRESSIVE GROWTH FUNDS—buy companies whose earnings are apparently rising fast. These funds are a blur of buy and sell, hopping on to stocks that are going up, hopping off stocks whose prices stall. Dividends are slim.

If all goes well: Aggressive growth funds shine in rising markets and most markets rise. So many of them have superior records over the long term. They usually bounce back strongly after a stock-market drop.

What to worry about: They get creamed when markets fall. You have to be prepared to suffer.

Who should buy: Crazy speculators. Market timers who want to try

---

* Brouwer & Janachowski invests $175 million of its clients' money in no-load mutual funds. Minimum account: $500,000.

their luck at buying into market rises and bailing out of market drops. Investors with nerve.

Some funds with good records: The Kaufmann Fund and RCS Emerging Growth Fund, both very small. For a slightly better record in down markets, look at General Aggressive Growth, a fund sponsored by the Dreyfus group.

2. SMALL-COMPANY FUNDS—growth funds that specialize in "small capitalization" stocks. Generally speaking, a stock is "small cap" when its share price, multiplied by the number of shares outstanding, comes to less than $250 million. Some small-cap funds buy big companies, too.

If all goes well: Over long time periods, the small caps do better than any other group of funds.

What to worry about: They're hammered in bad markets, and may do worse than the average fund for several years in a row. For example, they pooped out in the second half of the 1980s (which suggests that, in the 1990s, they may catch up).

Who should buy: Long-term, performance-minded investors who don't scare easily and will hold for at least five years.

Some funds with good records: Acorn, Columbia Special, Janus Venture, and Pennsylvania Mutual.

3. ASSET-ALLOCATION FUNDS—own several different types of assets—U.S. stocks, foreign stocks, bonds, money market instruments, real-estate stocks, gold stocks, and so on. A "fixed-mix" fund keeps a fixed percentage of your money in each asset—30 percent in U.S. stocks, 30 percent in bonds, 20 percent in foreign stocks, and so forth. A "flexible-mix" fund moves money from market to market, emphasizing the investments that it thinks will do best.

If all goes well: Your gains equal those of the average stock fund. But when the stock market falls, your fund shouldn't fall nearly as much.

What to worry about: The manager may allocate your assets poorly. Typically, you'll get some protection when the market turns down but won't do very well when the market turns up.

Who should buy: I'm not sure that anyone should. The jury is still out on whether asset-allocation funds will succeed. Don't equate their approach with individual asset allocation, where you choose investments to suit your objectives. These funds aim for competitive stock-market performance, which they may find tough to reach.

Some funds with good records: None. The few that have been around for a while are tilted toward inflation investments, which didn't serve them well in the 1980s. And the newer funds haven't been around long enough to judge.

4. SECTOR FUNDS—specialize in the stocks of a particular industry. They buy only housing stocks, or airline stocks, or health-care stocks, or biotechnology stocks—the sector list goes on and on. A fund will typically move up strongly, then stagnate or fall as buying interest moves to some other industry.

If all goes well: You will pick exactly the sector that's about to move up, and will sell your fund before that sector peters out. Then you'll hop to another sector that's about to move up. You'll do this successfully, over and over (pinch me, I'm dreaming).

What to worry about: You'll buy a fund after its big move up. As soon as you buy, it will go limp. You might catch the losses but not the gains.

Who should buy: Highly experienced investors who understand how various industries respond to changes in the economy and who have a good track record for picking individual stocks.

Some funds with good records: Forget it. None of these funds is a long-term hold.

5. INTERNATIONAL FUNDS—for foreign stocks. Every growth investor should consider them. (See Chapter 27.)

Some funds with good records: T. Rowe Price International Stock, and two Vanguard funds: Trustees Commingled–International Equity and Vanguard World International Growth Portfolio.

6. GROWTH FUNDS—invest in companies whose earnings are believed to be accelerating. They tend to buy larger companies than the more aggressive growth funds do. Dividends are a low priority.

If all goes well: You get superior long-term performance.

What to worry about: Bear * markets are bad for their health. And yours, too.

Who should buy: Long-term, performance-minded investors who can stomach market drops but don't want to run the higher risks of investing in small-company funds.

* Bear markets fall; bull markets rise.

Some funds with good records: Columbia Growth, Counsellor's Capital Appreciation, Gabelli Asset, Janus, Southeastern Asset Management Value Trust, SteinRoe Special, 20th Century Growth, and 20th Century Select.

7. GROWTH-AND-INCOME FUNDS—emphasize blue-chip companies. They grow steadily, sometimes splendidly, and pay good dividends. An index fund (page 588) is a growth-and-income fund. This group, and the following two, are excellent choices for the average investor.

If all goes well: You get more current income than growth funds pay, plus the potential for solid price appreciation. In some years, these funds have outdone the growth funds, thanks to the compounding effect of reinvested dividends.

What to worry about: What can I say? They're still stock funds, which means they go down when the market does—although generally not by as much as the growth funds do. The dividends help cushion the drop.

Who should buy: Investors who like blue chips, who want some income from their stocks, and who don't demand aggressive performance in rising markets. Growth-and-income funds make sense for beginning investors, conservative investors, people who will hold only a single fund, and people who want a conservative fund as a base for their more aggressive choices.

Some funds with good records: SAFECO Equity and Windsor II, a Vanguard fund.

8. EQUITY-INCOME FUNDS AND INCOME FUNDS—concentrate on companies that pay high dividends, even if they don't show terrific growth. Good examples would be electric utilities and telephone companies.

If all goes well: You get somewhat more income than the growth-and-income funds provide, and somewhat less growth. In declining markets, your losses shouldn't be too bad. Your income should keep up with inflation because these kinds of companies keep raising their dividends.

What to worry about: That some of your companies will quit raising their dividends, which would hurt the price of your mutual fund. As an industry, utilities aren't quite as solid as they used to be.

Who should buy: Conservative investors who want more income from their money while staying invested for modest growth.

Some funds with good records: Financial Industrial Income, T. Rowe Price Equity Income, and Vanguard Equity Income.

9. BALANCED FUNDS—buy common stocks, preferred stocks (which pay higher dividends than the common), and bonds. They may allocate fixed percentages of their money to stocks and to bonds—say, 60 percent stocks, 40 percent bonds. If that's the allocation you want, it's simple to let the fund do it for you.

If all goes well: Your fund emphasizes income without abandoning growth. When interest rates fall, balanced funds can grow smartly, because both their stocks and their bonds should rise. In a bear market, their interest and dividends will help support the price of the shares.

What to worry about: You're in trouble when interest rates rise. The value of both your stocks and your bonds will probably fall.

Who should buy: Income investors who don't want to foreclose on their chances for some capital growth.

Some funds with good records: CGM Fund and two Vanguard funds, Vanguard STAR and Wellington.

Where to Find all the Mutual Funds Listed

Acorn, Chicago; CGM, Boston; the Columbia funds, Portland, Oregon; Counsellor's Capital Appreciation, New York City; Financial Industrial Income, Denver; Gabelli Asset, New York City; General Aggressive Growth (Dreyfus), Garden City, New York; the Janus funds, Denver; Kaufmann, New York City; Pennsylvania Mutual, New York City; RCS Emerging Growth, San Francisco; SAFECO Equity, Seattle; Southeastern Asset Management Value Trust, Memphis; SteinRoe Special, Chicago; the T. Rowe Price funds, Baltimore; the 20th Century funds, Kansas City, Missouri; the Vanguard funds, Valley Forge, Pennsylvania.

Keep It Simple: Buy an Index Fund

How would you like a mutual fund that carries you right along with the market? It's never number one. On the other hand, neither will it ever fall much below average. In the 1980s, funds of this type outperformed more than two-thirds of all other stock-owning funds.

You don't have to sell your soul to the devil for such returns. You have only to buy an index fund. It's a way of winning the stock-picking game by deciding not to play it at all.

Indexers don't try to beat the market. They don't break their heads on stock analysis or economic trends. They simply buy the stocks (or a selection of the stocks) that make up a particular market average. Come what may, good markets and bad, your investments do just about as well as that particular market overall.

At this point, you may feel disappointed. Index funds sound dull, dull, dull. The thrill of investing is to find a fund that beats the market.

Ah, yes . . . but easier said than done. In the 1980s, a majority of mutual-fund managers fell behind the market averages.

How come so many hotshot stock pickers couldn't keep up? First, they own small stocks as well as large ones—and in the 1980s, small stocks lagged. Second, the market was incredibly speculative and many funds don't play that game. Third, in any kind of market mutual-fund managers have a massive burden to overcome—namely, their fees. A no-load (no-sales-charge) fund may levy a management fee of around 1 percent. It costs 2.5 percent in brokerage fees to buy and sell securities, and maybe more if the fund does a lot of trading. So a manager may have to do at least 3.5 percentage points better than the stock-market averages, just to cover his or her expenses. Throw in an upfront sales load plus annual 12b-1 fees and good performance melts away.

So here's the question: *If a majority of active mutual-fund managers can't beat the market on a regular basis, why should you pay them to miss?* Buy an index fund instead. Or put part of your money with an index fund and part with a manager whose record shows the possibility of beating the averages even after fees are subtracted.

Individual managers may do better in the 1990s, if the climate is less speculative and the smaller stocks catch up. Still, index funds have a strong appeal. Their "average" returns are exactly what everyone praises when they study how well stocks do over time. Any other fund may deliver good returns or bad ones. With an index fund, good performance is assured.

When you buy an index fund, only two things matter: What does it cost you and which index is it mimicking?

YOU WANT THE CHEAPEST POSSIBLE FUND. The less that's taken out in fees, the better an index fund performs. *Never* pay a sales load on an index fund; the biggest and best are all no-loads. At this writing, the cheapest index funds (costing around 0.2 percent annually) are offered by The Vanguard Group in Valley Forge, Pennsylvania (800-662-7447).

Some index funds try to tart up their performance by writing options or playing other nonindex games. Naturally, they charge more for this "service," which may or may not make you any money. Give these "index-plus" funds a pass. They contravene the very concept of indexing, by adding the fallible judgment of a manager to the mix.

You want an index that matches the market that best reflects the kinds of stocks you want to buy.

For larger companies—your fund should be tied to the Standard & Poor's 500-stock average. Less popular are the so-called Major Market Index funds that copy the Dow Jones Industrial Average.

For smaller companies—you need a broader index than the S&P. The Vanguard Index Trust–Extended Market Portfolio mirrors the Wilshire 4,500 index, which tilts toward the smaller companies.

For foreign stocks—performance is measured by Morgan Stanley Capital International's Europe, Australia, Far East index. The Vanguard Group has split that index in two. Under the umbrella of its International Equity Index Trust, you can buy a Europe fund, a Pacific fund, or a combination of both.

For income investors—bond funds copy standard indexes like the Salomon Brothers Broad Investment Grade Bond Index. But many non-indexed quality bond funds come pretty close to being indexed without even trying. That makes the indexed funds, like Vanguard's, even more attractive, because of their lower costs.

When to Sell a Mutual Fund

You should sell a mutual fund when:

• You have a better use for the money.

• You've held the fund for two years and it has always done worse than other funds with similar goals (page 527).

• Your life has changed and you want a portfolio with a different level of risk.

• You're going to need the money within four years and can't afford the risk that the market will fall and not recover in time.

• You've decided to keep a fixed percentage of your investment in stocks—say, 60 percent—and right now, your stock funds are worth more than 60 percent of your portfolio. You should sell enough shares to return to the percentage you want.

Timing the Market

You're a "timer" when you try to get into the market just before prices start to swing up and bail out of the market before it swings down.

For most investors, that's only a dream. Market timing won't work.

You can't do it. Your market-timing newsletter can't do it. Succeeding once doesn't mean you will succeed twice. You'll sell much too soon. You'll sell much too late. Ditto for your buying decisions.

Still, some of you can't resist market timing. So I offer here a few of the systems that timers follow. They all can work, although not consistently. They apply to the stock market overall, not to the shares of specific companies.

Here are the questions that timers have to ask themselves: Will the gains on your good calls outweigh the losses on your bad ones? What's the effect on your long-term returns of subtracting any commissions paid on trades and the taxes you may owe on your capital gains? After expenses, can market timers do well enough to beat the investors who buy and hold? (I doubt it, but go ahead and try.)

Some rules:

· *Buy when the economy is in recession.* That's when stocks are at their cheapest. But you have to buy early in the recession (if you can identify it; economists often can't). Toward the middle and end of an economic downturn, stocks are already leaping up.

· *Buy after a stock market crash.* The 1980s saw a crash (down 22.6 percent in a day) and a crashette (down 7 percent). After such an embarrassment, stocks typically bounce back by 50 percent. Where they go from there is anybody's guess.

· *Buy when the Federal Reserve has cut the discount rate twice in a row over a three-month period.* (The discount rate is what banks pay for short-term loans from the Fed.) Falling rates discourage money market investors, who switch their cash back into stocks.

· *Buy during year-end tax-selling time.* Prices often drop from October through December. Those may be good months for finding bargains, especially among smaller-company shares.

· *Buy when the volume of rising shares greatly outnumbers the volume of falling shares.* "Volume" means the number of shares traded. Watch the daily volume on the New York Stock Exchange, reported in *Barron's, The Wall Street Journal,* or your local newspaper. When "up" volume exceeds "down" volume by at least nine to one (not counting the stocks that remain unchanged), it's usually a buy. Market timer Martin Zweig says that two such days within three months is especially good news. (Any serious market timer should read Zweig's book, *Winning on Wall Street,* published by Warner Books.)

· *Buy when large numbers of stocks are advancing.* You can read this in the advance/decline (A/D) line—a running tally of the number of stocks that rise each day minus the number that fall. The tally appears in many financial publications, including *Barron's* and *Investor's Daily*. Says Zweig: When advances lead declines by two to one over a ten-day period, the market is strong.

• *Sell when dividends fall too low.* Check the average dividend paid by the companies in the Standard & Poor's 500-stock index (you can get it from a stockbroker or by checking the "Indexes' P/Es & Yields" table in *Barron's* every week). The market is at risk when the S&P dividend yield falls below 3 percent. It's a buy when the yield rises to 5 or 6 percent.

• *Sell when interest rates get too high.* Big deal. If I knew what "too high" was I'd believe in market timing. But it's indubitably true that, at a certain point, rising interest rates pull money out of stocks and the market falls. Here are some common clues to "too high": Business growth has run up for some years. The Federal Reserve has raised the discount rate three times in a row. The value of bond investments is plunging. If you had sold after the bond market crash of April 1987, you wouldn't have been trampled in the stock market crash the following October.

• *Sell when there's an inverted yield curve.* That's when short-term interest rates rise higher than long-term interest rates. When the curve is inverted for only a month or two, there may be no bear market. But if short rates keep climbing, stocks will probably fall.

• *Be skeptical of market-timing newsletters.* They don't count the effect of commissions and taxes when they boast about all the money they made. And you don't know how well their results compare with those of investors who buy and hold, which would be the only fair test.

Even if a letter pulls you out of the market at the right time, it may do badly getting you back in. There's no point selling at $10, watching the market drop to $8, but not buying in again until $11. That's just a whipsaw. Remember: Every successful switch requires three right calls, not just one. You have to get in, then out, then in again.

Even if a timer's record looks good, ask yourself if you really would have followed every change. If you'll pick and choose among the buy/sell recommendations, forget it. Your second guessing will spoil the system.

As an experiment, you might follow a market-timing newsletter with a small part of your money while leaving the rest in a growth mutual fund. After five years, compare performance. If your market-timed money isn't markedly higher than the buy-and-hold fund, it's not worth the risk.

• *Never try to time the bond market.* Anyone who claims to know the future of interest rates is certifiable.

I told you about timing because I had to. It remains my opinion that staying invested in mutual funds with good long-term records, and reinvesting dividends, will bring better long-term results than chasing after market turns.

Only one form of market timing strikes me as reasonable for the average investor. It's admittedly loosey-goosey. Still, it can yield good results.

Add to your mutual-fund holdings whenever stock prices are lower, much lower, than they were just recently. You will probably not luck into buying at a "market bottom." Prices will decline even further. But you'll get more shares for your money than if you had bought at a higher price—and eventually stocks will go back up. Buying on weakness is a money-maker, over time. Buying in recessions will make money for sure.

Similarly, when stocks are very strong sell some of your shares. You will probably not catch the market top. Prices will more than likely go higher. But you'll take some profits, which you might lose if you held too long. Put those profits into Treasuries or money market funds. Buy back into your mutual fund when stock prices swing down again.

This casual system leads you into buying and selling shares "too soon." But you can make good money that way. The losers are those who buy and sell too late.

BUYING INDIVIDUAL SHARES

Broadly speaking, individual shares move with the market, up and down. But they also have their own separate cycles. A stock might suddenly rise, or stall, or wander down in price while the rest of the stocks in its industry are doing something else entirely.

All this means that picking stocks is far more demanding of your time, knowledge, and persistence than picking mutual funds. Successful investors subscribe to investment publications, read company reports, and analyze industries. They devote many hours to study and research. They keep their eyes open to what's going on around them, how the world is changing, what neighborhoods and nations need.

Picking stocks is a serious business, but it's also an endless and colorful entertainment. A competitive sport. You are pitting your brains and your foresight against the collective judgment of millions of other investors, all—like you—seeking an edge. Next to horse racing, investing is the world's most exacting and unforgiving wager. (I put the stock market second to horse racing only because, sometimes, a stock can come around again.)

DON'T COUNT YOURSELF A STOCK PICKER IF YOU MERELY BUY STOCKS ON THE ADVICE OF A BROKER. Stockbrokers (or their firm's research departments) may have good ideas. But if you just nod and say, "yes, yes," you are a sheep. You need to develop a mind of your own.

The following pages are meant as a primer for new investors. You'll have to dig far deeper than this if you're going to be any good.

Some Definitions

When you buy the *common stock* of a corporation you are buying an ownership share. A tiny slice of the company belongs to you and you are owed a tiny slice of its profits. Your interest in the company is known as *equity*. Stockholders are also referred to as equity investors.

The company's executives (who run the show) take one of two attitudes toward your profits. They might pay them out to you in quarterly dividends. Or they might keep the profits and reinvest them in the business. Most companies do some of both.

When you buy a *growth stock* you aren't expecting dividends. You're expecting rapidly rising earnings and a higher stock price. When you buy a *blue chip*, on the other hand, you want dividend increases as well as steady share-price growth. An *income stock* leans more toward dividends and offers less growth. Utilities and real-estate investment trusts are income stocks.

In general, the higher the dividend, the less the share price tends to fall in bear markets and the less it tends to rise when markets go up. You usually have to trade income for growth.

Your bottom line is *total return*—your dividends plus your gain or loss on the price of the stock. Say, for example, that you bought a stock for $50 and saw it rise by $5 over the next 12 months, to $55. You also earned $2 in dividends. Your total return was $7, or 14 percent on your original, $50 investment. On a total-return basis, an income investor with a high enough dividend might do better than someone who gambles solely on growth.

When economic growth slows, you hear a lot about *defensive stocks.* They're supposed to fall less in bear markets than other stocks do. Food stocks and pharmaceuticals are good examples. But still, they go down. If you're going to sell shares to try to dodge a bad market, you'd be better off switching to a money market mutual fund than to a defensive stock.

When growth turns up, you hear a lot about *cyclical stocks,* whose earnings tend to rise (and fall) when the economy does. Steel, housing, automobiles, and airlines are cyclical industries.

A Mini Tour of the Markets

The biggest markets are the most liquid, the easiest to follow, and the least subject to price manipulation. As the markets and the size of the companies get smaller, prices get flakier and crooks find it easier to play games.

THE NEW YORK STOCK EXCHANGE—also known as the Big Board. Here's where most of the biggest and best-known companies trade. It's an "auction market," where prices are set, on the trading-room floor, by the competing bids of buyers and sellers.

THE AMERICAN STOCK EXCHANGE—also known as the Amex, where more medium-sized and speculative stocks are traded. This is also an auction market.

REGIONAL STOCK EXCHANGES—small exchanges found in Boston, Philadelphia, Cincinnati, Spokane, and Chicago (the Midwest Stock Exchange). The Pacific Stock Exchange in San Francisco and Los Angeles is also a regional exchange. They list local stocks as well as some stocks that are traded on other exchanges. Being listed is supposedly a guide to quality. But the Philadelphia exchange, for one, has been taking on some dubious penny stocks (page 679).

THE OVER-THE-COUNTER MARKET—also known as the OTC. This isn't an auction market. Instead, one or more dealers will "make a market" in a particular company. That means they'll buy its shares as they come up for sale, at prices they determine. And they'll sell shares to other dealers at whatever markup they can get. When several dealers make a market in a stock, you can assume that the price is fair. But when only one dealer makes a market, your buying price may be so high (and your selling price so low) that it's going to be hard to make a profit.

OTC stocks are said to be "unlisted," because they're not listed on a formal exchange. Companies with only a small number of shares outstanding are said to be "thinly traded." Some large and well-established companies trade over the counter. But this market is better known for its smaller and newer issues.

THE NATIONAL ASSOCIATION OF SECURITIES DEALERS AUTOMATED QUOTATIONS SYSTEM—also known as NASDAQ. This is where the better-known and more actively traded OTC shares are found.

THE PINK SHEETS—a volume published once a day, giving prices for more than 11,000 OTC stocks that don't appear on NASDAQ. An electronic OTC Bulletin Board fills in with more frequent quotes. Some of the Pink Sheet prices are firm; others are soggy (meaning that when you ask a dealer for a published price, and he or she changes it); others are blatantly manipulated. A few large companies trade in the Pink Sheets, including the American Depositary Receipts (page 706) of some large foreign companies that don't want to make the financial disclosures required for listing on an exchange. Most of the companies, however, are small.

A Mini Tour of Buying and Selling

An order to buy or sell a stock is placed with a stockbroker. Individuals generally give *market orders*, telling the broker to execute the order at the best price available at the time. A professional investor may give a *limit order*, telling the broker to stay within a certain price. As in, "Don't pay over $25 for that stock."

The *spread* is the difference between the *asked price* (what you pay when you buy) and the *bid price* (what you get when you sell). For example, a stock might be quoted at $10 asked and $9.75 bid, for a 25-cent spread. Actively traded shares have narrow spreads, maybe "an eighth" (12½ cents) or "a quarter" (25 cents) a share. Thinly traded shares have much wider spreads, especially if they're over the counter. The wider the spread, the greater the gain you will need in order to make a profit. You need an awfully good reason to buy an OTC share with a wide spread (offhand, I can't think of one).

A *round lot* is 100 shares of stock, which is the ideal minimum order. Anything less is an *odd lot*. Odd-lot orders can be pooled before the stock exchanges open for the day and executed at the regular price. If you insist on buying or selling odd lots later in the day, you'll pay a surcharge.

Learn to invest by degrees. When you find a stock you like, buy 100 shares. If the company continues to do well, buy another 100 shares. Step into it gradually. If something bad happens, you can quit right there. With this system, you never have to make an all-or-nothing buy decision, which helps investors who feel a bit uncertain. And it dollar-averages your cost (page 498).

It's also smart to sell by degrees: 100 shares this week, 100 shares next week, and so on. When prices have been rising sharply, spaced sales are a way of taking profits without getting out of the stock entirely. You can reinvest in a company whose price may have more room to run. Spaced sales also save you from making an all-or-nothing sell decision about a stock whose price has stalled. You can sell a bit, here and there, and then suddenly quit selling if a reason turns up to hold the company longer.

As a general rule, you should think about selling any stock that drops 10 percent from its peak price. Maybe that stock will suddenly turn and go up again. But 10 percent losses more often mean deeper drops ahead.

To force yourself not to hang on to a deteriorating stock, enter a *stop-loss order.* That tells your broker to sell the stock automatically if it drops to a certain price. If the stock moves up, set a new stop-loss order at 10 percent below the new, higher price. Stops can be made on stocks listed on the New York and American stock exchanges. Some big brokerage houses also offer them on some of the NASDAQ companies.

A stop-loss isn't a guarantee. In a free-falling market, your order may not be executed at the price you set. Normally, however, your broker will come pretty close.

Constant trading—buying and selling stock—costs a lot of money. Even with a discount broker, points out former Fidelity Magellan Fund manager Peter Lynch, your commissions may come to 1 to 2 percent. If you turn over all of your stocks once a year, you might pay up to 4 percent. To net just 11 percent on your stocks, you will have to gross 15 percent, before expenses. So the less you trade, the better your chance of making money.

Sad Stories I Have Heard (Or, What It Takes to Break Even)

You bought a stock and it's a dog. As soon as you bought it, the price started down. But you haven't sold it because you don't want to take the loss. You will wait until the price comes back.

YOU ARE CHERISHING FOUR ILLUSIONS.

1. You think that the price will come back soon, because you couldn't have been so wrong. (In fact, the price could stay down for years.)

2. You think that as long as you don't sell, you don't have a loss. (But a "paper" loss is just as real as the other kind. The stock is worth less than you paid for it. Period.)

3. You think that there's only one way of earning back the money you lost: by holding on to the stock you lost it in. (But you might earn that money back faster by selling the stock and reinvesting in something else.)

4. You think that gains come just as easily as losses.

The falsity of this last point needs an illustration. It's a simple matter of arithmetic. When a stock drops from $50 to $25, you lose 50 percent of your money. To get it back, your stock has to climb from $25 back up to $50—a rise of 100 percent. How many stocks do you buy, expecting a 100 percent increase in price? Not very many.

That's why it's so important to cut your losses before they get too deep. The farther your stock falls, the harder it becomes to earn the money back.

When a stock drops by	The gain you need to break even is	When a stock drops by	The gain you need to break even is
5%	5%*	55%	122%
10	11	60	150
15	18	65	186
20	25	70	233
25	33	75	300
30	43	80	400
35	54	85	566
40	66	90	900
45	82	95	1,900
50	100	99	9,900

* Rounded down from 5.2%. Even small losses require greater percentage gains in order to win your money back.
Source: American Association of Individual Investors.

IF YOU'VE HELD A STOCK IN A FALLING MARKET, BUT STILL LIKE IT, SELL IT FOR THE TAX LOSS. Losses are deductible in full against realized gains, and deductible at the rate of $3,000 a year against your ordinary income. After 30 days, you can buy the stock back. (If you buy any earlier, you lose the tax loss. And that's all you'll hear from me about taxes and stock portfolios. If God had wanted me to be J. K. Lasser, He'd have arranged it.)

A Short List of Stock-Picking Points

Every stock picker has a system. But it can't be packaged and delivered. You start by trying this and that, and pretty soon you've cleared a path. Since there are thousands of stocks that rise in the long run, one path may work just as well as another. In that eclectic spirit, I offer some ways of helping stock pickers get started. But the sooner you open your own path, the clearer your view of the market will become. *

You might start by attaching yourself to major trends. Maybe something political, like European unification or freer trade with Mexico. Maybe something economic, like the odds of falling interest rates in the 1990s. Maybe something demographic, like the growing need for health care for the elderly. Conversely, you might say, "All these big-picture trends are overpriced. What smaller industries are coming along that no one is paying attention to?"

Once you've found a likely industry, ask: Is it growing? Can it raise its costs without setting off price wars? Can it keep its labor costs under control? Can competitors easily enter this industry, or will the leaders keep their franchise for a while? Does it have any political troubles? Is it a steady grower, even during general recessions?

You then start looking for promising companies within that industry. Ask: Is the company an industry leader? Does it control a unique product or service? Does it dominate a profitable market? Does it have some new products coming along? Has management done a good job of raising the company's earnings and profit margins? That XYZ is a "good company" is not reason enough to invest.

Next, ask: How popular has this company already become with investors? One measure is its *price/earnings (P/E) ratio.* When a company carries a high P/E, its earnings have usually risen rapidly, *and* investors are betting that growth will still accelerate. At low-P/E companies, profits have grown more slowly or are in a slump. One theory of investing is: Pick low-P/E stocks, because they have more room to rise.

To calculate a price/earnings ratio, you divide the current market price by the company's earnings per share for the past 12 months. Or save yourself the trouble and look up the ratio in the stock tables printed

---

* Financial planner Lynn Hopewell of Falls Church, Virginia, comments: "Mostly useless, Jane! Laymen can't 'pick stocks.' Their choices wind up being all emotion." In my heart, I think he's mostly right.

in most newspapers. At this writing, P/Es in the 18 to 20 range and up are generally considered high. P/Es under 10 are considered low—and perhaps a good buy if the company is sound. P/Es under 5 suggest a company in trouble.

But every stock has its own P/E range. You should study its history, and the P/Es of other stocks in the industry, before deciding whether the stock price is attractive.

The P/E is also known as a "multiple." At a 15 P/E, a company is said to be selling at a multiple of 15 times earnings. Stock analysts may also refer to "a multiple of 15 times *estimated* earnings," meaning that they're judging the stock price by what they think the company will earn this year.

One important point about P/E ratios: The concept of "high" or "low" is a floating one. The current value of any investment depends on what competing investments have to offer. Stocks sell at somewhat lower P/Es when interest rates are high (because bonds are attractive alternative investments), and at higher P/Es when interest rates are low.

What is the company's *dividend yield?* To calculate it, divide the annual dividend by the stock's current market value. Income investors look for dividends in the 4 percent range. Blue-chip investors might take a little less. One of the most basic stock market strategies is to buy dividend-paying blue chips and hang on for the long term. (For more on dividends, see page 602.) Growth investors, by contrast, don't want big dividends. They look for growing businesses, and want most of the profits reinvested for even more growth.

If you're a growth investor, look at smaller companies—"smaller" meaning sales in the $50 million to $250 million range. Historically, smaller companies grow faster than the bigger ones do, and their stock prices have more bounce. They stalled in the 1980s, but won't stall forever. ("Smaller companies," in this context, are substantial businesses, *not* penny stocks—page 679.)

Look for good news in the annual report (page 613). Widened profit margins are good news. An especially good bet is a company whose low profit margins appear to be improving. Another friendly number is *operating income.* That tells you whether revenues from the company's basic business have grown.

The annual report also gives you the *earnings per share.* That's the company's total earnings divided by the number of shares outstanding. Investors like a company whose earnings have headed steadily up. But don't automatically write off a company whose earnings per share have declined. That might be good news, depending on the reason for it. For example, maybe the company made a major capital investment that should produce more earnings in the future. Or maybe a new, improved management group has arrived, and is writing off the mistakes of the old regime.

Look at companies whose own officers are buying stock. Insiders tend to buy more than usual before large price increases in the company's stock, and sell more than usual before large price decreases. The best price gains come in the first six months after the average insider purchase, with the biggest punch packed into the first month. So copycats have to move swiftly. Losses in these stocks occur more gradually.

Here are two newsletters that follow company insiders: *The Insiders*, 3471 N. Federal Highway, Fort Lauderdale, FL, 33306; and *Vickers Weekly Insider Report*, 226 New York Ave., Huntington, NY, 11743. But insiders are only one indicator; you have to study other aspects of the company. Furthermore, one or two insider purchases don't mean much. It's more significant if three or more insiders buy within a three-month period and no insider sells, opines market timer Martin Zweig.

If you're a beginner, play with no more than one-quarter of your money until you learn your way around. Start with the stocks of leading companies. Their prices are fair and you can always find a buyer when you want to sell. Stay away from the OTC market until you've learned a lot more about prices and values.

Always remember that you are not looking only for a *stock*. You are always looking for a *company* whose prospects you think are strong. When good, farsighted management creates a good, farsighted strategy, to grow a good company or rescue a troubled one, you've got a winner.

Remember This About Any Stock Price!

The stock market *anticipates*. The current price contains everything that investors know, or can reasonably guess, about a company's prospects. On the day you buy, you have paid in full for the expected value of any new product or service that the company has just announced. For the stock price to rise, prospects for that company have to *improve* beyond what investors can now foresee. Fortunately, prospects often do.

Dividends

A dividend is your cut of any profits that the company distributes to shareholders. It's declared and usually paid quarterly.

Rapidly growing companies pay low dividends or none at all. Profits are reinvested in the business, to help the profits and the share price grow. This suits investors who seek high capital gains.

Slower-growing companies, on the other hand, don't get the same high returns by reinvesting in their basic businesses. Sometimes they use their profits to buy other companies (for good or for ill). But they also pay dividends to shareholders. This suits investors who want income as well as reasonable growth.

If you're an income investor, look for companies that have paid dividends for 10 years or more, and whose dividends usually rise every year—because rising dividends help pull the stock price up. Stagnating dividends suggest that the company isn't going anywhere.

Even growth investors should think about owning some dividend-paying stocks. Investors tend to hold on to them in bear markets, so they don't drop in price as much as the growth stocks do. This helps to steady your portfolio. One smart use of dividends is to buy more of the company's stock. (For companies with dividend reinvestment plans, see page 576.)

Consider selling your shares, however, if your high-dividend company suddenly takes on a lot of debt. The need to make payments on all that debt will probably endanger your payout.

And beware the company whose percentage dividend payout is super-high. That means that the stock price is super-low—probably for a very good reason. With utility stocks, for example, a low price suggests that the dividend might be cut.

When timing your purchases and sales, watch out for stocks selling *ex-dividend.* That is the five-day period before a dividend is paid. If you buy during those days, you will not be recorded as a shareholder on the company's books, so you won't receive the dividend. If you sell any shares, however, the dividend follows you, because you are still the owner of record.

When a stock goes ex-dividend, the amount of the dividend is subtracted from the price. So the trading price should fall. If it doesn't, that means that the value of the stock has actually gone up.

All things being equal, you might as well buy when you can collect the dividend. A stock that's ex-dividend has an "x" next to its name in the stock tables published in the newspaper. Some companies pay part of their dividends in the form of new stock rather than in cash.

The Truth About Stock Splits

Nouveau investors think that stock splits make their shares worth more. Wrong, wrong, wrong. After a stock split, a company is worth exactly the same as it was before. Your $120 stock might be split into two $60 shares or three $40 shares, but the total value remains $120. In a reverse split, four shares worth $5 each may be combined into a single $20 share. After a split, all prior financial information will be restated to reflect the changed number of shares outstanding.

So the news that "they're splitting the stock" should not be a clarion call to buy. On the other hand, the stock *is* worth a look. Companies with high share prices usually don't split their stocks unless they expect stronger growth and higher dividends. If that indeed happens, the stock price will rise.

Sometimes, however, the company is merely drumming up more buying interest. Individual investors are more comfortable with share prices in the $40 or $50 range than with prices in the $200 range. So they may be willing to do more buying if the stock splits down to the level they like. But all you get out of that is a little flurry. The price will fall back if the company's prospects remain unchanged.

BEWARE OF THE LOW-PRICED COMPANY THAT SPLITS ITS STOCK. There's no reason for a $30 stock to split into two $15 pieces, except to hype itself to the innocent.

New Issues: For Gamblers Only

Stock markets will career from the heights of greed to the pits of fear and back again, until the last syllable of recorded time. And whenever the Greedometer hits new highs, new issues will come pouring out.

A new issue is a private company whose shares are being sold to the public for the first time. It's often called an IPO, which means—depending on your view of these things—Initial Public Offering or It's Probably Overpriced.

Some IPOs are genuine businesses, with real earnings and honest prospects. These are the only ones to entertain. On the fringes of the business are the startups—two guys and an idea. The idea may be great, but there's no proof they can grow a company out of it. Yet other IPOs are "blind pools." With a blind pool, an entrepreneur raises money in order to buy (he assures you) a profitable business, but you don't know what that business is going be. Don't just walk away from a blind pool. Run.

New issues bubble up on a hope and a hype. Speculators dream of copping a $10 stock that will be worth $15 within the week. The odds are actually better than even that an IPO will show a profit over the first 30 days. But what's your personal chance of buying into those winners? High, if you're a big player and give the broker a lot of business. Otherwise, low. The average Joe and Jane are there to take the mediocrities off the broker's hands. And even the high flyers may tank within a very few months.

For serious, longer-term investors, new issues are truly punk. In 1990, *Forbes* magazine took a look at nearly 2,000 companies that went public between January 1980 and May 1990. As a group, they did worse than Standard & Poor's 500-stock average. More than half were worth less than their offering price. A third sold at less than half of their offering price. Six percent had gone bankrupt. And these were the "better" IPOs. *Forbes* omitted trash issues—stocks offered at less than $5 a share.

So . . . don't buy IPOs. If one interests you, get the prospectus and watch the stock. If the company is real, with audited earnings increases, a reasonable P/E ratio, and genuine prospects, buy it later. You'll probably get it at less than the offering price. Genentech flew from $35 to $89 on its birthday in late 1980, but by 1982 it was selling at $26 a share. Apple Computer's first day took it from $22 to $36, but it bottomed out later at $10.75. Hot companies that go public at super-high price/earnings ratios (50 times earnings isn't unusual) are unrealized losses just waiting to happen.

If you cannot resist trying your hand at an IPO, look for a "senior issue"—a company that has been in business for three or four years, with palpable markets and rising earnings. The new money should be used for expansion, not for paying off bank debt or enriching the founders by buying their shares. If you can't get any shares at the opening, don't chase the price up. Wait for it to drop. If it doesn't, forget it. Another stock will come along.

THE PROSPECTUS—the legal document that accompanies the new issue of any stock, bond, or mutual fund—is chock full of pertinent information about the company and is, unfortunately, the least-read publication in America. Even *Undertaker's Weekly* has more fans.

Preferred Stocks: Old Dogs Don't Learn New Tricks

Preferred stocks sound tempting. They pay a fixed, high dividend, like bonds. If common-stock prices rise, preferreds might rise a little, too. So you have a good income plus some hope of growth.

But a lot more is wrong with preferreds than right.

1. If you're interested in growth, you'll get far, far more of it from the common stock than from the preferred. And the common may pay a dividend, too.

2. If you're interested in income, bonds are safer. In contrast to bonds, preferreds fluctuate more in price; they don't "mature," so there's never a point when you can expect your capital back; and your dividend isn't safe. With preferreds, the company always has the option of canceling payments for a while.

3. The moment a preferred succeeds (when prices are up and you're reveling in your high dividend payments), the corporation may call in the shares. Not only will you lose the stock but the call price may be to your disadvantage. You can exchange any convertible preferreds for a fixed number of common shares at a specified price. But they may not be terrific investments.

In short, I wouldn't suggest preferreds to anyone (except corporations, which get a tax break on the income). If you want income plus exposure to growth, buy bonds and dividend-paying common stocks.

Selling Short: For Sophisticates Only

To "short" a stock is to make a bet that the price will fall.

HERE'S THE IDEAL TRANSACTION.

1. You borrow 100 shares of stock from your broker and sell it at today's price—say, $50. As collateral, you have to put up a sum equal to 50 to 100 percent of the stock's current market value. If you put up only part of the price (which is typical), you borrow the rest of the money from your broker.

2. The stock price plunges.

3. Four weeks later, you "cover" your short by buying 100 shares at $10 and returning them to your broker. Your gross profit is $40 a share.

4. From that you subtract your buying and selling commissions; any

dividends paid by the stock during the time you held it, which you owe to the owner; and the interest you owe, if you borrowed any money from the broker (known as a *margin loan*). Occasionally, the broker might charge a premium for making the loan—usually $1 per 100 shares per business day.

HERE'S WHAT CAN GO WRONG.

1. The stock price can rise instead of fall. If you have to buy back the shares at $60 you'll lose $10 a share, plus commissions. The higher the stock rises, the more money you lose.

2. If you put up only part of the price, and the stock goes up instead of down, you might be asked for more collateral. That's known as a *margin call*. If you don't comply, part or all of your position will be sold, leaving you liable for any losses.

3. Even if you've sold out involuntarily, you will owe commissions and loan interest. Note, too, that no short sale pays dividends.

The average investor can't stand the tension of having a short sale run against him. It's different from owning a stock outright. When your own stock falls, you can comfort yourself with the thought that it will rise again. But when a stock rises, you can't feel dead sure that it will fall. You need a lot of experience (plus a fundamentally dark view of life) to get a kick out of a short sell.

The riskiest shorts * are popular companies that are overpriced. Happy campers may keep driving those prices higher. The safest shorts are stocks that already appear to be moving down.

To protect yourself, set a stop-loss limit. Tell your broker to close out your position if the stock rises by a certain amount, say 10 percent.

Remember: Short sellers potentially have more to lose than other investors. If you buy a $10 company that goes bankrupt, you cannot be out any more than 100 percent of your investment, or $10. But say that you short a $10 stock and the price goes to $30 before you cover. You've lost $20, which is 200 percent of your investment.

Free Money: Use It or Lose It

Sometimes securities are like lottery tickets. For some special reason your number comes up and you get a payoff you didn't expect—that is,

---

* A friend who read this said that the riskiest shorts are short shorts, but then he's sexist through and through.

if you're truly watching your investment (or your broker is). If not, you may lose money that should have been yours. For example:

WARRANTS. When you buy certain securities—such as new issues, or the preferred stocks or bonds of speculative companies—they might come with "warrants." They are a sweetener, to get you to buy an issue that otherwise might look like a dog. (It could still be a dog, but the warrants make it look like a much more valuable dog.) Warrants give you the right to buy a certain number of the company's common shares at a specified, higher price.

Say, for example, you buy the low-rated bonds of Jumpstart, Inc. They come with a warrant giving you the right to buy shares of Jumpstart at five dollars, any time over the next five years. The current market price is four dollars. Those warrants are worth money. If the underlying stock moves up, they're worth more money. If the stock price exceeds five dollars, your warrants are said to be "in the money."

You can sell your warrants through a stockbroker if you don't want to use them to buy the stock. But they generally have an expiration date. If you do nothing, warrants eventually become worthless. And that's just what happens when people don't pay attention. They forget about their warrants and let them expire, unsold and unused.

Warning: The modern, predatory company might cut the ground from under its warrantholders. Just when the stock is moving up nicely and you're expecting jackpot gains, the company will call in the warrants at, say, five cents each. You have 30 days either to sell the warrants at the current, higher price or exercise them and buy the stock. You shouldn't lose money on this transaction, but you'll lose the future gains that, as a warrantholder, you quite properly expected.

If you don't hear about the redemption (by reading your company mail or by getting a call from your stockbroker), you'll wind up with warrants worth only a nickel apiece. It's a dirty trick. Those warrants were your reward for taking extra risk. The company breaks faith with you by taking them away. Moral: Don't bother buying new issues with warrants. The company may not allow you to reap the gains you gambled for.

For speculators: Suppose that you own no warrants. You can still speculate in them, by buying them through a broker. If you're convinced that a stock will move up smartly, you get a higher percentage profit by buying the warrant than by buying the stock. If you're wrong, of course, you'll also swallow a larger loss. If you buy a warrant and the company suddenly decides to redeem, you could actually lose money on the transaction, even if you were smart enough to buy a warrant that should have been worth a lot.

SPINOFFS. A company may designate a subsidiary as a separate corporation and give it away to its shareholders. Your stock certificate will arrive automatically, by mail. But to know that you're now a shareholder in this new entity, you have to open your company mail. Unknown numbers of stock certificates get thrown away by people who simply aren't paying attention.

You don't run this risk if your stocks are held by your broker in a street name. The certificate goes to the broker, who will report its arrival on your monthly statement.

What if you don't tell your company that you've moved, and your stock is mailed to an old address? The company should get it back. You can claim it at any time in the future, plus any dividends that the spinoff might have paid. However, after three to seven years or more, depending on state law, the certificate will be turned over to the state as unclaimed property. You can still get it back. But you'll lose all further dividends and appreciation (assuming that the state sells the stock, which is common practice).

CONVERTIBLES. A company in trouble may give a current bondholder preferred stocks that are convertible into common stocks at a fixed price. If the company does well, you can convert at a profit. But many investors never realize that they have this right and lose out on that extra capital gain.

CALLS. A company "calls" a preferred stock or bond by ordering investors to turn it in for cash. If you don't get the word, you will lose money. You'll discover the call eventually, because you're no longer getting dividends or interest; you will then be given the securities' call value. But you've lost the money you could have earned by turning in the securities earlier and reinvesting the proceeds.

You might lose even more if you ignore a call on convertible bonds or convertible preferred stocks. The call value may be considerably lower than the value of the underlying common stock. If you don't convert into the common stock immediately, or sell your security to someone else, all that extra value will go down the drain.

CLASS ACTIONS. Sometimes the price of a stock suddenly collapses, and it turns out that management has been fudging. Maybe, for example, the most recent financial statements mixed some fiction with the facts. That lapse might trigger a class action lawsuit on behalf of everyone who owned shares at the time. You'll get a notice about the lawsuit (keep it). You'll get another notice if there's a settlement or judgment in your favor. To collect your money, you'll have to make a phone call, fill in a form, and—sometimes—follow up to be sure that you get your check. People who don't open their company mail, or can't be bothered filling in forms, are giving up found money.

STOCK RIGHTS. When a company sells new shares, it might give first dibs to its current stockholders. As an incentive to get you to buy, you'll be offered a discount on the price. This deal is offered to you by mail; the piece of paper guaranteeing your right to a discount price is called a "right."

Say, for example, that your stock sells at $10 and you're offered the right to buy more at $9. If you exercise that right, you'll save $1 per share—the difference between your discounted buying price and the market price. If you don't want to buy any more stock, you can sell that right—probably for slightly less than $1, after commissions.

Either way, you have to act within a specified number of weeks or the right will expire. If you throw out your company mail without reading it, your rights will vanish into a landfill. You may actually lose money because, once the period for exercising the right expires, the company's share price may fall by the worth of the rights that were issued. You have to exercise (or sell) your rights just to stay even.

Children can do their elderly parents a great kindness by keeping track of all these matters. Arrange for all company mail to come to you. The forgetful investor can easily lose substantial sums.

Mergers, Buyouts, and Tender Offers

Every year, thousands of shareholders lose money because they didn't respond to a tender offer for their stock. Shareholder Communications Corporation in New York City estimates, conservatively, that the 1980s mergers alone produced $150 million in tender-offer payments that haven't been claimed. Shareholders can retrieve this money after the fact, but will lose all the dividends and appreciation that they should have earned in the meantime.

If you're dragged into one of these corporate circuses, you'll need some definitions:

A MERGER is the voluntary combination of two companies under a new corporate name. Usually, the shareholders of both companies turn in their old shares for those of the new entity.

A TAKEOVER is the friendly purchase of one company by another. The dominant company usually offers cash, but occasionally offers securities, to the shareholders of the company it buys.

A HOSTILE TAKEOVER is an offer from a group that your company's management objects to. The company may counter with a higher bid of its own. It may restructure, sometimes offering you a big dividend. Or it may ask a more acceptable partner—a "white knight"—to bid for the company shares.

A MANAGEMENT BUYOUT is an offer from management to buy most or all of the company's common shares. Management borrows the money to make the offer, which is why these deals are called "leveraged" buyouts. When you use debt you are using leverage. Managements were buying out companies left and right in the 1980s, but so far in the 1990s, this business has quieted down.

A TENDER OFFER comes from anyone who wants to buy some or all of your shares, usually at a higher price than you could get in the open market. You are being asked to *tender* (surrender) your shares.

TENDER OFFERS DRIVE UP THE PRICE OF YOUR SHARES ON THE OPEN MARKET, ALTHOUGH NOT NECESSARILY QUITE AS HIGH AS THE TENDER PRICE. For example, a tender at $33.50 for a $25 share might push up the market price to $32. The discount allows for the risk that the deal might fall through. The greater the risk, the larger the discount.

In some cases, however, the share price might jump higher than the offer—say to $35. That shows that the pros expect a second bidder with a higher offer.

You have three ways of responding to a tender offer.

1. Sell your shares in the open market for a quick and easy profit. This is the surest way of making money. You'll get your profit even if, in the end, the takeover fails.

2. If it's a hostile takeover, consider holding on to your shares for a while. You're betting that more offers will be made and the stock will go even higher. Then you can sell. This, of course, is a gamble that you might lose.

3. Tender to the would-be buyer. The offer will probably be higher than the stock price. In a partial tender, where the buyer wants only, say, 50 percent of the shares, you'll have to respond within ten days to insure that at least some of your shares will be taken.

But there are some arguments against tendering. First, if the deal fails, you'll get your stock back and will have lost all those speculative market gains. Second, the value of the offer may not be firm. It might be announced at, say, $33.50 per share. But if that price includes preferred stock and bonds with payment gimmicks, the package may be cheaper than the bidder claims. Third, even if it's a good offer the payout may take months to accomplish. That's why, after all the bidding has stopped, a quick sale in the open market often looks more attractive.

After a merger or takeover, the stock price of the enlarged company usually goes nowhere for a while, or falls. So you might want to sell any shares you own and look around for a better stock. This is particularly true if the buying group loaded up your company with debt.

WHAT IF YOU FAIL TO SELL OR TENDER YOUR SHARES? This can happen if: you don't read the financial news; you ignore the mail you get from your company; you moved and never gave your company your new address; you (or your elderly parent) have forgotten that you own the shares; your broker, who is holding the shares, neglected to inform you; or you've been asleep for 20 years.

In a partial tender, your untendered shares still have value in the open market. But if the buyout or takeover was for all the shares, there will no longer be a public market for the shares you kept.

The ultimate value of those untendered shares will depend on the deal. Companies that make all-cash offers will set aside that money for you. It won't earn any interest, so its value will be demolished by inflation. But it's there, somewhere, if you suddenly wake up and claim it.

You may be luckier if the tender offer included securities. Those unclaimed securities will stay in your name, gaining or losing value as the market changes. Dividends will accrue (although the dividends won't earn interest). If you call up the company in a couple of years and ask about your shares, you may find them worth a handsome sum.

But your company isn't a permanent lost-property office. After three to seven years (longer, in some states), the money and securities due on untendered shares is turned over to the state as unclaimed property. You can get it back. But your securities will probably have been sold and you'll have earned no interest on the money.

Brokers have varying policies for handling tenders and other offers related to stocks they hold for you in street names. Ask about this when you open an account.

The brokerage firm may or may not inform you of tenders or impending expirations or redemption dates. A good firm will do so, but it's not required.

The firm may handle your securities in your best interest—for example, by selling rights or warrants that would otherwise expire worthless —even if you give no instructions to do so. The profits go into your account. However, you cannot count on your broker's picking up every single offer. You have to pay attention, too.

If you are not prepared to follow your investments closely enough to keep track of such things as tenders, spinoffs, and warrants, sell your shares and buy mutual funds.

Buying on Margin

You buy securities "on margin" when you borrow some of the money from your stockbroker. Why do it? Because a lucky margin buyer will make a bigger profit than someone who buys the same stock for cash.

Suppose that you're interested in a $50 stock. For $5,000 cash, you'll get 100 shares. If you borrow another $5,000 from your broker, you'll get 200 shares.

If that stock rises $5 in price, the cash buyer earns $500—a 10 percent return on his investment. But the margin buyer earns $1,000— a 20 percent return on his own $5,000. He also earns double the dividends, because he owns double the number of shares.

That's called *leverage*—increasing your profit by buying an asset with borrowed money. For stocks listed on the leading exchanges, and certain major over-the-counter stocks, you can borrow up to 50 percent of the cost, depending on the broker. Smaller loans, or none at all, may be allowed against smaller over-the-counter stocks.

Unfortunately, the margin buyer does not get to take all his profits home. Besides sales commissions, he has to repay the loan plus interest.

Brokers charge around 0.5 to 2.5 percentage points over the "broker call rate," which is the interest that the broker pays on money borrowed from the bank. The interest expense compounds in your brokerage account, and you generally pay it when the securities are sold. (That interest is deductible against investment income earned from your various investment securities.)

On the downside, margin loans can kill you. If the share price drops by $5, the cash investor loses 10 percent while the margin investor loses 20 percent. If the price drops by $12 a share, the cash investor is merely holding on to a loser. The margin buyer may have to put up more money or be partly sold out.

For all the details on margin loans, see page 225. I want to restate only two points here.

1. Interest charges and sales commissions can easily eat up the profits on securities held on margin for many months. Margin buyers make money only on securities whose price moves up fast.

2. If your stock drops too far in price, the broker will ask for more collateral, in the form of cash or securities. That's what's known as a *margin call.* If you don't have the money, some of your securities will be sold to cover the debt. You usually get a margin call if the value of your interest in all the securities in your account, net of the debt, shrinks to 30 or 25 percent of market value. To make margin calls less likely, borrow less than the maximum 50 percent.

Reading an Annual Report

Where do you start? Not at the front. At the back.

Turn to the report of the certified public accountant. This third-party auditor will tell you right off the bat if the report fairly represents the company's financial condition, according to "generally accepted accounting principles."

CPAs have been known to let some real howlers get by. But the auditors are the only "numbers police" an investor has, so you might as well see what they have to say. If the CPA qualifies his or her opinion in any way, or calls the report clean *only* if you take the company's word about a particular piece of business (which the CPA clearly didn't want to do), watch out. Doubts like these are usually settled behind closed doors, before the annual report is published. When they make it into print, it suggests that the company is a riskier investment than you might want.

Now go to the front, to the letter from the chairman. Usually addressed "to our stockholders," it reflects both the character and the well-being of the company. Is it stuffy or friendly? Straightforward or obfuscating? Proud or defensive? This letter should tell you how the business fared this year—its failures as well as its successes. Most important, it should tell you why. Candor builds confidence. Beware of sentences that start with phrases like "Except for" and "Despite the." They're clues to problems. Think about selling any stock whose chairman barely mentions that earnings fell.

On the positive side, the chairman's letter should give you some insight into the company's future and its stance on the economic and political trends that affect its business. You want a savvy letter, not a lot of boring doubletalk.

While you're up front, look for what's new in each line of business. Is management getting the company in good shape to weather the tough and competitive 1990s?

Next go to the footnotes of the financial reports. These are worth a try, even if you're not a numbers person, because they explain so much. A number that looks bad in the report itself may actually be good because of some special circumstance. A number that looks good may actually be bad.

For example, are earnings down? If it's only because of a change in accounting methods, that may be good. The company owes less tax and has more money in its pocket. Are earnings up? Maybe that's bad. There may have been a special windfall—like the sale of a business—that won't happen again next year. Does the company own shares in another company? The balance sheet may list those shares at original cost while the footnote says they're worth 20 times that amount. Does the company have a huge deferred tax liability? That means that the earnings aren't on as sound a footing as you might have thought. You need the footnotes to tell you whether the numbers in the main report present a fair picture of the company's finances.

If you're going to be a stock picker, you can't resist being a numbers person for very long. The key to a company's performance lies in its financial data, not in its press releases. You need to find the data that tell you what kind of a company you're dealing with.

Start with the *balance sheet*. It's a snapshot of where the company stands at a single point in time. On the left are *assets*—everything the company owns. Things that can quickly be turned into cash are *current assets*. On the right are *liabilities*—everything the company owes. *Current liabilities* are the debts due in one year, which are paid out of current assets.

The right-hand side of the balance sheet also shows you the *stockholder's equity*. That's the difference between total assets and total liabilities. It is the presumed dollar value of what stockholders own. You want it to grow from year to year.

The difference between current assets and current liabilities is *working capital*. You want to see a nice cushion here. It says that a company can pay its bills. Some analysts apply rules of thumb to the ratio between current assets and current liabilities—for example, that assets should be twice liabilities. That's known as a *current ratio*.

But holding that much working capital may not be a terrific idea. Why leave money sitting around that could be earning 20 or 30 percent if invested in the business? I raise this point to show you that "traditional" ratios aren't gospel. On the other hand, the stocks of companies with small amounts of working capital may be risky. What will management do if their business contracts? They need a clear strategy for paying their bills.

One important number to crunch is the company's *debt-to-equity-ratio*, including its preferred stocks. You get it by dividing long-term liabilities by stockholder's equity.

A high ratio means that the company borrows a lot of money to spark its growth. That's okay *if* the company is in a stable industry with reasonably predictable earnings—enough to cover debt service. One example would be regulated utilities. But high debt-to-equity ratios can bury a company that is vulnerable to cycles of boom and bust, like brokerage firms, retailers, or steel companies. The boom years are fine. It's the bust years that kill you. In general, analysts worry if the debt of an industrial company amounts to more than 25 or 30 percent of equity.

The second basic source of numbers is the *income statement*, or *statement of profit and loss*. It shows how much money the company made or lost over the year. And it comes with a brief analysis by management.

Most investors look first at the bottom-line number: *net earnings per share*. But it can fool you. The company's management might have boosted earnings by selling off a plant, changing the depreciation rules, or cutting the budget for research and advertising. (See the footnotes!)

So don't get smug about net earnings until you've found out how they happened. This much-watched figure is often manipulated to make companies look better or worse than they really are.

The *five-year summary of operations* gives you more perspective. Look for *net sales* or *operating revenues*. This is the primary source of money received by the company.

Ask yourself: Are net sales or operating revenues going up at a faster rate from year to year? If not, is the company cutting its rate of increase in costs? When costs rise faster than sales, profits may get mushy. Also ask: Are sales going up faster than inflation? If not, the company's real unit sales are falling behind. And ask again: Have sales gone down because the company is selling off a losing business? If so, profits may be soaring—which is great! And one time more: What's happening to *operating income* (income from the business, excluding unusual gains or losses)? Is it rising faster than operating costs? If so, *net profit margins* are widening—and that's usually Investor Heaven. Falling profit margins are not. Some companies help you with this analysis by breaking out net profit margins for you.

As a savvy investor, however, you have to be sensitive to the many other variables that affect profit margins. Say, for example, that margins are rising because the company raised prices. "Great," you say, and hold on to the stock. But the stock price falls and you wonder why. It turns out that your company's competitors held prices level. So your own company's sales and profits fell. Professional investors anticipated that the price increase wouldn't take and promptly drove the stock price down. (I never promised you that analyzing a company was going to be easy.)

One way of following *dividends* is to divide them by the company's total earnings. What percentage is being paid out to shareholders? You should get a fairly stable percentage payout over the business cycle, with dividends rising as earnings improve.

That brings up the most important thing of all. *One* annual report, *one* chairman's letter, *one* ratio won't tell you much. You have to compare. Is the company's debt-to-equity ratio better or worse than it used to be? Better or worse than industry norms? Better or worse at this point in the economic cycle than it was last time? In company-watching, comparisons are all. They tell you if management is staying on top of things.

Financial analysts work out many other ratios to tell them how the company is doing. You can learn more from specialized books on the subject.

But one thing you will never learn from an annual report is how much to pay for a company's stock. The company may be running well —but if investors expected it to be running better, the stock might fall. Or the company might be slumping badly—but if investors see better days ahead, the stock could rise.

You study the report to learn how well the company is handling its problems and opportunities, and whether it appears to know the difference. You study the market to get a feel for its price.

When to Sell a Stock

You can hold on to a good mutual fund forever. You may also find some stocks that look prettier every year. But most stocks should be sold from time to time as their potential peters out. Sometimes a whole industry gets into trouble because of foreign competition or unfavorable market trends. Sometimes an individual company comes under pressure because of a crippling legal liability or a misjudged merger. Sometimes a stock just dies in the water while other industries pass it by.

IN THE LONG RUN, IT IS MORE IMPORTANT TO AVOID BAD OR TUCKERED-OUT STOCKS THAN TO PICK GOOD ONES! Since the bias of the stock market is up, eliminating losers will, of itself, improve your performance.

The most amateurish of all mistakes is to hold on to a stock that sinks, because (you think) you couldn't have guessed so horribly wrong. Oh yes you could. But there's nothing wrong with making mistakes. That happens all the time in professional investing. The error lies in not correcting mistakes, by selling the stock while your loss is still small. Small losses can be canceled by small gains. Big losses drag down your performance for years (page 598).

CONSIDER SELLING WHEN:

· The reason for buying the company has passed, and no new reason is in sight. (The decision to hold a stock is virtually the same as a decision to buy. Does this company look better to you than other companies you might own?)

• Your stock did just fine for two or three years but its gains are now slowing. It's not doing as well as other stocks you own, or as well as other stocks in the same industry.

• Your company's industry will be hurt by a fundamental economic change. For example, stocks in the defense industries started to fall when it first appeared that peace was breaking out. (Any such companies become a buy again when conditions change or when they adjust their business to the new realities.)

• The financial reports aren't looking quite so good. Quarterly earnings are lower than last year's, or lower than expected for two quarters running. Profit margins have stopped widening and started to narrow.

• The stock price is down by 10 percent.

• In the annual letter from your company's chairman, he makes excuses for failing to reach last year's goals, and you see no plan for pulling out of the slump.

• Something odd is happening to the price. Perhaps it jumped 20 percent soon after you bought it, with no apparent explanation. Maybe you should take your lucky profits and run. Or perhaps the price suddenly dropped by 8 percent. Maybe someone knows something you don't.

• You think that prices are too high for stocks in general (see market timing, page 590). Furthermore, your stock's price/earnings ratio has ballooned to a much higher level than normal.

Please note that I said "consider" selling. Some of these stocks may still be good long-term holds. So do your selling slowly, to see what happens—dropping 100 shares this week, 100 shares next week, taking some profits, and watching the price. Maybe you will ultimately retain what's left of your investment. Once a price drops 10 percent or more from its peak, however, you should probably unload pretty quickly.

DON'T SELL A STOCK JUST BECAUSE IT HAS RISEN A FEW POINTS AND YOU DON'T WANT TO LOSE THE PROFIT. Maybe it will keep on going up. "Let your profits run," the old saw says.

Conversely, don't panic if the stock drops a point. That might be temporary. Resolve to sell if it drops 10 percent (or if you have a good reason to dump it earlier). Short of that, sit back and wait.

ONE FINAL POINT

Smart shoppers will drive 50 miles to a factory outlet to buy a new coat at 40 percent off. But when stocks go on sale at a big discount (because the stock market has gone down), many a shopper shies away. They feel safer buying stocks when they're expensive, rather than when they're cheap. And then they wonder why they don't make any money.

Buying stocks cheap is the *only* way to capture the superior performance that stocks deliver over time. So look at bear markets as if they were half-price sales, and buy.

25
HOW TO USE BONDS:

Income Investing—the Right Way and the Wrong Way

———

Seeking safe investments, people drop stocks
and buy bonds. Out of the frying pan
into the fire.

Properly used, bonds are safe and solid investments. But more often than not, they're improperly used. Investors seeking income may find themselves eaten up by inflation. Investors seeking safety may suffer serious capital losses. Our sense that bonds will be secure has not caught up with the truth of today's risky marketplace. Bonds and bond mutual funds can ride the same crazy roller coaster as stocks.

Bonds are enormously useful to almost any investment plan. But you have to know how to play them right.

A BOND IS . . .

. . . a loan. You lend money to a government or a corporation, and earn interest on the funds. After a certain period of time, the borrower pays the money back. When you "buy" a bond (through a stock broker or sometimes a bank), you are accepting an IOU. If the borrower repays at the end of the loan's full term, the bond is said to have "matured." If the borrower decides to prepay the loan, the bond is said to have been "called." Bonds come in three main types: *Treasuries,* issued by the U.S. Government; *corporates,* issued by corporations; and *tax-exempt municipals,* issued by cities, states, and other municipal authorities.

A BOND IS NOT . . .

. . . a high-rate certificate of deposit. Bond investors shoulder some risk. Usually, your principal and interest are paid on time—but they might not be, if the issuer goes bad. Furthermore, the underlying value of the bond goes up and down, as market conditions change. If you sell a bond before maturity, you might get less (or more) than you paid. A CD's value, by contrast, always remains the same.

A BOND MUTUAL FUND IS NOT . . .

. . . like a bond. You can hold a bond until maturity or until it's called and then get all your money back. But there's no special date when a mutual fund will pay you all your money back. The market value of the fund changes every day—sometimes rising, sometimes falling. How much you get when you sell your shares depends on market conditions at the time. Because of this uncertainty, bond mutual funds are generally more speculative than the bonds themselves.

WHY NOT STICK WITH A BANK CD INSTEAD OF BUYING A BOND?

Why not, indeed? Certificates of deposit are the very best choice for people who want total simplicity, no fees, and guaranteed principal at all times.

But bonds do have a couple of advantages: (1) Some are fully or partly tax free, whereas CDs are fully taxable. (2) Bonds often (not always) pay higher yields than CDs, even after brokerage commissions.

WHAT ARE BONDS GOOD FOR?

Use bonds to:

1. *Preserve your purchasing power.* For this, you want intermediate-term bonds (maturing in roughly 5 to 7 years), with all the income reinvested in money-market mutual funds. Your money won't grow very much, after taxes and inflation. But you'll hold on to the value of what you have. For details, see page 641.

2. *Reduce the risk of owning stocks.* You want short- to intermediate-term (2- to 5-year) Treasuries or short-term (2-year) bond mutual funds. When stocks tumble, bond prices may drop, too—but probably not nearly as much. If you need to raise cash, you can sell short-term bonds or bond funds for only small losses, without having to take big losses in stocks. But you must have easily salable bonds, which is why I specified Treasuries or mutual funds. Corporates and municipals aren't as liquid.

3. *Provide income to live on.* But exactly how to invest for income isn't as clear-cut as you might think (page 637). You should probably have a mutual fund withdrawal plan (page 524) as well as the interest income from bonds.

BONDS VERSUS BOND MUTUAL FUNDS

Whether to buy a bond or a bond fund is often a tough call. Whereas stock investors clearly belong in mutual funds, many bond investors may be better off owning bonds individually. Here are the issues. You decide.

THE CASE FOR BUYING INDIVIDUAL BONDS:

1. You can stack the deck so you won't lose money. Do it by buying top-quality bonds like Treasuries or AAA municipals that will mature when you'll need the funds. That spares you the risk of selling early and guarantees your principal back. For example, if you own tax-free municipals but will be in a lower tax bracket in retirement, you might buy bonds that will mature when you're 60, 63, and 65. You'll then have the cash to reinvest in higher-yielding taxable bonds, which will net you more income when your bracket drops.

By contrast, most mutual funds don't offer you a maturity date, so you can't control your risk of losing money. You may or may not get your principal back, depending on the fund's market value at the time you sell.

2. It's cheaper to buy individual bonds than mutual funds, as long

as you stick with bonds that are newly issued. With new bonds, you get the same price that the big institutions pay, and the issuer swallows the sales commission. At maturity or when the bond is called, you can redeem it through the issuer's paying agent, at no fee.

With mutual funds, on the other hand, you pay upfront or annual fees (often both), the amount depending on the fund you choose. These fees reduce your investment returns.

One warning: Your costs go up if you buy older bonds out of a stockbroker's inventory. The broker will be eager to sell, because these bonds carry lucrative price markups and sales commissions. But you're better off waiting for new-issue bonds that meet your maturity requirements. If you do buy an older bond, ask two different brokers to quote you a *net* yield, after sales commissions. If they know they're competing for your business, they may each offer you a better price.

3. You don't get much diversification when you buy individual bonds. But that doesn't matter if you invest mainly in Treasury securities. You should also be okay with a limited range of corporates or tax-exempt municipals, as long as you're buying top-quality (AAA or AA) bonds that will mature within 10 years or less.

The minimum investment on individual bonds is generally $5,000 for corporates and municipals, $5,000 on shorter-term Treasury notes, and $1,000 on longer-term Treasury notes and bonds.

Conclusion: Buy individual bonds if: (1) you'll buy new issues; (2) you'll buy Treasuries or other high-quality bonds, so default probably won't be an issue; (3) you'll hold the bonds until maturity; (4) you will reinvest every penny of your semiannual interest payments in a money market mutual fund, as long as you don't need the money to live on. Failing to reinvest your interest will greatly reduce your returns over the long run and reduce the purchasing power of your capital.

THE CASE FOR BUYING BOND MUTUAL FUNDS:

1. Your dividends can be reinvested automatically. To get a similar result with individual bonds, you have to reinvest each interest payment in a money market fund, which may not yield as much as a bond fund does. (However, if you plan to live on your bond income, reinvestment doesn't matter.)

2. You can invest small sums. The initial purchase may be $1,000 to $3,000, after which you can make small, regular contributions.

3. If you aren't sure when you'll want your money, a mutual fund is a safer buy. Fund shares can be redeemed at a better price than you'd get

for individual bonds, sold in advance of their maturity date. The market chops the price of small amounts of individual corporate and municipal bonds. Treasuries do better, but don't bring the price that's published in the newspaper. Fund shares do get the fair market price.

4. Funds are a good choice if you're speculating on a decline in interest rates. When interest rates fall, bond values rise—and you could sell your fund at a profit. The value of individual bonds would rise, too, buy they are not as easy to sell.

5. You can minimize costs by buying no-load (no-sales-charge) funds. The cheapest is the Bond Market Fund from The Vanguard Group, Valley Forge, Pennsylvania, which charges, at this writing, only 0.24 percent a year. Other no-loads may go as high as 1 percent. Loaded bond funds, with their imaginative range of charges, go even higher. Don't give loaded funds a single moment's thought.

6. You get a lot of diversification for a very small amount of money. This is critical to investors attracted by the higher yields on medium- to low-grade bonds. Some of those bonds will probably default. To minimize the loss, you need to own a piece of many different issues.

7. Fund managers try to limit your risks—for example, by selling bonds whose credit rating might decline. A mere cut in rating doesn't normally matter, if you plan to hold the bond until maturity. But it matters a lot if the bond is sliding toward default.

Conclusion: You should buy bond funds if: (1) You are speculating on lower interest rates; (2) you have only a modest amount of money (less than $10,000) and don't want to buy Treasuries; (3) you want to make regular, small contributions; (4) you aren't sure when you will need the money, and want to be able to sell at current market value at any time; (5) you want to speculate in lower-quality bonds, and therefore need broad diversification; (6) you want the discipline of automatic dividend reinvestment.

To me, the answer to the question "bonds or funds?" turns on these points: (1) Do you demand, to a high degree of certainty, that by a specific date you will get all your capital back, in addition to all the interest you have earned? If so, buy top-quality bonds, not funds. (2) Do you need a lot of flexibility, to sell intermittently and invest small amounts of money? If so, buy bond mutual funds.

Is there a case for buying bonds in a unit trust? I'm skeptical, although unit trusts are widely sold for this purpose. (Read more about them, starting on page 680).

THREE ABSOLUTELY WRONG THINGS TO DO WITH BONDS

1. Do not—repeat NOT—invest most or all of your pension-plan money in bonds, even tax-free bonds, when you're young or middle-aged. This is a waste of your precious youth. Adjusted for inflation (and, eventually, taxes), bonds may give you almost no growth at all. Younger and middle-aged people need significant holdings of stocks.

2. You should not—repeat NOT—assume that tax-free bonds are always the best for that portion of your portfolio devoted to bonds. Tax-free municipals yield less than taxable bonds. So to profit, you have to be in one of the higher tax brackets. (For more on this point, see page 657). If you're in a lower bracket, or are investing tax-deferred money like that in an Individual Retirement Account, go for taxable bonds, either Treasuries or corporates.

3. You should not—repeat NOT—put most or all of your money into long-term bonds at retirement, in order to live on the income. This advice may startle you, because buying bonds is the first thing many new retirees do. But they're typically aged only 60 to 65. Their bond income will wilt under current inflation rates. By age 70, they will be poorer and won't be able to restore the value of their capital, unless a deep deflation descends. You normally shouldn't shift principally into bonds until your mid-70s. (For more on investing at retirement, see page 810).

For an instant explanation of how best to use bonds for income, jump to page 637. But you'll have a much better understanding of this strategy if you first learn something about how bonds work.

THE BOND BUYER'S MANTRA

Repeat after me:

Falling interest rates are good. When interest rates fall, bond prices rise and investors make money.

Rising interest rates are bad. When interest rates rise, bond prices fall and investors lose money.

These basic principles of bond investing inform every paragraph of this chapter. So remember them.

There is just one exception (there is *always* an exception). This mantra is good for investments lasting 10 years or so. Over longer terms, investors in bond mutual funds might make some money even if interest rates go up. All that increased interest, reinvested in the fund, eventually overcomes your loss of principal. But for this to work out, you have to stick with the fund for a good long time—longer than many investors are willing, or able, to wait.

WHAT'S A BOND WORTH?

Bonds have several values.

THE PRINCIPAL. When you put up $1,000 for a new bond, you will get $1,000 back on the day the bond matures. That's your principal. The bond's face value is known as *par*.

THE PRICE. When you read that a bond costs 100, that means $1,000. It's "100 percent of the par value." When you read that a bond cost 95, that means $950, or 95 percent of the par value. To get the dollar price, you take the quote and add a zero. Some bonds are quoted in fractions, such as 98.6 percent of par value. To get the dollar price you move the decimal one number to the right—in this case, $986.

THE INTEREST. Most bonds pay interest semiannually on your money. This is called the *coupon*. A $1,000 bond paying $80 a year ($40 semiannually) has a coupon interest rate of 8 percent.

THE MARKET PRICE. If you want to sell your bond before maturity, the price will depend on market conditions. Remember your mantra. If interest rates have risen since your bond was issued, your bond is worth less than it was when you bought it. If interest rates have fallen, your bond is worth more. This is the most critical fact about bond investing, and the least understood. The interest payments you get from your bond remain the same. But the market price continually adjusts, so your bond always yields the return that investors currently demand. This makes no difference if you plan to hold your bond until maturity. But it makes a big difference if you want to sell ahead of time.

The table on page 627 shows how the market works. In the left-hand column, you'll see how the bond market might change. In the right-hand column, you'll see the effect of those changes on the price of the bond you hold.

HOW BOND PRICES CHANGE

What happens in the market

You buy a new 30-year bond. You pay its par value and earn an 8 percent coupon.

Immediately, market conditions change. Newly issued bonds now have to pay 8.5 percent in order to attract investors.

Immediately, market conditions change again. Newly issued bonds now have to pay only 7.5 percent in order to attract investors.

Thirty (zzzz) years later . . .

What happens to your bond

Your $1,000 bond, at 8 percent interest, pays you $80 a year.

The market value of your $1,000 bond drops to $946.* Its fixed $80 interest payment now produces an 8.5 percent current yield. You have an unrealized loss on your investment of $54. The bond is said to be priced at a discount.

The market value of your $1,000 bond rises to $1,060.* Its fixed $80 interest payment now produces a 7.5 percent current yield. You have earned $60 on your original investment. The bond is said to be priced at a premium.

You have collected a total of $2,400 in interest payments ($80 a year). The market value of your bond might have dropped to $900 in some years and risen to $1,100 in others. When the value was high you could have sold for a profit. If you didn't, you'll redeem it for $1,000— the 8 percent return you bargained for.

* I'm rounding these numbers.

KEEPING IT SIMPLE

When you buy individual bonds, always buy new issues. These are bonds newly offered to the public by government bodies or by corporations. The issuer pays the broker's commission. You get a prospectus, explaining what the money is being raised for and who is backing your interest and principal payments.

New-issue bonds come at an honest market price. No one can monkey around with the stated yield. On the whole, new-issue transactions are simple, sweet, and clean.

This is really all you need to know about buying individual bonds.

MESSING IT UP

What gets you into trouble is buying older bonds. Dealers have huge inventories of these bonds, so one can be found that exactly serves your purpose. Older bonds are part of the so-called "secondary market."

What's wrong with buying older bonds? In a word, *price*. All things being equal, an older bond costs more than a new one, because of the dealer's markup—the additional sum that is added to the wholesale price. Sometimes these markups are excessive.

The biggest markups (and sales commissions) are usually on longer-term bonds, zero-coupon bonds (page 661), and all the firm's garbage—bonds of poor credit quality or oddball bonds with virtually no resale market. So those are the bonds that many brokers push. Incidentally, these markups don't show on your confirmation statement. Any sales commission disclosed will represent only a portion of the markup you paid.

Many firms do enforce honest markups. In general, says former stockbroker Mary Calhoun, you are being overcharged if any retail markup or broker's commission exceeds two points ($20) per bond on long-term bonds or one point ($10) on intermediate-term bonds. Naive investors have been charged 6 to 8 percent and higher. Some dealers have been caught adding 15 percent markups to zero-coupon bonds.

If, for some reason, you can't wait for the right kind of new-issue bond and are forced to buy an older bond in the secondary market (where I would go only at gunpoint), try these strategies for uncovering the markup.

1. Ask your broker. He or she is supposed to disclose the markup, if the bond came out of the firm's own inventory. Ask specifically to see the inventory list, where markups are disclosed. They're written in code, so ask for the codebook.

2. If the bonds come from another broker's inventory, they will be listed in the daily Blue List of bonds for sale. Ask your broker for a photocopy of the page. (But those prices are "indication only." They frequently drop, when a sophisticated investor presses for better terms.)

3. Write down your broker's price quote. Then call a second broker and ask what you could sell that bond for today. (Remember my suggestion that you work with two brokers? Here's one reason why.) The difference between that day's buying price and selling price is the first broker's markup. If the first broker is overcharging you, confront him or her and demand a better price. Or ask the second broker to find you a more competitively priced bond.

4. Besides markup, ask the broker for the bond's current yield, the yield to maturity, and the yield to first call (these terms are all explained below). With a new issue, all these yields are roughly the same. But they

may all be different when you buy on the secondary market. An unscrupulous broker may quote you only the highest one.

5. When asked about markups, some brokers will pull a how-dare-you-mistrust-me act. Ignore it. Tell them it's just business. If they object, you have the wrong broker. Incidentally, your broker should be told that you always shop around for price.

THE BOND-BUYING BUZZWORDS

Once you stray off the straight-and-narrow path of new-issue bonds, you land in the tar pits. A few of the terms below apply to all bonds. But most of them describe the pricing of older bonds that are selling for more, or less, than their face value. To explain these terms, I'll use the examples I gave in the table on page 627, starting with a $1,000, 30-year bond paying 8 percent interest.

COUPON. The fixed interest payment made on each bond. A $1,000 bond paying $80 a year has an $80 coupon. Put another way, its "coupon rate" is 8 percent.

CURRENT YIELD. The coupon interest payment divided by the bond's price. A new-issue, $1,000 bond paying $80 a year has a current yield of 8 percent. If the price of the bond dropped to $946, the current yield—still based on an $80 interest payment—would rise to 8.5 percent. (Remember your bondspeak: At $946, the price would be quoted at 94.6.)

PREMIUM. The amount by which the market value exceeds the par value. A $1,000 bond selling at $1,060 carries a $60 premium. Bond prices can go to premiums when interest rates fall.

DISCOUNT. The amount by which the market value has fallen below the par value. A $1,000 bond selling at $946 is at a $54 discount. Bonds go to discounts when interest rates rise.

CALL. When the issuer decides to redeem a bond before its maturity date. For example, a bond maturing in January 2005 might be "called" in September 1995, and you'd have no choice but to surrender it. The earliest possible call date is generally specified in the bond contract.

TERM. Generally speaking, short-term bonds run for under three years. Intermediate-term bonds run up to ten years. Long-term bonds go longer than that.

YIELD TO MATURITY. What your bond would earn if you held it to maturity and reinvested every interest payment at the market rate at the time you bought. For example, if the broker says that your yield to maturity is 8.2

percent, that assumes that every single interest payment is reinvested at 8.2 percent. If you spend your interest payments, or reinvest them at a lower rate, you will earn less. That's not a big deal if you buy your bond at par ($1,000). If you reinvest at less than the bond interest rate, or not at all, your actual yield to maturity will be only slightly less than you were quoted (you'll have to trust me on this; that's how the professionals calculate). But if you buy an older bond, there may be a marked difference between the current yield and the true yield to maturity. Because of this difference, you might be flimflammed into buying a bond that yields less than you think.

For example, say that new, 10-year bonds are selling at 8 percent yields. Your broker calls you up one day and says, "hey, I have this nice little number at 8.5 percent." "Great," you say. "Buy." You think that your bond is beating the market. But your broker doesn't mention that the "8.5 percent" bond will cost you $1,034, a $34 premium. At maturity, you will redeem the bond for $1,000, taking a $34 capital loss. Your yield to maturity, counting that loss, should be 8 percent. So you're getting less than your broker claimed. If the bond is called before maturity (as bonds selling at premiums often are), you might get less than 8 percent. You'd also get less if the broker charged you more than $1,034 for the bond.

The reverse is true when you buy a bond at less than face value. Say you pay $946 for a $1,000 bond. At maturity, you'll have a $54 capital gain. Counting that gain, your yield to maturity will be higher than your current yield. Why would you deliberately buy a bond with a lower current yield? Because the issuer isn't likely to call it early. You accept less current income in hopes of hanging on to the bond's high yield to maturity, including its built-in capital gain. (I say "in hopes" because this strategy doesn't always work. If interest rates fall far enough, these bonds, too, may rise to premiums and be subject to a call.)

YIELD TO CALL. On a bond that is selling at a premium (that is, over $1,000), you will probably never bag a yield to maturity, any more than you'll bag a snark. In the paragraph above, I went through the math (or rather, Ian MacKinnon, senior vice-president for The Vanguard Group, did) just to demonstrate the principle. Those bonds will probably be called by the issuer well before their maturity date. They are high-interest bonds. The issuer wants to retire them fast. So the information you really need is the yield to the earliest date that these bonds can be called. That's your likeliest yield and holding period.

Using the example above, if you paid $1,034 for the bonds, and they were called the following year, your actual yield would be only 4.8 percent, because of that $34 capital loss. That's something your broker probably forgot to mention. Any time a broker offers you a bond with a high current yield, ask: (1) Is the bond selling above par (above $1,000), and if so, what is its yield to call, or (2) is it a junk bond (page 664)?

YOUR TOTAL RETURN. Ultimately, this is the only yield that matters! It's all the money you earn on the bond and it comes in two parts: (1) the annual interest and (2) the bond's gain or loss in market value.

For example, take a $1,000 bond with an $80 coupon and assume that bond prices go up. If you sell that bond for $1,050, your total return for the year (before brokerage commissions) is $130, or 13 percent—$80 from interest and $50 from the gain in the market price.

Or suppose that you pay $1,050 for a $1,000 bond with an $80 coupon, for a current yield of 7.6 percent. If you sell that bond one year later for only $1,000, you'll have taken a $50 loss. Your total return is $30 or 2.8 percent—$80 from the bond interest minus the $50 loss.

Out of all of these yields, brokers have created so many sophisticated fiddles that I couldn't begin to understand them all. Nor would I want to. Just give me a nice new-issue bond and leave me alone. If you *do* buy an older bond from a broker, the only way to know what you're getting is to ask for the current yield, the yield to maturity, and the yield to call.

MUTUAL FUND YIELDS

Many bond mutual fund managers fiddle, too, to make you think that you're earning more than is actually the case. Because of their sorry abuse of the public, the Securities and Exchange Commission wrote a rule, dictating how yields must be disclosed.

These rules cover advertising material and automated-quote services on telephone lines, but not what you're told by a stockbroker or financial planner. So ask the broker or fund salesperson specifically for the SEC yields. Any other yields may be misleading.

Here's what you should get: (1) the current yield for the past 30 days; (2) the yield to average maturity, which is the average maturity of all the bonds in the fund's portfolio, or the yield to average call, if there's a good chance that the bonds will be called before maturity; (3) the fund's total return for the latest 1-year, 5-year, and 10-year periods.

Funds with shorter lifespans have to disclose their performance from the day they began. "Total return" is their interest income plus or minus any gains or losses in the value of their shares.

YOU CANNOT COMPUTE YOUR ACTUAL YIELD FROM YOUR DIVIDEND CHECK. The check might not contain every penny of interest income. It might include income from writing options, or capital-gains distributions from bonds that were sold at a profit. You have to rely on the fund to tell you what it's yielding.

HOW RISKY ARE BONDS?

In certain ways, they are just as risky as stocks—especially the longer-term bonds. Bond risk comes in several forms,.

Market Risk

The market value of your bonds will rise and fall, as interest rates go down and up. If you sell, you might get more than you originally paid or you might get less, just as would happen if you sold a stock. This matters only if (1) you have to sell your bonds before maturity or (2) you own a bond mutual fund. Any time you sell a mutual fund, the price is set by market rates.

Short-term bonds are "safest," because they fluctuate the least in price. Intermediate-term bonds come next. Long-term bonds fluctuate the most.

To minimize market risk: Buy a "ladder" of short- to intermediate-term bonds, as explained on page 638.

Holding-Period Risk

The longer the terms of the bonds you hold, the greater the chance that you'll have to sell before maturity. You risk losing money when you sell, because market prices might be down.

To minimize holding-period risk, don't buy 20- and 30-year bonds. The odds of your holding that long are small. The average income investor should buy short- to intermediate-term bonds (no more than 10 years).

Inflation risk

As prices rise, both your principal and your interest lose purchasing power. Take that $1,000 bond with a coupon of $80 a year. After just five years of 4 percent inflation, your $1,000 principal will have a purchasing power of only $822 while your $80 interest check will buy only $65.75 worth of goods. Your standard of living has dropped by 21.6 percent. And what will happen over the next five years, and the five years after that, if inflation persists?

To minimize inflation risk, don't spend all the interest, if you can avoid it. Instead, reinvest enough to counter the inflation rate. For example, suppose that you own a $1,000 bond and inflation is running at 5 percent. In order to maintain its purchasing power, your $1,000 bond needs to rise in value by $50. If you're earning $80 in interest, you should reinvest $50 (to bring your principal up to $1,050) and spend only the remaining $30. In a bond mutual fund, reinvestment is easy. If you own individual bonds, put that $50 into a money market fund.

Takeover Risk

Management, old or new, may trample on the bondholders. Suppose, for example, that you're a conservative investor who buys only quality bonds. One day a raider attacks your company, or the company's own management does, and they load it up with debt. Your AA bond might drop to a junk rating and your bond will lose value in the marketplace. You have been, to put it technically, screwed.

To minimize takeover risk, sell without a moment's hesitation the bonds of any company mentioned as a takeover candidate. Or stick with bond mutual funds, where these catastrophes don't take such a bite out of your personal worth.

Call Risk

If interest rates fall, corporations and municipalities will "call in" their older, high-interest bonds, in order to finance at lower rates. Typically, you get 5 to 10 years' call protection from both corporations and municipalities. The call may come at par ($1,000) or par plus a small premium. But that's not much consolation. You will have been earning a high rate of interest. After the call, you'll have to reinvest at a lower rate. The rule on calls is: If it makes sense to the issuer, you can be darn sure that it won't make sense to you.

Most bonds are called through a *refunding*—the company issues lower-rate bonds and uses the proceeds to retire its higher-rate debt. You may also be parted from some of your bonds by a *sinking fund*—a lottery system for retiring a certain number of bonds each year (the sinking fund may take them from you or, if it's cheaper, buy them in the open market). A special or extraordinary redemption can occur in specified circumstances, such as changes in the economics of a project that make it unworkable.

Calls used to be one of the normal hazards of bond investing that you could hedge against successfully. Now, it's guerrilla warfare out there. Bond issuers tuck weasel words into the finest of print, to deceive you and your broker about how early a call could come. One reason not to be a bondholder (or to buy a mutual fund and let the fund manager worry about it) is that so many corporations and municipalities are playing fast and loose with your call protection.

What do you lose when your bonds are called? If you bought at par, your principal is returned intact (sometimes with a little sweetener). But you lose the capital gain you earned when the bond's value rose. If you paid more than the call price, you suffer an early capital loss. When a convertible bond is called, you'll lose the higher price it might have been selling for in the open market. And any call deprives you of the high bond income that would have kept you sitting pretty for many years.

To minimize call risk, the best advice is to buy newly issued U.S. Treasury notes and bonds, paying current dividends. They are almost always call-proof (or not callable until 25 years have passed, which, by me, is the same thing). A small number of intermediate-term corporate and municipal bonds are also noncallable, maybe.

If you buy in the secondary market, buy bonds with low interest payments, selling at discounts from par value. Your yield to maturity will equal that of higher-coupon bonds but your investment isn't as likely to be called. Or buy zeros that are callable only at par. If they're callable at their "accreted value" they're no better than garden-variety bonds.

Default Risk

The issuer might not pay the bond's principal and interest on time. For example, the company might go bankrupt or its loans might have to be restructured. U.S. government bonds have no default risk, but municipal issuers occasionally stumble. Most defaults are corporate.

To minimize default risk, buy only higher-qualify stuff—especially today, with credit so shaky. You sacrifice a little yield. A one-year AAA bond might pay 1.25 percentage points less than a BBB-rated bond, depending on the market at the time. A 20-year AAA bond might yield 2 percentage points less. But that's a pretty small price to pay, compared with the risk of losing your money.

The two most common bond-rating systems, from Standard & Poor's and Moody's, are shown on the table below. Admittedly, these systems aren't perfect. Companies occasionally default while they're rated A. But on the whole, the bond raters have done well at identifying winners and losers.

Credit Risk

If a company starts racking up losses, or a municipality admits to budget deficits, the credit rating on its bonds will fall. If you hold those bonds, your interest payments stay the same (as long as the issuer doesn't

	Risk	Standard & Poor's *	Moody's †
Investment-Grade Bonds	Champagne and roses	AAA	Aaa
	Good enough even for the queen	AA	Aa
	Probably fine, but down in class for a conservative investor	A	A
	Okay for now, but a white-knuckle buy for people who normally choose quality bonds	BBB	Baa
Junk-Grade Bonds	Junk with pretensions, or "junque"	BB	Ba
	The real stuff, and risky as heck	B	B
	Junk that's showing its true colors	CCC	Caa
	Junk that smells like old fish heads	CC	Ca
	Junk that isn't paying interest anymore: on life support	C	C
	Defaulted bonds: brain dead	D	C
	Unrated bonds: bonds that neither of the major rating services have touched; probably low junk, although some small municipalities may be of high quality.		

* A plus (+) or minus (−) from S&P indicates that, for a bond in that category, it's relatively strong or relatively weak.   † Moody's designates a strong bond with the numeral 1.

default). But if you have to sell before maturity, you'll take a beating on the price. When a company's or municipality's finances improve, its credit rating rises and so does the price of its bonds.

To minimize credit risk, check your bond's current rating *and* whether its rating is likely to change. Both Standard & Poor's and Moody's publish credit-watch lists of companies that might be downgraded or upgraded. These reports are carried regularly in the financial press. To find an issue's current rating and whether it's on a watch list, call the ratings desk at Moody's Information Center (212-553-0377) or the credit division of Standard & Poor's (212-208-1527), both in New York City.

Deception Risk

This now applies principally to unit trusts, although bond mutual funds are not immune. There are many different ways of making you think that you're earning more than is actually the case. Two examples:

1. A broker or planner may tell you that a fund's current yield (from interest and other income) is 11 percent. Terrific, you say. But that may not be the whole story. If interest rates rose, the fund might have lost, say, 9.5 percent in market value over the past 12 months. So its total return—11 percent in income minus 9.5 percent in market losses—was actually only 1.5 percent. Quite a difference.

2. A unit trust might buy a three-year, A-rated $1,000 bond that originally yielded 10 percent and now has only one year left to run. It's selling at a current yield of 9.7 percent, compared with only 7 percent on newly issued one-year bonds. The trust buys that bond in order to jack up its current yield. But it has to pay a fat $1,030 for it. On redemption, the trust takes a $30 loss, which drops the bond's actual yield to maturity to only 6.8 percent. Thus are customers duped.

To minimize deception risk: (1) Don't buy a bond mutual fund from a broker or planner. You are running the risk of being deceived and will doubtless be sold a fund with sales loads. Buy a no-load fund yourself, directly from the fund organization (page 531). (2) If you do buy a fund from a broker or planner, ask to see in the printed material all the SEC yields and the annual total returns (page 631). You can use these yields to compare one fund with another.* (3) Don't buy unit trusts (page

---

* Unfortunately, you can't compare bond-fund returns with the rates on bank certificates of deposit. The calculations don't mesh.

680). The rules that forced honest yield advertising on the mutual funds have not (at this writing) been applied to the unit trusts. So the advertised yields of many of these trusts are totally misleading. If you still want to buy, ask the salesperson whether the trust holds many bonds priced over par. If so, stay away. The true yield isn't as high as it sounds.

A BOND STRATEGY FOR INCOME INVESTORS

You are an income investor if you expect to live on the monthly checks that your capital produces. There's a right way and a wrong way to go about this.

The Wrong Way to Get Income from Your Bonds

The wrong way, in my view, is to lay in a lot of long-term bonds. This conclusion may surprise you, because "long bonds" usually pay the highest interest rates. The year you buy them, you'll earn some real spending money, even after inflation and taxes.

So you love Year One. Year Two, however, is not quite so terrific. Both your capital and your income lose purchasing power. By Year Three you are barely breaking even, after taxes and inflation. By Year Four, you are probably in the hole. Each subsequent year, your bond income buys you less and less. How much less depends on the inflation rate.

· If the rate of inflation holds steady or declines, you'll get poorer slowly, losing a modest amount of purchasing power every year. That may not matter, if you have a lot of capital and are in your late seventies or eighties. Your money may still stretch over your lifetime. (In the perfect lifetime financial plan, the check that's written to the undertaker bounces.) But you can't be sure. If your savings are small, you may have to reduce your standard of living. You will almost certainly have to cut back, if you switched all your modest savings into long-term bonds when you were still youngish—say, in your sixties. Ten or 15 years later, inflation may have eaten you up.

· If the rate of inflation goes up, the purchasing power of both your capital and your income will take a devastating hit. You will have to use your money at a much faster rate than you had planned or cut back sharply on your expenses. In an inflationary world, long bonds will kill you.

· Only if the country drops into true price deflation—as it did in the 1870s, parts of the 1880s and 1890s, and the 1930s—will you be in good shape. The purchasing power of your long bonds would actually rise (that is, if you owned noncallable Treasury bonds; corporates or municipals would be called in by their issuers, robbing you of your high-interest income).

So when income investors buy long-term Treasuries, they make a 20- or 30-year bet that inflation will promptly drop to zero or less. Believe me, I'm rooting for you. But if you're wrong, you've got no life preserver. If inflation keeps on running, it will lay waste to your capital. If interest rates rise and you have to sell a 30-year bond before maturity, you will take a loss. A mere one percentage point rise in interest rates lops 10.3 percent off the value of a 30-year bond (page 643).

Why take this risk when you can pursue a sensible income strategy with intermediate-term bonds instead? The extra yield you get from long bonds may be only 1 percent or less. That's a pretty skinny bonus for putting your money at such hazard.

The Right Way to Get Income from Your Bonds

Buy a mixture of intermediate- and shorter-term bonds. Here's why.

• They pay you a reasonable income. It's less than you'd get from a portfolio invested entirely in long-term bonds, but, depending on the market, maybe not a whole lot less.

• They give you inflation protection. If interest rates rise, your short-term bonds, when they mature, can be reinvested at a higher rate of interest. That will preserve some of your purchasing power. Unlike the owners of long-term bonds, you are not chained to a fixed income for the rest of your life.

• They protect you against the need to sell bonds before maturity, perhaps at a loss. With the right mix of bonds, you always have some that are reaching their maturity date, giving you fresh cash to use.

• Overall, the total return on intermediate bonds has been just as good as that on long-term bonds. Intermediates do a little better when inflation rises; long bonds do a little better when inflation falls. But the differences even out. So you can pursue this strategy without feeling that you're losing capital on the deal.

Here's how to carry the strategy out.

Buy bonds with maturities of 1 year, 2 years, 3 years, 4 years, 5 years, all the way up to 10 years. That's called "laddering" your investments. Altogether, your income might equal what you'd get from a 7-year bond.

A Treasury ladder will work for people with substantial assets. People with fewer assets can build this same ladder with bank certificates of deposit (page 67).

When your 1-year bond (or CD) matures, you have a choice. If short-term interest rates are uncommonly high, you can increase your income by reinvesting your capital for a 1-year term. Alternatively (and this is the usual case), long-term rates will be higher. So you'd increase your income by reinvesting that money in a 10-year bond. This helps offset the hole that inflation has left in your purchasing power.

The following year, your 2-year bond will come due. You'll again have a choice about where to reinvest for better returns. Again, it will probably be another 10-year bond. Or you might fill in a particular bond maturity that's missing.

Eventually, you will have a "ladder" of 10-year bonds, some of which are maturing every year. Result: a decent income plus some inflation protection. Every year, you will have fresh cash in hand that can be reinvested for higher income if interest rates rise. If you need that cash, you can spend it. You won't be forced to raise money by selling bonds early, perhaps at a loss.

What can go wrong?

Being no dope, you have already spotted the crack in my ladder. If interest rates decline, you lose. Every time one of your bonds matures, you might have to invest at a lower rate of interest. In that case, you'd have been better off putting all your money into long-term bonds. But that's strictly hindsight. Standing here, today, you don't know where interest rates will go. You have to be ready for anything.

If you emphasize long-term bonds, you're in good shape only if inflation and interest rates decline, and not just modestly. You need a drop that's steep and fast. You'll lose purchasing power if inflation declines just a little bit, holds steady, or rises. So the odds are three out of four that long bond investors will come up wrong. With a bond ladder, on the other hand, you're prepared for an inflation rate that is slower, steady, or higher. Your odds are three out of four of being right.

And even if interest rates truly fall, bond ladders don't necessarily lower your income right away. In the first year, for example, you would reinvest the proceeds of your 1-year bond in a 10-year bond. Assuming that 10-year rates are higher, your income might rise, even if rates in general are coming down. The risk of reinvesting at lower rates may not arise until most of your bonds are in the 7- to 10-year range.

Why not add some 30-year bonds to your ladder, to protect yourself against falling rates? You might—but strictly as a speculation (page 643). Long-term bonds should not be part of a locked-in program for producing income under a wide variety of circumstances.

Two Critical Backstops for Income Investors

First, don't put all of your money in bonds, regardless of their maturity. Going back to the table on page 627, you can see that an all-bond portfolio is too risky. At least 20 to 30 percent of your money belongs in dividend-paying stocks (maybe in an equity-income mutual fund).

That is one of your income hedges. If inflation slows and interest rates fall, the value of your stocks will probably rise. Those stocks should pay rising dividends, which will add to your income. You'll also earn some capital gains. Falling interest rates usually give an even greater boost to stocks than they do to bonds.

Remember: "Income" doesn't have to mean "interest" or even "dividends." If you cash in some of your stocks every year, that's "income," too. Bond interest can easily be supplemented by a monthly cash-withdrawal plan from a stock-owning mutual fund (page 524).

Second, you might add some zero-coupon bonds (page 661) to the mix. The financial advisor who figured out the following strategy calls it his "nursing-home bailout program." Pretend you're the client, and think about it this way.

"I'm 60, I own my house, and statistics say I have 24 years to live. I want to live well.

"I'll divide my capital into money to spend and money to save. The spending money will be deployed partly in short- and intermediate-term bonds and partly in conservative dividend-paying, stock-owning, no-load mutual funds. My savings will go into 24-year zero-coupon bonds and a small amount of stock-owning mutual funds.

"Over the next 24 years, I will consume every dime in my spending account—all the stocks and all the bonds. I'll tap the stocks through a monthly cash-withdrawal plan. I'll spend a certain percentage of my bonds as they mature. I have figured out a withdrawal rate that gives me a reasonable chance of maintaining a steady standard of living.

"If I'm still breathing after 24 years, I will turn to my savings account. There, my stocks will have gained and my zeros will have matured. That gives me a fresh pot of capital to sustain the remainder of my life. If I have to enter a nursing home, my stocks, my zeros, plus the value of my house should pay for quality care."

That's what I call a creative use of bonds!

Can you "ladder" with bond mutual funds? No, because most bond funds have no maturity date.

But you do get a similar effect by owning a combination of short- and intermediate-term funds. For the income you need, make regular, fixed withdrawals from each, on a monthly cash-withdrawal plan. That leaves the interest income with the fund, to be reinvested for the highest yields. (Mutual-fund cash-withdrawal plans are enormously useful to income investors, and insufficiently understood.)

These funds also give you some inflation protection. When interest rates rise, (1) their market price holds up better than that of long-term bond funds and (2) you should pick up some higher income immediately from your shorter-term fund. When interest rates fall, however, so will your short-term bond income—although your intermediate-term fund could continue to pay a fairly steady income for some period of time.

Among the no-load mutual fund groups that offer both short-term and intermediate-term funds: The Fidelity group in Boston and the Dreyfus Corporation in Garden City, New York, for both tax-frees and taxables; USAA in San Antonio and Vanguard in Valley Forge, Pennsylvania, for tax-frees; and T. Rowe Price in Baltimore, with an intermediate tax-free fund and both short- and intermediate-term taxable funds. Minimum investments are $1,000 to $3,000.

A BOND STRATEGY FOR PRESERVING PURCHASING POWER

If you don't need the income from your bonds to live on, you can use that money to maintain the purchasing power of your capital. Here's how.

Buy individual, high-quality, intermediate-term bonds. Consider five- to seven-year Treasuries. They're safe and you owe no state or local income taxes on the interest. Hold them until maturity (selling before maturity puts your capital at risk). Reinvest every dime that you earn in a money market mutual fund. Consider a money fund fully invested in Treasuries, because no state or local taxes may be due on the dividends (page 165).

Don't buy your Treasury securities all at once. Buy some this year, some next year, and some the year after, so you'll cover a range of interest rates. Your returns should equal inflation and federal taxes. Your money won't grow in real terms, but your purchasing power should be preserved. You can follow the same strategy with tax-exempt bonds, if you can find good prices at maturities of five to seven years. But you generally can't preserve purchasing power with short-term Treasury bills. Their returns may beat inflation over time, but after taxes you would fall behind.

Can you preserve purchasing power with bond mutual funds? Not reliably. You'll succeed if interest rates stay level or decline. But if interest rates rise, the value of your fund would drop. So with mutual funds, you run a risk. The guaranteed five-year Treasury strategy is the better choice.

A BOND STRATEGY FOR TOTAL-RETURN INVESTORS

Total-return investors want capital growth. They don't care if it comes from stocks, bonds, dividends, interest, or capital gains. They just want to make money on their money, after taxes and inflation.

You might think that bonds could be the ticket, especially some long-term bonds. If interest rates fall significantly, bond prices will rise, producing a handsome capital gain.

But if interest rates fall, stocks will probably rise even faster than bonds. So stocks are the main chance for anyone going for maximum yields.

Bonds play a supporting role. Use them to preserve part of your capital so you'll always have something to fall back on. That means owning some bonds of intermediate terms and reinvesting all the interest. With Treasuries or high-quality tax exempts in your back pocket, you can feel more confident about braving the near-term risks of stocks.

A BOND STRATEGY FOR INTEREST-RATE SPECULATORS

At last, I have something good to say for long-term bonds. They're a terrific speculation on the direction of interest rates over the short term.

Suppose that you're convinced that interest rates will drop by one percentage point over the next 12 months. Remember your mantra: Falling interest rates are good. Falling interest rates mean profits. To your mantra, add this corollary (no modern mantra is without its corollary): The longer the term of the bond, the bigger the profit when interest rates decline.

The table below shows exactly how much bigger. A one percentage point drop in interest rates would add only $95 to the market value of a $10,000, one-year Treasury bill, a gain of less than 1 percent. But it would add $1,247 to $10,000 in 30-year bonds, for a 12.5 percent gain. The potential gain on a 30-year zero-coupon bond is a huge 33.5 percent. Conversely, if interest rates rose, the longer-term bonds would lose the most.

Treasury security	The change in value of a $10,000 investment when interest rates:	
	Fall by 1%*	Rise by 1%*
1-year	$ 95	$ −94
5-year	416	−396
10-year	711	−650
20-year	1,067	−920
30-year	1,247	−1,032
30-year zero	3,346	−2,496

*Assuming an 8 percent yield on all issues.
Source: T. Rowe Price, Baltimore.

The nerviest speculators buy Treasury bonds on margin, putting up 10 percent of the cost and borrowing 90 percent. They go for zeros, where the price swings are biggest. You can make huge profits if your timing is right, and take huge losses if it isn't.

Take the 30-year zero shown in the table. Assume you bought it on 90 percent margin, putting up 10 percent of the cost and borrowing 90 percent from your broker. If, over the next year, interest rates fell by 1 percent, you'd earn a 345 percent profit before interest charges and commissions. But if rates rose 1 percent, you'd take a 331 percent loss.

You can also speculate on falling interest rates by buying the shares of long-term, no-load bond mutual funds, especially the zero-coupon bond funds run by the Benham Group (Mountain View, California), and Scudder, Stevens & Clark (Boston). If you go through certain discount brokers, you can even buy them on margin (page 530).

In a typical market cycle, bond prices rise before stock prices do. A speculator, then, would first swing into long-term Treasuries and then into stocks.

A BOND STRATEGY FOR HISTORIANS

Some speculators are gambling that, in the 1990s, long-term bonds will outdo stocks because—they say—deflation has arrived. Falling prices will hurt company earnings, hence stocks. But bonds thrive under falling interest rates. This bet is based on economic history.

"Normal" price inflation in this country is lower than many Americans imagine. From 1791 to 1989, prices rose at an annual compound rate of only 1.4 percent, and that included three periods of inflation greater than those we experienced in 1980.* Inflationary spasms are usually followed by periods of zero inflation or even deflation, when prices fall. Here's the record of American price changes:

U.S. PRICES, 1792–1989*	
Rate of price change	*How often those changes took place*
Over 1%	53% of the time
Under 1%	20% of the time
Stability	27% of the time

* Annual compound rate.
Source: The Leuthold Group, Minneapolis.

A few thoughts about this history lesson:

It is not imprudent to speculate on falling interest rates by owning a position in long-term bonds. In fact, investment advisor Steven Leuthold of The Leuthold Group in Minneapolis thinks it is imprudent not to. In the long run (maybe after we're all dead), inflation and interest rates will revert to their long-term trend. U.S. Treasury bonds have sold at yields of 5.5 to 6 percent and—some day—they will again.

* Those periods were the 1790s, 1860s, and 1910s, computed on a moving-average basis. For this data, my thanks to investment advisor Steven Leuthold, who, in 1980, published an insightful book called *The Myths of Inflation and Investing*. Among its little treasures was a 1,000-year history of consumer prices in the Western world. He found that prices rose about 60 percent of the time and fell about 40 percent of the time. The annual compound inflation rate ran at less than 1 percent—suggesting that, over time (sometimes over a lot of time), market economies stabilize themselves.

Even without deflation, the 10-year return from bonds sometimes beats out stocks—most recently in 1970–1979. After stocks' big run in the 1980s, they might slow a little in the 1990s, giving bonds a better chance to shine.

Speculators should buy only Treasury bonds. Unlike corporates or municipals, most Treasuries cannot be called away from you if interest rates decline. They will pay today's rates for 25 years or more. They also carry no credit risk, unlike corporates and municipals, which might default in a deflationary economy.

Don't buy Treasury bonds on margin (that is, with borrowed money). Who knows how long it will take for interest rates to get around to reading the history books? Rates might go up instead of down, throwing you for an enormous loss.

You won't be left at the church if you buy intermediate-term bonds (or construct a bond ladder, page 638) instead of buying long-term bonds. Intermediate- and shorter-term bonds also rise in value when interest rates fall. They just don't rise as much as long bonds do.

THE BOTTOM LINE ON BONDS

Speculators should buy long-term bonds and bond funds, especially the zero bonds. They're a bet on the direction of interest rates, just as stocks are a bet on dividends and profits. If interest rates fall, long-term bonds will yield high returns. Long-term Treasuries are a hedge against the worst stages of deflationary decline. If interest rates rise, however, long-term bonds will tank.

Income investors should look to a ladder of intermediate- and short-term bonds or CDs, or cash-withdrawal plans from intermediate- and short-term bond funds, backed up by dividend-paying stocks.

For investors still building their long-term retirement nest eggs, bond investments have a single purpose: to preserve the purchasing power of that portion of your capital that you want to keep safe (say, 20 to 40 percent of your money). By buying five-year Treasuries or other intermediate-term bonds and reinvesting the dividends, you provide yourself with a rock to stand on while the rest of your money is deployed for rowth.

A bond mutual fund is not a bond—a point absolutely essential for any fund investor to grasp! With a bond, you always get your principal and interest at maturity (as long as the issuer does not default). With a bond fund, however, you can never be sure of what you'll earn, because your fund's value fluctuates. When you sell, you may get more than your original investment, plus the interest it earned. Or you may get less, depending on market conditions at the time.

DECISION TIME: WHICH BONDS TO BUY? HOW TO BUY THEM?

You now have (I hope) a theory of bonds. You know why you want them and how you will use them. The next step is to choose the bonds that will serve you best.

When buying individual bonds, always look to the credit rating (page 635). AAA and AA are top quality, while A might be called a "businessman's risk." BBB is on the very cusp of investment quality. One slip and it's junk. Individual bonds are bought through discount brokers, full-service stockbrokers, or some banks. Treasury bonds can also be bought directly from the Federal Reserve.

When choosing an open-ended mutual fund, go through the selection process outlined on page 510. Also, take a look at the funds that are named below. They were picked in 1990 by the San Francisco firm of Brouwer & Janachowski, Inc., which invests $175 million of its clients' money in no-load mutual funds (minimum account, $500,000). All of these funds have good long-term records that won't, I hope, crack before this book goes to press. (For where these funds are located, see page 666. For some tips on closed-end bond funds, see page 540.)

Treasury Bonds

No bond is safer than a Treasury. Other bonds pay higher yields. But Treasuries' strong advantages may matter more.

TREASURIES, DEFINED:

Medium-term Treasury notes run from 2 to 10 years. Minimum investment for new issues: $5,000 for 2- and 3-year notes; $1,000 for longer terms. Treasury bonds are issued today at 30-year maturities, with a minimum investment of $1,000. You can buy them from the Federal Reserve or through a stockbroker or bank. (Treasury bills of one year or less are generally for savers, not investors; see page 169.)

When I say that Treasuries are "safe," I mean only that the interest and principal payments will always be made on time. Treasuries are exposed to the same market risk as any other bond. If you sell before maturity, you might get more or less than you paid, depending on market conditions at the time. You have to hold to maturity to be sure of getting exactly your capital back.

Treasuries don't pay as much income as other bonds of comparable maturities, but the interest is taxed only at the federal level, not by states and cities. So the net difference in income isn't as large as it seems.

WHY YOU MIGHT WANT A TREASURY:

1. With the financial system so unstable, you don't want to take any credit risks. Treasuries will never be downgraded or default.

2. Treasury bonds are noncallable, at least for the first 25 years. If you're speculating on declining interest rates and win your bet, these are the only high-rate bonds that you'll be able to hang on to. Corporate and municipal bonds will be called away (page 633).

3. Treasuries are liquid. If you have to sell before maturity, you get better prices on them than on other kinds of bonds.

4. You can buy Treasuries from the Federal Reserve, paying no brokerage commission.

THE DRAWBACKS:

1. In return for their safety and liquidity, Treasuries yield less than other bonds of comparable maturities. Still, their total return—yield plus capital gains or losses—has been competitive with corporate bonds, because their prices have been holding up better in the marketplace.

2. Taxpayers in top brackets net a lower current income from Treasuries than they would from tax-exempt bonds. But you might not care, in view of Treasuries' other advantages, especially their immunity to call.

If you choose a Treasury, would you buy . . .

INDIVIDUAL BONDS? Absolutely yes. You don't need to diversify, because Treasuries carry no credit risk. So there's no point paying a mutual fund's annual management fee. You can buy your Treasuries directly from a Federal Reserve branch or bank, paying no sales commission. If you buy through a broker or commercial bank, you'll generally be charged their normal bond commissions. Incidentally, although you can buy through the Fed and redeem your bond at maturity, you cannot sell through the

Fed before maturity. If you needed to sell early, the Fed would have to transfer your Treasury to something called the "commercial book-entry system" to make it accessible to stockbrokers. Anyone who expects to sell before maturity should buy through a broker or bank (for details, see page 177).

Always buy a newly issued Treasury, if you can get the maturity you want. When you buy existing bonds on the secondary market, the markup may be higher than you ought to pay, unless you take care to get competing bids (page 628). To deal in the secondary marketplace, you go through a bank, discount broker, or full-service stockbroker. Treasuries are ideal for the "ladder" suggested on page 638. If you don't need current income, reinvest all the interest you earn in a money market mutual fund in order to maintain the purchasing power of your capital.

A MUTUAL FUND? No. You'll net more money, more securely, by buying Treasuries individually. If you want government-insured securities in a fund go for one with higher yields, like a mutual fund that buys Ginnie Maes (below).

Don't fall for the funds that call themselves Treasury "Plus." They try to get you higher yields by pursuing fancy hedging tactics. In practice, they're usually at the bottom of the performance lists. If ever there were a plain-vanilla investment, it's a Treasury bond.

Ginnie Maes

A Ginnie Mae is a black-box investment whose workings you and I will never see. Its current yield is terrific. But you have to treat it carefully. Very carefully.

GINNIE MAES, DEFINED:

Ginnie Mae is short for Government National Mortgage Association. It's the highest-yielding government-backed security that you can get. New Ginnie Maes often yield 1 to 1.5 percentage points more than Treasuries of comparable maturities—and they're guaranteed by the full faith and credit of the U.S. government. Unfortunately, it takes at least $25,000 to buy a new issue. That's why so many investors buy their Ginnie Maes in the form of mutual funds or unit trusts (page 680).

A Ginnie Mae security is a pool of individual mortgages that are insured by the Federal Housing Administration or guaranteed by the Department of Veterans Affairs. Your own mortgage might be in a Ginnie Mae. Every time you make a monthly mortgage payment, your bank might subtract a small processing fee and pass the remainder to the investors in that pool.

Each investor gets a pro rata share of every homeowner's mortgage payment. When a homeowner prepays a mortgage, the investors get a pro rata share of that, too.

IMPORTANT! Ginnie Maes work differently from bonds. When you buy a bond, each semiannual check you get is pure interest income. At maturity you get your capital back. But with a Ginnie Mae, each monthly check is a combination of (1) interest earned and (2) a payback of some of the principal that you originally invested. At the end of the term, you'll get no capital back. It will all be paid out to you, over the life of your investment.

Suppose, for example, that you get a check for $237. Around $229 might be interest; $8 might be principal. That's an $8 bit of your original investment, returned to you. If you're living on the income from your investments, what should you do with this check? You can spend up to $229 of it, because that's interest income. But you must save the remaining $8. If you spend that $8, you are consuming your principal, which is something few Ginnie Mae investors understand. The statement that comes with your check should tell you how much is interest and how much is principal.

Each month, the amount of principal in your check will be a speck higher, and the amount of interest a speck less. Over the term of the Ginnie Mae, you will gradually receive all of your principal back. If you spend every check you get, all your principal will be gone. Conversely, if you save every check, including the interest, you will preserve the purchasing power of your capital, after inflation and after taxes.

ALSO IMPORTANT! If a broker says the fund is "government guaranteed," that means only "guaranteed against default." Principal and interest payments will always be made on time. But the Feds don't insure your investment result. How much money you make on a Ginnie Mae, or a Ginnie Mae fund or unit trust, depends on investment conditions and on how wisely you buy.

WHY YOU MIGHT WANT A GINNIE MAE:

1. You like its high current yield and its government-backed proof against default. Unlike Treasuries, Ginnie Maes are fully taxable by state and local governments, as well as by the federal government. So you

might choose them for the "safe" portion of your tax-deferred retirement fund.

2. If you're living on your savings, Ginnie Maes deliver attractive income to people in low tax brackets—for example, retirees with modest incomes.

THE DRAWBACKS (especially for investors in individual Ginnie Mae bonds and unit trusts):

Although the following list of horrors is formidable, plunge on. It has a happy ending.

1. The size of your check varies every month, depending on how fast the mortgages are prepaid. This can disconcert an income investor. Some months you get more, some months you get less.

2. You have to keep track of how much of your check is interest and how much is principal. When the principal payment is small, the best way to reinvest it at a decent rate of return is to stow it in a money market mutual fund.

3. You may be deceived by your Ginnie Mae's high current rate of interest. A unit trust, for example, might be paying 12 percent because it is packed with old, high-rate mortgages for which the trust paid more than face value. But those homeowners will rapidly refinance and the trust will take a loss on these loans. What you thought was an eight-year 12 percent investment might turn into a three-year 7 percent investment. Sic transit truth. Just as bad, you may never realize how small your return actually was, because yields on Ginnie Maes are so tough to calculate.

4. Any yield that's promised on a Ginnie Mae is only an estimate. Not until all the mortgages are finally paid can it be said with certainty what you earned. And no one will bother doing that calculation for you. So you'll never know.

5. If you have to sell your Ginnie Mae before maturity, the odds are that you'll lose money. These securities tend to rise very little in good markets and to plunge in bad ones.

6. The happy ending: You can get around most of these problems by buying Ginnie Maes in mutual funds (below).

If you choose a Ginnie Mae, would you buy . . .
AN INDIVIDUAL SECURITY? After that long list of drawbacks, how could I

recommend an individual Ginnie Mae? And in fact, I don't. Nor do I like the unit trusts, especially in view of the many trusts with deceptive yields (page 681). If you do buy an individual security, buy only a newly issued Ginnie Mae, for sale at face value. Then you can't be jerked around by a broker quoting a phony yield. Avoid at all costs a high-interest Ginnie Mae that's selling above its face value. Its true yield, after all the mortgage prepayments, will be much lower.

Sometimes older Ginnie Maes are good deals—and they sell for less than $25,000, because some of their mortgage principal has already been repaid. But you can't easily tell the good deals from the bad, so the safest thing is to stay away.

A MUTUAL FUND? In my view, this is the only way of buying Ginnie Maes. Leave it to the fund manager to worry about whether he or she is getting the right price. All your principal is reinvested for you, even those $8 bits. You can reinvest the income, too. You get quarterly and annual reports of how well your fund is doing. Minimum investments are often $1,000 or less. As with any other bond fund, however, you risk losing money if interest rates rise.

SOME GINNIE MAE FUNDS WITH GOOD RECORDS: Federated GNMA, Value Line U.S. Government Securities Fund, and Vanguard GNMA Portfolio.

Other Government Securities

There's an alphabet soup of government agencies that raise money from the public. Among the notes and bonds that are exempt from state and local taxes: those issued by the Federal Farm Credit System, which makes farm loans ($1,000 minimum); the Federal Home Loan Banks, which make short-term loans to savings and loan associations ($10,000 minimum), and the Resolution Funding Corporation, which is financing the S&L bailout ($1,000 minimum). These agencies aren't backed by the full faith and credit of the federal government, but they'd probably be bailed out in a pinch. Many agency securities have a credit line with the Treasury.

They pay a hair more than Treasuries—maybe an extra 0.25 or 0.35 percent. That's $25 to $35 a year on a $10,000 investment. If you're sure that you'll hold the note to term, maybe that extra fraction is worth it. But it's not if you might have to sell before maturity. You won't get as good a price for agency notes as you would for Treasuries, because the resale market isn't as broad.

Corporate Bonds

Corporates pay higher interest than Treasuries. But they're losing their following, because so many corporate executives have been treating their bond-holders with such contempt.

CORPORATES, DEFINED:

These bonds represent loans made to corporations, and come in a wide range of maturities. You need at least $5,000 to invest (that's five bonds at $1,000 each). You'll get the best price if you buy bonds newly issued to the public. You could easily be overcharged if you buy older bonds out of a stockbroker's inventory (page 627). Some corporate bonds are backed by some sort of collateral, like equipment or real estate—although, in a bankruptcy, that collateral can be tough for bondholders, to get their hands on. Most corporates are *debentures,* meaning that they're secured only by the executives' smiles.

WHY YOU MIGHT WANT A CORPORATE:

1. You're investing with tax-deferred money in your retirement plan and want more interest than Treasuries pay. Corporates are fully taxable, by federal, state, and local governments.

2. You're in the 15 percent federal tax bracket. At that level, you will net more, after tax, from taxable corporate bonds than from tax-exempts.

3. You want a utility bond, for its high and reliable interest payments.

THE DRAWBACKS:

1. You usually get only 5-year call protection on utility and telephone bonds. So if interest rates decline, you won't enjoy your high interest rates for very long. Industrial bonds may offer 10-year protection.

2. The interest on corporate bonds is taxed by every government in sight—federal, state, and local. That's why corporates are principally for low-bracket investors or tax-deferred pension plans.

3. Corporates are hard to sell before maturity at a decent price. If you buy, you should plan on holding them until maturity.

4. The bond's credit rating could be cut, which would lower its market value. This matters principally to investors who might have to

sell before maturity. Among the things that could hurt your bond's credit rating: Business goes bad, a takeover stuffs the company's balance sheet with debt, a regulatory commission doesn't let the utility raise its rates.

5. The company might default.

If you choose a corporate, would you buy . . .

AN INDIVIDUAL BOND? Maybe, if it were a top-rated, intermediate-term utility and you planned to hold it until maturity or until called. Or if it were a chip so super-blue that you felt it would never disappoint you. You might also ask your broker about high-rated *Yankee bonds.* They are issued in the United States, in American dollars, by foreign governments, banks, or corporations. Yankee bonds often carry higher interest rates than U.S. bonds of equal quality.

Otherwise, "quality" corporate bonds aren't what they used to be. RJR Nabisco was a blue chip until it announced its buyout plan; the price of its bonds promptly dropped by 20 percent. And there are dozens of other cases.

You simply cannot trust corporations to fulfill their obligations to bondholders. In a crisis, the managers may save cash for the stockholders (including themselves) while trying to dragoon the bondholders into taking less than they're owed. For this reason, you might want to give up on individual corporates and buy Treasuries, instead. Remember: You can buy Treasuries without paying sales commissions, and they're free of state and local income taxes. So compared with quality corporates, their net yield stands up pretty well.

A MUTUAL FUND? Absolutely yes. If you're going for corporates, a well-managed, diversified fund is a first-rate buy. Look for a no-load (no-sales-charge) fund with a portfolio made up largely of blue chips. It will probably include some of the higher-yielding government-backed securities, like Ginnie Maes. It may also own some slightly lower-rated bonds, in order to enhance your return. Always remember, however, that to buy a long-term bond fund is to bet that interest rates won't rise over the period that you expect to hold the investment.

SOME CORPORATE BOND FUNDS WITH GOOD RECORDS: Fidelity Intermediate Bond, Harbor Bond, T. Rowe Price New Income, Vanguard Bond Market, Vanguard Investment Grade Bond Portfolio.

Municipal Bonds

Munis are better than corporates, for people in high tax brackets. But diversify, diversify. Owning only your own state's bonds doesn't look as smart as it used to.

MUNICIPALS, DEFINED:

Municipal bonds are issued by cities, states, counties, or other local-government entities. Most of these bonds are taxed neither by the federal government nor, in most cases, by their own state and local taxing authorities. All states exempt from taxation the bonds of Puerto Rico, Guam, and the Virgin Islands. A few states levy no tax on any unearned income. At the other extreme, a few states tax even their own munis. But those are exceptions. In general, the states tax-exempt their own bonds when they're bought by state residents, and tax any interest that residents earn on bonds that were issued by other states. If you own an out-of-state bond in a mutual fund, that portion of your dividends will be state-taxed.

Munis come in the same short, medium, and long maturities as any other bonds. Minimum investment is usually $5,000. You should be able to get 10-year call protection, although some munis sneak in calls after 5 years or less.

If you own any munis issued before 1983, they might be bearer bonds, without your name on them. When interest is due, you clip off the interest coupon and take it to the paying bank, which will probably charge up to $10 or so for giving you your money.

Keep those bearer bonds in a safe place! If lost, they are difficult, even impossible, to replace. Anyone who finds the bonds can clip the coupons and collect the interest.

Another problem with bearer bonds: If the bond is called, you may not get the word on time. Your broker is supposed to alert you, if you keep the bonds at the brokerage firm—but he or she may not notice. If you keep the bonds yourself, you're unlikely to discover the call in the newspaper, because it will probably be printed, in flyspeck type, in a journal so obscure that not even the publisher's mother reads it. (Fortunately, *The Wall Street Journal* recently started printing major bond calls, but you might not read those, either.) You'll learn about the call eventually, when you present your semiannual interest coupon at the bank and the paying agent only laughs at you. When you turn in the bond, you'll get the principal you're owed. But once the call date has passed, your money will not have earned any interest.

Since 1983, all munis have been issued in registered form, either in your name or in the street name of your brokerage house. You may not get a certificate; your bond is often only a blip in a computer. There's no coupon clipping. The interest is mailed to you directly, if the bond is in your name, or to your broker if it's in a street name. The broker puts the money in your brokerage account. Many bearer bonds may be converted to registered bonds, at your request.

Munis may be sold as *serial bonds*, with a portion of the issue coming due every year. That lets you choose the maturity date you want. It's important to buy munis that will mature exactly when you'll want the money. If you try to sell before maturity, odds are you'll be offered an awful price.

MUNICIPALS COME IN SEVERAL TYPES:

1. *General obligation bonds*—backed by the taxes raised by the municipality itself. They are issued for public purposes like building schools and waste-treatment plants. "GOs" are the very safest munis. They rarely default. Even so, more GOs are seeing their credit ratings drop as state and local budget gaps get harder to close.

2. *Revenue bonds*—backed by revenues from the projects they were issued to finance. Some revenue bonds are of the very highest quality, especially when they're issued for essential services. If the proceeds of the bond are used to build a water main, for example, the bond interest may be covered by the very money that the residents pay to use the water. But revenue bonds used for hospitals, low-income housing, nursing homes, and retirement developments are the bond world's equivalent of the Irish Sweepstakes.

3. *Industrial-development and pollution-control bonds*—a form of revenue bond, used to finance buildings and equipment that will be leased to private companies. The interest on these bonds is paid out of the revenues from the leases, so the safety of the bonds depends on how well the private companies do. So far, defaults have been low—but these bonds can be risky. Municipalities often help back projects that private businesses wouldn't otherwise undertake on their own.

4. *Taxable municipals*—issued principally for private purposes. These may be exempt from state and local taxes, but not from federal tax. Individuals shouldn't get involved with them.

5. *Prerefunded municipals*—high-interest bonds that, for complicated reasons, are effectively backed by U.S. Treasury securities. At the
call date, these munis will be redeemed. If you own a muni that the
issuer decides to prerefund, its credit quality and price will rise. At that
point, you might want to sell the bond; you will lose your capital gain if
you hold to maturity. Alternatively, if the interest rate is rich enough,
you might want to keep on collecting it for as long as you can.

6. *"Black-box" bonds*—a shorthand term for bonds issued by state
and local agencies to get around state debt-limit laws. They're called
"black box" because no one, including the brokers who sell them, is
exactly sure how reliably all these bonds are backed. In a budget crunch,
would the issuing agencies have the authority to pay? Who knows?
Because of these uncertainties, black-box bonds sell at higher yields than
other munis. They're living proof that debt-limit laws make great ap-
plause lines for politicians but fundamentally don't work. When a government needs money, it will always find ways to raise it. Individuals
should avoid black boxes. Stick with old-fashioned GO and soundly
backed revenue bonds.

7. *Zero-coupon municipals*—see page 661.

WHY YOU MIGHT WANT A TAX-FREE BOND:

Why else but to earn a safe and steady tax-free income? If you expect
to drop to a lower income-tax bracket in retirement, time your munis to
expire by retirement day. If you don't need your tax-free income to live
on, reinvest every interest payment in a money market mutual fund.
Otherwise, your capital will lose purchasing power.

For the good of your nerves, pick high-grade, general-obligation
munis—AAA or AA. Low-grade issues pay more but may introduce
altogether all too much excitement into your life—like threatening
default. Bonds are for the no-worry portion of your portfolio. Save
your risk-taking for stocks, where the rewards are generally higher.
If you insist on speculating in low-rated munis, take a look at the
states and cities mired in the greatest credit problems. That's where
you'll make the most money, assuming that the bonds are eventually
paid.

Are You in the Right Bracket for Tax-Free Municipals?

For a tax-free bond to make any sense, you generally have to be
in the 28 or 31 percent federal bracket. Occasionally, however, inter-

est rates are high enough to interest even those in the 15 percent bracket.

Not so the tax-free money market mutual fund. Often, these funds yields so little that they make sense only for those taxed at 31 percent.

In a kind of financial flag burning, some low-bracket investors buy tax exempts purely to do the government out of a check. They don't care that their spite is costing them money. But that's chuckleheaded. Buy tax-frees only if they yield more than you'd get, after tax, from a taxable bond of the same credit quality and maturity. (And even then, you might prefer taxable Treasuries, for their call protection—see page 647.)

Here's a quick-check table for finding out whether tax-free or taxable bonds make more sense for you. When making comparisons, always use bonds, or bond mutual funds, of equivalent maturities and credit quality. Otherwise, you might make the wrong choice.

To use this table, find the yield (on the left) of the tax-exempt bond you're considering. Then read across to the column under your federal

If a tax-exempt bond yields . . .	. . . This is the minimum yield you need from a Treasury security to equal the tax exempt, in the following tax brackets		
	15%	28%	31%
3.5%	4.1%	4.9%	5.1%
4.0	4.7	5.6	5.8
4.5	5.3	6.3	6.5
5.0	5.9	6.9	7.2
5.5	6.5	7.6	8.0
6.0	7.1	8.3	8.7
6.5	7.7	9.0	9.4
7.0	8.2	9.7	10.1
7.5	8.8	10.4	10.9
8.0	9.4	11.1	11.6
8.5	10.0	11.8	12.3
9.0	10.6	12.5	13.0
9.5	11.2	13.2	13.8
10.0	11.8	13.9	14.5
10.5	12.4	14.6	15.2
11.0	12.9	15.3	15.9

Source: Goldstein Golub Kessler & Co., New York City.

income-tax bracket. That shows you the taxable yield you'd need to match the return from the tax exempt.

Note that this table works only for Treasury securities, where no state and local taxes are owed. If you're considering a corporate bond, your break-even yield will be a little higher. A short calculation in the Appendix shows you what a corporate would have to earn.

In the Appendix (page 885) you'll find calculations for (1) working backward from a taxable security, to see what tax-exempt yield you'd need to beat it; (2) checking the taxable equivalent of tax-exempt securities whose yields don't show on the table above; (3) finding tax equivalents for higher brackets than the three shown here; and (4) finding out whether you'd net more from a mutual fund that owns only your own state's bonds or a higher-yielding fund containing the bonds of several states.

SOME MUNICIPAL BONDS AND BOND FUNDS CARRY INSURANCE. If the insurer defaults, the insurance company will make all the interest and principal payments. Most of these bonds are of single A quality. Thanks to the guarantee, however, they're classified as AAA.

The insurance costs investors anywhere from 0.15 to 0.3 percentage points in yield. Even so, insured bonds may yield a bit more than their uninsured counterparts. That's because investors don't quite trust the insurance companies. In a couple of cases, the insurer's own credit rating has fallen, which brought down the ratings of the bonds it backed. Furthermore, none of the municipal insurers has been tested in a rash of major defaults. The extra yield on an insured bond delineates these risks.

Note that the insurer does *not* guarantee the bond's market value. You are not reimbursed if you sell before maturity and lose money because the bond's rating is down. You are protected only against default.

Some municipal bond mutual funds and unit trusts insure their whole portfolios. Five years ago, that smelled like nothing more than a marketing gimmick. Since the Great Depression, only around 1 percent of all munis are said to have failed. But lately, more bonds have gone into the drink. More credit ratings are moving down than are moving up. The failure of the Washington Public Power Supply System's bonds, which carried an investment-grade rating of Baa at default, turned investors especially queasy. I still think muni-bond insurance is a marketing gimmick. But nowadays, maybe it's worth paying for both belt and suspenders.

THE DRAWBACKS:

1. The liquidity is awful on individual municipal bonds. If you want to sell before maturity, you'll probably be offered such a terrible price that it wouldn't make any sense to take it.

2. If you live in a state with budget problems, your risks are compounded. Your bonds' credit ratings might be downgraded, which would make them even tougher to sell if you suddenly had to raise some money. Still, for gamblers low-grade munis are worth a flyer. If they don't default, they'll pay spectacular yields. For safety, however, put some of your money into Treasuries.

3. Unlike Treasuries, munis can be called, generally after 10 years. So you might get your principal back early. If interest rates have fallen, you will have to reinvest at a lower rate, which will lower the yield you earn on your capital.

4. If you're subject to the alternative minimum tax, be careful of which bonds you buy. You may be taxed on certain types of municipals, such as student-loan bonds and some industrial development bonds. Luckily for me, advanced tax advice is outside the mission of this book. See an accountant.

5. Municipalities are exempt from many of the laws on financial disclosure that rule corporations. Result: They sometimes publish rotten, misleading, and outdated financial information, and no one goes to jail for it. *Forbes* columnist Ben Weberman once reported on a $5 million bond issued by Pennsylvania, ostensibly to complete a hospital. The state failed to disclose that the hospital had no operating license. The bonds eventually went into default.

The level of disclosure is getting better but it's still not great. When a bond defaults, investors sometimes bring class-action lawsuits against their brokers, claiming that the broker didn't dig deeply enough into the issuer's true situation.

TWO ALTERNATIVES TO CONSIDER:

1. *Treasury bonds.* After tax, how many extra dollars are your munis really giving you? If the answer is "not much," you might be better off with safe, liquid, noncallable Treasuries.

2. *Bonds of other states.* You generally pay state and local taxes on the interest you earn on out-of-state bonds. But how much money are you talking about? It might be worth paying a little extra tax for the safety of diversifying into a multistate bond mutual fund. A one-state

bond portfolio leaves you totally at the mercy of that state's politics, budgets, industrial health, and natural disasters. Think of all the Californians living on, um, default line.

If you choose a municipal bond, would you buy . . .

AN INDIVIDUAL BOND? Absolutely, as long as you can afford to diversify over three or four issues and intend to hold until maturity. You pay no sales commission if you buy a new issue, and escape the loads or continuing fees charged by mutual funds and unit trusts. At maturity, you will get all your capital back (assuming no defaults). That's a promise that mutual funds can't make, because they have no maturity date.

But when you buy an individual muni, it should generally pass the following tests: (1) It's blue-chip quality—AAA or AA. (2) It doesn't yield more than other AAA or AA issues, which would indicate a special risk. (3) It's a general obligation bond, or a revenue bond for an essential municipal service. (4) It matures within ten years, so you're pretty sure of holding for the full term (which is not so likely with 30-year bonds). Alternatively, it is targeted to mature in exactly the year that you know you're going to want the money. (5) It doesn't have an early call date. (6) It's a new issue, so you get the same price that the professionals pay. If the broker sells you an older bond out of inventory, you may not get as good a deal. If only an older bond fits the maturity you need, ferret out the markup to see if the price is fair (page 628). Don't buy a low-rated or unrated muni under the illusion that, since it's a "government issue," it's safe. It isn't.

For help in buying individual munis and judging whether the price is fair, try a $90 six-month introductory subscription to the *Lynch Municipal Bond Advisory*, P.O. Box 25114, Santa Fe, NM, 87504. Annual subscription: $250.

A MUTUAL FUND? Yes, if: (1) You have only small amounts of money to invest. (2) You aren't sure exactly when you might need the money. Fund shares can be sold at any time, at a better price than individual bonds would bring if you had to sell them before maturity. (3) You believe that interest rates won't rise long term, so your bond shares won't lose value. If rates do rise, the value of your fund will fall—and there's no date certain when you know that your principal will be returned. (4) The fund keeps a high percentage of its money in high-quality bonds. Higher-yield (lower-quality) funds, concentrated in A or BBB bonds, could run into heavy weather if rising interest rates or a credit-quality panic roils the market. Some of their bonds might slip down to junk ratings, at great loss to their shareholders. (5) You've chosen a no-load (no-sales-charge) fund with low expenses, so your yield doesn't go through a meat grinder.

SOME MULTISTATE MUNI FUNDS WITH GOOD RECORDS: Dreyfus Intermediate Tax-Exempt Bond, Fidelity Limited Term Municipals, SteinRoe Managed Municipals, Vanguard Municipal Intermediate-Term Portfolio.

Zero-Coupon Bonds

Zeros are for extremists—wild speculators or sticks-in-the-mud.

ZEROS, DEFINED:

A zero bond has no current "coupon" or interest payment. Instead, you buy the bond at a fraction of its face value and wait. The interest (usually compounded semiannually) accumulates within the bond itself. At maturity, the bond is redeemed for its face value.

For example, suppose that in July 1990 you bought a 10-year, $1,000 Treasury zero yielding 8 percent. You'd have paid about $456. The following year, the bond would be worth about $493 thanks to accumulated interest. The year after that you'd have $533. And so on up. (The bond's value also rises and falls in response to market conditions, but that's another story.) In July 2000 you'll redeem that zero for $1,000.

Most people who buy zeros go for zero-coupon Treasury bonds, although you might be interested in municipal zeros. Corporate zeros are bought chiefly by institutions.

All the interest you earn will compound at the bond's own, internal interest rate—in the above example, 8 percent. A regular bond can't do that for you. With regular bonds, you get a dividend check every six months and have to reinvest the money as best you can (for example, in a money market fund).

Zeros sold under acronyms like LIONs, TIGRs, and CATS are brokerage-house promises-to-pay that are secured by Treasuries. I have no reason to believe that that arrangement isn't safe. But for a direct participation in a Treasury itself, buy the zeros known as STRIPs, which are the most widely traded. You have to buy them through a stockbroker. STRIPs aren't available directly from the Federal Reserve.

There are two different ways of buying zeros. You can get them when they're newly issued, or you can turn to the secondary market and buy an older zero out of a stockbroker's inventory. New issues are best. New-issue Treasuries can generally be had in a wide number of maturities. Among tax-exempts, however, your choice will be more limited.

If you buy on the secondary market, you'll probably have to use your two-broker system (page 628) to bargain for a good price. You will also complicate your income-tax return. In the year you buy the zero, only part of the taxable interest belongs to you. You'll need an accountant to sort it out.

Don't be so dazzled by the zero's apparent "low price" that you neglect two crucial strategic questions:

First, ask about the yield, net after commissions. It's no big deal to turn $456 into $1,000 in ten years. That's 8 percent, compounded annually. If you can get 8.5 percent in another investment, the latter is the better choice.

Second, ask yourself what $1,000 will be worth in ten years. After inflation and taxes, it might buy just about what $456 will buy today. Zero bonds can maintain the purchasing power of your capital. But unless inflation shrinks, the real value of your money will not grow.

WHY YOU MIGHT WANT A ZERO:

1. You want to guarantee that you'll have a fixed sum of money in a certain year. By paying $456 in July 1990, for example, you knew for sure that you'd have $1,000 in July 2000. Zeros are commonly used to accumulate money for college (a strategy that I don't much like, because it probably won't keep ahead of college inflation—see Chapter 20). But zeros are terrific for covering fixed-dollar obligations, like paying off your mortgage on the day you retire, assuring the payment of a balloon loan, or guaranteeing a future cash payout negotiated as part of a divorce.

2. You are speculating on falling interest rates. Recite your mantra: Falling interest rates are good. Falling interest rates mean profits. When rates decline, zeros move up faster in price than any other kind of bond. So they're the gambler's chip of choice.

THE DRAWBACKS:

1. If interest rates rise instead of fall, you'll lose more value in zeros than you would in other bonds. (For proof, see the table on page 643.) That's just how the market works.

2. Because of the risk of getting a bad market price, long-term investors should never buy a zero that they know they will have to sell before maturity. For example, don't buy a 30-year zero for a child who will be

off to college in 15 years. Buy a 15-year zero instead (if, indeed, you want to buy zeros at all). Your zero should always mature at the time when you know that you're going to need the money.

3. Comparison shop, to be sure that you're not overcharged. Stockbrokers tend to talk prices, not yields. For just $189, your broker might say, you'll have $1,000 in 20 years. What's the yield? On the surface, 8.5 percent—which might sound just fine. But if you're paying a commission of $25 per STRIP, your net yield drops to 7.86 percent. Another broker might charge you $189 plus only $10 per STRIP, for a fatter net yield of 8.24 percent. So always ask about yield to maturity, after commissions. (That net yield should show on your confirmation slip.) And call more than one broker, including a discount broker. I went through this exercise a few years ago and found a difference of $34 per $1,000 between the highest and lowest offers. That's a difference in yield of 3.4 percent—not chicken feed.

4. Income taxes are owed every year on the interest buildup inside a zero-coupon Treasury. But your bond doesn't pay any cash to help cover the tax. To avoid paying taxes on phantom income, put Treasury zeros into tax-deferred retirement plans or into the accounts of children who owe no tax. Otherwise, use tax-free municipal zeros.

5. New zero Treasuries are not callable. Neither are some zero municipals, but check. You don't want your bonds snatched away after 5 or 10 years if you had planned on holding them for 15. Noncallable municipals yield a little less than callable ones do. Early calls are doubly painful because a zero's big payoff comes during the final third of the bond's life. If a broker sold you a zero municipal priced at more than its current principal and interest value (it happens), you could lose principal on an early call. Beware of older Treasury zeros; a few of them are callable.

6. As with any other bond, zeros will probably not be as good a long-term buy as stocks. They serve some financial-planning purposes but aren't the key to real growth.

If you choose a zero, would you buy . . .

AN INDIVIDUAL BOND? Yes, if you plan to hold until maturity. It's the cheapest way of buying these bonds, assuming that you get a good price. You don't have to diversify when you're buying zero-coupon Treasuries.

A MUTUAL FUND? In most cases, no. The funds levy annual management fees, which reduce your yield.

Buy a fund only if you're speculating on falling interest rates. It's cheaper to trade mutual fund shares than to buy and sell zeros directly, and you'll get a fairer price on the bonds.

Unlike other bond mutual funds, zero-coupon funds have fixed maturity dates—for example, 1995, 2000, 2005, 2010, 2015, or 2020. On maturity day, all the bonds are redeemed and the investors paid. The further away the maturity date, the bigger your profit if interest rates fall (and the bigger your loss if rates fool you and rise). The no-load fund with the lowest expenses and the largest number of maturities to choose from is the Benham Target Maturities Trust.

High-Yield (Junk) Bonds

Junk investors take huge risks. Why would you bother, when there are so many "safer" ways of speculating?

JUNK BONDS, DEFINED:

I'm always astonished by the readers who tell me they wouldn't touch junk with an 11-foot pole (which is the pole they reserve for investments they wouldn't touch with a 10-foot pole). Then they ask what I think of their high-yield bond fund.

They're so blinded by the emotional power of words ("junk" sounding bad, "high-yield" sounding good) that they can't accept that the two are one and the same. But the higher the current yield, the junkier the credit rating. In the markets, there is no free lunch.

Junk-bond companies have poor credit ratings or none at all. The reasons vary. Some were great businesses once but have lost their touch. Some are smaller firms with good potential but not yet ready for prime time. Some were mauled by takeover artists—if not raiders, then their own management—and are now buried under debt. Some are true basket cases.

Municipal bonds get junk ratings if the project the bonds financed (such as a hospital or a bridge) isn't earning enough revenue to cover the debt reliably. Cities and states with intractable budget deficits may also wind up in the junk heap.

WHY YOU MIGHT WANT A JUNK BOND:

You wouldn't, because of the hazard. Junk-bond mutual funds did well in the early to middle 1980s. But by the end of the decade, they were coming in second-best to Treasury funds. Anyone who holds junk during the industry's first recession isn't an investor at all. He's a guinea pig.

THE DRAWBACKS:

1. If the company or project does badly, the bond will default and you'll lose your high interest income. In reorganization, you'd be lucky to get 40 percent of your principal back. You might be forced to exchange your bonds for preferred stocks, whose value may sink so low that you'll lose even more of your money. Take this as a given about most junk-bond companies: They do not want to pay you back!

2. If the company or project does well, the issuer will call in its junk bonds and refinance the debt at a lower rate of interest. So you don't get to keep those lovely high yields. After taking all the risks, you are robbed of some of the rewards.

3. If you want to sell a small number of junk bonds before maturity, it is almost impossible to get a decent price. Many junkers aren't salable at all.

4. Most junkers were issued in the 1980s. As a group, they are a veritable blimp of risk. The air leaked out of many of them, even during the good times. In a recession, scores of these Hindenburgs will crash and burn.

5. In a market panic, even "good" junk will go up in flames.

If you'd still choose a junk bond, would you buy . . .

AN INDIVIDUAL BOND? No, no, a thousand times no. Junk is too risky. If you're crazy enough to buy these bonds at all, you need a whole portfolio of them, in hopes that your winners will cover your losers. (A friend of mine did send his kids to college on a handful of junk bonds, but he was investing in the mid-1980s. I mention this only as a reminder that *someone* can make money in *anything*—although not necessarily you and me.)

A MUTUAL FUND? It's the only way to go. You are gambling that, with good management, the fund's high income will more than make up for the capital that you're losing through defaults or loss of market value. You are also gambling that a decent market for junk bonds will continue to exist, so that your shares can be sold at not-unreasonable prices. This is a bet for high rollers only. Do not use junk-bond funds as a source of current income. That income makes up for the losses you are taking on your underlying capital. If you spend the income, you are consuming your profits and leaving your losses to build up. All your income should be reinvested.

SOME HIGH-YIELD FUNDS WITH TOLERABLE RECORDS: Financial Bond—High Yield, T. Rowe Price High Yield, Vanguard High Yield Bond Portfolio. But I doubt that you should be buying junk funds at all.

Where to Find All the Mutual Funds Listed

Benham Target Maturities Trust, Mountain View, California; Dreyfus Intermediate Tax-Exempt Bond, New York City; Federated GNMA, Pittsburgh; the Fidelity funds, Boston; Financial Bond—High Yield, Denver; Harbor Bond, Toledo; the T. Rowe Price funds, Baltimore; SteinRoe Managed Municipals, Chicago; Value Line U.S. Government Securities, New York City; the Vanguard Funds, Valley Forge, Pennsylvania.

Convertible Bonds

Skip this section. It's here only because I'm obsessively tidy. Convertible bonds are widely marketed to retirees, but take my word for it: They're a waste.

CONVERTIBLES, DEFINED:
These bonds—like convertible preferred stocks (page 605)—are convertible into a fixed number of the company's common stock. You can make the exchange when the common stock reaches a certain price. In the meantime, you earn interest, although not as much as you'd earn from that company's regular bonds.

When the stock price rises, convertibles normally rise with it, although not by as much as the stock itself. You can either sell your converts at a profit or turn them into shares of stock.

When stock prices fall, converts don't drop as far as the underlying stock. Like a bondholder, you can sit tight and collect a regular income.

WHY YOU MIGHT WANT A CONVERTIBLE:
Beats me. Their definition, above, makes them sound niftier than they really are. Their admirers call converts the best of both worlds—a steady income plus price appreciation as the company grows. I see them as the worst of both worlds—paying less income than you'd get from regular bonds and earning less appreciation than you'd get from stocks.

As bonds, convertibles are supposed to protect you from falling markets. But in the 1987 crash, converts dropped almost as precipitously as stocks.

The ideal time to buy convertibles is when stocks are just about to rise and interest rates are about to fall. Just give me a jingle when you see that coming and I'll suggest that you invest.

THE DRAWBACKS:

1. A convert costs you more than the underlying stock is worth. So you're making a bet that the stock price will rise substantially. Pricing convertibles is a science too arcane for the average investor. If you overpay, it might take years to make the money you expected. Your bond might even be called by the company before you've had time to earn a profit.

2. Let's assume that you get lucky and the company's stock is running well. Your convert is moving up in price and you're collecting high interest payments. Suddenly, the bond might be called. That forces you to sell or to convert to the stock, like it or not. If you weren't following your investment and heard about the call too late, you'll still get the call value of the bond but will lose the extra value that the bond had gained in the marketplace.

3. If your company is taken over, the tender offer will probably eliminate your conversion rights.

If you choose a convertible bond, would you buy . . .

AN INDIVIDUAL BOND? No. You don't know how much to pay for it. And the risk is high, because so many converts are issued by companies with poor credit ratings.

A MUTUAL FUND? Yes, if you absolutely must. But any time I look at the mutual funds invested in convertibles, I usually find them behind the funds invested in plain-vanilla stocks or bonds. So why not buy a stock fund and a bond fund, instead of muddling along with a mediocre hybrid? There are always particular converts that do splendidly well. But investing is a game of odds and the odds aren't with them.

FOLLOWING YOUR BONDS

Daily bond prices don't matter to investors who plan to hold until maturity. But speculators can follow the prices of the major bonds in *The*

668   **MAKING THE MOST OF YOUR MONEY**

Wall Street Journal, Investor's Daily, Barron's, and the financial sections of many newspapers. You'll see, in abbreviated form, the company's name, the bond's coupon interest rate, the maturity date, the current yield (coupon divided by price), the number of bonds that traded that day (small, compared with stocks), the day's price action, and the change from the previous day.

The listings for Treasury securities show the coupon rate, the maturity date, the "bid price" (what investors would get if they sold their bonds), the "asked" price (what investors would pay to buy bonds that day), any change from the previous day, and the current yield based on the asking price. But these are wholesale prices, to large purchasers like mutual funds. As an individual buyer, you'll pay more than the newspaper shows; as a seller, you'll get less.

The prices of bond mutual funds, both the open-end and the closed-end funds, are carried in the same tables as those for the stock-owning mutual funds.

HEY, JANE, YOU FORGOT TO MENTION MONEY FUNDS

No I didn't. Money market mutual funds are not investments, they're variable-rate savings accounts. I love them (page 164) for your ready cash. They're terrific parking places for funds awaiting investment somewhere else. They're ballast for a portfolio with too much risk. But they are not long-term investments in themselves.

When you stash most of your assets in a money fund, you are robbing yourself of growth. You'll appear to stay even with inflation but, after tax, you'll fall behind. So your purchasing power will slowly shrink. This was true even in the heady days when money funds paid 16 percent, because inflation ran nearly as high. The *investment* alternative to money funds is the short-term, one- or two-year bond fund. It pays slightly higher yields, with small risk to your ready cash.

AND TAX-DEFERRED ANNUITIES

Check them out on page 763, along with all the other tax-deferred investment vehicles.

THE DIALOGUE OF STOCKS AND BONDS

Investors often act as if stocks and bonds live in separate worlds—one on Neptune, one on Mars, with orbits that will never cross. In fact, they are two sides of the same financial marketplace, always adjusting to each other's prices. Investors who follow their dialogue have a better feel for what's going on.

Stock and bond prices generally rise and fall in tandem. If stock prices are booming while bonds are fading, something's wrong. Either bonds will perk up or (more likely) stocks will turn down. Stock and bond prices do move in opposite directions for short periods of time. But they're never happy until they're once again on parallel tracks.

Bonds usually (but not always) lead stocks, which is why investors should pay more attention to what the bond markets are doing. The most spectacular recent example was 1987. The bond market crashed in April and May while stock investors were still reaching for the stars. Then, in October, stocks crashed, too.

The mediator between stocks and bonds is interest rates. Their influence on the market cycle is crystal clear.

At the start of a typical cycle, interest rates rise and bond prices gradually decline. For a while, stock investors pay no attention. But eventually, rates get so high that investors can't resist them. They move money out of stocks and into various fixed-income vehicles. Stocks start to fall. ("Usually," says Roy Neuberger of the investment firm Neuberger & Berman, "when both short-term and long-term rates start rising they tell the stock investor one story: Run for the hills.")

High interest rates also put a damper on business. The economy slinks into recession and demand for new credit slows way down.

This is when the cycle turns. Slow credit demand means that interest rates have room to fall, which causes bond prices to rise. Professional investors immediately switch some of their money out of interest-rate investments and back into stocks. Stock prices bottom out and soon are moving sharply up. Bonds have led stocks once again.

Typically, however, individual investors don't yet believe that anything has changed. They sit through the first 30 or 40 percent of the rise in stocks without lifting a finger to invest, thus losing some of the market's fastest gains.

Why do investors wait so long to buy? Usually because the economy is in the pits. They forget that markets *anticipate*. Falling interest rates signal easier credit, which will lead, eventually, to recovery—and that's what moves the markets up. Investors should anticipate, too, or else (my choice) stay in the market all the time.

Stocks and bonds have one more important relationship. They define the risks you choose to take and what your returns are likely to be. If you think you've been setting your sights too low, you'll reduce the percentage of bonds and other fixed-income investments you hold and raise your long-term commitment to stocks. If you think you've been taking unreasonable risks, you'll buy fewer stocks (or different ones), lower your holdings of long-term bonds, and move into shorter- and intermediate-term bonds. Either way, the balance you strike between stocks and bonds will determine the size of the nest egg you'll have when you come to the end of your working life.

26
THE CALL OF THE WILD:

Some Awful Investments, Plus a Word
About Gold

———

Wall Streeter Ray DeVoe calls it The Crack of
Doom. It's the point when you know, for sure,
not only that you are going to lose money, but
that you are going to lose a lot more money than
you can afford.

Quinn's First Law of Investing is
never to buy anything whose price you can't follow in the newspapers.
An investment without a public marketplace attracts the fabulists the
way picnics attract ants. Stock brokers and financial planners can tell
you anything they want, because no one really knows what's true.

The First Corollary to Quinn's First Law states that, even when the
price is in the newspapers, you shouldn't buy anything too complex to
explain to the average 12-year-old.

These rules proscribe some of Wall Street's most popular investments. They're "popular" not because you've been dying to own them
but because brokers and planners press them upon you. Not coinciden-
tally, they all carry higher sales commissions than surer, simpler invest-

ments do. I wouldn't touch any of them myself—and hope that you'll avoid them, too.

I won't even offer you "how-to" lists for finding gems among the dreck. Some gems exist but they're not worth the time it takes to do the research, or the risk that your broker will talk you into buying something that you shouldn't.

LIMITED PARTNERSHIPS: WHERE DID ALL THE MONEY GO?

The competition for "worst investment" is pretty stiff. But limited partnerships make the final cut. A limited partner is best defined as someone who gets a limited amount of his or her money back (if that).

Please don't send me letters about partnerships that delivered huge profits. Of course some did—notably, real estate in the late 1970s and cable TV in the late 1980s. You can't count on anything to be bad all the time. But these investments go bad a majority of the time. Getting a winner is bum's luck.

The textbook definition of a limited partner is someone who makes a passive investment in oil, real estate, nursing homes, cable TV, or any other venture. You're "passive" in that you make none of the business decisions. A general partner runs the business and accepts liability for any lawsuits. The limited partners get a pro rata share of the profits or losses. After a specified number of years, the investment is supposed to be sold (at a vast profit, you imagine) and the proceeds distributed— that is, if there are any proceeds. Around $130 billion was harvested from limited partners in the 1980s, at a minimum of $5,000 a pop. Much of that money vanished into failed deals or the pockets of the sharks who ran them. Sales for new partnerships are down but they're still substantial, as naive investors take their brokers' word that the new-breed ventures will make a fortune. As the great man said, you can fool some of the people all of the time.

Hook, Line, and Sinker

Limited partnerships were originally baited with tax deductions that reduced your ordinary income. But the write-offs grew so fraudulent that Congress put most of them out of business.

A tiny number of true tax-shelter partnerships remain: some oil-and-gas investments, historic rehabilitations, and—the ones with the biggest shelter—deals that invest in low-income housing. With them you might recoup (over a decade) 40 or 50 percent more than you originally invested, from tax savings alone. But to keep those write-offs you'll have to hold the properties for least 15 years (and maybe longer; the sponsor needs permission from a state agency to sell). That locks you into an investment fraught with risk. What if the government changes the rules on these shelters? What if the building goes into default and you have to repay the tax credits you took? What if you die or become disabled and your family needs the money? Will it be worth the sponsor's while, 15 years from now, to seek permission to sell the buildings? Like every other investment sold entirely on the basis of tax deductions and credits, low-income housing partnerships are probably an accident waiting to happen.

Today, most partnerships are structured as "income and growth investments." You still invest in oil, real estate, nursing homes, cable TV, and so on, but you expect current income from the business, plus a profit when the deal is sold. There's a bit of tax shelter in the mix, but only for income earned from this and other partnerships. You normally can't use the deal to tax-shelter any of your regular earnings. Stockbrokers and planners market these ventures to conservative investors who often think they're a no-lose proposition.

Where New-Breed Partnerships Tend to Fail

YOUR "INCOME INVESTMENT" MAY QUIT GENERATING INCOME. It's not uncommon for distributions to slow, then stop. The likely reason: The partnership overpaid for the property. The business cannot generate enough income to cover its expenses and pay you, too.

YOUR "PAYOUTS" MAY BE PHONY. The sponsor can delude you into thinking that you're earning money when you're really not. Suppose, for example, you pay in $5,000 and get a $400 payout. That could be an 8 percent return on your money. More likely, you got $400 of your original investment back, paid from a cash reserve kept for that purpose. You now have only $4,600 in the deal and haven't made a dime. When the cash reserve runs dry, your payouts will stop.

A variant on this game is the "guaranteed" distribution. You're promised, say, 10 percent a year for the first three years, and it doesn't occur to you that you're being paid with your own money. In any partnership, gimmicks like this should warn you away. The sponsor is merely collecting your money, taking a fee, and handing it back—without investing it for growth. Even worse, some sponsors won't be able to fulfill their guarantees.

YOUR YIELD MAY BE PHONY. You may not be getting as high a return as you think. To take just one example, consider the effect of a zero-coupon mortgage. The lender requires no current payments of principal or interest, which leaves more cash on hand to distribute to investors. Presto! A partnership with a high current return! But in five years, that mortgage plus the compounded interest has to be paid. It might absorb all your profits in the property, and then some. Real-estate pros call zero-coupon mortgages Pac-Man loans, because they eat up your equity. (I have lots of other examples of phony yields, but you get the idea.)

THE FEES MAY BE EXCESSIVE. Typically, investors pay 15 to 18 percent off the top. And that's only the start. Sponsors may hit their partnerships for millions of dollars in fees and expenses every year. Only an exceptional property can support such predation and still leave something for the investors. Had the sponsors curbed their greed, many of these deals would have worked out fine.

YOUR MONEY MAY STAY LOCKED UP IN THE DEAL BECAUSE THE GENERAL PARTNER (GP) WON'T LIQUIDATE. GPs earn fat fees by managing limited partnerships, even those that are in the red. When the time comes to sell off the properties and distribute the proceeds (usually after 7 to 10 years), they may find excuses to delay. Some limited partners have actually sued to force the general partner to sell.

In lieu of liquidation some GPs do "rollups," combining some of their better partnerships with some of their worse ones. The result: a new company, in which the partners are issued stock. The company is then listed on a stock exchange or opened for public trading over the counter. As "management," the GP hopes to collect a salary forever.

Limited partners generally vote "yes" on rollup proposals because they imagine that their stock will be valuable. Who tells them so? Who else but the brokers who sold them the deal in the first place? Brokers are motivated to support the rollups because the sponsor generally pays them for every "yes" vote they deliver. After a rollup, these stocks sometimes do okay. But not real-estate rollups, whose stocks have generally collapsed. When offered a rollup, you should probably vote "no." You might get more money if the properties were sold and the proceeds distributed to the limited partners.

SOME PARTNERSHIPS ARE STRICTLY TAX-DEFERRAL DEALS. You think you're saving taxes but you're only putting off paying them for a little while. To make money, you have to invest those tax savings during the years that you still have them.

The classic example of this is the leasing deal. You buy capital equipment (computers, airplanes, medical equipment), write off the cost on your tax return, and lease the equipment out. In general, the taxes you "save" are merely moved forward from one year to the next. Eventually, the bill falls due. So you achieve nothing unless you make a point of investing those savings to produce some income that you otherwise couldn't have earned. And even then, you might lose money at the end of the lease, unless the used equipment is sold for as much as the sponsors expected.

Investors may be drawn to equipment leasing by the size of the annual distributions, which sometimes reach 12 to 15 percent. But only part of that money is a real return on your investment. The rest is effectively a return of the capital you originally put up. If you spend the whole check, you are consuming some of your principal.

What Is Your Partnership Really Worth?

Who knows? In many cases, not even the sponsor does. Anything you're told may be totally off base. But here are your sources of information, flimsy as they are.

YOUR BROKERAGE-HOUSE STATEMENT. A purported value for your units may be printed on your statement, but that "value" probably bears no relation to reality. Some firms always carry your investment at its original cost (right up to the day that the partnership fails). Some may raise the "value" year by year, even when your units are selling in the marketplace for substantially less. In short, these statement are a fantasy (I'm being kind).

THE PARTNERSHIP SPONSOR. You'll get the same kind of valuation you get from your broker. Maybe even rosier. A few partnerships refuse to compute a value at all.

THE SECONDARY MARKET. More than a dozen firms buy and sell units of existing partnerships. For a free list of these firms, write to the Investment Partnership Association, Suite 500, 1100 Connecticut Ave., NW, Washington, DC 20036, and call around for some sample prices. These prices are low, but they reflect what you'd get if you had to sell.

PARTNERLINE, which is run by Robert A. Stanger & Co., Shrewsbury, New Jersey. It offers information on thousands of private and publicly registered partnerships—where the sponsors are located, what's happening to distributions, whether those distributions represent real earnings or just your own money back, the partnership's cumulative returns, and what the sponsors say the units are worth. If you want to sell, Partnerline can often tell you who's buying. It might even have some information on the price. Phone: 900-786-9600. Cost: five dollars a minute, so have your questions written out in advance. For an extra charge, Stanger will send a printed report.

THE STOCK MARKETS. You get truly accurate information only if your partnership shares are publicly traded. Open markets tell all.

How to Get out of a Rotten Partnership (Maybe)

TRY SELLING YOUR UNITS BACK TO THE PARTNERSHIP OR TO THE BROKERAGE HOUSE THAT SOLD YOU THE DEAL. They may have a list of other suckers, er, investors willing to buy. You probably won't get much of a price, but at least it's cash. The highest offers generally come from one of the national brokerage firms, such as Merrill Lynch, Shearson Lehman Brothers, and Dean Witter. (But if your partnership is rotten through and through, you won't get a nibble even there.)

TRY SELLING TO AN OUTSIDER. Around a dozen organizations find buyers for salable limited-partnership units. You can get a free list by sending a self-addressed, stamped envelope to the Investment Partnership Association (page 675). Call six or seven of the firms, to see how they work and the kind of deal you can get. Always ask if the price is solid; a broker might name a price that he or she is ultimately unable to get. Warning: None of these prices will be high. Partnership units sell at deep discounts. Many units don't fetch any bids at all. If fact, if someone else considers your partnership worth buying, entertain the thought that maybe, just maybe, it's worth keeping.

SEE A LAWYER. If the prospectus fraudulently oversold the deal, or didn't disclose everything that the general partner knew, you have a shot at recovering some money. But don't dawdle. Legitimate lawsuits are easiest to win if they're brought within a year of the time that a prudent person should have smelled a rat. Then, you have only to show that the prospectus was misleading. The longer you wait, the greater your burden of proof.

Your general partner (GP) may deliberately encourage you to dawdle by writing hearty quarterly reports. Bad news may be slipped into paragraphs that otherwise radiate good cheer. If you eventually go to court, the GP will argue that those wisps of bad news should have put you on notice years ago that the partnership was failing.

So read those reports with a lot of care. Underline every bad-news sentence, then call the sponsor and ask for details. Take notes of what the sponsor says. If the partnership isn't very old, there may have been problems right from the start that weren't disclosed to the investors. It's worth taking the prospectus and sales material to a securities lawyer for an evaluation. Ask your state bar association for the names of attorneys specializing in securities law, or ask your own lawyer for a referral.

To try to get your money back, your best route might be arbitration, especially if you feel that the partnership was too risky for someone in your circumstances (page 570).

Alternatively, you can launch a lawsuit. There are two ways of doing it: (1) Find a lawyer who will handle a class-action suit. You pay nothing up front and all the investors share the recovery. (2) Sue with a limited group of investors. The lawyer gets a retainer, probably 2 to 4 percent of your investment. His or her fee will be one-third of the recovery, plus expenses. Your group of investors will split the rest.

Occasionally, a "prospecting" attorney will write a letter to all the investors in a big public partnership that's under water. Each will be asked for a few hundred dollars, to cover the cost of determining whether there are any grounds to sue. Sometimes it's worthwhile to send the money, but sometimes not. It's hard to know when legal action is worth the price. Best bet: Get a second opinion from a securities lawyer who will not be a part of the case.

Partnerships Are a Special Risk for Older People!

I once heard from an investor who, at age 63, had put two-thirds of his capital into 10 limited partnerships. As he understood it, they would pay him an income right into old age. ("You'll get the income," his broker had said, "and your heirs will get the payoff.") Needless to say, many of his deals aren't paying a dime and many are bankrupt.

My opinion of the broker is beyond words. But I have plenty to say to the middle-aged and older investor.

DON'T BUY LIMITED PARTNERSHIPS! They are typically designed to last for 5 to 10 years or longer. At age 63 or even age 55, you cannot risk having your capital frozen for so long a period. What if you retire early? What if you die or become disabled and your family needs the money? By the time you near retirement age, you should be holding liquid (that is, readily salable) investments. Furthermore, nothing binds general partners to the specified exit date. If they don't want to liquidate the investment, for whatever reason, they have every right to hold on to it longer.

Some partnerships tell investors that they plan to go public in two years. But again, the GPs can change their minds, leaving you with no way to sell.

It's especially dangerous to put limited partnerships into tax-deferred retirement plans. After age 70½, you *must* start withdrawing money from these plans or face a serious penalty (page 794). If the GP won't sell, and you bought your units with Keogh funds, the penalty will decimate your investment. You have an escape hatch only if you bought the partnership for an Individual Retirement Account *and* have other IRAs as well. The law lets you take money from other IRAs to cover the withdrawals due from the one that's tied up.

Adding insult to injury, your GP may put a valuation on the partnership that is arbitrary and unrealistic. For example, many sponsors tell investors that their investment is worth what they originally paid when in fact the property's value has dropped. Yet for purposes of an IRA or Keogh withdrawal, the broker's valuation is gospel. If penalties are owed, they'll be based on what the broker says the deal is worth.

If You Still Want to Buy a Partnership . . .

Buy a "used" unit. First decide which partnership you'd like to own. Then call the sponsor to see if it has any units for sale. If not, ask Partnerline who's selling (page 676). Or call the Investment Partnership Association (page 675) for the list of firms that buy and sell. Ask each firm what it's charging for the units you want. Find out who gets the partnership distributions during the weeks or months it may take to transfer the units into your name. Compare each firm's fees, and ask whether it belongs to the National Association of Securities Dealers (not all do; NASD membership gives you some protection against a broker who takes your check and doesn't deliver). Don't buy from the major brokerage houses. Their prices are too high.

Look for a seasoned partnership (at least three years old) that is doing well. Its cash flows should be covering its costs, with some money left over for the investors. Don't bet on troubled properties that you think might turn around. Even sophisticated players have lost their shirts on some of these. Visit the properties, evaluate their past performance, and talk to management. If you can't, or won't, do the homework, invest somewhere else. Buying blind from a broker or financial planner is just as bad the second time around as it was the first.

PENNY STOCKS: FOR SUCKERS ONLY

A penny stock comes from a new and untested company and is sold to the public for five dollars or less per share. Often, it's under one dollar a share. Not all cheap stocks are bad. But almost all the rotten issues are cheap. The state securities commissioners call penny stocks today's number-one investment fraud. They're peddled, by phone, by Hole-in-the-Wall Gangs who transfix their victims with the claim that the investment "cannot lose." With automatic dialing, a penny-stock broker can place 200 calls a day.

If you're ever tempted by the pitch, here's what will happen. You'll buy the stock and, lo and behold, the price will rise. So you'll put up more money for another stock that rises, too. It feels like luck, but actually the broker manipulates the price. You keep getting good news while the broker milks you for all the money he or she thinks you've got.

Then things change. Suddenly, one of your stocks goes down. You want to sell, but discover you can't. In crooked penny-stock schemes, the brokers will not process your order unless you use your "profits" to buy another stock. They keep rolling your money into other ventures until they finally wipe you out.

Many penny-stock schemes are "blank checks" or "blind pools." (One state securities commissioner calls them "deaf pools," as in: "Give me your money and you'll never hear from me again.") Here's how they work. You buy shares in a hollow company that does no business of its own. When it gets your money, it goes looking for small, private companies to buy. Some of these companies are legitimate, like a printer or a bakery. Others are frauds. Gold is a popular line to pretend to be in; so is claiming to have a cure for AIDS.

Once there's a business—real or apparent—publicists send out lyrical reports predicting a brilliant and profitable future. Brokers hit the telephones and start pushing the stock. They create excitement by quoting higher and higher prices which are literally plucked out of thin air. The insiders make money by selling their shares to all the deluded innocents who think that the company is real.

As soon as the scamsters have scored their gains, they drop the stock and switch to another one. The price collapses to its true value, which may be only a few cents a share.

In certain circumstances, a penny-stock broker is supposed to get proof that you, the investor, are financially able to shoulder the hazard of buying these shares. You'll be asked about your income and net worth and will have to sign a "suitability statement." New investors also have to sign a purchase order; you can't be held to an okay that you gave by phone. But brokers may tell you that the forms are "just paperwork," "routine," and "not worth reading." If you believe them, it's your loss. These statements alert you to the risk.

You don't even have to sign these forms if you've bought penny stocks before, if you initiated the purchase, if the broker doesn't make a market in the stock (meaning that the broker doesn't control the price), if the stock is listed on a formal exchange (the Philadelphia Exchange has been accepting pennies), or if it's on the National Association of Securities Dealers Automated Quotations system (page 596). These loopholes keep penny-stock scams in business.

If you're called by a penny-stock broker who strong-arms you to buy, hang up. If this advice comes too late, tell your broker to sell your shares and send you the cash. If he or she won't, threaten to call the state securities commissioner. That sometimes works. And carry through with the threat (for where to get the phone number, see page 555). Your complaint might help shut that boiler room down.

UNIT TRUSTS: THE MYSTERY DEALS

Imagine a house with an elephant in the basement. It's been said that the animal holds up the house. Grateful for the constant support, the householders feed their elephant richly. But no one ever goes down with a flashlight to see what the beast is really doing.

That pretty much defines the bizarre faith engendered by unit investment trusts, a multi-billion-dollar industry directed especially to conservative investors. You buy unit trusts for their "steady income" and "locked-in yields." Stockbrokers like to claim, based on no visible evidence, that the trusts do better than comparable mutual funds.

But no one has ever gone down with a flashlight to look. I know of no other major investment for which so little performance data is available. It's impossible to tell whether unit trusts are better than, or even as good as, competing mutual funds. I do know, however, that some of the claims made for unit trusts are simply not true.

In general, a unit trust is a fixed portfolio of securities—usually municipal bonds or Ginnie Maes, but sometimes corporate bonds or stocks. A package of securities is assembled. You buy an interest in the package for a minimum of $1,000. Those securities are supposed to be held virtually unchanged until the trust expires, in anywhere from six months to 30 years. Securities are occasionally sold out of the trust, but no new ones are added. The sales commission runs in the area of 3 to 5 percent and you'll pay a trustee up to 0.2 percent annually, but there are no annual management fees.

You get a pro rata share of the trust's interest or dividends, mailed to you monthly, quarterly, or semiannually. As the securities mature, you'll also receive a pro rata share of the proceeds. Take, for example, a $20,000 investment in a municipal-bond unit trust. Initially, you might earn $117 a month in bond interest. Five years later, a block of those bonds may mature. You'd then get a check for $2,034, representing your share of the proceeds. That $2,034 is a return of some of the capital you invested. After that, your monthly check might drop to $105, because there are now fewer bonds in the trust. Each check specifies how much is interest and how much is principal.

Ginnie Mae unit trusts are a little more complicated. They invest in mortgages, so every check you get is a combination of mortgage interest and principal—the latter being a partial return of your own capital. Every time a homeowner prepays a mortgage, the proceeds are distributed to the trust's investors (for more on Ginnie Maes, see page 648).

The distributions you receive from unit trusts cannot be reinvested in the trust itself. But the sponsor may arrange for them to be reinvested in a money market mutual fund.

In theory, the trust remains in existence until the last bond matures. In practice, the sponsor often sells the remaining securities and distributes the proceeds when the trust's principal value has shrunk to perhaps 25 or 20 percent of its opening value.

You can usually sell your shares back to the unit trust sponsor before maturity. If the sponsor won't buy them, you may be able to redeem the shares directly through the trustee. Depending on the state of the market, you might get more or less for the units than you originally paid.

THE QUESTION FOR INVESTORS IS WHETHER THEY WILL REALLY EARN THOSE LOVELY YIELDS THEY READ ABOUT IN THE SALES LITERATURE. There is no way of telling. No independent service tracks the performance of unit trusts to find out what they actually pay.

Any investment whose claims can't be checked invites abuse. I find the following soft spots in the unit trusts.

THEIR ALLEGEDLY SUPERIOR RETURNS AREN'T PROVEN. Unit trusts claim that they outperform comparable mutual funds because they charge no management fees. More of your money is supposedly left in the trust to compound.

But you pay a sales load up front, which you don't with a no-load mutual fund. And because unit trust portfolios are more or less fixed, the sponsors may be slow to weed out investment mistakes. Until someone starts charting the trusts' performance relative to mutual funds, you should disregard this claim.

YOU MIGHT LOSE MONEY IF YOUR TRUST DOESN'T LAST UNTIL ITS STATED MATURITY DATE. Trusts have the right to cash you out early if calls and redemptions shrink their assets by a specified amount. But if the remaining bonds are sold, what price will they bring? Some unit trusts have been dumping grounds for bonds that the sponsors otherwise couldn't sell. At liquidation, investors in these trusts would almost certainly take a loss.

THE INCOME ISN'T STEADY. Unit trusts are most often bought for their alleged "steady stream of income." The payments, your broker may say, are "fixed." But payments are not fixed. They might stay the same for a couple of years, but then your trust could start melting at the edges.

Here are four ways that your income might shrink.

Shrinker One: Some high-interest bonds will probably be called before maturity or retired through a sinking fund. This usually lowers your final yield. Calls have already bled many unit trusts that were sold in the early 1980s. During the early 1990s, huge numbers of securities in municipal-bond unit trusts will be called—to the shock of the people now living on that income. Unit trusts try for call protection on their bonds of at least 5 years and sometimes 10. But on a 30-year trust, that's a far cry from a "steady stream of income." If long-term, guaranteed income is your objective, buy noncallable Treasury bonds instead.

Shrinker Two: Some securities will be sold out of the trust in order to cover early redemptions. If the amount of bonds sold exceeds the sum redeemed (as sometimes happens), the leftover money will be distributed to investors—returning them a small share of their principal whether they want it or not. In choosing which securities to sell, the trusts try to hold your yield steady. Sometimes they can; sometimes they can't.

Shrinker Three: The credit quality of some bonds will slide. If a bad bond has to be sold out of the portfolio, you lose some of your principal. If a bond defaults, you lose interest and, generally, part of your principal (although some residual value will remain). Says former stockbroker Mary Calhoun, "There are fantastic safety problems with certain unit trusts. . . . Some of the sponsors put in poorer-quality bonds because they're desperate to get the yields up."

Junk-bond unit trusts are double trouble. Their better-quality bonds get called (because those issuers will be able to borrow at lower rates). The poorer bonds remain in the trust. After the calls, you lose some of your "steady" income and you're stuck with the issues most likely to default.

Shrinker Four: Some trusts are smoke and mirrors. They pay a higher income than you'd get from other bond investments, which makes you think you're earning a superior yield. But in fact, you're earning a normal yield and are running an abnormal risk of loss.

Here's how that happens: the trust buys a lot of older bonds that carry higher interest rates than are available today. So investors get more current income—say, 10.4 percent tax free. But to get those irresistible rates the trust had to pay a premium—say, $1,150 for each $1,000 bond. Those bonds will almost certainly be called before maturity at their $1,000 value, leaving the trust with a $150 loss per bond. After the call, your actual yield might be only 6.6 percent, vastly less than you thought you were earning.

But that's only Step One in the deception. Step Two is to disguise the loss. The trust does that by buying zero-coupon bonds. Zeros pay no current income; each year's interest is added to the value of the bond itself. The gains from the zeros are supposed to balance the losses you take on the bonds that are called.

That's the theory, anyway. In practice, these trusts are time bombs. Follow what is going to happen: (1) You will lose your tax-free income when your high-rate bonds are called. (2) You will take a capital loss on the money used to buy those bonds. (3) Much of the money that's left in the trust will be tied up in zeros, which pay no current income and won't mature for another 20 years. (4) If you sell your trust you will lose money. You won't come out whole unless you hold the zeros to maturity.

So much for the "high yield" unit trust that was supposed to pay a steady income!

Older unit trusts, which some stockbrokers have been peddling furiously, can run you into a similar trap. You're attracted by the high current income. But when those bonds are called, your income will drop and you'll be left with a capital loss.

SOME YIELDS CAN BE CHECKED BEFORE YOU BUY, thanks to some requirements promulgated by the Securities and Exchange Commission.

On new unit trusts, the sponsor must disclose the estimated long-term return instead of the current return, if there's a material difference between the two. Often, the sponsor will disclose both.

On old unit trusts, no disclosure rules are yet in effect (although the SEC is working on them). If you're buying such a trust, here's how to investigate it: (1) Ask the broker for both the current yield and the estimated long-term yield and get it in writing. Those two figures should be about the same. If they're not, you've got a weasel trust. If the sponsor won't disclose the long-term yield, assume the worst and walk away. (2) Check the list of securities in the trust's portfolio. If it contains a lot of zero-coupon bonds, you're buying into a potential disaster. Your income may not last very long and your capital will be tied up in zeros. (3) If a broker offers you a unit trust that apparently yields more than the new bonds coming to market, laugh hysterically and change the subject. More money may be lost in the stretch for extra yield than in any of the straight-out market scams. "If you want a high yield real bad, that's what you'll get," a friend of mine says. "A real bad high yield."

SOPHISTICATED INVESTORS IN TAX FREE SECURITIES RARELY BUY UNIT TRUSTS. They buy high-quality, new-issue, intermediate-term bonds instead. There's no upfront sales commission on new issues, intermediate-term bonds may be noncallable, and the income really *is* steady. Unit trusts, with their misleading yields, are pitched to smaller investors who know less about how the bond market works.

A unit trust invested in Treasury bonds (as some are) is a pure con. You're paying a 3 to 5 percent sales commission to buy securities that you can get yourself, commission-free, from the nearest Federal Reserve bank (page 178).

COMMODITIES: A LOSER'S GAME

For those of you eager to lose money on commodities, let me count the ways.

Commodities Funds

Public commodities funds are actually limited partnerships. They buy and sell tangible investments like metals and agricultural products; they also trade foreign currencies, as a hedge against the dollar. Typically, it costs no more than $2,000 to $5,000 to buy in. Sponsors may hold out the hope of gains as high as 90 percent a year.

But that's a joke, as studies of the public commodity funds have found. On average, they have yielded lousy returns for their investors—on the order of 4 to 10 percent annually, depending on the time period and the fund. And they've been a poor hedge against inflation. (These conclusions come from work by Professors Edwin Elton and Martin Gruber of New York University and Joel Rentzler of Baruch College.)

There are two worms in the commodities apple.

1. *Costly mistakes.* Fund managers trade furiously, trying to catch quick changes in trends. They "go long" some commodities, betting that prices will rise, and "go short" others, betting that prices will fall. So inflation itself is no guarantee of profit. Your manager has to be on the right side of each bet.

2. *Kleptomaniacal fees.* If one counts management fees, performance fees, and brokerage commissions, investors in commodity funds between 1979 and 1985 paid an average of 19 percent a year just to have their money managed, as opposed to around 1 percent in stock-owning mutual funds. In recent years, expenses have dropped but not by much. So even when your manager rides the price trends right, the fees leave large portions of the profits sticking to his or her fingers rather than yours.

During various time periods, some funds do show sensational gains. But there's no reliable way of identifying these funds in advance. A manager's performance this years says nothing about how well he or she is going to do next year.

On new funds offered to the public, the managers' past performances look consistently superb. The money they made for previous clients may be reported at 50, 60, even 70 percent a year. But those astonishing track records are a clever form of fiction. They're not wrong, exactly, but they're biased and misleading.

There are two slugs in the performance cabbage.

1. *Luck.* The law of averages says that, in any period, some of the country's 2,000 commodity managers will do spectacularly well for their private clients. They're not geniuses; they've just hit a hot streak. At the height of their streak, they're picked to run a public commodities fund. But soon their performance reverts to average and their funds poop out.

2. *Guile.* In the prospectus, managers are required to show their track record for at least the past three years. But they can show more if they want to. That allows them to pick the time period that creates the most attractive record.

Fighting their bad reputation, the commodities funds have come up with a gimmick. It's a performance guarantee—a no-risk offer, safe even for my sainted grandmother. At the end of five years or so, the brokers say, you will get back at least as much as you invested, and much, much more if the fund succeeds.

How is this miracle achieved? Part of your money buys a zero-coupon bond; the remainder goes into commodities. After five years, the zero is worth your original investment. (Some funds use bank letters of credit for this guarantee.)

But the price of security comes high. Just to net 8 percent, your "guaranteed" fund might need gross returns on its commodity investments of anywhere from 15 to 23 percent a year to cover its expenses and offset the money invested in the zero. If it earns less (and it probably will) your investment is a bust.

Besides, what's the big deal about getting your money back after five years? It will have earned no interest. At 4 percent inflation, your purchasing power will be down by 33 percent.

Commodities Futures

This is the world of futures contracts: a contract on June gold; a contract on December wheat; a contract on March soybeans. You put up perhaps 5 or 10 percent of the cost of the contract to bet on the price of a specific commodity on a specific date. Prices are moved by rumor, politics, war, scientific discoveries, business announcements, economic developments, and international weather and crop reports, and they move fast. You can "go long" (a gamble that prices will rise) or "go short" (a gamble that prices will fall). Winners may earn many times their investment. But if prices run against you, you can lose far more money than you put up—perhaps tens of thousands of dollars more. In fact, you are liable for up to the contract's full value. Fortunes can be lost or made within a few days or even a few hours.

End of lesson. The only other thing you need to know is that an estimated 75 percent of commodities speculators lose money. I would bet that 99.9 percent of *amateur* commodities speculators lose money.

The record is probably no better for plungers who buy *options* on futures. A call option gives the holder the right to buy the underlying futures contract at a specified price within a specified time; it's a bet that the price will rise. A put option gives the holder the right to sell and is a bet that the price will fall. If you pay, say, $1,000 to buy an option and prices move in your direction, the value of your option will rise. But if prices run against you, you can never lose more than the $1,000 you put up.

There are two main differences between options and futures.

1. When you buy or sell a future, you are contracting to buy or sell the commodity itself. If you don't close out a purchase (at a profit, you hope) before the contract's delivery date, you'll literally have bought the farm. You'll own warehouse receipts for a silo full of soybeans or wheat. By contrast, when you buy an option on a future, you are buying the right to the contract's change in value over a limited period of time. If you don't sell or exercise your option, it will expire worthless.

2. With futures, you can lose much more than the money you put up. The same is true if you sell an option. Both carry unlimited risk. If you *buy* an option, however, your losses can't exceed your original investment. For this reason, commodities traders say that buying options is "safer" (although the risk of losing 100 percent of my investment isn't on my comfort list).

To the ruin of many a trusting buyer, options on futures have been a staple of get-rich-quick TV shows. Some slick salesperson shows up on the tube to say there's a shortage of oil or a drought in the Middle West and that oil or wheat prices will soar. (For more information, call 800-555-GYPP.)

The options are real enough but the prices you pay are hugely inflated. As much as 40 percent of your "investment" may be taken off the top in sales commissions and hidden costs. Any price moves in oil or wheat would have to be enormous to cover these costs and yield a profit.

Any customer with a modest income and few assets who was fast-talked into buying options on futures has a good chance of winning an arbitration case against the broker. There's no way these investments are suitable for anyone with a low net worth. For arbitration procedures, see page 570. To get your money back from firms that deal exclusively in futures, try the arbitration service of the National Futures Association, 200 West Madison St., Suite 1600, Chicago, IL 60606. Or use the reparations service offered by the Commodity Futures Trading Commission, Office of Proceedings, 2033 K St. N.W., Washington, DC 20581. A reparations hearing resembles arbitration except that its procedures are more formal and the result can be appealed. If your broker's firm belongs to a stock exchange, you can use stock-exchange arbitration.

STOCK-INDEX OPTIONS AND FUTURES

You can book bets on stocks without ever owning one, by buying and selling stock options and futures. They're a speculation on the future prices of some of the major market averages. If you think you know where the Standard & Poor's 500-stock index will be next month, here's the place to make your fortune.

During the years of the Great Bull Market, when higher stock prices felt ordained, options players made astonishing profits on very small amounts of cash. But the morning after the '87 Crash, those same investors woke up to learn that they'd lost many times their original stake. An Indiana teacher, who thought he was risking only $5,000, found himself $100,000 in debt (the firm settled this case in arbitration.) A stockbroker in Oklahoma, after losing a large arbitration case, admitted to his clients that options confused him. "I never should have messed with them," he said. A Florida broker who suffered huge losses in his own account took his brokerage firm to arbitration, arguing that his boss should have realized that he, the broker, was in over his head.

If the brokers didn't understand what they were doing, you can imagine where their customers stood. Here's a glimpse of the complexities of stock-index trading, just to show you what you're up against.

STOCK-INDEX OPTIONS, DEFINED: When you buy or sell any option, you're securing the right to profit (you hope) from the change in price of the underlying commodity. Here, that commodity is stocks. You're betting that the stock index will rise or fall by a specified amount within a limited period—typically one to four months.

Buying a call is betting that the index will rise. Buying a put is betting that the index will fall. (Conversely, *selling* a put is a bet that the index will *not* fall, which is different from betting that it will go up. Selling a call is a bet that the index will not rise.) The cost of an option is known as its *premium*. You also have to pay brokerage commissions.

A winning option can be held until maturity and settled for cash, or it can be sold at a profit ahead of time. To cut your losses on a losing option, try to sell it before it expires. If you don't sell, or can't, that money is gone. Options are offered on a variety of stock market indexes, but the most popular is the Standard & Poor's 100 (100 blue chip stocks), which is traded on the Chicago Board Options Exchange.

When you *buy* an option, your risk is limited to the money you put up. When you *sell* an option, however, your risk is unlimited. Many investors and their brokers failed to grasp this crucial difference and were selling put options on the eve of the '87 crash. That's why their losses were so big.

STOCK FUTURES, DEFINED: When you buy or sell futures, you are contracting to buy a particular commodity. In this case, the commodity is a stock market index, the most popular being the S&P 500-stock index. You put up about 10 percent of the contract as collateral. If stock prices move in the right direction (either up or down, depending on your bet), you can sell the contract at a profit. Or you can take a cash settlement at the end of the contract's term. Either way, you get your collateral back. If the market runs against you, you will be asked for more collateral. Your losses could be substantially more than you put up.

OPTIONS ON STOCK FUTURES, DEFINED: You can buy the right to profit from any futures contract, on any commodity, without contracting to take delivery of the commodity itself. With respect to stocks, this means betting on the value of a futures contract on a stock market index. You can buy or sell either puts or calls. Either way, you will own a piece of paper that speculates on the changing worth of another piece of paper, neither of which has any tangible value. (If you're not with me, that's proof that you shouldn't be with an options broker, either.)

The prices of options on futures swing more widely and wildly than the prices of options on the stock indexes themselves. So of these three super-risky investments, buying futures options combines the highest potential for gain with "limited" losses (*only* 100 percent of your investment could go down the drain).

A PRUDENT USE OF STOCK-INDEX OPTIONS IS TO HEDGE AGAINST AN ANTICIPATED MARKET DROP. If you own a large and diversified stock portfolio, but don't want to sell for tax or other reasons, you can buy puts on an index that resembles your holdings. In a market decline, you'll lose on your stocks but make money on your puts. Your losses may not be fully covered by your gains, but at least you'll have limited the shock. If the market doesn't fall, consider the puts a small price to pay for peace of mind.

A SPECULATIVE USE OF STOCK-INDEX OPTIONS IS TO BET ON WHICH WAY THE MARKET WILL MOVE. Minor changes in the index produce big percentage gains or losses on the money you put up. But to win this game, you have to get three things right: (1) The market has to move in the right direction; (2) the index has to rise or fall by more than enough to cover your costs; and (3) the change has to come within a short, and specified, period. That's market timing with a vengeance. It shouldn't surprise you to hear that the majority of options buyers lose. But their brokers win. At a full-service firm, your combined buying and selling commissions generally run in the area of 5 to 8 percent of your invested capital, although they can go both lower and higher.

Just as you can speculate in puts and calls on the market as a whole, you can do so on individual stocks, such as General Motors or IBM.

A conservative, money-making use of options is to sell calls against blue-chip stocks you own—an action known as "writing covered calls." If you own IBM, for example, you can sell someone the right to buy it from you at a specified higher price (the "strike price"). The money you collect is called a premium. If IBM doesn't rise above the strike price, you keep the premium and the stock—so you eat your cake and have it, too. If the price does go up, your IBM stock will be called away, costing you the capital gain. So you earn extra income by writing options but will give up a lot of stock profits, over time. As soon as they come to understand this, individuals tend to lose interest in covered calls.

A hugely high-risk use of options is to sell them against stocks you don't own, a strategy known as "writing naked calls." Suppose that you write such a call against General Motors. As long as the price of GM doesn't rise above the strike price, you win. If it does, you lose. You would have to buy GM in the open market, whatever its price, to deliver to the person who bought the call. Alternatively, you might write naked puts. As long as the stock doesn't drop below the strike price, you win. If it does, you will have to swallow the stock at a higher price than it's selling for in the open market.

Some speculators are substituting options for stocks. If you feel in your gut that IBM will go up pretty soon, it's cheaper (and potentially more profitable) to buy a three-month call on the stock than to buy the stock itself. If your gut was just registering indigestion, however, you'll be out the money.

When the speculators are Wall Street pros, I couldn't care less. Professional investors are action junkies and options are an easy fix. Ditto for economists and other interest-rate experts who often gamble on Treasury-bond futures. But no individual seriously trying to build net worth should use options, period. Even if you win at the start you will lose in the end.

CHICKEN FUNDS: THE ULTIMATE PLUCKING MACHINE

Chicken funds (mostly unit trusts) flourish after any stock market scare. Sponsors package a "safe" zero-coupon bond with a speculative or growth investment like gold, stocks, or real estate. The pitch is: "Come back to the market, my dear departed ones. I'm positive that your money will grow. To calm your nerves, I will guarantee that, whatever happens, you will get your money back."

Salespeople call chicken funds "balanced investments." I call them humbug. The zeros don't lower your investment risk, any more than they did with commodities funds.

Here's what's wrong with chicken funds.

Over five to eight years, the zero will mature—eventually paying the money you originally put in. But it will have lost a lot of purchasing power. Also, you may have paid taxes every year on the interest building inside the bond. To keep up with inflation and taxes and earn a real return on your money, you are counting on the other part of your investment—the gold or the real estate—to succeed. So the zero hasn't shielded you from risk at all.

You're at double jeopardy if you want to sell. You'll lose money unless both parts of your packaged investment did well. Had you held, say, your gold and your zeros separately, you'd be able to sell just one or the other, as market conditions dictate.

MARKETS ARE NOT "SAFE." ZEROS WILL NOT MAKE THEM SO. When you buy a zero combined with any other kind of investment, you are really making a three-part bet: that your growth investments will succeed; that you will hold to maturity; or that interest rates will fall, so that if you sell before maturity, the zero will show a profit, not a loss. That's a lot of ifs. Furthermore, you pay a higher commission to buy zeros packaged with growth investments than you would if you bought them separately through a mutual fund or discount broker.

A FEW MORE THINGS YOU MAY REGRET IN THE MORNING

1. Any new investment touted as "safe" with a higher-than-normal yield. This field is so jammed with hopefuls that I had trouble picking just one to tell you about. Anyway, for your delectation, here's the story on "plastic bonds."

Plastic bonds are high-rated, intermediate-term bonds (lasting four years or so), backed by consumer credit card debt owed to major institutions like Citibank or Sears Roebuck. Wall Street has been selling these bonds in $1,000 lots to folks who like a higher yield. But is the extra yield worth it? First, it's fully taxable. Second, it might run only 0.4 percentage points above comparable Treasuries (that's an extra $20 a year on a $5,000 investment). Third, the resale market isn't so hot. You might find it hard to sell before maturity at a decent price. New products like these need some market seasoning so that people can learn what the downside is. Don't be the guinea pig.

2. Any mutual fund calling itself Something Plus—as in Government Plus. Such a name implies higher yields at no increase in risk. That's never true. There is always risk. "Plus" means "We'll try to squeeze out some extra money by hedging with index options, zloty futures, plastic bonds, and puts on Imelda Marcos's shoe collection." Mark these funds a minus.

3. Anything advertised on late-night, get-rich-quick TV shows. No-money-down real estate deals. Options on grain or oil futures. Penny stocks. Investment tapes and books of any kind.

4. Anything hyped by phone, by a salesperson you don't know. Even if the firm is honest, this is no way to pick an investment. If the firm is dishonest, you're being set up to lose serious money. The bigger the profit the broker promises, and the greater the pressure to make a decision, the worse the investment is going to be.

5. Any fancy new way of holding investments that worked okay the old way. Here, too, there are a lot of entrants. The winner, to my mind, is the collateralized mortgage obligation known as a CMO. CMOs, touted to people who might otherwise buy Ginnie Maes, are said to have more predictable paybacks. You can opt to get your money back over a

variety of short-, medium-, and long-term periods. But the repayment rate isn't absolutely certain. The securities are hard to sell before maturity. The yield (so firmly announced) is only a rough estimate. There's no way of telling whether you've been offered the fairest price. And the highest yields go with the longest maturities, which can also lose the most in price. So who needs them?

6. Diamonds and other precious gems. Wholesale prices are rigged. Markups are huge. Price indexes are unreliable. Prices depend on subjective judgments about the "quality grades" of the stone, which is an invitation to cheat. Even if the dealers all agree on a stone's grading (and it's backed by a certificate from the Gemological Institute of America), you could still get burned by paying too much. But it's a free country. Go ahead and buy. Investment-grade stones are usually kept in their own soft bags, in vaults. The stones in jewelry are of lesser grade and speculation rarely affects their price. By the time a stone is set, it may retail at more than double the value of the gem itself.

7. Smaller stocks that trade over the counter in limited amounts. Brokers may take huge markups on these issues. You may need a 20 percent increase in price just to cover the overt and hidden costs. Buy a smaller OTC stock only for a sound, fundamental reason, and plan to hold it a long, long time.

8. Rare, or "numismatic," coins. These are strictly for specialists. Among coin collectors, the condition of a coin is critical and you're in no position to judge. Two coins of the same apparent grade could sell for different prices, depending on who graded them. A coin might be graded up when you buy, in order to make it more expensive. When you sell, a different dealer might grade it down, which lowers its price.

Coin dealers are trying to bring order to this chaos. Instead of relying on a dealer's eye to establish a grade, several services now grade coins according to what they say are standard criteria. These coins, known as "certified coins," are sealed in a plastic container called a "slab." A coin slabbed by a particular service is theoretically a standard, tradable item in the rare-coin market, because everyone supposedly agrees on the value of that service's grade. For this protection, you might pay an extra $25 to $30 over the cost of an unslabbed coin.

In practice, however, the grades haven't always been as standard as the services proclaim. Furthermore, they don't all agree on grades, some being harder markers than others. So even the prices of slabbed "MS65s" (MS meaning "mint state"), which are just about tops, will vary according to who certified and slabbed them. So it's still a slippery market. To buy well, you have to know your way around. Some quite ordinary coins are being sold to the credulous at excessive prices, just because they've been slabbed.

Many wannabe investors are seduced into buying coins by the staggering rise in the widely quoted Salomon Brothers "Index" of rare-coin prices. But that index is a bit of a crock. You're not getting a measure of actual buying and selling prices, only one dealer's estimate of the current value of 20 leading coins. More than likely, the index vastly overstates the long-term gains in average prices.

By all means collect rare coins as a hobby. Start visiting dealers and auctions. Subscribe to *Coin World,* published in Sidney, Ohio, which has good coin-price indexes of its own. If you really get smart about your hobby, your passion could become your investment. Otherwise, it's a waste of money.

9. Collectibles of all kinds—stamps, art, porcelain, rare books, maps, antiques, rare wines, Oriental rugs, baseball cards, Mickey Mouse ears. None is worth a moment of your time. They yield their treasure only to dedicated collectors, who study them, admire them, and understand their value. Buy a lithograph because you love it, not because you think it will make you rich.

GOLD: THE ULTIMATE WORRY BEAD

For some, it's the supreme inflation hedge. If the U.S. dollar is ever carted off in wheelbarrows, there will be gold.

For others, it's a trauma defense. Let the Middle East mushroom into darkest night, let South Africa flame into civil war, there will be gold. (But gold for whom? Back when Lebanon first fell apart, rich people rushed to their banks to retrieve their gold, only to be robbed of it by gunmen at the door. The gold hoards of many Kuwaitis were similarly seized by Iraqi troops.)

For yet others—the less zealous investors—it's a speculation on changes in the rate of inflation, real interest rates, and other economic factors. For them, there will occasionally be gold, depending on the price.

As an investment that beats inflation, gold is a bust. From the end of 1974, when it again became legal for Americans to own gold (then nearly $200 an ounce) through the end of 1989, the price has risen almost exactly by the inflation rate. That's a zero percent real return. What's more, gold paid no income and cost an investor money to insure and store. If you're satisfied with a zero real return long-term, you might as well buy Treasury bills because after taxes and inflation they pay zero, too.

So why all hoo-ha about gold? Partly because so many small investors bought gold coins at $700 or $800 an ounce during the manic weeks of 1981 and are dreaming of getting their money back. And partly because rich people can afford to worry about everything.

Gold will protect you against a hyperinflation or currency collapse. But those risks are remote, hence not worth the average investor's time and money. You need to grow your assets for college tuition and retirement. You cannot afford to prepare yourself for Armageddon, too. For everyday-inflation protection, you are well enough hedged by owning your own home, common stocks, and short-term Treasury securities.

Once your net worth reaches the $500,000 range, however, you have enough money to extend your field of worry. So you might start building toward a gold cache worth 5 percent of your assets, dollar-averaging your purchases over time.

"Insurance buyers" hardly care if their gold goes up in price. They own it for ultimate protection, not for capital gains. But "investment buyers" seek profits, and may own gold for diversification. Gold and gold stocks often behave differently from other major assets—for example, rising in price when the stock market goes down. That makes gold a legitimate holding even for those who are not inclined to hedge against the end of the world. Every investment has its day and so, periodically, will gold.

What moves gold prices? Who knows? Demand may suddenly explode for a wide variety of geopolitical reasons, none of them predictable. But surprises aside, gold is thought to move up on the expectation of higher inflation ahead and move down on the expectation of level to lower inflation—that is, unless there's a competing inflation investment that looks even better. Lately, investors have been perfectly happy in short-term government securities rather than gold.

If you're still interested in owning gold, here are the various ways to buy.

GOLD-MINING STOCKS AND MUTUAL FUNDS. There are two ways of using these funds, one aggressive, one conservative.

Gunslingers swing into mutual funds when they think that gold prices are going to rise. The stocks of gold-mining companies move up faster and higher than gold itself. Conversely, the stocks suffer faster and deeper losses when gold prices drop, so speculators may not own them long. Some mutual funds avoid stocks in South African gold mines; others buy whichever stocks look good.

For conservative investors, no-load gold mutual funds are a simpler and cheaper inflation hedge than coins. Also, they earn some dividends. To avoid the funds' roller-coaster price risks, invest a fixed amount of money regularly, every month, for several years. You'll wind up with a long-term precious-metals position at a reasonable average cost. Consider a gold "index fund," which invests in a broad range of companies that mine, fabricate, and process gold. Two such (both no-load funds): the Benham Gold Equities Index Fund, Mountain View, California, and the Rushmore Precious Metals Index Plus Portfolio, Bethesda, Maryland. (Yes, I hate the "Plus" part—page 692.)

GOLD BULLION COINS AND BARS. These are for "insurance buyers," who hold gold against the risk of some frightful (but not unthinkable) disaster. Coins can also be moved from one place to another, quickly and privately, for purposes that this book wouldn't dare delve into.

A "bullion" coin is traded almost entirely on the basis of its gold content. It has no numismatic interest. You pay a modest premium over its gold value, to reflect the cost of the coin's manufacture and distribution. True investors stick with one-ounce coins. The smaller coins (half-ounce, quarter-ounce, and so on) are more heavily weighted with sales and manufacturing expenses, so it's harder for buyers to earn a profit. You'll see small coins in jewelry, not in safe deposit boxes.

Of the many bullion coins now on the market, the most widely sold are the U.S.-minted American Eagles and the Canadian Maple Leafs. South African Krugerrands, although no longer being imported, do trade, but at lower prices than other coins.

Premiums change on bullion coins, reflecting daily supply and demand. For a small order of one-ounce coins, you might pay 3.5 to 6 percent over the gold price, depending on the dealer, plus a 1 percent sales commission. There may also be a shipping charge.

Here are some cost data to help you gauge the fairness of the prices you're offered on a purchase of 5 to 10 gold coins: The U.S. and Canadian mints sell coins to primary wholesale dealers for the current auction price of gold plus 3 percent. The primary wholesalers mark up the price by about half a percentage point and sell to retailers. The cheapest retailers add another half point, so their coins sell at the price of gold plus 4 percent. Other retailers price up from there. Costs are typically higher if you buy just one coin and lower on a larger order. You may owe sales taxes unless you store your gold hoard out of state.

When you resell a coin, you might be offered two to three percentage points over the auction-market price, minus a 1 percent sales commission—with the lowest bid coming from the so-called "discount brokers." Suggestion: Buy from a discounter, if the price is truly low, and sell to a full-service dealer, who may offer you more. Gold might have to rise by 3 percent or more in price for you to break even after costs.

The best way to compare prices is to call several dealers and ask for "the market"—both the buying price and selling price for an order of the size you're interested in—plus the commission, shipping charges, and any other fees. Don't tip your hand in advance by indicating whether you mean to buy or sell.

Bullion bars are generally fabricated for wealthy investors who buy their gold in major league amounts. Small bars are poured, too, but often by little-known companies whose bars are not readily accepted for resale. To protect your investment, stick with the majors. The dominant small bar traded in the United States is made by Credit Suisse, sealed in plastic, and sold with a certificate of authenticity. Two other well-known fabricators: Engelhard and Johnson Matthey. For safety and simplicity, however, small investors should stick with bullion coins.

GOLD-CERTIFICATE OR ACCUMULATION PLANS. These serve investors who don't care about running barefoot through their gold. They want only to own it, no muss, no fuss. So they buy a share in a large gold bar that's held in storage by a dealer. You might make a single purchase, for a minimum of $1,000 to $2,000. Or you might begin an "accumulation plan," investing, say, $100 a month. With accumulation plans, you dollar-average your purchases—some at a higher price, some at a lower one—which usually gives you good value over time. There's a modest monthly storage charge.

Whether it's cheaper to buy by certificate or to own the coins themselves depends on what each dealer is charging. Certificate and accumulation accounts are offered by a few major banks and brokerage houses, among them Shearson Lehman Brothers, the Rhode Island Hospital Trust National Bank in Providence, and the discount broker Ben-ham Certified Metals in Mountain View, California. Buy only from a well-known institution. Small gold-certificate deals may be cons.

Be absolutely sure that your gold is in a segregated account so that the bank or broker can't use it. Check that it's insured, even to the point of writing to the insurer for confirmation. You don't want any arguments if the bank or the brokerage house fail. Refuse any arrange-ment that lets the brokerage firm use your gold.

Warning: Gold-certificate accounts are for holding, not for moving. If you ever wanted the gold delivered, you'd have to pay shipping costs, maybe sales taxes in your state, and the cost of fabricating your gold into smaller bars (because the dealers buy their gold in bulk). Certificate holders can sell only to the dealer they bought from, which prevents you from shopping for a better price. If your dealer goes out of business, your worries are: (1) Is the gold really there? (2) How long will it take to get my investment out? For liquidity and total control of your investment, coins are best.

GOLD-STORAGE ACCOUNTS. Here, you buy an individual gold position, in coins or bars, and the dealer arranges to store it for you. It might be stored in a segregated account run by the dealer or in a personal account under your name. These accounts are favored by people who buy and sell gold frequently and don't want to pay the price of shipping it around.

SILVER DOESN'T CARRY THE SAME CACHET AS GOLD. The price may indeed rise in times of rising inflation and high political risk. But silver more often trades as an industrial metal, responsive to changes in the photography, dentistry, and electronics industries. A rule of thumb is that silver shouldn't trade at a ratio to gold any lower than $50 to $1. But it does, often enough and long enough to make that rule a poor investment guide. The coin of choice for silver investors is the one-ounce American Eagle. It sells at about 1.25 to 1.5 percent over the price of silver, plus a 1 percent sales commission, for lots of 100 to 400 coins.

PLATINUM coins have been getting a lot of press. Platinum costs more than gold, per ounce. Like silver, platinum's primary use is industrial—especially in auto antipollution devices. The classic coin is the Noble, from the Isle of Man. Newer coins are being fabricated by Australia and

Canada. Platinum prices are jumpy and erratic, however, and the jury is out on whether this metal will ever be considered a store of value.

THE IMPOSSIBLE TRIPLE PLAY

The bad investments pretend to be all things to all people. "Buy me," they whisper, "and you'll get your three wishes—no risk, high income, and high growth." Some throw in a fourth wish, tax deferral, just for spice.

But no single investment can make all your wishes come true. Each one leans principally in a single direction. When you go for high income, you give up some safety and growth. When you go for high growth, you give up some safety and income. When you go for safety, you lose growth and income. You have to decide which matters most. Any investment that promises all three is leading you down the garden path. The financial press is loaded with warnings from saddened investors who fell for one slick promise too many. Study their stories. Better an object lesson than a learning experience.

27
AIMEZ–VOUS GROWTH?

The Case for Putting Some Money Abroad

———

The question is no longer whether Americans
should invest abroad. It's only what to buy and
how much.

By the twenty-first century, Ameri-
cans will be investing abroad as comfortably as they do at home. Thousands of you do already. But to most investors, foreign markets still feel
like too much of a gamble.

I'd like to change your mind.

There are four strong reasons for putting maybe 10 to 20 percent of
your money abroad.

1. *To own a piece of other countries' growth.* At this point in world
history, Australia, much of Europe, and parts of Asia and Latin America
are growing faster than the United States. So their stock markets should
do better. In a number of industries, the world's strongest companies are
based abroad.

2. *To invest in currencies other than the American dollar.* U.S. investments are fine when the dollar is strong, but lose ground against foreign

investments when the dollar is weak. In the 1980s, the dollar rose sharply against most other currencies, then declined by almost as much. Adjusted for those changes, markets in five major foreign countries beat ours during the 1980s (Japan, Holland, the United Kingdom, France, and Germany, in that order).

3. *To invest in the world's strongest economic trends.* These include the consolidation of Western Europe and its emergence as an economic superpower; the rebuilding of Eastern Europe, if political trends remain favorable; Latin America's new appetite for private investment; the growth of affluent consumer markets in Asia, as its armies of workers rise to the middle class; and rapid economic development in any low-wage country whose government encourages private foreign investment. In the 1990s, many foreign countries will be growing strong while the United States spends the decade mud-wrestling with its debts.

4. *To reduce the risk to your investments overall.* This surprises many investors, who assume that foreign stocks carry greater risks. Individually, they may. But not in combination with U.S. stocks. Foreign markets are often strong when U.S. markets are weak, and vice versa. When one market drops, another may go up. If you're invested in several countries, your risk is less than if you were in one alone.

THE DOLLAR CONNECTION

When you invest in foreign securities, two factors influence how much money you will make: First, how well the foreign markets perform. Do stocks rise or fall? Are bond interest rates going up or down? Is the political or economic climate good or bad? Second, how well the U.S. dollar does. This is the part of international investing that leaves many investors confused.

SOMETIMES THE DOLLAR DECLINES ON INTERNATIONAL MARKETS. American currency is worth less while foreign currency is worth more. The result: Foreign securities rise in value, in dollar terms. As an example, take a $100 German stock whose price in Germany remains unchanged. If the dollar drops by 5 percent against the German mark, the dollar price of that stock rises to $105.

SOMETIMES THE DOLLAR RISES ON FOREIGN MARKETS. American currency is worth more while foreign currency is worth less. Result: Foreign securities fall in value, in dollar terms. If you buy a $100 German stock and the dollar rises 5 percent against the mark, your stock will be worth $95.

In a nutshell, then, your foreign investments are helped by a falling dollar and hurt by a rising dollar.

The dollar may rise against one currency while it's falling against another, depending on such things as comparative rates of inflation and whether each country's interest rates are moving up or down.

Every investment gain or loss in foreign markets comes in two parts —changes in the market itself and any changes in currency values. Both contribute to your total yield. The table below shows how that worked for the 12 months ending in June 1990.

If you invested in	The local stock market rose (fell) by	The local currency rose (fell) by *	American investors gained (lost)
Austria	32.6%	1.2%	34.2%
Norway	15.2	2.9	18.5
Italy	4.6	3.9	8.7
Germany	6.0	1.8	7.9
United Kingdom	−1.9	8.3	6.3
Singapore/Malaysia	1.5	3.3	4.8
France	0.5	3.5	4.0
Spain	−3.7	7.0	3.1
United States	1.8	—	1.8
Australia	−6.6	0.4	−6.2
Canada	−9.9	−0.6	−10.5
Japan	−21.2	−5.1	−25.2

* Against the dollar.
Source: Morgan Stanley Capital International. The percentage change in U.S. dollars is not directly equivalent to the percentage change in the local markets plus the percentage change in currency values.

DO YOURSELF A FAVOR: BUY MUTUAL FUNDS

It's hard to pick foreign stocks and bonds successfully. To do so, you have to follow foreign economies, tax laws, financial news, and interest rates; the outlook for each foreign currency relative to the dollar; each company's growth, profitability, and prospects; and the vagaries of each foreign stock market.

That's a lot. What's more, you have to do your corporate research without access to as much financial information or stockmarket data as is available in the United States. You're more dependent on investment-advisory services and the recommendations put out by the research departments of brokerage firms.

Or you could buy mutual funds.

If ever there were an argument for mutual funds, it's for buyers of international securities. Sit back, relax, and let the fund managers handle everything. A *global* funds buys worldwide, including the United States. An *international* fund buys securities everywhere but the United States. A *regional* fund sticks to a small group of countries, such as Europe or the Pacific Rim. A *single-country* fund buys just that. And so does a *foreign-bond fund.* You can choose among a huge variety of *open-end funds* (defined on page 504) and *closed-end funds* (page 538).

Single-Country Funds

Most single-country funds are closed-end. Like any other closed-end fund, they should generally be bought only when they trade at a deep discount to the value of the securities in the fund's portfolio (say, a discount of 10 to 15 percent or more). If you buy at a premium over the net asset value, you are usually setting yourself up for a loss. Ditto if you buy when a closed-end fund is first offered to investors.

The exceptions are funds in desirable markets where the government sharply limits the number of investment vehicles. Two examples, at this writing: the Korea Fund and the Taiwan Fund. Closed-ends like these tend to rise to premiums and stay there. However, competition is expected soon for both of these funds, which will probably reduce the premium that investors are willing to pay.

Even at a discount, any single-country fund carries extra risk. If that country's market hits a downdraft, so does your investment—and the manager can't shift his or her money to a more profitable part of the globe. If new closed-end funds for that particular country are introduced, investors may neglect the older funds, causing their prices to fall. That doesn't happen with open-end funds, which are always priced according to the value of the securities they hold, no matter how many funds are offered.

On the other hand, closed-ends are terrific for investing in developing countries, where the stock exchanges are relatively small and not very liquid. The fund manager can invest as he or she pleases, without worrying about what shares to sell if a lot of investors want to cash out. You might choose a closed-end for Mexico, for example, which during most of the 1980s, had the world's most profitable market.

Global, International, and Regional Funds

Most of the mutual funds in these categories are open-end. I prefer them for the average investor because you never have to worry about premiums or discounts, as you do with the closed-end funds. You always buy and sell at the net asset value of the securities in the portfolio. I also like widely diversified funds. The more countries you own, the less likely you are to take a bath in a particular market gone sour.

Global funds switch your money back and forth among American and foreign securities, depending on where they find the strongest markets and stocks. As much as one-third of their assets could be invested in the United States. For this reason, globals should beat the pure international funds when the American market is especially strong, because international funds don't buy U.S. stocks. By contrast, internationals should excel when foreign markets are especially strong.

For the average small investor, I don't see a strong reason to favor global funds over internationals or vice versa. But choose an international fund (or maybe a regional fund) if, at all times, you want to keep a specified percentage of your assets in foreign stocks.

To tap into average worldwide stock performance, try the international index funds offered by the no-load Vanguard Group in Valley Forge, Pennsylvania (800-662-7447; minimum investment, $3,000). An index fund matches the performance of a particular market by owning the stocks that make up its published price index. Vanguard mimics Morgan Stanley Capital International's Europe, Australia, Far East stock-index average, known as EAFE. There's a European portfolio and a Pacific portfolio. If you invest in each, you'll have a stake in most of the major foreign markets in the world.

Foreign-Bond Funds

Unsuspecting investors buy foreign-bond funds in hope of securing a higher-than-normal income. They don't understand the currency risk. You'll get a fine yield if the dollar stays level or declines, but your income will shrink if the value of the dollar goes up.

Some funds try harder than others to stabilize their dividend payouts, by hedging currencies and placing other arcane bets. But at bottom, you cannot count on a foreign-bond fund for steady income. The gyrations of the dollar dictate the size of your dividend check.

Foreign-bond funds, in short, are better for speculators than for income investors. If you think the dollar is going to decline, you might play your hunch with a foreign fund. Ditto if you think that foreign interest rates will drop (which means that bond prices will rise).

But remember: There is usually no free lunch in the interest-rate market. If an Australian bond is paying 14 percent in U.S. dollar terms, when similar American bonds are at 8 percent, it means that the market is expecting a 6 percent rise in the American dollar. That would equalize the yields. You'll make extra money only if the market guessed wrong and the American dollar doesn't rise that far. And, indeed, the market often guesses wrong, but you can't count on it.

All this assumes a pretty sophisticated knowledge of foreign economies, not to mention a high tolerance of currency risk. Changes in the dollar weigh more heavily on bonds than on stocks. A foreign stock fund can do reasonably well even if the dollar runs against you, because the capital gains you earn may more than offset your currency losses. But bond funds don't earn gains of that magnitude, so currency losses hit them harder.

In short, if you depend on your capital for a steady income, home-grown bonds are best. If you do choose a foreign-bond fund, make it a no-load (because you don't want sales charges cutting into your total return) or a closed-end fund selling at a decent discount.

Foreign-Currency Mutual Funds

Take care. Some advertise themselves as "money market funds" because they buy foreign money market instruments, such as short-term government securities and certificates of deposit. But the value of your shares isn't fixed at one dollar, as is the case with real money market funds. Instead your investment will fluctuate with changes in the dollar value of foreign currencies.

Although these mutual funds earn interest, they are principally currency plays. Some buy just a single currency, some buy several. They'll do well when the dollar declines and badly when it rises. Their expenses are high, which takes a big bite out of their potential yield. To me, they're a risky game in a roiling market. But if you have a yen for adventure, take a look at the currency funds of the Fidelity group in Boston, Massachusetts.

WARNING: It costs more to buy foreign securities than American securities. You have to pay for currency conversions as well as the higher expenses of investing abroad. So global and international mutual funds generally charge higher fees than comparable domestic funds.

For how to account for foreign taxes paid by your fund, see page 538.

MANY U.S. MUTUAL FUNDS INVEST A SMALL PORTION OF THEIR MONEY ABROAD. Check your prospectus to see if your fund has the right to do so. Check your quarterly reports to see if any foreign shares have actually been bought.

If your fund routinely keeps 10 or 20 percent of its assets in foreign stocks, you don't have to buy an international fund in order to diversify. Your American fund has done it for you.

But, but, but. Will the fund's managers, who specialize in the American market, do equally well when they train their sights abroad? Or are you better off with 80 percent of your equity money in a pure U.S. fund and the remaining 20 percent in a fund specifically geared to foreign opportunities? I'd guess the latter, until proven otherwise. A separate foreign fund is also best if you want to be sure that a portion of your money stays abroad. An American fund may dump its foreign shares at the first sign of trouble, while a foreign fund will prowl the world for other opportunities.

SOME OTHER WAYS TO JOIN THE PARADE

If you're willing and able to do your own securities and currency research, there are several other roads to foreign investing.

U.S. MULTINATIONAL CORPORATIONS—an armchair way for your money to travel. Look for major U.S. companies that earn a large percentage of their profits abroad. Just a few examples: IBM, Coca-Cola, Minnesota Mining & Manufacturing, Microsoft, Procter & Gamble, and McDonald's. Owning them gives you a stake in international growth as well as a currency play. Their foreign earnings are worth more when the dollar declines and less when the dollar rises.

CANADIAN STOCKS—the only foreign shares to be listed directly on U.S. exchanges, thanks to reciprocal agreements allowing American shares onto Canadian exchanges. Some 200 Canadian companies trade here.

AMERICAN DEPOSITARY RECEIPTS (ADRs)—the easiest way of buying all other foreign companies. ADRs represent foreign shares that are held in the vaults of a custodian bank. You buy and sell the receipts as if they were the stocks themselves. At this writing, more than 800 ADRs trade in this country, up from about 150 in 1961. Some are listed on the New

York and American stock exchanges, or on the National Association of Securities Dealers Automated Quotations system (NASDAQ). The majority trade through the Pink Sheets, where you might not get as good a price as you would on an exchange.

More than one-fourth of the ADRs are "sponsored" by the companies themselves. They give you American-style financial information (although not as quickly) and pick up the cost of administering the securities. The remaining ADRs are "unsponsored," meaning that they're managed by a bank without company involvement. With unsponsored ADRs, you usually get no financial reports. The administration cost (maybe two to four cents a share) is deducted from your dividends. The ADRs of some well-known companies are unsponsored, including, at this writing, Deutsche Bank, Mitsubishi Electric, B.A.T. Industries, Club Méditerranée, and Olivetti. Most ADRs represent one share each, but some represent bundles of five or ten shares or fractions of a single share. The Nestlé ADR, for example, is one-fortieth of a Swiss share.

Many of the listed ADRs attract a lot of buyers. But Pink Sheet issues are often illiquid. When you sell them, you're apt to take a haircut on the price. Generally speaking, investors should stick with sponsored ADRs, listed on NASDAQ or the exchanges, that trade actively all the time.

FOREIGN BONDS—absolutely not for the average buyer. They carry high minimum investments—often $25,000 to $50,000 or more. And it's hard to make money on them after paying all the transaction costs, including currency conversion, brokerage commissions, and the profit that the brokerage house tacks on to the price. Bond lovers should buy mutual funds, instead.

FOREIGN-CURRENCY BANK ACCOUNTS—offered by a small number of banks. You can get interest-paying money market funds and certificates of deposit denominated in Japanese yen, German marks, Canadian or Australian dollars, French or Swiss francs, British pounds, and other currencies. Interest is paid in those currencies, and so are the fees charged.

At present, these accounts are used principally by companies that do business abroad and by travelers locking up the cost of their foreign vacations. For example, if you're going to Germany six months from now and buy a six-month, mark-denominated certificate of deposit, your vacation fund will be insulated from any drops in the value of the dollar.

By the twenty-first century, however, more investors will be using foreign-currency accounts as a hedge against U.S. inflation and other economic risks.

Both foreign-currency bank accounts and mutual funds are sometimes described as being for "conservative investors." I disagree, because currency movements can be so sudden and sharp. I'd say they were for "knowledgeable investors," who know if they're getting a good exchange rate and who can afford to hedge every possible risk.

IF YOU CAN'T BEAT 'EM, JOIN 'EM

The American Century is over. Our growth is slowing, while growth in Europe, Asia, and Latin America is picking up. Happily, prosperity anywhere in the world creates vast new markets for American goods and services, so we'll get a piece of their new wealth. And so will every investor who is wise enough to buy.

28

REAL ESTATE – THE NEW

WINNING SYSTEMS:

Finding the Properties That Pay

———

Everyone said, "You can't lose money in real
estate, because they're not making any more of
it." Hmmmm. Where did everyone go wrong?

To make money in real estate today,
you need a system. Any one of a score of systems will do. Successful
investors are following their fortunes along more tracks than I have the
space to write about. You'll find 17 of their strategies starting on page
712. Unsuccessful investors are mostly on one of two tracks, both of
them so popular that I want to dismiss them before getting down to
serious business.

HOW TO LOSE MONEY IN REAL ESTATE

The most widely desired loser today is the single-family rental house.
I'm speaking of houses that are rented for less than their carrying cost.
You dip into your pocket to help cover the expenses. But you believe
that you'll more than earn that money back when you finally sell. This

strategy worked fine in the 1970s and part of the 1980s, when speculation and the baby boomers lit a firecracker under housing values. But nowadays, it's hard to sell for the price you need. That splat you're hearing from coast to coast is the sound of the property bubble bursting. Even if prices drift gently up—for example, at an average of 4 percent a year—most rental houses aren't good deals. After expenses, you'd probably do better with nice, quiet tax-free bonds. And tax-free bonds never call to complain that the windows leak or the furnace whines.

Investors in rental condominiums are doing even worse. Condos are chronically overbuilt, which holds down their rents and resale values.

The other popular strategy in trouble is the "cosmetic" fixer-upper. You buy a house with a few minor problems and put some money into repairs. A few months later, you try to resell at a higher price. But *everyone* wants that perfect little fixer-upper, so it's not cheap. The price you need to make a profit will probably exceed the property's current market value. So, for a year or more, no one will buy. To pick up some money, you'll take a tenant whose rent won't cover your carrying costs. That brings you back to the failed strategy I mentioned first.

YOU MAY NOT EVEN REALIZE THAT YOU'RE LOSING MONEY ON THE PROPERTY! As long as you sell for more than you paid, you might think that you came out ahead. You'll then be encouraged to get yourself into another terrible real-estate deal. So do yourself a favor and find out the truth. Determine what you made or lost on any venture you tried in the past, stating your profits as an annual compounded rate of return. And don't buy into anything new without a businesslike projection of what it will take to make a profit.

HOW TO MAKE MONEY IN REAL ESTATE

Active real-estate investing is practically a part-time job. You're a dealmaker, an entrepreneur. You're running your own small business. The successful investor will:

· Work up a personal investment system. (For some overlooked approaches, see pages 712 to 716.)

· Spend a lot of time looking at properties. You might do a deal for every 50, or 100, or 1,000 you consider. You won't actually visit 1,000 properties, but you might look at 1,000 deeds in the courthouse. If even reading this sentence bores you, forget active real-estate investing. Buy real-estate investment trusts, instead (page 725).

• Develop strict financial criteria. For example, you should decide in advance the maximum you will pay for a property relative to its rents and expenses (page 722), and the minimum projected profit you will accept. These rules tell you quickly whether a proposal is any good. Investors who fail either lack criteria or lack the discipline to follow them.

• Have a large enough line of credit to carry a good investment through a bad market or a period when it cannot be rented. Otherwise, you may be forced to sell at a give-away price.

• Look for properties that my friend Jack Reed * calls "lepers." Neither the seller nor other potential buyers see much value in them. But thanks to your X-ray vision, you might. Some leper strategies are given below. One of your criteria: Buy only properties that you can get at 20 to 30 percent below what you believe is their true market value. That's not an easy job, but real-estate investing isn't easy anymore.

TOMORROW IS YESTERDAY—AND A GOOD THING, TOO

To discover how rental real estate will be played in the 1990s, put away all your books by Donald Trump. Have a chat with your grandfather instead. For people who plan to hold properties for the long term, real-estate investing is reverting to an older style. Instead of depending almost entirely on tax benefits and capital gains, rental-property investors of the 1990s will stand or fall by the annual income they get from rents. A good rental investment has to generate real cash. Every year. Year in, year out.

Investors in single-family rental homes won't find many deals that meet this test. The price of the average house is too high, relative to the rent you can get. But in some cities and neighborhoods, it still pays to be a landlord. You can also pump value out of unorthodox properties that other investors might not even bid on.

Alternatively, forget about rentals and look for properties that—for one reason or another—can be had at a bargain price. You buy low, solve the property's problem (if there is one), then resell immediately at fair market value. But be warned that these ventures don't always work

* Jack tracks down profitable investing strategies for his newsletter, the *Real Estate Investor's Monthly* ($99; 342 Bryan Dr., Danville, CA, 94526). Send him a self-addressed, stamped, business-size envelope and he'll send you a free copy.

out. You may misjudge the property and overpay. Vandals may strike. A buried heating-oil tank in the yard may be found to be leaking, socking you with a cleanup cost. There may be asbestos in the house. And that's just the start of the stories I've heard. Many properties are indeed bought and sold on short schedules. But you should always be prepared for a longer haul.

HOW TO FIND RENTAL PROPERTIES THAT PAY

A property "pays" if its rents cover all your costs plus 5 to 10 percent. That extra money is both profit and cushion against the risk of unexpected costs. Here are seven strategies to try:

LUCK INTO LIVING IN A LOW-PRICED CITY. In a few neighborhoods, in a few cities, you can still buy a house in the regular way and rent it profitably.

BUY IN WORKING-CLASS NEIGHBORHOODS. Homes and apartment houses there are far less likely to be overpriced than they are in the classier sections of town. And working-class homes rise just as much in value, maybe even more.

BUY A HOUSE WITH A PROBLEM THAT TRAUMATIZES THE SELLER. Maybe asbestos was blown onto the ceiling. Maybe the foundation has dropped four inches and the floors tip. Whatever the problem, investigate the cost of solving it, then offer a low enough price to make the repair and guarantee yourself a substantial profit. The seller may accept, just to get the monster off his or her hands. (This strategy, incidentally, is a variant on buying a house that needs only cosmetic repairs. By going beyond cosmetics, you may truly get a bargain price.)

BUY A ONE-BEDROOM HOUSE. There aren't many of these left, but they're dandy investments. They sell cheaply because hardly anyone wants to own one. And they rent dear, because they appeal to single people and childless couples. If the house has an enclosed space that you can inexpensively turn into a second bedroom—an attic, a breakfast room, a sun porch, an attached garage—you have a real winner. (But check out the neighborhood before converting the garage. In some areas, houses without garages are tough to resell.)

BUY TWO HOUSES ON ONE LOT—one of them in the other's backyard. Few homeowners want them, so the second house goes for about two-thirds off. But most tenants don't mind the proximity. You get normal rents and a fine cash flow. You might also take a look at the profit in moving one of the houses to a lot of its own.

BUY A HOUSE WITH EXTRA LAND—a little more land than the zoning requires but not enough extra to subdivide into a separate building lot. Sell that extra eighth or quarter of an acre to a neighbor, for a garage, a swimming pool, or a green space for planting shrubs and trees. You'll still have to go through a formal subdivision, but the extra money you get from the sale can turn a breakeven property into a winner.

RENT YOUR HOUSE WITH AN OPTION TO BUY. This strategy works especially well when rents are sagging and real-estate prices are going nowhere. Put an ad in the paper reading "$4,000 moves you in" or "Buy a house, no money down," depending on what you want up front. You then strike a deal that will let the tenant buy the property, typically within one to five years. The tenant pays the monthly rent plus something more, which is credited toward his or her down payment. If the normal rent is $800, the lease-option rent might be $1,200. At the end of the term the tenant can buy, at a price defined by the contract. There are no rules for lease-options. They're all custom deals and should be drawn up by an experienced real-estate attorney. Warning: They may have nasty side effects, like triggering the clause requiring you to prepay the mortgage.

Lease-options greatly improve your cash flow by paying you more than you'd get from rents. If the tenant ultimately can't buy, you get to keep all the extra money. Fairness demands that you work with tenants who will have a good shot at making the down payment and qualifying for a mortgage. It's dirty pool to take lease-option money from people who will probably not be able to buy.

PROPERTIES JUST WAITING TO BE SQUEEZED FOR CASH

Here are some properties that can be "flipped"—bought at a low price and sold pretty quickly at a profit.

A TEARDOWN. Buy a house or a duplex that is going to be torn down. Don't pay any more than $1,000 for it. Hire a professional to move the house to another lot. Your goal is to sell the property for twice the money that you have in it.

ABSENTEE OWNERS. Do some research at the county records office. Write to everyone who owns land locally but lives somewhere else. Ask what they would sell their property for. Maybe one out of 200 will name a price that's half the real value. That one you buy. (The flip side of this advice: If you ever get such a letter, don't answer it before calling a local real-estate agent to find out what the property is worth.)

TAX-SALE REDEMPTIONS. In some states, former owners have a right of redemption if their homes were seized for nonpayment of property taxes and sold at auction. Call or write such people, if their houses sold for substantially less than market price. They usually have several months to redeem their homes for the sale price plus interest. If that's utterly beyond their means, you might make a deal. Put the redemption money into an escrow account; let the former owner use the account to redeem the house and sell it to you at the same low price; pay the former owner a reasonable premium, and resell the house at full market value. (There is no flip side to this advice. For the former owner, it's all found money. He or she might even advertise for someone to do this deal with.)

Houses sold at IRS seized-property sales carry redemption rights all over the country. But each state has its own rules for local tax or foreclosure sales. Some states allow no redemptions at all.

EXPIRING OPTIONS. Look for people who are renting a house with an option to buy at something less than the current market value but haven't got the money to proceed. You can buy their option, take over the house at the low option price, and resell for a higher price. Valuable real-estate options are expiring all the time, unused. Where do you find them? Advertise—"We buy options to purchase real estate." Or write to the tenants of any real-estate investor who does a lot of lease-option deals. Or write to tenants against whom eviction notices have been filed, to see if they have an option for sale. Or see if any lease-option memorandums have been filed with the county clerk. Some investors buy valuable options and resell them to someone else rather than taking title to the property (because of the environmental risks—page 719).

TENANCIES IN COMMON. A person who owns property as a tenant in common (page 85) may want out. But the other owner might refuse to sell and decline to buy the defector's interest. That person can always start a lawsuit to require a sale. But he or she may be constrained by personal considerations, or else may want the money fast. In this situation, an investor can often buy the defector's interest at a low price and then force a buyout or a sale. You can advertise for these opportunities—"We buy the interests of tenants in common"—or go through deed records and compile a mailing list of tenants in common. These opportunities often arise when Great Uncle Peter leaves a plot of land to all three of his nephews, who hold different views on what should be done with it.

PROBATE SALES. Estates will sometimes (not often) sell real estate at a low price to buyers who pay cash. This usually happens when heirs are pressing for their money and are not using a real-estate agent. To find these properties, send a letter to the executors of every estate filed for probate. You might send out hundreds of letters a month, leading to one deal every three months on the terms you want.

CLOUDED TITLES. Attorneys, paralegals, and specialists in title searches, in particular, might invest in properties with clouded titles. The owners may be glad to sell at almost any price. Buy only when you can cure the title and resell the property for full market value.

HOUSES GOING TO FORECLOSURE. Send a letter every ten days to people whose houses are scheduled for foreclosure. Offer to buy immediately for cash. Not many people respond at first, because they're still hoping to save their homes. But they become more interested once they accept the inevitability of the loss. Foreclosures often result from divorce. Anger, spite, and a shortage of cash may have stopped the mortgage from being paid. With an offer in hand, the couple may decide that selling the house is the best way out. Do a thorough title search before buying the property. It may be encumbered by several liens. The records may not show how much is currently owed on the liens, so work with the owner to find out.

One advantage of buying from the owner is that you usually get a low price. One risk is that the owner may go bankrupt, which could tie up the house in court. Many states have laws regulating preforeclosure sales, so check them out.

FORECLOSURE SALES. For details on foreclosure sales, see page 398. But you have to be a lot pickier when you buy for investment than when you're looking for a home of your own. A 5 percent discount from market price may be great if you plan to live there. Professional investors, however, require discounts of at least 20 percent. You might check addresses on hundreds of houses, drive by scores, and enter bids for dozens just to purchase one or two at the price you want. These houses, too, may be encumbered by liens of unknown current balance.

It takes a lot of experience to buy well at foreclosure sales, especially when you can't inspect the house in advance. New investors should generally buy after a foreclosure, or before.

FORECLOSED HOUSES HELD BY A BANK. By following foreclosure sales, you'll learn which lenders have bought particular properties that interest you. Call the bank officer in charge. Make an offer on the property that's at least

20 percent below market value. The bank will generally say no. Call the following week with the same offer. The bank will keep saying no and no. But if the property doesn't sell, and you persist, one day the bank may suddenly say yes. Investors get perhaps one out of every 25 properties they pursue this way, but that house is a real bargain. Incidentally, if the bank says a property has been sold, ask if the deal has actually closed. If not, keep calling. Sometimes sales fall through.

HOW MUCH LEVERAGE SHOULD YOU RISK?

Real-estate profits are greatly magnified by *leverage,* defined as the amount of debt you carry relative to your investment. Take a $100,000 house which rises $3,000 in value. If you bought the house for cash (no leverage), you made only 3 percent on your money. If you bought with a $20,000 down payment, you made 15 percent. With a $5,000 down payment (high leverage), you made 60 percent. Conversely, if prices turn down, the higher your leverage the larger your percentage loss.

But it's not the wipeout I worry about as much as the cash flow, which is the income you get from the property, after expenses. The lower your down payment, the bigger your mortgage and the larger your monthly payments. With big payments, it's impossible to cover all your costs with rents. You'll have negative cash flow. You'll be reaching into your pocket each month to help support your investing habit. What happens if you lose your job or are forced into early retirement? If your salary was supporting your real-estate investment, you may have to sell the property fast, maybe for 10 to 15 percent less than its actual value. When you have a big mortgage to repay, your profits may evaporate.

The wise investor arranges for rents to cover his or her costs. Working backwards, that generally means getting the house at a bargain price or making a down payment in the area of 25 percent.

HAVE YOU THE NERVE TO BE A LANDLORD?

Before buying any rental property—a single-family home, a duplex, a fourplex—ask yourself: Do I have the guts to evict? To demand the rent on time? To demand the rent at all, if someone gives me a sob story? Can I throw out an illegal pet? A sweet mutt just saved from extinction at the pound? A mutt adored by a crippled four-year-old?

If you can't answer all these questions with a hard-boiled yes, don't even try to be a landlord. In this game, nice guys get their clocks cleaned. You may set out to be the first decent landlord in history and discover, too late, that you were merely incompetent. Buying any sad story, from any tenant, could cost you not only your profit but your principal.

I don't mean to be harsh on tenants, having once been one myself. Most tenants are fine. They take care of your property and pay on time. Other tenants start out fine, then turn into monsters. They bounce checks. Make excuses. Break rules. When it becomes clear that you're going to evict, they may sell your stove and refrigerator, break all the windows, and punch holes in the walls.

Before even getting into this business, get up to speed on your local eviction procedures. Find out how fast you're allowed to act and how easy or hard it is to protect your property. Send an eviction notice if the rent is even one day late. A good tenant may be furious, but will pay on time from that day forward. Bad tenants you want out sooner, not later.

Never take tenants without checking them out: a credit check, personal calls to the tenants' past two employers, and personal calls to the past two landlords (the current landlord might lie, just to get rid of them). If bad tenants slip through your screen, move against them decisively. Enforce all rules to the letter. Demand money orders from anyone who ever bounced a check. Evict anyone who violates the lease. Grrrrr.

THE ACCIDENTAL LANDLORD

Some homeowners try to sell and can't (or can't sell for any price they will accept). So they move to a new house and find tenants for the old one. What happens?

If you have a recent mortgage, you probably can't charge enough rent to cover your expenses. So the house may keep on leaking money. You get a small tax break: All rental expenses can be written off against rental income. When you finally sell, you should be able to treat the property as a "temporary rental," which lets you tax-defer the profit. *Don't let the house become a permanent rental!* If that happens, you will owe a capital gains tax on the property when you sell. Worse, your taxable profit will encompass all the gains that you deferred from previous properties. How do you hang on to the status of "temporary" landlord? Keep offering the house for sale, don't give a lease, and pray that you won't have to rent it for very long.

Best advice: (1) Don't get into this box in the first place. Owning two homes can be Bankruptcy City. Always sell your own house before buying another. If you take a new job in another city, live in a rented room until your house is sold, even if it means leaving your family behind. It's the lesser misery. (2) Sell on a lease option (page 713). You can usually strike a fair deal with an individual buyer, who will pay a fair rent plus something extra toward the down payment. But a professional real-estate investor, aware of your anxiety, might offer only rent and demand that the entire payment go toward the purchase. Whatever you decide, try not to let the option run for more than a year or two. Never sign a lease-option contract without the advice of an attorney who specializes in real estate. (3) Slash the price on your unsold house, just to get rid of it. It might even be worth selling for less than its mortgage value, if you can arrange with the bank to refinance the remaining debt.

THE HUGE RISKS IN RAW LAND

Generally speaking, it's not smart to buy land and sit on it, waiting passively for its price to rise. Prices may rise slowly, and in the meantime empty land devours money. You'll owe real-estate taxes, liability-insurance premiums, and maybe loan interest, if the seller financed your purchase.

Raw-land owners also face enormous political risks. For example, your town might decide that it's growing too fast and downzone your land from commercial to residential or from multifamily use to single-family use. That sharply reduces your property's value. Or a new town environmental officer may declare part of your property a wetland, which restricts its use. In other parts of the country, you may be unable to get water rights. *Anything* can happen to a piece of raw land, and three-quarters of what can happen is bad.

It's that last quarter that's interesting. When a land deal is good, it often is very, very good. Consider investing when:

• You have reason to believe that you can, within a reasonable period, make the land more valuable. For example, you might subdivide it into building lots, or get its zoning raised from residential to commercial, or get a road approved for a plot that was previously inaccessible. Any of these changes will raise the land's value.

• You believe that you have some inside information about where roads will go or where a major company plans to move. In real estate, it is usually legal to trade on such tips. Your risk is that the tip was wrong.

• You can buy on an option. With an option, you pay the owner for the right to purchase the land, at a stated price, within a certain number of months or years. During that period, you do the rezoning or subdividing and line up a buyer. Then you take possession of the land and flip it to your buyer on the same day. If your plans don't work out, however, your option will expire. The landowner gets to keep both the property and your option money.

WHEN YOU DO A RAW-LAND DEAL: The checklist is long. Can the property be built on? What are the town's environmental rules? What's the present zoning? How will water and electricity get to the site? Where will the town allow roads to be built? What about sewage systems? Can foundations be dug or will a developer have to blast? Where does the town stand, politically, on development? How fast does the planning board act on proposals brought before it? Arm yourself with a good, local real-estate development lawyer. If you plunge into raw-land development, you are going to need one.

THE HUGE NEW ENVIRONMENTAL RISKS

Any real-estate investor—from the owner of a single-family house to a major-league developer—faces extraordinary liabilities under the rapidly changing laws on environmental protection. You may say, "I have no problem with my property." But a year from now, a new substance may be found to cause cancer and be added to the government's "horribles" list. Surprise! That substance may be found in your roof. Unless you replace the roof, your investment may go down the tubes.

You think this far-fetched? Consider the retired California couple who invested in a mortgage on a pear orchard. The borrower defaulted and they foreclosed. Two fuel tanks were found buried on the property. So far, they have had to pay $30,000 toward the cleanup and the state may force them to spend $100,000 more. And consider the Indiana homeowners who lived near an area where the state stored road salt. The salt got into the ground water and contaminated the wells. The water was drinkable, but the homeowners' pipes and appliances corroded. Their property values plunged.

And consider that nice piece of land you just bought. Fifty years ago, it might have been the site of a factory that left toxic chemicals in the soil. Or tomorrow night, two guys in dark clothes may use it as a dump for leaking drums of industrial waste, leaving you responsible for the cleanup. If you don't have city water, and the chemicals leach into your ground water, you're cooked. You're also in trouble if you own a building that's found to have asbestos in it. The law may not force you to remove it, but no one will buy or finance the building as long as the asbestos is there, so your investment has been damaged.

Professional investors won't buy a property anymore without first getting an environmental audit. The auditor tests the property for buried oil tanks, chemicals, pesticide residues, asbestos, and other substances that impair its value. Individuals should get audits, too, especially if you're buying open land, land next to an old gas station, a commercial or industrial property, farmland, or an apartment building. In fact, your lender may require it. Probable price range for small investors: $500 to $30,000, depending on the property. Before rejecting the expense of an audit out of hand, think what you'd lose if you bought a contaminated piece of real estate that had to be cleaned up.

Three other reasons to check for toxic waste: (1) If you buy a property and wastes crop up later, you may not be forced to pay for the cleanup as long as you made "all appropriate inquiry" before buying. "Appropriate" hasn't been defined, but an audit should do it. (2) Even if the government has to pay for cleaning up your property, it might not do the job for years. In the meantime you're holding a worthless investment. (3) Anyone who buys your property will probably subject it to an environmental audit. If wastes are found, it may kill the deal and will certainly reduce its price.

In short, the risks of investing in real estate have risen sharply. The average investor has not yet caught up with these new environment dangers, which are lopping billions of dollars off property values in America today.

WHAT IT TAKES FOR SUCCESS IN HIGH-RISK CONDITIONS

FULL-CIRCLE, 360-DEGREE AWARENESS. You should follow real estate constantly, to track the ever-changing political and financial risks. The new environmental hazards, for example, might persuade you to lean toward the shorter-term investing ideas. Some investors don't even want their names on a chain of title, lest they get hit for part of a property's cleanup costs. So they're finding ways to trade property interests without ever owning the real estate themselves. One idea: options. You can trade them without taking title to anything.

PATIENCE. You may have to look at dozens of properties in person, and hundreds on paper, to find one that meets your investment specifications. Many a seller is lying in wait for an idiot who will overpay.

TOUGH-MINDEDNESS. You have to be firm with tenants, firm with buyers, firm with sellers. Not mean, but firm. Real estate is a deal-making business with fewer rules that the average consumer is used to. That's why your investment criteria are so important, and your discipline in following through.

FLEXIBILITY. A truly superior investor brings his or her technical knowledge of real-estate contracts and finance to bear on a single critical point: the special needs of the person you're negotiating with. What can you give him or her to secure the terms you want? If there's no way to reach your minimum criteria, however, bow out and go on to another deal.

QUICK DECISION MAKING. When you first start to think about real estate, take a lot of time to study up. Read some books on real-estate finance. Learn about local property values. Analyze your area's economy—are jobs and people moving in or out? Check the environmental hazards. Choose some investment niches to investigate. Set some yardsticks for yourself (page 722). But once you step into the arena, be prepared to move quickly. No one leaves money lying on the table for very long. If you have to think and think and think and *think* about it, someone else will buy.

AN IRON GUT. In almost every deal, something goes wrong. Price estimates are bad. Somebody dies. The town passes new laws that change the rules. Your lender drops out. The seller tries to change the terms. A tenant sets fire to an apartment. Most of the problems can be worked through. But it will take time, your nerves will fray, and you might not make as much money as you thought. That's how real-estate investing goes. If you can't handle pain, buy Treasury bills.

TIME. Direct investing in real estate is a part-time business. To make money, you have to be personally involved: inspecting properties, evaluating prices, negotiating, arranging for tenants, seeing to repairs, going to zoning hearings, lining up financing, living your deal in a dozen ways. If you don't have the time, don't even think about trying to buy.

CLEAR FINANCIAL YARDSTICKS. Before you begin your real-estate investment career, draw up some yardsticks for yourself. Measure every opportunity against them. If they fit, follow up. If they don't move on. Find out quickly if a deal falls within your financial parameters, so you won't waste your time on something that can't produce a large enough return. These yardsticks will change as you gain experience, but they should always be written clearly on your cuff. They act as a discipline against the all-too-human tendency to buy that pretty house or lot just because it's there.

SOME RULES OF THE ROAD

No set of financial parameters fits every investment or every investor. But here are some guidelines to start with.

• Don't make improvements to a house or building you own unless you can get two dollars of increased market value out of every dollar you spend.

• A rental property is worth its risk when its rents run 5 to 10 percent over all your known costs. Fifteen percent is even nicer. This cushion is for profit, for unexpected expenses, or for an unexpectedly high vacancy rate. Don't pay more for a property than it can earn. That means forgoing most traditional rental properties today.

• On rental properties that you plan to hold, focus on the "capitalization rate," which is the rate of return on your invested capital. You have a 10 percent cap rate if your net operating income comes to 10 percent of the price of the property. (Net operating income is the rental income from the property minus expenses such as insurance and repairs but before mortgage payments.) Many buyers go with low, 4 or 5 percent cap rates, counting on the property's capital gain to raise their returns. But those are often poor investments. Tougher-minded buyers won't accept cap rates lower than 10 percent.

• Given all the risks in rental real estate today, you should be shooting for a combined annual return of 25 percent, in appreciation, amortization, cash flow, and tax savings. To calculate a one-year rate of return, add the dollar amounts of those four items and divide by the money you invested. There are fancier ways of calculating returns, but for individuals, this will do.

• Another way to figure: You want a current cash return on your investment of at least 10 to 15 percent. Your cash return is your net income after all expenses (including mortgage payments) divided by your down payment and closing costs.

· Bargain-price deals, such as buying in foreclosure or buying out of probate estates, are measured by the discount you can get from current market value. Professionals demand 20 to 30 percent discounts. If they can't get that price on a particular deal, they move on to the next one. When they buy a property they expect to resell almost immediately.

· All things being equal, invest close to home, in neighborhoods you know—but only if prices are reasonable there. If they're not, you have two choices: Forget about real estate or buy in another part of the state or the country where you think you can make a profit. Long-distance rental-property ownership is no big deal, as long as you have some local help. Bargain purchasing—buying a teardown, for example —can easily be done anywhere. Foreclosure buying, however, requires a close understanding of state law.

· Consider assuming the seller's mortgage, if the lender will allow it. Sometimes the mortgage carries a low fixed interest rate. Sometimes it's an adjustable loan with a low lifetime cap. In either case, it's cheaper to take over a mortgage than to get a new one, because you don't pay points and closing costs. If you're the seller, make sure that the buyer assumes all responsibility for your mortgage, and that the lender releases you from liability, in writing, You don't want to find yourself back on the hook if the buyer defaults. If the lender won't release you (and many won't), you may not want to agree to the assumption, unless the buyer puts so much money into the property that you feel sure he won't walk away.

AS LITTLE AS POSSIBLE ABOUT TAXES

YOU CAN DEDUCT YOUR RENTAL COSTS, including depreciation, against your rental income from this and similar projects. Any excess expenses can tax-shelter some of your regular income, if you meet the income limits explained on page 417. If you don't, all your unused tax deductions are allowed to accumulate. You can use them against rental income in future years, or to reduce the size of your taxable profit when you finally sell.

INVESTORS IN RAW LAND GET VIRTUALLY NO TAX BREAKS, because land isn't depreciable. If you borrowed money to buy the land, you might not even be able to write off the interest. Such interest can normally be deducted only against income from other investments, such as stock dividends. (The loan interest becomes deductible, however, if you borrowed on a home-equity line of credit.)

YOU CAN DEFER PAYING TAXES WHEN YOU DISPOSE OF AN INVESTMENT PROPERTY, by doing a "1031" tax-free exchange. Instead of selling the property, you exchange it for another one. You don't even have to do a direct, two-way swap. You can set up a three-cornered trade (or more). For example, suppose that Sally wants your rental property and you want Sam's. You can each deed the house to the proper person, noting that the agreement is part of an overall plan to accomplish an exchange. These exchanges aren't a do-it-yourself project. You will need an attorney to dot the *i*'s, cross the *t*'s, and keep you within the time limits set by the IRS.

CAN YOU GET RICH ON VULTURE INVESTING?

Not yet. "Vultures" buy properties at carcass prices. But *everybody's* into vulture investing, which means that prices are still too high. For example, it's hard to buy a single-family house where expenses can be covered by rents, because buyers expect to make their money on capital gains. They won't, but they don't know that yet. When they do, prices will drop and vulture investing will become profitable.

CAN YOU GET RICH BUYING SECOND MORTGAGES?

A second mortgage is a second loan against a home. It makes a tempting income investment because it pays a lovely yield. And it normally doesn't require property management, as direct real-estate investing does. But you face huge risks if the borrower defaults.

When you buy a second mortgage, you are betting that that borrower is going to make his or her payments on time—and, in fact, most do. You advertise for these loans ("We buy second mortgages") or find them through real-estate brokers and lawyers. They are usually bought at a discount from face value, in order to increase your yield.

Before buying, put the borrower through a credit and employment check (don't count on the broker to do it for you). Some of these borrowers are perfectly sound but others are flakes whom normal lenders wouldn't touch.

You want a loan that comes due within a short period—say, two or three years. It should be collateralized by real estate, usually by the property itself. The borrower should have substantial equity in the property and a history of making all payments on time. In general, the house should be worth at least 30 percent more than all the loans against it. Raw land should be worth at least 60 percent more, because of the risk. Many investors won't buy second mortgages against raw land.

If the borrower defaults, he or she will probably default on the first mortgage, too. If the first mortgagor forecloses, your interest will probably be entirely wiped out. You might have to make the first mortgage payments for a while, or bid on the house at the foreclosure auction, in order to salvage your investment. Talk about these risks with a real-estate attorney before getting into second mortgages. In a shaky economy, with so many homeowners losing their jobs, these are riskier buys than they used to be.

CAN YOU GET RICH BY LISTENING TO TV GURUS?

No—you can only get poor. Poor, by spending your hard-earned money on the windy books and tapes they flog. Poor, if you try to follow their half-baked schemes, which will cost you money with small chance of reward. Really poor, if you can't afford the deals you get into. They set you up for default, personal bankruptcy, and even jail.

I studied a group of these programs once, talked to the gurus, and got their materials. I found them misleading, fantastical, false, and in some cases, flatly illegal. The dream they sell—that you can buy profitable property with no credit, no job, no experience, even with a bankruptcy behind you—shouldn't pass anyone's first-round BS test. Gurus earn their Rolls-Royces and their diamond pinky rings not by extracting value from real estate but by extracting cash from *you.*

FOR THE PASSIVE INVESTOR

If dealing with tenants or bidding at auction is harder work than you had in mind, consider the real-estate investment trust (REIT). It's for people who want to own properties without ever leaving their Barcaloungers.

REITs do your investing for you. They buy and manage properties, or buy mortgages, and hold them for the long term. REITs trade like stocks on a stock exchange. Their prices rise and fall, in line with their dividends and the changing values of their properties. You buy them through stockbrokers, paying normal brokerage commissions. Some

REITs are faltering, as the end-of-the-decade property bust keeps rolling on. Others are outperforming the average stock. As with any other investment, you have to learn how to make a good choice.

By law, virtually all of a REIT's earnings have to be paid out every year, so their current yields are generally high. For this reason, they appeal strongly to income investors. An especially high yield, however, is always suspect. It means that the REIT has dropped in price—maybe because some of its properties are failing or because its dividend may be cut. REITs turned in a strong performance in the 1980s. But with so many real-estate projects crashing today, REIT investors should narrow their focus to the very strongest companies that have paid out top returns for years.

REITS COME IN FOUR TYPES.

EQUITY REITS—your best long-term bet, for steady growth and dividends. Equity REITs buy apartment buildings, hotels, shopping centers, and office buildings. Some specialize in certain types of properties or invest in certain parts of the country; others are widely diversified. Some invest passively in developers' deals; others buy, develop, and manage properties themselves. In general, the most profitable REITs are those that specialize and that do their own developing,.

To investigate a REIT, get the company's annual report. Find out what it buys and how it's doing. Check the history of its stock price and dividend payouts. Are its dividends growing? Most important: Is its dividend being covered by cash from operations? Or is the REIT paying investors by selling properties or dipping into reserves? If the latter two, avoid it. In general, you should stick with the big, actively traded REITs that are listed on the major exchanges. Among those most widely followed on Wall Street: Federal Realty Investment Trust, New Plan Realty Trust, Pennsylvania REIT, United Dominion Realty Trust, Washington REIT, Western Investment Real Estate Trust, and Weingarten Realty Investors.

Over the short term, equity REITs tend to behave like stocks, rising and falling with the market. But over the long term, they behave more like real estate, following the values of their underlying properties. So if long-term real-estate values rise, well-managed REITs should, too.

MORTGAGE REITS—don't have as good a performance history as equity REITs. Instead of buying properties they invest in mortgages and, sometimes, construction loans. They usually have some sort of equity or income participation in the property, so they're not straight income investments. Still, they behave more like bonds than stocks. If your aim is to diversify into real estate, mortgage REITs won't do it.

HYBRID REITS—combination equity and mortgage REITs. But for real-estate participation, the equity side is the only one that counts.

FINITE-LIFE REITS (FREITS)—an investment to avoid. They're the same crummy real-estate limited partnerships that cost investors so much in the 1980s, marketed under a new name. FREITs have a "finite" life—meaning they plan to dissolve in 7, or 10, or 15 years, just as the limited partnerships intended. Whether they actually will dissolve, and whether they'll get good prices for their properties, remains to be seen. FREITs have big upfront and continuing management fees—not quite as dreadful as the fees charged by some limited partnerships, but pretty close. When a stockbroker or financial planner suggests a REIT it may be a FREIT, so be sure to check.

INITIAL PUBLIC OFFERINGS (IPOS)—these are also poor investments, for new REITs as well as FREITs. You have no idea how the properties will perform or how well the REIT is going to be managed. Most FREITs don't even own any real estate yet; they're just raising money and will buy properties later. There's no point risking an IPO when you can buy a well-established REIT that has been making profits and paying dividends for years. Furthermore, an IPO's offering price is usually puffed up by hype and sales expenses. A few months after the offering period, the REIT or FREIT will probably sell for less.

WATCH OUT FOR REITS WITH CONFLICTS OF INTEREST! A mortgage REIT that lends to its sponsor has its sponsor's best interest in mind, not yours. An equity REIT "advised" by a developer may be buying that developer's properties at too high a price. Or it may be buying from a company owned by its sponsor. REITs that invest in nursing homes may be controlled by the operators of the homes. Look for these interlocking relationships in the REITs' annual reports and proxy statements. They should warn you off. You want an independent REIT, preferably one whose management holds a significant interest in the company. Managers like that are investing with you, not against you.

WHY BUY REAL ESTATE AT ALL?

Investors buy real estate to make a buck. They study the market, see an advantage, and go for it. But it's riskier than, say, a no-load, stock-owning mutual fund. Real estate *in general* may do well, eventually. But if your *particular* property comes a cropper—because of an environmental hazard, a lawsuit, a difficult tenant, a change of zoning—your loss can be huge. You can't easily trade out of it, the way you can a stock.

The classic argument for owning property is diversification. Real-estate prices may go up at a time when stocks are going down. Carefully chosen real estate is a better inflation hedge than stocks.

But if diversification is the only draw, the average investor needn't bother. You may own your own home. You may also own a vacation home. Odds are that a substantial percentage of your assets are tied up in these properties. Your next logical step would be stocks rather than another piece of property.

The lure of real estate, however, isn't always logical. An aroused investor is obsessed by properties—tromping through them, judging them, reshaping them, haggling over them. They're not like mutual funds that you can buy and forget. You have to give real estate your soul.

RETIRE-MENT PLANNING

Nowadays, retirement planning is critical even for the young. It didn't used to be. When I came up, you thought about it later. You had children in your twenties and by your early fifties you had written your last tuition check. That left you ten or more good years, at the peak of your earning power, to put aside money for yourself.

But the world today is a different place. Couples are waiting until their thirties to start having children. That means they'll be writing tuition checks in their early sixties. They'll have no time left to save money for themselves. The same is true for people who divorce, remarry, and start second families. Adding to the pressure is the corporate push for early retirement. Older parents may lose their paychecks while their children are still young.

This change in pattern calls for a brand-new plan of attack. You should save for retirement in small bites, over all your life.

29

HOW TO RETIRE IN STYLE:

The Tax-Deferred Route to Easy Street

———

It's daring and challenging to be young and
poor, but never to be old and poor. Whatever
resources of good health, character, and
fortitude you bring to retirement, remember,
also, to bring money.

Are you old enough to remember
Harvey? Harvey was America's most famous rabbit, a giant of his kind,
a star of his own eponymous movie. He was invisible. Only his co-star,
Jimmy Stewart, could see him. But despite Harvey's handicap, his performance was so riveting that he stole the show.

You might well wonder what this has to do with a chapter on retirement savings, other than the fact that only gray-hairs will remember the
film at all. But I think of today's inflation as Harvey. Even though it's
big (in the 5 percent area, as I write), today's workers treat it as invisible.
Only 5 percent inflation; nothing much. I've seen some guides to retirement savings that barely mention inflation at all.

The rule of thumb for retirement income is that you can live comfortably on 80 percent of your preretirement earnings. But that's for the first year. In the second year, your purchasing power will have shrunk a bit, and so will the value of your fixed capital. In the third year you'll start to notice it, and more so in the fourth. At 5 percent inflation, every $100 you have now will be worth $60 in ten years, so by then you'll be living on just about half of your preretirement income. In the following decade, your standard of living may drop by another half. That's Harvey for you. Invisible but riveting.

HOW MUCH MONEY WILL YOU REALLY NEED?

Plenty.

Social Security benefits (yes, doubters, you will get Social Security —see page 776) rise with the consumer price index, and so do many government pensions. But private pensions usually are fixed. So is the income from most annuities and the interest on bonds and certificates of deposit. You have to be clever to stare down inflation in retirement.

Still, you can do it. Here's how.

✓ Save enough money to offset your pension's steady loss of purchasing power. Plan to dip into your capital every year, to make up for those losses to inflation. Acquiring this money may be less of a struggle than you think. To find out how much to save, sharpen your pencil and fill in the worksheet "How Much Should I Save for Retirement? (Long Form)," in the Appendix (page 884).

✓ If you're saving for retirement *and* for college for your kids, put retirement first. Fully fund every tax-deductible old-age plan available. Any money left can go into college savings. Retirement accounts earn money faster than anything else, because of their tax deferral. If worse comes to worst, you can borrow against them for tuition payments. For a strategy that combines college and retirement savings, see page 456.

✓ Own your own home. A house gives you inflation protection over long periods. It stabilizes your living costs. In old age, your home gives you extra equity to live on. For example, you might sell the house, buy something smaller, and bank the surplus. Or you might use a reverse-mortgage plan (page 817).

✓ Invest a substantial portion of your long-term retirement savings for growth. That generally means stock-owning mutual funds. Bonds and their ilk keep you running in place. You are wasting your youth (by which I mean all the years under 60) if you keep most of your retirement money in fixed-income investments.

✓ Don't kid yourself about early retirement. It takes a fortune to quit at 50 and keep yourself going for another 40 years. Even if you quit at 65, you're likely to want some part-time earnings.

✓ Take every advantage of every tax-deductible, tax-deferred corporate or individual retirement plan that comes your way. Company savings plans usually match any money you put in. That's like finding gold in the street. All you have to do is bend over and pick it up.

✓ Even when you retire, keep a portion of your retirement savings invested for growth—which means conservative equity-income or growth-and-income mutual funds. If you switch all your money into fixed-income investments at age 60 or 65, and live on the interest, inflation is going to eat you up.

WHERE YOUR RETIREMENT FUNDS WILL COME FROM

Your retirement security generally stands on three legs: a pension, Social Security, and personal savings.

PENSIONS are paid to government employees and employees of most corporations. Only at the very smallest companies do employees go without. The size of your retirement benefit may depend on your age and the number of years you worked there, or it may depend on how well the money was invested. Either way, the longer you stick with a company, the larger your benefit should be (page 736).

But pensions are changing, even for "lifers." A growing portion of your retirement income may be linked to money you pay into the plan voluntarily. If you choose not to contribute, your pension will fall short.

If your company is reorganized or taken over, your pension might be frozen in its tracks and replaced with a plan that offers less. Pensions remain critical to retirement planning, but you can't be dead sure that they will always pay as planned.

SOCIAL SECURITY will be with us always. But the monthly checks mailed in the twenty-first century won't replace as much of a beneficiary's working income as checks do that are mailed today.

PERSONAL SAVINGS are growing more critical to your security in old age. With both Social Security and your employer stepping back, you'll have to depend more on what you put aside for yourself.

The best way to build a retirement fund is through automatic-payment plans. You want money to slip out of each and every paycheck and into tax-favored retirement accounts without your even seeing it.

Many employees can use corporate payroll-deduction plans to roll pretax dollars into 401(k)s or 403(b) tax-sheltered annuities. Or you might roll post-tax dollars into thrift plans whose earnings are tax-deferred.

If you own a mutual fund, you can arrange for a monthly payment to be taken out of your bank account and invested through the fund's deductible Individual Retirement Account or Keogh plan. Nothing could be simpler. All you have to say is yes.

WHAT YOU SHOULD BE SAVING NOW

For a down-and-dirty estimate of the annual savings that you need, take a look at the Short Form retirement planner on page 735. Those aren't reliable numbers. They're a wake-up call, meant to get you up and moving. I'll explain in a minute how to find out exactly what to save. But first, let me tell you what the Short Form can do for you.

It's a quick-check savings target for two kinds of working couples, one with company pensions, one that's funding Individual Retirement Accounts, instead. They have no other savings, they qualify for Social Security, their wages are rising at an annual rate of 5 percent, and they'll retire at age 65 on 75 percent of their preretirement earnings.

Two points stand out: (1) The older you get before you start saving, the tougher it is to acquire the money you need. (2) If you have a company-funded pension, you're a heck of a lot better off than if you don't.

The Short Form makes no allowance for the Harvey Effect—the inflation that will nibble away at your income. On the other hand, neither does it account for any investments you have already. The remaining sum you need to save might actually be smaller than what's shown here.

The only way to know for sure is to turn to the Appendix, page 884, where you'll find a first-rate mini-workbook called "How Much Should You Save for Retirement? (Long Form)." Fill it in. As far as your finances are concerned, it may be the most profitable hour you will ever spend. That workbook tells you exactly how much of your income you should be putting aside, not only for yourself but for Harvey as well. To encour-

HOW MUCH SHOULD YOU SAVE FOR RETIREMENT?
(SHORT FORM)

Current salary	Current age	Needed to invest annually*	
		With a company pension	With a double IRA but no pension†
	30	$ 3,660	$ 4,000
$35,000	40	4,360	5,990
	50	6,000	9,970
	30	$ 7,590	$ 8,350
$50,000	40	8,940	11,790
	50	12,280	17,950
	30	$15,270	$18,050
$75,000	40	17,890	23,220
	50	24,730	33,700

* Assuming an 8 percent gross return on investment taxed in a combined state and federal bracket of 35 percent.
† Including $4,000 a year for the double IRAs.
Source: Ernst & Young.

age you to use it, I'd have moved the Long Form right to this page if it weren't so, well, *long.*

Before you can tell what to save for yourself, you need to know what is being saved *for* you. That's where your company pension comes in.

YOUR PENSION: THE EMPLOYER'S PART

You *must* understand your corporate plan. If you don't know how much of your retirement income is guaranteed and how much isn't, you won't have a clue as to what you ought to be saving now. You're entitled to an Individual Benefit Statement once a year, showing the size of your pension credit (ask for the statement in writing if you don't get it automatically). Don't burst out laughing when it comes. Pension credits always start small. To understand where these credits lead, drop by the employee-benefits office for a full-dress explanation.

Corporate plans come in two basic types: defined-benefit plans and defined-contribution plans.

Defined-Benefit Plans

These are the classic, old-fashioned pensions. You get a fixed, lifetime income at retirement, the amount generally depending on how long you worked and how much you earned. Typically, you pay nothing into the plan. It is financed entirely by your employer. Unlike other kinds of plans, defined-benefit pensions guarantee the size of your retire-ment income. The value of your monthly payment will be eroded by inflation, because private pensions rarely make cost-of-living adjust-ments. Still, you know in advance what your monthly benefit will be.

Regrettably, many companies have been pronouncing defined-bene-fit plans too expensive and cutting them back in the following ways.

• New payment formulas are reducing the relative size of pensions given to long-term employees, especially those in the middle and upper-middle salary ranges.

• Fewer pension credits are now offered as a "signing bonus" to workers hired in middle age. These credits make up for a worker's late arrival in the retirement plan. If your credits go down, your retirement income won't be as large.

• Some plans are terminated. When that happens, your benefits to date are funded with an insurance-company annuity. But pension credits build faster as you move toward retirement, whereas annuity payments are fixed. What's more, the safety of your pension now depends on the solvency of the insurance company, not on your employer or on the federal pension-insurance plan (page 738). In this game, employees are always the losers.

HOW TO GET THE MOST FROM A DEFINED-BENEFIT PLAN

1. Don't job-hop too readily. Defined-benefit pensions generally re-ward the workers with the longest service.

You may think it's okay to leave the company after only a few years, because you can take your vested benefit with you (you "vest" when the money in your pension account becomes yours to keep). Full vesting may come in three, five, six, or seven years, depending on the plan. But in that short period, what are you vested *in?* Only a peanut payment. You have to stay 20 or 30 years before you are looking at real money.

What if you move through three or four different companies, taking a small vested benefit each time? All things being equal, they will not add up to the same size pension that you'd get by staying with a single employer.

This fact shows up clearly in the table on page 737. You see what happens to two brothers, earning the same starting salaries ($20,000) pegged to 6 percent wage inflation and working for companies with exactly the same pension rules. Itchy Brown worked for four different companies, 10 years each. His brother, Boring, spent 40 years with the

THE JOB-SWITCHER'S RISK

	Itchy Brown	Boring Brown
First-job pension	$ 3,582	$82,286
Second-job pension	6,414	N/A
Third-job pension	11,487	N/A
Fourth-job pension	20,571	N/A
Total annual pension	$42,054	$82,286

Source: Federal Reserve Bank of Boston.

same company. Boring's pension is twice as large. Plans with different rules might produce a narrower difference, but the principle is the same.

I'm not arguing that you should chain yourself to the first desk you ever occupy, only that job changing carries a price. The new offer has to be sharply better than the job you've got before it's financially smart to quit. Had Itchy Brown earned a lot more money at his other jobs, he'd have beaten boring Boring Brown hands down.

The closer you come to middle age, the more critical this risk-reward analysis becomes. What will your new salary be? What salary increases lie ahead? What level of benefits, and what vesting, does the new pension carry? Will the company pay you a "signing bonus" to cover the future credits you're losing by leaving your old pension plan too soon?

American mobility highlights your need for a "portable pension" that you can carry from job to job. That portable pension is all of the money that you save yourself, in 401(k) plans, Individual Retirement Accounts, thrift accounts, and similar tax-favored retirement plans.

2. If you do quit the company, squeeze the maximum good from your vested benefit. You may have a choice between taking your money in a lump sum or leaving it in your old company's plan. If you leave it, the benefit will be frozen. If it's worth $1,000 a month at age 65, that's what you'll get—even though, by the time you're 65, the purchasing power of that money may have dropped by two-thirds. Alternatively, you could take a lump sum and roll it into an Individual Retirement Account or the pension plan of your new employer. But consider this: That lump sum will have to be invested at a certain interest rate (known as the "discount rate"), merely to yield the same $1,000 at retirement that you'd get from the pension plan! So ask the plan what discount rate it's using. If you think you can earn more, take the lump sum; otherwise, leave it with your old employer, if you can. (For more on this, see page 790). *Do not* take this money and spend it. You will never make it up.

3. If you hate your new job, you can go back to your old employer

without losing all your pension and vesting credits, provided that you weren't away for too many years. Ask your employee-benefits office exactly where you stand. You can also maintain your pension with part-time work—at least 501 hours of work per year. (But part-time work at the very end of your career may diminish your pension, if the pension formula focuses on your pay in your final years. Again, check with your employee-benefits office.)

You won't lose past credits if you quit for a while to have (or adopt) a baby. You accrue no new benefits while you're away, but you hang on to your old ones for up to 501 hours' worth of maternity leave.

4. Know what all your benefits are. As you approach middle age (or if you're thinking about a new job), ask the employee-benefits office to estimate what your actual pension is likely to be. Walk through the calculation step by step. (If you think that the pension-plan administrator is making a mistake, you can appeal.)

5. Many companies "integrate" their plans with Social Security, meaning that your pension check will be reduced by part of your Social Security benefit. This has a greater effect on lower-paid workers than on higher-paid ones. Ask the person in charge of employee benefits to calculate what integration will mean to your total retirement income. You need this information, to help determine how much more money you'll need to save personally.

6. Don't let your spouse lose any benefits due. Ask the company for its Survivor Coverage Data, which will explain it all. As long as you're partly or fully vested, and have reached early retirement age, your spouse can usually get something out of your pension, even if you die before actually retiring. (For more on spouse protection, see page 796.)

7. Don't worry. Defined-benefit pension plans are at least partly insured by the industry-funded Pension Benefit Guaranty Corporation (PBGC), which insures the basic pensions owed by plans that fail. Both you and your survivor are covered. The 1991 ceiling: $2,250 a month for a single, 65-year-old worker. Younger retirees, and married retirees with joint-and-survivor pensions, receive less. The maximum payment for workers in newly failed plans goes up each year.

But the PBGC doesn't cover everything. If your company or pension plan failed, here are some of the benefits you would lose: (1) the amount of your pension that exceeds the PBGC ceiling; (2) collateral benefits, such as life and health insurance, severance pay, disability pay, and recent improvements in the plan; (3) any payments arising from a defined-contribution plan (see below). The PBGC also doesn't insure the defined-benefit plans of government entities; some plans run by churches and fraternal organizations; the plans of professional-service employers (for example, doctors and lawyers) that haven't covered any more than 25 active workers at any time; and worker's compensation and unemployment insurance.

8. Do worry, if you earn a high income. Your pension doesn't have anywhere close to total PBGC insurance. It may not even be fully contained in your company's formal pension plan. A significant portion might be in a supplemental plan instead. Supplemental plans are often backed by nothing but the company's good health. If the company failed, part of your pension would probably be uncollectable.

Top-level executives usually know how much of their pension is guaranteed and how much isn't. In fact, their excess benefits may be guarded against some contingencies by a trust. But some employees with medium-high incomes may also have had some of their money pushed into the uninsured supplemental plan without their knowledge.

Many employers disclose, on your annual Individual Benefit Statement, how much of your retirement account is secured by the pension plan and how much isn't. But others don't volunteer this information. To find out exactly where you stand, ask your employee-benefits office: (1) What percentage of the pension plan is "funded"—meaning what portion of the benefits could it afford to pay today? A strong plan is 100 percent funded, or nearly so. (2) How much of your combined pension, profit sharing, and 401(k) savings are covered by the pension plan? (3) If you're in the supplemental plan, what stands behind it? If the answer is "nothing," your future may be less secure than you thought. Solution: Try to save more money outside the plan.

Defined-Contribution Plans

The number of defined-contribution plans has exploded because, for employers, they're no-risk deals. Instead of promising you a fixed lifetime pension, the company promises only to contribute a certain sum toward your retirement every year. It takes no responsibility for the size of the pension you ultimately get.

The contribution might be in cash or in stock. It might be a fixed percentage of your salary (known as a money-purchase plan) or a fixed percentage of profits (known as a profit-sharing plan). The company might also match any contributions you make to a company-savings plan.

All this money is invested—some at the company's discretion, some at yours. By retirement, you should have a sizable sum. You can generally take it in a single check, leave it with the company to manage for you, or turn it into a fixed income for life.

How large will your retirement income be? Who knows? The size of your check depends on how much was contributed each year and how well those funds were invested. *You bear all the risk.* Maybe you'll retire on far more than a defined-benefit plan would have paid. Maybe, on the other hand, you'll get less. For a graphic example of what can happen, compare the pension of the person who retired in August 1987—just before the big stock market crash—with that of the person who retired in November. The post-crash retiree might have gotten one-third less.

No cost-of-living raises come with defined-contribution plans. You have to create your own inflation hedges, with your own investments.

How to get the most from a defined-contribution plan.

1. Some companies perch a defined-contribution plan on top of a defined-benefit plan. So you have to understand both plans and how they work together. Typically, the defined-benefit plan will carry less and less of the load as times goes by. Responsibility for delivering a decent pension will be shifted toward the riskier defined-contribution plan. Both plans carry the same vesting schedule. Check the details, and the current size of your benefit, in the plan documents: the Summary Plan Description and the Individual Benefit Statement. The company is required to give them to you.

2. It's less costly to job hop when you're backed by defined-contribution plans. Your new employer may not cover you for the first year. But after that, you'll participate in full. Unlike defined-benefit pensions, these plans are not tipped to favor employees with longer service. All things being equal, 40 years of work should net you only a slightly smaller sum from four different employers than you'd get from one, assuming that you stay at each company long enough for the benefits to vest.

3. If you want to quit, establish your "escape date"—the earliest you can leave the job with your full retirement account in hand. Your own contributions, plus the money they earned, are always yours for the

taking. But you usually have to have worked for a while before you're vested in your company's matching contributions. (Some companies, however, vest you in their contributions immediately.)

4. Job-switchers should reinvest their lump-sum pension payouts in an Individual Retirement Account or in the new employer's pension plan. If you spend the money, that chunk of your pension savings is permanently gone. You will never make up its loss. Besides losing your nest egg and the value of years of tax deferral, you will have to pay income taxes on the money plus a 10 percent penalty if you're under age 59½. Spending your pension cash is nuts.

5. Don't fail to contribute to a tax-deductible 401(k) plan, if it's offered (page 743). Your company assumes that you'll make the maximum contribution, when deciding how much additional money to put into your account. Together, your money and the company's is supposed to add up to an acceptable retirement income. If you don't put in your share, your nest egg will fall short.

6. You absolutely must learn something about long-term investing. This new responsibility is something that most pension savers haven't gotten their minds around yet. Professionally run pension funds invest heavily in stocks because, over time, they produce the very largest returns. Yet individuals tend to go for lower-yielding fixed-income investments. If you put all your 401(k) money into fixed-income plans, the size of your pension is probably going to disappoint you. (For more on investing 401(k) plans, see page 761.)

Employee Stock Ownership Plans (ESOPs)

Of all the defined-contribution plans that you might be offered, an ESOP is by far the riskiest. Its name is wonderfully evocative, suggesting a company bursting with zeal, eager to serve, with every man and woman a capitalist. The better the company does, the richer the stock-owning employees get. And in fact, if your little company grows big, you could strike it rich. But some companies go bankrupt, taking their ESOPs— and your pension—with them. ESOPs are not insured by the Pension Benefit Guaranty Corporation.

Some ESOPs diversify a bit. Most, however, are made up entirely of the company's own stock. Each employee holds an ESOP account, to which stock is added periodically. But those shares are frozen; you cannot sell them. You get the stock's value—in shares or cash—when you leave the company or retire.

If the shares trade publicly, you at least know exactly what they're worth. But if your company is closely held, the shares are worth what an appraiser says they are—and who's to know if the price is right?

Dozens of new ESOPs are set up each year, not because employees are clamoring for them but because they offer so much to management. ESOPs provide companies with special tax breaks; they're a captive buyer for a retiring owner's closely held shares; and they defend management against a hostile takeover, because the ESOP trustee won't tender those shares to a raider.

Lately, some companies have been substituting ESOPs for retiree health plans. Your stock is supposed to grow so much in value that you can buy all of the health care you'll need. If it doesn't, that's your lookout, not the company's.

It's unfair for a company to construct its only (or major) pension plan as an ESOP. No employee should be asked to stake his or her entire future on whether, at retirement, the company's stock will be up or down. The firm should also offer a defined-benefit pension plan or a broadly diversified defined-contribution plan. If there's a 401(k) or other company savings plan, use it to the max to acquire other pension investments.

If you are stuck with only an ESOP, look for another job. Or make superhuman efforts to save money for yourself. If your company fails, your personal money is all you'll have. Also, take full advantage of two escape hatches that your ESOP is required to offer by law.

1. When you reach age 55 or more, and have been in the plan for at least 10 years, you can order that 25 percent of your ESOP money be invested in other assets. This switch can be made all at once or over five years. Do it, even if the company's stock is going up. You might retire early, and who knows where the stock price will be then? You need a more diversified portfolio.

2. In the sixth year (you'll usually be age 60 or 61), you can order that half of your money be switched out of your company's stock and into a broader range of investments (that's 50 percent of the ESOP minus the percentage you took out before).

Sometimes, you can diversify through the company's own defined-contribution plan. Alternatively, you'll be given cash, which you can roll into an Individual Retirement Account and invest yourself. Either way, diversify to the fullest. It's the very safest thing to do.

Top-heavy Plans

This phrase refers to pension plans that benefit, disproportionately, the highest-paid people in small companies, usually the owners. A lot of law now exists to force owners to offer their employees a fairer shake. Advising on these plans is a job for your friendly certified public accountant, not me. I mention them only to remind the top-heavies that they might lose their tax benefits if their plans don't follow 5 zillion rules.

YOUR PENSION: THE DO-IT-YOURSELF PART

Pension savings are not optional for anyone who hopes to escape genteel poverty in old age. The sufficiency of your retirement income will depend increasingly on how much you are putting by for yourself.

The earlier you start the better. A dollar today is always worth more than a dollar tomorrow, thanks to the unflagging power of interest, dividends, and profits left alone to compound. Compounding is a true perpetual money machine. No force (except early withdrawals!) can ever stand in its way.

401(k) Savings Plans: The Best Deal in Town

You'll find these wonderful 401(k) salary-deferral plans at almost every large company and many smaller ones. Each may give its plan a special name, like the Super Saver or the Pot-of-Gold Account. Details differ from firm to firm. But at bottom, they are all the same unbeatable deal.

Many young people avoid these plans because they "can't afford" them. But you gain so much in tax savings and free employer contributions that it's crazy not to join. If you don't, you'll look back 10 years later and kick yourself.

Here are your 401(k) questions, answered.

HOW DOES THE PLAN WORK? You agree that part of your salary will be set aside every year for your retirement. That money is exempt from current income taxes (although not from Social Security taxes). The earnings on your contributions—interest, dividends, and capital gains—accumulate tax deferred. You are taxed only when the funds are withdrawn.

Your plan may also allow for after-tax contributions. You get no deduction for saving this money but the earnings will accumulate tax deferred.

HOW DO I CONTRIBUTE? By payroll deduction, which is doubtless why 401(k) plans work so well. These dollars slip into the plan without your even seeing them go. You live on the net paycheck you receive, forgetting the portion that was set aside. Ignored, your 401(k) money sits there peaceably and grows.

HOW MUCH CAN I PUT IN? Your own maximum tax-deductible contribution is some percentage of salary (set by your company) up to a legal ceiling that rises with inflation every year. In 1991, it was $8,475.* After-tax contributions go on top of that.

The maximum annual contribution to all of your company savings plans, including what your employer puts in (below), is 25 percent of your net salary after subtracting your own 401(k) contributions, up to a ceiling of $30,000. Higher-paid employees, however, may not be able to fill their plans right up to the top. They are not allowed to save a substantially higher percentage of pay than lower-paid employees do.

You should fund these plans to the absolute maximum of your ability. Start small, if you must, and step up your commitment every year. If you change jobs several times in your life, this may be the only significant pool of retirement money that you'll ever have.

DOES MY EMPLOYER CONTRIBUTE? Usually yes. You might get 25 cents or 50 cents—sometimes even $1—for every pretax dollar you put in, up to a certain percentage of pay. If you make after-tax contributions, some companies will match them, too. Sometimes the match is made with company stock instead of cash. *This is free money!* Any employee who doesn't contribute is throwing a huge profit away.

WHAT HAPPENS TO THE MONEY? You invest it in one or more investment vehicles provided by the company. These might include stock-owning mutual funds, guaranteed-investment contracts at a fixed rate of interest, money market mutual funds, and the company's own stock. The trend is toward a larger number of choices. (For more on retirement-plan investments, see page 76.)

CAN I SWITCH FROM ONE INVESTMENT TO ANOTHER? Absolutely. Most plans allow it. You can also divide your money among the various funds—so much in stocks, so much in fixed-income deals. Exactly when you can switch investments depends on your plan. Some set fixed dates—for example,

* This is your total, annual pretax contribution, even if you work two jobs with two 401(k) plans. However, if you also have a tax-qualified 403(b) annuity (for employees of schools, hospitals, and certain other institutions), you can put up to $8,475 into the 401(k) plus enough extra into the annuity to bring your total contribution to $9,500.

quarterly or annually. Some allow a fixed number of switches per year that you can use any time you want. (But there may be penalties for early withdrawals from certain fixed-income investments, to discourage hot money from moving around.) In general, it's best to set up a long-term plan and stick with it rather than seek to cadge extra points by making quick switches. When it comes to trying to time the markets, you are more likely to lose than to win.

HOW DO I KNOW HOW MY INVESTMENTS ARE DOING? You get a written performance report at least once a year. Some companies go a lot further than that, distributing monthly or quarterly reports. If you bought a mutual fund, you may be able to follow its progress in the newspaper. You may also receive the fund's regular reports to shareholders.

CAN I TAKE ALL MY MONEY FROM THE PLAN IF I LEAVE? You can take every dime that you contributed plus all the income it has earned. How much you get of the company's contribution depends on the plan. Some companies give you everything regardless of how long you worked. Others give you nothing unless you stayed in the plan five years, or vest you gradually starting from the third year. In all cases, however, you will be fully vested after seven years. To avoid paying taxes on your 401(k) money, and to keep your cache building, roll it into an Individual Retirement Account within 60 days, or into the retirement plan of your new employer, if that plan allows.

CAN I MAKE CASH WITHDRAWALS FROM THE PLAN WHILE I'M STILL AT WORK? Yes, at a majority of companies. But younger people should raid their plans only as a last resort. First, this is retirement money, not to be messed with. Second, withdrawals are usually expensive. You have to pay income taxes on the funds, except for withdrawals of any after-tax money you contributed, and a tax penalty of 10 percent if you're under age 59½ (for the rules on when this penalty is waived, see page 759). Third, you lose the tax-deferred interest that all that money would have earned in the future.

If you're under age 59½, you can't even ask for a withdrawal unless you face financial "hardship." Typically, that means huge medical expenses, buying a principal residence, a college tuition bill due immediately, a threat of eviction, or a similar "immediate and heavy financial need." ("Needing" a new boat is not a hardship, unless perhaps you're in the shrimping business.)

What's more, you have to have exhausted all other possible sources of funds. Has your bank turned you down for another loan? Have you borrowed all you can against your 401(k) account? If you finally make it over the "hardship" hurdle, you may withdraw any tax-deductible sums that you personally contributed, plus the earnings on them up through 1988. All the earnings on your money after 1988, however, cannot be withdrawn, no matter how tough life gets.

There is no hardship test for withdrawing any of the after-tax money you put in or the earnings on it. After two years, you may also start withdrawing some of the employer's contribution, if the plan allows. And, of course, you'll get all of this money when you leave the company. On departure, your 401(k) funds will be handed over in a lump sum.

Some further wrinkles in the cash-withdrawal rules:

· At some companies, workers making hardship withdrawals may not contribute to their 401(k)s for at least the next 12 months. When you start up again, your maximum contribution will be reduced.

· When you take any after-tax money you stored in the plan, no further taxes are owed. But what about the earnings on that money, that have been building tax deferred? (1) On contributions made up through 1986, you may be able to specify that the earnings stay in the plan. Ask your company about it. (2) On contributions made since, your withdrawal has to include the earnings, on which taxes and, perhaps, penalties will be owed.

· Withdrawals are much easier after age 59½. There is no 10 percent tax penalty. And companies usually impose no "hardship" requirements.

· A very few companies allow no withdrawals at all, for any purpose or at any age, until you leave work.

CAN I BORROW FROM THE PLAN? A majority of companies say yes. So this is your end run around the "hardship" question. Instead of making a withdrawal, you take a loan. There is normally no credit check. You can borrow your own contributions and the money they've earned. You may also be able to borrow the employer's contributions and the money they've earned. Some plans allow loans for any purpose whatsoever; some allow them only for certain purposes, like buying a house or paying tuition; some allow no loans at all, generally because they don't want to bother with the paperwork.

HOW MUCH CAN I BORROW? The size of your loan depends on the value of the account. On accounts of $20,000 or less, you can get up to $10,000. With larger accounts, you can borrow 50 percent of the value, up to a legal maximum of $50,000. (Some plans impose lower maximums.) If you already have one or more loans against your plan, your further borrowing is reduced. Your account must be loan-free for a full 12 months before you can borrow the maximum again.

DOES MY SPOUSE HAVE TO AGREE TO THE LOAN? No, not if your plan meets the no-consent rules outlined on page 796.

WHAT ARE THE LOAN TERMS? You pay market interest rates, probably equal to the bank prime lending rate. Whether you can tax deduct the interest depends on the purpose of the loan and which funds you borrow against. When you borrow against your own *pretax* contributions and the money they've earned, the interest is never tax deductible. But if you borrow against your *after-tax* contributions plus earnings, or the employer's contributions plus earnings, and use the money to make investments, part or all of the interest may be deductible (page 231). That is, unless you're a "key employee," whose 401(k) loans are never deductible at all. *

Most loans have to be repaid within five years, although longer periods (10 to 30 years) may be allowed for loans taken out to buy a principal residence. Repayments are usually made by payroll deduction.

WHAT IF I STILL HAVE A LOAN WHEN I LEAVE MY JOB? You generally have to repay it. Most companies want payment right away, or within three months at the latest. So you may have to refinance with a bank. A few companies let you repay over a year, or over the loan's full life. If you cannot repay, the loan is treated as a withdrawal. You'll owe income taxes on the money and a 10 percent penalty if you are younger than age 59½.

WHAT HAPPENS TO MY MONEY WHEN I RETIRE? You get it all. You can take it then or later. You can take it in installment payments or a lump sum. (For your payout options, see page 791).

HOW TO GET THE MOST FROM A 401(K) PLAN

1. Make the maximum contribution, or as close to it as you possibly can. A 401(k) is the richest deal you'll ever find. Contributions are tax deductible; the earnings are all tax deferred; the plan may offer several investment choices; and your employer will probably match what you save. In an emergency, you can usually borrow some of the funds.

2. If the plan allows it, consider adding some extra money, after tax. The earnings will build tax deferred. Counting what your employer puts in, your total annual contribution can reach the lesser of $30,000

---

* The law is unsettled on several of the points above. According to Harry Gross, a partner in Kwasha Lipton, an employee-benefits consulting firm in Fort Lee, New Jersey, strong legal opinions hold that *no* 401(k) loans are eligible for interest deductions, for any employee.

or 25 percent of your net salary, after subtracting your deductible contribution. (Let your employer contribute first; then you top the plan off.)

3. My advice about funding your plan to the maximum applies, without reservation, to savings plans that let you borrow money if you need it and are reasonable about hardship withdrawals. But what if you have a true "lock-up" plan, that won't give you a penny until you leave the company? In that case, I'd still fund the tax-deductible 401(k) portion in full. But I might not invest after-tax money, too. Some of your savings should be on tap for emergencies.

4. Invest a good part of your retirement money in the plan's stock-owning mutual fund rather than in fixed-income contracts. Over the long term, stocks yield the best return by far. But don't buy much of your own company's stock. You don't want both your job and your retirement fund riding on the fortunes of a single firm, no matter how good. Diversify, diversify.

5. Although 401(k)s are designed for retirement, they're also worthwhile for college savings, as long as there's a loan provision. Why save for college outside the plan, where there's no tax deduction or employer match? A loan from your plan does not deplete your retirement savings, as long as the interest you pay is no less than the plan was earning on its other investments, and as long as you repay the money.

Here's how to decide whether to take a bank loan or a loan against your retirement plan: A bank home-equity loan is better, because the interest will be tax deductible. If the bank loan will not be tax deductible, however, make the decision strictly on the basis of whether the bank or your retirement plan offers the better interest rate and repayment terms.

6. Don't borrow from the plan at all if you can avoid it, except to make investments that promise an exceptionally high return. If you do borrow for investment, borrow the employer's contribution, not yours. The interest may then be tax deductible. (For more on borrowing from 401(k)s, see page 228.)

7. If you need some money and you're at least age 59½, consider a withdrawal instead of a loan. At this stage of life, you might not want to start running up new debts. You'll owe income taxes on the withdrawal but no 10 percent tax penalty.

Keogh Plans: Almost Unbeatable for the Self-Employed

Keogh plans are for anyone with self-employment income. Obviously, that includes people who work for themselves: consultants, artists, professionals, and owners of small unincorporated businesses. Not so obviously, it covers employees who moonlight. Suppose, for example that you're a magazine editor, participating in your company's pension and 401(k) plan. But you also teach journalism on the side. Your teacher's pay can be stashed in a Keogh plan. A partnership can set up a Keogh, but only in the name of the partnership, not for the partners individually.

When you work for yourself, do not fail to set up a Keogh or similar plan. No Kindly Big Corporation will send you a check at age 65. Your own savings are all that stand between you and the penury of Social Security.

So which Keogh? They come in four basic styles, to suit three levels of income. Here's what they're called and who might want them.

• A *profit-sharing Keogh.* This is usually the plan to start with. You can contribute, and tax deduct, up to 13.04 percent annually of your self-employment earnings,* to a maximum contribution of $30,000. But how much, or how little, you add every year is always your call. You can make any percentage contribution below the ceiling, or none at all.

• A *money-purchase Keogh.* This plan is for higher-income people who are sure that the money will keep rolling in. Contributions can run as high as 20 percent of your self-employment earnings each year, to a maximum contribution of $30,000. You have to pick a percentage contribution and stick with it. If you can't make the specified payment, you'll owe a penalty. The IRS might let you change the level of your contributions, if you plead bad business conditions. However, anyone having trouble making payments should generally drop the plan and roll the money into an Individual Retirement Account.

• A *combination Keogh.* You use both of the plans explained above. That gives you the right to the largest possible contribution, while allowing you to pull back in any year when money is short. Here's how: (1) You set up a money-purchase plan with a guaranteed annual payment of 8 percent. That's your floor. (2) You set up a profit-sharing plan to

---

* Your maximum contribution will go down a bit, as a side effect of deducting one-half of your self-employment (Social Security) tax. In 1991, the total earnings counted toward your contribution were $222,220; that ceiling rises every year.

receive whatever you can afford above 8 percent. In a good year, your maximum contribution would be 12 percent, for a total of 20 percent in all (up to a maximum of $30,000). People often start with a profit-sharing Keogh and later add the money-purchase plan.

• A *defined-benefit Keogh*. This provides you with a fixed annual income at retirement. It's for high-income people around 50 or older with a fondness for hanging around actuaries. You pick the annual pension you want, then contribute (and tax deduct) whatever sums are needed to reach that goal. Your contributions could be quite large. In 1991, you were allowed to build a kitty big enough to yield a pension as high as $108,963, starting at age 65. This figure is indexed to inflation.

Each year, your plan has to be checked by an actuary. He or she will update it for any changes in the law, tell you how large a contribution you should make, and send you a bill. The service isn't cheap: It may cost $2,500 to set up the plan and $750 a year or more to administer it. If your income drops, a defined-benefit Keogh can be stopped in its tracks and the money rolled into an Individual Retirement Account.

If you have employees, they have to be included in your Keogh, too. Contributions go to 15 percent for employees in profit-sharing plans and 25 percent in money-purchase plans. Yes, that's right. Higher than yours. Anyone with employees should talk with an accountant before starting a pension plan.

How you start a Keogh depends on where you want to invest. Do you want only certificates of deposit? Call a bank, S&L, or credit union and ask for its Keogh application form. Do you want an annuity? Call an insurance company. Do you want mutual funds? Call the mutual fund organization (page 531). You can contribute to several different Keoghs, as long as your total contribution doesn't exceed the annual ceiling. But administratively, it's a whole lot easier to maintain a single account.

If you want to choose your own stocks and bonds, as well as CDs and mutual funds, call a brokerage firm (full-service or discount) and establish a self-directed Keogh trust. Name yourself as trustee. All your contributions then go to the trust, to be invested wherever you like.

KEOGH PLANS VERSUS CORPORATE PLANS

As a self-employed person, you might decide to incorporate. The business reasons for making that choice go beyond the edges of this book. In terms of personal money, however, there are two advantages to incorporation and one to having a Keogh.

• You can borrow from corporate pension plans and can't from Keoghs. So Keogh owners generally can't make use of their money penalty free.

• Corporations can tax deduct all the premiums on their medical insurance. The self-employed can deduct only 25 percent. (The remaining 75 percent is counted toward deductible medical expenses).

• Profit-sharing and money-purchase Keoghs are far easier to administer than corporate plans. They save you large sums in accounting and actuarial bills. Not so defined-benefit Keogh plans. They cost just about the same as corporate pension plans.

How to get the most from a Keogh plan.
1. Hold down your paperwork and centralize your investing by having just one plan. For the greatest flexibility, open a plan with a mutual fund group. Or, if you do your own stock picking, establish a self-directed Keogh trust with a discount or full-service stockbroker.

2. Set up a plan for making automatic deposits, which guarantees that you'll really save money. The simplest way is to have a fixed amount of money withdrawn from your bank account each month for investment in a mutual fund. Any time you get a windfall payment, add a piece of it to your Keogh.

3. If you don't now have a Keogh plan, start one by the end of the year, even if you only put $100 into it. As long as the paperwork is done by year end, you can make a contribution, and deduct it, all the way up to the due date of your tax return (including extensions).

4. Don't use a Keogh at all. Use a near-Keogh, known as a Simplified Employee Pension plan, or SEP.

SEPs: Truly Unbeatable for the Self-Employed
I told you all about Keoghs because that's what most people use. But if you have no employees, and can't stash a whole lot of money each year, I'd vote for a Simplified Employee Pension, or SEP, instead.

SEPs work like profit-sharing Keogh plans. The contribution limits are the same—13.04 percent* of self-employment earnings, up to a maximum contribution of $30,000. You can add to your plan each year or not, depending on what you can afford. But SEPs are handled as

---

* Or less, as a side effect of deducting one-half of the self-employment tax.

Individual Retirement Accounts, which makes them a whole lot simpler to administer than Keogh plans.

You get a SEP at all the same places that offer Keoghs: banks, S&Ls, credit unions, mutual funds, brokerage houses. There are only three differences with SEPS, all minor. There's no tax break on lump-sum withdrawals as there are with Keoghs. You can't put life insurance into the plan. If you take a job with a company, you can't roll your SEP into the employer's retirement plan. Big deal. To me, their administrative simplicity beats all. SEPs are easier than Keoghs for small businesses with employees, too. But Keoghs make it simpler to exclude lower-paid employees, if you're of a mind to do so.

Other Retirement Plans Not to Be Missed

403(b) PLANS—tax-deferred plans for employees of religious, charitable, or educational organizations. Most of them are funded with insurance annuities, but growing numbers of organizations offer mutual fund shares, too. Your annual, tax-deductible contributions are subject to ceilings so complicated I wouldn't dream of trying to explain them here. Suffice it to say that the maximum is usually the lower of $9,500 or 25 percent of pay. You can make your contribution through an automatic payroll-deduction plan.

FEDERAL THRIFT SAVINGS FUND—for federal government employees. You're allowed the same tax-deductible contribution as employees with 401(k)s.

SECTION 457 PLANS—for state and local government employees. Your normal contributions are the lesser of $7,500 or one-third of includable compensation.

INDIVIDUAL RETIREMENT ACCOUNTS

Don't give up on the Individual Retirement Account! Ever since it lost its universal tax shelter (and banks and mutual funds quit selling it so aggressively), folks seem to have consigned it to limbo. I see no last-minute scramble at tax time to get an IRA investment together.

That's a mistake. IRAs are still fully tax deductible for millions of American savers. And they're partly deductible for millions more. The tax writeoff gives long-term savers a huge leg up. If you're eligible for this deduction, grab it.

If you can't deduct most or all of the contribution, however, IRAs become a personal call. Your earnings still build tax deferred—always an advantage. But nondeductible contributions complicate your tax returns. If you do your own taxes, you might not want to bother with them. Here are the IRA rules.

WHO CAN TAX DEDUCT THE CONTRIBUTION?

1. You can deduct a full IRA if you don't participate in any company retirement plan. If you're married, your spouse can't be a participant, either. You "participate" if you're eligible for your company's defined-benefit plan (page 735), even if you're not yet vested. But if you're covered only by a defined-contribution plan (page 739), you don't "participate" until money goes into the plan on your behalf—which may not happen in the first year of your employment. So for that first year, you'd be entitled to take a tax-deductible IRA.

2. You can deduct a full IRA if you participate in a company retirement plan but your adjusted gross income isn't too high. The limits: $25,000 if single or $40,000 if married. If your income is larger, you get a partial deduction. The more you earn, the smaller your IRA writeoff. It phases out at $35,000 for singles and $50,000 for marrieds.

HOW MUCH CAN I CONTRIBUTE?

Individuals can put away up to $2,000 a year out of earnings or alimony. One-income couples can add an extra $250 for the at-home spouse. "Spousal" IRAs needn't be split 50-50. As much as $2,000 a year can be deposited in the name of either spouse. Two-income couples can save up to $4,000—$2,000 for each.

Some savers think that it's $2,000 or nothing. Not so. That's just the ceiling. Contribute a lesser amount, if that's all you can afford. You can even skip a year (although that would be a pity). If you earn less than $2,000, you can contribute every penny of it to your IRA (net of expenses, if you're self-employed).

HOW DO I HANDLE NONDEDUCTIBLE IRA CONTRIBUTIONS?

You file a special form (Form 8606) with your tax return.

HOW DO I HANDLE IRA WITHDRAWALS WHEN I'VE MADE NONDEDUCTIBLE CONTRIBUTIONS?

With desperation in your eye or with gratitude to your accountant. These contributions make a mess out of every withdrawal.

Suppose for example, that you've made $20,000 in IRA contributions. Of that, $2,000 was nondeductible. It can be retrieved tax free. The other $18,000 was deductible, so taxes are owed on it at withdrawal. The entire $20,000 has been earning tax-deferred interest, which is also taxable when withdrawn. Suppose further that, through careful investing, your IRA is now worth $40,000. You take out $1,000. What happens?

You are taxed on the portion of each withdrawal that equals the percentage of tax-deferred money in all of your IRAs. In this example, your $2,000 nondeductible contribution comes to 5 percent of the $40,000 total. So 5 percent of your $1,000 withdrawal ($50) passes income-tax free. The other $950 is taxed. You have to redo this calculation every time you take money out.

Many taxpayers feel that it's just not worth it. They'd rather forgo a nondeductible IRA than mess with the taxes. That's a pity, especially for those of you who could get partial tax deductions. Over the years, that money really builds up.

Here are three ways of making the nondeductible life a little easier.

1. Put all your nondeductible IRA contributions in separate accounts from your deductible ones. That makes them easier to keep track of.

2. At tax time, turn the whole mess over to an accountant and let him or her solve it for you.

3. Keep all of your 8606 forms to the last syllable of recorded time. They tell you what nondeductible contributions you made, hence what taxes are owed on withdrawals. If you can't prove the size of your nondeductible contribution, you may have to pay a tax on everything.

WHY WOULD I WANT A NONDEDUCTIBLE IRA? Four possible reasons. (1) Your income is just over the deductible-IRA limit. You can still write off most of the contribution. (2) You're a terrific investor and make huge gains by trading stocks rapidly. The IRA defers the taxes due. (3) You aren't buffaloed by the fact that your tax return will be more complex. (4) You intend to leave your IRA to your spouse, have reason to believe that you'll die before you pass age 70½ or soon thereafter, and you won't be making many withdrawals. The IRA can pass to your spouse with its tax shelter intact.

HOW DOES A NONDEDUCTIBLE IRA COMPARE WITH OTHER TAX-FAVORED, NONDEDUCTIBLE INVESTMENTS?

1. Commercial tax-deferred annuities generally don't do as well, because of the higher expenses they carry. Over time, a comparable IRA from a bank or no-load mutual fund should yield better returns.

2. Series EE Savings Bonds give you tax deferral but not a particularly high yield. You'll do better, long term, with a nondeductible IRA invested in intermediate-term U.S. Treasuries or stocks.

3. With tax-exempt municipal bonds, your interest is entirely tax exempt, not just tax-deferred. IRAs still do better for investors in the lowest bracket. But in the higher brackets, IRAs excel only if kept entirely in stocks and held for 20 years or so. Otherwise, munis come in first.

HOW DOES A DEDUCTIBLE IRA COMPARE WITH OTHER DEDUCTIBLE INVESTMENTS?

1. Company 401(k) plans always beat IRAs, for employees who are eligible for both. The 401(k) permits larger contributions and may allow loans. What's more, the employer usually matches the money you put in.

2. Keogh plans usually beat IRAs, too, because you can put more money into them. The IRA wins, however, if your earnings are small. Every penny of an annual paycheck of $2,000 or less can be stashed in an IRA to accumulate tax deferred, whereas only a portion of it could be put into a Keogh plan.

HOW DO I SET UP AN IRA? Decide where you want to invest your retirement fund, then ask an appropriate institution for its IRA account forms. Fill out the papers, send in the money, and you're up and running.

For certificates of deposit, you'd choose a bank, S&L, or credit union. Setup fees are minimal or zero. For an annuity, you'd choose an insurance company. For a diversified portfolio of stocks and bonds, you might take a mutual fund. Funds, insurers, and some banks charge a small annual maintenance fee. If you want to pick your own stocks, bonds, CDs, and other investments, get a "self-directed" IRA from a brokerage house. With these accounts, you can also buy American Eagle gold and silver coins—but no other coins, no gems, no gold bars, no art, and no collectibles. You're charged a setup fee for a self-directed IRA, plus an annual maintenance fee payable separately and deductible as part of your miscellaneous tax deductions. Brokerage commissions, however, are subtracted from your IRA money. Tip: You'll save a lot of money on both fees and commissions by dealing with a discount broker (page 546).

You're allowed to have as many IRAs as you want—for example, one at a credit union, one at a bank, and one at a mutual fund. But whether you have one IRA or ten, your total annual contribution can't exceed the $2,000 or $2,250 ceilings.

Do not, incidentally, use your IRA to buy municipal bonds or muni funds. You don't need tax deferral for these investments because they're tax exempt already. What's more, if you put them in an IRA, their interest becomes taxable at withdrawal.

CAN I CHANGE MY IRA INVESTMENTS? Yes, as far as the tax laws are concerned.

You can switch from one investment to another within the same institution, or to another institution entirely. With a self-directed IRA, which is just like a regular brokerage account, you can change investments as often as you care to pick up the phone.

There are two ways of switching from one institution to another: (1) a direct IRA-to-IRA transfer, which can be done as often as you want; (2) a payout to you, which you must roll into the new IRA within 60 days. Each IRA can be rolled over only once a year.

Sometimes, however, you're thwarted by the institution that you leave behind. Some drag their heels on transferring your investments. Some charge an exit fee. A few brokerage firms can actually prevent you from leaving, because the agreement you originally signed locks your money up. Moral: Don't open an IRA without first checking your escape routes. And get a list of all the fees.

CAN I MAKE WITHDRAWALS FROM AN IRA? Yes, if you're willing to pay the price. First come income taxes. Second, there's usually a 10 percent penalty if you're under age 59½. Third, if your IRA is in a bank certificate of deposit or an annuity, you may owe an early-withdrawal penalty.

CAN I AVOID THE TAX PENALTY FOR EARLY WITHDRAWAL? Yes, in four ways, only the last of which I'd recommend. You're off the hook if the early withdrawal is due to: (1) your total disability; (2) your death; (3) your need to pay deductible medical expenses that exceed 7.5 percent of your adjusted gross income; or (4) setting up a schedule of substantially equal lifetime payments. Take a look at that last point, which is fully explained on page 759. It's a dandy idea for middle-aged people in need of funds.

HOW LONG CAN I CONTRIBUTE? As long as you have earnings, up to the year before you reach age 70½. Then you have to stop. But you can keep on depositing up to $2,000 a year for an at-home spouse who is under age 70½.

WHAT IF I GET DIVORCED? As part of the divorce agreement, some or all of the IRA money may go to your former spouse. Anything taken out of the account is treated as a rollover (below). The funds have to be transferred to a new IRA within 60 days or taxes and penalties will be due.

HOW DO I HANDLE AN IRA ROLLOVER? Rollovers are for lump sums coming out of pension plans. Maybe you retired. Maybe you quit. Either way, you might be handed a single check that represents your entire accumulated pension.

If you spend the money, you'll pay taxes on it and won't have the income in old age. The smarter choice is to roll it into an Individual Retirement Account (or into the retirement plan of a new employer, if the plan allows). That preserves your retirement savings and keeps your tax shelter intact. With smaller checks, a rollover sometimes doesn't seem worth it. But $1,500, at an untaxed 8 percent, grows to $7,000 in 20 years without your having to lift a finger, and to $15,500 in 30 years. That's worth it.

The rollover rules:

• The money has to go into the IRA (or the new employer's plan) within 60 days. Don't wait until the last minute. If the bank or the mutual fund misses a beat, and your funds aren't deposited by the 60-day deadline, the money is taxed.

• You can roll over all of the money or some of it, as you choose.

• You have to roll over the very same assets that came out of your old pension plan, with two exceptions. You can sell an asset and roll over the cash instead. Or you can spend some of the cash you took out of the plan and replace it with other cash.

• Rollovers are only for pretax money. If you made any after-tax contributions to your pension plan, those have to be removed. If you want to keep this extra money in a tax-deferred investment, consider a nondeductible IRA.

• For your money to qualify for rollover treatment, you have to get all of it out of the plan within the same calendar year. If the plan doles out some of your assets in December and some in January, you're generally stuck. Exceptions exist, however, if some of your pension-plan assets are frozen by litigation or bankruptcy.

• Don't add your rollover funds to an existing IRA. Always segregate this money in an IRA of its own. Rollover money in segregated accounts can be rolled into a new employer's retirement plan, if you ever want to do so. Funds from other IRAs can't.

CAN I BORROW FROM, OR AGAINST, AN IRA? No dice. But if you have a truly short-term need for money—for example, a bridge loan, while waiting for a mortgage to come through—you could tap your IRA through the rollover rule. The rule lets you take money out of your IRA and use it, as long as you put it back within 60 days. When you're using one IRA, you're allowed to do this once a year.

If you still need the money after 60 days, you could roll an equivalent sum into a second IRA, leave it there one day, then draw it out for another 60 days. At the end of that period, you could roll the money though a third IRA and a fourth—until you got sick of it or didn't need the loan anymore.

HOW TO GET THE MOST FROM AN IRA.

1. Put yourself on a regular monthly contribution plan with a bank or mutual fund. That should guarantee you the maximum $2,000 deposit every year. Savers who wait until the last minute may come up short. It's okay to deposit less, but that lost amount can never be made up.

2. If you didn't make monthly contributions, all is not lost. You can open an IRA on the very eve of the day that your tax return is due, deposit up to $2,000, and still deduct it for the previous year.

3. If you have a scattering of IRAs at many different institutions, consolidate them. They add to your paperwork, and maybe to your maintenance fees. Better to have all the money under one roof—with a mutual fund group or in a self-directed IRA. You should also be able to wring a higher return from a single lump sum than from a clutch of separate, disorganized accounts.

4. If you're a TWOI-some—two workers, one income—use a spousal IRA to build up the assets of the at-home spouse. Put the bulk of your annual deposit (up to $2,000) into his or her name.

5. As a general rule, you shouldn't tap your IRA until retirement. If you're a homeowner and need money, take a home-equity loan, instead. You will probably earn more on your IRA investment than you will pay for the home-equity loan, after tax. But if you're in serious need of cash, and are under age 59½, take a look at Loophole Six on page 759. It's a way of using your IRA funds without paying the 10 percent early-withdrawal penalty.

6. Buy a commercial tax-deferred annuity only for a tax-*deductible* IRA, so you can write off the contribution. Otherwise, buying the annuity is a waste; it's tax deferred anyway, with or without the IRA wrapper. Don't buy tax-exempt municipals, either. Use the IRA to shelter investments that would otherwise would be taxable.

7. When you take a lump sum out of a qualified retirement plan, invest it in a segregated IRA of its own. Don't add it to an existing IRA. Rollover funds from a segregated IRA can be rolled back into the retirement plan of a new employer. Funds from other IRAs can't.

8. If you want to move your IRA from one institution to another, there are two different ways of getting the job done: transfers or rollovers. Which you choose will depend on your character and your needs.

• *A transfer is the sure and easy way.* The new institution does most of the work and every dime of your money is reinvested. The drawback is that transfers sometimes take weeks. That could be damaging, if there's a particular investment that you want to make at present prices. (Tip: Ask your old institution if there's an exit fee and pay it promptly. That sometimes gets the ball rolling faster.)

• *A rollover is the quicker way.* Ask the old institution to close your account, which should be accomplished within five days. You then hand that money to the new institution. The success of any rollover, however, depends on your self-discipline. You may be tempted to tweak out a few thousand dollars while the money passes through your hands. So your IRA may not be reinvested intact. Furthermore, you have to accomplish the rollover within 60 days. If you miss the deadline, you'll have made a permanent withdrawal on which taxes and maybe penalties are due.

9. If you're moving to a mutual fund group and aren't yet sure which funds you want, put your IRA into its money fund and choose investments later. If you dither around trying to pick a stock or bond fund, you might let the 60-day deadline get by.

GETTING AWAY WITH IT

Whether you have a 401(k), a Keogh, a retirement annuity, an Individual Retirement Account, or a SEP, it usually costs you an extra 10 percent to withdraw your money if you're younger than 59½. But loopholes dot any government rule. The penalty may be waived in the following circumstances.

1. You're totally disabled.

2. You're dead, and the money is going to your beneficiary.

3. You've taken early retirement and are at least age 55. (This particular loophole works for all plans but IRAs.)

4. The money is going to a divorced spouse pursuant to a court decree. (This doesn't work for IRAs, either. To avoid penalties, roll the money into a new IRA.)

5. You need the money for deductible medical expenses that exceed 7.5 percent of your adjusted gross income. Here, there's a catch. Taking money out of your pension plan raises your income, which reduces the size of the medical deduction you can take. Thank you, Uncle Sam.

6. You set up a payment schedule for withdrawing the money over the rest of your life.

Loophole Six sounds restrictive on the surface, but it is, in fact, the most interesting flexible one of all. It applies to IRAs as well as to all the other plans.

LOOPHOLE SIX. This escape route is so useful that I want to spend a few paragraphs telling you about it. It lets you avoid the 10 percent early-withdrawal penalty if you're under age 59½. You just set up a regular withdrawal schedule that, if followed faithfully, would lead to "substantially equal" periodic payments for the rest of your life (or for the joint life expectancies of you and your spouse or another beneficiary).

But here's the beauty part: The payments don't have to last for life, if your need for money is short term. Once you start withdrawing, you must keep to the schedule for at least five years and until you reach age 59½. After that, you can change your mind. You might decide on larger withdrawals or smaller ones. Or you might take no more money at all. Withdrawal rules don't begin again until you pass age 70½ (page 794).

I can think of several problems that Loophole Six might solve. For example, you might tap the fund to help pay for your child's college degree. Once those bills are behind you (and five years have passed, and you're age 59½), you can stop the withdrawals and let your remaining money grow. Or you might have lost your executive job and replaced it with a job paying less. A withdrawal plan could provide the extra income you need. It might also be a way of paying alimony.

This loophole, however, works best for the middle-aged, who may not have to use it for any more than five years. Young people should forget it. Their monthly payments would be pretty small. And, once started, withdrawals must continue at least until age 59½. That would pretty much run down the fund.

THERE IS ONE IMMUTABLE LAW OF FINANCIAL PLANNING THAT THIS LITTLE GAME RUNS UP AGAINST. God punishes anyone who uses loopholes. In this case, your trials are actuarial.

There is more than one way of calculating "substantially equal" payments, and the method chosen makes a huge difference to the size of your income. I ran one example for a 55-year-old woman. She had a Keogh worth $150,000 that was earning a 9 percent rate of return. Depending on which calculation she chose, her first-year payment could have been as little as $5,245 or as much as $15,490. Alternatively, she could have divided her money into two separate $75,000 Individual Retirement Accounts, drawing $7,735 a year from one of them and leaving the other one to accumulate. Or she could have split the IRAs into different sizes. The possibilities are endless.

The IRS's free publication on Individual Retirement Arrangements —Publication 590—leads you through all the numbers. If you find them too complicated (most people do), ask an accountant for advice. If you get the size of your "substantially equal" withdrawals wrong, tax penalties may be due.

WHICH INVESTMENTS BUILD THE BEST RETIREMENT FUND?

That's easy. A preponderance of stocks or stock-owning mutual funds, held for the long term. No financial investment does better than stocks, despite their occasional alarming dips. No financial investment so soundly outperforms inflation. When stocks are down, people treat them like lepers. But in fact, that's the very best time to buy. Well-chosen bonds and certificates of deposit take the edge off your losses during those months when stocks decline. So it's worth owning some of them, too. But only stocks give you real long-term growth. For a full explanation of this position, see Chapter 21. The young and middle-aged who invest their retirement money in stock-owning mutual funds will wind up much wealthier than those who don't.

Unfortunately, this message isn't getting through. Individuals, nervously seeking "safety," tend to settle for the fixed-income stuff. They're "safe" from the stock market's scary wastes. But, after inflation and, eventually, taxes, you might as well have put your money in a mattress. In real terms, it doesn't grow.

The largest amount of 401(k) money, by far, lies in the mattress known as a guaranteed-investment contract (GIC). GICs are fixed-income contracts. Investors usually buy them one year at a time. Each year, you're offered a new interest rate, either higher or lower. The GIC is usually guaranteed by one or more insurance companies, so find out their names and whether they've been rated A-plus by the A. M. Best insurance-rating service. Your GIC is not guaranteed by your employer (although, as a practical matter, the employer might find itself in court if the insurer failed and GIC investors lost money). Some GICs are guaranteed by banks and backed by federal deposit insurance.

After GICs, employees tend to choose other forms of fixed-interest investments, such as bond funds and government securities. But while they're earning, say, 8.5 percent "safe," their colleagues in stock-owning mutual funds will walk away with 10 to 12 percent long term, despite all the dips they took along the way.

Over long periods (which is an appropriate measure for retirement funds), stocks run about 7 percent ahead of inflation, compounded annually, while intermediate-term government bonds run about 1.8 percent ahead, reports Ibbotson Associates in Chicago. After taxes, you make money on stocks but practically nothing at all on bonds.

Moral: When looking at your investment choices for long-term retirement funds, take a deep breath, hold your nose, and go for a diversified selection of stocks. Or at least go substantially for stocks.

The only exception to this rule is stock in the company you work for. Life is long and bad things happen even to good companies. I'd hate to stake my entire financial life—my retirement fund as well as my income and health plan—on the fortunes of a single firm. By all means buy the stock when you, as a close observer, know that the price is right. But diversify away from it by periodically selling it off.

What about real estate as a retirement-plan option? Some 401(k) plans offer shares in real-estate funds that are managed by insurance companies or banks. In general, I rate them a lousy idea because the properties are illiquid. If a lot of employees suddenly wanted their money out—for loans or withdrawals, or to switch to another investment—the real-estate funds might not have enough cash on hand. In 1989, in fact, one such fund shut down. Its sponsor (a bank) bailed out all the 401(k) investors. But you can't always count on a happy ending. If you love real estate, buy it separately, not in your 401(k).

When investing retirement-plan money, don't look at it in a vacuum.

I've heard people say, "I divide my money half and half, between stocks and fixed-income investments." That sounds reasonable until you see what's really going on. Their retirement funds might indeed be divided just as they said. But when you look at all their other savings— their money market fund, the Series EE bonds in their children's college account, the utility bonds their grandfather left them—it turns out that, at age 35 or 40, only 25 percent of their total available assets are truly invested for growth.

Please, folks. Line up *all* your investments, before deciding what to do about any one or two of them. Set a single, total risk level for yourself (page 495), and spread it over every savings and investment account you own. Give the larger risks (more stocks) to your retirement plans, because this is money you will leave alone for 10 to 30 years. Buy lower-risk investments for pools of funds that you will tap sooner.

Would I write these same words if I knew in advance that, when you read them, the stock market would be in a tailspin? You bet I would. That's what stocks do from time to time, and when it happens they're great buys. You'll never get the market's superior gains unless you have the nerve to buy during recessions when Wall Street reluctantly throws a half-price sale.

Nor would I say anything different if, when you read this, stocks were roaring up. Long-term investors shouldn't give a thought to where stock prices will be next week. Your horizon is 20 years, by which standard prices today are *cheap.*

AUNT JANE'S SINGLE MOST IMPORTANT SECRET FOR ACCUMULATING HUGE POTS OF MONEY FOR YOUR RETIREMENT, REVEALED HERE FOR THE FIRST TIME

When you get a payout from any pension plan, and you haven't yet retired, put all of the money back into another plan. Don't spend it. Don't even think of spending it. Don't think even of spending part of it. Give it a kiss and put it back.

The sum that you want to spend may seem small. But it's not just the loss of that money that hurts. It's the loss of all the money that that money would have earned over the next umpty ump years, plus the loss of the shelter that protected that money from tax.

Steady deposits in tax-favored retirement plans is only the beginning of wisdom. You also have to *leave that money alone.*

TAX-DEFERRED ANNUITIES

So potent are the words "tax deferral" that, in their presence, otherwise strong minds turn to pudding. Analysis flies out the window. Of all the unexamined premises of financial planning, one of the most dangerous is that tax deferral is always smart.

Which brings me to tax-deferred annuities.

I am not speaking here of tax-*deductible* annuities, bought by teachers and others for pension savings. They're as valid a vehicle as any other retirement plan and should be funded to the maximum.

The subject before us is commercial tax-*deferred* annuities, bought by conservative savers with after-tax dollars. In certain circumstances, they make sense. But a lot of hogwash accompanies the sale of tax-deferred annuities. You need to know how to step around it.

All commercial annuities have two main things in common. (1) You get no tax deduction for the money you put up. (2) Inside the annuity, your money compounds tax-deferred.

Beyond that, each annuity has its own cost structure, gimmicks, and rate of return. Annuities are sold by bankers, stockbrokers, financial planners, insurance agents, mutual funds, even by forces of telephone salespeople. But regardless of who makes the sale, an annuity is always backed by an insurance company—so you'd better buy from an A-plus company that is likely to last as long as you will.

Here's what the industry has to offer.

An *immediate annuity* pays you a lifetime income, starting now (for the scoop on immediate annuities, see page 803). A *deferred annuity* accumulates money for the future. Some retirees buy both kinds (a deal known as split funding)—an immediate annuity for current income and a deferred annuity to build more capital for later years.

Deferred annuities come in two types, depending on how you want to invest. A *fixed* annuity pays an interest rate that isn't really fixed at all; it changes whenever the company says, which may be often. But it's still a straight interest-rate investment. A *variable* annuity lets you put your money in stocks, bonds, or money market mutual funds and gamble on what the outcome will be.

A *single-premium* annuity is bought with a single sum of money. Minimum purchase: $2,000 to $10,000, although buyers typically put up much larger sums. A *flexible-premium* annuity takes smaller amounts or irregular amounts. You might pay $100 a month, or dump in $3,000 every now and then. A handful of companies have added a clause that lets you draw on your deferred annuity without penalty if you enter a nursing home.

When you decide to quit accumulating money and start spending it, annuities offer another range of choices. You can take monthly payments for the rest of your life. You can make periodic withdrawals. You can take the money in a lump sum. You can roll your savings into another annuity tax free (for more information on withdrawals, see page 800).

You Don't Date an Annuity, You Marry It

An annuity isn't a mutual fund that you buy today and sell tomorrow. Nor is it a certificate of deposit, ready for any new use at maturity. When you buy an annuity, you are making (or ought to be making) a 15- or 20-year commitment, at least. You can move your money from one annuity to another. But it's expensive to quit the investment altogether. How expensive? Read on. There are IRS rules and penalties when you withdraw the money, and insurance-company rules and penalties.

THE IRS SAYETH:

1. Income taxes are owed on your tax-deferred earnings whenever you take the money out.

2. There is normally a 10 percent penalty on earnings withdrawn before age 59½. So this isn't a short-term savings vehicle for the young. The penalty is waived only in limited circumstances, among which are death and disability. You can also dodge the penalty by setting up a lifetime withdrawal schedule.

3. If you make regular, periodic withdrawals (say, in monthly payments over your lifetime), part of each withdrawal is treated as taxable income. The rest is the nontaxable return of your own capital.

4. If you make occasional withdrawals, subject to no particular schedule, the entire withdrawal is treated as taxable income. Taxes are levied until you have taken all of the interest your money earned. After that, you can start withdrawing your original investment, tax free.

THE INSURANCE COMPANY SAYETH:

1. You usually have to pay a surrender fee for quitting the annuity too soon. Often, it's 7 percent the first year, 6 percent the second, and so on until, after 7 years, the penalty finally dribbles away. A few companies charge a fee if you leave any time within 10 or even 20 years. Drawn-out exit fees are designed deliberately to lock customers in. At the other end of the scale, some annuities release you after only one year, with a penalty of six months' interest for leaving any earlier.

2. An annuity with a long-term lock-in doesn't cut you off from your cash entirely. Usually, you can withdraw 10 percent of the policy's value every year without paying a surrender fee. But you'll still owe income taxes on any money you take out, and maybe a 10 percent penalty, too. If you think you might need to retrieve your funds, you shouldn't be buying a tax-deferred annuity in the first place.

The Big Fakeroo

Certain kinds of annuities work just fine for certain financial-planning purposes. I am troubled, however, by the way these investments are so often sold. You may be misled about what they are actually likely to yield.

The typical brochure extolls the glories of tax deferral. On a slick little chart, you'll see a fat line zipping up to Heaven. That represents how fast your money grows untaxed. Inching up from the very bottom of the chart is a thin, sluggard line. That supposedly shows the pitiful returns earned by simps whose investments are taxed every year.

But those pretty charts may greatly exaggerate what an annuity actually yields. First, they often "forget" the tax you owe when you finally cash the annuity in. So they're comparing apples and oranges: the pretax return from an annuity is contrasted with the after-tax return from, say, a certificate of deposit. Once taxes are subtracted, the annuity doesn't look nearly as good. Second, the brochures for variable annuities may leave out certain fees and other expenses that will lower your returns.

When you adjust for all fees and taxes, the picture changes—sometimes drastically.

A fixed annuity, initially paying just the same as a certificate of deposit, may take 6 or 7 years to equal the CD's return after taxes, because of the surrender fees. If you invest for 10 years, you may do fine, but if you pull out after 5 years, you're a loser.

A variable annuity shows even worse results because of its high expenses. Take an insurer who charges 1 percent on top of the usual investment fees. For an investor who will eventually cash out and pay the tax, the annuity might take 12 to 15 years to equal the return from a no-load mutual fund, even if both investments yield the same gross rate of return. If the insurer charged 1.25 percent, as many do, it would take much longer for the annuity to come out ahead. If you're in a low income-tax bracket, the fees may entirely overwhelm the value of the tax deferral.

Many salespeople argue that there's no point showing the annuity's final value after tax because that's not the way to take the money. Instead of cashing out, you should stretch your payments—and your taxes—over a lifetime. But in fact, most annuity holders *do* cash out. And even if they didn't, stretching out the tax doesn't make that much difference to the comparison. The sales brochure is still misleading.

Fixed Annuities

If you're gong to buy an annuity, go for one with a so-called "fixed" interest rate. It's easier to analyze than a variable annuity and it usually carries fewer expenses.

Fixed annuities guarantee you an interest rate for a specified period of time. New customers may be offered one, three, and five-year rates. After that, the rate may change once a year, or several times a year, as the insurer decrees. If all goes well, you will always earn a competitive yield, tax deferred.

Your risk is that the company won't pay a competitive yield. It may treat new customers to a one-year ride in a golden coach. But then you'll be demoted to scullery maid. A typical riches-to-rags return: a fat 11 percent to start, a leaner 8 percent the second year, then down to 6.9 percent, and a huge surrender charge if you rebel and want to leave. The bigger the surrender charge, and the longer it lasts, the freer the company is to drop your rate. It's got you where it wants you: padlocked in.

How to Lower Your Interest-Rate Risk

1. Never buy from a company whose interest rate is markedly above average. Such a rate is sure to drop, probably to subnormal levels. (Why would your agent tout you onto such a company? Probably because it's paying an extra-high sales commission.)

2. Never buy from a company whose exit fee is unreasonably high. A standard surrender charge in the industry starts at 7 percent and declines by one percentage point every year. The baddies charge fees for as long as 10 or 20 years.

Read the contract closely for other costs. A few companies (known as "two-tier" companies—see page 768) impose an *increasing* surrender charge. If you quit, they will lower your interest rate from the very first day you put your money in. By me, that's practically racketeering.

3. Ask the salesperson the following questions: What interest rate did the company pay on this particular annuity (or one similar to it) six years ago? When its interest-rate guarantee ran out, what renewal rates did the customers get in each subsequent year? During those same years, what interest rates were being paid to brand-new buyers of this annuity?

You are looking for: (1) a company that pays the same rate to old customers as to new ones, or (2) a company that pays old customers no more than 0.75 percentage points less than new ones (assuming that interest rates remained unchanged), or (3) a company that, in an unchanging interest-rate environment, drops the second-year interest rates on its annuities by no more than 0.3 percentage points. That would constitute fair treatment, in the opinion of Timothy Pfeifer, a consulting actuary at Tillinghast, a Towers Perrin Company, in Chicago.

What you don't want to see: (1) An annuity that paid 12 percent for the first two years, then rapidly dropped to 8 and 7 percent, or (2) a company paying new customers 10 percent while renewing old customers at 8 percent.

If you are buying a flexible-premium annuity, ask what rate was paid on new deposits as opposed to the rate paid on old deposits over the past six years.

These interest rates, incidentally, are readily available. In the course of researching this chapter, I spoke to two insurance-company actuaries, both of whom pressed a button and called up all the rates on their computer screens. If your agent, or the company, won't supply the information you asked for, assume the worst. If your agent says that your particular annuity hasn't been sold for the past five years, ask for the rates on a similar policy. If the agent says no, you say no, too.

Here's a first-rate piece of advice one actuary urged me to pass along: *"Tell your readers to make their agents disclose the annuity's past interest-rate history. Many agents won't bother as long as their customers don't insist. And because of that, a lot of bad annuities get sold. But agents are a dime a dozen. If more people quit doing business with uncooperative agents, maybe this industry would start telling more truths."* Amen.

4. Don't pay much attention to the computerized "illustration" that purports to show what your annuity will be worth in 20 years. Among other sins, it projects current interest rates, which are not guaranteed. And it may include undisclosed "bonus" rates, which you'll get only if you stay with the company for 20 years. Some of these gimmicks may be disclosed in the footnotes, but they probably won't mean much to you. As an aid to your buying decision, this illustration is virtually useless.

5. Stay away from a "two-tier" company. Such an insurer pays a higher interest rate to savers who stay but a much lower one to savers who leave. To earn the higher rate, you generally have to stay for life! If you take your cash at retirement, instead of converting to a lifetime annuity, you'll get a lower interest rate from the first day you bought, even if you've been with the company for 30 years. The difference may be huge: say 9 percent for stayers but only 6.75 percent for consumers

who take their money somewhere else. In short, you are handcuffed to the company, even if its rates are not as good as they used to be.

The computerized illustration that you'll get from the agent may show only the top-tier rate of interest. So you may not realize that you're being locked in for life. Always ask whether you're dealing with a two-tier company. If so, end the discussion right there. What's wrong with such a company as long as it pays a high interest rate and you plan to stay? First, you don't know that it will always pay a high rate. Second, if you want to convert to a lifetime annuity at retirement, you might get a much better income from another company (page 803)—that is, if you were free to take it.

6. Look for a company that is dedicated to the annuity business long term. One measure: it should write at least $50 million in annuities per year. A company that is only dabbling in annuities is much more likely to write bait-and-switch contracts that give you a princess rate the first two years but a scullery rate the third.

7. Two new annuity products purport to offer higher rates. In return, you shoulder higher risks.

The "market-value-adjusted" annuity may pay a high, guaranteed rate for a specified period—say, three or five years. Any money withdrawn earlier, however, is adjusted for changes in interest rates. The adjustment may give you a little more money than originally projected, or a little less, depending on what the insurer is paying.

Another type of annuity has no interim cash surrender value. You get a high interest rate after, say, three or five years. But you cannot make withdrawals in between. You can take loans, however, so you're not entirely without liquidity. If you die, your beneficiary receives the annuity's accumulated value.

Either of these approaches might interest long-term investors, assuming that the interest rate is really competitive. But they're risky for people who think they might need some cash in advance.

8. Annuities guarantee a "floor" below which your interest rate won't fall. The floor is so low—usually 4 to 6 percent—that it probably doesn't count for much. But if you need a tie-breaker, choose the company with the higher guarantee. You never know.

9. Make sure that your annuity's annual statement discloses your yield as a percentage rate. Some statements show only what you earned in dollars, which can conceal many sins. If you see only dollars, ask your

agent for a letter from the company disclosing the true interest yield. You're entitled to know.

Do You Want a Walkaway Clause?

Some fixed annuities let you quit, at no surrender charge, if you're not happy with your renewal rate. You typically have 30 to 60 days to find an annuity you like better. Walkaway clauses give a company a strong incentive to stay competitive. The downside is that the first-year rates on these annuities aren't as high as others pay.

Walkaway contracts are of two types.

1. *Bailout annuities.* You have a one-time chance to quit if the interest rate drops by a certain amount over a specified period. For example, your bailout might be triggered by a one-percentage-point drop from your starting rate over a period of four years. Insurers don't send out announcements when their annuities drop below the bailout threshold. If you don't notice it, too bad. Typically, you have 30 to 60 days to move. Low bailout rates—1.5 to 2 percentage points under your starting rate—generally aren't worth paying for.

2. So-called *CD annuities,* * also known as certificates of annuity. These are often sold in banks, by salespeople who say, "they're just like certificates of deposit, only tax deferred."

They are *not* just like certificates of deposit. They carry no federal deposit insurance. There is no maturity date. You may owe tax penalties for withdrawing the money before age 59½. So add "CD annuities" to your growing list of insurance products pushed deceptively.

The pity of it is that these annuities can be a decent buy, as long as you know what you are getting. The banks and insurers could probably sell them even if (horrors!) they told the truth. You choose a rate of interest for one, three, or five years. At the end of the period, you're offered a new set of interest rates. If you don't like them, you can leave. You pay a surrender penalty only if you quit the annuity midterm.

What do these walkaway clauses cost? In late 1990, single-premium deferred annuities with bailouts were paying around half a percentage point less than those without. That's a pretty big haircut, compounded over many years. One-year certificates of annuity were around 1 percentage point less.

---

* A deceptive name. Minnesota and North Carolina don't allow the term to be used in advertisements, because of its potential to mislead.

Should you pay for a walkaway? No, if you're a careful shopper. Over the long term, you will earn more from a good insurance company with a history of paying competitive interest rates and treating its older customers well. At such a company, rates may fall—but only if the general level of rates declines. In that case you wouldn't use the bailout anyway, because other companies would all be paying about the same. Get a walkaway only if you won't take the time to shop. It's a guarantee that your company won't drop your renewal rate by four percentage points and exit laughing.

Consider a short-term certificate of annuity, however, if you're older than 65 or 70 and don't want to lock up your money for a seven-year term. Alternatively, consider one of the low-load annuities named below, because their surrender charges don't last long.

How to Shop for a Fixed Annuity

Several services list the companies with the most competitive rates.

For $10, get a copy of the *Annuity Shopper,* from United States Annuities, 98 Hoffman Rd., Englishtown, NJ, 07726. It lists anywhere from 10 to 35 of the top-paying companies for deferred annuities (both single-premium and flexible, with and without bailouts), certificates of annuity, and immediate-pay annuities. For each company, you get the latest interest rate, the guarantee period, the bailout rate, the surrender fees, and the safety rating. You can call USA for more information about an annuity (800-872-6684) or to buy an annuity by phone. When shopping, throw out the handful of top-paying companies. They're the most likely to drop your rate. Shop among the companies just below the very top.

For current quotes on certificates of annuity, you can call Term-Quote in Dayton, Ohio, 800-444-8376 (which also sells term life insurance by phone).

Consider a company that designs products with low sales expenses. One such: USAA in San Antonio, Texas (800-531-8000). A USAA single-premium deferred annuity paying 10 percent in 1984 was renewing customers at 8.7 percent in 1989, reports Glenn Daily, author of *The Individual Investor's Guide to Low-Load Insurance Products.* A competing company that was touting 12 percent in 1984 dropped its customers to 7 percent just three years later and kept them there. USAA's surrender penalty is $25 plus 4 percent for the first three years, and $25 a year thereafter. Two other low-load annuities, John Alden Life's Pioneer

Annuity and Lincoln Benefit Life's Futurist II, are sold only through financial planners who charge fees for their services (page 832).

For the interest rates on the top 100 flexible and single-premium deferred annuities, send $20 for two successive copies of the *Comparative Annuity Reports Newsletter*, P.O. Box 1268, Fair Oaks, CA, 95628. They rebut the agent who says, "The 7.5 percent now being paid on my Central Reliance American Plan is the highest in the country," when in fact it doesn't even come close. One letter will show you each company's "accumulation values"—meaning the amount of money that might be built up over 10 years. The other will shows the "withdrawal values"—what you'd get if you quit. Withdrawal values show the effect of surrender charges, especially on the annuities sold by two-tier companies (page 768).

Buy only from a company with top ratings from at least three of the four insurance-rating companies: A-plus from A. M. Best, and AAA or AA from Standard & Poor's, Moody's, and Duff & Phelps. These ratings are voluntary, but any serious annuity writer should have gone to the trouble of getting them. An annuity may be a lifetime commitment. You can't afford anything less than the very best. If your company's safety rating slips, switch to another company's annuity, in a tax-free exchange.

Buy only from a company licensed to do business in New York State. Its insurance department imposes some tough tests of solvency that aren't required in other states.

Consider purchasing the *Best's Retirement Income Guide,* at this writing $53 a year (two issues, April and October), from A. M. Best's Customer Service, Oldwick, NJ, 08858. It shows the current interest rates, expenses, accumulation values, and surrender values for a large number of annuities. The October issue also shows what the companies have been paying on single-premium and flexible-premium deferred annuities over the past five years. (If you're in the market for an immediate annuity, check *Best's* for the monthly income that the various companies are paying on a $10,000 investment. Actual rates may be a little better for bigger contracts.)

How do you ditch a company whose interest rate or safety rating is too low? You do a tax-free "1035 exchange" into another annuity. But beware the salesperson who keeps encouraging you to switch. Yes, you might get a higher interest rate somewhere else; and yes, it might compensate you for the surrender charge. But when you change annuities, your surrender-charge period starts all over again. So you have locked yourself back in.

Agents may be offered commissions of 10 or 11 percent in order to induce their customers to switch. So that's what's in it for them. I am not sure what's in it for you. Those high commissions have to come from somewhere. The new company probably charges high surrender penalties and, down the line, will drop your rate. If you switch, look for a sound company with a history of treating its older annuity holders well.

Never buy from an agent who claims that the annuity is "no-load." All agents earn sales commissions, and all customers pay them, in one way or another. The costs are built into the annuity's structure. Any salesperson who deceives you on this point will deceive you on others.

On a classic single-premium deferred annuity, a 4 to 5 percent commission is pretty standard. On certificates of annuity, the commission may be 1 percent, plus another 1 percent each time you renew. No knowledgeable customer will deal with agents who collect 10 or 11 percent commissions. Such agents pick annuities in their own interest, not yours. The traditional declining-surrender-charge annuities sold at banks often contain 10 percent commissions, by the time the bank, the insurance company, and the salesperson take a cut.

WHO MIGHT WANT A FIXED ANNUITY?

· A middle-aged person saving for retirement, who doesn't need current income from his or her capital, doesn't care that fixed-income investments don't *grow*, after taxes and inflation, and feels sure that the money can remain untouched at least until age 59½. Before even considering an annuity, however, put every nickel you can into tax-deductible savings and investments: 401(k) plans, Keoghs, and deductible Individual Retirement Accounts. *Any* tax-deductible investment is worth more, in the long run, than investments that are merely tax deferred.

· Someone who insists on tax deferral. But look first at municipal bonds. Their current yield may be a little lower than annuities pay. But that yield is good until maturity, whereas the interest rate on annuities will change. Furthermore, munis are permanently tax exempt. After taxes, it might take a deferred annuity 15 years or more to equal the net income you'd get from a muni bond.

· A deeply conservative investor, in middle to late-middle age, who keeps his or her savings in a six-month CD, rolls it over regularly, and never touches the interest income. For this person, an annuity might truly be a better deal, because the money will accumulate tax deferred. The annuity should pay a quarter of a percentage point more than the CD (to start with, anyway; be sure to check on how well the insurance company treats its customers at renewal). You should be older than age 59½, in order to avoid income-tax penalties on early withdrawals. To avoid insurance-company penalties, you should feel sure in your heart that you won't need the income until the required number of years have passed.

BUT BE CAUTIOUS ABOUT FIXED ANNUITIES IF:

• You are elderly and the insurer's surrender fees run for several years. You might suddenly need the money and get stuck with a withdrawal penalty.

• You have a big certificate of deposit that represents most of your retirement money. If you put it all in a tax-deferred annuity, you'll have nowhere to turn for ready funds (except, perhaps, for an annual 10 percent withdrawal). Consider investing part of your money in an annuity while keeping the rest of it free to help pay your expenses.

• All of your retirement money has been invested in fixed-income securities. You don't need more of the same. Life is long and inflation steady. Some portion of your money should be invested in conservative stock-owning mutual funds, for growth.

Variable Annuities

How about investing for growth through a variable annuity? You can put your money into stock funds, bond funds, or money-market instruments, which might outperform the old-fashioned fixed annuities.

I say no. Variable annuities do offer you an abundance of investment choices. You can switch your money from fund to fund, or ask the investment manager to allocate your assets for you.

But it's hard to make money in variable annuities, because they're so loaded with fees. You pay an extra 1 to 1.5 percentage points for the annuity wrapper, plus assorted extra charges. To cover them, your fund needs consistently superior returns. Take a look at the fee table in the front of any variable-annuity prospectus. It's awesome.

You might assume that the tax deferral more than makes up for the extra costs. It doesn't, except for high-bracket investors whose funds yield superior returns and who plan to hold their annuities for many years. If you buy at age 55 and cash out at 65, you would probably have done better, after tax, in a plain-vanilla, no-load mutual fund. As measured by Lipper Analytical Services, variable-annuity stock and bond funds generally run behind other funds—doubtless because of the expenses. The performance shown in *Best's Retirement Income Guide* is also unimpressive.

If you put your money into a variable annuity's money market fund, you are dead certain to come out behind. Its yields are too low to compensate you for the costs. The bond fund is marginal, and so is the fixed-income fund. That leaves stocks as your only reasonable bet.

If you have only a small sum to invest—$2,500 to $5,000—variable annuities are truly a waste. Insurers levy $20 or $30 annual fees that chop 0.5 to 1 percent off your returns.

WHO MIGHT WANT A VARIABLE ANNUITY?
An investor who:

1. Has a substantial sum on hand—at least $25,000.

2. Is in a high income-tax bracket where tax deferral matters more.

3. Will keep *all* of his or her money in stocks. Only stocks have a chance of growing by enough to cover the fees and still return a decent profit.

4. Will stick with the annuity for at least 15 years.

5. Has chosen an annuity whose stock fund manager has shown consistently superior returns (although the past is no guarantee of the future).

But why put your money into any investment that has to fight so hard to cover its costs? I'd stay away from variable annuities until someone figures out how to sell them cheaper.

Should You Buy Single-Premium Life Insurance Instead of an Annuity?

This is a question for older people with plenty of money.

Suppose for example, that you have a big certificate of deposit that you keep rolling over. You intend that the money pass to your children. If you put your CD into an annuity, all the interest will accumulate tax deferred.

But it might be smarter to buy single-premium life insurance, instead (page 276). Your children will get even more money, because of the insurance payout. Insurance proceeds aren't taxable to your beneficiaries, while annuities are. If you need any money during your lifetime, you can always borrow against the policy. The loans will be treated partly as taxable income, but so what? So would occasional withdrawals from a tax-deferred annuity. In this particular circumstance, life insurance seems the better choice.

SOCIAL SECURITY

You *will* get a Social Security check when you retire. If you doubt me, just look around and count the votes. How many among us will vote to abolish the Social Security system? What is the future of any politician who proposes to eliminate it?

That said, however, Social Security benefits won't be worth as much in the future as they were in the past. They will replace a smaller percentage of your working income. They will probably be fully taxed. And today's young people will have to work up to two more years (to age 67) before they can retire on their full Social Security check. Retirees today get full benefits at 65.

That's why it's so important to save more money for yourself. You won't get as much out of Social Security as your parents and grandparents did.

The next chapter—on deploying your money at retirement—tells you how and when to claim Social Security benefits. The question here is how to create the largest benefit you can.

HERE'S HOW TO GET THE MOST FROM YOUR SOCIAL SECURITY ACCOUNT

1. Pay your tax! Kids who float from job to job may think it's clever to work "off the books." But, like everyone else, they will eventually knock at Social Security's door. When figuring your benefit, Social Security looks at how much (or how little) you paid into the system during the years you were old enough to work. If your record shows several years of zero participation, your retirement check will be dragged down. It's sometimes fun to be young and poor but never to be old and poor. So pay the tax.

2. Make sure that your account shows all the tax that you have paid to date. More often than you think, records go awry. Your employer might err when reporting your earnings to Social Security, or fail to report them at all. Social Security might err in transferring that record to your account. You might err when giving your Social Security number. In 1990, the Social Security Administration was sitting on a cumu-

lative $67 billion * worth of reported wages, some of it dating back to 1940, whose owners have never been identified.

Here's how to make sure that you'll get every dime that's coming to you: Right now, and every three years thereafter, check your Social Security record. Call toll-free 800-234-5772, and ask for Form SSA-7004—a Personal Earnings and Benefit Estimate Statement (PEBES). Fill it in and mail it to Social Security.

Within four to six weeks, you'll get a statement showing how much was credited to your Social Security account each year. You may see a zero in the most recent year because Social Security hasn't posted your current wages yet. But if there are zeros in earlier years, and shouldn't be, call Social Security right away. Maybe it can correct the error without specific information from you. All the same, look for old tax returns, and W-2 forms to prove that you really did pay taxes that year. If your old company is still in business, ask it for a letter confirming that year's salary.

Incidentally, if you've written in the past for your Social Security earnings record and found it unhelpful, you were right. The old form was stingy with information and tough to decode. But the new PEBES form is terrific. It clarifies your earnings record and gives you highly detailed information on the size of the benefits you can expect.

3. Find out if you qualify for Social Security benefits at all, and if not how close you've come. A woman who worked many years ago, then dropped out to have children or to take care of an elderly parent, may find that—with just a couple more years of full- or part-time work—she'll qualify for a Social Security check. The PEBES form tells you how many more work credits you need. Having her own account may not matter to a woman who can collect on the account of her present or former spouse (page 134). But it matters a lot to someone who doesn't have that to fall back on.

4. Make your personal planning decisions in light of what Social Security is likely to pay. Here, too, the PEBES form will help. It discloses: (1) your estimated monthly retirement benefit (in today's dollars), for the age that you want to retire and for age 70; (2) the likely survivors' benefits for your family, if you die in the current year; and (3) what you might get in disability pay, if you become totally and permanently disabled.

---

* That's a big number, but it represents only 0.3 percent of all posted wages.

The deeper you move into middle age, the more critical this information becomes. Once you know how much income you can count on, you'll get a better fix on how much more you have to save.

5. Keep on truckin'. The longer you work, the more money you'll have and the fatter your Social Security check will grow. Today, you can get full benefits at age 65—but a bonus is paid for each year you delay your retirement, up to age 70. By contrast, if you quit at age 62 (normally the earliest Social Security retirement age), your benefit will be reduced by 20 percent.

That's the rule for the 1990s. Starting in 2000, the age for getting full retirement benefits starts creeping up. For example, I won't qualify until I reach age 65 and four months. If you were born in 1960 or later, full benefits won't be payable until age 67. You will still be allowed to claim Social Security as early as age 62, but your check will be cut by 30 percent.

Early retirement seems to make sense, if you count only your Social Security income. Those extra three years of payments, from age 62 to 65, come to a sizable amount. If you wait until age 65 to retire, it might take 12 years or more for the extra money in your larger checks to equal what you'd have received from those three years of early retirement pay.

But when you're at work, you are earning much more than your retired colleagues get. Furthermore, your steady paychecks should add to the size of your Social Security benefit. So later retirement brings you more money overall.

6. Don't retire if there's any chance that you'll have to return to work part-time. In 1991, retirees aged 62 to 64 could earn only $7,080 free and clear. Over the amount, every $2 in earnings cut $1 off their Social Security checks. Retirees 65 to 69 could earn up to $9,720, but were docked $1 for every additional $3 in earnings.* Your income plus the other expenses of returning to work may all but eat up your Social Security check.

Before retiring early, ask an accountant to lay out a likely cash-flow plan for the rest of your life (page 785). If the plan looks marginal, and you have the option of keeping your job, do it. Don't retire until you're pretty sure that you won't have to exceed the Social Security earnings

---

* These ceilings rise with inflation every year. Special rules in your first year of retirement apply the ceiling on a monthly basis instead of annually.

ceiling in order to survive. At age 70, however, you get your full Social Security benefit, no matter how much money you earn.

These income ceilings, incidentally, refer only to earnings. You can pull down all the interest, dividends, royalties, and capital gains you want, without losing a dime of your Social Security check. The purpose of the earnings limit is to define who has "retired" and who has not.

7. If you do retire early, then return to work, consider suspending your Social Security check entirely. At age 65, your retirement age will then be refigured, so you won't be stuck with a lower benefit for the rest of your life. (For more on this point, see page 808).

Would you be better off dropping out of Social Security?

Many people imagine that they'd have more money if they could ditch Social Security. "Just give me my contribution and my employer's, and I could invest for a higher income," they say. I doubt it. To begin with, you probably wouldn't invest it all. You'd spend some. Some would be thrown away on bad investments, like many of the real-estate limited partnerships. Some might be invested too conservatively, in low-interest passbook savings accounts. In the end, you would probably fail to build the enormous sum you'd need to pay yourself a Social-Security-equivalent income that kept up with the inflation rate. You'd also lose the disability and life-insurance benefits that come in the Social Security package.

Compulsory Social Security protects part of your old-age income against the hazards of life and judgment, and we should all be grateful for it. Without it, many more of our elderly would live poor.

30
MAKING IT LAST:

Still Living Rich, at 99

If you ever needed a plan for your money, you
need it now. You earned it. You saved it. Now
it's time to spend it well.

Here you are, at the very lip of retire-
ment or beyond. You have pretty much defined your standard of living
by the pension you earned and the money you saved and invested years
ago. But it's not over yet! You still have plans to lay and choices to
make. How you handle your pension and investments will make a huge
difference to your comfort for years to come.

EARLY RETIREMENT: THE AMERICAN DREAM

You may have no choice about when you retire. Your job may be
reorganized right out from under you.

Or you may have an apparent choice. An early retirement bonus
may be offered to anyone willing to take the leap (page 784). If you say
no, your job may continue as usual. But then again, it may not.

Or you may jump yourself, without being pushed. Some people point their entire savings and investment programs toward bailing out of the workforce at age 50 or 55.

The Truth Is, You Can't Retire at 50

Correction: You *probably* can't.

It takes a tremendous amount of money to be able to quit early—far more than you think. Until you sit down with a calculator (or accountant or financial planner), you won't appreciate how much capital you're going to need, especially when future inflation is factored in.

If you have no children to educate, and have been saving 20 percent of your income for years, and have liquid savings and investments worth $1 million or more, and will live modestly, maybe you can do it. Especially if you expect a big inheritance.

Short of that, you should figure on staying at work. Even if you retire on an inflation-indexed government pension, you will probably need another job.

The very earliest that most employees can even consider shaking loose is age 55. You will probably get a company pension (half the size, or less, of what you'd receive at age 65). You will get penalty-free access to many of your own retirement plans, such as Keoghs, 401(k)s, and company thrift plans. You can tap your IRA at an even earlier age (see page 736).

But will this money really last for the rest of your life?

To Retire Early . . .

Here's what you need for the life of leisure you intend.

1. *Health Insurance,* to carry you to age 65 and Medicare. Corporations may pay for stopgap medical-insurance plans. If not, you can usually stay in the group plan, at your expense, for up to 18 months (page 299). After that, however, you will have to find your own individual plan.

2. *A pension.* If early retirement is your overriding goal, stay with the same employer for all of your working life. Job-hoppers lose significant benefits (page 736). A government pension would serve you best, thanks to its cost-of-living increases. Corporate pensions usually come in fixed dollars that erode from the day you start collecting. Social Security starts at age 62. But if you haven't been working for several years, your check will be lower than if you had stayed on the job.

3. *A large nest egg.* Elephant size. Enough to provide money to live on *and* to reinvest each year, to keep your capital even with inflation. By this rule, what sounds like plenty may turn out to be paltry.

Suppose, for example, that you have $225,000 and feel rich. Your money is earning 8 percent pretax, but inflation is running at 4 percent annually. You're single, with a small pension and an effective federal tax rate of 15 percent. Here's your situation.

Your $225,000 is earning $18,000—$15,300 after tax. To preserve your purchasing power, you must reinvest 4 percent of your capital, or $9,000, bringing your nest egg up to $234,000. That leaves you with $6,300 to spend (less, if you also owe state and local taxes). For another way of feeling sick, look at the table on page 789. If you invest $225,000 at 8 percent, withdraw 7 percent of your capital the first year to live on ($15,750), and continue drawing that same amount plus an extra 4 percent annually to counter inflation, your money will last 20 years. If your life expectancy is 30 years, what then?

The answer is to look at the table another way. Assuming that you're earning 8 percent on your money and it has to last for about 30 years, you can afford to take about 5.5 percent of your capital the first year. That puts your basic income at $12,375, plus 4 percent increments to keep up with inflation. So although $225,000 looks like a lot, it's not nearly enough to sustain an early retiree, unless you have income from other sources.

How about a $450,000 nest egg—does that mean you're rich? Not if you have little else to live on. Assume that you're single, paying an effective federal rate of 28 percent, and earning 8 percent on your money pretax ($36,000). Inflation is running at 4 percent and you have a modest pension. Your capital produces $25,920 after federal tax, but you have to reinvest $18,000 to keep up its purchasing power. That leaves you with only $7,920 to spend, if you want to keep your capital intact. Not a life with a lot of laughs. If you take 6 percent of your capital the first year ($27,000), plus an extra 4 percent annually for inflation, your money will last for 25 years. (To play this game with other rates of inflation, see the Appendix, page 893.)

4. *No kids at home.* All the expenses of raising and educating your children should be behind you.

5. *Life insurance,* if you're married. Your spouse may not be able to live on the reduced pension and Social Security that you will leave behind if you die first, especially if you're forced to eat into your capital.

6. *Low housing expenses.* Sell your house, buy a smaller one or a condominium, and invest the proceeds that remain. Or move to a low-cost part of the country. Or move to Mexico or Buenos Aires. At age 55 and up, the first $125,000 of the profit on your house comes tax free. If you buy a cheaper house, you can put a significant profit in the bank (page 814). One money-making idea, if you think you'd be a successful landlord: Buy a two-family house, live in one half, and rent out the other half (but check the rent-control laws, first).

7. *Low living expenses.* Early retirees need simple tastes. Cheap entertainments. Only one car (or no car at all—use a taxi and buses). Life in the country where real-estate taxes are low. I don't mean to make this sound like a downer. But you have to be very clear in your mind that quitting work means keeping to a slender budget.

8. *A job.* Forget "early retirement" in its classic, freebooting sense. Think about earning enough money to fill the gap between your pension income and your expenses, so you can leave your capital alone to grow. Some companies rehire their own retirees for temporary work on specific projects. Many senior-citizen centers keep lists of companies that seek older people for occasional work. If the job is covered by Social Security, so much the better. That beefs up the retirement benefit that you'll get at 62.

9. *A spending and investment plan* worked out with an accountant or financial planner. Don't try to doodle this down by yourself on a yellow pad. Taxes, inflation, interest rates, the size of your savings, and the sources of your income all have a bearing on whether you can afford to retire. If you do quit work, you need to know quite specifically what your savings must earn to keep you afloat, what you have to earn, and what you can afford to spend. That's a job for a professional.

A Dangerous Complacency

People who dream of retiring early are dangerously complacent about inflation. They shrug off 4 or 5 percent increases as if they were zero. But if that keeps up, you'll need $1,480 to $1,629 worth of income 10 years from now for every $1,000 you have today, just to preserve your standard of living. In 20 years, you'll need $2,191 to $2,653 for every $1,000 you have today. Where are you going to get that kind of money? Especially if you're living off capital rather than adding to it.

The Golden Boot

Not all early retirees have a choice.

You may arrive at work one morning to learn that your company has opened an early-retirement window for everyone age 50 and up. Typically, you have 30 to 90 days to jump out the window (or be politely shoved). If you leave, you'll get bonuses not normally available. Should you take the offer?

As you sit at your desk, with your heart beating a little faster, ask yourself the following three questions.

QUESTION ONE: Do I really want to retire? If the answer is yes, see an accountant and work out the arithmetic. This window may fit in perfectly with your plans. If the answer is no . . .

QUESTION TWO: What happens if I stay? In the bosses' minds, all employees are divided into "greenwood" and "deadwood." Some of you they want to keep; others they want to sweep away. But they can't walk down the hall saying, "You, you, you, retire early," without running afoul of the age-discrimination law. So it's up to you to guess their intentions.

Take it for granted that deals have been cut with particularly valuable employees ("stay, and you'll get the bonuses you'd have gotten if you left"). If nothing like that has come your way, drop by your boss's office for a chat. What's the future of your department? Is your job subject to reorganization? What's your next promotion? Is your boss going to stay or go? If the vibes say "stay," you might want to chance it. Someone has to keep the shop open. If the vibes say "go," don't hesitate. You may lose your job anyway, and without the cushion of a good-bye bonus.

QUESTION THREE: Where do I get advice? Don't try to figure out the finances yourself. Your company's employee-benefits office may have an explainer on the staff. Alternatively, see an accountant or a financial planner who is capable of analyzing the offer objectively (not all are—page 786). You may have to choose between taking a higher pension or taking severance pay, and only savvy calculating will reveal the better offer. You may have to choose between taking a lump sum and investing it yourself or letting the company invest it for you. Often, it's better to leave it with the company. (Beware the biased planner, who urges you to take the money and invest the proceeds in mutual funds and partnerships that the planner recommends.)

Anyone given the Golden Boot might be offered several incentives.

Typically, they include a higher pension than you've actually earned; a cash bonus to help you make the transition to civilian life; a supplemental monthly income of maybe $400 to $500, paid until age 62 when Social Security starts; a modest life insurance policy; and health insurance until you're eligible for Medicare.

Despite all these goodies, an early retiree gets the short end of the money stick. Even if you're 60, and are offered the pension of a 65-year old, you've lost five years of salary, which would have paid a lot more than the pension does. But a Golden Boot is a leg up for anyone with other work in mind. Taking this income as a base, you can write a book, start a business, or accept a lower-paying job that offers you more satisfaction.

YOUR RETIREMENT SPENDING PLAN

Early retirement or late, you now face the ultimate reality test. Your capital and life circumstances are pretty much known. What can be squeezed out of your resources? How much can you afford to spend each year, so that you won't run out of money?

These simple questions involve some extraordinary choices, which will affect your personal comfort for the rest of your life. You have to decide:

· What's the best way of taking money out of your various retirement plans—in annuity payments or in a lump sum?

· When should you swallow the income taxes on your tax-deferred investments?

· How should your retirement savings be invested?

· Who should invest those savings for you?

· Should you keep your present house or sell it?

· What rate of inflation should you assume?

None of these questions has just one answer. You need to test one set of possibilities against another, to see how the alternatives play out. With only a couple of choices to make, you can probably reach the right decisions without help. But for multiple possibilities, I don't recommend it. God hasn't made enough erasers and yellow pads for you to work this out yourself.

Fortunately, God has made more than enough certified public accountants (CPAs), who practice in every town in the country. Go see one. Ask for advice. A CPA can lay out each and every choice: What net income you'd get from various types of pension-plan distributions.

How much capital you can round up to invest. What yield you will need from your capital, in order to support your standard of living. Whether it pays to sell your house. What inflation will do to your purchasing power. Don't begrudge the expense of the analysis. At this stage of life, it's the best investment you could make. Some financial planners could help you, too.

I ask only that you not bring these questions to a CPA or financial planner who earns commissions by selling financial products. Salespeople may be biased toward lump-sum withdrawals from pension plans, because that gives you money to buy the investments they sell. But what if those investments fail? Can you afford to take the risk? Your best choice may be to leave your money right there in the pension plan, for the company to manage for you.

Once you've nailed down your income and assets, you have to shape a budget to match. Chapter 8 should help you go about it. When listing your outlays, don't look back at your old life, look ahead to your new one. The differences are going to surprise you.

Retirement spending is totally unlike workaday spending. Your house may be paid for. Your children are gone (one devoutly hopes). The fires may no longer burn in your breast for classier furniture, showoff cars, or drop-dead parties. You no longer need disability insurance if you have no earnings to replace. With sufficient savings (or no dependents), you may not need life insurance, either—which saves you the price of the insurance premiums. You'll buy more sneakers and sweatshirts and fewer dresses and suits. Instead of keeping two cars, you may drop to one.

Celebrating their freedom, the newly retired often travel. But after a while, that impulse usually quiets down. One critical expense is a good health-insurance policy, the price of which will escalate. Even so, you may find that your real expenses, after inflation, gradually fall. The older you get, the less purchasing power you are likely to need. So your capital will last longer than you might think.

Once you have assembled all your resources and all your expenses, ask an accountant or planner the following question: "Assuming a reasonable investment return on my savings, and assuming that I want my income to keep up with inflation every year, how long will my present resources last?"

The news might be good.

"Ms. Certain," your accountant might say, "assuming that your savings earn 7 percent and assuming that you want to maintain the purchasing power of a $35,000 income, your money will easily last until your death, with a nice chunk left over for your heirs."

With that comforting knowledge, what might Ms. Certain do?

· She might feel free to donate some money to charity.

· She might roll her lump-sum pension distribution into an IRA and leave it alone to grow.

· She might travel, throw parties, and live it up.

· She will most certainly relax. She knows for sure that, at life's end, she won't be a bag lady on the streets.

On the other hand, the news may be bad.

"Mr. Hopeful," your accountant might say, "assuming that your savings earn 7 percent and assuming that you want to maintain the purchasing power of a $35,000 income, you will run out of money in 14 years." That will startle Mr. Hopeful, whose life expectancy might be 24 years. But at least he knows his situation and can start to adjust.

· He might try to increase his return on investment, by holding less money in passbook savings and more in certificates of deposit and equity-income mutual funds.

· He might take part-time work.

· He might reduce his expenses and live on, say, $25,000 a year.

· He might sell his house, buy something smaller, and use the re-maining equity to build up his nest egg.

· He might accept his son's invitation to move into the small apart-ment over the son's garage—if not now, then maybe 10 years from now.

· If he has a choice, he might change his mind about retiring and stay at work a little longer.

Knowing the limits of your savings gives you tremendous power over your future. You'll know exactly what to do in order to make your retirement work.

For Do-It Yourselfers

If your finances are pretty simple, you can work the budget out yourself. The table on page 788 shows how to do it (I've given an example on the right). All these calculations are pretax.

HOW LONG WILL YOUR SAVINGS LAST?

The table on page 789 shows how long your savings are likely to last in a world of 4 percent inflation. It assumes that you'll maintain your

YOUR RETIREMENT SPENDING PLAN

Example

1. Basic income
   - *Social Security* — $ _____ — $ 8,000*
   - *Pension* — $ _____ — $ 19,000
   - *Lifetime annuity* — $ _____ — 0
   - *Earnings* — $ _____ — $ 2,800
   - *Other income†* — $ _____ — 0
   - Total Income — $ _____ — $ 29,800

2. This year's expenses, including taxes — $ _____ — $ 37,000

3. Gap between this year's income and expenses‡ — $ _____ — $ 7,200

4. Total savings, in banks, retirement plans, mutual funds, and so on — $ _____ — $120,000

5. Percent of total savings needed to fill the gap between this year's income and this year's expenses — _____ — 6%

6. The return on investment that your savings are earning — _____ — 8%

7. Using the table on page 789,§ find out how long your savings will last. — _____ — 25 years

* Social Security benefits rise with inflation, so this calculation has a small spending cushion built in.
† Don't count income from your savings. That is included later.
‡ If there isn't a gap, go read a murder mystery.
§ Assumes an annual 4 percent inflation rate. For other rates, see page 892.

purchasing power by drawing enough extra money out of your savings to match the annual rise in prices. For example, for every $1,000 you take in the first year, you'll take $1,040 in the second year, $1,081.60 in the third year, and so on. In the Appendix, starting on page 892, you'll find tables with different inflation rates. Here's how to compute.

Add all the capital that you are free to draw on: bank accounts, mutual funds, stocks, bonds. Decide what percentage of your capital you will need this year, and find that percentage in the left-hand column. Read across that line to the column showing the average rate of return your money is earning. That shows how many years your capital will last.

Taking the example used in the table above, you have $120,000 earning an average of 8 percent annually. You need $7,200 to meet your expenses, or 6 percent of your total capital. At an initial 6 percent withdrawal rate, and allowing for 4 percent annual inflation, your capital will last for 25 years.

THE 4 PERCENT SOLUTION

Percent of capital withdrawn in the first year	4%	5%	6%	7%	8%	9%	10%	11%	12%	13%	14%
				Will last this many years, if the original withdrawal rises by 4 percent annually and your money is invested at the following average rates of return							
2%	50	68	151	#	#	#	#	#	#	#	#
3%	33	40	52	96	#	#	#	#	#	#	#
4%	25	28	34	42	69	#	#	#	#	#	#
5%	20	22	25	29	36	53	#	#	#	#	#
6%	17	18	20	22	25	31	43	#	#	#	#
7%	14	15	16	18	20	23	27	35	#	#	#
8%	13	13	14	15	16	18	20	24	30	65	#
9%	11	12	12	13	14	15	17	19	21	26	40
10%	10	10	11	12	12	13	14	15	17	19	23
11%	9	9	10	10	11	11	12	13	14	16	17
12%	8	9	9	9	10	10	11	11	12	13	14
13%	8	8	8	9	9	9	10	10	11	11	12
14%	7	7	8	8	8	8	9	9	10	10	11
15%	7	7	7	7	8	8	8	8	9	9	10

* Assumes a single withdrawal at the start of the year. All the numbers are rounded.
Source: John Allen of Allen-Warren, Arvada, Colo.

Notes to the table
1. Look up your probable life expectancy on the table in the Appendix, page 901. Think about how long your parents and grandparents lived. Pick a likely lifespan for yourself and add five years. That's the period over which you need your money to stretch.
2. The average rate of return on your nest egg assumes that some investments earn more and some less. Over time, for example, your stock investments may earn 11 percent, your bond investments 8 percent, and your money-market mutual funds 6.5 percent. Keep the money you need for each year's living expenses stashed in a money fund. Invest the rest of your nest egg for longer terms.
3. Recalculate as inflation changes, based on the current value of your nest egg and the amount you need for expenses. The Appendix contains tables for inflation rates from zero to 9 percent.
4. What if it appears that your savings will run out before you do? You can lower your living expenses, raise the returns you're getting from your investment (a plausible answer for anyone holding every dime in cash), or try to earn more money.

HOW TO TAKE MONEY OUT OF YOUR PENSION PLANS

Given a fixed and final retirement sum, the size of your income will depend on two things: (1) the kind of pension plan you have and (2) the system you choose for taking money out. Some plans are easy; they offer you no choice at all. More likely, you will have several choices— some of them better for you than others. Here's how to get the most from your pension, taking it plan by plan.

Your Defined-Benefit Plan

This is the classic pension plan. You get a fixed, taxable, monthly income for the rest of your life. At retirement, your payment looks generous (or adequate, or stingy, as the case may be). Ten years later, it looks worse, because price increases have eroded your purchasing power. Occasionally, corporations cough up a cost-of-living benefit for retirees. But not often. Anyone tied to a defined-benefit plan had better come armed with a separate pool of savings and investments, to make up for your pension's unstoppable losses to inflation.

Beneficiaries of a defined-benefit pension plan may face two choices.

1. *Should the pension cover you alone or you and your spouse?* You get a larger monthly check if you take the pension for your lifetime only. But at your death, the pension stops and your spouse gets nothing. That's okay, as long as your spouse doesn't need your pension or if you have good reason to believe that your spouse will die first. But if your spouse will depend on that money, it should cover both your lives. A two-life pension (joint and survivor) is much smaller, but at least your spouse won't be left empty-handed.

If you do opt for spousal protection, you generally face another choice. Should you leave your spouse the same size check you got as a couple or a smaller check? If this income is critical to your spouse's welfare, take the largest check your spouse can get. (For more on this issue, see page 797.)

2. *Should you take your pension as a monthly income or in a lump sum?* Generally, monthly payments are your only choice. But some employers offer lump sums, too. If you doubt that your company is sound, take the lump sum, unless your pension is fully insured by the Pension Benefit Guaranty Corporation (page 73). Otherwise, here's how to decide which choice is best.

• If you're highly dependent on this money, take the monthly pension. A pension lasts for life, even though it's eroded by inflation. If you take the lump sum and invest it, you might not be able to make it last.

• If you're an inexperienced investor, take the monthly pension. A financial planner might show you, on paper, that by taking the lump sum and investing it, you'd wind up with a higher income. But what if the planner's investments fail? You lack the knowledge to judge whether you're getting good advice.

• If you're a terrific investor, consider the lump sum. But first, ask what "discount rate" of interest the company used to decide how much money you should get. This rate is critical! You have to invest your entire lump sum at that same rate, just to *match* what you'd get from the company over your life expectancy. To *improve* your income, you have to invest at a higher rate. Unless you're strongly convinced that you can beat the discount rate, you're better off with the monthly pension.

• If you have other sources of income, take the lump sum. You can roll that money into a tax-deferred Individual Retirement Account and let it accumulate for your older age. That gives you inflation protection.

• If you're rich enough not to need a pension, take the lump sum. Roll it into an IRA, or use it to buy single-premium life insurance (page 276) and leave the money to your kids.

• If your health is so poor that you don't expect to live very long, take the lump sum. You can tap it for larger payments than you'd get from a pension because it doesn't have to cover a full life expectancy.

For ways of handling a lump sum, if you choose it, see page 793.

When you take a lump sum, you may actually want only a small part of the money, to repay debts or buy an RV for retirement travel. The rest of the cash gets put away—but you might not invest it very well. To help you avoid this risk, a few companies offer split withdrawals. Part of the money can be taken in cash; the rest is left in the pension plan to provide you with a lifetime income.

Double-check the size of your pension, if it is "integrated" with Social Security. The check you're getting may be too low.

A pension is integrated when the monthly check you get from your corporation is reduced by a portion of your Social Security benefit. When making that reduction, companies *estimate* what your benefit will be. If they estimate too high, they wind up paying you too little.

Get a copy of your Social Security earnings history (page 777), then ask the company what it assumed when it cut your check. If its assumptions were incorrect, show proof of your earnings. The company will refigure your pension, giving you a larger check.

Your Defined-Contribution Plan

At retirement, you're owed a lump sum of money. Period. No promises have been made about the size of this sum or how long it will last. Maybe it will see you through a comfortable retirement. Then again, maybe it won't. These plans include profit sharing, 401(k)s, stock-bonus plans, and Employee Stock Ownership Plans.

There are various ways of taking this money. The lump sum can be tax deferred, but the income you get is taxable when received.

YOU MIGHT CHOOSE A LIFETIME ANNUITY—a fixed monthly pension, covering you alone or you and your spouse (or a beneficiary). Your employer buys the annuity from a commercial insurer. Find out which one, and what the monthly payment will be. Often you can get a higher monthly income by taking your money to a different insurer (page 803). The risk: Every year, your fixed payment will buy less and less. In general, annuities are smarter for the old-old than for the young-old.

YOU MIGHT CHOOSE PERIODIC PAYMENTS—an income that lasts a specified number of years. You get higher payments than you would from a lifetime annuity. But at the end of the period, those payments stop. The risk: Your other income may not be enough to live on. Periodic payments suit someone who expects another source of income (like a payout from a trust fund) or someone in poor health who doesn't expect to live very long. If you die before collecting all your pension money, the remainder goes to a beneficiary.

YOU MIGHT LEAVE SOME OR ALL OF YOUR MONEY IN THE COMPANY PLAN—a terrific idea for people who won't need the income right away. You get professional money management and can make withdrawals as you need them (at times specified by the plan). Your company will manage your 401(k) money, too. To get this service, however, your total retirement account must be worth at least $3,500. Otherwise, you'll be cashed out. The risk: The pension-fund manager might not do very well. But he or she will almost certainly outinvest the average retiree.

YOU MIGHT MANAGE SOME OR ALL OF THE MONEY YOURSELF—by taking a lump sum and investing it. Penalties may apply if you're younger than age 59½, unless you meet one of the exceptions outlined on page 759. One of the exceptions is early retirement at 55 and up. The risk: You may invest the money badly.

If your company has both a defined-benefit plan and a defined-contribution plan, play it this way.

1. Don't touch the money in the defined-contribution plan. Leave it alone to grow tax deferred.

2. Live on your monthly defined-benefit pension, Social Security, and other savings for as long as you reasonably can.

3. When inflation has eroded your fixed pension so much that you're

starting to feel the pinch, start using the money in your defined-contribution plan. That fund should have gained enough in value to restore your purchasing power.

The Lump-Sum Withdrawal

When you take all the money out of your pension or profit-sharing account, there are two things you can do with it.

1. *Roll some or all of the funds into an Individual Retirement Account.* You can leave it alone to build tax-deferred (no withdrawals are required until you pass age 70½). Or you can tap it as needed for living expenses, paying income taxes on the money you take. There is usually a 10 percent penalty on withdrawals prior to age 59½, unless you go for Loophole Six (page 759). Note that rollover IRAs are only for money that you or your employer contributed *pretax,* plus all of the money you earned tax-deferred. You cannot roll over any after-tax contributions that you might have made to the company's thrift plan. If you want a tax-favored investment for this money, too, consider tax-deferred annuities or municipal bonds.

2. *Take all the money as straight income, pay taxes currently, and invest the remainder.* If you go this route, you'll save taxes on any lump sum under $447,000 by using a calculation known as five-year averaging. But that's relevant only when full withdrawals make sense in the first place. Usually, it's smarter to defer the tax by rolling the money into an IRA.

Your Keogh Plan

With a profit-sharing or money-purchase Keogh (page 749), you follow the rules that I just laid out for defined-contribution plans. You can tap the Keogh (or not tap it) at any rate you like. Or you can take a lump sum. No withdrawals are required until you pass age 70½. Defined-benefit Keoghs, by contrast, work like any other defined-benefit plan. You take the monthly pension you planned on, or take the money in a lump sum.

Your IRA or Simplified Retirement Plan (SEP)

This money is normally available starting at age 59½, or earlier if you use Loophole Six (page 759). When you pass age 70½, withdrawals become compulsory. IRA- and SEP-holders cannot use five-year tax averaging, if they take all their money in a lump sum. But you probably wouldn't choose lump-sum withdrawals, anyway.

After that Magic Age . . .

For most of us, 70½ is the witching age. You have to set up a lifetime plan for removing all the money in your corporate and individual retirement accounts.

Your first withdrawal must occur no later than April 1 of the calendar year following the year you reach age 70½. After that, each year's required amount must be taken no later than the close of the calendar year. That could give you two payments the first year—one after reaching age 70½, which you can defer until April of the following year, and one for age 71, which must be completed by the end of December. You have to start using your retirement fund even if you're not yet retired and are still putting money in. (You can keep on contributing to Keoghs and 401(k)s after age 70½ but not to IRAs or SEPs.)

HOW MUCH DO YOU HAVE TO TAKE OUT EACH YEAR? Enough so that, if you continued at that rate, you would empty all your retirement plans over (1) your lifetime, (2) the joint lifetimes of you and your spouse, (3) the joint lifetimes of you and a designated beneficiary, or (4) any shorter period you designate. If the beneficiary is young, the payments are figured as if he or she were no more than 10 years younger than you are. If your spouse is young, however, you use his or her actual age.

As to life expectancy, you have two choices. You can calculate it once and use it for all subsequent withdrawals. That pulls more of your income into the earlier years. Or you can recalculate your life expectancy (and that of your spouse) every year. That pushes more income into the later years, where it might benefit a surviving spouse. Once you decide to recalculate annually, you aren't allowed to change your mind.

How do you figure your withdrawals? It's easy—and I say this as one who's allergic to arithmetic. The steps are:

1. What was the balance in your IRA last December 31? (Look at the December 31 before you turned 70½, if this is your first withdrawal.)

2. What is the life expectancy, for you or for you and a beneficiary? You'll find the single-life table in the Appendix, page 901. For joint lives, consult the IRS's free Publication 590, *Individual Retirement Arrangements,* an indispensable guide to how these plans are taxed.

3. Divide the balance of the IRA by the life expectancy. That gives you the minimum withdrawal.

4. Do this for each IRA you have. Add up the results. That's the amount that must be withdrawn. You can take it from one IRA or from several, as long as the total dollar amount is met.

5. Go through the same steps for each Keogh or other retirement plan you own. Under the law, the proper amount has to be taken from each plan separately. You cannot use withdrawals from one Keogh to cover the money due to come out of another one. That argues for combining all your Keoghs into a single plan—for example, through a self-directed trust (page 750). Then you can cash in whichever investments seem the most appropriate.

If you can't figure out the proper withdrawals yourself, the trustee for your retirement plan might help. Or ask an accountant.

Banks generally require that withdrawals be made from a money market deposit account, not a certificate of deposit, so you may have to shift your savings around. Mutual funds will put you on a regular monthly withdrawal plan. Some savers buy an immediate-pay annuity (page 800), to put their withdrawals on automatic pilot.

IT IS CRITICAL THAT YOU TAKE THE RIGHT AMOUNT EACH YEAR. If you withdraw too little, you'll be socked with a 50 percent penalty on the sum that you should have taken but didn't (unless you can convince the IRS that it was an accident; you were just all thumbs with the life-expectancy tables).

Conversely, you can't withdraw too much. At present, you are normally not allowed more than $150,000 a year, or $750,000 in a lump sum, from all your retirement plans collectively. If you take any more, you'll owe a 15 percent "too rich" penalty on the excess.

This creates a pretty problem for the self-employed whose pension funds grow to elephant size. Your required minimum withdrawal may put you in the "too rich" category, costing you 15 percent. But if you stay within the $150,000 limit, you may withdraw too little, at a penalty of 50 percent. Corporations solve this problem by creating supplemental plans for their top dogs, but the self-employed don't have that option.

At age 45 or 50, sit down with your accountant and play some "what if" games. How large is your current retirement fund likely to grow? How long will you live? How big might the excess-withdrawal penalties be? Based on what you learn, you might decide to quit making pension-fund contributions. Instead, you'd pay taxes currently on your earnings and invest the remainder outside the plan. Conversely, you might get so much from your pension fund's tax deferral that a 15 percent penalty is a small price to pay. This is strictly a numbers decision, so take a look.

SPOUSE PROTECTION

The law worries a lot about widows, and so it should. Wives usually live longer than their husbands and generally wind up with far lower incomes. So an automatic "survivor annuity" has been written into all defined-benefit and many defined-contribution pension plans. It protects men as well as women, but it matters more to women. Here are the spouse-protection rules for the various kinds of plans.

WITH ALL DEFINED-BENEFIT PLANS AND DEFINED-CONTRIBUTION PLANS WHERE THE EMPLOYER HAS TO PUT IN A FIXED PERCENTAGE OF YOUR SALARY EACH YEAR—when you reach your company's earliest retirement age, the company might offer a "preretirement survivor's annuity." If it does, and you die in harness, your spouse will receive a lifetime income. It's worth half of what your own benefit would have been if you had chosen to retire early.

Your spouse can waive this right, however. If he or she does, and you live to retire, you'll have a larger pension check. But if you die, says Peat Marwick's Peter Elinsky, "The pension goes right into the box with you." The spouse gets no pension from the company, ever.

I once got a sad letter from a widow. She waived her preretirement benefit thinking that it covered only the years before her husband retired —and indeed, the company's form letter was none too clear on this point. When he died unexpectedly, she was horrified to learn that she had lost his "postretirement" pension, too. So don't waive the preretirement benefit if you'll need your spouse's pension income to live on.

Pension plans offer yet another form of spouse protection. If you live to retire, and then die, your spouse automatically gets a lifetime income worth at least 50 percent of what you were getting before your death (and up to 100 percent benefits, usually at your expense). That's called a "joint-and-survivor" payout.

Your spouse can waive this benefit, too, which would give you a larger check each month. But when you die, the pension stops and your spouse gets nothing. That's okay, as long as your spouse has an adequate income. If not, a single-life pension is usually a mistake. (Nevertheless, some insurance agents urge this choice upon you. "Take the larger pension," they say, "and protect your spouse with an insurance policy, instead." That is almost always a bad idea. For the reasons why, see page 798.)

Some pension plans let you take your benefit in a single lump-sum payout. Again, your spouse has to agree.

The protection here is absolute. In one case, a female executive was retiring and wanted to take the maximum pension lasting for her life alone. Her husband was in jail for assaulting her. She had to visit him to ask if he'd forgo his joint-and-survivor check, and he refused. Solution: Divorce.

WITH PROFIT-SHARING PLANS, INCLUDING EMPLOYEE STOCK OWNERSHIP PLANS AND 401(K)S—spouses get some protection but not as much as traditional pension plans provide.

If you die before retirement, and you're married, all vested benefits in the account normally have to go to your spouse. Your spouse can waive this benefit, however. For estate-planning purposes, you might rather pay the assets to the children or into a trust.

If, at retirement, you decide to convert your plan into a lifetime income, your spouse still is protected. The annuity has to cover both of you, unless the spouse specifically agrees that the pension will cover your life only.

However, if the plans allows it, you can take all your money in a lump sum and your spouse has no say. You can spend it on a gigolo. You can roll it into an IRA and leave it to the zoo. You cannot be compelled to provide a retirement income for your spouse. Most people do, but it's optional.

WITH PLANS YOU SET UP YOURSELF—IRAs and SEPs offer no specific spouse protection. You're not required to create a survivor annuity. The assets in the plan can be left to any beneficiary you name.

Keoghs mimic corporate plans. With a defined-benefit Keogh, spouse protection is required. With a profit-sharing or money-purchase Keogh, you follow the rules for corporate profit-sharing plans (above).

A SPOUSE CAN SIGN AWAY HIS OR HER RIGHT TO YOUR PENSION.

In some cases, this makes sense. A continuing pension may not matter if: (1) Your spouse has a good pension of his or her own; (2) your spouse is ill unto death and not likely to outlive you; (3) you have so much money that your spouse doesn't need the pension to live on. The consent has to be in writing and notarized, so the company knows that your spouse really did agree. If your spouse waives the preretirement benefit, it can be reinstated at any time (provided that you're still alive). But waiving a joint-and-survivor benefit at retirement is an irrevocable choice. Once a spouse says bye-bye to his or her share of the pension, it's gone forever.

BEWARE PENSION MAX.

One of the tragedies of our time is that so many widows are being talked out of their pension protection by an army of insurance agents and financial planners. These salespeople are "experts in their own minds" about pensions and believe—incorrectly—that they've found a better way. They call their product "pension maximization," pension max for short.

They advise you, the worker, to take the higher, single-life pension. You use that higher income to buy a life-insurance policy. If you die first, the proceeds of the policy can be used to create an income for your spouse. If your spouse dies first, you have your higher pension for the rest of your life.

Sounds neat—especially when it's laid out in a slick, computer-generated presentation. But many such presentations mislead. After paying for the policy, the couple may have less to live on, after taxes, than if they had taken the joint-and-survivor pension. More distressingly, if the husband dies, the insurance policy may not be large enough to provide the promised income for the wife.

After I aired this opinion in a newspaper column, angry insurance reps peppered me with dissenting letters. I invited them to prove the glories of pension max at retirement age. Ten of them took up the challenge; their work was analyzed by two financial planners using two different systems.

Only one proposal worked passably well, and it turned out to be a ringer. It was constructed by a computer-software company, using an Ameritas life-insurance policy that carried a minimal sales commission. All the proposals sent in by insurance agents (based on policies with normal commissions) were off the mark. Some ignored taxes, to make the couple's income look higher than would actually be the case. Some lowballed the amount of insurance needed, which gambled with the widow's income. Some suggested policies that cost more than the couple would gain in extra pension benefits. Some started the program well before retirement but didn't include those early costs in their "proofs" of how well the idea worked.

A luckless client is not likely to find the holes in pension max proposals. I couldn't have found them either, without expert help. Many a widow will discover her error only on learning she won't have all the after your death. Half your check? Two-thirds of your check? The same size check? The more you leave, the smaller your check while you're still alive and vice versa.

INSTALLMENT PAYMENTS. You sign up for a fixed number of payments, over the period of your choice. You may outlive the income. Conversely, if you die, before getting all the money, what's left in your account goes to a beneficiary.

APERIODIC PAYMENTS. You withdraw money from time to time, as it suits you. Normally, the company lets you do this until age 85. Then you may have to set up a withdrawal plan. If you die, all the money left in your account goes to a beneficiary.

A HYBRID. You allocate part of your money to lifetime payments. The rest can be left to accumulate or to be tapped for aperiodic payments.

VARIABLE PAYMENTS. You link your monthly income to the investment results of a variable annuity. Some people imagine that this choice will keep them ahead of inflation. But that depends on how well the investments do. The substantial fees attached to variable annuities will probably undercut your goal (page 774).

A LUMP SUM. You take the money and run. The usual reason is to buy a lifetime income from another insurance company, because it pays more than your present insurer does (page 804). But first find out if you're in a "two-tier" company. If so, and you leave, the interest you've earned on your annuity over the years will be sharply reduced. Two-tier deals are a disgrace, but once you're hooked it generally makes sense to stay.

SYSTEMATIC WITHDRAWALS. This option has a lot of uses. But it's especially dandy for people using Loophole Six (page 759) or who have reached age 70½ and have to start taking minimum withdrawals from IRAs and other pension plans. Instead of receiving a straight-life annuity, you can establish an income based on your life expectancy. At age 65, for example, you will—on average—reach age 85. So you draw on the IRA as if you had 20 years to live. By age 75, however, your life expectancy will have lengthened to 87½, which changes the size of your monthly payment.

With this system, your income is annually being adjusted to provide you with substantially equal payments over a *lengthening* lifetime. If the annuity also covers your spouse, payments can be rejiggered to reflect your changing joint life expectancies. You can take extra payments from time to time. If you die, the account generally goes to a beneficiary, not to the insurance company. If, at any time, you decide that you want a level income for life, you can usually switch to a straight annuity then.

Two points about systematic withdrawals: (1) Your interest rate isn't locked in. Each year, you get the company's current rate, which may be higher or lower than you had before. (2) You start out with smaller monthly payments than you'd get from a straight-life annuity. But for many years your income and principal should rise, assuming no sharp drop in interest rates (and depending on the system you use for calculating life expectancy). Rising payments help you offset inflation.

Not all insurers provide systematic withdrawals. But anyone who chooses an insurance company for his or her retirement savings should consider one that offers this option. The first such program in the insurance world came from SAFECO Life Insurance, in Seattle, Washington.

WARNING: *If you buy a tax-deferred annuity late in life, you may face surrender charges on some of your withdrawals.* Typically, you have to keep the annuity for seven years or longer before the surrender charge expires. Ask the insurance agent about this before you buy.

How Your Payouts Are Taxed

IF YOU TAKE A LIFETIME ANNUITY OR PAYMENTS OVER A FIXED PERIOD: Each check is a mix of taxable income and a tax-free return of your original capital. At the end of the year, the insurer will tell you (and the IRS) how much taxable income you received. If you started these payouts before reaching age 59½, and they're projected to last for your lifetime, there's no 10 percent tax penalty on early withdrawals.

IF YOU TAKE A LUMP-SUM WITHDRAWAL: You're taxed all at once, on all of your earnings over the years. There's also a 10 percent penalty, if you're under age 59½. However, you can roll your money into another company's annuity, in a tax-free exchange. Your insurance agent will show you how.

IF YOU MAKE OCCASIONAL WITHDRAWALS: They are treated entirely as taxable income, until you have taken out all the money that your investment ever earned. Any further withdrawals are a tax-free return of your own principal. (But different rules apply to annuities bought before August 14, 1982. Withdrawals attributed to money put in then can be treated as a tax-free return of principal until all the principal has been taken. After that, all your withdrawals are taxed in full.)

IF YOU DIE: The tax depends on the type of annuity and its status. (1) If you're collecting income from a straight-life annuity, and die before recovering all the money you paid into it, the loss is reported on your final tax return. (If you recover more than your original investment, it is taxable as received.) (2) If you're collecting income from an annuity designed to last for your lifetime plus a "period certain," die before the period expires, and leave the payments to a beneficiary, the beneficiary pays taxes on the income received. (3) If you're still accumulating money in the annuity and die, it passes to a beneficiary. When the beneficiary withdraws money, he or she pays taxes on the difference between what you invested and what the annuity is now worth.

How to Get the Most from Annuity Payouts

1. Leave the money alone for as long as you can. The longer it sits and multiplies, the more comfortable your old age will be. Insurers generally don't require you to start taking payments until you reach age 85.

2. Holders of IRAs and other retirement plans should consider the systematic withdrawal program, outlined above. Note, however, that you can follow this plan in any event (page 759). You don't need an insurance company to handle it for you.

3. If you go for fixed lifetime payments, start them as late as you possible can. Any fixed income will be chopped by inflation every year. The fewer years inflation has at you, the stronger your finances will be.

4. If you need extra money, consider occasional withdrawals. Or increase your withdrawals every year, to keep up with inflation. You pay more taxes on each withdrawal than you would if you took a straight lifetime annuity. But you're able to control the rate at which the money is used, and assure that any funds left after your death go to your heirs.

5. Don't take the money in a lump sum and invest it yourself. You won't get as much income, after tax, as a lifetime annuity would pay.

6. You can often get a much higher income just by switching your money to a better-paying insurance company. The differences can be truly amazing. As I write, I am looking at a price list for 34 companies. With $100,000 cash, a 70-year-old man can buy an income as small as $636 a month or as large as $1,150 a month, depending on the company he chooses.

How to Buy the Very Best Lifetime Annuity

You buy a lifetime, or "immediate," annuity from an insurance company. In return for a lump sum of money—perhaps from an insurance payout, a certificate of deposit, a tax-deferred annuity, or a retirement account—the insurer guarantees you a fixed income for life. Finding the best such annuity is the easiest job in personal finance. First, you buy the right publication. After that, the process takes four steps and five minutes.

The right publication is the *Annuity Shopper,* at this writing $10 from United States Annuities, 98 Hoffman Rd., Englishtown, NJ, 07726, (800-872-6684). It surveys 30 or more companies for their prices on various immediate annuities. (For a more comprehensive survey, get *Best's Retirement Income Guide,* A. M. Best's Customer Service, Old-wick, NJ, 08858—at this writing, $53 for two issues. But the shorter publication will do just fine.)

Prices are quoted in terms of monthly incomes. A price of $9.03, for example, means that, for every $1,000 you give the insurance company, it will pay you $9.03 a month for life. If you have $50,000, that's $451.50 a month (50 multiplied by $9.03), which comes to $5,418 a year. If you have $250,000, that's $2,257.50 a month or $27,090 a year.

You can buy the annuity directly through United States Annuities, which will answer your questions and handle your order by phone. Or take the list to your insurance agent or financial planner and tell him or her to get cracking. Here's the procedure.

1. Check the *Annuity Shopper* (or *Best's Retirement Income Guide*) for the companies that pay the five highest monthly incomes per $1,000 invested.

2. Starting from the top of your list, find out if that company has been rated A-plus by the A. M. Best insurance-rating service for at least ten years. A Standard & Poor's, Moody's, or Duff & Phelps rating should be AAA. Top quality is critical. You can't switch out of a lifetime annuity once you've started receiving the income. If your insurer fails, you risk losing your money. Current A. M. Best ratings are in the *Annuity Shopper.* Ask your agent for the company's previous Best safety ratings and for the ratings issued by the other services. If the insurer with the best price also meets your quality standards, go no further.

3. If you've been saving money in a tax-deferred annuity at a top-rated insurance company, ask that company for its quote on immediate-pay annuities. Insurers often give current customers better rates than they offer to customers buying in from the outside.

4. Go with the quality company that pays the most. To spread your risk, buy annuities from two or more companies. You might even buy one annuity this year, another next year, and another the year after

that. You'll then get a range of interest rates—advantageous if interest rates go up, although disadvantageous if they fall.

The Charitable Alternative

Here's a way of earning an income from your money while serving others, too. Forget about buying an annuity from a life-insurance company and letting the insurer walk away with anything left over. Give that money to a charitable organization instead. A college. A hospital. A museum. A church. Many such organizations stand ready to offer you a lifetime income from cash and other types of gifts. The gift triggers an immediate deduction on your income-tax return. If you give appreciated property, you'll save on capital gains taxes, too. The institution invests the money, paying you (and a beneficiary, if you like) an income for life. After your death (and the death of your beneficiary), the institution collects.

If you have a cause that you care about, explore this alternative before signing up with an insurance agent. Many institutions have planned-giving offices, which can explain the mechanics to you. You won't get as large an income as insurance companies pay. But you'll have the pleasure of knowing that you've done some good.

WHEN SHOULD YOU START DRAWING SOCIAL SECURITY?

That decision isn't always obvious. You have several choices, especially when you're married. Go over all the options with a Social Security representative (page 809) before deciding exactly when to claim your check.

If you're single, you have only one question to consider: At what age should you retire?

Ask Social Security how large your check would be at various ages, starting at 62. From 62 to 70, benefits ratchet up each year. Starting at age 70, however, you get no further credit for waiting. (These calculations assume no additions from salary. Your benefit may rise further because of your extra payroll taxes.)

Retire at age 62 if your health is poor. Personal considerations aside, early benefits provide larger total payments to anyone who doesn't expect to live for many more years. How many years? Until about age 75.

Retire at 65 or later if you're earning a good income and like your job. Your salary is much higher than a Social Security check would be, and your payroll taxes add to the size of your final Social Security benefit.

Retire at age 65 if your family history suggests that you'll live well past age 75. The longer you live, the greater the value of the maximum Social Security check. You might also delay payments until 65 if your Social Security benefit will be taxed.

If you're married, the optimal retirement age depends on your health, your respective ages, your income, your expected lifespans, and the size of each spouse's Social Security account.

Here are the basic rules.

If only one spouse has a Social Security account, the other is entitled to a benefit on that account. You get up to 50 percent of your spouse's benefit while you're both living and up to 100 percent after your spouse dies, depending on what age you retire.

If both spouses have a Social Security account, you each get your own separate benefit. But when your own benefit is less than you'd collect as a spouse, you get an extra payment to bring you up to the "spousal" level.

You can retire on your own account whenever you want. But you cannot retire on your spouse's account unless your spouse has also retired. Exception: An eligible divorced spouse can collect on his or her "ex's" account even if the "ex" has not retired—see page 134.)

Here are the various ways that this game can play out.

• *When the wife* * *has no benefit of her own:*

1. The husband may retire as early as age 62 on a reduced benefit. At age 62 the wife may also take a reduced benefit. She gets 37.5 percent of whatever her husband would have gotten at full retirement age. If he dies, she gets 100 percent of whatever benefit he was receiving.

2. The husband can retire as early as age 62 while the wife waits until she's age 65. That gives the wife 50 percent of what her husband would have gotten at full retirement age. You may conclude, however, that the difference is too small to be worth the wait. At the husband's death, the wife will still get 100 percent of whatever he was receiving. So waiting to age 65 will add to her income as a wife but not as a widow.

* These rules are the same for a husband with little or no Social Security earnings who applies for benefits on his wife's account. But using "wife" as "spouse" tells the story in its most typical way. I could use the word "spouse" everywhere, but you'd never figure out which spouse I was talking about. Try it and see!

3. The longer the husband waits to retire, the larger his benefit and the larger his spouse's benefit, no matter when she retires. He also improves his spouse's income after his death.

• *When the wife has a benefit of her own, but it's less than her spousal benefit:*

1. She can retire at any time from age 62 on, using her own benefit, even though her husband is still working.

2. When her husband retires, she can also receive her spousal benefit, to raise her Social Security income to a higher level. If she's under 65, she may apply for a reduced spousal benefit immediately or wait for a full spousal benefit at age 65. Normally, the difference is so small that it doesn't pay to wait.

3. If her husband retires first, and then she retires, she gets the spousal benefit for her age at the time. She doesn't have the option of waiting until age 65.

• *When the worker dies, and the widow has a widow's benefit as well as a benefit of her own:*

1. She can start her widow's benefit as early as age 60. Starting at age 62, she can switch to her own Social Security benefit, if it will be higher. Or she can wait until age 65.

2. She can take the widow's benefit and keep it, if that will always be the higher amount. Her payments will be higher if she applies at age 65 than if she applies earlier. But again, it may not pay to wait.

• *When the wife has a benefit of her own and it's better than her spousal benefit:*

1. She can retire on it at any time, from age 62 on, and will keep it. She will never switch to a spousal benefit.

2. If her husband's benefit is small, he may get more money by claiming a spousal benefit on his wife's account.

• *When one spouse has a government pension, and also qualifies for Social Security benefits on the account of the other spouse:* Don't expect to collect much Social Security, if any. You generally get only the amount of your Social Security benefit that exceeds two-thirds of your government pension. That is usually zero.

• *When you have an eligible child at home:* Your family is entitled to additional Social Security benefits. But you're subject to a maximum monthly benefit, no matter how many eligible members there are in your family.

How Much Can Widows and Spouses Earn and Still Get Benefits?

All Social Security benefits are subject to the retirement test ex-plained on page 809. Whether you receive benefits as a retiree, a spouse, a widow, a widower, or a child, your check goes down if you exceed the earnings limit. A 62-year-old widow, employed at good wages, may find that she earns too much to collect much of a widow's benefit. In that case, she'd be smarter not to claim it. Let it build up until she actually retires, when the check will be larger.

Can You Unretire?

Sure. If you quit work, start getting Social Security, and then take a job again, you can simply put a halt to your benefits. Some workers choose to repay all the Social Security money they have received. That cancels any reduction they took for retiring earlier than age 65. They are treated as if they never retired at all.

Alternatively, you can tell Social Security to suspend your benefits. When you retire again, your retirement age will be refigured, based on the number of Social Security checks you previously received. For ex-ample, if you received the equivalent of six full checks, you'll be treated as having retired at age 64 and six months. Your check, however, won't be refigured until you reach age 65, so if you reretire earlier you will have to wait.

Applying for Social Security benefits.

You can apply as early as three months before you want your benefits to start. Otherwise, benefits generally start in the month when applica-tion is made. If you apply after age 65, you can—if you want—claim back payments for up to six months (but because of your late filing, you might lose a month of Medicare protection—see page 322).

Before okaying your benefits, the government will want your Social Security number, originals or certified copies of your birth certificate and the birth certificates of anyone else applying for benefits (no photocopies allowed), and proof of how much money you made last year. If you don't have all these documents and can't get them, don't worry. Social Secu-rity will suggest some acceptable substitutes. All Social Security benefits are indexed to the inflation rate. You get your higher checks each Janu-ary.

How to Get Paid

Your Social Security check can be mailed to your address. Or—easier and faster—you can have the money sent directly to your bank. Social Security will wire it to your checking account or your savings account, as you prefer.

How to Talk to Social Security

If you like to deal in person, check the Yellow Pages under U.S. Government to see if one of Social Security's 1,300 offices is anywhere near you. Unfortunately, budget cuts have all but eliminated the staffers who visited shut-ins, set up shop once a week at senior-citizen centers, and circuit-rode to rural areas. You can telephone Social Security toll-free (800-234-5772), Monday through Friday, from 7:00 A.M. to 7:00 P.M. The best time to get through is between 7:00 A.M. and 9:00 A.M. or 5:00 P.M. and 7:00 P.M. on Wednesdays, Thursdays, and Fridays of the second, third, and fourth weeks of the month.

Got it?

What if You Earn over the Social Security Limit?

If you earn too much, your Social Security check goes down. In 1991, retirees aged 62 to 64 could earn only $7,080 free and clear. Over that amount, every $2 in earnings cut $1 off their Social Security checks. Retirees 65 to 69 could earn up to $9,720, but were docked $1 for every additional $3 in earnings. These ceilings rise with inflation every year.

At the start of each year, anyone under age 70 who expects to exceed the earnings limit should report that fact to Social Security. Estimate how much extra you are likely to earn. Your monthly check will be adjusted accordingly.

The following year, at tax time, you have to report your earnings to Social Security as well as to the IRS. Send in Form SSA-777 (available from a Social Security office), a copy of your tax return, or just a letter.

If you earned more than you originally expected, your Social Security checks will have been too big. You'll have to return the extra money. You can send a single check or repay in installments. If you don't file an earnings report, and were over the limit, Social Security will hit you with a penalty. How does Social Security find out? It gets copies of the W-2 form that your employer sends.

Conversely, if you earned less money than you expected, Social Security will restore any benefits due.

How Your Social Security Benefits Are Taxed

Retirees with middle incomes and up will owe federal income taxes on up to half of their Social Security benefits. Taxes click in for singles with incomes from all sources (pension, dividends, royalties, even municipal bond interest) of $25,000 or more, and for married couples with $32,000 or more. Some states also tax Social Security income, but most don't. At year end, you'll be mailed a Social Security Benefit Statement, showing how much money you received. Use that to figure out whether taxes are owed.

How Should You Invest for Retirement?

The investment rules in Chapter 21 are as good for age 65 as for age 35. But there are several points that retirees, in particular, should think about.

1. *You are not dead!* You will probably live for another 20 years or more, during which time inflation may rage. You will impoverish yourself if you put all your money in bonds, certificates of deposit, money market mutual funds, tax-deferred annuities, or other fixed-income investments. You *must* keep some portion of your capital invested for growth—for example, in equity-income mutual funds.

2. *"Safe" investments aren't!* Take the person who insists on owning only 8 percent government bonds. In 15 years (when he or she will almost surely still be alive), and assuming 4 percent inflation, the purchasing power of those bonds will have been cut in half. Put another way, you are choosing an investment guaranteed to drop in value by 45 percent. How "safe" is that?

3. *Paying taxes won't kill you!* When investing, pursue an appropriate total return and pay your taxes as they fall. If you look at the tax angle first and the investment angle second, you are going to make some lousy decisions. For example, if you're a low-bracket investor, municipal bonds will yield you almost nothing, after inflation.

4. *It's too late to start over!* Hordes of entrepreneurs troll for early retirees who dream of beginning another life. They'll hold out a dream of riches, if you'll just invest your severance pay or lump-sum pension payout in their guinea-hen farms or solar go-carts. Don't do it. You are holding the only serious money that you will ever have. If you want to start another business, grow it yourself, out of personal experience and the contacts you have. Put your pension money into a prudent array of stocks and bonds.

5. *There's more than one way to skin a cat!* "Income investors" usually focus on interest income—from bonds or certificates of deposit. But stock dividends are income, too. With a portion of your money in dividend-paying stocks, you're getting income and some growth. Furthermore, "growth" is income, too. Whether you're getting 8 percent from a $10,000 bond or by selling 80 shares of a $10 stock, you're collecting $800 to spend.

HERE ARE MY BEST IDEAS FOR A YOUNGER RETIREE SEEKING INCOME.

1. Invest a part of your money for growth. Put it in conservative mutual funds that buy dividend-paying stocks. Reinvest all your dividends. Then set up a monthly withdrawal plan (page 524). With this plan, the mutual fund will mail you a monthly check, of whatever size you need. You can increase that check once a year, to keep your purchasing power level with inflation. Ten years later, you may have as much capital as you started with, because of your mutual fund's increase in value.

2. Invest part of your money in a collection of short- and intermediate-term bonds. They offer more protection against inflation than long-term bonds do (page 638). Spend the income and reinvest the capital as your bonds fall due. Or buy short- and intermediate-term bond mutual funds and reinvest the dividends. Set up a monthly withdrawal plan with your bond funds, too.

WHEN SHOULD RETIREES GIVE UP STOCKS?

Never, if you're mentally active, well-to-do, and can afford to outwait the market's cyclical declines. You probably won't have to use all your money during your lifetime. So you can risk keeping some of your capital invested for growth. You may not get all the benefit, but your heirs will.

My advice changes if you expect to spend most of your capital during your lifetime. During early retirement, you still need stocks to increase the value of your capital and stay ahead of inflation. In late retirement, however, you can't afford the risk of a prolonged market downturn. So take a look at your own statistical life expectancy in the Appendix (page 901), and modify it by the age your parents died. Roughly five years before, consider selling all your stock-owning mutual funds and moving entirely to fixed-income investments. Sell stocks even earlier if your health is poor. Keep six month's worth of living expenses in a money market mutual fund. With the rest of your capital, build a ladder of short- and intermediate-term bonds or certificates of deposit (pages 638 and 67). Spend all of the income from your bonds or CDs, and as much principal as you need from each bond or CD that matures. The tables on page 789 and in the Appendix (page 892) will help you determine how long your capital can last. Aim for a spending plan that will carry you five years past your life expectancy. If you own a house, you can always release that capital, too—by taking a reverse mortgage, or by selling and moving into an apartment or senior-citizens' complex.

At the end of your life, you shouldn't be saving money anymore. It's time to spend. These are the years you accumulated all those savings *for*.

31
RETIRING ON THE HOUSE:

How to Tap the Equity You've Built

———

Your home is your piggy bank. You have only
to shake it and money will fall out.

A lot of money rides on your house.
It's usually your biggest asset. When you retire, should you pull out that
money or leave it alone? If you pull it out, what's the best way to do it?

These questions focus on where you'll live and how much debt you'll
want to carry. The decision may ultimately be swung by things that have
nothing to do with money: your health, your community ties, the
weather, where your kids live, and your feelings about the house you're
in. But the money issue has sharpened, now that so many cities have
seen house prices fall. Should you sell right now, lest you lose some of
your equity? Or should you hang tight? Suddenly, in retirement, you've
become a housing speculator.

SHOULD YOU MOVE?

DON'T MOVE if you're happy in your house, can afford to keep it, and
don't care if its value rises or falls. The money you have in home equities

is not material to your welfare, at least not now. If you run short of cash sometime in the future, you can think of selling then.

BUT MOVE IMMEDIATELY if you're counting on the *current* value of your house to help support you in retirement. Maybe your house will be worth more next year—but then again, maybe it won't. You can't afford to take the risk. In fact, you might even sell up to two years before you actually retire. Put the money in a bank and find a place to rent. As long as you buy a new house within two years, you can defer the income tax on any profit you're carrying forward.

HERE'S HOW TO MAKE MONEY ON A MOVE:

1. Go to a lower-cost part of the country. Not only will a new house or condominium cost less but your other living expenses will usually be lower, too. That leaves you more money to invest, to get a higher retirement income.

2. Stay in your community but trade down to a smaller place. You'll pay less for taxes, insurance, and upkeep, and will have money left over to invest. Why be house poor in retirement? Shake loose that cash and enjoy it, instead.

3. Sell your house and rent. (For a look at this option, see page 821.)

4. Move to a lower-cost part of the world. Even when the dollar declines, it can be cheaper to live in certain countries abroad. Your pension and Social Security checks will follow you, but Medicare won't. So check the local health services, and whether Blue Cross or another private policy will cover you both at home and abroad. Three other issues critical to expatriates are taxes (U.S. and foreign), the inheritance rules in the country you've moved to, and investments that hedge against a dollar decline.

The Government Practically Pays You to Move

Locked up in your house lies a beautiful pot of tax-free money, reachable only if you move. It represents all the profits you've ever made on the homes you've owned. Every time you sold, you probably rolled those profits over, tax deferred. Age 55 (for either you or your spouse) marks the Great Escape from taxes due. Up to $125,000 of all those profits can now be realized tax free, *if* you decide you want to sell.

In some states, counter-tax-breaks may encourage you to stay. In California, for example, people who don't move pay lower property taxes than people who do. But that's the exception. For the majority of Americans, moving pays.

As an example, assume that you paid $20,000 for your first house 25 years ago. The house you own today can be sold for a net of $170,000.* Over your lifetime, you've made $150,000 in taxable profits. When you sell, $125,000 of that profit comes tax free. Only the remaining $25,000 is taxable, and even that tax can be deferred if you buy yourself another house (below).

This $125,000 tax break, incidentally, applies only to your principal residence, not to your vacation house. And you have to have owned and lived in the house for at least three of the past five years.

How to Get the Most from the 55-Plus Tax Exclusion

1. This tax break is offered once in a lifetime. So use it only to cover a sizable profit. If you take it against a $25,000 gain, you've shot your wad. You can't claim another exclusion for the $100,000 you wasted. When you have smaller profits, roll them over into a new house and continue to defer the tax.

2. If you buy a new house costing less than you sold the old one for, a tax falls due on a portion of the profits you've deferred. If the tax is modest, go ahead and pay it. Don't waste your big, one-time tax exclusion on a peanut gain. Wait until you sell for good—to move to an apartment, your child's house, or a nursing home. That's the profit this tax break was born to save.

3. What if you use the maximum exclusion and still have a taxable profit left over? You can continue to defer the tax, even if you move to a cheaper house, as long as you meet the following test: Your new house costs at least as much as you sold the old one for, minus the gain you took tax free. The example below shows how that works out, assuming that you took the full $125,000 tax break.

What you sold the old house for, after various adjustments:	$175,000
Minus your age-55 tax exclusion:	125,000
The minimum your new house has to cost to allow you to defer all the remaining taxable gain:	$ 50,000

* I'm leaving out everything that complicates this example. But remember that real-estate commissions, home-improvement expenditures, and fix-up costs within 90 days of the sales will all reduce your taxable profit.

4. Older people who plan to marry should play their tax status like chess. If only one of you has used the exclusion,* the other will be barred from it from the moment you say "I do." So the person still entitled to the $125,000 tax break might consider selling his or her house before the ceremony. That tax-free gain would be a dandy dowry. If neither of you has used the exclusion, and you plan to buy a new house together, you might both sell your houses before the wedding and claim two exclusions. You can do this even on a joint tax return, as long as the houses were sold before you married.

5. What if you use the tax exclusion and later come to regret it? You have three years to change your mind and amend your return.

YOUR ALTERNATIVES TO MOVING

For many retirees, trading down to a less expensive house or condominium is so practical that it should top their list of retirement solutions. But if you want to hang on to your house despite the fact that money is short, you have several alternatives.

• You might take in a roommate or a boarder. A house too costly for one to maintain might be duck soup for two. Some mortgage lenders make special loans available to homeowners who want to add a senior-citizen apartment. But don't make a move without checking the following points. (1) Does your zoning allow you to take in boarders? (2) Are you subject to rent control, or are rent-control laws on your town's agenda? If so, your tenant might gain the right to occupy that apartment forever, at a fixed or slowly rising rent. (3) Is the boarder covered by your liability insurance? (4) Have you taken a lesson in how business properties are taxed? For example, if you sell, you can't tax-defer the profit on the portion of your house that was used as a rental apartment. (5) Have you a written lease? Without one, you may have no grounds for evicting a bad tenant.

• You might sell the home to one or more of the children and lease it back from them for life. Here's how that deal works: (1) The children give you a 10 or 20 percent down payment. (2) You take back a mortgage

---

* You have used your exclusion if you took it alone or while married to your late spouse or former spouse. You have *not* used your exclusion if *all* of the following statements apply: (1) You never took the tax break yourself or in a former marriage, (2) you were temporarily ineligible for the exclusion because you married someone who had taken it previously, but (3) you are no longer married to that person.

from them for the rest of the money. (3) The children send you a mortgage payment every month. (4) You pay your children a monthly rent, which, at the start, is smaller than the mortgage payments you receive. So taking back the mortgage adds to your income. (5) The children pay the insurance and taxes. For them, the house is a rental property, so the mortgage interest, taxes, insurance, and depreciation are all deductible business expenses. These deductions shelter their rental income and possibly some of their ordinary income, depending on how much money they make (see page 417). (6) The children see to maintenance and repairs, which for them are also tax deductible. You usually pay the utility bills. Work out this transaction with a lawyer. The house price, the mortgage interest rate, and the current and future rent must all be set at fair market value or your children will lose their tax deductions. Your risk with a sale/leaseback is that, if the kids get greedy or decide that you're not taking care of the house, they might try to evict. Remember King Lear. You can also do a sale/leaseback with an outside investor, but that's even riskier. Outsiders could really push you hard, if they wanted their money out.

· You might reduce expenses by using local programs available to low-income homeowners. For example, you may be able to defer your real-estate taxes or get a home-repair loan that needn't be repaid until your house is sold. Ask about these and other forms of financial assistance at your local senior-citizens' center.

· If you own your house free and clear, you might give it to a charity or an educational institution. Talk to the charity about the kinds of arrangements it will make. You'll get an immediate tax deduction and the right to live in the house for life. You pay the real-estate taxes, insurance, and maintenance. At your death (and the death of your spouse, if the gift covers both of you), the house passes to the charity. This solution pays the most if you're older and your tax bracket is high.

· You might take a reverse mortgage (details below).

Reverse Mortgages: A Good Idea That's a Long Time Coming

Reverse mortgages (also known as home-equity conversions) are in their infancy. They've been in their infancy for 10 years or more. For all I know, they may still be in their infancy 10 years hence. But recently, the federal government took up their cause, which makes it more likely that this baby industry will grow. The Federal Housing Administration (FHA) is now making government-insured mortgages available to all

10,000 institutions that offer FHA loans. So far, however, only a small fraction of banks have signed on. To find one, you'll still have to hunt.

REVERSE MORTGAGES, DEFINED:

With a reverse mortgage, you can tap the cash locked in your house without having to move. Different lenders offer different programs, but generally speaking, the deal works like this.

1. A lender agrees to make you a loan against the value of your house. But the loan agreement normally doesn't set a maximum amount. Instead, you get a check a month.

2. The size of your check depends on your age, the age of your spouse, and how much equity you have in your house. For example, say that you're 70 years old. Your home equity is worth $100,000 and the loan interest rate is 10 percent. An FHA lender might give you $276 a month for life. If you took out the loan at age 85, you might get $604 a month for life. Private lenders generally offer larger amounts (page 820).

3. Those checks keep coming for as long as you live in the house. So how much you ultimately borrow is dictated by how long you stay there.

4. You pay no cash up front. All closing and insurance costs are included in the loan.

5. You pay no interest currently on the money you're borrowing. The interest compounds, to be paid off when the loan is settled.

6. When you die or leave your house, it will be sold and the proceeds used to repay the loan, plus interest. Many lenders also take a piece of the home's appreciation. In fact, it's not uncommon for most of the money to wind up in the lender's hands. If you want to save some of the proceeds for yourself or your heirs, look for a lender who offers an "equity reserve." With a reserve, you always retain a fixed portion of the equity—say, 10 or 20 percent. You pay for this reserve by taking lower monthly checks.

7. If the loan builds up to something more than your house is worth, the lender normally swallows the loss (but check this out before signing up).

Although regular monthly checks are the usual way of receiving the money, the lender may offer up to three other options: a fixed number of checks, a lump sum, or a line of credit that you can draw on whenever you want. I especially like the line of credit, because it lets you borrow as much or as little as you need.

Each check looks and feels like income. But it is not income, it's a loan. So it doesn't raise your income tax or affect your eligibility for Social Security. Nor will it hinder your access to programs for the low-income elderly in most states, as long as you borrow only enough to cover your expenses.

THE REWARDS:

• With most reverse mortgages, you can stay in your house as long as you're able, thanks to the income they supply.

• The monthly checks help you finance home health care, which may keep you out of a nursing home.

• The checks also help you keep the house in good repair.

THE RISKS:

• You pay huge rates of interest if you leave your house soon after taking out the loan. The fees assume normal lifetime occupancies, not shortened ones. And even at normal occupancies, this loan is expensive.

• When you quit the house, you may have little or no equity. How, then will you finance new housing or home-health expenses? So as not to lose everything, consider a reverse-mortgage credit line that you can draw on lightly. Or take a mortgage with an equity reserve that gives you some percentage of the money when the house is sold.

• For young retirees, the monthly checks are far too small. Don't even consider this program until you're 75 or older.

• You might take out a fixed-term loan, lasting anywhere from 3 to 10 years. Such loans may make sense for people who are already wait-listed for a subsidized senior-citizens' apartment, who can move in with a child, or who believe they won't outlive the loan. But if their expectations fail, they'll be forced out of their homes before they're ready. In general, you should stick with loans of indefinite term.

• You may misunderstand the loan's permanence. A "lifetime" loan doesn't necessarily last a lifetime. It lasts only as long as you stay in your home. The contract defines the end of that term and you should study its every nuance. Can you spend three months in a nursing home and then return? Can you be evicted if the lender believes that the property isn't being well kept?

• A reverse mortgage may seduce you into keeping your house when you shouldn't. It might be wiser, socially as well as financially, to sell your house and move into an apartment, condominium, or senior-citizens' home.

Three private companies write reverse mortgages that will last as long as you stay in your home. They generally pay larger monthly checks than you'd get from an FHA lender, especially on higher-priced homes (but note: These firms may not lend if the market is poor).

1. The Individual Reverse Mortgage Account, Mount Laurel, NJ (800-233-4762; in New Jersey, 800-233-4762). It lends in California, Connecticut, Delaware, Maryland, New Jersey, Ohio, Pennsylvania, and Virginia.

2. The Home Income Security Plan in Louisville (800-942-6550; in California, 800-431-8100), lending mostly in the metropolitan areas of California, Illinois, Kentucky, Maryland, North Carolina, Virginia, and just starting up in Florida. It also offers a home-equity line of credit.

3. The Providential Home Income Plan in San Francisco (800-441-4428), offering loans and home-equity lines of credit in California, Florida, Illinois, Minnesota, and Wisconsin.

A number of state and local housing agencies also make reverse mortgages, usually to low-income homeowners and for limited purposes, such as paying property taxes or keeping the house in good repair. Some nonprofit agencies offer programs for specified terms, such as 10 years. Two firms are working on true lifetime loans that would act like annuities.

For free information on where to find all these reverse-mortgage programs, send a self-addressed, stamped, business-size envelope to the National Center for Home Equity Conversion, 1210 East College Dr., Suite 300, Marshall, MN, 56258. For an excellent free booklet explaining reverse mortgages send for *Home-Made Money, a Consumer Guide to Home Equity Conversion,* from the American Association of Retired Persons, 1909 K St. N.W., Washington, DC, 20049.

CONTEMPLATING THE PAID-UP HOUSE

If you have enough cash to pay off the mortgage, should you or shouldn't you? This is one of those questions that can only be answered "it depends."

If you're rolling in money, pay off the loan. A paid-up house stabilizes your living costs, saves you the price of interest payments, and makes you feel secure. You don't give a hoot about locking up capital because you have all you need.

If you're rolling in money that is earning more than the cost of your mortgage, you might decide to keep the loan. But even in these situations, I see people paying off their mortgages, for the pleasure of owning free and clear.

If you are definitely *not* rolling in money, hang on to your mortgage. If you pay off the loan, your precious liquidity will be lost. You'll be house rich but cash poor. You might even be forced to sell the house just to get your capital back out. For you, paying interest on a mortgage is the price of financial flexibility.

If you paid off the mortgage and regret it, you can (1) try for a home-equity credit line from your bank (hard to get, however, if your income is small); (2) sell your house, buy something smaller, and add the extra capital to your bank account; (3) consider a reverse mortgage.

SHOULD YOU RENT OR OWN?

When you retire, security is what matters most. You want an easy style of life you can comfortably afford. If your present house is eating up too much of your income, you have two choices: (1) trade down to something smaller, perhaps in a cheaper part of the country. That will free up spending money. (2) Sell your house, invest the proceeds for a higher retirement income, and rent an apartment.

To figure out which way is best, estimate the net sum of money you'd have on hand if you sold your present house. Call that your kitty. To make it as large as possible, assume that you'd take the tax break for people 55 and up (page 814). Then make the following comparison.

IF YOU BUY A NEW HOUSE:

1. Reduce your kitty by the amount you'd invest in the house. Do this calculation two ways—once assuming a mortgage and once assuming that you bought the house for cash. Estimate how much income you would get from your remaining kitty, after tax.

2. Add up your monthly housing expenses—principally mortgage (if any), taxes, insurance, utilities, and a reserve for repairs. Take a deduction both for mortgage interest and for real-estate taxes.

3. Subtract your net housing expenses from the monthly income your kitty throws off. If the kitty won't cover all your costs, subtract the remaining expenses from the rest of your after-tax retirement income. What's left is the net you have to live on.

IF YOU RENT:

1. Reduce your kitty by any taxes you'll owe on the sale of your home, after using the $125,000 tax exclusion. Estimate how much income you would get from the remaining kitty, after tax.

2. Add up your monthly housing expenses, principally rent, utilities, and insurance.

3. Subtract your expenses from the monthly income you'd get from the kitty. If it won't cover all your housing costs, subtract the remaining expenses from the rest of your after-tax retirement income. What's left is the net you have to live on.

OTHER CONSIDERATIONS:

This rough comparison tells you which choice is cheaper now. But it leaves out some intangibles. On the homeowner's side of the ledger, the house might rise in value, which provides more equity for a retiree's later years. Young retirees might want to own; older retirees might want to rent. Furthermore, homeowners' costs are pretty stable. So your income won't get eaten up by housing inflation. Taxes may rise, but that increase is small compared with the potential rise in rents.

On the renter's side of the ledger lies a much larger pool of capital, thanks to all the money that was liberated from the house. With wise investing, that capital might gain more in value than if it were still tied up in home equities. Rents will probably rise every year. But renters can dip into capital if their income should run short.

So the question of renting versus owning also gets answered: "It depends." Work out the numbers and see how you feel about it. The odds are, however, that if you own your own unmortgaged home, you won't find any cheaper way to live.

THE PIGGY BANK

Older people count themselves lucky if they enter retirement with a home, especially a paid-up home. It's worth the effort when you're young if it points you toward freedom as you age.

8 MAKING IT WORK

This book, I hope, has been moving you to pick up the phone and make decisions. First you have to study and learn but then you have to follow up. A plan that stays in your head is a daydream. What adds to your wealth are the actions you take and whether you manage to take them in time.

At the end of this chapter, you'll find the broad principles that give shape to financial plans. Tackle them one after the other. Flesh them out with safe and sane financial products (many of which I've named in this book). You'll get more ideas as you go along.

Occasionally, your goals will change, as both successes and mistakes refine your knowledge of yourself. But having made one plan, you can easily make more and better ones. No activity is more comforting, in risky times, than drawing a circle around your finances and pronouncing them sound.

32

BE YOUR OWN PLANNER:

The Secret, Revealed

———

You've been waiting for 31 chapters for the
secret to handling money well. Here it is. Use
common sense. The simplest choices are the
best ones. Impulse is your enemy, time your
friend.

Most of us don't need professional fi-
nancial planners. We don't even need a full-scale plan. *Conservative
money management isn't hard.* To be your own guru, you need only a list
of objectives, a few simple financial products, realistic investment expectations, a time frame that gives your investments time to work out, and
—to keep you from falling for rascally sales pitches—a well-tempered
humbug detector. Don't put off decisions for fear you're not making the
best choice in every circumstance. Often, there isn't a "best" choice.
Any one of several will work fine.

Occasionally, however, you do want an expert opinion—usually to
address a narrow question. I can think of a handful of circumstances
when you'd be glad for professional help.

1. You earn good wages but cannot manage to save a dime. You need a strong reality lecture. Someone has to show you—in dollars and cents—how little you'll have at the end of your life unless you shape up. Most of us shape ourselves up. But if you can't, get help.

2. You face a question that can't be answered without some technical expertise. For example, your company may have made a general early-retirement offer and you want to examine your alternatives. (Many technical questions, however, can be answered with the tools that you'll find in this book—questions like how much to save for college or retirement or how much life insurance you need.)

3. You're following a personal plan but wonder if an expert can improve it. Arrange for a meeting at an hourly fee (minus sales commissions, if you eventually buy any products). Throughout the conversation, ask yourself whether you're hearing helpful or predatory advice. Make no decisions until you've gone home and thought about it. If the words "limited partnership" escape the planner's lips, run for your life. You're there to talk long-range strategies, not to listen to sales pitches for high-commission products.

This meeting will have one of two results: (1) You'll stumble into a wonderful planner who makes suggestions you're grateful for. (2) You'll feel more confident that your own decisions have, in fact, been the right ones. In the latter case, turn up the volume on your humbug detector. You may need to be saved from buying some of the planner's lousy investment products.

Don't go near a planner if you've just come into a lot of money (an inheritance; an insurance settlement) and don't know what to do with it. Clients with loose cash and weak convictions are fresh meat, ready for roasting. A self-interested planner may urge you to buy high-commission investments that serve his or her objectives better than yours. And you won't be able to tell the difference.

Before you set foot in the office of a stockbroker, insurance agent, or financial planner, learn the basics yourself. Sock your money into bank certificates of deposit or Treasury securities. Then study up. Take all the time you need to work out an approach that you're comfortable with. Six months; one year; the wait doesn't matter. During that period, your money will be earning a decent rate of interest and isn't at risk. The only expert it's safe to visit is a certified public accountant who doesn't sell financial products. An accountant can advise you on taxes, answer technical questions, and make some general suggestions as to how to allocate your money. Should you pay off debt? Raise your standard of living? Set aside a college fund?

When you're ready to invest, try it yourself—a little in this mutual fund, a little in that one. Give it a year, see how it feels, then invest some more. It might take two or three years to deploy your money, but that doesn't matter. Life is long. By taking pains, you can preserve your capital and make it grow.

If you truly hate making investment decisions, you have two choices: (1) With a large sum of money, consider a professional investment advisor or bank trust department. For a middling sum, try the trust department's pooled fund. (2) Ask a financial planner to pick out some appropriate mutual funds. Pay the sales commissions willingly. They're a fair charge when you've sought advice. But don't touch any exotic products and don't do business—not even mutual-fund business—with a planner who urges exotic products upon you.

Never give a stockbroker a sum to manage for you. He or she may manage it in half.

WHICH KIND OF PROFESSIONAL TO SEE

SEE A CERTIFIED PUBLIC ACCOUNTANT—for tax planning, budget planning, small-business advice, and long-term income and savings projections. Some CPAs have expanded their practice into personal financial planning, too (page 831). Enrolled agents, who are licensed to represent you before the IRS, and licensed public accountants also have tax practices.

SEE A TAX ATTORNEY—for complex wills and estate planning.

SEE AN INSURANCE AGENT—to buy an insurance policy, although some policies you can buy yourself.

SEE A STOCKBROKER OR CALL A DISCOUNT BROKER—to buy stocks and bonds. Mutual funds you can buy yourself.

SEE A FINANCIAL PLANNER—to answer more general questions about how your finances fit together.

WHAT ABOUT "THE PLAN"?

"The plan" is the vast written tome that financial planners love to tout, a thick, loose-leaf binder that tells you how to behave from cradle to grave. Forget it. Such plans are artifacts of the 1980s. No client's plan survived the first change in the tax laws.

You do need a very general plan, outlining your financial objectives, spending limits, fallback positions, and investment strategy. To make it real, write it down. In your head, a plan is only a vague hope that things will turn out well. On paper, it's an action project.

This plan will cover just a few sheets of your ever-faithful yellow pad. Keep in it your file and pull it out once a year, just to see that everything's on track. If your circumstances change, so will the numbers you've written down. Such plans, drawn up on your dining-room table, are far more valuable than the big-book schemes that planners, banks, and brokers sell, because they're *yours*.

THE PLANNER PROBLEM

In theory, a financial planner is a one-stop money pro. This paragon knows a little something about everything. He or she will uncover your past financial crimes, help you formulate new goals, and draw a map to get you there. Under a planner's loving care, your scattered savings and investments will blend miraculously into a blueprint for a prosperous future (background music: trumpets, crashing cymbals, tonic chords).

Sometimes that even happens.

More often it doesn't.

The majority of planners are delivery systems for prepackaged financial products. They make their living selling limited partnerships, insurance policies, tax-deferred annuities, unit trusts, loaded mutual funds, and other high-commission investments. They cannot escape the taint of bias. Most planners have to sell or starve.

Horror stories abound: life-insurance policies sold for two-year-olds, limited partnerships sold to elderly retirees, "pension maximization" plans that will backfire on widows. All the caveats that I've written about stockbrokers also apply to financial planners, and in spades.

HOW DO YOU FIND A PLANNER WORTH HAVING?

This question is a hard one. In almost all states, absolutely anyone can hold himself or herself out as a financial planner. No tests are required, no licensing done. I worry even about offering you guidelines, because of the tremendous range of competence and honesty within the field. But there *are* some terrific planners in this country. Here are some ways of tracking them down.

1. Turn back to page 551, where I list ways of finding a stockbroker. Most of those rules will also help you find a good financial planner, so I won't repeat them here.

2. Ask about the planner's professional background; he or she should have a printed handout. Avoid "planners" who are basically insurance agents or stockbrokers. Look for broader experience: maybe they worked in business, or are accountants or tax lawyers.

The planner should be registered as an investment advisor with the Securities and Exchange Commission. Ask for his or her SEC Form ADV, which discloses education, business background, fees, and investment methods. Also, check the planner's CRD form, to see if there's a disciplinary history (page 555). Don't do anything more than the simplest kind of business with an unregistered planner.

Some schools give certificates in financial planning, most notably the College for Financial Planning in Denver (a Certified Financial Planner designation or CFP) and the American College in Bryn Mawr, Pennsylvania (the Chartered Financial Consultant designation or ChFC). The American Institute of Certified Public Accountants offers an APFS tag, for Accredited Personal Financial Specialist. A number of colleges and universities also give financial-planning degrees. These diplomas attest that the planner has passed a number of exams, in such things as taxes, insurance, investments, and estate planning. But a certificate is only a starting point. It doesn't say whether the planner is any good.

3. How long has the planner been in business? Skip any new kids on the block, including career-switchers who have been practicing only for couple of years. Go for 10 years of experience, at least. What kinds of clients does he or she have? Planners often specialize—in doctors, entrepreneurs, entertainers, teachers, or young, upper-middle-income families. The more experience the planner has with people like you, the better.

4. Ask for the names of five clients you can speak with, who have been with the planner for at least three years. If the planner says that all names are confidential, assume that he or she has no long-term clients or can't trust them to be uniformly complimentary. That's your sign to take a hike. When you do speak with a planner's clients, ask how much better off they are, thanks to what the planner did.

5. Don't pick a planner just because he or she gets quoted in the newspapers. The paper doesn't check on how good a planner is, or

whether his or her ideas work out. If enough phone calls, or ideas, or press releases arrive at the newspaper, the reporter may eventually pick up the phone—and one quotation almost inevitably leads to more. Courting the press is one way planners advertise. It says absolutely nothing about their honesty or expertise.

6. Don't pick a planner just because he or she gives investment seminars. That's a form of advertising, too. A San Francisco planner named Lawrence Krause once told his trade secrets to a magazine called *CALUnderwriter:* "You don't have to know as much as you think you have to know in running a seminar," he said. "All you have to know is more than your audience, and your audience doesn't know your subject. . . . You also have to remember that you're not there to educate. You're there to sell. The purpose of a seminar is twofold: one, to confuse your audience; and two, to create dependence. . . . As long as you are going to confuse them, do a good job of it. Then you ask for the order, so that they'll come to see you afterward."

Now you know.

7. A planner should be willing to advise you on a narrow point without demanding that you take the total service. If you just want some tips on college investing, the answer should be "Sure." Many planners argue that, because money decisions interlock, they can't help with college savings unless they draw you a lifetime plan. But that's nonsense. Narrow plans are effective, too. On specific projects, planners should work for hourly fees or flat fees per job. They might waive the fees if you buy a product on which they earn a sales commission.

8. If you work successfully with a planner on a narrow point, maybe you'll decide to go further. All planners stand ready to rip up your dining-room-table program and insert a fancier one of their own. Personally, I'd rather hear a planner's ideas one at a time and think about whether they're worth following. The big-book plan may tilt toward selling products rather than advancing your personal goals.

What if you pay $500 or $1,000 for what turns out to be a risky or unsuitable plan? Some clients execute it anyway (or at least part of it), because they don't want to "waste" the money they've invested. That attitude plays right into the planner's hands. I say: Walk away. You're lucky that you've lost only the money you spent up front and not all the rest of the money that might have followed.

9. Ask the planner, "How are you paid?" This question is critical. A planner should hand over a schedule that discloses his or her compen-

sation in full. Planning fees, hourly fees, the sales commissions on various products (front-, middle-, rear-end, and renewal commissions), continuing fees from the firms that package the financial products the planner sells, fees from the lawyers or accountants he or she refers you to, fees for managing money.

Ask specifically what percentage of the firm's income comes from commissions on insurance products, annuities, mutual funds, limited partnerships, stocks, bonds, and other investments. That tells you where the planner's interests lie. If 60 percent of the income comes from insurance products, you have an insurance agent. If 60 percent comes from limited partnerships, you have a hyena.

If the planner claims not to know where all the income comes from, he or she is either running a lousy business or fibbing. Either way, you don't want to deal. You should also ask whether the firm owns an interest in any of the investments it recommends. Get a "no" answer in writing. If that's a fib, too, it will help you with your lawsuit.

10. Several organizations will give you the names of financial planners in your area.

• The National Association of Personal Financial Advisors (NAPFA, 1130 Lake Cook Rd., Suite 105, Buffalo Grove, IL, 60089, call 800-366-2732). Members charge no sales commissions. They are all fee-only planners (see below).

• The American Institute of Certified Public Accountants (AICPA Personal Financial Planning Division, 1211 Avenue of the Americas, New York, NY, 10036). It will mail you the names of local CPAs who have taken the courses needed for the Accredited Personal Financial Specialist designation. Most APFSs charge no sales commissions on products, but some do.

• The International Association for Financial Planning (IAFP Registry, Two Concourse Parkway, Suite 800, Atlanta, GA, 30328, call 404-395-1605). Most of its members charge sales commissions, in all their infinite variety. In general, the planners listed in the Registry have better qualifications than some other planners.

• The Institute of Certified Financial Planners (7600 E. Eastman Ave., Suite 301, Denver, CO, 80231, call 800-282-7526). It gives you the names of local members, for better or for worse. These planners, too, charge sales commissions.

Whatever the source, follow the same rule: Check 'em out, check 'em out, check 'em all out!

HOW FINANCIAL PLANNERS ARE PAID

There are five ways for planners to make a living.

1. *Commission only.* These planners don't make a cent unless they sell you something that carries a sales commission. So don't expect much "planning" time. They have to sell, and will probably recommend the highest-commission products going (see page 561). Commission-only planners are sometimes insurance salespeople in disguise.

2. *Fee and commission.* This is probably the most common arrangement. The planner charges a fee for basic advice and earns commissions on any products you buy. Commissions may or may not be deducted from the upfront fee.

But make no mistake about it: Sales commissions are the driving force and produce the same biases you see in commission-only planners. About half the planners disclose their commissions to clients, according to a study by the Securities and Exchange Commission. The rest leave you in the dark unless you press for information. Some certified public accountants are also fee-and-commission salespeople—so always ask.

Many of these advisors press you to start with an overall financial plan, generated by computer and costing anywhere from $250 to $1,500. "Asking" a computer for advice makes the planner seem more objective. But who sets up the rules that the computer has to follow? The planner, of course. And who builds the basic computer programs? Firms in thrall to financial-product companies and to the planners who do the selling. So biases are programmed in. Skip these plans—they're selling tools.

I am not suggesting that you can't get good service and wise advice from fee-and-commission planners. But in judging any proposed investment, keep in mind that it was chosen with an eye to the planner's needs as well as yours. A bias toward high-commission products is easy to spot. More subtle is the bias to sell you *something* in cases where nothing would have served.

3. *Fee offset.* These planners set a fixed fee for their advice. You might pay by the hour, by the job, or by the month. You might pay a percentage of the money the planner manages for you. Any sales commissions the planner earns are subtracted from your basic fee. So the planner has no strong incentive to urge you to buy risky high-commission products. Either way, you pay the same.

4. *Fee only.* These planners charge only for advice. As with fee-

write a palpable check. Even the insurance policies don't carry commissions (or only minor ones). Instead, the planner charges for the time spent analyzing your insurance needs and handling the policies' purchase. By contrast, of the money paid to the fee-and-commission planner, you see only the upfront cost. The rest of the planner's compensation slides gently out of the checks you write for insurance premiums or mutual funds. The fee-and-commission planner feels cheaper, but you have actually paid him or her more.

	The amount charged by a	
	Fee-only	Fee-and-commission
Product	planner	planner
Financial plan	$6,000	$ 1,500
Life-insurance premium: $1,500	750*	975
Disability-insurance premium: $2,000	750*	1,300
Mutual funds: $150,000	1,500†	9,000
Total cost	$9,000	$12,775

* At $150 an hour.
† At 1 percent a year for money management.
Source: Lynn Hopewell CFP, Falls Church, Virginia.

If you want a planner, look first for one with a fee-only or fee-offset practice who will work on narrow problems at an hourly rate. I can't say whether fee planners are more or less competent than commission planners, but I feel they're on my side.

If you choose a fee-and-commission planner, discuss what you need, ask for an hourly rate, and suggest that if you buy any products, the commission be deducted from the hourly rate. That way, the planner gets paid for his or her time whether you buy anything or not—which might relieve the planner's compulsion to sell.

Whoever you work with, accept only advice that seems *appropriate* to you. If you're uncertain about the alternatives a planner presents, you have only to mumble and hesitate until the session is over. If you think you'd like to work with a particular planner, but don't feel experienced enough to judge the advice, start small. Follow one or two of the planner's recommendations and see what happens. Leave most of your money in the bank until you feel that both of you know what you are doing.

offset planners, their fee structures vary—hourly charges, monthly retainers, fees per job. Any products they sell are entirely no-load—meaning that no sales commissions are attached. Some fee-only planners (especially certified public accountants) sell no products at all. They give you advice, then turn you loose. In that case, take care to buy no-load products without any further help. Otherwise, you will pay double: once for the plan and once for the services of a stockbroker or insurance agent.

Incidentally, fees charged for tax and investment advice can be written off on your income-tax return. They're part of that bagful of miscellaneous expenses that are deductible to the extent that they exceed 2 percent of your adjusted gross income. Sales commissions are not similarly deductible up front; they're used to reduce your taxable profits when you sell.

5. *Salary and bonus* (or commission). This is typical of the financial planners employed by some banks and S&Ls. Generally speaking, they design plans around bank-sold products: certificates of deposit, money market deposit accounts, and mutual funds. They may also act as agents for insurance companies, in which case tax-deferred annuities and insurance products rise to the top of their list.

ONE WAY OR ANOTHER, YOU PAY, YOU PAY

Which type of planner is more expensive—one who charges sales commissions or one who charges fees?

Superficially, fee-only or fee-offset planners seem more expensive. You pay more for The Plan, if you want one. You pay hourly fees for analysis and advice. You may pay monthly retainers, or a fixed percentage of your assets that the planner keeps under management. What you *don't* pay is sales commissions. Any products that the planner buys for you should be no-load (no-sales-charge).

By contrast, fee-and-commission planners might charge $250 to $1,500 for The Plan. All the rest, they say, is "free." But it's not free. The planners earn sales commissions, which come out of the money you pay for insurance policies, limited partnerships, mutual funds, and other products. Because you don't write a separate check for these commissions, you may not realize how large they are.

THE TABLE BELOW SHOWS YOU WHAT THE TWO TYPES OF PLANNERS MIGHT EARN FROM AN ACTUAL JOB. Everything paid to the fee-only planner is visible. The client has to

WHEN A PLANNER DOES YOU WRONG

In the largely unregulated industry of financial planning, no formal body sets the rules and punishes the rulebreakers. You can complain to the International Association for Financial Planning in Atlanta or to the schools that grant the financial-planner designations (page 831). But all they can do is yank the offender's professional certification or membership—hardly an onerous penalty, since he or she can go on practicing without it. Furthermore, these groups will probably not lift a finger until a planner has been found guilty in another forum. To take just one example, the College for Financial Planning revoked the CFP degrees for two of its graduates only after a federal court sentenced them to prison.

Here's a sampling of the complaints typically brought against financial planners:

· Misrepresenting the tax benefits and investment outlook for limited partnerships.

· Failing to tell the truth about how large a fee the planner was earning.

· Failing to diversify a client's investments to minimize risk.

· Selling "rare" coins at hugely inflated values.

· Roping clients into outright frauds: nonexistent investments, Ponzi schemes, misrepresentations of every sort.

· Putting clients into investments unsuitable for someone of their age and circumstances.

· Giving bad tax advice.

· Failing to disclose that the planner had a financial interest in the investment being sold.

· Exaggerating an investment's likely yield, while failing to disclose the risks.

· Failing to process a client's investments or insurance properly, resulting in a loss of money.

· Ignoring a client's specific investment instructions and goals.

If you think you have grounds for suing your planner, start by trying to work out a settlement personally—either with the planner or with the firm. Often, a letter from your lawyer helps. If you're stonewalled, your next step depends on the nature of the planner's business. If the planner is a stockbroker, call your state's securities commission (get the phone number from the information operator in your state's capital or call the North American Securities Administrators Association, 202-737-0900). Or you can go to arbitration (page 570). For an insurance-agent planner, call the state insurance commission. Your state might also be able to help with planners who aren't brokers or insurance agents. Otherwise, you'll have to sue. If the deal was a fraud to begin with, however, there may not be any money left to recover.

TO PROTECT YOURSELF

When doing business with a planner, proceed in the same orderly way that you would with a stockbroker (page 563)—with written goals, notes of conversations, and so on. In a confrontation, you might find that the planner kept his or her own notes, which a court or arbitration board might consider more credible than your memory.

If the planner tells you that a specific investment is low risk, ask for a letter confirming that diagnosis. This is the kind of "paper trail" that supports a winning lawsuit. It may also encourage your planner to proceed with more caution and exactitude. If you get a letter from your planner confirming an investment strategy, and it differs in any way from your recollection, call the planner immediately, then send a letter laying out the course that you want taken.

AUNT JANE'S LAST RECIPE: A DO-IT-YOURSELF FINANCIAL PLAN

Over the next eight weeks, take the following eight steps to success.

MAKE A LIST OF SPECIFIC OBJECTIVES.

The list might read: "a college education for Sarah and Emily, a down payment on a house, graduate school for Josh, hockey camp for Eric next year, Heather's wedding, two weeks in France year after next, a retirement income worth $40,000 a year." Put down exactly what you want. Your objectives will change as your life does, but you should always know what you're working toward.

DRAW UP A SPENDING PLAN.

This isn't a big deal. You've known about budgets all your life, and if you've forgotten, there's always Chapter 8.

CALCULATE WHAT YOU HAVE TO SAVE.

This isn't a big deal either, once you've specified what you're aiming for. Ask yourself, "How much will each objective cost?" and "When am I going to need the money?" Then point your savings toward those goals. In the Appendix, you'll find tables for figuring your long-term college and retirement savings. Short-term savings can be plotted in your head. You want to go to France year after next? Take this year's price, divide by 24, and put away that much per month. Nothing complicated about it.

You *will* have to coordinate your savings with your spending plan, which is the hard part. But if you didn't intend to try, you never would have bought this book. (You say that your mother bought this book for you? Oh, well. Try anyway.)

SECURE WHAT YOU HAVE.

This is your safety net: life, health, disability, homeowner's, and auto insurance. I've looked for inexpensive coverage, where it exists. Do-it-yourselfers can buy some policies by phone. Or ask an insurance agent to buy them for you.

DEVELOP A RISK PLAN.

Decide on a prudent level of risk for someone of your age, goals, and circumstances. On this point, Chapter 21 should steer you right.

FOLLOW THROUGH WITH AN INVESTMENT PLAN.

You will do splendidly with a few no-load mutual funds, chosen yourself and held long-term, plus some Treasury securities, tax exempts, or certificates of deposit.

CHECK OUT A TAX PLAN.

Tax planning isn't nearly the gold mine it used to be, now that so many deductions have been eliminated. You can't be tempted by foolish tax-shelter partnerships because most of them have gone out of business. Chiefly, you need a tax-deductible retirement plan (Chapter 29) and, if you're in a high bracket, municipal bonds. What could be easier? If you have a high net worth, however, you'll be forced to deal with estate taxes, trusts, executive-compensation contracts, and all the other tax entanglements that wealth is heir to. *That's* when you need professional help—and only a handful of the most experienced planners can serve.

More likely, your outriders will include a clutch of highly specialized professionals: tax lawyer, accountant, actuary, investment advisor.

A RETIREMENT PLAN.

The savings part you can do yourself. For how much to save, see Chapter 29 and the Appendix (page 884). When retirement day comes, however, you may need professional advice. Chapter 30 gives you a look at the landscape. Then ask an accountant to lay out the consequences of all your tax and pension choices. You can't afford to make a mistake. Once you've worked out your total retirement resources, the accountant can project a spending and investment plan that will carry you through the rest of your life. Or you can use the tables in this book to do that job yourself.

And that's it. The planning process from first sharpened pencil to final phone call. A project you can handle, step by step, just by applying some basic, down-home common sense.

For generations, most Americans have managed their money themselves and done a pretty good job of it. And they still can. The only trick is to turn your back on today's insanely complex financial marketplace and buy the simple things that you can analyze yourself. Trust me on this one. In the world of money, one or two clear and strong ideas, persisted in, will make you richer in the end.

AFTERWORD

Many people have contributed to this book but none so much as Virginia Wilson. Virginia has been my associate for many years, both at *Newsweek* and for more than a decade of newspaper columns. Her expertise is unparalleled. She took on the burden of fact checking this book and found errors that even some of the specialists missed.

Lynn Kane, also of *Newsweek,* keeps my office and professional life together, against great odds. She hunted up material I needed and stood off the world when I hunkered down to write.

The chapters were read and commented on by experts in many fields. I greatly appreciate the time they spent and the pains they took to set me straight.

To the following collaborators, a toast.

John Allen of Allen-Warren, Inc., Arvada, Colorado, a financial planner who loves precision and accuracy above all things; Richard Anderson, vice-chancellor for administration and finance, Washington University in St. Louis; Neal Blaher, of the Orlando, Florida, law firm of Duckworth, Allen, Dyer & Doppelp (Bob Dyer instructs me on securities arbitration); William G. Brennan, partner, Ernst & Young; Kathleen Brouder, director of the College Scholarship Service's information bureau, of The College Board in New York City; Kurt Brouwer of Brouwer & Janachowski, Inc., in San Francisco, managers of mutual-fund accounts; Mary E. Calhoun, consultant to securities lawyers and expert witness in securities cases; William P. Cantwell, a partner in the law firm of Sherman & Howard in Denver; Mark Coler, president, Mercer, Inc., in New York City, which keeps track of discount brokerage firms; Glenn Daily, independent insurance consultant in New York City and author of *The Individual Investor's Guide to Low-Load Insurance Products;* Peter Elinsky, partner and national director for compensation, employee benefits, and tax, KPMG Peat Marwick (for some parts of this book, Peter is practically co-author), and Nick Zieser, also of Peat Marwick; Phil Gambino, press officer for the Social Security Administration; Harry Gross, partner in Kwasha Lipton, employee benefit consultants, Fort Lee, New Jersey; from the Health Insurance Association of America, Jon Gabel, Geza Kadar, Harvie E. Raymond, and Susan Van Gelder; Thomas J. Herzfeld, president of Thomas J. Herzfeld Advisors, Inc., a Miami investment firm specializing in closed-end mutual funds; Judy Hole of CBS News, who found the story line in a couple of chapters when I'd lost it; and Lynn Hopewell, Certified Financial Planner, Falls Church, Virginia.

Also, James Hunt of the National Insurance Consumer Organization; Allan B. Hunter, partner, Neuberger & Berman; Sheldon Jacobs, of the *No-Load Fund Investor,* Hastings-on-Hudson, New York; David Kahn and Stuart Kessler, partners in the New York City accounting firm of Goldstein Golub Kessler & Co.; Christine Carter Lynch, managing editor of the *Lynch Municipal Advisory Letter* in Santa Fe, New Mexico; John Markese, director of research for the American Association of Individual Investors; Wesley G. McCain, chairman of Eclipse Financial Asset Trust and of Towneley Capital Management, Inc., in New York City, managers of institutional, individual, and mutual-fund accounts; Drs. Richard W. McEnally and Richard J. Rendleman, Jr., professors of finance at the University of North Carolina's Business School at Chapel Hill, specialists in securities options and futures; Alexander Miller, president, Shareholder Communications Corp., New York City; Richard L. D. Morse, professor emeritus, Kansas State University, who can see beneath the surface of any advertised interest rate; Jeffrey O'Connell, the father of no-fault auto insurance and professor of law at the University of Virginia School of Law; Timothy Pfeifer, consulting actuary for Tillinghast, a Towers Perrin Co., Chicago; from the no-load mutual-fund group T. Rowe Price in Baltimore, Steven Norwitz and Jane White of public relations, who produced tables tirelessly, Preston G. Athey, vice-president and portfolio manager specializing in emerging-growth companies, Edward A. Wiese, vice-president and portfolio manager, fixed-income division, and associate portfolio manager Christy DiPeitro.

Also, John T. Reed, editor of the *Real Estate Investor's Monthly,* Danville, California; Kenneth Scholen of the National Center for Home

Equity Conversion, Marshall, Minnesota; Muriel Siebert, president and chairperson of the discount brokerage firm of Muriel Siebert & Co., Inc., New York City; Harold Skipper, professor of risk management and insurance at Georgia State University; Edward Snitzer, partner, Prudent Management Associates, Philadelphia; Deborah Summerlin, manager, insurance lines, at the American Association of Insurance Services; from USAA Life Insurance Co., Kenneth McClure, vice-president of life and health sales, and Richard Jones, director of health sales; from USAA, Laurens Jockers, vice-president, auto insurance, and Robert Brakey, senior vice-president, property and casualty underwriting; from The Vanguard Group of no-load mutual funds, in Valley Forge, Pennsylvania, Ian MacKinnon, senior vice-president of the fixed-income group (I also stole a couple of Ian's jokes), and Jeremy Duffield, senior vice-president for planning and development; Luis Vigdor, gold-coin expert and head of the Industry Council of Tangible Assets in Washington, D.C.; Barry Vinocur, editor-in-chief of *Stanger's Investment Advisor* in Shrewsbury, New Jersey; Timothy B. Walker, of counsel at the law firm of Cox, Mustain-Wood & Walker, Littleton, Colorado; and Lawrence W. Waggoner, a professor of law at the University of Michigan Law School.

Many of the readers and critics above produced tables to illustrate useful points, as did Larry Siegel, managing director of research, and economist Paul Kaplan, both of Ibbotson Associates in Chicago, and James Floyd, senior research analyst at The Leuthold Group in Minneapolis. Dozens of other specialists—regrettably, too many to name—talked me through knotty problems and helped me put issues into perspective.

Making this book happen were Mort Janklow, who truly deserves the sobriquet Superagent, and Alice Mayhew, my wizard editor at Simon & Schuster, whose patience *does* know an end. My old friend Ed Engberg suggested the title. My husband, David, read everything and made suggestions. Dolly Howard kept our household functioning. My wonderful friends listened to my troubles, murmured sympathetically, and took David out to dinner during the weeks when I clapped myself into book jail to get chapters out.

Warmest thanks to all.

APPENDIXES

1. THE BEST INSURANCE PLANNER YOU WILL EVER FIND

Here's the professional way of establishing how much life insurance you need. All it demands of you is blind obedience. Follow the directions and you'll get the right answer.

You'll be doing a "present value" calculation, which accounts for the fact that a dollar received or spent right now is worth more than a dollar received or spent in the future. In professional lingo, you will be "discounting" future income and expenses to find out what that money is worth today.

The easiest way to explain this concept is with an example.

Assume that you owe your landlord $1,000 tomorrow. To make that payment, you need $1,000 in hand right now.

But if that $1,000 payment isn't due until next year, you need only $934.58 today, invested at 7 percent. If the payment isn't due until 10 years from now, you need only $508.35, also invested at 7 percent. That's what "discounting" means. That's the "present value" of a future $1,000 payment.

What if inflation is running at 4 percent, so that 10 years from now your $1,000 rent will have grown to $1,480? Present value analysis can handle that, too. In this case, you'd need $752.48, invested at 7 percent.

To do the calculations, you need a yellow pad, a sharp pencil, a hand-held calculator, and a trusting heart. Your reward is knowing that the size of your life-insurance policy will be exactly right.

All credit for this presentation goes to financial planner John Allen of Arvada, Colorado. He offered me the method and then fussed with my prose until we got it right.

Step One

PICK AN AFTER-TAX RATE OF RETURN THAT YOU THINK YOU CAN PROBABLY EARN ON YOUR MONEY. Keep it reasonable. For 1991, a good number is 6 to 7 percent. I'd call 8 percent aggressive and 5 percent conservative. You will use this rate of return at key points in the following calculation. It is also known as the "discount rate."

After-tax rate of return or discount rate _____%

Step Two

WHAT SOURCES OF MONEY WOULD YOUR SURVIVORS HAVE IF YOU DIED TODAY? List all available income and savings. Don't include the value of your house, if your spouse will continue to live there. Home equity should be counted only if your spouse would sell the house and live on the net proceeds.

· Your spouse's wages.	$_____
· Social Security "family benefits" (payable to your spouse and children until the youngest child reaches age 16). *	$_____
· Social Security "survivor's benefits," payable to your spouse from your Social Security account, usually starting when your spouse reaches ago 60.†	$_____
OR	
Your spouse's own "retirement benefit," payable from his or her own Social Security account, starting as early as age 62.‡	$_____
· Any portion of a pension you are currently receiving that would be paid to your spouse.	$_____
· Any pension due your spouse from his or her own earnings.	$_____
· The value of your cash savings.	$_____
· The value of your investments.	$_____
· Life-insurance proceeds.	$_____
· Other lump sum payments.	$_____
· Other usable assets, such as real estate.	$_____

---

* To find this payment, see page 777. Your unmarried children are due their own Social Security payments up to age 18 (19, if they're still in high school, and perhaps for life if they're disabled). I've left these extra years of payments off the chart, just to make your life a little simpler.
† To find this payment, see page 777. Younger spouses can get payments if they're disabled or if they're caring for eligible children.
‡ To find these payments, see page 777.

Step Three

HOW SOON DOES YOUR FAMILY GET THIS MONEY, AND HOW LONG DO THEY HAVE IT? For each of the money sources listed above, list: (1) the likely annual payment they will get; (2) the probable rate of growth, which can be different for each item; (3) the net discount rate; * (4) the number of years they have to wait before the money becomes available;† (5) the number of years over which the money will be paid.‡

Money source	Current payment	Rate of growth	Net dis- count rate	How soon available	How long paid
1. _____	$_____	____%	____%	_____	_____
2. _____	$_____	____%	____%	_____	_____
3. _____	$_____	____%	____%	_____	_____

4. _____	$_____	____%	____%	_____	_____
5. _____	$_____	____%	____%	_____	_____
6. _____	$_____	____%	____%	_____	_____
7. _____	$_____	____%	____%	_____	_____
8. _____	$_____	____%	____%	_____	_____
9. _____	$_____	____%	____%	_____	_____
10. _____	$_____	____%	____%	_____	_____

* The net discount rate equals the discount rate chosen in Step One, minus the rate of growth selected for this item in the table. For example, if your discount rate is 7 percent and your rate of growth is 5 percent, your net discount rate is 2 percent.

† The first year your spouse will receive the money. Use 1 for any funds available within a year of your death. Use 2 for money payable the year after your death. For example, if you die in 1992 and a certificate of deposit is payable in 1993, the answer to "How Soon Available" is 2. If you die in 1992, and your spouse will get Social Security in 2002, that money becomes available in year 11—the year of your death plus 10 years.

‡ The number of years your spouse will receive the money. Begin with the year the payment starts. For lifetime payments, use the spouse's life expectancy (tables on page 901) plus a cushion of three years or so.

Here's how to enter your various sources of money onto the table. I've assumed a surviving wife aged 45, with two college-bound children aged 15 and 18.

The net discount rate is the discount rate chosen in Step One—for this example, 7 percent—minus the rate of growth you choose for each particular item. (For the life expectancy table, see page 901.) I haven't illustrated every money source; just enough of them to give you the idea.

1. WAGES. *Current payment*—your spouse's current income after tax. *Rate of growth*—the annual raises your spouse expects (say, 5 percent). *How soon available*—put down 1, because wages are payable currently. *How long paid*—until your spouse will quit or retire, say until age 62 (which means through age 61). That's 17 years. (Use this same method for figuring the value of any pension you are currently receiving that would be payable to your spouse.)

Money source	Current payment	Rate of growth	Net dis- count rate	How soon available	How long paid
Wages	$30,000	5%	2%	1	17

2. SOCIAL SECURITY FAMILY BENEFITS. *Current payment*—what your family would receive this year, in spouse's and children's benefits. *Rate of growth*—Social Security normally rises by the inflation rate, so say 4 percent. *How soon available*—put down 1, because payments would begin immediately. *How long paid*—until the youngest child reaches age 18 (meaning through the 17th year). That's three years more.

Money source	Current payment	Rate of growth	Net discount rate	How soon available	How long paid
Social Security family benefits	$13,000	4%	3%	1	3

3. SOCIAL SECURITY RETIREMENT BENEFIT. *Current payment*—the amount your spouse will receive when benefits start. *Rate of growth*—Social Security normally rises by the inflation rate, so say 4 percent. *How soon available*—the year your spouse will retire, say at age 62. *How long paid*—starting in the retirement year and lasting until life expectancy, plus, say, three years. For a 45-year-old woman, life expectancy is 83; adding three years brings you to age 86. That means payments *through* the 85th year, stopping when the 86th year begins—for a total of 24 years of payments.

Money source	Current payment	Rate of growth	Net discount rate	How soon available	How long paid
Social Security retirement benefit	$9,000	4%	3%	18	24

4a. SPOUSE'S PENSION, PAYABLE IN THE FUTURE, WITH NO COST-OF-LIVING ADJUSTMENT. *Current payment*—the estimated size of your spouse's pension in the first year. Your spouse's employer can help make the estimate. *Rate of growth*—enter zero. *How soon available*—the year your spouse will retire, say age 62—18 years away. *How long paid*—starting in the retirement year and lasting until life expectancy. For a 45-year-old woman, life expectancy is 83; adding three years brings you to age 86. That means payments *through* the 85th year, stopping when the 86th year begins—for a total of 24 years of payments.

Money source	Current payment	Rate of growth	Net discount rate	How soon available	How long paid
Pension	$12,000	0	7%	18	24

4b. *SPOUSE'S PENSION, PAYABLE IN THE FUTURE, WITH A COST-OF-LIVING ADJUSTMENT.* Apologies. This one is a little more complicated. Fortunately, you don't have to understand it. Just fill in the blanks and it will come out okay.

First, find out from your spouse's employer what he or she is likely to receive at retirement, and what the cost-of-living adjustment is. Then enter here: *First-year pension payment:* _____. *The number of years before it will be paid:* _____. *The cost-of-living adjustment:* _____.

Then go to the Accumulated Capital Table (page 860). Go down the left-hand column until you reach the number of years before the pension will be paid. Follow across the row to the percentage representing the cost-of-living adjustment, and enter here the factor you find there. *Factor:* _____. Divide the first-year pension payment by the factor, and enter the result: $_____. This is today's deflated value of that first-year pension payment.

Example: Assume a $24,000 pension, payable in 18 years with a 3 percent cost-of-living adjustment. The factor from the Accumulated Capital Table is 1.16. Divided into the pension, you get $20,690.

Now you're ready to fill in the table on page 845. *Current payment* —the deflated value of your future pension payment, as calculated above. *Rate of growth*—the cost-of-living adjustment. *How soon available*—the year your spouse will retire, say age 62, 18 years away. *How long paid*—starting in the retirement year and lasting until life expectancy. For a 45-year-old woman, life expectancy is 83; adding three years brings you to age 86. That means payments *through* the 85th year, for a total of 24 years of payments.

Money source	Current payment	Rate of growth	Net discount rate	How soon available	How long paid
Pension	$20,690	3%	4%	18	24

4c. *SPOUSE'S PENSION, PAYABLE CURRENTLY, WITH A COST-OF-LIVING ADJUSTMENT.* This is for couples who have already retired. *Current payment*—the first-year amount your spouse will get after your death (from the spouse's own pension, or the survivor benefit payable from your pension, or both). *Rate of growth*—the cost-of-living adjustment (say, 2 percent). *How soon available*—immediately, so enter 1. *How long paid*—life expectancy plus a cushion. If the wife is 69, life expectancy is 17 years. That's to age 86. Adding a three-year cushion brings you to 89. So payments continue through the 88th year, stopping in the 89th—for a total of 20 years of payments.

Money source	Current payment	Rate of growth	Net dis-count rate	How soon available	How long paid
Pension	$12,00	2%	5%	1	20

5. *FIVE-YEAR CERTIFICATE OF DEPOSIT. Current payment*—the full amount of the CD at maturity. *Rate of growth*—the net the CD is earning, after tax (say, 6 percent). *How soon available*—when the certificate matures. *How long paid*—enter 1, because it is paid all at once.

Money source	Current payment	Rate of growth	Net dis-count rate	How soon available	How long paid
Five-year CD	$20,000	6%	1%	5	1

6. *MUTUAL FUNDS. Current payment*—the current value of all your funds. *Rate of growth*—use the discount rate (after-tax rate of return) that you chose in Step One, even if your funds are, at the moment, growing at a higher rate. You chose the discount rate for long-term planning purposes. *How soon available*—right away, so enter 1. *How long paid*—the money is available all at once, so enter 1.

Money source	Current payment	Rate of growth	Net dis-count rate	How soon available	How long paid
Mutual funds	$30,000	7%	0%	1	1

7. *LIFE-INSURANCE PROCEEDS. Current payment*—the proceeds of the policy if you died tomorrow. *Rate of growth*—use the discount rate (rate of return) that you chose in Step One, which is the after-tax rate your investments are expected to earn. *How soon available*—right away, so enter 1. *How long paid*—the money is available all at once, so enter 1.

Money source	Current payment	Rate of growth	Net dis-count rate	How soon available	How long paid
Life insurance	$150,000	7%	0%	1	1

Step Four

WHAT IS THE VALUE OF EACH MONEY SOURCE IN TODAY'S DOLLARS? To find out, you do a present value calculation. It shows you what all your resources—income, savings, wages, investments, Social Security benefits, and future pension—would be worth today, if you had all the money to finance them in a single lump sum.

To get the right answer, you'll have to consult the table you filled in on page 845 and punch up a few numbers on a hand-held calculator. On the left, below, I show you the steps. On the right, an example.

The example calculates the present value of your spouse's earnings over the next 15 years. I've assumed that the spouse is currently earning $30,000 after tax, and will get 5 percent raises every year. The discount rate (from Step One) is 7 percent. The net discount rate (7 percent minus your spouse's 5 percent raises) is 2 percent.

This isn't hard! Just follow the bouncing ball.

The bouncing ball		The example
A. Go to the first source of income on your table (in Step Three).	$_____	$30,000
B. Take the net discount rate.	_____ %	2%
C. Take the number of years over which the money will be paid.	_____	17
D. Go to the Discount Table on page 864. Read across the top to find the net discount rate. Read down the left-hand side to find the number of years over which the money will be paid. Enter the factor you find where these two lines intersect.	_____	14.58
E. Multiply the current payment by that factor.	$_____ × _____ $_____	$30,000 × 14.58 $437,400
F. Stop. Do some deep knee bends. Get a glass of beer. Stare out the window.		
G. Take the net discount rate again.	_____ %	2%
H. Look at how soon the money will be available.	_____	1
I. Go to the Accumulated Capital Table on page 860. Read across the top to find the net discount rate. Read down the left-hand side to find how soon the money will be available. Enter the factor you find where these two lines intersect.	_____	1.00
J. Enter the number you got in E above. Divide by the factor you got in I.	$_____ ÷ _____	$437,400 ÷ 1.00
Present value:	$_____	$437,400

Run through this calculation for each source of money on your table. (Time-saving tip: Anything available immediately and payable all at once is worth exactly its current value. If your mutual funds are worth $30,000, put that down. If your life insurance is worth $150,000, put that down. Ditto for savings accounts, money market mutual funds, and stock portfolios.)

Add everything up. You'll get a single lump sum, representing the present value of all of the resources you expect to have in the future.

Money source	Present value
1. _____	$_____
2. _____	$_____
3. _____	$_____
4. _____	$_____
5. _____	$_____
6. _____	$_____
7. _____	$_____
8. _____	$_____
9. _____	$_____
10. _____	$_____
Total	$_____

Step Five

WHAT WOULD IT COST YOUR FAMILY TO LIVE AFTER YOUR DEATH? Go by your spending plan (page 146) and eliminate any expenses related to you. If you count yourself in the middle class, your survivors should be able to pay their daily bills with 75 to 80 percent of your current after-tax income.

On separate lines, enter any temporary or unusual expenses, such as your funeral and your kids' college. For college, use the current one-year cost of the kind of school you want each child to attend: tuition, room, board, books, transportation, and incidentals.

Throw in a contingency fund to cover the accidents of life. A good figure might be 10 percent of your income.

An extra lump sum does double duty. It provides more principal for your spouse to live on. At the spouse's death, it becomes a legacy for your children.

· Daily expenses while the children are young.	$_____
· Daily expenses after the last child leaves home.	$_____
· The mortgage.	$_____
· Other expenses.	$_____
· The cost of your funeral and other final expenses.	$_____
· College expenses for Child One.*	$_____
· College expenses for Child Two.	$_____
· Other lump sums payable, such as estate taxes.	$_____
· A contingency fund.	$_____
· A legacy for your children.	$_____

* Enter each child separately. They will attend school at different times, so their expenses carry different weights.

Step Six

WHEN WILL THESE DOLLARS BE NEEDED, AND FOR HOW LONG? For each expense, put down: (1) The total one-year cost, today; (2) the rate at which you expect that particular price to rise; (3) the net discount rate;* (4) the number of years before the expense begins;† (5) the number of years the expense will continue.‡

Expense	Current cost	Inflation rate	Net dis- count rate	Starting year	How long paid
1. _____	$_____	_____%	_____%	_____	_____
2. _____	$_____	_____%	_____%	_____	_____
3. _____	$_____	_____%	_____%	_____	_____
4. _____	$_____	_____%	_____%	_____	_____
5. _____	$_____	_____%	_____%	_____	_____
6. _____	$_____	_____%	_____%	_____	_____
7. _____	$_____	_____%	_____%	_____	_____
8. _____	$_____	_____%	_____%	_____	_____
9. _____	$_____	_____%	_____%	_____	_____
10. _____	$_____	_____%	_____%	_____	_____

* The net discount rate equals the discount rate chosen in Step One, minus the rate of growth selected for this item in the table. For example, if your discount rate is 7 percent and your inflation rate is 5 percent, your net discount rate is 2 percent.
† The first year this bill will have to be paid. Use 1 for any expenses that start immediately or within a year of your death. Use 2 for expenses that start the year after your death. For example, if you die in 1992 and your child starts college in 1993, the "Starting Year" is 2. If you die in 1992 and college won't begin until 2002, that cost arrives in year 11—the year of your death plus 10 years.
‡ Begin with the year the payment starts. For lifetime payments, use the spouse's life expectancy (tables on page 901) plus a cushion of three years or so.

Here's how to enter your various sources of money onto the table. I've assumed a surviving wife aged 45, with two college-bound children aged 15 and 18.

The net discount rate is the discount rate chosen in Step One—for this example, 7 percent—minus the rate of growth you choose for each particular item. For life-expectancy tables, see page 901.

1. DAILY EXPENSES WHILE THE CHILDREN ARE YOUNG.

Expense—the annual cost of living for your spouse and children until the last child gets out of school. *Current cost*—75 to 80 percent of what you budget today. *Inflation rate*—pick a likely average rate (say, 4.5 percent). *Starting year*—these expenses start now, so put down 1. *How long paid*—through the youngest child's 21st year. For a 15-year-old, that's the current year plus 6 years, 7 in all.

Expense	Current cost	Inflation rate	Net discount rate	Starting year	How long paid
Daily expenses while the children are young	$39,000	4.5%	2.5%	1	7

2. DAILY EXPENSES AFTER THE LAST CHILD LEAVES HOME.

Expense—the annual cost of living for your spouse alone. *Current cost*—often, one-third less than the family expenses when the children were home. *Inflation rate*—pick a likely average rate (say 4 percent). You can assume a lower (or higher) inflation rate in your future than you picked for the years that the children were small. *Starting year* —these expenses start in the year the last child leaves home; for this example, in the eighth year from now, when the spouse is 52. *How long paid*—for the rest of the spouse's life. Figure life expectancy plus a cushion of three years or so. For a 45-year-old woman, life expectancy is 83; adding the cushion brings you to 86. So these expenses will last *through* the 85th year, stopping when the 86th year begins. That's 34 years of costs, from age 52 through age 85.

Expense	Current cost	Inflation rate	Net discount rate	Starting year	How long paid
Daily expenses after the last child leaves home	$26,000	4%	3%	8	34

3. MORGAGE. *Expense*—the annual mortgage payment. *Current cost*—how much you pay each year. *Inflation rate*—zero for a fixed-rate mortgage. For simplicity's sake, use zero for an adjustable-rate mortgage; even though payments rise in one year they may fall the next. *Starting year*—1, because payments have to be made right now. *How long paid*—the number of years until the loan is paid off.

Expense	Current cost	Inflation rate	Net dis-count rate	Starting year	How long paid
Mortgage	$17,500	0%	7%	1	12

4. FUNERAL AND FINAL EXPENSES. *Expense*—the cost of the funeral and settling the estate. *Current cost*—funeral home, lawyer's fees. *Inflation rate*—zero, because these costs are paid immediately. *Starting year* and *how long paid*—both 1, because all the expenses fall within the first year. Estate taxes are handled the same way.

Expense	Current cost	Inflation rate	Net dis-count rate	Starting year	How long paid
Funeral and final expenses	$7,000	0%	7%	1	1

5a. COLLEGE EXPENSES FOR CHILD ONE. *Expense*—the full cost of one year at college today (tuition, room, board, books, transportation, incidentals). *Current cost*—if you expect no college aid, put down the full amount for the school your child will attend. If your family will qualify for college aid, turn to page 428 to calculate how much of the college bill you might have to pay. *Inflation rate*—college costs are rising faster than other costs; for this example, I used 8 percent. *Starting year*—if the child will start school this year, or is in school already, put down 1. Otherwise put down the number of years before the first tuition bill is due. *How long paid*—put down the number of years until the child graduates: up to four years for undergraduates; more, if you want to finance graduate school.

Expense	Current cost	Inflation rate	Net dis-count rate	Starting year	How long paid
College expenses for Child One	$12,000	8%	−1%	1	4

5b. *COLLEGE EXPENSES FOR CHILD TWO.* *Expense*—the full cost of one year at college today (tuition, room, board, books, transportation, incidentals). *Current cost*—if you expect no college aid, put down the full amount for the school your child will attend. If your child will qualify for college aid, turn to page 428 to calculate how much of the college bill you might have to pay. *Inflation rate*—college costs are rising faster than other costs, but state schools generally rise at a lower rate than private ones; for this example, I've put the second child at a state school. *Starting year*—the number of years before the first tuition bill is due. *How long paid*—put down the number of years the child will be in school: up to four years for undergraduates; more, if you want to finance graduate school.

Expense	Current cost	Inflation rate	Net dis-count rate	Starting year	How long paid
College expenses for Child Two	$4,000	6%	1%	3	4

6. *A CONTINGENCY FUND.* *Expense*—your cushion, in case expenses are higher than you figured. *Current cost*—put down any sum that seems reasonable. *Inflation rate*—zero. This sum is treated as if it were paid all at once. *Starting year*—now, or 1. *How long paid*—immediately, or 1.

Expense	Current cost	Inflation rate	Net dis-count rate	Starting year	How long paid
Contingency fund	$10,000	0%	7%	1	1

7. *LEGACY.* *Expense*—the sum you would like to leave to your children. Your spouse can live on the income from this sum during his or her lifetime. *Current cost*—whatever you want to leave. *Inflation rate*—zero, because it's treated as paid all at once. *Starting year*—the year your spouse will probably die, which means life expectancy plus the cushion you have been using. In this example, the 45-year-old spouse will die after 41 years, so the legacy will be paid in the 42nd year. *How long paid*—all at once, or 1.

Expense	Current cost	Inflation rate	Net dis-count rate	Starting year	How long paid
Legacy	$100,000	0%	7%	42	1

Step Seven

WHAT IS THE VALUE OF ALL YOUR EXPENSES, IN TODAY'S DOLLARS?

Bad news.

You have to follow Step Four all over again. So I'm restating it here.

The example on the right in the table below shows how to figure the present value of the 45-year-old widow's $26,000 in annual living expenses, growing at the rate of 4 percent a year. She needs this money from the time her last child leaves home (in the eighth year from now, when she's 52) until her death (upon reaching age 86, after 34 years have passed).

A. Go to the first expense on your table in Step Six.	$	$26,000
B. Take the net discount rate.	%	3%
C. Take the number of years the expense will run.		34
D. Go to the Discount Table on page 864. Read across the top to find the net discount rate. Read down the left-hand side to find the number of years before the money will be paid. Enter the factor you find where these two lines intersect.		22.49
E. Multiply the current payment by that factor.	$	$26,000
	×	× 22.49
		$584,740
F. Stop. Watch a soap opera. Make some waffles with maple syrup. Jog around the block.		
G. Take the net discount rate again.	%	3%
H. Enter the number of years before the expenses start.		8
I. Go to the Accumulated Capital Table on page 860. Read across the top to find the net discount rate. Read down the left-hand side to find the number of years before the expenses start. Enter the factor you find where those two lines intersect.		1.23
J. Enter the number you got in E above.		$584,740
Divide by the factor you got in I.	÷	÷ 1.23
Present value:	$	$475,398

Run through this calculation for each expense on your table. Add everything up. Result: A single lump sum, representing the present value of all the expenses you expect to have in the future.

1._____ $_____

2._____ $_____

3._____ $_____

4._____ $_____

5._____ $_____

6._____ $_____

7._____ $_____

8._____ $_____

9._____ $_____

10._____ $_____

Total _____

Step Eight

DO YOU ALREADY HAVE ENOUGH MONEY? Compare the present value of all of your sources of money (Total, Step Four) with the present value of all your future expenses (Total, Step Seven).

Present value of all resources $_____
Minus: Present value of all expenses $_____
Difference (plus or minus) $_____

If your family's resources are greater than their expenses, throw away your worksheets and pour yourself another beer. You're in great shape. You don't need any more life insurance.

If your family's expenses will be greater than their resources, you do indeed need life insurance. So go on to . . .

Step Nine

HOW MUCH MORE LIFE INSURANCE DO YOU NEED? Buy enough to cover the total deficit shown in Step Eight. If you're $150,000 short, buy a $150,000 life-insurance policy.

Your immediate needs can probably be covered by inexpensive term insurance (page 252). Redo this calculation every three to five years, to see how you're doing.

If, at middle age, you decide that you'll want to carry life insurance into older age, start converting some of your term insurance into a cash-value policy (page 262).

NOTES TO THIS CALCULATION.

• I've assumed that the surviving spouse will use up all the money you left behind. Principal will be tapped for college expenses and other lump sums listed in Step Five, as well as for daily living expenses. If you want your spouse to live mostly on the income from principal, you will have to provide extra money—under "legacy," Step Six. This expense will probably have to be funded with additional life insurance.

• Assume a good salary for the widow only if she is already employed. If she starts work after her husband's death, her salary will probably be low.

• The trickiest part of this calculation is knowing how many years to count, because the answer isn't obvious. How many years before a particular benefit will begin? How many years will it be paid? There are two points to remember: First, *count the current year.* If your child is 15, and will be at home until graduating from college at age 21, that's 7 years from now: this year (your child's 15th), plus 6 years. Second, *when finding the number of years you have to wait for a benefit, don't count the year that a benefit begins.* Suppose you're 45 and will retire at age 62. You have 17 years to go—the current year plus 16 years, taking you through age 61. Age 62 isn't counted. What's the easiest way to count the years? Use your fingers. And toes.

• When both spouses work outside the home, the life insurance has to be done twice (two yellow pads) to find out how large a policy each of you needs. Do it once assuming that the husband dies first, and again assuming the wife dies first.

• Recheck your insurance every three to five years, or when something changes in your life—a new baby, an inheritance, or divorce. Maybe you'll need more coverage, maybe you'll need less.

2. THE ACCUMULATED CAPITAL AND DISCOUNT TABLES

ACCUMULATED CAPITAL
(in percentages)

Beginning of Year	−3.00	−2.50	−2.00	−1.50	−1.00	−0.50	0.00	0.50
1	1.00	1.00	1.00	1.00	1.00	1.00	1.00	1.00
2	0.97	0.98	0.98	0.99	0.99	1.00	1.00	1.01
3	0.94	0.95	0.96	0.97	0.98	0.99	1.00	1.01
4	0.91	0.93	0.94	0.96	0.97	0.99	1.00	1.02
5	0.89	0.90	0.92	0.94	0.96	0.98	1.00	1.02
6	0.86	0.88	0.90	0.93	0.95	0.98	1.00	1.03
7	0.83	0.86	0.89	0.91	0.94	0.97	1.00	1.03
8	0.81	0.84	0.87	0.90	0.93	0.97	1.00	1.04
9	0.78	0.82	0.85	0.89	0.92	0.96	1.00	1.04
10	0.76	0.80	0.83	0.87	0.91	0.96	1.00	1.05
11	0.74	0.78	0.82	0.86	0.90	0.95	1.00	1.05
12	0.72	0.76	0.80	0.85	0.90	0.95	1.00	1.06
13	0.69	0.74	0.78	0.83	0.89	0.94	1.00	1.06
14	0.67	0.72	0.77	0.82	0.88	0.94	1.00	1.07
15	0.65	0.70	0.75	0.81	0.87	0.93	1.00	1.07
16	0.63	0.68	0.74	0.80	0.86	0.93	1.00	1.08
17	0.61	0.67	0.72	0.79	0.85	0.92	1.00	1.08
18	0.60	0.65	0.71	0.77	0.84	0.92	1.00	1.09
19	0.58	0.63	0.70	0.76	0.83	0.91	1.00	1.09
20	0.56	0.62	0.68	0.75	0.83	0.91	1.00	1.10
21	0.54	0.60	0.67	0.74	0.82	0.90	1.00	1.10
22	0.53	0.59	0.65	0.73	0.81	0.90	1.00	1.11
23	0.51	0.57	0.64	0.72	0.80	0.90	1.00	1.12
24	0.50	0.56	0.63	0.71	0.79	0.89	1.00	1.12
25	0.48	0.54	0.62	0.70	0.79	0.89	1.00	1.13
26	0.47	0.53	0.60	0.69	0.78	0.88	1.00	1.13
27	0.45	0.52	0.59	0.68	0.77	0.88	1.00	1.14
28	0.44	0.50	0.58	0.66	0.76	0.87	1.00	1.14
29	0.43	0.49	0.57	0.65	0.75	0.87	1.00	1.15
30	0.41	0.48	0.56	0.65	0.75	0.86	1.00	1.16
31	0.40	0.47	0.55	0.64	0.74	0.86	1.00	1.16
32	0.39	0.46	0.53	0.63	0.73	0.85	1.00	1.17
33	0.38	0.44	0.52	0.62	0.72	0.85	1.00	1.17
34	0.37	0.43	0.51	0.61	0.72	0.85	1.00	1.18
35	0.36	0.42	0.50	0.60	0.71	0.84	1.00	1.18
36	0.34	0.41	0.49	0.59	0.70	0.84	1.00	1.19

1.00	1.50	2.00	2.50	3.00	3.50	4.00	4.50
1.00	1.00	1.00	1.00	1.00	1.00	1.00	1.00
1.01	1.02	1.02	1.03	1.03	1.04	1.04	1.05
1.02	1.03	1.04	1.05	1.06	1.07	1.08	1.09
1.03	1.05	1.06	1.08	1.09	1.11	1.12	1.14
1.04	1.06	1.08	1.10	1.13	1.15	1.17	1.19
1.05	1.08	1.10	1.13	1.16	1.19	1.22	1.25
1.06	1.09	1.13	1.16	1.19	1.23	1.27	1.30
1.07	1.11	1.15	1.19	1.23	1.27	1.32	1.36
1.08	1.13	1.17	1.22	1.27	1.32	1.37	1.42
1.09	1.14	1.20	1.25	1.30	1.36	1.42	1.49
1.10	1.16	1.22	1.28	1.34	1.41	1.48	1.55
1.12	1.18	1.24	1.31	1.38	1.46	1.54	1.62
1.13	1.20	1.27	1.34	1.43	1.51	1.60	1.70
1.14	1.21	1.29	1.38	1.47	1.56	1.67	1.77
1.15	1.23	1.32	1.41	1.51	1.62	1.73	1.85
1.16	1.25	1.35	1.45	1.56	1.68	1.80	1.94
1.17	1.27	1.37	1.48	1.60	1.73	1.87	2.02
1.18	1.29	1.40	1.52	1.65	1.79	1.95	2.11
1.20	1.31	1.43	1.56	1.70	1.86	2.03	2.21
1.21	1.33	1.46	1.60	1.75	1.92	2.11	2.31
1.22	1.35	1.49	1.64	1.81	1.99	2.19	2.41
1.23	1.37	1.52	1.68	1.86	2.06	2.28	2.52
1.24	1.39	1.55	1.72	1.92	2.13	2.37	2.63
1.26	1.41	1.58	1.76	1.97	2.21	2.46	2.75
1.27	1.43	1.61	1.81	2.03	2.28	2.56	2.88
1.28	1.45	1.64	1.85	2.09	2.36	2.67	3.01
1.30	1.47	1.67	1.90	2.16	2.45	2.77	3.14
1.31	1.49	1.71	1.95	2.22	2.53	2.88	3.28
1.32	1.52	1.74	2.00	2.29	2.62	3.00	3.43
1.33	1.54	1.78	2.05	2.36	2.71	3.12	3.58
1.35	1.56	1.81	2.10	2.43	2.81	3.24	3.75
1.36	1.59	1.85	2.15	2.50	2.91	3.37	3.91
1.37	1.61	1.88	2.20	2.58	3.01	3.51	4.09
1.39	1.63	1.92	2.26	2.65	3.11	3.65	4.27
1.40	1.66	1.95	2.32	2.73	3.22	3.79	4.47
1.42	1.68	2.00	2.37	2.81	3.33	3.95	4.67

(continued on page 862)

ACCUMULATED CAPITAL
(in percentages)
(continued from page 861)

Beginning of Year	5.00	5.50	6.00	6.50	7.00	7.50	8.00
1	1.00	1.00	1.00	1.00	1.00	1.00	1.00
2	1.05	1.06	1.06	1.07	1.07	1.08	1.08
3	1.10	1.11	1.12	1.13	1.14	1.16	1.17
4	1.16	1.17	1.19	1.21	1.23	1.24	1.26
5	1.22	1.24	1.26	1.29	1.31	1.34	1.36
6	1.28	1.31	1.34	1.37	1.40	1.44	1.47
7	1.34	1.38	1.42	1.46	1.50	1.54	1.59
8	1.41	1.45	1.50	1.55	1.61	1.66	1.71
9	1.48	1.53	1.59	1.65	1.72	1.78	1.85
10	1.55	1.62	1.69	1.76	1.84	1.92	2.00
11	1.63	1.71	1.79	1.88	1.97	2.06	2.16
12	1.71	1.80	1.90	2.00	2.10	2.22	2.33
13	1.80	1.90	2.01	2.13	2.25	2.38	2.52
14	1.89	2.01	2.13	2.27	2.41	2.56	2.72
15	1.98	2.12	2.26	2.41	2.58	2.75	2.94
16	2.08	2.23	2.40	2.57	2.76	2.96	3.17
17	2.18	2.36	2.54	2.74	2.95	3.18	3.43
18	2.29	2.48	2.69	2.92	3.16	3.42	3.70
19	2.41	2.62	2.85	3.11	3.38	3.68	4.00
20	2.53	2.77	3.03	3.31	3.62	3.95	4.32
21	2.65	2.92	3.21	3.52	3.87	4.25	4.66
22	2.79	3.08	3.40	3.75	4.14	4.57	5.03
23	2.93	3.25	3.60	4.00	4.43	4.91	5.44
24	3.07	3.43	3.82	4.26	4.74	5.28	5.87
25	3.23	3.61	4.05	4.53	5.07	5.67	6.34
26	3.39	3.81	4.29	4.83	5.43	6.10	6.85
27	3.56	4.02	4.55	5.14	5.81	6.56	7.40
28	3.73	4.24	4.82	5.48	6.21	7.05	7.99
29	3.92	4.48	5.11	5.83	6.65	7.58	8.63
30	4.12	4.72	5.42	6.21	7.11	8.14	9.32
31	4.32	4.98	5.74	6.61	7.61	8.75	10.06
32	4.54	5.26	6.09	7.04	8.15	9.41	10.87
33	4.76	5.55	6.45	7.50	8.72	10.12	11.74
34	5.00	5.85	6.84	7.99	9.33	10.88	12.68
35	5.25	6.17	7.25	8.51	9.98	11.69	13.69
36	5.52	6.51	7.69	9.06	10.68	12.57	14.79

8.50	9.00	9.50	10.00	10.50	11.00	11.50	12.00
1.00	1.00	1.00	1.00	1.00	1.00	1.00	1.00
1.09	1.09	1.10	1.10	1.11	1.11	1.12	1.12
1.18	1.19	1.20	1.21	1.22	1.23	1.24	1.25
1.28	1.30	1.31	1.33	1.35	1.37	1.39	1.40
1.39	1.41	1.44	1.46	1.49	1.52	1.55	1.57
1.50	1.54	1.57	1.61	1.65	1.69	1.72	1.76
1.63	1.68	1.72	1.77	1.82	1.87	1.92	1.97
1.77	1.83	1.89	1.95	2.01	2.08	2.14	2.21
1.92	1.99	2.07	2.14	2.22	2.30	2.39	2.48
2.08	2.17	2.26	2.36	2.46	2.56	2.66	2.77
2.26	2.37	2.48	2.59	2.71	2.84	2.97	3.11
2.45	2.58	2.71	2.85	3.00	3.15	3.31	3.48
2.66	2.81	2.97	3.14	3.31	3.50	3.69	3.90
2.89	3.07	3.25	3.45	3.66	3.88	4.12	4.36
3.13	3.34	3.56	3.80	4.05	4.31	4.59	4.89
3.40	3.64	3.90	4.18	4.47	4.78	5.12	5.47
3.69	3.97	4.27	4.59	4.94	5.31	5.71	6.13
4.00	4.33	4.68	5.05	5.46	5.90	6.36	6.87
4.34	4.72	5.12	5.56	6.03	6.54	7.09	7.69
4.71	5.14	5.61	6.12	6.67	7.26	7.91	8.61
5.11	5.60	6.14	6.73	7.37	8.06	8.82	9.65
5.55	6.11	6.73	7.40	8.14	8.95	9.83	10.80
6.02	6.66	7.36	8.14	8.99	9.93	10.97	12.10
6.53	7.26	8.06	8.95	9.94	11.03	12.23	13.55
7.08	7.91	8.83	9.85	10.98	12.24	13.63	15.18
7.69	8.62	9.67	10.83	12.14	13.59	15.20	17.00
8.34	9.40	10.59	11.92	13.41	15.08	16.95	19.04
9.05	10.25	11.59	13.11	14.82	16.74	18.90	21.32
9.82	11.17	12.69	14.42	16.37	18.58	21.07	23.88
10.65	12.17	13.90	15.86	18.09	20.62	23.49	26.75
11.56	13.27	15.22	17.45	19.99	22.89	26.20	29.96
12.54	14.46	16.67	19.19	22.09	25.41	29.21	33.56
13.61	15.76	18.25	21.11	24.41	28.21	32.57	37.58
14.76	17.18	19.98	23.23	26.97	31.31	36.31	42.09
16.02	18.73	21.88	25.55	29.81	34.75	40.49	47.14
17.38	20.41	23.96	28.10	32.94	38.57	45.15	52.80

DISCOUNT TABLE
(in percentages)

Payment Period	−3.00	−2.50	−2.00	−1.50	−1.00	−0.50	0.00
1	1.00	1.00	1.00	1.00	1.00	1.00	1.00
2	2.03	2.03	2.02	2.02	2.01	2.01	2.00
3	3.09	3.08	3.06	3.05	3.03	3.02	3.00
4	4.19	4.16	4.12	4.09	4.06	4.03	4.00
5	5.32	5.26	5.21	5.15	5.10	5.05	5.00
6	6.48	6.40	6.31	6.23	6.15	6.08	6.00
7	7.68	7.56	7.44	7.33	7.22	7.11	7.00
8	8.92	8.76	8.60	8.44	8.29	8.14	8.00
9	10.20	9.98	9.77	9.57	9.37	9.18	9.00
10	11.51	11.24	10.97	10.71	10.47	10.23	10.00
11	12.87	12.52	12.19	11.88	11.57	11.28	11.00
12	14.27	13.85	13.44	13.06	12.69	12.34	12.00
13	15.71	15.20	14.72	14.26	13.82	13.40	13.00
14	17.19	16.59	16.02	15.47	14.96	14.47	14.00
15	18.73	18.02	17.34	16.71	16.11	15.54	15.00
16	20.31	19.48	18.70	17.96	17.27	16.62	16.00
17	21.93	20.98	20.08	19.24	18.45	17.70	17.00
18	23.61	22.52	21.49	20.53	19.63	18.79	18.00
19	25.34	24.09	22.93	21.84	20.83	19.88	19.00
20	27.13	25.71	24.40	23.18	22.04	20.98	20.00
21	28.96	27.37	25.89	24.53	23.26	22.09	21.00
22	30.86	29.07	27.42	25.90	24.50	23.20	22.00
23	32.81	30.82	28.98	27.30	25.75	24.32	23.00
24	34.83	32.61	30.57	28.71	27.01	25.44	24.00
25	36.91	34.44	32.20	30.15	28.28	26.57	25.00
26	39.05	36.33	33.85	31.61	29.56	27.70	26.00
27	41.26	38.26	35.55	33.09	30.85	28.84	27.00
28	43.53	40.24	37.27	34.59	32.17	29.98	28.00
29	45.88	42.27	39.03	36.12	33.50	31.14	29.00
30	48.30	44.35	40.83	37.67	34.94	32.29	30.00
31	50.79	46.49	42.66	39.24	36.19	33.45	31.00
32	53.36	48.68	44.53	40.84	37.56	34.52	32.00
33	56.01	50.93	46.44	42.46	38.93	35.80	33.00
34	58.74	53.24	48.39	44.11	40.33	36.98	34.00
35	61.56	55.60	50.38	45.78	41.74	38.16	35.00
36	64.47	58.03	52.40	47.48	43.16	39.35	36.00
37	67.46	60.52	54.47	49.20	44.59	40.55	37.00
38	70.55	63.07	56.59	50.95	46.04	41.76	38.00
39	73.73	65.69	58.74	52.73	47.51	42.97	39.00
40	77.01	68.37	60.94	54.53	48.99	44.18	40.00

0.50	1.00	1.50	2.00	2.50	3.00	3.50
1.00	1.00	1.00	1.00	1.00	1.00	1.00
2.00	1.99	1.99	1.98	1.98	1.97	1.97
2.99	2.97	2.96	2.94	2.93	2.91	2.90
3.97	3.94	3.91	3.88	3.86	3.83	3.80
4.95	4.90	4.85	4.81	4.76	4.72	4.67
5.93	5.85	5.78	5.71	5.65	5.58	5.52
6.90	6.80	6.70	6.60	6.51	6.42	6.33
7.86	7.73	7.60	7.47	7.35	7.23	7.11
8.82	8.65	8.49	8.33	8.17	8.02	7.87
9.78	9.57	9.36	9.16	8.97	8.79	8.61
10.73	10.47	10.22	9.98	9.75	9.53	9.32
11.68	11.37	11.07	10.79	10.51	10.25	10.00
12.62	12.26	11.91	11.58	11.26	10.95	10.66
13.56	13.13	12.73	12.35	11.98	11.63	11.30
14.49	14.00	13.54	13.11	12.69	12.30	11.92
15.42	14.87	14.34	13.85	13.38	12.94	12.52
16.34	15.72	15.13	14.58	14.06	13.56	13.09
17.26	16.56	15.91	15.29	14.71	14.17	13.65
18.17	17.40	16.67	15.99	15.35	14.75	14.19
19.08	18.23	17.43	16.68	15.98	15.32	14.71
19.99	19.05	18.17	17.35	16.59	15.88	15.21
20.89	19.86	18.90	18.01	17.18	16.42	15.70
21.78	20.66	19.62	18.66	17.77	16.94	16.17
22.68	21.46	20.33	19.29	18.33	17.44	16.62
23.56	22.24	21.03	19.91	18.88	17.94	17.06
24.45	23.02	21.72	20.52	19.42	18.41	17.48
25.32	23.80	22.40	21.12	19.95	18.88	17.89
26.20	24.56	23.07	21.71	20.46	19.33	18.29
27.07	25.32	23.73	22.28	20.96	19.76	18.67
27.93	26.07	24.38	22.84	21.45	20.19	19.04
28.79	26.81	25.02	23.40	21.93	20.60	19.39
29.65	27.54	25.65	23.94	22.40	21.00	19.74
30.50	28.27	26.27	24.47	22.85	21.39	20.07
31.35	28.99	26.88	24.99	23.29	21.77	20.39
32.20	29.70	27.48	25.50	23.72	22.13	20.70
33.04	30.41	28.08	26.00	24.15	22.49	21.00
33.87	31.11	28.66	26.49	24.56	22.83	21.29
34.70	31.80	29.24	26.97	24.96	23.17	21.57
35.53	32.48	29.81	27.44	25.35	23.49	21.84
36.35	33.16	30.35	27.90	25.73	23.81	22.10

(continued on page 866)

DISCOUNT TABLE
(in percentages)
(continued from page 865)

Payment Period	4.00	4.50	5.00	5.50	6.00	6.50
1	1.00	1.00	1.00	1.00	1.00	1.00
2	1.96	1.96	1.95	1.95	1.94	1.94
3	2.89	2.87	2.86	2.85	2.83	2.82
4	3.78	3.75	3.72	3.70	3.67	3.65
5	4.63	4.59	4.55	4.51	4.47	4.43
6	5.45	5.39	5.33	5.27	5.21	5.16
7	6.24	6.16	6.08	6.00	5.92	5.84
8	7.00	6.89	6.79	6.68	6.58	6.48
9	7.73	7.60	7.46	7.33	7.21	7.09
10	8.44	8.27	8.11	7.95	7.80	7.66
11	9.11	8.91	8.72	8.54	8.36	8.19
12	9.76	9.53	9.31	9.09	8.89	8.69
13	10.39	10.12	9.86	9.62	9.38	9.16
14	10.99	10.68	10.39	10.12	9.85	9.60
15	11.56	11.22	10.90	10.59	10.29	10.01
16	12.12	11.74	11.38	11.04	10.71	10.40
17	12.65	12.23	11.84	11.46	11.11	10.77
18	13.17	12.71	12.27	11.86	11.48	11.11
19	13.66	13.16	12.69	12.25	11.83	11.43
20	14.13	13.59	13.09	12.61	12.16	11.73
21	14.59	14.01	13.46	12.95	12.47	12.02
22	15.03	14.40	13.82	13.28	12.76	12.28
23	15.45	14.78	14.16	13.58	13.04	12.54
24	15.86	15.15	14.49	13.88	13.30	12.77
25	16.25	15.50	14.80	14.15	13.55	12.99
26	16.62	15.83	15.09	14.41	13.78	13.20
27	16.98	16.15	15.38	14.66	14.00	13.39
28	17.33	16.45	15.64	14.90	14.21	13.57
29	17.66	16.74	15.90	15.12	14.41	13.75
30	17.98	17.02	16.14	15.33	14.59	13.91
31	18.29	17.29	16.37	15.53	14.76	14.06
32	18.59	17.54	16.59	15.72	14.93	14.20
33	18.87	17.79	16.80	15.90	15.08	14.33
34	19.15	18.02	17.00	16.08	15.23	14.46
35	19.41	18.25	17.19	16.24	15.37	14.58
36	19.66	18.46	17.37	16.39	15.50	14.69
37	19.91	18.67	17.55	16.54	15.62	14.79
38	20.14	18.96	17.71	16.67	15.74	14.89
39	20.37	19.05	17.87	16.80	15.85	14.98
40	20.58	19.23	18.02	16.93	15.95	15.06

7.00	7.50	8.00	8.50	9.00	9.50	10.00
1.00	1.00	1.00	1.00	1.00	1.00	1.00
1.93	1.93	1.93	1.92	1.92	1.91	1.91
2.81	2.80	2.78	2.77	2.76	2.75	2.74
3.62	3.60	3.58	3.55	3.53	3.51	3.49
4.39	4.35	4.31	4.28	4.24	4.20	4.17
5.10	5.05	4.99	4.94	4.89	4.84	4.79
5.77	5.69	5.62	5.55	5.49	5.42	5.36
6.39	6.30	6.21	6.12	6.03	5.95	5.87
6.97	6.86	6.75	6.64	6.53	6.43	6.33
7.52	7.38	7.25	7.12	7.00	6.88	6.76
8.02	7.86	7.71	7.56	7.42	7.28	7.14
8.50	8.32	8.14	7.97	7.81	7.65	7.50
8.94	8.74	8.54	8.34	8.16	7.98	7.81
9.36	9.13	8.90	8.69	8.49	8.29	8.10
9.75	9.49	9.24	9.01	8.79	8.57	8.37
10.11	9.83	9.56	9.30	9.06	8.83	8.61
10.45	10.14	9.85	9.58	9.31	9.06	8.82
10.76	10.43	10.12	9.83	9.54	9.28	9.02
11.06	10.71	10.37	10.06	9.76	9.47	9.20
11.34	10.96	10.60	10.27	9.95	9.65	9.36
11.59	11.19	10.82	10.46	10.13	9.81	9.51
11.84	11.41	11.02	10.64	10.29	9.96	9.65
12.06	11.62	11.20	10.81	10.44	10.10	9.77
12.27	11.81	11.37	10.96	10.58	10.22	9.88
12.47	11.98	11.53	11.10	10.71	10.33	9.98
12.65	12.15	11.67	11.23	10.82	10.44	10.08
12.83	12.30	11.81	11.35	10.93	10.53	10.16
12.99	12.44	11.94	11.46	11.03	10.62	10.24
13.14	12.57	12.05	11.57	11.12	10.70	10.31
13.28	12.70	12.16	11.66	11.20	10.77	10.37
13.41	12.81	12.26	11.75	11.27	10.83	10.43
13.53	12.92	12.35	11.83	11.34	10.89	10.48
13.65	13.02	12.43	11.90	11.41	10.95	10.53
13.75	13.11	12.51	11.97	11.46	11.00	10.57
13.85	13.19	12.59	12.03	11.52	11.05	10.61
13.95	13.27	12.65	12.09	11.57	11.09	10.64
14.04	13.35	12.72	12.14	11.51	11.63	10.69
14.12	13.42	12.78	12.19	11.55	11.65	10.71
14.19	13.48	12.83	12.23	11.69	11.19	10.73
14.26	13.54	12.88	12.28	11.73	11.22	10.76

3. SHOULD YOU BUY OR RENT?

Which is more profitable: To buy a $100,000 house for $20,000 down *
and hold for seven years? Or rent instead, investing your down payment
and other upfront costs in seven-year Treasuries? † To decide, go to the
table below and pick a likely rent from the column on the left. Then
read across to the column representing your best guess for the home's
annual appreciation rate. Where those lines intersect you'll find the
compound annual rate of return that you'll earn on your equity, if you
choose to buy instead of rent.

   1. You're better off renting when rents are unusually low. But if
rents are anywhere near average (typically, 1 percent of the market price,
which is $1,000 a month on a $100,000 house), you do better owning,
even if housing inflation is slow.

   2. You may want to rent instead of own if you think that prices will
stay pretty flat, not just this year but over several years. At gains of zero
or 1 percent, ownership generally yields poor investment returns. You
might get these low yields from condominiums, whose prices are chronically weak, or from houses in cities that are losing population. But house
values in thriving areas should tag along with the general inflation rate,
which makes homeowning highly attractive.

   3. Even at modest rates of housing appreciation, homeowners make
big gains on their investments. That's because of the value of their tax
deductions and their leverage. A small gain in value for the house overall
translates into a large gain in value on the 20 percent you put down.

   4. This table can give you a general feel for your potential gains in
other housing situations. Say you buy a $150,000 house renting at
$1,050 a month, which is 0.7 percent of market value. The equivalent
0.7 percent for the $100,000 house on the table is $700 a month. You
will get a slightly higher yield on the more expensive house (and a
slightly lower yield on a less expensive house). On down payments
smaller than 20 percent, your potential for profit or loss is much greater
than the table shows. So you'd be more inclined to buy than rent.

Monthly Rent	The homebuyer's profit or loss if rents and real-estate values change by‡:					
	−2%	0%	2%	4%	6%	8%
$ 500	loss	loss	loss	0.6%	7.6%	13.4%
$ 600	loss	loss	loss	5.2	11.2	16.9
$ 700	loss	loss	0.5	8.6	14.9	20.4
$ 800	loss	loss	5.1	12.6	18.7	24.0
$ 900	loss	0.2	9.8	16.8	22.6	27.7
$1,000	loss	5.8	14.4	21.0	26.6	31.4
$1,100	loss	11.3	19.1	25.3	30.6	35.3
$1,200	6.8	16.8	23.9	29.7	34.7	39.2

* A 30-year mortgage at 10 percent interest.
† Assuming $4,262 in net closing costs and Treasuries at 8.8 percent. Taxes in the top bracket and other expenses considered.
‡ Compounded annually for seven years.
Source: Real Estate Center at Texas A&M University

4. THE BEST-GUESS COLLEGE PLANNER (LONG FORM)

Who knows exactly what college will cost in the future? Who knows what you'll be earning when the axe falls on your bank account? You have to make guesses—good guesses—to set up a reasonable college investment plan.

That's what this worksheet is all about. It's a four-step system for figuring out how much you ought to save each month, courtesy of the T. Rowe Price mutual fund company. The answer isn't guaranteed to provide every penny you need. But it's close enough.

What I like about this worksheet is that it tells you what *percentage* of your after-tax income you should be saving every year. Conventional college planners (including the Short Form on page 469) advise you to save fixed sums—for example, $500 a month. That's unrealistic. Right now, $500 a month might be much more than you can afford. Ten years from now, however, it might be pocket change. If you save a fixed percentage of income—for example, 5 percent a year—your college contributions can start low and rise as your salary does.

Go through the calculations separately for each child. If you save all this money, you'll win a silver cup for the Best Prepared Parent in the class.

Step One

WHAT WILL COLLEGE COST WHEN YOUR CHILD FINALLY GOES?

THE EASY WAY: Check the table on page 425, which gives you a four-year estimate for the average school. All costs are included: tuition, room, board, books, supplies, transportation, and spending money.

Total Average College Cost $_____

THE BETTER WAY: Take the current one-year cost for the exact school, or type of school, that you expect your child to attend. Include everything: tuition, fees, room, board, books, supplies, transportation, spending money. *College cost:* $_____.

Pick a plausible college inflation rate (at this writing, 6 to 8 percent). *Inflation rate:* _____%.

Put down the number of years from now that your child will start school. Count the current year as 1. For example, an eight-year-old who will start at age 18 has 11 years to go—this year plus 10 years. *Number of years to matriculation:* _____.

Put down the number of years until your child's sophomore, junior, and senior years. If your eight-year-old starts school in 11 years, the next three years would be numbered 12, 13, and 14. *Years to the child's sophomore, junior, and senior years:* _____, _____, _____.

Then go to the MiracleGrow table on page 875. Look down the left-hand column to find the number of years from now that college starts. Read across to the college-inflation rate you chose. Where those lines intersect, you'll find a "compounding factor." *Compounding factor:* _____. Multiply the college cost by that factor. The result is the likely cost of your child's freshman year.

Go to the next number down the column, representing your child's sophomore year, and do the same. Ditto for the junior and senior years. Add those four numbers together for the total college cost.

Freshman year	$_____
Sophomore year	$_____
Junior year	$_____
Senior year	$_____
Total college cost	$_____

If you have no college savings to speak of and expect no student aid, jump directly to Step Four. I'm sorry that you're broke, but you've saved yourself a lot of calculating.

Step Two

HOW MUCH HAVE YOU SAVED ALREADY? Put down the size of your current college savings fund (plenty, right?), then go to the MiracleGrow table on page 875. Go down the left-hand column to find the number of years to matriculation day.* Read across to the row that best represents the return you think your money will earn pretax.† For reference, the long-term return from stocks has been about 10 percent (although the roaring '80s saw 17 percent).

Where those lines intersect, you will find a "compounding factor." Multiply your savings by that factor. The result: What your current savings will be worth when college starts. Subtract this amount from the total college cost to find out how much money you're still missing.

If you have no college savings at all, put a zero here, clear your throat, and move on.

The savings you have now	$_____
Multiplied by the compounding factor	×____
Gives you: The future value of your savings	$_____
Your total college cost	$_____
Minus the future value of your savings	$_____
Gives you: The missing money	$_____

* Include the current year in your count. A 10-year-old child who will start school at age 18 has nine years to wait—this year plus eight years.
† This calculation assumes that you pay any taxes due on your college account from other income.

Step Three

HOW MUCH STUDENT AID CAN YOU EXPECT? If your income falls in the $60,000 to $70,000 range, you'll probably get no help. If you're earning around $40,000, you'll get help at an expensive private college but maybe not at a state university. Anyone who expects no substantial aid should skip to Step Four.

If you think you might qualify for student aid, here's a very, *very* rough guide.

1. Pick a likely college for your child and put down its total cost in 1991–92.

2. Go to the Parental Contribution table on page 428 and figure out about how much you'd have had to pay in 1991–92. Add $700 if the student is a freshman and $900 if he or she is a sophomore, junior, or senior. Subtract 20 percent, just to be conservative. That's your total family contribution. Subtract it from the college's cost.

3. Divide the result by the same 1991–92 college cost that you started with. That gives you the percentage of the bill that you can hope for in college aid. Use this as a proxy for the aid you might get in the future.

Cost of college in 1991–92	$_____
Minus your parental contribution	$_____
Gives you: Aid you might get	$_____
Divided by the cost of college in 1991–92	$_____
Gives you: The percentage of aid available	_____%

4. Enter the total college cost you found in Step One and multiply it by the percentage of the cost that might be covered by student aid.

Subtract that sum (plus any gifts you expect) from the missing money that you calculated in Step Two.

Total college cost	$_____
Multiplied by the percent covered by student aid	$_____
Gives you: Hoped-for student aid	$_____
The missing money	$_____
Minus hoped-for student aid	$_____
Minus anything Grandma will kick in	$_____
Gives you: Cash still to come	$_____

Step Four

HOW MUCH MORE WILL YOU HAVE TO SAVE TO MEET YOUR CHILD'S COLLEGE BILLS? Here's how to figure the percentage of income you should set aside.

Estimate the general rate of inflation you expect in the future. A nice round number is 4 percent. Subtract that from the rate of growth you expect on your investments (you used this rate in Step Two). The result is your inflation-adjusted rate of return.

Expected return on investments	_____%
Minus: Expected rate of inflation	_____%
Gives you: Inflation-adjusted rate of return	_____%

Enter the cash still to come, which you found in Step Three. Divide it by the compounding factor you used in Step Two. This is the current value, in today's dollars, of the money you still need for college expenses.

Cash still to come	$_____
Divided by the compounding factor	÷ _____
Gives you: Current value of what's needed	$_____

Then go to the Best Guess table on page 876. Read down the left-hand column to the number of years to matriculation day.* Read across to the row that shows the net rate of return you expect on your investments, *after inflation*. Where those lines intersect you will find an "inflation adjustment factor." Divide the current value of what's needed (calculated above) by that factor. That tells you how much you should save in the first year of your investment plan.

Divide your first-year savings by your current gross income and multiply by 100. That leads you, finally, to the percentage of income you

have to save each year in order to meet your college costs. (This calculation assumes that your income rises by the inflation rate you used when
you estimated the inflation-adjusted rate of return on your investments,
above.)

The current value of what's needed	$
Divided by the inflation adjustment factor	÷
Gives you: First-year savings amount	$
Divided by current gross income	$
Multiplied by 100	× 100
Gives you: Percent of your income to be saved annually	%

* Include the current year in your count. A 10-year-old child who will start school at age 18 has
nine years to wait—this year plus eight years more.

Afterword

If you follow this plan, you will have all the money in hand by the
time your child enters college. If you miss a few contributions and your
savings fall short, you can make up the slack out of your current income
during the years that your child is in school. If your savings and income
aren't enough, you can exercise your borrowing power. Some parents
deliberately plan to save, say, three-quarters of the sum they need and
borrow the rest.

What if, despite all your calculations, it appears impossible to pay
the freight? You have three choices: (1) make a lot more money (a
nonworking spouse might get a job); (2) improve your borrowing power
(by buying a house and trusting it to appreciate); (3) send your children
to less expensive schools.

MiracleGrow: The Joy of Compounding

This compound-growth table tells you what any sum of money will rise to in any year in the future, if it compounds at a given rate. Look down the left-hand column, for the number of years into the future that you're looking. Read across to the rate of increase you expect. Where those lines intersect, you will find a compounding factor. Multiply that factor by the sum you started with, to see what it will rise to in the years ahead. Use this table to estimate the price of college in the future, or to estimate what your current college savings will be worth in a given year.

The number of years from now that college starts	4%	5%	6%	7%	8%	9%	10%	11%	12%
1 *	1.00	1.00	1.00	1.00	1.00	1.00	1.00	1.00	1.00
2	1.04	1.05	1.06	1.07	1.08	1.09	1.10	1.11	1.12
3	1.08	1.10	1.12	1.14	1.17	1.19	1.21	1.23	1.25
4	1.12	1.16	1.19	1.23	1.26	1.30	1.33	1.37	1.40
5	1.17	1.22	1.26	1.31	1.36	1.41	1.46	1.52	1.57
6	1.22	1.28	1.34	1.40	1.47	1.54	1.61	1.69	1.76
7	1.27	1.34	1.42	1.50	1.59	1.68	1.77	1.87	1.97
8	1.32	1.41	1.50	1.61	1.71	1.83	1.95	2.08	2.21
9	1.37	1.48	1.59	1.72	1.85	1.99	2.14	2.30	2.48
10	1.42	1.55	1.69	1.84	2.00	2.17	2.36	2.56	2.77
11	1.48	1.63	1.79	1.97	2.16	2.37	2.59	2.84	3.11
12	1.54	1.71	1.90	2.10	2.33	2.58	2.85	3.15	3.48
13	1.60	1.80	2.01	2.25	2.52	2.81	3.14	3.50	3.90
14	1.67	1.89	2.13	2.41	2.72	3.07	3.45	3.88	4.36
15	1.73	1.98	2.26	2.58	2.94	3.34	3.80	4.31	4.89
16	1.80	2.08	2.40	2.76	3.17	3.64	4.18	4.78	5.47
17	1.87	2.18	2.54	2.95	3.43	3.97	4.59	5.31	6.13
18	1.95	2.29	2.69	3.16	3.70	4.33	5.05	5.90	6.87
19	2.03	2.41	2.85	3.38	4.00	4.72	5.56	6.54	7.69
20	2.11	2.53	3.03	3.62	4.32	5.14	6.12	7.26	8.61

* Use 1 if your child is 18 and will matriculate this year. Use 2 if the child is 17 and will matriculate next year. You always have to count this year plus the remaining years until college starts.

The Best-Guess Table

Use this table to help figure out what percentage of your income you have to save to reach your college goal. Look down the left-hand column for the number of years before college starts. Read across to the net rate of return you expect on your investments, after inflation. Where those lines intersect, you will find an inflation-adjustment factor. Divide the amount of money you will need by that factor. That tells you how much to save in the first year of your investment plan.

The number of years from now that college starts	Rate of return, after inflation							
	1%	2%	3%	4%	5%	6%	7%	8%
1 *	1.00	1.00	1.00	1.00	1.00	1.00	1.00	1.00
2	1.99	1.98	1.97	1.96	1.95	1.94	1.93	1.93
3	2.97	2.94	2.91	2.89	2.86	2.83	2.81	2.78
4	3.94	3.88	3.83	3.78	3.72	3.67	3.62	3.58
5	4.90	4.81	4.72	4.63	4.55	4.47	4.39	4.31
6	5.85	5.71	5.58	5.45	5.33	5.21	5.10	4.99
7	6.80	6.60	6.42	6.24	6.08	5.92	5.77	5.62
8	7.73	7.47	7.23	7.00	6.79	6.58	6.39	6.21
9	8.65	8.33	8.02	7.73	7.46	7.21	6.97	6.75
10	9.57	9.16	8.79	8.44	8.11	7.80	7.52	7.25
11	10.47	9.98	9.53	9.11	8.72	8.36	8.02	7.71
12	11.37	10.79	10.25	9.76	9.31	8.89	8.50	8.14
13	12.26	11.58	10.95	10.39	9.86	9.38	8.94	8.54
14	13.13	12.35	11.63	10.99	10.39	9.85	9.36	8.90
15	14.00	13.11	12.30	11.56	10.90	10.29	9.75	9.24
16	14.87	13.85	12.94	12.12	11.38	10.71	10.11	9.56
17	15.72	14.58	13.56	12.65	11.84	11.11	10.45	9.85
18	16.56	15.29	14.17	13.17	12.27	11.48	10.76	10.12
19	17.40	15.99	14.75	13.66	12.69	11.83	11.06	10.37
20	18.23	16.68	15.32	14.13	13.09	12.16	11.34	10.60

* Use 1 if your child is 18 and will matriculate this year. Use 2 if the child is 17 and will matriculate next year. You always have to count this year plus the remaining years until college starts.

5. YOUR PERSONAL PERFORMANCE INDEX

How well are you doing with your investments? Here's a simple system for finding out.

Start a Quarterly Performance Notebook, set up like the one on the following page. On the left, list all your investments and their current value. Then list their value at the end of the quarter.

Each quarter's ending values should include all interest and dividends that you reinvested. Make a separate notation of any interest and dividends that you spent, instead.

Enter, as shown, any net new money added to your investments for the quarter, or any net withdrawals. Add the unreinvested interest or dividends to your withdrawals. After the portfolio, you will find the instructions you need for calculating your own pretax investment returns.

The Sample Portfolio shows only stocks, bonds, and money market mutual funds. But you can use this system just as easily for gold, real estate, and other assets, as long as they can be evaluated quarterly. For this Performance Index, and the example, my thanks to John Markese of the American Association of Individual Investors.

YOUR SAMPLE PORTFOLIO

	First Quarter		Second Quarter	
	Beginning*	End*	Beginning*	End*
Money market mutual fund	$ 10,000	$ 16,300	$ 16,300	$ 11,600
Stocks	50,000	49,000	49,000	54,000
Bond mutual fund	40,000	42,000	42,000	44,000
Total value	$100,000	$107,300	$107,300	$109,600
Added (or withdrawn) for the quarter†	$6,000		($5,000)	
Quarterly return	1.26%		6.97%	

	Third Quarter		Fourth Quarter	
	Beginning*	End*	Beginning*	End*
Money market mutual fund	$ 11,600	$ 7,800	$ 7,800	$ 14,000
Stocks	54,000	49,000	49,000	48,000
Bond mutual fund	44,000	41,000	41,000	40,000
Total value	$109,600	$97,800	$97,800	$102,000
Added (or withdrawn) for the quarter†	($4,000)		$6,000	
Quarterly return	−7.25%		−1.79%	

Annual return −1.33%‡

* Current market value, including reinvested dividends and capital gains.
† New investments and funds withdrawn.
‡ Sorry it's negative! The example just turned out that way. Yours will be positive. I promise.

So how do you figure the quarterly and annual returns? Here is the answer, step by step. The calculation is explained on the left. An example (using the portfolio on page 878) is on the right.

The first quarter shows a period of net additions to your portfolio, and a positive return.

	First Quarter
1. Multiply your net contributions for the period (excluding reinvested dividends and interest) by 0.5.	$6,000 \times 0.5 = 3,000$
2. Subtract the result from the value of your portfolio at the end of the period.	$107,300 - 3,000 = 104,300$
3. Again, multiply your net contributions for the period (excluding reinvested dividends and interest) by 0.5.	$6,000 \times 0.5 = 3,000$
4. Add the result to the value of your portfolio at the start of the period.	$100,000 + 3,000 = 103,000$
5. Divide line 2 by line 4.	$104,300 \div 103,000 = 1.0126$
6. Subtract 1.00 from line 5.	$1.0126 - 1.00 = 0.0126$
7. Multiply line 6 by 100. The result is your quarterly yield.	1.26%

The second-quarter calculation shows how to handle a period of net withdrawals from your portfolio, but still with a positive return.

	Second Quarter
1. Multiply your net withdrawals for the period (including unreinvested dividends and interest) by 0.5.	$-5,000 \times 0.5 = -2,500$
2. Ignoring the minus sign, add the result to the value of your portfolio at the end of the period.	$109,600 + 2,500 = 112,100$
3. Again, multiply your net withdrawals for the period (including unreinvested dividends and interest) by 0.5.	$-5,000 \times 0.5 = -2,500$
4. Subtract the result from the value of your portfolio at the start of the period.	$107,300 - 2,500 = 104,800$
5. Divide line 2 by line 4.	$112,100 \div 104,800 = 1.0697$
6. Subtract 1.00 from line 5.	$1.0697 - 1.00 = 0.0697$
7. Multiply line 6 by 100. The result is your quarterly yield.	6.97%

In the third quarter, sad to say, you had both net withdrawals and a negative return.

	Third Quarter
1. Multiply your net withdrawals for the period (including unreinvested dividends and interest) by 0.5.	$-4,000 \times 0.5 = -2,000$
2. Ignoring the minus sign, add the result to the value of your portfolio at the end of the period.	$97,800 + 2,000 = 99,800$
3. Again, multiply your net withdrawals for the period (including unreinvested dividends and interest) by 0.5.	$-4,000 \times 0.5 = -2,000$
4. Subtract the result from the value of your portfolio at the start of the period.	$109,600 - 2,000 = 107,600$
5. Divide line 2 by line 4.	$99,800 \div 107,600 = 0.9275$
6. Subtract 1.00 from line 5.	$0.9275 - 1.00 = -0.0725$
7. Multiply line 6 by 100. The result is your quarterly yield.	-7.25%

In the fourth quarter, you had net additions with a negative return.

	Fourth Quarter
1. Multiply your net contributions for the period (excluding reinvested dividends and interest) by 0.5.	$6,000 \times 0.5 = 3,000$
2. Subtract the result from the value of your portfolio at the end of the period.	$102,000 - 3,000 = 99,000$
3. Again, multiply your net contributions for the period (excluding reinvested dividends and interest) by 0.5.	$6,000 \times 0.5 = 3,000$
4. Add the result to the value of your portfolio at the start of the period.	$97,800 + 3,000 = 100,800$
5. Divide line 2 by line 4.	$99,000 \div 100,800 = 0.9821$
6. Subtract 1.00 from line 5.	$0.9821 - 1.00 = 0.0179$
7. Multiply line 6 by 100. The result is your quarterly yield.	-1.79%

Once you have figured your yield for each quarter, you can calculate your annual return. Do it this way:

1. Divide the first quarter's percentage return by 100 and add 1.	1st Q: 1.26 ÷ 100 = 0.0126 + 1 = 1.0126
2. Do the same for each subsequent quarter.	2nd Q: 6.97 ÷ 100 = 0.0697 + 1 = 1.0697 3rd Q: −7.25 ÷ 100 = −0.0725 + 1 = 0.9275 4th Q: −1.79 ÷ 100 = −0.0179 + 1 = 0.9821
3. Multiply each of the quarterly returns in sequence.	1.0126 × 1.0697 × 0.9275 × 0.9821 = 0.9867
4. Subtract 1.00 from line 3.	0.9867 − 1.00 = −0.0133
5. Multiply line 4 by 100. The result is your annual yield.	−1.33%

What if you want to figure only annual returns, not quarterly ones? Start with your portfolio's market value when the year began. If you made net additions to capital over the year, use the formula shown for the first quarter. If you made net withdrawals, use the formula shown for the second quarter. The result is your annual return. It's not quite as accurate as the quarterly returns, but it's pretty close.

6. TAXABLE VERSUS TAX-FREE BONDS

Here's how to calculate the taxable equivalents to tax-free bonds, for interest rates and state and local tax brackets not illustrated on the table on page 657. You can also use it for calculating higher tax brackets. On the left are the instructions. On the right, an example of how the numbers work. I've picked an investor in the 35 percent federal and state bracket, looking at a tax-exempt bond yielding 8.1 percent. It turns out that he'd need a 12.46 percent taxable yield to equal his return from the tax-free bond.

When using this calculation, always use bonds, or bond funds, of equivalent credit quality and maturity. Otherwise, you won't have the right information.

		Example
1. What is your maximum tax bracket?	_____%	35%
2. Subtract your maximum tax bracket* from 1.00.	_____	0.65
3. What is the yield on the tax-free bond you're considering?	_____%	8.1%
4. Divide the tax-free yield by the number on line 2. This gives you the taxable yield you'd need to net the same return you'd get from the tax-free bond.	_____%	12.46%

* For all calculations, use the decimal. In the example, line 1 would be 0.35.

Here's how to calculate how much you'd need from a tax-free bond in order to match a taxable bond that you're considering.

		Example
1. What is your maximum tax rate?	_____%	35%
2. Subtract your maximum tax rate* from 1.00.	_____	0.65
3. What is the yield on the taxable bond you're considering?	_____%	12.45%
4. Multiply the yield on line 3 by the number on line 2. This is the tax-free yield you need to earn the same net return you'd get from the taxable bond.	_____%	8.1%

* For all calculations, use the decimal. In the example, line 1 would be 0.35.

Here's how to decide between a mutual fund specializing in the bonds of your state and a mutual fund containing the bonds of several states. You might assume that the single-state fund is always best because it's entirely tax exempt. But that's not necessarily so. If a multistate fund offers a higher yield, it might net you more despite the state tax on the out-of-state bonds. A multistate fund also carries less risk, because its managers can diversify.

		Example
1. What is your maximum state tax rate?	____%	8%
2. What percentage of the interest from the multistate fund is taxable in your state? *	____%	80%
3. Multiply the tax rate † on line 1 by the percentage on line 2 to determine your effective state tax rate.	____%	6.4%
4. Subtract your effective state tax rate from 1.00.	____	93.6
5. What is the average yield on the multistate tax-free fund you're considering?	____%	7.0%
6. Multiply the yield on line 5 by the number on line 4. This is the average yield you need from a mutual fund invested in the bonds of many states, in order to match your return from the single-state fund. ‡	____%	6.55%

* This generally covers the interest on all out-of-state bonds, except those from Puerto Rico and other U.S. possessions.
† For all calculations, use the decimal. In the example, line 1 would be 0.08 and line 2, 0.8.
‡ This does not count the deduction you get on your federal tax return for the extra state taxes paid.
Source: Goldstein Golub Kessler & Co., New York City.

7. HOW MUCH SHOULD YOU SAVE FOR RETIREMENT?
(Long Form)

This miniworkbook answers three critical questions: (1) How much money will you need for a comfortable retirement? (2) How much have you got already, counting pension, Social Security, and personal savings? (3) How much more will you need to save, starting today?

I chose this particular retirement planner because—unlike so many others that I studied—its feet are planted in the real world. For example, it faces the fact that fixed pensions don't carry you very far in an inflationary time. You need enough savings to overcome your income's gradual loss of purchasing power. This workbook also reminds you that your home equities can add to your retirement standard of living, and counts the value of any inheritance you're due.

Most usefully, it doesn't project a flat amount per month that you ought to save (although you can calculate one if you want). Flat amounts are unrealistic. In today's dollars, they are much too large—probably more than you can afford. In the dollars of the twenty-first century, however, they are much too small.

A savvier approach is to figure out what percentage of gross income you ought to be putting away each month. Your retirement savings will then rise right along with your income, in order to produce the sum you'll need.

To use this miniworkbook, you will first have to round up some basic financial information (all good stuff, that you ought to know). (1) Get a projection of your probable Social Security retirement benefit (available free, see page 777). (2) Get your projected pension benefit, available from your company's employee-benefits office. Ask whether your pension has an annual inflation adjustment after retirement, and how much your employer contributed last year to your pension or profit-sharing plan. (3) Get the amount of money in your current tax-deferred retirement savings plans, such as 401(k)s, profit-sharing plans, Keogh plans, and Individual Retirement Accounts.

This worksheet was developed jointly by the accounting firm Coopers & Lybrand and the no-load mutual fund group T. Rowe Price in Baltimore. Although the reasoning is sophisticated, the actual steps are easy to follow. To help you, I've shown a specific example on the right. The whole exercise should take you just about an hour.

For a free copy of T. Rowe Price's excellent *Retirement Planning Kit*, which includes investment suggestions as well as this do-it-yourself financial planner, call T. Rowe Price at 800-638-5660. Tell them Jane sent you.

Step One

YOUR WORKING ASSUMPTIONS

		Example
General assumptions		
1. The average rate of inflation you expect.	_____	4%
2. The annual rate of return you expect on your investments, pretax.	_____	9%
Assumptions for your working years		
3. The inflation-adjusted rate of return on your investments (subtract line 1 from line 2).	_____	5%
4. Your federal, state, and local income-tax bracket.	_____	35%
5. Your after-tax bracket (subtract line 4 from 1.00). *	_____	65%
6. The after-tax rate of return on your investments (multiply line 2 by line 5).	_____	5.85%
7. Your inflation-adjusted after-tax rate of return (subtract line 1 from line 6).	_____	1.85%
8. Number of years to retirement.‡	_____	20
Assumptions after you retire †		
9. Your federal, state, and local income tax bracket.	_____	35%
10. Your after-tax bracket (subtract line 9 from 1.00).	_____	65%
11. The after-tax rate of return on your investments (multiply line 2 by line 10).	_____	5.85%
12. Your inflation-adjusted after-tax rate of return (subtract line 1 from line 11).	_____	1.85%
13. The number of years you expect to be retired (life expectancy, page 901, plus a few extra years—you pick the number).	_____	25

---

* All calculations used the decimal. For example, 0.35 subtracted from 1.00 leaves 0.65.
† These results will differ from the preretirement rates only if your tax bracket drops in retirement.
‡Use year 1 if this is the retirement year, year 2 if you'll retire next year, and so on.

Step Two

LINING UP THE FACTORS *

14. *Factor A:* Use the Accumulated Capital Table on page 860. In the left-hand column, find the number of years to your retirement (line 8). Read across to your assumed inflation rate (line 1). Enter the factor you find there.	_____	2.19

15. *Factor B:* Use the Accumulated Capital Table on page 860. In the left-hand column, find the number of years to your retirement (line 8). Read across to the assumed rate of return on your investments (line 2). Enter the factor you find there.   5.6

16. *Factor C:* Use the Accumulated Capital Table on page 860. In the left-hand column, find the number of years to your retirement (line 8). Read across to the after-tax rate of return you expect from your investments during your working years (line 6). If you don't see your exact rate of return, round down to the closest one. Enter the factor you find there.   2.92

17. *Factor D:* Use the Discount Table† on page 864. In the left-hand column, find the number of years you expect to be retired (line 13). Read across to the after-tax rate of return you expect from your investments in retirement (line 11). If you don't see your exact rate of return, round down to the closest one. Enter the factor you find there.   14.15

18. *Factor E:* Use the Discount Table on page 864. In the left-hand column, find the number of years you expect to be retired (line 13). Read across to the inflation-adjusted after-tax rate of return you expect from your investments in retirement (line 12). If you don't see your exact rate of return, round down to the closest one. Enter the factor you find there.   21.03

19. *Factor F:* Use the Discount Table on page 864. In the left-hand column, find the number of years to your retirement (line 8). Read across to the inflation-adjusted after-tax rate of return you expect to achieve during your working years (line 7). If you don't see your exact rate of return, round down to the closest one. Enter the factor you find there.   17.43

20. *Factor G:* Use the Discount Table on page 864. In the left-hand column, find the number of years to your retirement (line 8). Read across to the after-tax rate of return you expect to achieve during your working years (line 6). If you don't see your exact rate of return, round down to the closest one. Enter the factor you find there.   12.61

21. *Factor H:* Use the Discount Table on page 864. In the left-hand column, find the number of years to your retirement (line 8). Read across to the inflation-adjusted rate of return you expect to achieve during your working years (line 3). Enter the factor you find there.   13.09

---

* You will need these factors for making all your calculations. Once you've lined them up, you can simply slip them in where needed.

† Use year 1 if this is the retirement year, year 2 if you'll retire next year, and so on.

Step Three

YOUR RETIREMENT COST OF LIVING

22. *The easy way*—and the best one for younger workers. Enter 80 percent of your current after-tax income. That's a close estimate of what it will take to maintain your present standard of living.   _____ $31,200

23. *The more accurate way*—best for people nearing retirement. Look at the spending plan on page 146 and redo it for your likely expenses in retirement. Enter your probable annual expenses, in today's dollars.   _____ $30,000

Step Four

YOUR ANNUAL INCOME IN RETIREMENT

Your net Social Security income

24. Enter your projected Social Security retirement benefit. *   _____ $17,500

25. If your Social Security income will be taxable (page 809), enter one of the following tax rates.
    - If your state taxes your Social Security benefits: Subtract one-half of your combined tax bracket from 1.00.†   _____   0.825
    - If your state doesn't tax Social Security, and you are in the 28 percent federal bracket, enter 0.86. If you're in a different bracket, use the calculation given above.   _____   _____

26. Multiply your Social Security retirement benefit (line 24) by the tax rate (line 25). The result is your net Social Security income.   _____ $14,437

Your net pension

27. Enter the projected annual benefit from your defined-benefit plan (not a defined-contribution plan, profit sharing, or 401(k)). If you don't have a defined-benefit plan, enter zero.   _____ $18,000

28. Enter your postretirement after-tax bracket (line 10).   _____   65%

29. Multiply line 27 by line 28. This is your pension income after tax.   _____ $11,700

Any other income

30. Enter any other sources of income, such as earnings, royalties, and trust-fund income, but not income from savings. If there will be none, enter a zero here and on line 32.   _____   0

31. If you have any such income, enter your postretirement after-tax bracket (line 10).   _____   65%

32. Multiply line 30 by line 31. This is your other income
after tax. _____ _0_

33. Add lines 26, 29, and 32. This is your basic after-tax
retirement income. _____ $26,137

* See page 777 for how to get your free estimate. Couples using a joint benefit should remember
that that income will drop when one of you dies.
† Here's how to do this calculation in the combined state and federal 35 percent tax bracket:
Divide 0.35 by 2, which gives you 0.175. Subtract that from 1.00 to get 0.825.

Step Five

IS YOUR BASIC RETIREMENT INCOME ENOUGH?

34. Enter your retirement expenses, from line 22 or 23. _____ $30,000
35. Enter your basic retirement income, from line 33. _____ $26,137
36. Subtract line 34 from line 35. This is your annual
current shortfall or surplus. * _____ −$3,863
37. Enter Factor A from line 14. _____ × 2.19
38. Multiply line 36 by line 37. This is your gross annual
shortfall at retirement, taking future inflation into
consideration. _____ −$8,460
39. Enter any income that you will get from a fixed annuity
at retirement. If there will be none, enter a zero here
and on line 41. _____ _0_
40. Enter your postretirement after-tax bracket (line 10). _____ 65%
41. Multiply line 39 by line 40. This is your annuity income
after tax. _____ _0_
42. Subtract line 41 from line 38. This is your net annual
income shortfall in retirement. _____ −$8,460
43. Enter Factor E from line 18. _____ × 21.03
44. Multiply line 42 by line 43. This is the amount of capital
you will need at retirement to meet your annual income
shortfall. _____ $177,914†

* If you show a surplus, skip down to line 44 and enter a zero. But complete this worksheet
anyway. You may not have a lifetime surplus, if your pension income isn't indexed annually to
inflation.
† Depending on your situation, this can look like a very big number indeed. But remember that
it's expressed in future dollars at retirement, so it's never as bad as it looks.

Step Six

THE VALUE OF YOUR SAVINGS AT RETIREMENT

The value of your tax-deferred savings plans
45. Enter the current value of all your tax-deferred savings:
401(k)s, IRAs, Keoghs, SEPs, profit sharing, and other
company plans. _____ $15,000
46. Enter Factor B from line 15. _____ × 5.6
47. Multiply line 45 by line 46. This is the pretax value of
your tax-deferred savings, at retirement. _____ $84,000

48. Enter the sum you expect your employer to contribute to your defined-contribution retirement plan this year. (Exclude your own contributions, if any, and any money your employer puts up to match those contributions.)   _____ $4,800

49. Enter Factor H from line 21.   _____   × 13.09

50. Multiply line 48 by line 49.   _____ $62,832

51. Enter Factor B from line 15.   _____   × 5.6

52. Multiply line 50 by line 51.   _____ $351,859

53. Add lines 47 and 52.   _____ $435,859

54. Enter your working-years after-tax bracket (line 5).   _____   65%

55. Multiply line 53 by line 54. This is the potential value of your tax-deferred savings, after tax. *   _____ $283,308

The value of your after-tax savings

56. Enter the current value of all of your taxable savings and investments. Use the after-tax value of mutual funds, stocks, investment real estate, and other assets on which you'd owe capital gains taxes if you sold today. Exclude fixed annuities, which were covered on line 39.   _____ $10,000

57. Enter Factor C from line 16.   _____   × 2.92

58. Multiply line 56 by line 57.   _____ $29,200

The value of your total savings

59. Add lines 55 and 58. This is what you can expect to realize from all of the retirement savings you hold today.   _____ $312,508

---

* This assumes that you take a lump-sum distribution and pay taxes on it. It's a conservative assumption. You will more likely defer taxes by leaving at least some of the money in the plan or by rolling it into an IRA.

Step Seven

HOW MUCH CAPITAL WILL YOU NEED AT RETIREMENT?

60. Enter the amount of capital needed from line 44.   _____ $177,914

If your company pension is not indexed to inflation *

61. Enter your annual after-tax pension (line 29).   _____ $11,700

62. Enter Factor A from line 14.   _____   × 2.19

63. Multiply line 61 by line 62.   _____ $25,623

64. Enter Factor E from line 18.   _____   × 21.03

65. Multiply line 63 by line 64.   _____ $538,852

66. Enter the value from line 63.   _____ $25,623

67. Enter Factor D from line 17.   _____   × 14.15

68. Multiply line 66 by line 67.   _____ $362,565

69. Subtract line 68 from line 65. This is the extra money you'll need at retirement to maintain the purchasing power of your fixed pension income.   _____ $176,287

To pay off your mortgage and other debts †

70. Enter the mortgage balance you will still be carrying at retirement, as well as other long-term loans you are likely to have.   _____ $45,000

To cover any other capital needs

71. Enter a lump sum, in today's dollars, to cover any other financial responsibilities you will have in retirement: tuition for a grandchild, funeral expenses, an emergency fund for yourself.   _____ $50,000

72. Enter Factor A from line 14.   _____   × 2.19

73. Multiply line 71 by line 72, to determine the future value of these lump sums at retirement.   _____ $109,500

Your total capital needs at retirement

74. Add lines 60, 69, 70, and 73. This is the sum you will need to achieve all the purposes you have in mind.   _____ $508,701

The capital you have already

75. Enter the value of your current retirement savings from line 59.   _____ $312,508

76. Enter, in today's dollars, any other sources of capital. You might be due an inheritance. Or you might plan on selling your house at retirement, investing some of the proceeds and moving into a smaller place.   _____   0

77. Enter Factor A from line 14.   _____   × 2.19

78. Multiply line 76 by line 77.   _____   0

79. Add lines 75 and 78. This is the future value of all of the capital you have amassed so far.   _____ $312,508

80. Subtract line 79 from line 74. If you have a surplus, congratulations. But check on it periodically to be sure that you're still keeping up. If you have a shortfall, this is the sum that you still have to accumulate.   _____ $196,193

* If you have an indexed pension, enter zero on line 69 and go on to line 70.
† This plan tries to take you into retirement debt free.

Step Eight

HOW MUCH MORE DO YOU NEED TO SAVE?

81. Enter the shortfall from line 80.   _____ $196,193

82. Enter Factor C from line 16.   _____   ÷ 2.92

83. Divide line 81 by line 82. This is the current value, in today's dollars, of the extra capital you need.   _____ $67,189

84. Enter Factor F from line 19.   _____   ÷ 17.43

85. Divide line 83 by line 84. This is how much you should invest this year to reach your goal.   _____ $3,855

86. Enter your current gross income.   _____ $60,000

87. Divide line 85 by line 86. This is the percentage of your gross annual income that has to be invested annually to meet your retirement goal, assuming that your income keeps pace with inflation. Adjust your savings every year, to keep up with this percentage amount. *   _____   6.4%

If you would rather save a fixed amount each year

88. Enter the sum on line 83. _____ $67,189

89. Enter Factor G from line 20. _____ ÷ 12.61

90. Divide line 88 by line 89. This is the fixed sum of money
    you would have to save every year to meet your goal. _____ $5,328†

---

* To be conservative, we assumed that this money went into after-tax savings where the earnings are taxed every year.

† This shows graphically how much harder it is to follow a fixed-sum savings program. In the first year, you would have to save $1,473 more than if you saved a fixed percentage of your annual income.

8. HOW LONG WILL YOUR CAPITAL LAST?

The following tables show how many years your capital will last at varying rates of withdrawal. For annual withdrawals of equal size, use the first table. The remaining tables assume that you'll take enough extra money each year to keep up with the inflation rate. At 4 percent inflation, for example, a first-year withdrawal of $5,000 grows to $5,200 the second year, $5,400 the third year, and so on.

To use these tables, choose a likely inflation rate, up to 9 percent (the table showing 4 percent inflation is on page 789). In the left-hand column, find the percentage of your capital that you will withdraw in the first year. If you withdraw $5,000 from a $125,000 nest egg, for example, you have taken 4 percent. Read across to the pretax rate of return that you're expecting to earn on your money. Where those lines intersect, you will find the number of years your capital will last. I've assumed that the money is taken at the start of each year. The # symbol means that, at that rate of withdrawal, your capital will never be exhausted.

(The source for all the tables in Appendix 8 is John Allen, J.D., of Allen-Warren, Arvada, Colorado.)

EQUAL-SIZE WITHDRAWALS

Percent of original capital withdrawn annually	Will last this many years, if invested at the following average rates of return										
	4%	5%	6%	7%	8%	9%	10%	11%	12%	13%	14%
2%	#	#	#	#	#	#	#	#	#	#	#
3%	#	#	#	#	#	#	#	#	#	#	#
4%	83	#	#	#	#	#	#	#	#	#	#
5%	37	62	#	#	#	#	#	#	#	#	#
6%	26	32	49	#	#	#	#	#	#	#	#
7%	20	23	28	40	#	#	#	#	#	#	#
8%	17	19	21	25	34	#	#	#	#	#	#
9%	14	15	17	19	23	29	#	#	#	#	#
10%	12	13	14	16	18	25	45	#	#	#	#
11%	11	12	12	13	15	16	18	22	32	#	#
12%	10	10	11	12	12	14	15	17	20	26	#
13%	9	9	10	10	11	12	13	14	15	18	22
14%	8	9	9	9	10	10	11	12	13	14	16
15%	8	8	8	8	9	9	10	10	11	12	13

ASSUMING 1 PERCENT INFLATION

Percent of capital withdrawn in the first year	Will last this many years, if the original withdrawal rises by 1 percent annually and your money is invested at the following average rates of return										
	4%	5%	6%	7%	8%	9%	10%	11%	12%	13%	14%
2%	#	#	#	#	#	#	#	#	#	#	#
3%	111	#	#	#	#	#	#	#	#	#	#
4%	44	78	#	#	#	#	#	#	#	#	#
5%	29	37	59	#	#	#	#	#	#	#	#
6%	22	26	32	47	#	#	#	#	#	#	#
7%	18	20	23	28	39	#	#	#	#	#	#
8%	15	17	18	21	25	33	#	#	#	#	#
9%	13	14	15	17	19	22	28	#	#	#	#
10%	12	12	13	14	16	17	20	24	39	#	#
11%	10	11	12	12	14	16	18	22	27	#	#
12%	9	10	10	11	12	12	13	15	17	19	25
13%	9	9	9	10	10	11	12	13	14	15	17
14%	8	8	9	9	9	10	10	11	12	13	14
15%	7	8	8	8	8	9	9	10	10	11	12

ASSUMING 2 PERCENT INFLATION

Percent of capital withdrawn in the first year	Will last this many years, if the original withdrawal rises by 2 percent annually and your money is invested at the following average rates of return										
	4%	5%	6%	7%	8%	9%	10%	11%	12%	13%	14%
2%	168	#	#	#	#	#	#	#	#	#	#
3%	63	105	#	#	#	#	#	#	#	#	#
4%	34	43	75	#	#	#	#	#	#	#	#
5%	25	29	37	57	#	#	#	#	#	#	#
6%	20	22	26	32	46	#	#	#	#	#	#
7%	17	18	20	23	28	38	#	#	#	#	#
8%	14	15	17	18	21	24	32	#	#	#	#
9%	12	13	14	15	17	19	22	27	52	#	#
10%	11	12	12	13	14	15	17	20	24	35	#
11%	10	10	11	12	12	13	14	16	18	21	28
12%	9	9	10	10	11	12	12	13	15	16	19
13%	8	9	9	9	10	10	11	12	12	13	15
14%	8	8	8	8	9	9	10	10	11	12	13
15%	7	7	8	8	8	8	9	9	10	10	11

ASSUMING 3 PERCENT INFLATION

Percent of
capital
withdrawn
in the
first year

*Will last this many years, if the original withdrawal
rises by 3 percent annually and your money is invested
at the following average rates of return*

first year	4%	5%	6%	7%	8%	9%	10%	11%	12%	13%	14%
2%	68	158	#	#	#	#	#	#	#	#	#
3%	40	52	100	#	#	#	#	#	#	#	#
4%	28	34	43	72	#	#	#	#	#	#	#
5%	22	25	29	36	55	#	#	#	#	#	#
6%	18	20	22	26	31	44	#	#	#	#	#
7%	15	17	18	20	23	27	36	#	#	#	#
8%	13	14	15	17	18	21	24	31	#	#	#
9%	12	12	13	14	15	17	19	22	27	44	#
10%	10	11	12	12	13	14	15	17	19	23	33
11%	9	10	10	11	12	12	13	14	16	18	21
12%	9	9	9	10	10	11	11	12	13	14	16
13%	8	8	9	9	9	10	10	11	11	12	13
14%	7	8	8	8	8	9	9	10	10	11	12
15%	7	7	7	8	8	8	8	9	9	10	10

ASSUMING 5 PERCENT INFLATION

Percent of
capital
withdrawn
in the
first year

*Will last this many years, if the original withdrawal
rises by 5 percent annually and your money is invested
at the following average rates of return*

first year	4%	5%	6%	7%	8%	9%	10%	11%	12%	13%	14%
2%	41	50	67	145	#	#	#	#	#	#	#
3%	29	33	40	52	92	#	#	#	#	#	#
4%	23	25	28	33	42	67	#	#	#	#	#
5%	18	20	22	25	29	35	52	#	#	#	#
6%	16	17	18	20	22	25	30	42	#	#	#
7%	13	14	15	16	18	20	23	27	35	#	#
8%	12	13	13	14	15	16	18	20	24	29	53
9%	11	11	12	12	13	14	15	17	18	21	26
10%	10	10	10	11	12	12	13	14	15	17	19
11%	9	9	9	10	10	11	11	12	13	14	15
12%	8	8	9	9	9	10	10	11	11	12	13
13%	7	8	8	8	9	9	9	10	10	11	11
14%	7	7	7	8	8	8	8	9	9	10	10
15%	6	7	7	7	7	8	8	8	8	9	9

ASSUMING 6 PERCENT INFLATION

Percent of capital withdrawn in the first year	* Will last this many years, if the original withdrawal rises by 6 percent annually and your money is invested at the following average rates of return										
	4%	5%	6%	7%	8%	9%	10%	11%	12%	13%	14%
2%	35	41	50	67	139	#	#	#	#	#	#
3%	26	29	33	40	51	89	#	#	#	#	#
4%	21	23	25	28	33	42	65	#	#	#	#
5%	17	18	20	22	25	29	35	50	#	#	#
6%	15	16	17	18	20	22	25	30	41	#	#
7%	13	13	14	15	16	18	20	22	26	34	#
8%	11	12	13	13	14	15	16	18	20	23	29
9%	10	11	11	12	12	13	14	15	16	18	21
10%	9	10	10	10	11	12	12	13	14	15	17
11%	8	9	9	9	10	10	11	11	12	13	14
12%	8	8	8	9	9	9	10	10	11	11	12
13%	7	7	8	8	8	9	9	9	10	10	11
14%	7	7	7	7	8	8	8	8	9	9	10
15%	6	6	7	7	7	7	8	8	8	8	9

ASSUMING 7 PERCENT INFLATION

Percent of capital withdrawn in the first year	* Will last this many years, if the original withdrawal rises by 7 percent annually and your money is invested at the following average rates of return										
	4%	5%	6%	7%	8%	9%	10%	11%	12%	13%	14%
2%	31	35	41	50	67	135	#	#	#	#	#
3%	24	26	29	33	40	51	87	#	#	#	#
4%	19	21	23	25	28	33	41	63	#	#	#
5%	16	17	18	20	22	25	29	35	49	#	#
6%	14	15	16	17	18	20	22	25	30	40	#
7%	12	13	13	14	15	16	18	20	22	26	33
8%	11	11	12	13	13	14	15	16	18	20	23
9%	10	10	11	11	12	12	13	14	15	16	18
10%	9	9	10	10	10	11	12	12	13	14	15
11%	8	8	9	9	9	10	10	11	11	12	13
12%	8	8	8	8	9	9	9	10	10	11	11
13%	7	7	7	8	8	8	9	9	9	10	10
14%	7	7	7	7	7	8	8	8	8	9	9
15%	6	6	7	7	7	7	7	7	8	8	8

ASSUMING 8 PERCENT INFLATION

Percent of capital withdrawn in the first year — Will last this many years, if the original withdrawal rises by 8 percent annually and your money is invested at the following average rates of return

Percent of capital withdrawn in the first year	4%	5%	6%	7%	8%	9%	10%	11%	12%	13%	14%
2%	28	32	36	41	50	67	131	#	#	#	#
3%	22	24	26	29	33	40	51	84	#	#	#
4%	18	19	21	23	25	28	33	41	61	#	#
5%	15	16	17	18	20	22	25	28	34	48	#
6%	13	14	15	16	17	18	20	22	25	30	39
7%	12	12	13	13	14	15	16	18	20	22	26
8%	10	11	11	12	13	13	14	15	16	18	20
9%	9	10	10	11	11	12	12	13	14	15	16
10%	9	9	9	10	10	10	11	12	12	13	14
11%	8	8	8	9	9	9	10	10	11	11	12
12%	7	8	8	8	8	9	9	9	10	10	11
13%	7	7	7	7	8	8	8	9	9	9	10
14%	6	7	7	7	7	7	8	8	8	8	9
15%	6	6	6	7	7	7	7	7	7	8	8

ASSUMING 9 PERCENT INFLATION

Percent of capital withdrawn in the first year — Will last this many years, if the original withdrawal rises by 9 percent annually and your money is invested at the following average rates of return

Percent of capital withdrawn in the first year	4%	5%	6%	7%	8%	9%	10%	11%	12%	13%	14%
2%	26	29	32	36	41	50	66	127	#	#	#
3%	20	22	24	26	29	33	40	51	82	#	#
4%	17	18	19	21	23	25	28	33	41	50	#
5%	14	15	16	17	18	20	22	25	28	34	47
6%	13	13	14	15	16	17	18	20	22	25	29
7%	11	12	12	13	13	14	15	16	18	20	22
8%	10	10	11	11	12	13	13	14	15	16	18
9%	9	9	10	10	11	11	12	12	13	14	15
10%	8	9	9	9	10	10	10	11	11	12	13
11%	8	8	8	8	9	9	9	10	10	11	11
12%	7	7	8	8	8	8	9	9	9	10	10
13%	7	7	7	7	7	8	8	8	9	9	9
14%	6	6	7	7	7	7	7	8	8	8	8
15%	6	6	6	6	7	7	7	7	7	7	8

9. PENSION MAXIMIZATION: WILL IT WORK FOR YOU?

At retirement, you have two ways of taking your pension: (1) *Lifetime only.* You get a higher monthly income, but it stops when you die. (2) *Joint-and-survivor.* You get a lower income, but it lasts for the lifetimes of you and your spouse.

A "pension max" salesperson will propose that you take the lifetime-only pension. To protect your spouse, you buy a life-insurance policy. At your death, the proceeds of that policy can provide your spouse with a lifetime income.

This plan is potentially workable if: (1) your net lifetime pension, after paying the insurance premium, is *greater than* you would have received had you chosen the joint-and-survivor pension; and (2) after your death, the insurance proceeds are sufficient to buy your spouse a lifetime income *at least equal to* what the joint-and-survivor pension would have paid for life. Most proposals fail one or both of these tests!

Are you looking at a plan that works? This worksheet will tell you, *if you are starting pension max at retirement.* *

You and the salesperson should fill in the following blanks.

---

* This worksheet is not effective for plans started earlier than retirement. For such plans, the salesperson should compare the cost of the insurance premium with the after-tax pension benefits expected—adjusting for the fact that the costs come now and the benefits later.

Worksheet prepared by John Allen, J.D., Allen-Warren, P.O. Box 5597, Arvada, CO, 80005.

Have You Really Maximized Your Pension?

---

1. Your monthly pension, if paid for your life only. .... $_____
2. Your monthly pension after all taxes.† .... $_____
3. Your monthly pension if you take a joint-and-survivor option. .... $_____
4. The joint-and-survivor monthly pension after all taxes.† .... $_____
5. Your spouse's monthly pension after your death, if you take the joint-and-survivor option. (This may, or may not, be the amount you reported on line 3). .... $_____
6. Your surviving spouse's monthly pension after all taxes.† .... $_____
7. The midpoint between lines 5 and 6. Use this as a first, rough target for the monthly annuity your spouse should get if you choose pension maximization.‡ .... $_____
8. The cost of buying your spouse an annuity after your death, figured for your spouse's age when you retire.‡

The "annuity rate" tells you, in dollars and cents, how much
monthly income can be bought for every $1,000 of life-insurance
proceeds.

Spouse's age: _____

Annuity rate: $_____

9. The life-insurance proceeds needed to provide the monthly income.
   To calculate this, divide the target income (line 7) by the annuity
   rate (line 8) and multiply by 1,000. $_____

10. Monthly life-insurance premium required to secure the proceeds
    shown on line 9. $_____

11. Subtract the monthly premium (line 10) from the after-tax income
    you'd get from a single-life pension (line 2). This gives you the
    disposable income that you, as a couple, would have left to live on. $_____

    Compare this with the income you'd get from a joint-and-survivor
    pension, after tax (line 4). $_____

† Federal, state and local. Do the exact calculation. Don't just estimate 15, 28 or 31 percent.
‡ A professional planner will be able to target the amounts in lines 7 and 8 exactly.

If your income after pension max is less than you'd get from a joint-and-survivor pension, stop here. It usually makes no sense to use the insurance scheme.

If pension max provides you with more income as a couple, continue
the calculation to see if it protects your spouse.

Have You Left a Large Enough Annuity for Your Spouse?

12. Your spouse's "life expectancy," based on his or her age when you
    retire.† The number comes from an IRS table, and is called the
    Expected Return Multiple—see page 901.   _____

13. The portion of the spouse's annuity income that will be excluded
    from income taxes. This is called the Exclusion Ratio.‡ Carry it to
    three decimal places.   _____

14. Subtract the Exclusion Ratio from 1.000.   _____

15. Enter the monthly annuity income you targeted, from line 7. $_____

16. Multiply line 15 by line 14. This tells you how much of the spouse's
    annuity income is subject to tax. $_____

17. Subtract income taxes§ from the spouse's annuity income (line 15) $_____
    and enter that income after tax.

18. Enter the actual amount of net spousal income you need to protect
    (line 6). $_____

† For safety, refigure for 5, 10, and 20 years ahead. Each year the spouse lives, his or her life
expectancy improves.
‡ To get the Exclusion Ratio: Multiply the spouse's monthly annuity income by 12. Multiply the
result by the Expected Return Multiple (line 12). Divide the result into the proceeds of the life-
insurance policy (line 9).
§ Federal, state and local. Do the exact calculation. Don't just estimate 15, 28 or 31 percent.

If line 18 is larger than line 17, you need more life insurance to protect your spouse. Redo the worksheet using a larger policy. If the cost of the larger policy reduces your income as a couple to less than you'd get from the joint pension, pension max doesn't work.

If you start pension maximization earlier than retirement, you'll also need a "present value" analysis. This recognizes that $1,000 spent on insurance today is worth much more than $1,000 received in higher pension benefits in the future. A present value analysis tells you whether those extra pension benefits are worth their cost. Don't buy from an insurance agent or planner who won't (or can't) do this calculation for you.

This worksheet does not consider the value of pensions with cost-of-living adjustments. But you can simulate the analysis by estimating what your pension will be in 5, 10, and 20 years, and using this sheet to see if the life insurance will indeed supply a comparable pension for the spouse.

All pension-max proposals with cost-of-living adjustments should also be subjected to present value analysis. So should any proposal where insurance premiums or death benefits vary.

The Risks of Choosing Pension Maximization

If your pension has a cost-of-living benefit, you will need to purchase a much larger amount of insurance (or a rising amount of insurance) in order to provide your spouse with a similar amount of income. And even that might not be enough, if inflation explodes.

If you buy a universal-life policy or an interest-sensitive whole-life policy and interest rates decline, your plan may not work out. You might have to pay a higher insurance premium or accept a lower death benefit. Ask the agent to show you what happens to the pension-max plan, if interest rates drop to 7 percent, or to the policy's minimum guaranteed rate.

If you buy a policy with a "vanishing premium" and interest rates fall, your plan may not work out. You figured on paying premiums for a limited number of years, but will have to pay them longer. That might reduce your standard of living.

At your death, annuity rates may have dropped. Your spouse may not be able to buy as high an income as you expected. Ask the sales rep to show you how large an annuity could be obtained in an interest-rate environment of 6 or 7 percent.

Inflation or unexpected expenses may eat away at your income. At some point in the future, you may not be able to afford the life insurance. If you have to cancel the policy, and die, your spouse will lose that part of his or her income.

If you become forgetful, your insurance might accidentally lapse—leaving your spouse to do without. If the marriage goes bad and the husband owns the policy, he might cancel it or change the beneficiary.

Your spouse may get health benefits from your pension plan, which could be lost when you die and your pension stops. Even if no health benefits are paid now, they may be added in the future, especially in public-sector plans. It is generally unwise to sever all connection with a public-sector plan.

The spouse's money might run out, unless the life-insurance proceeds are used to buy a lifetime annuity. But choosing an annuity means that you won't have a lump sum of money for your heirs. Both goals—a legacy and a lifetime spousal income—cannot be guaranteed.

The Advantages of Pension Maximization

If your spouse dies first, the insurance can be canceled—leaving you with more disposable income.

If you want to continue paying for the insurance after your spouse dies, you'll have a larger estate to leave to your heirs (although, if leaving a larger estate is important to you, you can carry extra life insurance without using pension max).

If there's a divorce, the pension-holder could cancel the policy (although the divorce settlement might require that the policy be kept in force).

If you and your spouse live for many years, you can—at some point—withdraw some cash from the policy. You will shrink the death benefit left for your spouse. But at later ages, less money is needed to provide the spouse with a lifetime income.

10. LIFE EXPECTANCY (EXPECTED RETURN MULTIPLE)

These are the unisex life expectancies used by the Internal Revenue Service for such things as deciding how much of an annuity is taxable income.

If you are this old	The IRS expects you to live this long	If you are this old	The IRS expects you to live this long
10	71.7	44	38.7
11	70.7	45	37.7
12	69.7	46	36.8
13	68.8	47	35.9
14	67.8	48	34.9
15	66.8	49	34.0
16	65.8	50	33.1
17	64.8	51	32.2
18	63.9	52	31.3
19	62.9	53	34.0
20	61.9	54	29.5
21	60.9	55	28.6
22	59.9	56	27.7
23	59.0	57	26.8
24	58.0	58	25.9
25	57.0	59	25.0
26	56.0	60	24.2
27	55.1	61	23.3
28	54.1	62	22.5
29	53.1	63	21.6
30	52.2	64	20.8
31	51.2	65	20.0
32	50.2	66	19.2
33	49.3	67	18.4
34	48.3	68	17.6
35	47.3	69	16.8
36	46.4	70	16.0
37	45.4	71	15.3
38	44.4	72	14.6
39	43.5	73	13.9
40	42.5	74	13.2
41	41.5	75	12.5
42	40.6	76	11.9
43	39.6	77	11.2

If you are this old	The IRS expects you to live this long	If you are this old	The IRS expects you to live this long
78	10.6	89	5.3
79	10.0	90	5.0
80	9.5	91	4.7
81	8.9	92	4.4
82	8.4	93	4.1
83	7.9	94	3.9
84	7.4	95	3.7
85	6.9	96	3.4
86	6.5	97	3.2
87	6.1	98	3.0
88	5.7	99	2.8

INDEX